TRUE MYTH

BLACK VIKINGS OF THE MIDDLE AGES

Nashid Al-Amin

Order this book online at www.trafford.com
or email orders@trafford.com

Most Trafford titles are also available at major online book retailers.

Printed in the United States of America.

ISBN: 978-1-4669-6003-9 (sc)
ISBN: 978-1-4669-6004-6 (e)

Library of Congress Control Number: 2012923568

Trafford rev. 10/02/2014

 www.trafford.com

North America & international
toll-free: 1 888 232 4444 (USA & Canada)
fax: 812 355 4082

For my mother,
Jacqueline Weber

Thanks to Pam and Jim Knowles, Scott Mosier and Michael Thomas for their contributions.

Dedicated to all human beings seeking an honest assessment of our dispersal around the earth and history since our emergence in Africa.

CONTENTS

FOREWORD

Europe, we are told, has always been the domain of white-skinned people, classified variously as Caucasians, Whites, Nordics, Aryans, Indo-Europeans—white people. So, when we read or hear of any particular people inhabiting Europe, we assume—because of what practically all historians and scholars have impressed upon us for roughly three centuries—that the people under discussion were white or Caucasian. The Vikings, or Norsemen, are one such group of people and, perhaps, 98% of books written about them make the claim that they were white, blond, blue-eyed "Nordics"—often without offering a shred of proof. We—all people—assume this *must* be true. Eurocentric scholars (those who extol the ingenuity, civilization, uniqueness and purity of all things European over all other races) have repeatedly asserted this. The physical appearances of Scandinavians today seem to validate this, so the same must have been so one, two, three millennia ago—which seems only reasonable since we also have been told that light or white skin is necessary in far northern regions of our planet. Black-skinned people could never have survived in such frigid conditions.

Not having a computer or access to the Internet until fairly recently, the first two drafts of this work were done on an electric typewriter. After someone gave me a computer about three years ago, I did a third draft of the book as I typed it into my computer chapter by chapter. Except for an Internet article someone printed out and gave me several years ago, I did not, myself, check "Black Vikings" on the Internet until after this work was completed, finding that there were articles written on black Vikings and other European black peoples—some offering quotes from sources cited in the work you are about to read. These Internet articles also post commentary from readers—some insisting that Vikings or Norsemen could not have been black because white skin was essential to survive the frigid weather conditions of northern Europe, and that only so-called *Nordics* had ever inhabited northern Europe. It is an assumption that has been drilled into us through the works of Eurocentric scholars and scientists. This book will demonstrate, however, that this assertion is flawed—perhaps a deliberately conceived fallacy devised to preclude any notion of black-skinned people ever occupying northern Europe.

This book will demonstrate to the reader that the Vikings, Norsemen or Scandinavians—particularly those of the so-called "Viking Age" (i.e., c. 800-1100 AD)—were a predominantly black- and dark-skinned, non-Caucasian people, and that Blacks, whether of African or Asian descent, were not strangers to any part of Europe in ancient *or* historical times. Although the word *race* has been fairly debunked over the last two decades or more, the world has endured three or four centuries of racial conditioning, the effects of which still remain imbedded in our psyches and still affect the quality of life for millions of people around the earth.

Within most of the world's nations—large or small—there are often ethnically divergent peoples suffering discrimination from the ruling class or the predominant race in their particular countries. Some recent or current examples are the Ouighurs and Tibetans suffering discrimination from the majority Han Chinese in China; Aborigines treated as second class citizens by the majority white population of Australia; Palestinians suffering the contempt of their Israeli overlords; Gypsies persecuted and marginalized in eastern Europe and many countries they reside in; African immigrant populations in Italy and Spain suffering ostracism by the majority populations; Muslims discriminated against in France, the country having officially banned Muslim women from wearing headscarves in public and Muslim girls banned from wearing them in schools; Sudanese Blacks being set upon, killed and driven from their towns by Arab government forces who are—judging by what is seen on television—nearly as black-skinned as the Blacks they are persecuting. The above are only the most commonly heard incidences of oppression, persecution and—in the case of the ongoing Israeli-Palestinian conflict—protracted genocide, though many lesser known but similar situations can be cited, like the passage of a recent Arizona law authorizing police to question anyone they feel is an illegal alien (aimed primarily at Mexicans), or the killing in Sir Lanka of untold thousands of ethnic Tamils which has elicited charges of genocide from major "rights" groups and which the United Nations is considering looking into.

A greater and more enduring form of oppression is that waged against practically every nation of the world with predominantly black- and dark-skinned populations by the Western powers—Europe and the United States—which has been in evidence for roughly 500 years, but whose origins date back at least two millennia—to about the time of the rise of Rome (which I term "new" Rome, to be discussed later), which sought to conquer the known world. Generally speaking, there are no indications that race or racism played any part in the Roman quest for world domination, that race or racism played any part in the many wars that took place in the archaic world which preceded the advent of Rome. At least the chroniclers of those days and times made no allusion to race, per se, and did not denigrate enemies or nations in racist-tinged commentary. Nevertheless, the seeds of the racism we know today, of supposed white superiority and the inferiority of the dark-skinned races, unnoticed and unremarked upon by Eurocentric chroniclers, is an ongoing plague loosed upon the world when white European nations finally overcame the domination of an older, dark-skinned world which had held them in check almost until the onset of the 16th century—a world which Norsemen, or Vikings, were a significant factor in during the Viking Age—roughly spanning the years 800-1100 AD.

The unleashing of European, or "white," racism, rapine and slaughter would directly and negatively impact the indigenous populations of the Americas, Africa, southern Asia, and eventually Australia, China and the island nations of the South Pacific. The effects of this racism, which has infected practically the entire planet, still haunt us, affecting international relations and influencing the way we regard fellow human beings within nations or in other areas of the world. It is this European—white vs. black, superior vs. inferior—brand of racism which will be discussed now and again throughout this work.

We know what we know of history what we have been taught, what has been presented to us, impressed upon us, embedded into our consciousness through repetition and visual imagery, fortified by the assumed infallibility of the Eurocentric intellectual and scientific authorities that present us with information. And for the past two centuries or more Eurocentric, Western scholarship has dominated our view of what we know of history—from the Americas to India and in all the areas of the world once colonized by European nations. Although the standing armies which once subjugated these various nations are gone, legacies of European colonialism yet remain: the Christian religion; the European languages spoken by the populaces of non-European nations; the necessity of the vast majority of these populaces to speak those European languages (i.e., English in Ghana, Nigeria, Kenya, and India; French in Haiti, Senegal and Niger; Spanish throughout South and Central America, and so on) since the educational systems of these nations are chiefly based on what the colonizers established and which, in some cases, the former colonial powers still administer. So, the education received by the populaces is unavoidably *westernized*—be it Literature, Physics, Psychology or, most important for our understanding, History. The history most of the world has inculcated is a Eurocentric version, which most of us have come to accept as truthful, absolute. In most instances, none of these adjectives can or should be applied to what Eurocentric writers have presented to us regarding the history of the world—from the most ancient past to the present.

While the main focus of this work is the Vikings or Norsemen, I find it necessary to begin with an overview of man's beginnings and the peopling of the earth. Though I adhere to conventional time frames for the most part, I do feel that man has been roaming the earth far longer than Eurocentric scholars and historians admit and that ancient Egypt is more ancient than we have been lead to believe. Here and there

I break with convention and pursue a course the reader may not at all have considered before, but I will not do this without valid justification. Even the "experts" are not always in agreement on particular points, like the age of the Great Pyramid or the Great Sphinx, the years particular Egyptian dynasties began and ended, whether the Trojan War actually occurred or was totally mythological, or whether modern man mated with Neanderthals. My own study of history has led me to certain conclusions that may not be in accord with standard views, and I ask the reader to contemplate what I have to say and, in all instances, employ his or her own common sense and logic.

My Masters degree is in English, not history or anthropology. I have been an adjunct English professor for twenty-seven years, teaching essay and research writing as well as Literature. However, I began a personal study of history more than forty years ago, after reading J.A. Rogers' *Sex and Race vol. 1*. I sought out books on African history, anthropology, Native Americans and race, building my own modest library and pursuing my own areas of study. I also pursued an acting career, got married, wrote poetry and began a novel before entering college at age 30, where I eventually decided that I wanted to teach college level English. But I continued to read historical material, absent any historical discipline or approach as I might have had to do had I formally pursued a degree in history or anthropology.

While I consider myself a minor historian, the reader might consider me a mere researcher or historical neophyte. I have read the works of a number of historians, some prominent, some less so, all of whom I consider more conversant and informed than myself, although I may not totally agree with their theories and conclusions. I have never examined ancient artifacts first-hand, gone on archeological digs, or visited most of the areas I discuss in this book. I can only trust in the research, theories and writings of those who have devoted much of their lives to the subjects they discourse upon, contrast their conclusions with others presenting theories regarding the same subjects, consider, contemplate and weigh what I have read, then add, subtract, and re-order impressions and visions in my mind as I synthesize the material and arrive at my own concepts, beliefs and conclusions about the subject in question. My opinions are formulated according to what seems most reasonable, most accurate, most probable.

Just as any other writer or researcher of history, I utilize the sources that best allow me to achieve my objectives and validate my assertions. Some readers, of course, might not open themselves to what I present and stubbornly cling to the outline of history they are most comfortable or familiar with, an outline practically devoid of any contribution by black-skinned participants in world history. And any notion that the cherished Vikings were not blond, blue-eyed Aryans will strike them as outlandish, impertinent or abhorrent. European writers—Eurocentric writers, including white, American writers—have elevated the Vikings into demigods just as they have the ancient Greeks, Romans, Germans, popes and almost any notable individual or people who appeared on the European continent. Doing so lends credence to the assumption of superiority that most Whites seem to feel and often exhibit toward the darker races of mankind. Their historians have repeatedly told them that *they* gave civilization to the world, shaped and ordered it, spread it, spawned the inventions, sciences, arts and exploration that improved human conditions. One practice Eurocentric historians have used to practically write black-skinned people out of history is to subsume the ancient Egyptians, Sumerians, Indians and other non-Caucasian peoples into the Caucasian race, thereby transforming the innovations, civilizations, architecture and achievements of these peoples into the works of Caucasians, Whites and, by association, peoples we know today as Europeans!

I am a Viet Nam Era veteran but, thankfully, did not serve in Viet Nam. I spent almost two-and-a-half years of my three-year U.S. Army service in Europe—almost two years in France, my last seven months in Germany—spending time in or passing through five other countries—Luxemburg, Belgium, Italy, and Switzerland. Using up the last of my leave time before returning to the States in two months, I spent two weeks in Copenhagen, Denmark. This now distant period represents the bulk of my travel anywhere and, although I did not know what I know now about the history of Scandinavia and the Vikings, two realizations remained with me as I rode the train back to my post in Germany: all Danes were not blond-haired (maybe 40% of those I saw in Copenhagen), and—speaking here as an African-American—the Danes were the friendliest Europeans I had encountered. I remember asking myself again and again on the train ride back to my post: "Why are they so *friendly?*"

Denmark is north of Germany, where 80 or so years ago Hitler extolled the superiority of the blond Aryan (there is a much smaller percentage of blonds in Germany than in Denmark), so when I visited Copenhagen just 22 years after the end of World War II, I did not expect to be openly welcomed by what I imagined would be super-Aryan Danes who were surely purer Whites than the Germans. But no: though Europeans generally showed more respect and acceptance toward me than American Whites ever had, I remember the Danes as the most friendly and urbane of Europeans. I mention my sojourn in Copenhagen only to inform the reader that I did spend time in a Scandinavian land, saw the broad coast of Sweden only a few miles away across a strait separating Zealand (the island upon which Copenhagen is situated) from Sweden called The Sound, and experienced the sun coming up before 2 a.m. after only about four hours of darkness.

I believe the average reader will find what I present revelatory. I utilize reputable sources, some historians long forgotten or deliberately overlooked by more modern writers of Viking history. Most of the sources I utilize are not difficult to find, and a number of Icelandic sagas—easily accessible in libraries or bookstores—provide information on a number of Norsemen who are described as "black," "dark" or "ruddy" complexioned. Although black Vikings or black Norsemen are the focus of this work, I find it is necessary to begin our journey from remote times to show that black-skinned people were not strangers to this western extremity of Asia and that they—as black Egyptians and other Africans, and as black-skinned Asians—called Europe home even into fairly recent historical times, as will be seen.

This book is not intended as a comprehensive work presenting detailed information about Viking weaponry, religion, dress, customs, ship-building techniques, succession of rulers, and so forth. The reader can consult many Viking books in libraries or lining the shelves in bookstores for these particulars. A number of these areas will be touched upon, of course, but the primary focus of this work is the racial make-up of the people called Norsemen, an issue the more popular and accessible books do not honestly delineate or even mention, invariably asserting that these northern warriors were blond, blue-eyed Caucasians of the "Nordic" race. Evidence will be presented demonstrating that the Norsemen of Scandinavia were predominantly black-skinned during the so called Dark Ages, Viking Age and into the Middle Ages—and were often referred to as "black pagans," "black heathen," "black devils" and Moors in the British Isles. This fact is almost never mentioned in popular books on the Vikings, and the few sources which *do* mention the blackness of the Vikings do so fleetingly, on a page or two, and almost never afterward.

When the adjective *black* is used to describe the racial makeup of a member or members of the human family, most people equate it to a black or sub-Saharan *African* with Negroid features. My use of the term black will include such people but will also imply people with black skin outside of Africa who may not exhibit the typical African features that we are familiar with—people from south India, Myanmar (Burma), Bangladesh, Indonesia, or the dark-skinned people in areas of the Near East and the Arabian Peninsula. My use of the term black or *dark-skinned* should not be confused with Caucasians—people with white or colorless skin, long, wavy hair, less prominent cheek bones, a segment of whom may be blond and have blue, gray or green eyes.

Along with Africa, Asia, itself, was once a *dark continent*—with black and much darker-skinned populations than it exhibits today—as will be discussed. It is not my intent at all to disrespect people of the above listed areas of the world who do not think of themselves in terms of color or race, or people who may think of themselves as Caucasians because they have embraced the classifications of Eurocentric writers who have classified them as such. Irregardless, we live in a world that generally abides by what Europeans have outlined, defined and classified, and while today's trend is to debunk racial theories or declare that there is no such reality as race, we cannot easily undo the four to five centuries of racial conditioning which most of humanity has been impelled to inculcate.

This work must necessarily be written in the racial vein we have come to understand so that we can also understand how Eurocentric historians and scientists have used race and racial classifications to their advantage, especially in declaring this people or that Caucasian—ancient Egyptians, Indians, Australian Aborigines, Norsemen and many others—to glorify white Europeans and diminish the achievements of black- and dark-skinned humanity.

Since almost any encyclopedia will inform the reader that the Vikings or Norsemen arrived on North American shores roughly 500 years before Christopher Columbus dropped anchor in the Bahamas, there must be a tangible reason for the Western world to select him over the Vikings as the "discoverer" of America. That reason may be a simple one: Racism. Perhaps the Eurocentric Brotherhood of Academia long ago realized that a little too much information was extant regarding black Norsemen to accord them this achievement. Not that the Norsemen were the *actual* first visitors to American terrain. They weren't. Outside of early Native Americans, who must be considered the first, there is evidence that black African, Chinese, Egyptian, Phoenician, Carthaginian and Irish visitors came to areas of North America prior to the Vikings—some of whom will be touched upon on this work, some more than others. Also discussed in adequate detail will be the origins of black Vikings, their expansion and influence in Europe, names of Norse individuals which indicate their probable racial makeup—like Thorstein the Black and other "the Blacks"—and individuals whose names do not denote complexion but who are *described* as black-skinned in the Icelandic sagas, like Thorhall the Hunter or Huntsman, who was the chief navigator for Eric the Red (*Red*, more than likely an indicator of a dark or brown complexion, perhaps resulting from mixed parentage), Egil Skallagrimsson and other Viking explorers, warriors and chieftains.

While the notion of black Vikings or Norsemen might surprise or offend the reader who has never heard of or imagined Blacks even inhabiting Europe—much less Scandinavia—evidence does exist showing this was so, and that the Norsemen of the Viking Age were *styled* black by presumably white populaces of areas they overran, particularly those of Ireland, Wales, and what would become England, where learning and literacy had not totally succumbed to the atrophy of the Dark Ages in Europe (i.e., 500-1100 CE). Sources mentioning black Vikings are not abundant, nor are sources mentioning other black- and dark-skinned peoples who made their home in Europe. Works by more modern or popular historians most often totally ignore older works by reputable authors who did not attempt to portray Europe as an eternal Caucasian homeland. I utilize several of these older sources in this work as well as more modern ones which, I think, will present a balanced, plausible and revelatory synthesis of the information extant. This is not to say that I have explored every source available; I have not. I have not spent hours in dimly-lighted research libraries poring over archival materials. And, as mentioned, I did not search the Internet, writing this book the old fashioned way, typing the first two drafts on an electric typewriter. So, I am certain there are beneficial sources that I have missed because—writing essentially part-time, teaching and correcting papers, and working non-teaching part-time jobs to make ends meet—I simply did not have time for extensive research. But what might become apparent to the reader is that even the perusal of more accessible works have, however briefly, offered spoonfuls of evidence that black- and dark-skinned peoples have participated in the affairs of Europe, despite efforts by what I call the Eurocentric Brotherhood of Academia to obscure this reality.

Presenting an intelligible narrative of European history is an extremely difficult undertaking. Eurocentric historians have littered their works with a multitude of tribes and peoples, some major, some not, emigrating, settling among, displacing, and contending with numbers of other tribes and peoples with assorted nomenclatures—most presumed to be racially, culturally or phenotypically different, but invariably white. A scan of a historical atlas of Europe during the height of the Roman Empire, the Dark Ages or the 9th century will bear this out. Or look at the number of peoples occupying ancient Greece; 5th century Britain; 10th century Germany in historical atlases. Consider also that Europe is a mere extension of Asia, and that the *whole* of *Western Europe*—the tourism mecca with its Alps, numerous countries, expansive Riviera and world-famous cities—is, essentially, no larger than the than the *Arabian Peninsula*—even tossing in the British Isles! Writers of European history present nearly all these tribes as distinct, some emigrating from points farther east or from Asia, itself, nudging themselves into this west Asian extremity (supposedly already occupied by Caucasians); yet, Eurocentric historians, anthropologists, writers, educators and film-makers would have us believe that *all* the peoples and tribes who made their home in, or emigrated into, Europe were and have always been white or *Caucasian*—the term German-born Johann Blumenbach first coined in the early 19ᵗʰ century to describe people of European or supposed white ancestry.

Our journey must necessarily begin with an overview of man's spread around most of the earth after leaving Africa, with statements from respected historians attesting to his negritude. We will look at the possible origins of white people or Caucasians and their spread into Europe. I dispense with Biblical references, as some scholars have employed, to outline the differentiation and dispersion of major racial groups of people, relying instead on historical and anthropological data in most instances. We'll discuss the ancient black populations of Asia and then steadily begin to focus on Europe and the ancient intermingling of people there, moving into historical times. A half dozen middle chapters will concentrate on black Vikings or Norsemen and include a listing of individuals whose names denote blackness or who are described as black or dark-skinned in early chronicles and in the Icelandic sagas. A chapter on Columbus and Europeans coming to the Americas, films, and two chapters discussing DNA science, will follow. And then we will try to make sense of what we have discussed and see how the Europe we know today gained the ascendancy it maintains (with the assistance of the United States) and what that ascendancy has wrought upon the rest of the world.

I must add that when I began my research into the Vikings, I did so believing they were the blond, blue-eyed "Nordics" I had always heard they were. It was 1991 and the buildup for the quincentenary of Columbus arriving in America had begun. Why, I asked myself for the hundredth time, aren't the Vikings credited with America's discovery? I wrote a 20-page research paper that did not answer the question. It was when I wrote a second draft, coming across a modern source asserting that the Vikings were *black*, that I found a focus, expanding my research paper to 65 pages. A couple of years later, I felt I had enough information to begin a book whose purpose now is to demonstrate that the Vikings of the Dark and Middle Ages were predominantly black- and dark-skinned peoples, not the blond-haired Caucasians more modern historians have long claimed they were.

Whether Norsemen ever wrote their own histories or chronicled particular events, invasions, expeditions or religious practices is, regrettably, unknown, or else hidden from us. Most of what we know of them is derived from Scandinavian or Icelandic poems and tales recorded two or three centuries after the individuals and the events they were involved in took place. More revealing, though, are chronicles recorded by Irish, English and Welsh historians (I have not pursued French, Italian or other European sources which may be in existence) written during or nearer to the times under discussion, offering a more visceral depiction of Vikings and the fear they evoked in British populaces although these are often tinged with prejudice and deliberate distortions. In regard to race, however, distortion cannot be blamed for descriptions referring to Viking Age Norsemen as "black heathen," "black Strangers" or "black devils" in chronicles of the period, written by men who were, presumably, white. We will also see that some later historians—those most ignored by more modern writers—called other tribes of Europeans or Asians who entered Europe "black," including tribes generally classified as Germanic as well as peoples who were part of Classical Greece.

To repeat: Eurocentric historians and scientists have littered history with dozens of tribes sprouting out of nowhere, seemingly dissimilar in character, appearance and culture, yet "Caucasian"—or so we would surmise since, concerning Europe, little effort has been made by historians to describe these peoples in racial terms—although Europeans were the originators of racial divisions and theories. Rather, Eurocentric historians and scientists (and I always include white Americans in the term *Eurocentric*) more often employ non-racial terminologies to obscure the achievements of darker peoples, or dismiss black- and dark-skinned peoples from history itself, though these were the earliest human beings to spread around the earth and establish the world's earliest civilizations which Europeans borrowed from to begin their own.

In this work the term *black* refers to people with significant melanin content giving their skin a black or brown appearance irrespective of their hair texture, physiognomy (body type, skull shape, nose shape, eye color). For whatever reason, Eurocenric scientists have long classified black- and brown-skinned Indians (from India) and black-skinned Australian Aborigines as Caucasian. I consider these people, on the whole, quite *black*, as well as the ancient peoples of North Africa, the Near East, central and southern Asia and the island nations of the Pacific. A relatively recent book, *The History and Geography of Human Genes*, by several DNA scientists, continues the Eurocentric practice of subsuming black- and dark-skinned peoples into the Caucasian family, which will be discussed in two later chapters.

I do not claim to have all the answers to every topic raised in this work. While I demonstrate that some of the hodge-podge of peoples on historical atlases were black- and dark-skinned, like the *Goths*, who are always styled Germans, for lack of clear information, I have not done this with all the European groups mentioned. I make every effort to combine my assertions with the statements of historians and scholars who have done far more research in various areas than I have—even those I may generally disagree with. I do think the reader will see a much different picture (and a more honest one) of Europe than the picture Eurocentric historians have presented over the last three centuries or so—allowing us to understand that the theory of so-called "racial purity" is transitory, deceptive, and illusory for the most part. Although, for many of us this theory is most associated with the era of Hitler and Nazism, racial purity and the emotions it evokes has been long ingrained in the white European psyche and remains rampant in the psyches of white Americans today. The sooner we dispense with the notion of racial purity, the by-product of which is the racial superiority most Caucasians have long felt toward Blacks and people of color in general, the better the human family will be able to commingle on our fractious planet.

CHAPTER 1

THE ANCIENT WORLD RECONSIDERED

When we hear the term "Viking," the image that comes to mind most readily is that of a tall, blond, broad-shouldered, bearded white man dressed in animal skins, wearing a rounded helmet with horns protruding from either side of it. Many books written by Western scholars present illustrations of Norsemen thusly attired, and the few Viking films that have been made reinforce this image, although Vikings rarely, if ever, wore such helmets, or *never* actually wore them. Numerous books have chronicled the exploits of these vigorous peoples, also called Norsemen and Northmen, who swooped down from Scandinavia to wreak havoc on civilizations from the British Isles to Spain, Italy, France and Russia. That these Vikings or Norsemen left an indelible impact on the territories they scourged is undeniable; that they were all members of the white or "Nordic" race, however, is questionable, for ample evidence—evidence heretofore *not* unknown, strongly confirms that a substantial number of these peoples were black or dark-skinned.

Black-skinned will not always denote "African" in this work, although most people, especially Caucasians, seem to associate blackness of skin exclusively with Africa. However, there are numerous black-skinned Indians (from India), Indonesians, Burmese, Pacific islanders and Southeast Asians and, as will be shown, several millennia ago the earth's population was comprised of many more black-skinned peoples in these areas, as well as in Asia and Europe, generally. White historians and anthropologists have classified the populations of some of the aforementioned areas—including the black-skinned, so-called Aborigines of Australia—*Caucasian* by methods only they seem to understand, which has only added to confusion in those of us unacquainted with their intricate methods of categorization. Even new DNA technology has not clarified the issue, somehow arriving at the same conclusions that pre-DNA historians and scientists have asserted for two centuries or so in regard to race. The new DNA science has forced Eurocentric scholars and historians to grudgingly admit that the origin of Homo sapiens, or modern man, was Africa, but a number of them (although this theory is at least two centuries old) are still uncomfortable with this notion and continue to seek ways to revise it, rework it, disprove it to fit the Eurocentric racial models they have so long cherished.

I reject the classifying of obviously black-, brown-, and dark-pigmented people as Caucasian or white, as Eurocentric historians and scientists do the Aborigines, Indians, and historic peoples like the ancient Ethiopians and Egyptians. And the reader who wishes to understand this humble work needs to understand that an element of the white race—or people who considered themselves "white," different, and perhaps *superior* to the dark races of mankind—introduced the theory of race, nurtured it after invading the territories of the darker races all over the earth, destroying civilizations and countless human beings in the process. They then wrote the books that most of us read depicting these deeds and assigning this or that people to one race or another. A plague arose, and continues to afflict most of the world: racism. Racism is the dominant malady infecting today's world—more than crime, drugs, pollution, weapons of mass destruction, poverty, cancer and war. Race and racism, in fact, seem to be at the root of most wars fought over the last thousand years or so, perhaps longer, obviously (at least to this writer) a factor in the first Crusade in 1096 when Christian Europe, with the blessing of Pope Urban II, invaded the Holy Land to wrest Jerusalem from the *Infidels*—dark-skinned, Muslim Turks and Saracens. European and American historians of course cite other causes for the wars Europeans have waged since the decline of Greece and the fall of Rome at the end of the 5th century, but even a cursory look at wars fought by Europeans outside the European continent would show them to have been expansionist and waged (when European countries were not fighting each other) against dark-skinned peoples.

Except, perhaps, for World War I and the Revolutionary War, race has been a factor in all of America's wars, beginning with the subjugation and near-genocide of Native American peoples in establishing what would become the United States.

Eurocentric historians and scholars almost never mention racism—that is, *a collective white racial hatred toward non-white peoples*—in their assessments of European colonization and warfare. They have excused European trespasses and the destruction of numerous non-Caucasian cultures and peoples as mere acts of economic necessity (for Europeans) or strategic utilitarianism or necessary evil, exhibiting not the slightest regard for the lives of the affected populations in the areas overrun: Europe needed trade; Europe needed spices; Europe (or a particular European country) needed a trade route to the East; Europe needed raw materials; Europe (or particular European countries) needed slaves; Europe needed oil to maintain its industrial growth. The people who suffered the loss of their lands, way of life, resources, lives or particular civilization are less important than the needs of European nations. Their resultant fates go unnoted, or are mentioned in a brief afterthought at the end of a historian's chapter.

The most profitable pursuits by Europeans for trade, resources, slaves and other riches were into areas of the world populated by dark-skinned people—Africa, the Middle East, southern Asia, South America, the Caribbean, China, the isles of the Pacific. Yet, racism—the dehumanization of dark-skinned people in the minds of Europeans; their bold, and often undesired, intrusions into areas inhabited by dark-skinned populaces; their use of more modern weaponry to subdue these populaces; the guiltless slaughter of untold numbers of people—is never mentioned by historians who write of the events that we ingest in schools, universities and our own private readings which invariably present a one-sided picture: the European side.

We have become used to this presentation of history without realizing that another whole side is missing, practically unrecorded, unknown. Whether we like it or not, the vast majority of inhabitants in Europe, Canada, India, South and Central America, the Caribbean, Africa and the United States—whatever our individual race or racial background—are *westernized* and attuned to Eurocentric thought and values. Most of the dark races of the world have not totally kicked free of the shackles of colonization, slavery, imperialism, fear and subjugation that they have lived under for the last five centuries. And the Whites of Europe and North America—having shaped our modern world and mores, having benefited from the injustices their ancestors wrought and continue to effect against the darker races of the world—have not let go of the racial animus that consumed their forefathers, no matter how enlightened, liberal or tolerant some may feel they are.

The scholars who write the histories we read are predominantly white and Eurocentric, and their writings present a Eurocentric view of history offering very little information on the contributions of black- or dark-skinned people to civilization. One method employed by Eurocentric historians to erase dark-skinned people from history is to declare them *white*, assert that this or that people were Caucasian—as they have done with the ancient Egyptians, Indians, Ethiopians, Australian Aborigines and others, which will be discussed further on in this work. It will also become apparent that Western scholars have ignored the presence of black- and dark-skinned, non-Caucasian people *in Europe* so that we think of Europe as always having been a continent inhabited exclusively by white-skinned people.

*   *   *   *   *

To assert that the Vikings or Norsemen were primarily black-skinned must cause the average reader to smile at this writer's naivete, a naivete certainly attributable to the publication of fairly recent books and scholarly articles by African-American and other non-white scholars who have emerged over the last three or four decades to challenge the oft-repeated assertions of white historians whose numerous works have shaped the consciousness of most of the world for the last several centuries. Our nurturing by historians and scientists has been masterfully accomplished and we believe, for instance, that Asia has always been inhabited by Mongoloid or "yellow" people; Europe has always been inhabited by Caucasoid or white people; and that Africa has, for the most part, always been inhabited by Negroid or black people who, the analyses contend, have never contributed much of anything to civilization. We look at the present distributions of races over the continents they dominate today and assume that these distributions have always been constant—especially the Caucasian presence in Europe. Blacks, scholars and scientists have drilled into us, could not have survived the colder climates of Europe and northern Asia.

While the writers of scientific and historical treatises seem to be caught up in the trend of moving away from racial considerations in their writing, enlightened by the new science of DNA and what the science reveals about racial intermixing, so much damage has been done by the centuries-old focus on race by Eurocentric scholars that suddenly replacing this focus with a supposed race-free veneer would merely increase the damage and confusion wrought by three centuries of Eurocentric, race-based scholarship. Blacks and other dark-skinned people who have been written out of history would still not find themselves in it. Whites or white nations who perpetrated crimes against them could not be singled out and condemned in absentia for racial crimes against humanity. Eurocentric writers whose racial theories we have inculcated, whose often deliberate fabrications have obscured the blackness of some civilizations, would go unexposed and unvilified. An expression that has become popular in the United States over the last two or three decades is "Let's move on"—an aphorism implying that the past is done and the present should be concerned with forging a new future. But to simply move on would not rectify the damage that has been done over the past several centuries or reveal the falsehoods and omissions by the majority of Eurocentric scholars.

So this work will discuss race in terms we have come to understand, referring to the black, brown, red, yellow and white races that Eurocentric scholars originated and have drummed into us for three centuries that we have become accustomed to and which most of us still abide by. Only then, after considering what is presented in this work, might we be able "move on."

History should show us that the races of man have been constantly in flux and that over many millennia various peoples have migrated from one territory to another vanquishing, settling among and intermingling with the races they encountered, often spawning new races and acquiring or imposing new languages, customs and lore. Over the last two decades (although such a theory has existed for two centuries) it has been universally acknowledged by most scholars that true man first evolved in Africa and then migrated over untold millennia to nearly every part of the earth—including northern climes. His movement out of the Mother Continent was made easier during the last great ice age (Wurm glacial), beginning roughly 2,500,000 years ago (the Pleistocene Epoch) and lasting until about 10,000-12,000 years ago. Ocean and sea levels fell significantly and land-bridges were formed, connecting the Iberian Peninsula to North Africa; Italy with Sicily, and Sicily with North Africa, or close enough to North Africa that the two continents were separated by a narrow channel of water between them; northeastern Asia formed a wide land-bridge connecting with Alaska; and southeast Asia and Indonesia were joined in a more solid landmass which may have stretched to Australia. As well, many Greek isles were larger and there was a land-bridge connected to Asia Minor (i.e., Turkey); the Greater and Lesser Antilles (i.e., the Caribbean islands stretching from Cuba to Trinidad) may have been a solid landmass stretching from the Yucatan Peninsula of Mexico to northern South America; Japan and the Philippines may have merged with China; northern Japan may have been joined to Sakhalin Peninsula and northeastern Russia; the Red

Sea and Persian Gulf may not have existed, joining Africa and southwestern Asia in one solid landmass, with Arabia sandwiched between them. The whole of northern Europe was covered by glacial ice as was much of northern Asia, and this was the prevailing condition on earth for more than two million years, until the glacial ice finally melted—raising sea levels and producing the present formations of continents and island land masses—only 10,000 to 12,000 years ago.

In 1989, a theory was developed by the late Allan C. Wilson of the University of California, Berkeley, strongly suggesting that the first "anatomically modern human beings" evolved in Africa 166,000 to 249,000 years ago (*Washington Post,* 27 Sep. 1991, "New Evidence of 'Eve'"). This was the controversial study which asserted that all human beings are ancestors of a single, African woman. Dr. Wilson's theory is hardly new. He and his colleagues compared a special DNA type passed down through the maternal line. Changes or mutations that DNA undergoes can be counted, and analysis showed that "the trunk of the tree was African" (op. cit.).

A rival theory insists that man did not evolve into Homo sapiens in Africa but left Africa as Homo erectus and evolved into true humans simultaneously in different parts of the earth (op. cit.). But whether Homo erectus or Homo sapiens walked out of Africa is not essential at this point. What *is* is that for as long as we have studied it, we've seen that the masses of humanity that flowed out of Africa have been *black*-skinned, and common sense should tell us that earliest man must have remained so for many millennia after he reached various territories in Europe, Asia, Australia and the Americas before climate or other still to be determined factors caused him to differentiate into other races which, over time, predominated in the regions he found himself in.

These earliest Homo sapiens, short and pygmy-like, are often referred to as "Negritos." These first humans spread from Africa (probably East Africa) to nearly all parts of the earth, and we must assume that they resembled, in complexion and physiognomy, the present-day pygmies of central Africa. They would have emerged during the Paleolithic Period or Old Stone Age if man were in existence 249,000 years ago, accepting Dr. Wilson's conclusion (although some believe that man has existed much longer). It must also be considered that the physiognomy of man began to differentiate—in musculature, dexterity, limb length, waviness of hair and skin tone (i.e., jet-black, dark-brown, blue-black, reddish-black, copper-colored, reddish-brown, and so on)—brought about by the inexorable forces of African nature which first brought true man into existence, and not by naturalistic forces outside of the African continent—although these must also be considered. However long these genetic alterations took to produce each physically altered human type (there is evidence of a Mongoloid characteristic in one or more present-day southern African tribes) and for each type to migrate out of Africa to some other part of the earth, those humans were essentially black-skinned and remained so for many millennia afterward in the areas they eventually settled.

We can fathom the extent of black-skinned humanity around the earth in the statements of historians and scholars who have long written of this reality, although their works and comments are largely overlooked today. In *Why We Behave Like Human Beings,* George A. Dorsey states:

> Open your atlas to a map of the world. Look at the Indian Ocean: on the west, Africa; on the north, the three great southern peninsulas of Asia; on the east, a chain of great islands terminating in Australia. Wherever that Indian Ocean touches land, it finds dark-skinned people . . . . (44-45)

In a work entitled *India,* H.G. Rawlinson notes that German anthropologist Baron E. von Eickstedt—

> . . . considers the oldest stratum, going back to an early post-glacial period [in India] to have been a dark-skinned group *akin to the early Negroid stocks of Africa and Melanesia. These Indo-Negrids once covered the whole peninsula . . .* (*my emphasis* 9)

In *The Arabs*, Bertram Thomas states:

> The original inhabitants of Arabia . . . were not the familiar Arabs of our own time, but a very much darker people. *A protonegroid belt of mankind stretched across the ancient world from Africa to Malaya.* (*my emphasis*, 339)

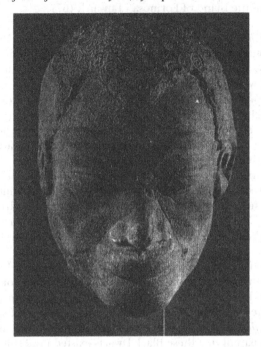

Fig. 1A. A negroid head or mask from ancient Sicily. Curled hair, wide nose and thick lips denote an individual of African phenotype that would be classified as a "Mediterranean" type or "dark white" by Eurocentric anthropologists.

Fig. 1B. Depiction of a Willendorf Venus Statuette with kinked hair and large breasts. Statuettes of this type were first unearthed in Austria in the latter part of the 19th century and subsequently unearthed in other areas of Europe and Asia usually 4"-6" high.

The remnants of the black-skinned Australoids, who once overspread much of the earth, whose remaining representatives today are most clearly seen among the people known as the *Aborigines* in Australia, are believed (after a fairly recent find) to have occupied the continent of Australia for at least 62,000 years, entering the continent by the now submerged Sahul Shelf, or else island-hopping in rafts and other watercraft among the stretch of Indonesian islands that lead to it. New Guinea, Tasmania, New Zealand, the islands of Melanesia and others further east into the Pacific Ocean were settled by the same race of people, although Eurocentric scholars have developed theories that some of these peoples belong to different races—even the Caucasian race.

There is also evidence of a predominant Australoid presence in Europe, which remained evident into modern times. In *The Racial History of Man*, anthropologist Roland B. Dixon notes that the Angles, whom most have classed as *Germanic* along with Saxons, "have an unexpectedly large element of the Proto-Australoid type . . . prominent in Mecklenburg [northern Germany] in Neolithic times" (67). So there is the probability that the Australoid or Proto-Australoid human type once overspread most of Asia *and* Europe.

The earliest inhabitants of the Philippines were the short, black-skinned Negrito type who may, as well, have been of Australoid stock. China and southern Japan also show evidence of a Negrito strain. J.A. Rogers, in *Sex and Race, vol. I*, quotes French anthropologist H. Imbert, who states:

> The Negroid races peopled at some time all the south of India, Indo-China, and China . . .
> Skulls of these Negroes have been found in the island of Formosa [Taiwan]. (67)

Further, Imbert notes that a classic text, the *Tcheu-Li*, composed during the Tcheu [Chou] Dynasty (1122-249 B.C.), "gives a description of the inhabitants with black and oily skin" (op. cit.). The reader should note that here we are speaking of a Chinese text that was composed two to three thousand years ago discussing a China we have been led to believe was always populated by "yellow" people.

Obviously, there were "other" Chinese people, probably people who were the remnants of an original black-skinned Chinese type that mutated into a lighter-skinned type, or else intermixed with an albino element in a *White Forest* area (see Chapter 2) in central or northeastern Asia from which the present Chinese type evolved—although very dark-skinned Chinese were still in evidence in southern areas of China even at the opening of the 20th century. In an article entitled, "African Presence in Early China" (*African Presence in Early Asia*, Editor, Ivan Van Sertima), James Brunson notes that numerous Neolithic Negroid skeletal remains have been unearthed at sites south of the Yangtze River in the provinces of Szechwan, Kwangsi, Kwangtung, Shensi, Yunnan and others. Brunson cites Carrington C. Goodrich (*A Short History of the Chinese People*) who notes that, "Negritos whom the Chinese call 'Black Dwarfs' are reported in the mountainous districts south of the Yangtze," and that they occupied this region as late as the Chin Dynasty (Brunson 121).

We are still some distance away from Europe and the Vikings, but it is necessary to travel the prehistoric world so that when we arrive at our intended destination and central subject it will be easier for us to visualize black-skinned people in northern Europe. In fact, we will find "Black Dwarfs" in Scandinavia, as well. They are mentioned in the *Prose Edda* and the Icelandic sagas, often possessing magic and special abilities. And while they are often relegated to *mythological* beings in Scandinavia, Germany, the British Isles and other areas of the world, it will become apparent that these Black Dwarfs existed (and still exist) in the diminutive peoples—our earliest Homo sapiens ancestors—who migrated out of Africa in remotest times and spread around the earth, their presence constituting a *true myth* or actuality.

For the present, the reader should understand that for untold millennia black-skinned people exclusively predominated in that "protonegroid belt of mankind"—the wide band of land and sea between 40% N. Latitude and 40% S. Latitude around the earth. Eventually, taller physical types of men and women developed in Africa over more millennia, with different sub-divisions, hair textures, complexional variations, head shapes and bone densities. These too, for whatever reason, would find it necessary to migrate out of Africa in waves over more millennia, populating that 6,000 mile wide band of land and sea around the earth, encroaching upon longer settled Negritos (or Australoids) and forcing them to more remote regions of the planet. Since these taller types of men out of Africa were essentially black-skinned (black to brown to reddish-toned, etc), it should not be surprising that black-skinned people were the earliest inhabitants of Europe.

Cro Magnon man is promoted as the first modern human in Europe arriving, according to most, roughly 30-35,000 years ago. It is widely proclaimed that he was Caucasian or white-skinned by a vast body of anthropologists who laud his larger brain, pronounced chin, straighter forehead and artistic abilities. He is said to have succeeded *Neanderthal man*, a pre-human type in Europe and Asia believed to have "died out" shortly after *true man* or Homo sapiens spread to those continents. Neanderthal man, more than likely the same pre-human type as *Homo erectus*, is thought to have migrated into Europe and Asia beginning about 300,000 to 250,000 years ago. If so, he would have arrived around the onset of the Wurm glaciation which would have prevented him from occupying the more northerly regions of those continents, although some anthropologists opine that pockets of Neanderthals survived in glaciated areas.

Neanderthals are believed to have still been occupying most of Europe and Asia when modern man migrated into these areas, but soon afterwards their populations began to diminish rapidly. Modern man had superior tool and weapon-making abilities, could hunt more efficiently, had better-organized tribes and societies. The prevailing theory is that modern man impinged on Neanderthal man's food supplies and game hunting, driving them out of areas they had long occupied as more moderns poured into their territories. Others believe that there was open warfare and that modern man's superior weapons—spears that could be launched with accuracy, more advanced hand-axes, better communication and fighting tactics—eventually decimated Neanderthal populations everywhere.

Over the last century, the unearthing of both human and pre-human bones has made it abundantly clear that Africa was the cauldron of man's origin and physical maturation. There is no reason to believe that any human type to emerge out of Africa was other than black-skinned—including Neanderthal man who, along with Cro Magnon man, is characterized as white by most Western historians. If Neanderthals originated in Africa, they must have originally been black-skinned, although they may have been more hirsute than modern humans. They would have endured nearly the whole of the Wurm glacial, which would have been long enough to have contributed to the loss of their originally black skin although, as I will discuss later, climate might not have been the sole contributor to their loss of pigmentation. A recent article alleges that "at least some of these extinct hominoids [i.e., Neanderthals] *could have had fair skin and red hair*" ("Primitive Makeover," *New York Daily News*, 26 Oct. 2007, *my emphasis*), and briefly reports: "Researchers studying the DNA of Neanderthals found a mutation in two individuals that can affect skin and hair pigmentation . . . reported in yesterday's online issue of the journal *Science.*"

While 20th century researchers (as well as films, documentaries and commercials) discussing Neanderthals promote the belief that Neanderthals were white-skinned, this minor article, stating that Neanderthals "*could have had fair skin and red hair,*" is a tacit admission that they were *not* originally so.

Scholars and anthropologists continue to speculate about the reason for the disappearance of Neanderthals as well as whether modern humans ever mated with them.

I will not spend more time here on pre-human hominids but will return to the question of possible interbreeding between modern humans and Neanderthals in the next chapter.

Another type of modern man is mentioned as being the first Homo sapiens to enter Europe, preceding Cro Magnon man. A number of anthropologists assert that *Grimaldi man* was the first modern human to trod European soil, like author Legrand Clegg II, who asserts that *Grimaldis* "were black people who probably invaded Europe as early as 40,000 B.C. and thereby became the first *human beings* to occupy this continent" ("The First Invaders," *African Presence in Early Europe*, Editor, Ivan Van Sertima, 23). Grimaldis entered Europe at the end of the Early Paleolithic period, according to sources, as glacial ice had receded to the southern edge of the North Sea but still covered most of Britain, the North Sea itself, and all of Scandinavia, extending eastward into northwest Russia.

Two complete Grimaldi skeletons at a Grimaldi cave near Menton, in the southeast corner of France near the Italian border, place the Negroid Grimaldis in Europe at least 40,000 years ago. Pre-human Neanderthals would still have been present and would be for at least another 5,000 years or so when Cro Magnon man appeared about 35,000 years ago. So it would seem that all three types of sapiens were contemporary. For the Eurocentric historian, it is paramount that the presence of a white race be established as early as possible, so Cro Magnon man—whose skeletal remains were unearthed in southwest France in 1868—continues to be touted as being Caucasoid, or white. The two *complete* Grimaldi skeletons, unearthed in southeast France in 1901 and immediately classified as Negroid were, and continue to be, ignored by the Eurocentric scientific community. The Grimaldi relics, as of this writing, are estimated to be at least 40,000 years old, 5,000 years older than the Cro Magnon remains, but it is probable that they are both the same type and that claims of Cro Magnon man's supposed whiteness are spurious.

In *Men Out of Asia*, Harold S. Gladwin, speaking of the dispersal of Negroid strains in Asia and the Pacific islands, quotes Sir Arthur Keith ("New Discoveries Relating to the Antiquity of Man") as stating:

"We meet with the same 'negroid' features amongst members of the Cromagnon race . . . the deepest and oldest burials in the Aurignacian strata of the Grimaldi cave . . . ." (Gladwin 26), revealing that Cro Magnon man is not universally accepted as belonging to the Caucasian race, even by some white scholars. And if we know that modern man emerged out of Africa and spread, in his blackness, around the earth, the following commentary from Cheikh Anta Diop, author of *Civilization or Barbarism*, is instructive:

> The Grimaldi Negroids have left their numerous traces all over Europe and Asia, from the Iberian Peninsula to Lake Baykal in Siberia, passing through France, Austria, the Crimea, and . . . *there is no other variety of Homo sapiens that precedes the Grimaldi Negroid in Europe or in Asia.* (*my emphasis,* 15)

Diop asserts that the first white person or Caucasian appeared somewhere around 20,000 years ago in Cro Magnon man and that Cro Magnon "is probably the result of a *mutation* from the Grimaldi Negroid due to an existence of 20,000 years in the cold climate of Europe at the end of the last glaciation" (*my emphasis* 16).

There is also the possibility that Cro Magnon man and Grimaldi man are the representatives of only a single type of human and that their classification as separate types is due to scientific misinterpretation. When Cro Magnon remains were unearthed in 1868, the vast majority of Europeans were white, and European scientists assumed that the bones could be of no other type. When the two complete Grimaldi skeletons were unearthed in 1901 the field of anthropology was more advanced and craniological examination would have left no doubt that the skulls and perhaps limb measurements were Negroid. But racist thought in the scientific world was firmly set by then, and the majority of European scientists touted Cro Magnon man as the first human to enter Europe into the 20th century—a belief which is still prevalent.

Other scientists and scholars have found too many similarities between the two to consider them to have been separate types, and Diop makes this clear when he states that there were "intermediate types between the Negroid [Grimaldi] and the Europoid [Cro Magnon], without any occurrence of interbreeding . . . [and] the osteology of the very first Cro-Magnons is Negroid, which seems normal" (49, 51). In clearer words, the bone structure and density of even the earliest unearthed Cro Magnons is Negroid or African, and natural variations occur in this single African type, which have been misidentified as Caucasoid. Therefore, the first modern humans to enter Europe (and other areas in the world) were Grimaldi Negroids at least 40,000 years ago—a date, I am certain, that will be pushed back considerably some time in the future.

If the reader has not heard of Grimaldi man before, it is only because the vast body of Eurocentric historians has opted not to mention him in their works on prehistoric Europe, preferring instead to uphold Cro Magnon man and his presumed whiteness. But long before Diop, African-American historian J.A. Rogers asserted that Grimaldi Negroid relics "may be found from Italy to Russia and as far north as Scandinavia" (*Sex and Race, vol. I,* 31). And long before J.A. Rogers, in a work published in the same year Grimaldi man was unearthed (1901), G. Sergi states:

> The types of Cro-Magnon, L'Homme-Mort, and other French and Belgian localities, bear witness to the presence of an African stock in the same region in which we find the dolmens and other megalithic monuments . . . . (*The Mediterranean Race, 70*)

It is likely that Grimaldi man had not yet been unearthed when Sergi's *The Mediterranean Race* was published in 1901, but the above quote indicates that G. Sergi was at least one European scholar who had noted the Negroid characteristics of Cro Magnon man and connected this African type with the erecting of megalithic (huge stone) structures. Besides North Africa, these structures are found throughout most of western Europe, from the Iberian Peninsula (i.e., Spain and Portugal) to Scandinavia and will be discussed in a later chapter.

It was the Grimaldis who brought with them well-made flint instruments, the bow and arrow, improved spears and spear-points and art, characterized by wall paintings and statuettes. These appeared in what has been termed the Aurignacian age, which began about 35,000 years ago (according to present assignments of particular "ages" or "periods" of man) around the onset of the Later Paleolithic period. Among the most notable art artifacts were statuettes of Negroid females of carved limestone. The first of these relics was unearthed in present-day southern Austria in 1909 and was designated *Venus of Willendorf* after the town near which it was discovered. This earliest find stood 4 ½ inches, with large breasts, steatopygia (excessive fat on the buttocks) and what many scholars have called "pepper-corn" hair. Scholars at the time likened it to the women of the Hottentot tribe in south Africa. Since the initial discovery, statuettes of these Venuses have been found at Grimaldi sites all over Europe and Asia. Most scholars consider the oldest of these to be the very first human sculptures.

Grimaldi cave art during the same period depicts the types of fauna the Grimaldi hunted—reindeer, bear, mammoth, horses—often engraved on stones that could fit in the palm of a hand. Art, implements, hunting weapons, sewing and jewelry-making continued to evolve toward the end of the Later Paleolithic period and, by 20,000 BC, had expanded throughout the most habitable areas of the earth. Legrand Clegg II says it is possible that Grimaldi artists "created virtually every known form of prehistoric art including decorative costume pieces (such as bracelets, necklaces, buttons, rings and headbands), decorated tools, amulets and . . . ritual objects" (*Invaders* 25), and remarks that their revered Venuses are found "as far away as the center of Southern Siberia" (op. cit.).

And Diop states unequivocally: "Negroids survived everywhere in Europe until the Neolithic period [i.e., c. 12,000 years ago]: Spain, Portugal, Belgium, the Balkans, etc." (54).

It is believed that by 20,000 BPE (before the present era) several races of mankind had evolved or were evolving—Caucasoids and intermediate types between Grimaldis and Caucasoids—with Grimaldi Negroids (or Cro Magnon Negroids, if you like) still numerous in Europe. By this time the Wurm glacial ice sheet had nearly receded so that Grimaldi Negroids could trek into southern Scandinavia and other areas of northern Europe and Asia. The British Isles were detached from continental Europe, and the landbridges that had for many millennia joined Europe and Africa were now submerged. The twin lakes once separated by the Italian peninsula became the Mediterranean Sea we know, stretching from the Iberian Peninsula to the Levant.

Almost no European historians mention the undeniable presence of Blacks or Grimaldi Negroids (who were of the Australoid type) in Europe, crediting Grimaldi arts, crafts and societal achievements to the ostensibly white-skinned Cro Magnon man. We should realize by now that virtually all the inhabitants of Europe to the onset of the Paleolithic period were African or Grimaldi Negroids who supposedly "vanish" in Europe by about 12,000 BPE. By then, many had differentiated into other types or "races" who occupied general territorial areas. Natural forces like environment or mutation had produced varying complexions and other physical alterations in humans occupying these areas and, having altered over millennia, interbreeding between physically altered groups produced still other types who multiplied in the areas they found themselves inhabiting.

Pygmy-like Grimaldis had altered over many millennia and, having spread over most of the earth, did not "vanish" everywhere. Some anthropologists call them *Negritos*, among the earliest inhabitants of the Philippines, Malaysia, Indonesia southern Asia and islands stretching into the Pacific. Other groups who have been likened to Grimaldis or Negritos are the Arctic Twa or Lapps of the northern areas of Scandinavia and the *Picts* (whom we will hear more about later), who are mentioned in the early history of the British Isles, most notably in Scotland. The *Australoid* type had spread from eastern Europe into southern Asia and Australia looking, we must assume, as black-skinned and wooly-haired as the so-called Aborigines whom 19th century English and Irishmen found occupying Australia. Whether through interbreeding with some unknown type or natural mutation, it is fairly certain that *Mongolians* developed out of Australoids as did the Chinese. Diop contends the first Homo sapiens in China evolved c. 17,000 BPE and that the present Chinese type developed c. 6,000 BPE (53). The reader has already been presented with evidence that the early Chinese were very dark-skinned, if not black, and the reader has already been offered evidence that some portion of the Chinese had "black and oily skin" (Rogers 67) just over 2,000 years ago.

In volume 1 of *Anacalypsis* the eminent Godfrey Higgins makes a case for a black nation in Asia, citing Sir William Jones, who claims that "a great nation of Blacks formerly possessed the domain of Asia" (52). Higgins states that these people were the *Cushites* described in Genesis and that the story of this empire has never been told.

Higgins then speaks of two Ethiopias in ancient history, one branch in southern Egypt (present-day Ethiopia), the other in Arabia (Felix) or, more likely, India. He notes that Herodotus and Eusebius place one branch of this ancient nation in India and that the religion of Buddha is very ancient. Of Buddha, Higgins states:

> In the most ancient temples scattered throughout Asia, where his worship is yet continued,
> he is found *black as jet*, with the flat face, thick lips, and curly hair of the Negro. (52)

According to Higgins, the religion of Buddha was dominant throughout the ancient and far-reaching territory of Ethiopia from Egypt or Ethiopia to the Indus, including the areas of present-day Arabia, Syria, Jordan, Iraq, Iran, Afghanistan, Pakistan, India and, perhaps, the western fringe of China. Sidon, at the eastern end of the Mediterranean in present-day Lebanon, was the ancient capital of this great black nation known as Ethiopia and, Higgins informs us, "the figures [of the God Buddha] in the caves in India and in the temples of Egypt, are absolutely the same" (57)—that is, black-skinned, thick-lipped, flat-faced, with crisp, curly hair.

We have looked at human origins in Africa and traced man's earliest movements out of that continent into Europe and Asia. This writer's belief is that Grimaldi man and Cro Magnon man were the same—Negroids, African Blacks—who entered Europe at least 40,000 years BPE (but probably much earlier) to become the first human beings, or Homo sapiens, to inhabit that continent. It is only Eurocentric historians' focus on Cro Magnon man, whom they have long asserted was Caucasoid, that keeps the matter of Europe's original inhabitants unsettled. But if Cro Magnon man was black-skinned and Negroid like Grimaldi man and not Caucasoid or white, the obvious next question to grapple with is where did white people come from?

Unless Caucasians arrived on earth from another planet (which a number of occult works actually allege), or are the descendants of Neanderthal man, then they must have evolved out of black-skinned Grimaldis or another type of earthly Homo sapiens. If—as most anthropologists who have grappled with the question allege—the earliest human beings were Grimaldis, out of which other types of humans evolved, then Caucasians likely developed through *albinism*, or albino-ism—which seems most logical.

In *The Isis Papers*, Dr. Frances Cress Welsing mentions an interview in the Winter 1976 issue of <u>Black Books Bulletin</u> in which Cheikh Anta Diop states: "There is absolutely no doubt the white race which appeared . . . during the upper Paleolithic . . . was the product of a process of depigmentation" (Welsing 25). This modern-day assessment mirrors what the esteemed 19th century philosopher, Arthur Schopenhauer, stated a century and a half ago:

> The white color of skin is not natural to man . . . and thus there is no such thing as a
> white race . . . but every white man is a faded or bleached one. (op. cit.)

Western scholars and scientists never seem to discuss the matter of Caucasian origins, content to have us believe—because Whites predominate in Europe today—that all inhabitants of Europe have always been Caucasian—Neanderthals and Cro Magnon man included. Diop contends that the Caucasoid race appeared 33,000 years BPE—referring to its initial branching off from Grimaldi man, or when a period of depigmentation took place—although there is no actual consensus regarding Caucasian development. Diop estimates that by 20,000 BPE Caucasoids developed to the point of producing exclusively Caucasoid or white offspring absent the racial characteristics of their Grimaldi Negroid ancestors, classifying this new type of human Cro Magnon (*Civilization or Barbarism* 53).

Dr. Frances Cress Welsing, noted scholar and geneticist, opines, in *The Isis Papers*, that Grimaldi albinos were cast out of Grimaldi settlements and relegated to areas separate from the black masses and that this alienation was responsible for the "destructive and aggressive behavioral patterns . . . by white people towards all non-white peoples" (18). She explains what she calls a "reaction formation" as a "response that converts (at the psychological level) something desired and envied but wholly unattainable, into something discredited and despised" (5). Since alienated albinos or Whites were unable to attain the skin color that they coveted, they (psychologically) "claimed that skin color was disgusting to them, and began attributing negative qualities to color—especially to blackness" (op. cit.).

When this ethos developed—whether it occurred during the early stages of mass albinism, or later, after several thousands of Grimaldi albinos saw themselves as a distinct group dominating a large territory—cannot be ascertained with accuracy. What does seem certain is that by the early Neolithic age man had differentiated into several racial types, which included Caucasoids, and the great Grimaldi culture was in decline, losing cohesion or simply intermingled with newer types of mankind in territories they had long dominated. However, in no way did Grimaldis, or Australoids, simply vanish.

The murkiest period of human development are the millennia between 12,000 BPE and the rise of the first civilizations anterior to our present time, when the earliest agricultural societies arose c. 6,000 to 4,000 BPE in the Nile valley in northeast Africa.

Mesopotamian agricultural societies may have been developing at the same time along the Euphrates and Tigris rivers in ancient Sumer—present-day Iraq—as well as along the Indus, the eastern portion of the great Ethiopian Empire that Higgins made a case for a century and three-quarters ago. These above time periods are in accordance with dates most often asserted by Eurocentric historians, but it is possible agricultural societies are older than the generally accepted 8,000 years—especially when one considers the antiquity of Egypt (by which I mean the entire northeast quadrant of Africa—Egypt, Cush, Ethiopia, Punt and Nubia). Higgins asserts that what I will henceforth refer to as *Greater Ethiopia* extended from Egypt to India, its inhabitants—"Cushitic Negroes"—sharing a similar culture, religion and language. Higgins is not precise in regard to the time period Greater Ethiopia flourished, but it surely would have been from c. 7,000 to 4,000 years ago, a millennium or less before the world's cradle of advanced civilizations began to be plagued by racially different invaders and foreign ideas. But perhaps Greater Ethiopia endured to a later date. However, we can derive a sense of Higgins' Ethiopian Empire from several more contemporary works.

In *Stolen Legacy*, George G.M. James mentions that Greek historian Diodorus, and Egyptian High Priest Manetho relate a tale about two columns found at Nysa, Arabia. One was a column commemorating the goddess Isis, the other commemorating the god Osiris. On Osiris' column, states James:

> . . . the God declared that he had led an army into India, to the sources of the Danube, and as far as the ocean [unidentified, but probably referring to the Black Sea]. This means of course, that the Egyptian Empire, at a very early date, included not only the islands of the Aegean sea and Ionia, but also extended to the extremities of the East. (11)

James is not precise in regard to time, but the cult of Osiris is extremely remote in Egyptian antiquity, far older than the First Dynasty. What follows is a statement, which has not been seriously considered by Eurocentric historians. In *Signs and Symbols of Primordial Man*, Albert Churchward offers this riveting assertion:

The Osirian religion is at least 20 thousand years old, and may be 50 thousand for aught any Egyptologist knows to the contrary. This has been proved by the recent discoveries at Abydos, showing that the Osirian doctrines existed there in all their glory and perfection more than 15 thousand years ago, and before this the Egyptians had the doctrine of Atum . . . . (302)

And to give further credence to the god Osiris' column in Nysa, Arabia, commemorating the extent of Osiris' exploits, outlined by George G.M. James above, historian Charles S. Finch III, M.D., in *The Star of Deep Beginnings*, tells us that—

It can be said that what is known as the Near East is more properly thought of as Africa's "Northeast Extension," because geologically and geographically that is in fact what it is. It was the main corridor of human migration out of Africa into the rest of the world beginning 100,000 years ago and it makes sense to find that the earliest definable Near Eastern Neolithic populations . . . are indisputably Africoid . . . . [We] are looking culturally at a "province" of Neolithic Africa. (14)

Speaking of the "yogic tradition" that the world today understands as the "Light of the East"—which Eurocentric scholars have always insisted had its origin in India—author Ra Un Nefer Amen, in *Metu Neter, vol. 1*, informs the reader that yoga and the yogic tradition, "in reality . . . is a modification of the Light taken by the Blacks from Nubia into the Tigris, and Indus Valley in prehistoric times" (44). Nefer Amen states that yogic principles as well as Buddhism have an African origin and did not originate in India. As well, the black-skinned populaces of Nubia (Egypt, Ethiopia), Arabia, Sumer and India were essentially the same type of people, whether one refers to them as Nubians, Cushites, Ethiopians or *Dravidians* (i.e., the ancient blacks of India).

Only four or five decades ago it was a common practice for European and American historians and anthropologists to state that Egyptians, Ethiopians, Indians (of India) and Australian Aborigines were members of the Caucasian family despite the black or dark complexions most have always been known to possess. The practice continues to this day and is so patently absurd I will not waste time mounting a detailed refutation. What the reader has read so far should be refutation enough. However, the reader might want to consider the following: In which of these *Caucasian* populaces did white Europeans recognize their kinship with the above-mentioned peoples? In which of these *Caucasian* populaces did white Europeans not indiscriminately kill the inhabitants during the era of colonialism, when even relatively minor disputes arose? In which of these *Caucasian* populaces did European Whites, recognizing their Caucasian kinship with these populaces, not undermine the social, religious or cultural stability of their respective countries or attempt to subjugate them wholly? In which of these territories occupied by *Caucasians* did white Europeans not attach demeaning names to the populaces—*brutes, savages, beasts, niggers, apes, beasties, coolies, burrheads,* and others long forgotten—in all their respective countries?

For Eurocentric historians, draping a cloak of whiteness over the above peoples enhanced their efforts to inject whiteness into the earliest, most dynamic civilizations. Their written works have intentionally promoted white superiority and the false notion that Caucasians were involved in the building of ancient architectural wonders and that white-skinned people authored all works of art found sprinkled in archaic ruin throughout the territories these *Caucasian* people inhabited. They could claim that Caucasians were the builders of the Great Pyramid and the other Wonders of the World, claim that Caucasians charted the constellations, built the intricately designed buildings and temples of India, sailed the seas into the Pacific, peopling them and promoting civilization. More importantly, they could enhance their presence on earth as civilizers and innovators when, in truth, European Whites attained civilization relatively recently, in historical terms, *and only after contact with the black-skinned world*—more of which will be discussed in later chapters.

These comments are not meant to demean, insult, vilify, or diminish in any way what people referred to as Caucasians or Whites have accomplished since their ascension to world dominance. The beginnings of this ascension, however, can be narrowed to a general historical time frame, with all the elements of civilization already present and extant from Iberia (i.e., Spain) to India—the most advanced centers found in Egypt, Sumer and the Indus Valley, or Greater Ethiopia. The ascension of Europe roughly six centuries ago would eventually engender a European or Eurocentric recounting of world history and a diminution of the participation of black-skinned people in it—anciently or otherwise. In their writings, Eurocentric or Western historians have disconnected the relationships of the ancient world, for instance, separating Greater Ethiopia into Egyptian, Sumerian and Indus Valley, or Indian, civilization, setting them at odds with each other—culturally, chronologically, architecturally, racially, religiously, linguistically—so that we cannot fathom their ancient interrelationship. And it was only *after* invading areas of this more ancient world that Caucasian or white civilization began to develop.

In regard to this ancient black-skinned world, some scholars even make a case for a single, original language spoken by ancient man. If such a universal language existed, it is logical it would have to have been extant in that vast "protonegroid belt of mankind that stretched across the ancient world" or, perhaps, in Greater Ethiopia. A number of historians, including Godfrey Higgins and Sir William Jones, have remarked upon an early universal language, and author John Phillip Cohane presents a detailed study in *The Key*, offering striking similarities between words in many present languages which point to a single origin. Cohane notes that despite corruptions the same words may be deciphered in the names of mountains, lakes, volcanoes, towns, rivers, islands, regions and waterfalls around the earth, showing that—

> . . . sufficient evidence . . . indicate[s] a strong likelihood that in ancient times, before the Phoenicians, the Carthaginians, the Egyptians, the Greeks, and the Romans, certain key names and words were taken out in all directions from the Mediterranean, in some instances by water . . . and these same names and words can still be found . . . . (18)

Cohane points out that <u>don</u> is a name indicating water or a river, and cites *The Concise Oxford Dictionary of English Place-Names*, which states:

> Don is an old river-name, Brit [British] <u>Dana</u>, which is related to the name Danube and is really an old word for "water", found in Sanskr [Sanskrit] danu, "rain, moisture." (45)

Cohane cites the frequency of <u>Don</u> in rivers in the British Isles, Eastern Europe, Russia (the Russian Don, Dneister, Dnieper, Dan), and India (Dhan, Dhon, Dhansiri). There are many other examples he presents, too numerous to spend more time on, like Jor<u>dan</u> or <u>Dan</u>aus of Greek mythology (who will be mentioned in a later chapter). Cohane also states, "In Scandinavian and Teutonic mythology—<u>Donar</u> was the forerunner name for the <u>Great</u> <u>Thor</u> (hence our words 'thunder' and 'Thursday')" (46), explains how the word <u>Dan</u> is related to the Danaid legend; how Dan happens to be the father of the god Odin; and that a still current rendering of the country Denmark is <u>Dan</u>mark (255), a point he does not elaborate but which the reader might keep in mind for later.

It is not precisely known how long man has traveled by sea, but by land and sea black-skinned men and women journeyed to the British Isles, Belgium, France, Denmark, Russia, India, China, Indonesia and the rest of the world in remote times, which the reticence of Eurocentric scholars is unable to completely obscure. I have mentioned Egypt often in this chapter, and Egypt will be mentioned a number of times more as we proceed because it has figured more prominently in world affairs than Eurocentric scholars have revealed. It was the gateway to the world, sending colonies out everywhere in remote antiquity long after Grimaldi man had initially populated the earth. Egyptians closer to our own epoch probably overspread Europe, and we will see that their occupation of this continent included the British Isles and Scandinavia. And despite Eurocenric historians' efforts over the centuries to whiten the ancient Egyptians, they were black-skinned people who, under various names, brought civilization to Europe, dominated it for millennia and had a continued presence there into our present historical age. We will come to understand that such people, including those who became known as Northmen and Vikings, were described as black-skinned as late as a millennium ago, a fact that *cannot be unknown* to European scholars who have read the Norse sagas and other writings concerning these so-called "black heathen" who dominated Europe for centuries after the complexions of most Europeans had whitened.

Asiatic peoples also ventured into Europe, many of them *black-skinned* Asians, mingling their blood with the Africoid men inhabiting the continent. So, whether Norsemen resembled the archetypal Negroids of Africa that we are familiar with or the straight-haired, smaller-nostriled, shorter Indian or Mongolian, is left to the reader to surmise. However, it is reasonable to presume that a blending of such people would produce men and women of varying physiognomies—heights, hair-textures, body types—with predominantly black or dark skin. A degree in DNA science is not necessary to understand this.

Evidence that the Vikings were predominantly black-skinned peoples is not abundant, but there is enough extant to make a case as well as demonstrate that Eurocentric historians who have spoon-fed us history have deliberately misrepresented facts and lied outright in their historical works, especially regarding black-skinned people in Europe. My primary motivation for beginning research on the Vikings two decades ago was to fathom why Christopher Columbus is credited with the discovery of America even though most people know or have heard that the Vikings or Norsemen sailed to areas of North America five-hundred years earlier. When I began this investigation, I had no idea that Vikings, or Norsemen, had been other than the blond, blue-eyed, bearded Whites history books and films had long contended they were.

This work, using primarily English-language sources, is the fruit of that early research which, I trust, will provide the reader with enough evidence that Norsemen—specifically those of the Viking Age (c.800-1100 AD)—were black- and dark-skinned, which is more than likely the primary reason they have not been credited with America's discovery. My intent is also to show that a number of other dark- or black-skinned peoples occupied Europe and to offer a more realistic picture of Europe than, perhaps, ever has been presented.

But our journey has only just begun; we still have a ways to go before we begin looking at the Vikings. Before arriving in Scandinavia, we will look at ancient European peoples and invaders into Europe that some historians (historians who took the time to discuss race) assert were black or dark-skinned. We will revisit ancient Greece, ancient Rome and Britain and discuss peoples who occupied western Europe before or at the time of Rome's rise, like the Etruscans and Phoenicians. Much of what is said in ensuing chapters may be new to the average reader, even unbelievable. If, however, the reader has appreciated the citations of reputable scholars in this first chapter, understand that further assertions will be equally supported.

In this first chapter, we have seen that the earliest humans who departed Africa and spread around most of the world—including those who entered Europe—were essentially black-skinned, and remained so for untold millennia. Now, I think it is time we consider a subject Eurocentric scholars never to get around to discussing: How did *white people* evolve?

CHAPTER 2

THE GREAT WHITE FOREST

As far as is commonly known, there are no written records of the period between 12,000 BC, when Grimaldis supposedly vanish, and 6000 BC, after agricultural societies had sprung up along the great rivers which saw the emergence of the earliest civilizations—the Nile, Tigris, Euphrates and Indus. The millennia between 12,000 and 6000 BC seem to be the haziest period for scholars and scientists to accurately decipher, although a number of Western historians have commented on this period with seeming assuredness. By this time humans had differentiated into three basic races—Negroids or Australoids, dispersing Grimaldis in Europe and southern Asia;.a Mongoloid race or type in central Asia, related to Australoids; and a Caucasoid, or white, type in Eurasia, a territory north of the Caucasus Range, between the Black and Caspian Seas, comprising what is today the southern portion of Russia. The boundaries of this territory might have extended northward to the vicinity of Moscow, eastward to the Ural River, and westward to the Desna River in the vicinity of Kiev. Let us consider these boundaries the primary region of Caucasoid evolution. There may have been several smaller "White Forest" areas, but the area whose boundaries are outlined above will henceforth be referred to as the Great White Forest in this work.

There is often disagreement among scholars as to the age of this or that monument, the race of this or that people, the year this or that Egyptian Dynasty began, and even those we consider experts in any particular discipline are often not in accord—even when considering the same artifacts or information. Many of those who discuss Grimaldi man (or Cro Magnon Negroids) at *all* state that this earliest human "vanished" after 12,000 BC. But he—beginning his migrations out of Africa at least 100,000 years ago—was the first true human being anywhere; so it would seem logical that all other human beings anywhere on earth had to come from him. Therefore, how could he have vanished as a physical entity while mankind still survived?

He did not vanish. His culture, which once spread around the earth, perhaps became outdated and did not allow him to dominate the areas he once had. Later types of man, evolving out of Grimaldi man, along with later migrants from Africa, modified and improved upon the older culture, superimposing a newer culture in the same areas that Grimaldi man had once dominated. Humans would continue to evolve, bifurcating into new types of man—initially, perhaps, in Africa, but also in the areas they had settled in outside of the Mother Continent and, like Grimaldi man before him, spread around most of the earth. Humans were still black-skinned but over many millennia would differentiate into still other types in the areas of the earth they eventually populated. And for long millennia all humans remained black- and brown-skinned.

Somehow, white-skinned humans evolved, and most Westrrn scholars and scientists attribute their emergence to dark-skinned people spending many millennia in the cold, northern regions of Asia and Eurasia. These regions, the analyses contend, offered less direct sunlight in near-Arctic weather conditions during a time when Wurm glacial ice still blanketed the northern regions of the planet. To survive the climate, dark-skinned humans lost their ability to produce melanin—the pigment in the body responsible for dark complexions, hair and eye color—which prevents the body from absorbing the sun's UV rays. This adaptation, the analyses contend—the whiter skin, lighter hair and eyes—allows the body to absorb nutritional benefits from diminished direct sunlight, and this genetic adaptation is what most Western scientists contend produced—over untold millennia—the people we refer to as Caucasians.

However, this long-asserted scenario may be partially true, but is not be the only explanation for the emergence of Caucasoids. There is no universal agreement as to when humans lost the ability to produce melanin, but living in a cold, sunless climate is not the only prerequisite for the genetic disorder called *albinism* or albino-ism to take place. The theory of this writer (and others who will be mentioned) is that a significant outbreak of albinism took place in humans in some long ago epoch leading to the emergence of the so-called Caucasian race. A cold, sun-starved climate was not necessary for this to occur, and what will be outlined below seems far more reasonable than the commonly accepted explanation—which, in all honesty, is nothing more than an oft-repeated theory.

Why this mass albinism began is not precisely known, and may not necessarily have begun in frigid northern climes. Albinism could have begun—and indeed occurs—in *warmer* climes, and Charles S. Finch, in "The Evolution of the Caucasoid" (*African Presence in Early Europe*), makes it clear that albinism "is a well-documented disorder in Africa in which the body is unable to produce melanin, leaving the skin and hair a stark white to whitish-yellow color . . . [the] irises of the eyes . . . [a] gray blue" (20).

It has long been conjectured that the ancient Libyans were a light- or near-white-skinned people strongly opposed to the rule of Egypt immediately to the east of their territory. In Egyptian hieroglyphic wall paintings, Libyans are often depicted as white-skinned and have been described as a "Semitized-Negroid" people, as states James Brunson in "The African Presence in the Ancient Mediterranean Isles and Mainland Greece" (*African Presence in Early Europe*), who notes that "[s]ome of the earliest settlers of Crete are recognized as Libyans of North Africa" (36). Cheikh Anta Diop, in *The African Origin of Civilization*, alludes to the whiteness of Libyans, citing 18th century historian Cornelius de Pauw, who states that in the delta regions surrounding the future Alexandria, "Egypt was almost saturated with foreign white colonies," Arabs, Libyans, Babylonians and Jews (5).

That the delta region of Egypt became heavily populated by light-skinned or white peoples is well established; but Caucasian penetration and colonization of northern Egypt—and the spill-over of Caucasians into Libya—was a much later historical development in Egyptian history, occurring after invasions of supposedly Caucasian peoples from the Near East and from Greece who intermixed with or drove away the indigenous black-skinned inhabitants who had always lived there. Eurocentric Western historians have exploited this presence of Caucasians in northern Egypt and Libya to imply that Caucasians were indigenous to North Africa. Western historians have taken every opportunity to declare a population or civilization *white* or Caucasian, even if the civilization or population was black—a point that will be expanded upon later.

If Libyans were white or near-white, it is probable that this was the result of a significant *albino* population and that Libya was a White Forest area in North Africa. Chancellor Williams, in *The Destruction of Black Civilization*, assures us: "Libya was once so nearly all black that to be called a Libyan *meant* Black" (*my emphasis*, 118). How or when Libyans were transformed into a white race is not certain and may be merely an overblown conjecture of Eurocentric writers. For instance, in *A Book of the Beginnings, vol. 1*, Gerald Massey explains that the Egyptian word *Tamahu*, a term designating Libyans in the ancient Egyptian language, literally means "'Created white' people" (27), lending credence to the probability that ancient Libyans were *albinoids*—more than likely originally black-skinned people of Egyptian origin but rejected and cast out of Egyptian (Ethiopian or Kushitic) society because of their unseemly complexions. Diop, for instance, cites Herodotus who states that to the Egyptians "the Libyans remained on the lowest rung of civilization" (*African Origin* . . . 68).

The aforementioned regarding the whiteness of the ancient Libyans does not necessarily connect them with the Caucasoids of Eurasia; it is presented to demonstrate that a mass depigmentation or albinization of people need not be brought about by a cold, sun-starved environment, as most theories regarding the evolution of Caucasoids suggest. North Africa offered abundant heat and sunlight, yet somehow albinism was triggered in a black-skinned population there as well as in Eurasia where the emergence of Caucasoid peoples is generally thought to have occurred.

Something disrupted or interfered with ancient man's genes to the point where one in every two or three babies born was albino, a shock to early humans who had seen no other complexion than black or dark-brown. This disorder, this contagion, must have continued for several centuries, perhaps a millennium or two, with albinos being separated, kept far away from the societies of the *normals* to somehow limit its spread. Albinos might have been killed, or else were taken or driven far away, left to fend for themselves, without the accouterments of village life—a sturdy hut, a warm fire, tribal protection, the love of family and relatives. Ancient black peoples may have had a name for the distant, uncultivated, lonely expanse of territory (or territories, since there were probably several smaller ones) they were banishing infected members to, but that name is unknown. But the largest of these territories where albinos from Asia, the Near East and Europe were taken to and abandoned—that expanse of territory north of the Caucasus mountain range between the Black and Caspian Seas—is the area that most scholars believe Caucasians or white people, emanated from: the Great White Forest.

The reader may consider what follows speculation, but it is no more or less speculative than other theories on man's origins and divergence into differing types or races. While Western scholars have liberally opined on man's origins and divergence, they have been reticent on the origin of white people (except for the abovementioned, commonly accepted *cold climate* theory)—even though most have grudgingly come to accept that man's origin was Africa, the Mother Continent. Although Eurocentric historians offer long-winded assertions about racial origins and races emanating from such and such a racial group, they have not detailed the origin of Caucasoids. They present Caucasoids as if they were always here—eternal denizens of Europe or Eurasia, eventually invading this or that territory to produce such and such a people (who then became, ostensibly, Caucasian). No explanation required as to *specific* Caucasian origins.

In view of this omission, what is presented below is tempered by an honest desire to account for the development and expansion of white-skinned people, taking into consideration human longings, maternal instinct and survival imperatives that our specie has exhibited throughout our existence. The reader is asked to take a few long, deep breaths, relax and allow his or her mind to drift back in time.

*   *   *   *   *

Considering what was outlined above, almost nothing would have been more distressing to ancient black humans than to produce children with colorless complexions, blond or whitish hair and light-colored eyes. Such children would have been extrtemely abnormal, considered diseased, cursed, and the children, and possibly their parents, would have been quarantined or banished to limit the spread of the contagion. If, say, one of every two or three children born to parents were afflicted with this disorder, albinism would have soon become so prevalent that afflicted children (and perhaps their parents) would have been banished, taken hundreds of miles away to remote areas and deposited in them during seasonal hunting expeditions or migrations.

It is difficult to imagine mothers voluntarily abandoning their children, whatever their condition, so it is reasonable to assume that many black Grimaldi, Australoid or Mongoloid mothers accompanied their albino children to these areas and stayed with them—at least until they were older and able to fend for themselves. The mothers, themselves, may have been banished along with their albino children (and, perhaps, their normal *black*-skinned offspring) to White Forest areas where they would live out the remainder of their lives. It is not unreasonable to assume that some husbands accompanied their wives and children to these territories where the number of albinos would become numerous after many centuries or a millennium or two of intermarrying with other albinos to produce albino children when the number of individuals with similarly defective genes increased.

Along with the indignity of banishment, a sense of alienation developed in these albinoids because of the rejection they felt over their expulsion from the company of the tribe or society. Dr. Frances Cress Welsing, in *The Isis Papers,* lists a number of attendant manifestations of alienation developing, such as "child abuse, psychosis, suicide, neurotic depression, delinquency, psychosomatic disorders, prejudice . . ." (20-21). Over the centuries, a hatred toward Blacks developed because albinoids, or Whites, could not redeem the black coloring they had lost and return to the societies that rejected them. So, they began to despise all people of color. According to Dr. Welsing:

> The destructive and aggressive behavioral patterns displayed throughout the world by white peoples towards all non-white peoples is evidence of the inner hate, hostility and rejection they feel towards themselves and of the deep self-alienation that has evolved from their genetic inadequacy. (18)

Welsing states that this is why "Black males' testicles were the body parts that white males attacked in most lynchings: the testicles store powerful color-producing genetic material" (7).

The process that Welsing calls *reaction conversion* was the psychological mechanism that transferred the Whites' self-hatred into hatred for Blacks. This must be the reason why white scholars have done everything possible to diminish or ignore the evidence that true man evolved in Africa and established the earliest civilizations; they would rather give Asia the credit because we have been conditioned into believing that Asians were generally much lighted-skinned than Africans, and there is more evidence of Whites (in ancient times) mingling their blood with Asians in Asian territories than with Blacks in Africa. Western historians, generally, have even asserted that ancient Asian peoples—Hyksos, Babylonians, Sumerians, and others—*were* Caucasians, Aryans, Whites, merely because Whites intermingled with the predominantly black populations in these territories.

Diop and a few other historians theorize that the Chinese were produced from a mixing of early Caucasoids and Asiatic Blacks, although I have yet to hear of any historian calling the Chinese Caucasians. While black-skinned Asians (Asia's earliest inhabitants) may have absorbed Caucasian blood, Whites—true Whites—behaved with savage, negative aggression in Asia as well as Africa when they became powerful enough to seriously encroach on territories within those continents. In sum, as stated by Welsing:

> The white personality, in the presence of color, can be stabilized only by keeping Blacks and other non-whites in obviously inferior positions. The situation of mass proximity to Blacks is intolerable to whites because Blacks are inherently more than equal . . . Always, in the presence of color, whites will feel genetically inferior. (9)

However the people we know as Caucasians or Whites evolved, their numbers were burgeoning during the Late Neolithic in the Great White Forest area, from eastern Poland into southern Russia north of the Caucasus range. Their eastern limit was probably the Ural Mountains, and on the western and eastern fringes of this territory, Whites must have eventually had some contact with the towns and trade routes of their black-skinned and now-distant relatives, acquiring better tools, weapons, clothing and other implements from them which improved the lives of a relatively small number.

The great masses of them lived in desperate privation in rude hovels or cavesites where squalor and disease abounded. Around 10,000 BC northern Europe and Asia saw the retreat of Wurm glacial ice, and swampy expanses stretched from modern-day Poland into Russia. And while most scholars agree that Neanderthals had completely "died out" by 35,000 years ago, it is probable that many of these pre-Grimaldi humans still lingered in Eurasia (perhaps, after 250,000 years, having lost their original dark pigmentation) and that Grimaldi albinoids, driven into the Great White Forest, intermingled extensively with remaining Neanderthals, "since," opines Michael Bradley in *The Iceman Inheritance,* "the Neanderthals very recently occupied the part of the world which is the cradle of the Caucasoid race, and the most extreme Neanderthals occupied the part of Europe which has produced the most extreme manifestations of Caucasoid aggression" (67).

Bradley places most of his Caucasoid "cradle" in western Europe, present-day France and Germany, which does not negate the existence of several relatively small White Forest areas, in addition to the Great White Forest of Eurasia, a subject that will be revisited later in this work. Satisfied that Cro Magnons were Caucasoids, western scholars are completely silent as to how they developed, their most regurgitated explanation being the long millennia they spent in the colder climate of Europe and the need to absorb more vitamin-D because of reduced sunlight or less intense UV-rays, which sunlight provides.

In the face of evidence and DNA research that all human beings had an African origin, modern scholars who do speculate on the development of Caucasoids out of black-skinned people seem to infer that the primary difference between Blacks and Caucasians is the loss of melanin in the Caucasian and, according to some, the Caucasian's higher intelligence. But there are physical differences that need to be considered, indications that Caucasoids are not merely depigmented Blacks with superficial differences in hair texture, eye color and nostril width. There are differences in skull shape and in physiognomy, Caucasians possessing more pronounced chins, less prominent cheekbones and brow-ridges. Their frontal lobes (foreheads) are generally higher, and Caucasian males are more thickly built with generally thicker waistlines, larger calves, ankles and wrists than Blacks and other non-white peoples. They are generally more hirsute, with longer body hair, hair often covering the arms, backs, buttocks, chests and legs of males. The reader would not have to consult a scientific text to find that these observations are accurate.

Neanderthal man was reputedly large-limbed, hirsute and extremely aggressive, and while scholars have long asserted that Neanderthals and humans never interbred, that humans advancing into Europe killed them off, recent evidence has emerged to contradict this long-held belief. In an article published in *USA Today* ("Neanderthals and humans interbred, fossils indicate," 7 May 2010), author Dan Vergano reports that new DNA fossil analysis reveals that "people of European and Asian descent inherited a small amount, an average of 1% to 4% of their genes, from the extinct species." Samples from the bones of three Neanderthals who lived 38,000 to 45,000 years ago were compared with the genetic background of five living humans from different parts of the world, and the report was published in the journal *Science* (not consulted for this work). The *Science* report revealed that Neanderthals and Africans last shared an ancestor 500,000 years ago but that Neanderthals were still present in Europe and the Near East as late as 30,000 years ago. So, it is quite probable that Africans migrating into the Near East, Asia and Europe beginning 100,000 years ago encountered remaining Neanderthals—who were not markedly different from Homo sapiens.

In a *National Geographic* article entitled "Last of the Neanderthals," by Stephen S. Hall (Oct. 2008), the author quotes Ed Green, head of biomathematics in a Leipzig study group, who states: "We know that the human and chimpanzee [gene] sequences are 98.7% the same, and Neanderthals are much closer to us than chimps . . . [S]o the reality is that for most of the sequence, there's no difference between Neanderthals and [modern] (sic) humans." The size of the Neanderthal brain matched our own, so the demise of this specie of human may have come about for relatively insignificant reasons, like modern man's ability to effectively adapt to new or changing situations and, according to Kate Wong, in a *Scientific American* article entitled "Twilight of the Neanderthals" (Aug. 2009), diet. Wong notes that studies estimating the metabolic rates of Neanderthals conclude that they required "significantly more calories to survive" than modern humans did. Although humans were essentially hunter-gathers, they adapted to the changing circumstances of their environments and were able to incorporate plants and grains into their diet and "outcompeted Neanderthals simply by virtue of being more fuel-efficient: using less energy for baseline functions meant that moderns could devote more energy to reproducing and ensuring the survival of their young" (Wong).

The last known Neanderthals, according to evidence so far uncovered, lived in seaside caves at the southern tip of Gibraltar (southern Iberia) 28,000 years ago, long after Grimaldi man had entered and occupied Europe. However this writer is certain that evidence of their continued existence in Eurasia and elsewhere until at least as late and later than 28,000 years ago, will emerge, as well as evidence of a higher percentage of intermingling between Neanderthals and humans.

My humble suggestion is that the albinoid outcasts of ancient black-skinned humans—Grimaldis, Australoids or later types—were driven away or banished to White Forest regions where bands of Neanderthals were still present. Early contact might have been contentious affairs—Neanderthals fighting to hold onto their diminishing territories; rejected albinoids trying to secure territories for themselves because they could not return to their black-skinned tribes and societies. Neanderthals may have been aggressive enough in their dwindling numbers to rout some albinoid groups from some areas, perhaps kidnapping a number of them, especially females, in fierce skirmishes throughout White Forest areas. It is unlikely albinoid males would have found Neanderthal women attractive and wholesome enough to mate with; Neanderthals would not have paid a lot of attention to hygiene and cleanliness, and the stench of their abodes would have been extremely offensive to those albinoids who may have remembered the more civilized life of their tribes and villages and who, in fact, had brought the higher civilization of their tribes along with them in their exodus. But captured albinoid women could not have avoided their fate, and it is more likely the earliest interbreeding between the two groups would have taken place between Neanderthal men and albinoid women. However, men being the way they are, it is not unlikely that albinoid men impregnated Neanderthal women as well. It remains to be discovered how widespread interbreeding was between the two groups, but they will likely be found to have interbred more extensively than current data has so far revealed.

In *The Iceman Inheritance,* author Michael Bradley (writing before DNA technology was developed), referring to Caucasians as *Neanderthal-Caucasoids,* suggests that humans and Neanderthals mated far more extensively than is generally thought. And he unremorsefully decries Caucasian aggression, stating:

> It seems reasonable to suppose that we Caucasoids are an identifiable group because of the "primitive" and "bestial" physical characteristics we inherited through Neanderthal genetic input . . . If the Neanderthals were originally somewhat "closer to the apes" as a relatively primitive hominoid, it might be justifiable to speculate that our Caucasoid aggression may mirror the apes' lower frustration tolerance. (105, 106)

While Bradley does not discuss man's African origins, seeming to infer a European origin for Caucasians, the reader has been presented with sufficient evidence demonstrating that Africa was the cauldron out of which modern man emerged. Agreeing with Bradley that humans interbred far more extensively with Neanderthals than is currently believed, I suggest (along with others mentioned above) that rejected and banished albinoids, interbreeding with still existing Neanderthals—primarily in the Great White Forest, but in smaller White Forest areas in Europe and Asia as well—evolved into the people we call Caucasians.

Albinoid Grimaldis would have had a more advanced language than Neanderthals, sewing and tool-making skills, more efficient weapon-making skills and implements. Neanderthals would have been more familiar with the terrain, better adapted to a colder climate, knew the seasonal migrations of the various animals they hunted for food and clothing. Although it might have taken a hundred generations and numerous forest skirmishes, a coalescencing of the two groups, considering an increase in albinoid-Neanderthal types through interbreeding, would have been beneficial to both. Tribes would form, and interbreeding would have produced albinoid-Neanderthal offspring whose women were more pleasing to the eyes of albinoid males, making interbreeding more commonplace, while purer Neanderthal types continued to die off. However, Neanderthal genes and traits had been passed down to this emerging Caucasoid race whose development continued at a slower pace in White Forest areas because contact with their now distant black-skinned ancestors and relatives was essentially severed. While their existence was not unknown to ever-expanding Grimaldi, Africoid or Egyptian peoples continuing their migrations to various parts of the earth, there was no concern for their rejected progeny, and civilization, in that Proto-Negroid belt of mankind from Spain to India and beyond, would continue to advance without them.

Moving forward to about 12,000 years ago, Eurocentric scholars make a case for a Caucasian presence in Europe by designating the population of southern Europe—from Spain to the Balkans—*Brunet people, Iberians, Mediterraneans* or *dark whites,* or as Wells refers to them in *The Outline of History, vol. 1,* "the Mediterranean or Iberian division of the Caucasian race" (111). However, in his very next sentence, Wells states: *"It is very hard to define its southward boundaries from the Negro"* (*my emphasis,* op. cit.). Not to single out Wells (for his *The Outline of History* seems to have been honestly intended), but his attempt to establish a white presence in the southern half of Europe is typical of Eurocentric historians who discuss ancient Europeans. They insert a Caucasian race in Europe, finding *whiteness* in people living in a wide expanse of territory whom they refer to by nomenclatures inferring *blackness*—Brunet people, and the oxymoronic "dark whites." Brunet, of course, implies brown or black, as any decent dictionary will reveal; Mediterranean and Iberian are geographic terms, but are applied to the same people. Wells, at least, intimated, or insinuated, that these southern Europeans were Negroid, or extremely close to "the Negro" in appearance. But by insisting these southern Europeans were Caucasian, and through repetition in serious publications over two or more centuries, Eurocentric scholars placed Caucasians in southern and western Europe far earlier than they arrived and—along with their claims that Cro Magnon man was Caucasian—established Europe as an exclusively white continent that Blacks had never inhabited.

Most high school and college history texts begin ancient history with an overview of the "Pre-Hellenic" world: a chapter about ancient Egypt; a chapter about Sumer or Mesopotamia, with an insinuation that the populations of these areas were not black-skinned or Negroid but Asian, and Caucasian, thereby "whitening" both the people and their achievements. They never say that the ancient *Egyptians* were black; they insinuate an Asian connection and dissociate Egypt from "black Africa" to the south, thereby disconnecting Egypt from the African continent in many readers' minds. Then follow a couple of chapters espousing Greek architecture, philosophy, art, mythology; profiles of Socrates, Aristotle and Plato; culminating in the conquests of Alexander the Great, laying a cloak of whiteness over Greece, Egypt, and the whole area of the Greater Ethiopia discussed in the first chapter. And the accompanying map depicting Alexander's empire at its greatest extent leaves the impression in the reader's mind that *all* the inhabitants living within this vast territory were Caucasian!

A fuller examination of the evidence (*not* offered in school or college texts) clearly demonstrates that the Greeks did not bring civilization to the world, not even the Western world, and raises serious questions as to their supposed whiteness. Regarding the early Greeks, Wells informs us: "These Hellenic tribes [Greeks] conquered and largely destroyed the Aegean civilization that *preceded* their arrival; upon its ashes they built up a civilization of their own" (230). The Aegean civilization Wells refers to were composed of the essentially black- and dark-skinned people Eurocentric historians styled Iberians, Mediterraneans, Brunets and dark whites—nomenclatures intended to disguise the fact that black- and dark-skinned Africoid peoples were predominant in Europe *as well as* Greece at the onset of the historical era (i.e., 2000 BC). So, an older, highly civilized people or peoples were supplanted by what Wells says were "barbaric Greek herdsmen raiders" who overran the area, a point we will revisit in more detail further on. For now, the reader should understand that a highly advanced civilization (or civilizations) had flourished in Greece, on many of its islands, and in Crete long before Hellenes—barbaric, Caucasian Greeks—flooded the area. Wells further informs us:

> Shipping and agriculture, walled cities and writing were already there. The Greeks did not grow a civilization of their own; they wrecked one, and put another together upon and out of the ruins . . . At first they lived in open villages outside the ruins of the cities they had destroyed, but there stood the model for them, a continual suggestion. (232)

The contention of this work is that Africoid peoples, many of them Egyptian, made up the preponderant population in Europe, especially western and southern Europe. These populations had inhabited Europe for millennia before invading Caucasoids, pouring out of the Great White Forest in Eurasia, laid low their civilizations, just as barbaric Greeks largely destroyed the Aegean civilization flourishing around the eastern Mediterranean and Aegean Seas, beginning c. 1500 BC or a little before.

There are a few more foothills to climb before heading north to Scandinavia and the Vikings, but when we arrive there, the reader will have been provided with enough evidence of black-skinned people in Europe to understand their presence in the northern reaches of the continent, which Eurocentric historians have always asserted was the domain of blond, blue-eyed Caucasian populations. If the reader understands that the first modern human beings anywhere originated in and migrated out of Africa, that they were black-skinned and moved into Europe over the Iberian and Italian landbridges (quite obvious migration routes that Eurocentric historians and DNA researchers are reluctant to discuss), it should not be a shock that the earliest populations of Italy, Spain, Austria, Britain, France and the Balkans were black-skinned and Africoid.

Also never mentioned is that Alexander's empire lasted barely a dozen years, or that black-skinned Indians chased his army out of India and into Afghanistan where dark-skinned Afghanis sent it reeling back to the west; that his army in the Hindu Kush region was nearly destroyed by cold and frostbite that killed many of his troops, and that Alexander died in Babylon, not making it back to Greece alive. The only part of Alexander's empire to endure for a time was in Egypt where the Ptolomys would rule for three centuries (from 332 to 30 BC) building the city of Alexandria as their capital.

Greece is touted as the first *Western* civilization, but was at one time lauded as the first *ever* civilization—or so it seemed from the way it was presented in history books of the first half of the 20th century. But even then more honest historians were emerging, and a fuller examination of the evidence clearly demonstrates that the Greeks did not bring civilization to the world—not even the Western world.

Our understanding of the prehistoric and historic populations of Europe, the belief that these populations were white-skinned, are based largely on the fact that Whites dominate the continent today. The popular, more accessible historical works insist that Whites have occupied Europe from Paleolithic times to the present. All the more recent historical peoples of Europe—Gauls, Celts, Goths, Britons, Slavs, Etruscans, Iberians, Lombards, Danes, and such—were white by implication, and very little, if anything, is mentioned regarding the probability that some of the abovementioned peoples—perhaps all—were black-skinned, or non-Caucasian. So when we look at a historical atlas of Europe with these peoples and others splashed across the European landscape, we assume that all of them were Caucasian, Aryan or white based on what most historical works have left us to imply. These histories are strengthened by attendant scientific claims that Blacks or dark-skinned people could not have flourished in the colder climate of Europe, especially northern regions.

In *Ancient and Modern Britons,* however, a work published in 1884, David MacRitchie informs us that the *Picts,* who inhabited areas of Britain and Scotland when the Romans invaded what would become England, were *blackamoors.* The Picts are often referred to as the *Painted People* in many histories, designated so by the Romans because they supposedly tattooed their entire bodies or, more commonly heard, "painted themselves blue." But the general assumption is that the Picts were a Caucasian people, which even more modern histories have made no effort to correct. MacRitchie and a handful of other historians wrote of the Picts being *blackamoors* (black-skinned men) as far back as the early 19th century, yet a modern work, like *The Picts and the Scots,* by Lloyd and Jenny Laing, a work published in 1998, makes no mention of race, leaving the reader to assume, as Eurocentric writers have habitually hoped we would, that the people being discussed were Caucasian since, of course, Europe has always been inhabited by Caucasians. But neither assumption is true, and at the beginning of Chapter 7 of his work, MacRitchie poses the question: "Could they [black Picts] have been related to the *Scandinavians,* as some aver?" (*my emphasis* 110). He goes on to cite a Mr. Keightley, who states that the Picts were "akin to the Scandinavians," and a Mr. Martin, who states:

> It is generally acknowledged that the Picts were originally *Germans,* and particularly from that part of it bordering upon the Baltic Sea. (*my emphasis,* op. cit.)

In the Picts, we are speaking about a people who occupied the northern half of Britain's main island long prior to the Roman invasion, which commenced in 43 AD. How long they had lived there is unknown, but there is no mention of any people occupying northern Britain prior to the Picts. And if, as abovementioned, they were known as Germans and crossed to Britain from northern Germany, it would seem that Germany (i.e., the *territory* that would become known as Germany) was home to the bulk of these black-skinned people, who were—or were related to—Scandinavians, which also raises questions regarding the *Germans* the Romans fought against when they invaded the area of the Rhine c. 133 BC.

There were other tribes and peoples in the British Isles who are described as black or dark-skinned by a handful of historians and scholars who, like MacRitchie, published books and articles which defied the 19th century trend of ignoring the presence of Blacks in Europe. Their views must have been extremely unpopular, a time when the enslavement of Africans by Europeans and Americans was several centuries old and popular historical and scientific works were claiming that Blacks (i.e., Negroes, sub-Saharan Africans, African-Americans) were inferior to Whites. The belief that Negroids were intrinsically inferior to Whites would expand to all peoples of color—East Indians, Chinese, Melanesians, Australians, people of color anywhere—in the European mind as European countries, having grown militarily and economically powerful, continued to pursue policies of colonialism and imperialism within territories of black- and dark-skinned peoples around the world.

The mass of humanity we have come to know as Caucasians developed in White Forest areas—perhaps in two areas in both western Europe and Asia, and in the Great White Forest of Eurasia, described above. The initially albinoid human rejects shunted into these areas probably mingled more extensively with declining Neanderthal populations still inhabiting them than current data suggest. Michael Bradley (*The Iceman Inheritance,* Pub. 1978) wrote of such interbreeding (between Neanderthals and Caucasians, not homo sapien *albinoids*) during a time when the scientific world considered such mating biologically impossible—more than a decade before DNA science was developed. Bradley contends that certain Neanderthal traits were passed on to Caucasoids, the most significant being "the characteristic or capacity we call 'aggression,'" going on to state:

> I find it difficult to believe that any objective observer, or even a subjective one, viewing the world's history, can deny that there *is* this difference [i.e., aggressive behavior] between Caucasoids and other kinds of men. (61)

Both Michael Bradley and Dr. Frances Cress Welsing (*The Isis Papers*) detail the psychological causes of the aggressive nature of Caucasians, Welsing more particularly in Caucasian behavior towards Blacks and peoples of color—which will be made more clearly obvious further on. For now, let us understand that several millennia of interbreeding between albinoids and Neanderthals ("normal," or black-skinned humans may also have entered the mix) eventually brought about the evolution of the Caucasian race, that Diop believes emerged 20,000 years ago.

To the south and west of the Great White Forest, the civilization of n*ormals*—black Africoid civilization—was expanding, its most dynamic aspects spreading outward from the northeast quadrant of Africa. Caucasoids, confined to the Great White Forest and smaller White Forest areas, languished in a deprived, barbaric state bereft of anything that could be called civilization. Even 5,000 to 6,000 years ago, there is no evidence to show that the general condition of Caucasoids had changed. But some areas of the

Great White Forest's outer fringes would begin to come into tenuous contact with civilized people, as the expanding Proto-negroid belt of humanity spread and their populations increased.

Venturing beyond their own overcrowded confines, Great White Forest inhabitants skulked near enough to glimpse passing caravans of better dressed, confident, laughing black-skinned people journeying to unknown destinations. These people would have seemed almost god-like in their flowing, colored raiment, driving flocks of sheep, goats, cows and cattle, flanked by shepherds keeping the animals in order. Great White Forest tribes eyed them from safe distances, hunger pangs stabbing their guts whenever they thought about sinking their teeth into a freshly-killed lamb, while they fought the impulse to charge into the procession and make off with one or two animals and escaping back into the hills from where they watched, and slicing into the flesh of the beast with their crude stone implements.

They knew their crude stone hand-axes could bash the skulls and bodies of the animals' owners, but they knew the black men in the caravan had dangerous weaponry, long, thin spikes with sharp, penetrating tips that could be hurled long distances, penetrate their bodies, leave them writhing in agony, unable to pull them out without more pain, or even death. The fleet footed strangers would run them down and pierce them with short, black spikes, sharper than any substance they knew. They had witnessed the deaths of bolder tribe members who had grabbed a small animal and tried to flee with it and did not want to suffer the same fate. So most of the time they watched the dark strangers in awe until they passed out of view, wondering where they were going and when the next procession would pass by.

They envied the strangers, sometimes imitating the strutting gaits of the black men they had seen when they returned to their village, to the amusement of tribe members. But mostly, they seethed with anger. Gradually, they approached closer to the strange processions, waved at the people in it who sometimes waved back, but more often ran threateningly at them, chasing them back into the hills where they lived. But sometimes, driven by hunger and their sorry state, they approached the haughty black-skinned strangers and begged, by sign and gesture, for food, clothing, sometimes weapons—sometimes offering their young daughters or sons to them for something that would make their lives more bearable. Even when the strangers offered to trade a cow or food or weapon for a few young children or animal hides, the white-skinned barbarians fumed when their initial exuberance over the newly acquired possession abated. Then a feeling of hatred for the strangers would consume them back in their lairs, even as they enjoyed the notoriety their daring contact with the passing black strangers brought them back in their villages.

When night fell, the faces of the daughters or sons they had traded for food or their new possessions drifted starkly into their minds. They remembered the looks of utter bewilderment in their children's eyes as they were led away by the strangers—the way they kept looking back, believing their fathers would gesture for them to come back and that the strangers would simply release them. Then, in the dark of their lairs, men would scream out in the night, hating themselves, hating what they had done—but hating the black-skinned strangers even more for agreeing to such a bargain. But they had more children to feed and, besides the few furs and trinkets they could manage to part with, they had nothing more valuable to trade than their older children, whom they knew would be living in improved circumstances despite any hardships they might have to endure. Maybe one day they would come back.

Hatred toward the black-skinned strangers persisted, even though the next year or the year after that they would approach another caravan and trade more furs and trinkets, or more children, receiving in return a few goats or sheep, a cow, a few wondrous weapons tipped by what the black strangers called *metal*, or implements to stitch together furs for more durable garments. Slowly, very slowly, their wretched condition improved, less of them died of hunger and disease, and their birthrate improved because black fe—male strangers had told their women about cleanliness and isolation from the group, and given them herbs to ease childbirth—most waving off any trade-goods in return, even though these were offered.

Even so, they could not shake a general feeling of anger toward these black-skinned people, believing in their souls that the possessions of these Blacks were somehow owed to them, should be given without recompense because the Blacks had so much. Great White Forest dwellers were unable to rid their minds of the unexplained abhorrence and anger they held toward the black strangers. *"One day,"* they thought, often telling other men in their tribe or group what they felt. *"One day . . ."* This feeling of ill will gradually spread throughout the Great White Forest as, over the centuries, Great White Forest tribes moved about and mingled with other tribes. Eventually as news of the black strangers and their incredible towns far to the south spread throughout most of the Great White Forest—reported by tribe members who had followed a caravan to its destination at a safe distance, or by a few traded children who eventually returned as adults—a burning question gnawed at the minds of the more aggressive denizens: Why can't *we* have all the things the black strangers have?

CHAPTER 3

THE ICEMAN RETURNS

Eurocentric scholars and scientists have long made a case for a Caucasian presence in post Wurm glacial Europe, designating ancient northern Caucasians *Nordics,* while referring to the ancient populations of southern Europe, from Spain to the Balkans as <u>Brunet people</u>—equally referred to as <u>dark whites,</u> <u>Iberians</u> and <u>Mediterraneans</u>—or, as H.G. Wells calls them in *The Outline of History, vol. 1,* "the Mediterranean or Iberian division of the Caucasian race" (111). However, in his very next sentence, Wells states: "It is very hard to define its southward boundaries from the Negro" (op. cit.). I believe that Wells made an honest attempt to present a truthful rendering of history and do not mean to single him out, *per se,* when I say that his attempt to establish a white presence in the southern half of Europe is typical of Eurocentric historians and scientists who discuss ancient peoples in the continent.

They carve out a Caucasian race in Europe, drawing whiteness out of people they call Mediterranean, Iberian or, most incongruously, *dark whites,* living in a wide expanse of territory which surely must have been populated by black-skinned, Africoid peoples from remote times who were still present 10,000 to 12,000 years ago. Brunet, of course, implies brown or black, as any decent dictionary will reveal. And <u>dark whites</u>? Interesting_wordplay. But through repetition in serious publications over two centuries or more, white scholars placed Caucasians in southern and western Europe far earlier than they seem to have actually arrived.

Readers have long been obliged to accede to Eurocentric assertions, since there has long been a dearth of serious non-Caucasian scholars who possessed the monetary resiliency to travel to various locales, effectively investigate artifacts, assess their findings, or have their views widely published by reputable publishers to countervail assertions presented to us as unassailable. However, a fairly recent find two decades ago, in the same general area that the first Venus of Willendorf statuette was discovered, has seemingly unhinged the Eurocentric scientific brotherhood. It was a startling find, quite unexpected, confounding, beguiling in the manner of its untoward appearance—suddenly shaking the foundations of Eurocentric historiography and science.

In September, 1991, a German couple, Helmut and Erica Simon, stumbled upon a body frozen in the ice while hiking in the Austrian Alps. The couple were skirting the Italian border at 10,000 feet up the mountain, and it would later be determined that they, and the body they had chanced upon, were actually in Italy, a mere hundred yards from the Austrian border. They notified the police, believing the body to be that of a hiker who had only recently succumbed to the cold and snow at that altitude. A wooden axe with a metal blade was still clutched in one of the corpse's hands, and other possessions of this man were later found around his body which, again, looked like a recent casualty of severe weather. A *Washington Post* article, "Bronze Age Corpse Found in Glacier," (27 Sep. 1991), stated that the man had lived 4,000 years ago, but further tests would reveal that the find was much older.

A flint knife, a bead, a leather pouch, an unfinished bow and a leather quiver containing 14 arrows were also found in remarkably good condition. Presented on PBS Channel 13 (in New York City) in the fall of 1992, the *Nova* documentary "Iceman" chronicled the unearthing and preliminary examinations of "the most important discovery in modern archeology." The skin of the corpse was still tautly stretched over the full skeleton of the man, skin that one examiner described as "brown and leathery . . . like a mummy." To this writer, the face and skull certainly appear to be Africoid—like that of a modern Ethiopian. According to the documentary, subsequent radiation and carbon (C-14) dating put the Iceman's age at 5,300 years, making him a dweller of the Late Neolithic age in Europe.

I had no doubt—looking at the Iceman's facial structure, physique and still dark skin—that the Iceman was African (or Africoid), although I was sure at that time that the "experts" would somehow arrive at some other conclusion in the hope of whitening him. They might question the quality of the film, the quality and reliability of television signals. But the Iceman's skin is dark, a medium-dark, reddish-brown, which leads me to conclude that 5,300 years ago it must have been quite black, although the experts would certainly have something to say about this presumption, as well.

So it is strange that despite the documentary's "brown and leathery" commentary as well as the Iceman's physical appearance, an ensuing publication, *The Man in the Ice,* by Konrad Spindler, would skirt the issue of race. In the fifth chapter Spindler cautions against discussing the Iceman through *methods of classical anthropology!*—stressing that scientifically, the Iceman constitutes only one individual and that there is "no adequate information on the population to which . . . he might belong" (214). Please! Conclusions regarding man's ancestry and racial classifications were drawn by Eurocentric scientists on far less evidence—a piece of a skull, a thigh bone, teeth—than a fully preserved, skin-covered body like the Iceman; yet this scientist cannot even venture to even *suggest* what racial type the Iceman *appears* to be. Instead, Sprindler states:

> *Suitable comparable samples are lacking over extensive areas of his cultural background.* But quite regardless of that lack of data, we should avoid *burdening the Iceman* with the *long outdated and discarded racial labels of the late nineteenth and twentieth century,* which might have assigned him to some Mediterranean, Dinaric or Nordic racial type. (*my emphasis,* 214)

I should add that Spindler is the leader of the scientific team investigating the body and is described as an *expert* in medicine, anthropology and archeology. Yet he needs "comparable samples . . . over *extensive* areas" to determine the Iceman's "cultural background" because racial classifications are no longer in vogue? After three centuries of classifying mankind in racial terms and by racial types, right up to the end of the 20th century, when did racial classifications become outdated? If Spindler were to find the samples and data he claims to need, how might he then classify the Iceman if not by race?

How would human types different from the Iceman be classified if not by race? And would the scientific community then go back and reclassify all human types previously classified by race—which we have come to understand—and bestow them with non-racial nomenclatures, give them cultural or territorial sobriquets, perhaps? Will we have Arabian Man, Kenyan Man, Mammoth-killing Man, Austrian Alps Man, Pottery-making Man, Cold Weather Man, and so forth?

Europeans developed the whole system of classifying the varied types of humanity by race, elevating *themselves* to the highest, most dynamic human type in the process. It is primarily the works of European historians, scientists, anthropologists, archeologists and paleontologists that give us our history of the past, despite the flaws, misrepresentations and lies that have been discerned over the last half century. But we have gotten used to the classifications, seen patterns we could follow and generally rely on, found truths, exposed spurious assumptions, arrived at fresher understandings because the basic concepts of racial classifications became familiar and dependable to us after three centuries of conditioning. We came to believe after centuries of indoctrination that Europe has always been inhabited by Caucasian people, assertions based on bone fragments, skulls, and the lengths of skeletal arm and leg bones. Based on these finds, European scientists declared Cro Magnon man white and the earliest human to enter Europe, even after two *complete* Grimaldi skeletons were unearthed more than a century ago that were declared older than Cro Magnon by a score of other European scientists, who also pointed out definitively Negroid traits in Cro Magnon remains. But the more influential Eurocentric scientists, those I like to refer to as the European Brotherhood of Academia, then and afterwards, continued to ignore Grimaldi finds.

And now cometh the Iceman. Now the lead scientific investigator of the team examining the *complete* body of an immensely ancient Late Neolithic European inhabitant decries classifying the Iceman by race despite his training in classical anthropology (i.e., old-school anthropology) and the fact that Europeans have always done so. Spindler now needs to know the population the Iceman derives from and his cultural background, which Eurocentric scientists never needed to know before. And Spindler doesn't want to "burden" the long deceased Iceman with suddenly discarded racial classifications. When were they discarded? It is quite apparent that they were discarded when the Iceman—in all his obvious Africanness—made his unexpected appearance.

Fig. 2
The Iceman in situ during first recovery attempt, September 20, 1991. Note his still dark skin, indicating that 5,300 years ago this individual was black-skinned.

No. A racial analysis would burden *Spindler* and all Eurocentric scientists and historians who continue to stubbornly reject any notion that black-skinned people once occupied the whole of Europe—particularly its southern regions, which the return of the Iceman strongly establishes. By their own long-established classifications and assertions, the Iceman should at least be assigned to the Mediterranean, Iberian, Brunet or dark white race—obscure terms Eurocentric historians and scientists have used to avoid saying *African* and admitting that black men and women once overspread not only southern Europe, but the whole of it. Now that a complete, fully preserved specimen of a *Mediterranean* is unearthed, an event so far completely unprecedented in the study of mankind, described as "the most important discovery in modern archeology," an "expert" in medicine, archeology and anthropology refuses to classify the Iceman by any of the commonly understood racial categories Eurocentric scholars have employed for at least two centuries which he, trained in classical anthropology, is conversant in. Now, he needs more information to even *suggest* a racial analysis, which he calls antiquated.

The Iceman, perhaps returning to his village (inhabited by people like himself), was caught in a sudden, violent blizzard. As the PBS documentary illustrates through computer technology, he took refuge in a small depression in the rocks of the mountain and was covered up by several feet of snow. How long he survived is unknown, but he was buried by snow, unable to leave the depression or gully. Although the Wurm glacial was long over, glacial icing still occurred on mountain peaks. A capping of glacial ice overspread the mountaintop, growing in thickness to several feet, perhaps a dozen, spreading downward and partially retreating when the weather warmed and reforming in the winter over the millennia—dragging rocks and reshaping the terrain while the Iceman inside the small gully remained in place, untouched by the forces of nature.

In 1990 a powerful sandstorm in the Sahara Desert blew sands northward across the Mediterranean Sea, much of which wafted high into the air and settled on Alpine mountaintops, including the mountaintop which had long concealed the Iceman.

Covered by a coating of sand, the sun's rays made the mountain glacial ice melt faster during the spring and summer of 1991, uncovering the corpse of the Iceman, presumably for the first time in more than five millennia. With the advance and retreat of mountaintop glacial ice year after year, it seems improbable that the corpse would not have been uncovered at least once, or several times, in 5,300 years. Examination would show, however, that the corpse did not suffer erosion by the elements and had not been attacked by birds or other animals, something that, to this writer, betokens the intercession of the Divine in the Iceman's reappearance. This has nothing to do with any established religion. Whatever Force, Universal Truth or Supreme Being that created the vast universe, brought all life on earth and elsewhere into existence, allows our planet and countless other heavenly bodies and suns to continue their eternal revolutions, sidereal interactions and internal atmospheric properties is responsible for the Iceman being uncovered at this time in our history.

Our world has been dominated for the last two millennia by a people who seem—collectively—to have no real love or compassion for the dark-skinned majority of mankind on our planet, people who, having risen from a forlorn, uncivilized, wretched existence, brought destruction, pain and death to the lands of every non-white people they came into contact with, including the lands of the very people who authored civilization and were directly responsible for their *own* rise. Eurocentric historians write the books we read, inserting themselves into ancient civilizations they had no part in shaping, yet they refuse to acknowledge any other presence in Europe but their own—despite considerable evidence to the contrary. The Iceman's return discredits one of their biggest lies.

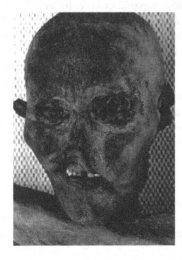

Fig. 3
Face of the Iceman discovered at 10,000 feet on an
Alpine mountain on the Italy-Austria border. Note
still dark skin and Ethiopian facial structure.

The gully the Iceman took shelter in allowed him to remain unscathed by advancing and retreating glacial ice, which would have shredded his corpse into bits, scattering its parts among the soil and rock detritus of the peak. The corpse became mummified, giving the skin its leathery texture, unblemished by the elements, untouched by scavengers and fortuitously stumbled upon by a hiking couple after sands from a Saharan storm settled onto Alpine peaks causing glacial ice to melt faster and more completely than it had in 5,300 years. The Iceman's medium-to-dark-brown skin denotes that he had most likely been black-skinned when he lived—that millennia in the glacial ice lightened it. In the scheme of Universal Truth, the Iceman was *meant* to be revealed at this time in history revealing, to those who ponder such things, that black-skinned people were still inhabiting Europe as recently as 5,000 years ago—which Eurocentric historians never even suggest in their works.

A further note regarding the Iceman is that his penis and testicles were missing, presumably lost when he was initially unearthed because police and rescue-workers, who were not scientists, were unaware of the importance of the find, believing the corpse was that of a hiker who had only recently succumbed to the elements, so well was the corpse preserved. This seems reasonable, however I have a nagging suspicion that some European authority or scientist recovered them; if they were mangled in unearthing, they still should have been nearby. And when the significance of the find was discovered, it seems that an intensive search for them would have been undertaken, even if it would have taken a month. Spindler mentions that a private individual in Munich accused him of having stolen the penis, while others speculated that the Iceman came from a culture "in which castration rites were practiced for religious reasons" (Spindler 174).

Spindler comes across as basically honest in his writing of the discovery and examination of the Iceman, including his discussion regarding the genital puzzle. Perhaps my suspicion is unwarranted, fueled by the knowledge that white men—certainly American white men—have always been fearful of black males because, as Dr. Welsing notes, "[b]lack males' testicles were the body parts that white males attacked in most lynchings . . . [because] the testicles store powerful color-producing genetic material" (7). There is also the jealousy and fear exhibited by white males of black male sexual power—a by-product of white racism—to consider in this regard.

Although Spindler may be technically correct when he states that the Iceman represents *one* individual and that there is no information as to what population he might have belonged to, his reluctance to be more forthright on the race of the Iceman only illustrates the centuries-old unwillingness of white scholars to acknowledge the presence of Blacks in Europe. Eurocentric scholars have generally claimed the Egyptians were Caucasian. If a *white-skinned* mummy, or a comparatively preserved white-skinned corpse was unearthed in Egypt, would the Eurocentric body of scientists exercise such restraint in identifying the corpse as Caucasian? I think not. News of the discovery would dominate the media for weeks, months, and the corpse's unearthing would be proclaimed as proof that the ancient Egyptians were, indeed, Caucasian. One or two dozen scholarly books would be published within a year or two based on the unearthing of *one* individual without regard for "comparable samples." And one hundred earth-excavating cranes would be flown into Egypt and northeastern Africa in an attempt to unearth another such body, a project that would be jointly funded by several European countries—perhaps, along with the United Nations—and continue feverishly for at least a decade.

In the case of the Iceman, experts won't even offer a tentative finding regarding his obvious race and physiognomy, and Spindler needs "comparable samples over extensive areas of his cultural background" before offering even a *suggestion* as to the Iceman's race. Racial classification is suddenly a "long outdated" system of human identification, even though European and American scholars and scientists developed the system, employed it up until the end of the 20th century and, to date, have not presented an alternative system by which to classify or differentiate human types.

Since the initial fanfare surrounding the Iceman's discovery in 1991, not much has been heard about him—nothing, at least, that has filtered down to the general public.

Why the relative silence now? Are Spindler and other Eurocentric scientists expecting to uncover similarly preserved individuals in the Alps? And if two or three such individuals were unearthed, would their blindness regarding the Iceman's race be restored as suddenly as it descended upon them? Probably not. They would concoct some other classification to place the Iceman into and continue to obfuscate the fact that black-skinned people were inhabiting Europe only 5,000 years ago, before Caucasians arrived there in any significant numbers.

Our perception of the prehistoric and historic populations of Europe, the belief that these populations were white-skinned, are based largely on the fact that Whites dominate the continent today—along with the assertions of Eurocentric historians and scientists. All the major peoples and tribes of Europe—Gauls, Saxons, Celts, Britons, Slavs, Etruscans, Iberians, Danes, Lombards, and such—are, therefore, white by implication, and very little, if anything, is mentioned regarding the probability that some of the abovementioned peoples were black-skinned. So, when we look at a historical atlas of Europe with these tribes and others dotting the landscape, we assume that all of them were Caucasian, Aryan or white based on what most historical works have left us to imply. These historical works are strengthened by attendant scientific claims that Blacks or dark-skinned people could not have flourished in the cold climate of Europe, especially the northern regions of the continent. Yet, there is a surprising amount of evidence to the contrary, which we will consider further on.

The Mediterranean basin, from the Pillars of Hercules in the west to the Levant, Palestine, Egypt and the western portion of Asia, was the scene of land and sea migrations of people for commerce, raw materials and living space for at least three millennia before the time of the Iceman, or since about 8,000 BPE. Western scholars rarely discuss this epoch honestly, a time when Egyptians and other African peoples were still migrating out of Africa to other areas of the world. Since ancient Egypt had by far the most advanced civilization in the world even 8,000 years ago (more evidence of which will be presented in a later chapter), common sense should make it obvious to the reader that ancient Egyptian seafarers would have touched down in many areas of the Mediterranean—North Africa, the Balearics, Sardinia, Corsica, Crete, Cyprus, the Greek Isles, Sicily and Italy—in their quest for raw materials and ores that may have been rare or non-existent in their homeland.

Again, Egypt here is meant to designate peoples who generally occupied the northeastern quadrant of Africa—Egyptians, Nubians, Cushites (same as Kushites), and Ethiopians—peoples Eurocentric historians have continually divided by language, supposed racial differences, cultural and religious practices, and insisted were in contention with each other. In remotest times, Ethiopia—extending over a much larger territory than it does today—seems to have been the dominant nation and driving force of migrations and civilization in the area. A racially and culturally alike people once spanned a vast territory stretching from Ethiopia—including present-day Egypt—to India and possibly China, discussed earlier, and I am referring to this racially and culturally akin people when I refer to Egypt, which has become more prominently known than Ethiopia. A people called *Garamantes* were inhabiting North Africa c. 9,000 years ago whose territory extended to the northwestern portions of the continent and south to the Sahara and beyond to which the ancient Libyans and Berbers may have been related to.

While it may be thought of as remarkable (or impossible) that men were making long voyages in the Mediterranean 8,000 or 9,000 years ago, the reader might consider that the last leg of the Aborigine migration through southeast Asia to Australia at least 62,000 years ago was over water. The watercraft the Aborigines used may not have been large ocean or sea-going vessels but demonstrates that in that remote period man had at least begun taking to the water. The melting of Wurm glacial ice 10,000 to 13,000 years ago raised sea-levels significantly. In *Underworld*, author Graham Hancock states, "the rise in sea-level of 120 metres . . . between 17,000 and 7000 years ago is large enough to have engulfed entire cities forever" (59). One hundred-twenty metres is roughly 400 feet, the height of a 40-storey building. Hancock has explored a number of sites now under sea and ocean levels in various parts of the world and spends considerable time discussing a megalithic temple and other undersea megalithic structures around Malta, a small island south of Sicily, which had been adjoined to Sicily when Sicily was adjoined to Italy, forming a long land-bridge which once connected to North Africa (although Hancock does not imply this). Hancock asserts that as Wurm glacial ice melted fully about 10,000 years ago, Atlantic Ocean waters flooded the Mediterranean basin, turning the earlier-mentioned twin lakes into one elongated sea extending to the shores of the Levant.

Whatever cities and structures were once above water were flooded and submerged under 400 feet of sea. Hancock and others suggest this submergence—which probably did not take place all at once, but over a relatively short span of time, like a century or two—was the basis for the myth of Atlantis' sinking beneath the sea and the *Gilgamesh* and Biblical Noah's Flood legends.

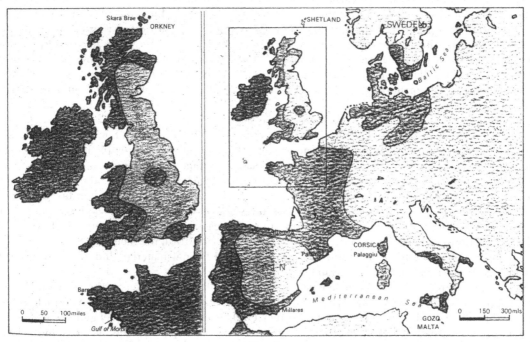

Fig. 4

Extent of megalithic structures in Western Europe. Dark shading indicates oldest megaliths dating to at least 4000 BC. Lighter shaded areas denote megalithic structures dating from about 3500-2500 BC and extended to southern Sweden. Several authors in this work assert that only ancient Egyptians had the ingenuity to cut, transport and erect these huge stones and structures.

My math isn't great, but I believe a rise in sea level to 400 feet in 200 years averages out to an annual two-feet rise in sea level, four feet annually in 100 years. In either case, it constitutes a tremendous rise in sea level (which possibly could have occurred in even less time) over a historically short period of time. The inhabitants of any towns or settlements at the lower levels of the Mediterranean basin would have frantically attempted to block the rapid inundation by erecting sea-walls around their towns, but their efforts would have proved almost fruitless as the water level continued its rapid rise—an inch or more daily over a 100-year span. They would relocate their towns 200 feet higher on the hills, only to face the same misfortune a few decades later, and they would have had to move again. This is assuming the inundation occurred slowly. A significant breach in the Pillars of Hercules barrier which had adjoined Europe and Africa for millennia would have brought about a frightening surge of Atlantic Ocean water into the Mediterranean basin, catching some basin dwellers unawares and drowning many in the sudden inundation. But more than likely the inundation of the Mediterranean basin took place more slowly, over a two or three-century span, allowing most inhabitants time to relocate to higher ground as the sea level continued to rise.

Previously accessible settlements or towns were now more distant—if they had not been entirely erased by inundation. Some survivors would have founded new settlements on newly formed islands, fearful of the still rising waters that had forced them from their former towns—waters that now submerged all but the highest points of land they could once traverse on foot. Settlements that could once be reached in a few days' march over land, or reached in a day or two by boat, had vanished under unpredictable seas. For the early Africoid civilization nestled around the twin lakes of the Mediterranean, the end of the world had come.

The survivors needed to construct larger vessels to obtain the necessities to restart their interrupted civilization—food supplies, lumber, building stones, pottery, linens, domesticated animals, farming implements—and perhaps new trading partners to obtain them from. Familiar trading partners, relatives and allies, had either disappeared or managed to re-establish themselves further inland along the new shorelines of North Africa in the south, southern Europe in the north and west, or on Italy. Far to the east of Italy, the once solid landmass connecting Greece to Asia Minor had been inundated, leaving a string of islands, the largest of which were Crete, Cyprus and Peloponnesus—upon which the city-states of Mycenae, Corinth, Argos and Sparta would emerge many millennia in the future.

Perhaps man's greatest characteristic is his desire to survive, so it is reasonably certain to believe that the disastrous flooding of the Mediterranean basin soon brought about a surge in shipbuilding and sea-travel, countering the unforeseen forces of nature—or the Gods—that threatened the world he knew and meant to preserve. And while Eurocentric scientists and historians ignore mentioning the race of the people who established the earliest settlements, commerce, religions, monuments, maritime exploration, megalithic structures, and other enduring archeological constructions, the evidence points to Africa as the source—with Egypt the primary civilizing engine before and after the Great Deluge.

After the Wurm glacial meltdown ending 10,000 years ago, only 10-15 miles of water separated Africa and Europe at the Pillars of Hercules, now known as the Strait of Gibraltar. Africans on either side of the strait would have had to build watercraft to take them back and forth between the two continents; on the European side, those who had lived there would—as populations expanded, territorial disputes arose, and weaker tribes were compelled to move—have journeyed farther inland, perhaps reaching the English Channel and crossing it into Britain where they would have come into contact or conflict with the more primitive Grimaldi people, who would have been the earliest people to settle there (perhaps crowding out remaining Neanderthals) soon after the retreat of glacial ice, and may have inhabited Britain only a millennia or two before the repercussions of the Great Deluge drove taller, modern humans to settle there. Possibly the meeting of these divergent peoples was initially peaceful. But successive influxes of settlers into continental Europe would beget conflict, and the taller, more organized newcomers would eventually drive these earlier Africoid people still occupying Europe to less hospitable areas just as Grimaldis had driven Neanderthals away and into virtual extinction. But Grimaldis did not die out in the sense that Neanderthals may have. They reestablished their lives and settlements in the hinterlands of Britain and other areas of western and northern Europe that newer settlers encroached upon, while in some areas of northern Europe they remained largely unaffected by the new influx of migrants for a time.

Ancient Egyptians (Nubians, Ethiopians, Kushites), though, were already the world's most advanced civilized people 9,000 to 10,000 years ago. Of course, most Eurocentric historians and Egyptologists do not affirm such an early date for these earliest advanced populations; the estimates of their ascendancy, beginnings of Dynastic Egypt, the construction of stupendous monuments generally reduced to half of what other scholars—those who do not conform to the Eurocentric Brotherhood of Academia standard—contend, including European scholars who insist, for instance, that the Great Sphinx, standing guard before the Great Pyramid and the two smaller ones near it just outside of Cairo, is at least 10,000 years old.

In *Lost Cities of Atlantis, Ancient Europe & the Mediterranean*, author David Hatcher Childress cites the 1993 documentary "Mystery of the Sphinx," in which the presenter, John Anthony West "and his researchers sought to prove that the Sphinx had been severely waterworn and was over 9,000 years old!" (11). And some explanation for the probable greater antiquity of the Great Sphinx is offered in *Voyages of the Pyramid Builders*, by Robert M. Schoch, Ph.D., who explains that the Gizah pyramids exhibit weathering by sand-blown desert winds "which scours the limestone like a sandblaster, leaving a horizontal . . . steplike pattern" (11). But the Great Sphinx displays another kind of weathering, says Schoch, "a rolling, undulating surface with deep vertical fissures, or runnels . . . . Water, not wind, does this" (op. cit.).

While most Egyptologists and historians date the Great Sphinx to c. 2,600-2,500 BC, Schoch, for good reason, cannot accept this relatively late date for the monument, stating:

> The water-weathering pattern on the Sphinx makes sense only if the structure had been carved at a time when the Egyptian climate was much wetter than it is today. This indeed was the case at the end of the last Ice Age, circa 12,000 years ago . . . . (11-12)

Twelve-thousand years ago, of course, coincides with the melting of Wurm glacial ice in the northern latitudes, the rising of global sea levels, the flooding of the Mediterranean basin, and the submergence of towns and settlements in the basin and coastal areas in western and southern Europe as well as North Africa. Citing research by himself and seismologist Thomas L. Dobecki, Schoch feels certain that the Sphinx was carved sometime between 7,000 and 5,000 BC (12). It is entirely possible that the whole Nile Delta and many more miles inland were flooded by the rise in sea level forcing nearly all inhabitants to evacuate the entire area for several centuries, perhaps, and submerging the lower portion of the Great Sphinx in ten to fifteen feet of water so that for a century or two, before the steady northward flow of the Nile pushed enough soil and silt down (the Nile flows south to north) to create the Nile Delta, the Great Sphinx reposed in patient majesty—a singular, silent sentinel in the center of an expansive lake as Mediterranean tides coursed and ebbed around it. To an onlooker on a distant shore it would have looked like a strange human protuberance, an Enigma that, even in moonlight, seemed to be slowly wading eastward to an unknown, but anticipated, destination.

The rapid rise of sea levels and increased distances that now needed to be traveled for lumber, building stones, commodities, trade and commercial endeavors must have necessitated the construction of larger, more sea-worthy vessels as Mediterranean communities and larger metropolises recovered and steadily expanded. How long man had sailed the twin lakes of the pre-Deluge Mediterranean is unknown; megalithic structures and towns lie sunken off present-day shorelines, which cannot be outlined in more detail here. After the Deluge, however, man resumed his expansion, and carried the erection of megaliths farther than he had previously. With the opening to the Atlantic Ocean at the Pillars of Hercules, Egyptian mariners in larger vessels gained access to the western coastline of continental Europe, which previously could only be reached by overland routes. And just across a channel of water lay the large islands of Britain and Ireland, where early settlers erected villages and megalith-building would eventually begin.

The megalithic structures and standing stones in western Europe, Britain, Ireland and Scandinavia attest to the presence, a considerably heavy presence, of Egyptians in these areas—the only known people in ancient times who possessed the knowledge of how to erect and transport huge stones. So it would have to have been primarily Egyptians and other Africans who were responsible for megalithic sites erected *before* the great Deluge as well as after, and Childress points out that:

> Sunken structures of megalithic proportions have been found off Morocco and Cadiz in Spain . . . . It is an archeological fact that there are more than 200 known sunken cities in the Mediterranean. Egyptian civilization, along with the Minoan and Mycenaean in Crete and Greece are, in theory, remnants of this great, ancient culture. (30)

Just a sampling of the multitude of megalithic structures littering western Europe—built as places of worship, fertility monuments, tombs, living quarters and towns, etc. Fig. 5A (Above left) is a burial chamber in Sweden. Fig. 5B (Above) is a partial view of extensive rows of dolmens at Carnac in Brittany (France). Fig. 5C (at left) standing stones in northwestern Ireland.

The Greece referred to by Childress is not the Greece lauded by Western scholars as the first European civilization inhabited, presumably, by Caucasians. It is a more archaic Greece, still inhabited by *Africoid* peoples, like those who established the Mycenaean and Aegean civilizations—whose culture was derived from Egypt and, as Wells informed us earlier, was laid low by barbaric Hellenistic Greeks who arrived much later.

Of the areas where dolmens and megalithic structures are found, Carnac, in Brittany (northwest France), is most mentioned after Stonehenge and Avebury in Britain. According to most scholars, megalith-building took place from about 3,500-1,500 BC, ranging, says the Reader's Digest publication, *The World's Last Mysteries,* from "single natural boulder to grandiose structures which would have demanded complex architectural planning and the labor of tens of thousands of men for centuries" (65).

In Malta, the temple of Hagar Qim is a megalithic city with windows, chambers and corridors and is considered the most complex of European megaliths. Dolmens, menhirs and megaliths are connected to those of southern Russia north of the Black Sea that would be dominated by Scythians for long centuries and to similar constructions throughout the Middle East, Mesopotamia, Persia (present-day

Iran), India and Cambodia. Although numerous sources inject Aryans or "dark whites" into these areas—like the pictorial history *The World's Last Mysteries*, that calls the megalith builders of Europe "a sturdy folk, probably dark-*haired*" (*emphasis mine*, 66), the reader, I'm sure, can see that the description of the builders is a contrivance to obscure the reality that they were black- or dark-*skinned*; of what significance is dark-*haired*? Eurocentric scholarship is littered with similar wordplay, which the reader should more easily be able to identify now. Wordplay, misrepresentation and outright lies on the part of Eurocentric historians and scientists have long been employed to conceal the fact that Blacks were the originators of the world's earliest cultures and civilizations: megalith-builders, architects, scientists, artists, cartographers, writers, inventors, religionists, lawgivers, physicians, explorers, empire-builders, navigators and teachers.

The Neolithic Mediterranean and Egyptian peoples we have been looking at were black- and brown-skinned peoples, part of that earlier-mentioned black belt of mankind stretching from Spain to India and beyond—people we today would in no way consider Caucasian. If the reader finds this difficult to fathom, that black-skinned people predominated in the pre-archaic world, it is only because Eurocentric historians have omitted Blacks from it in their works, injecting Caucasians where there were none through wordplay and an unproven assumption that Caucasians had always inhabited the whole of Europe. If they were there, precisely where were they? Where—in France, Germany, Scandinavia, the Czech Republic or Austria—are the monuments, buried cities, ruins and artifacts that establish a distinct, culturally independent Caucasian civilization during the period we have been discussing?

Caucasians *were* in existence. But the reader should by now understand that the obscure terms Iberians, Brunets, dark whites and Mediterraneans have for two centuries been used to conceal the actuality that these peoples were, in effect, Africoid. In southern Europe along Mediterranean shores, later tribes and peoples would be identified as Basques, spread over a much larger territory than they occupy today; Ligurians, whose home territory was east of the Iberian Peninsula in present-day France, who show evidence in linguistic constructions, that they may have at one time spread into Switzerland, northern Italy and valleys of the Rhine. And in *A History of Gaul*, Fr. Funck-Brentano cites one Auguste Longnon suggesting that Ligurian territory once reached "as far as the North Sea" (17). Fr. Funck-Brentano notes that ancient writers call Ligurians a dark-*haired* race (there's that dark *hair* again), adding that they were "of short stature, extraordinarily robust and . . . . [i]n running the light-footed Ligurian knew no rival" (19). The home territory of the Iberians was the whole Iberian Peninsula, but there is also evidence that they once occupied a more extensive area. The later Aquitanians were a branch of Iberians, who were occupying the whole of western Gaul or France during the first century BC.

Most of the above people are generally put under the Brunet/dark—white/Mediterranean umbrella, but they were without doubt black- and dark-skinned Africoid peoples occupying probably *all* of western Europe in the 6th century BC—prior to the rise of the Roman Empire, or rather, the *new* Roman Empire, which will become clearer shortly. I left out Britain in the above mix of early peoples because much of the next chapter and later chapters will discuss the British Isles. But even this area of western Europe shows evidence of early occupation by Africoids, not Caucasians. In *Signs and Symbols of Primordial Man*, Albert Churchward notes, "Professor Sergi, from his anthropological studies, confirms our opinion that the Druids and inhabitants of these Isles came from an African stock originally" (180).

Moving forward in time, a people called *Etruscans* became dominant in Italy around 750 BC, although they may have been there far longer. Also referred to as *Tyrrhenians*, most Western historians trace their origin to Asia Minor, some claiming that they were a tribe of Trojans fleeing the aftermath of the Trojan War in which they had fought against the Greeks. Barbaric, Hellenistic Greeks began invading the Greek mainland and many of its islands sometime around 1,500 BC from the Balkans. These were the first Caucasians of note to enter the Mediterranean arena in any significant numbers.

Troy—anciently known as Ilium—was a fortified city in the northwest corner of Asia Minor (present-day Turkey) and the epic poem, *The Iliad*, contends that the Trojan War began when Prince Paris of Troy abducted the beautiful Helen, wife of King Menelaus of Achaea, so that she could be his bride. Enraged over the abduction, Menelaus enlists the help of Greek allies and a great fleet is assembled to bring war upon Troy and secure the return of Helen to her lawful husband. *The Iliad*, with its heroes, gods and goddesses, may not be an accurate depiction of the events of the war, but a great war was indeed fought between Greeks and Trojans over a ten year span from 1194-1184 BC.

According to most historians discussing the Etruscans, after Troy fell to the Greeks, a large group of defeated Trojans (Etruscans?) eventually established themselves in central Italy, establishing a civilization reputed to be greater than any Europe had seen up to that time. What is questionable about this theory is the length of time it took for the Etruscans to reach Italy—seemingly a 430-year-long span of time that historians seem not to have traced. Where did they go after Troy fell? What route did they take to get to Italy? A few historians contend that the Etruscans fled a great famine in Asia Minor that took place *4,000 years ago*—which would have been 2,800 years *before* the Trojan War! If that was the case, did they actually do battle at Troy?

Whatever the reason for their supposed departure from Asia Minor, historians nearly always refer to the Etruscans as a "mysterious" people because of the uncertainty of their true origin, but they note the affinity between their burial customs, written letters, pottery and metalwork to peoples of the east and Asia Minor. More than one author has commented on their physiognomy which, from their pictured pottery and friezes, show them to have been dark-skinned. Commenting on the Etruscans, David Hatcher Childress statess:

> Curiously, Etruscan statuary often shows the Hindu "tika" or third-eye mark on the forehead between the eyes. The Etruscans also made masks and statuary of Gorgons . . . . Gorgon images are common in Hindu mythology and commonly seen as far east as Bali in Indonesia. (167)

Greek historian Strabo states that the Tyrrheni or Etruscans were of Lydian stock and came from Asia Minor, and Ivar Lissner, author of *The Silent Past*, states, "Andalusia [Iberian Peninsula] has a number of Etruscan place names which come from the Lydian home of the Tyrrhenians" (164).

Dionysius of Halicarnassus, though, was convinced that the Etruscans "were a very ancient indigenous people who 'do not resemble any other in its language and its customs'" (qtd. in Childress 169). Childress agrees with Dionysius that the Etruscans were indigenous to Italy, which should not be surprising since black, Africoid peoples—Grimaldis, ancient Basques, Iberians, and people classified as *Capoids*, and *Alpines*, like the Iceman—had long been present in western and southern Europe.

If Etruscans were indigenous to Italy, it should not be a surprise to researchers that their statuary masks and burial customs were the same as peoples living further east or in India since the inhabitants of Greater Ethiopia—before it began to disintegrate, perhaps between 1,500 and 1,700 years ago BC—were physically similar people with similar cultural practices. The onset of its disintegration began with invasions of Caucasian peoples streaming out of the Great White Forest of Eurasia and their barbaric intrusions into civilized lands. But Caucasians had yet to enter *western* Europe, and cultural practices there would have remained essentially the same, or similar to the Indian or Asian portion of Greater Ethiopia.

Eurocentric historians have always emphasized differences between peoples of the ancient proto-Negroid belt of mankind and Greater Ethiopia, discussing Asians as being different from Africans or Africoid peoples so that we fail to see the general connectedness the peoples once had. In assigning the Etruscans an *Asian* origin, historians obscure the reality of an African or homogeneous one—removing a prominent black- or dark-skinned, essentially African group from a western Europe that had always been Africoid—like the vast majority of the inhabitants of the "black belt' of mankind (i.e., Greater Ethiopia).

In *Anacalypsis, vol. 1*, Godfrey Higgins notes one Mr. Franklin, who declared that the Etruscans "*had the countenances of Negroes*, the same as the images of Buddha in India" (*my emphasis*, 166), which, if true, does not dismiss their possible origin in Asia Minor or somewhere farther east, but rather strengthens the assertion that the peoples of Greater Ethiopia—west and east—physically resembled each other more closely than they may now.

The *Carthaginians* rose to prominence in North Africa about 814 BC, establishing the city-state of Carthage in the area of what is now Tunis, in Tunisia. Carthage began as a settlement established by Phoenicians from the Levant, or what is now Lebanon. The Phoenicians enter history as seafarers but, as we will see later, did most of their sailing for Egyptians and may have been a colony of Egyptians given autonomy in the region of the Levant. They established a string of colonies along the north coast of Africa, but Carthage quickly became their jewel. It was a beautifully built city, and a harbor was constructed unlike any ever seen before. For trade and alliance purposes, Phoenician royalty intermarried with the royalty of nearby black African and Berber tribes.

Phoenicians are another people Eurocentric historians generally whiten for their insidious purpose of removing Blacks and achievements of black-skinned people from history. Phoenicians may not have been as black as typical Africans; Caucasians had begun impinging on black-skinned societies in the Near and Middle East, spawning warfare and intermingling with the inhabitants around the same period Hellenistic Greeks had descended on Mycenae on the mainland and various other Greek isles. Caucasian intermingling with black- and dark-skinned Asiatics in Persia and Mesopotamia resulted in lighter-skinned Asiatics—who still retained dark- to light-brown complexions, but nevertheless, lightening the general complexions of the people in the area. These intermixed people are the ones Eurocentric historians have labeled *Caucasian*, Caucasian merely because they had an admixture of Caucasian blood, though their physiognomy still exhibited their Negroid or Ethiopian origins. Living in the area, Phoenicians—some Phoenicians—eventually were dominated by these lighter-skinned dark people, tribes of whom became known as Assyrians, Babylonians, Hittites—all of whom Eurocentric historians style *Caucasian*.

When the Etruscan Empire began to blossom, Carthage developed strong and ongoing commercial ties with Etruria (modern Tuscany, but a much larger territory in 750 BC). This relationship would endure over several centuries. The Carthaginians had a large naval fleet and guarded the Pillars of Hercules, preventing rivals like the Greeks and Phocaens from gaining access to Carthaginian-controlled areas in Spain and to the Atlantic Ocean. Etruscans, however, were not so restricted and "came to Spain for metals in accordance with a commercial bargain made with the Carthaginians," according to Pierson Dixon in *The Iberians of Spain* (42). The Etruscans even wore purple garments similar to the famed royal garments of the Carthaginians, and there was intermarriage between members of the two nations.

It must be pointed out and stressed that the Etruscans were the original founders of the city of Rome. Most historical atlases locate the Etruscan Empire north of the Tiber River, stretching into central Italy and north to the Po Valley. But their empire and influence spread to the foothills of the Alps in the north as well as south of the Tiber where they traded with Italic peoples—Latins, Samnites, Volscians—and with Greeks around Naples and Cumae. The Italic peoples were little more than illiterate farmers and herdsmen living in rude huts but, according to Werner Keller, in *The Etruscans*, "central Italy under the Etruscans was like an oasis transplanted from the east . . . . Everything about it [i.e., Etruria] was new to Italy, its whole civilization and culture, its technology and architecture" (98).

Keller's statement that Etruscan civilization was "new" to Italy is misleading, seeming to imply that Italy had been long established and Etruscans arrived *afterwards*. If so, the Italian peoples occupying the south of the peninsula would have observed the arrival of the Etruscans and, presumably, have witnessed the flowering of this "new" civilization and its technology—perhaps even participating in it. This was not the case. When Greeks, Phocaeans and Latins—presumably Caucasian émigrés from areas in and around Greece—*arrived* in southern Italy and expanded northward, Etruscans were already there, their civilization already established. If they had fled there after the Trojan War, as some Western historians allege, the Caucasian settlers in southern Italy would undoubtedly have known of them, or heard of them or of their migration to Italy, since Greeks (who had settlements in southern Italy) had participated in the Trojan War.

However, the Etruscans and their civilization were "new" to the presumably Caucasian settlers of southern Italy, lending strong credence to Dionysius' belief that the Etruscans were, indeed, indigenous. In *The Etruscan Cities and Rome*, H.H. Scullard mentions that Dionysius had two reasons for his belief:

> First, he could find no similarity between the Etruscans and Lydians [of Asia Minor] of his own day in language, religion or institutions . . . His second reason is . . . that Xanthus of Lydia, who lived about the same time as Herodotus [i.e., 450 BC] and wrote a history of his country, showed no knowledge of a Lydian ruler named Tyrrhenus nor of any settlement of Lydians in Italy. (35)

So, the Etruscans were "new" to Greeks and Italic Caucasians in the sense that they "discovered" Etruscans and their civilization already established in Italy—which seems more reasonable and accurate than Keller's observation that Etruria "was new to Italy." Etruria was there first.

It was the Etruscan ruler Lucius Tarquinius Priscus who was the founder of the Rome that would come to rule the world centuries later. Around 607 BC Etruscans spread southward from their original territory and Tarquinius ordered the draining of the swamps all about the hills that would become the center of Rome. Buildings began to be erected, regular streets were laid out, and the Circus Maximus was built in which, says Keller:

> The varied program included horse racing and chariot racing, athletics such as track events, and wrestling and boxing. Sporting contests, which had long been highly popular in the city-states of Etruria, were something quite novel to the Tiber settlers. (128)

Keller asserts that the pomp and circumstance of Rome was of Oriental origin and that the ceremoniousness begun by Tarquinius began to spread through Europe "in symbols, insignia of sovereignty, badges of office" (130). For more than three centuries Rome grew in size and fame until the Caucasian Latin tribes, who would become the *new* Romans, turned against the Etruscans, and between the 4th and 3rd centuries, drove them out of Rome, destroying their cities, and burning many to the ground. By 264 BC, the onset of the first Punic War against Carthage, Etruria was largely desolate, its once proud people humbled, slain or enslaved by the most powerful, predominantly white-skinned people the world had known to that time. I say predominantly white-skinned because we need to understand that race-mixing has always taken place when people of varying types warred, traded extensively or lived in close proximity. This certainly was the case in Italy between Italic peoples, Etruscans and Greeks, people who often occupied the same cities and inter-married for political and commercial advantage.

Why the new Romans turned on the old, their benefactors, is a bit confusing and will be touched upon later. But the new Romans usurped or appropriated most of their culture and civilization from the Etruscans, who more than likely *were* indigenous to Italy, a powerful contingent of an older black-skinned world that once overspread Europe.

The engineering feats of the Etruscans are too numerous and detailed to delineate here, but a few lines from Keller should inform the reader of the consummate skills they introduced to western Europe:

> They knew the methods of digging channels and building dams. They knew the Phoenician system of land drainage . . . of installing elaborate networks of underground tunnels . . . . Surviving hydraulic installations from later days suggest that *Etruscan engineering skills were drawn on by the Romans* for works which still command admiration today. (*my emphasis*, 54)

It was Etruscan ingenuity that led to the production of every kind of crop being grown in Italian soil and, according to Keller, "it was the Etruscans who introduced the grape to Italy and established it there" (56). And while the Romans are lauded for the aqueducts they built transporting water to towns or areas in need of irrigation, Keller notes:

> The Etruscan constructions can stand comparison with the much later Roman aqueducts, which became so famous . . . The much more complicated underground systems built by the Etruscans to provide their cities with drinking water fell into decay and were completely forgotten . . . . It was thanks to the initiative of Etruscan experts that the experience and sophisticated techniques . . . were transmitted to the West and first put into practice there [i.e., Italy] on a large scale. (57-58)

This is enough for now regarding the Etruscans who according to one historian, "had the countenances of Negroes"; were Asiatic according to many others; and were "mysterious" people according to some who, however, generally restrain themselves from designating them Caucasian. This is because there is enough evidence extant indicating that they were *not*, and to do so would be seen as a too obvious falsification of historical fact. But Eurocentric historians are extremely reluctant to style them black, for that would locate black-skinned people on the continent of Europe—violating an unwritten taboo kept in place for two centuries by the Eurocentric Brotherhood of Academia, whose mission seems to have always been to expurgate any notion of a black or African occupation anywhere on the continent.

The return of the 5,300 year old Iceman should be heralded by an honest scientific body truly dedicated to reconstructing our past. But for some, his return is bittersweet. When the world should be receiving periodic updates in journals and respected newspapers with revelations of what this ancient ancestor is revealing about our past life, habits, tools, occupations and journeys, the world has received—outside of a handful of books that continue to be reticent about the Iceman's race—virtual silence. The excitement and fanfare has long simmered and died.

The Eurocentric Brotherhood of Academia retains its power to influence what should be disseminated and what should remain concealed, unmentioned. Absent, it seems, are the genuinely candid and forthright historians and scholars of the past—even European ones—who, in the face of reprobation by the powers that were, fearlessly challenged prevailing historical and scientific models in their day that the majority of their colleagues upheld—especially regarding the racial classifications of mankind, past and present. But now that the full-bodied, skin-covered, Ethiopian-looking Iceman made his miraculous, unprecedented return, racial classifications are suddenly outdated, passé, an antiquated practice from a bygone era.

If the reader should have understood anything in these first three chapters—and understood the implications of the quotations I have included from noteworthy historians and anthropologists—it is that much truth has been deliberately withheld from the history we have been presented with in regard to the presence of black- and dark-skinned people in Europe. And the more I think about a day 5,300 years ago when a man, who had wandered too far from his village in search of game, was slammed by a blizzard more severe than he anticipated, the more I am convinced that a Divine hand drove him to seek shelter in that small gully he was found in more than five millennia later. Had he not been found, had glacial ice shredded his body and bones; had wolves, mountain lions, bears or sharp-eyed, carnivorous eagles located him and ripped apart his body; had the several feet of snow that blanketed him melted away too quickly and exposed his body to parasites of earth and air, leaving only a fragment or two of rib-bone that might never have been found, then those who have written our history, writing of a purely Caucasian Europe that black men never trod upon could continue indoctrinating us with fallacies.

The Iceman persevered, though he perished, died but actually lived because his life, unbeknownst to him, had a higher calling, a Divine purpose. He is a living relic from an epoch which most Western historians describe as pretty much the beginning of our present history, the dawn of civilization, supposedly a time before the first Egyptian Dynasty was established, or the first of many pyramids was erected. We will see further on that Egyptian civilization is far older than Western scholars have told us and shatter the widespread assertion that the Great Pyramid was built without the use of metal tools (the Iceman, remember, had a knife with a *metal* blade). But for our immediate purpose, we can be assured that the Iceman's discovery destroys an assertion that Eurocentric scholars thought would remain unchallenged: The Iceman "lived" to prove to a world long deceived that there were, indeed, black-skinned people occupying Europe—and that they were still present only 5,000 years ago.

CHAPTER 4

AFRO-ASIATIC REALMS—PART I

Most Viking historians have written about Scandinavia and the Viking peoples with chapters of their works titled Viking Settlements, Viking Religion, Viking Graves, and so forth, without offering a shred insight into their racial makeup. They often suggest an Asian origin, mentioning the Aesir of the sagas, reputedly an Asiatic race; but the Aesir are never described in racial terms, merely as *heathen*—whether men or deities. The reader, already convinced from years of indoctrination that ancient Scandinavians were blond, blue-eyed Caucasians, is left to conclude that white-skinned Scandinavian peoples had, perhaps, an admixture of Asian or yellowness added to their white complexions, which would have had only a negligible impact on the complexion of Norsemen and soon disappeared.

The intention of this work is to demonstrate that the Vikings who made Europe tremble throughout the first half or more of the Middle Ages were actually black-skinned people of predominantly Africoid descent, inhabiting northern regions of the continent only a millennium ago. The average reader's reluctance to accept such a notion is understandable, but the evidence that will be presented should be sufficient enough to confirm this, as well as attest that this information has been long known and ignored by nearly all Western writers to this day. Hopefully, the preceding chapters have demonstrated that Blacks, African Blacks, were the first modern human beings to enter and settle Europe, and it will be shown that they inhabited the continent from remote into historic times.

Asiatic Blacks migrated to the continent in later epochs and had to have mingled with the Africoids already there. There is ample archeological evidence that both types inhabited the whole of Europe, and I suggest that northern Europe, particularly Germany and Scandinavia, was a major melting pot and that the Black Norsemen of the Viking Age were the progeny of these anciently intermingled people who had developed a fierce warrior-culture over many centuries prior to Viking assaults in the British Isles and other areas of Europe.

Europe was in no way the pastoral, united Caucasian entity that Eurocentric historians have always seemed to suggest. At the opening of the 9th century (i.e., 800 AD), there was no Europe as we think of it today. There was the idea of a unified Europe, an idea dashed by the fall of the western Roman Empire in the late 5th century—which had been brought down by Hunnish and Gothic invasions, of which more will be said later. But the Huns, asserts David MacRitchie in *Ancient and Modern Britons, vol. I,* "are described as being of a dark complexion, *almost black*" (*my emphasis,* 35), a particular almost never touched upon in works by Western historians.

In the middle of the 5th century under Attila, the Hunnish Empire—Attila's empire—stretched from eastern Mongolia and China to Gaul (France). The Huns were repulsed in 451 AD in a massive battle outside Orleans (or Chalons) in western Gaul, and it is estimated that from 252,000 to 300,000 Huns and their allies were slain and left on the battlefield. Although accounts vary as to the actual number of Huns slain (the above figures are probably inflated), the Battle of Chalons, as it is usually referred to, is credited with saving western Europe from domination by the Black Huns and becoming part of the Hunnish Empire. Even without Gaul, Attila's empire included a vaster territory than that of the aforementioned Alexander the Great, whose "empire" lasted a mere decade.

To illustrate how insignificant and undeveloped Europe was in the mid-5ᵗʰ century, Richard Gordon, in an article entitled "Stopping Attila: The Battle of Chalons," says of Attila's onslaught:

> Town after town was destroyed, including Metz, Cambrai, Strasbourg, Rheims, Amiens and Worms. Paris was saved only because the Huns considered it too small to be worth the trouble of a siege. (*Military History* 35)

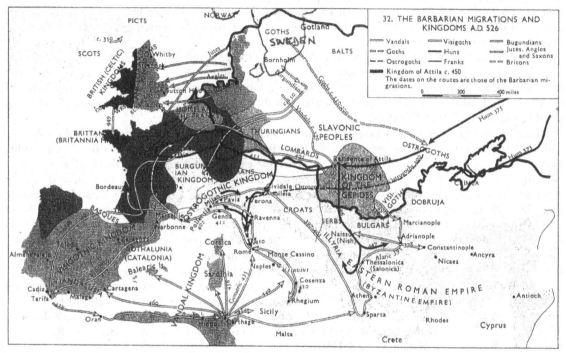

Fig. 6
Hunnish and Barbarian invasions of 4ᵗʰ and 5ᵗʰ centuries. Kingdom of Attila is denoted by dark outline. Note that Attila's territory includes all of Denmark and Southern Sweden.

Even after its fall before the close of the 5ᵗʰ century (c. 476 AD), Rome would remain Europe's largest and most developed city. Paris and London were essentially cow towns and would remain fairly insignificant for several centuries more—except as population centers and seats of ruling powers for surrounding areas.

The Hunnish invasions of the 4ᵗʰ and 5ᵗʰ centuries precipitated what may be called a "domino" effect in western Europe, sending one tribe reeling into another, spurring Germanic tribes, like Goths and Vandals, fleeing in all directions to avoid them. Or, so we have been told. A number of historians have asserted that Goths, Alans and Vandals were, themselves, Hunnish peoples and, therefore, would likely have been "dark . . . almost black" like Attila's Huns. The Vandals flee west-southwest through Iberia to North Africa in a 30-year period, from where they begin assaulting Rome and her colonies from the area of long-fallen Carthage five years later. During the same period, Gothic tribes—as Ostrogoths, Visigoths and Black Huns—are engaged in assaults on Rome and her territories in the general area of Italy. So, while a historical atlas of Europe during the 5th century seems to illustrate presumably white-skinned Germanic tribes fleeing in disorder and confusion throughout western Europe, part of a domino effect, a more careful perusal of the map in Fig. 6 might suggest another inference.

The assaults on Rome, Italy and the Roman Empire's areas of influence take place from about 400 to 460 AD by Vandals, Ostrogoths, Visigoths, Huns and less well known tribes. Historians single out Huns (omitting any mention of their blackness) as the primary invaders, outsiders who send Gothic Germanic tribes (presumably Caucasian) stumbling about Europe. But if (as has been asserted here, for which more evidence will be offered later) Goths were, like Vandals, Alans and other Hunnish tribes, black- and dark-skinned Asians entering Europe around the same period, might not the relatively swift Vandal departure for North Africa have been part of a planned flanking maneuver to assault the Roman Empire?—a probability I have never heard suggested by Western historians, but which seems obvious looking at Fig. 6 above. Could the Hunnish invasion of Europe have been much broader and purposeful than we have been informed?

Also note in Fig. 7 that the Kingdom of Attila includes a sizeable portion of what is now Russia, northeastern Germany and all of Denmark. The reader can note in Fig. 7, below—minus many of the details of Fig. 6, above, that Denmark is part of the Kingdom of Attila. Fig. 7, a map presented in Richard Gordon's article, shows, in addition to Denmark, that the Hunnish Empire extended westward as far as the Rhine in northwestern Germany.

In Fig. 7, also dated as 451, the Empire of Attila shows a different configuration with nebulous details, and does not place southern Sweden within the Hunnish Empire as other maps clearly do. (If the reader looks closely, he or she will see a Kingdom of Iberia just east of the Black Sea in the Caucasus region. Was this Iberia in any way connected to the Iberians of the Iberian Peninsula who are rumored to have extended into Asia?) The Jutes, Angles and Saxons, as depicted in Fig. 7, left (fled?) Jutland (Denmark) for Britain during the period of Hunnish domination of the territory. We assume these to have been more Caucasian peoples fleeing the onrush of the Hunnish incursion into the Jutland Peninsula, but who were they, really? We have discussed the presence of black-skinned people in Scandinavia and Germany for several millennia prior to this epoch, with no indication that any significant Caucasian element had entered the Jutland Peninsula—although Caucasians may have migrated into areas of Germany in significant numbers by this time. Historical atlases show Jutes, Angles and Saxons entering eastern and southeastern England in the early 6th century, but might these have been dark-skinned Hunnish elements extending themselves into England—designated Jutes, Angles and Saxons to obscure a black-skinned, Afro-Asiatic invasion of Britain? Might the Angles at least, who settled farther north and gave their name to England, have been a branch of Black Huns?

Although the works of Western historians seem to smoothly outline the events of European history and seem to be in general agreement, they are not always in total accord. What they do seem to be in total accord on is eliminating the presence of black- and dark-skinned people from the history of Europe—from Grimaldi man to the predominantly African invasions (or reinvasions) of Europe by Hannibal in 219 BC; the Moors in 711 AD; and the periodic onslaughts by black- and dark-skinned Hunnish peoples, discussed just above. Except for a bold minority, Eurocentric historians have written black-skinned people out of Europe, whitewashing European history to have us believe that Blacks never played a role in its development. But if the reader has fathomed the line of reasoning presented here, it seems obvious that European Blacks—like early Scandinavians, Black Celts and Picts of Germany, Britain and Gaul, who might all be considered components of an extensive Iberian populace—should be regarded indigenous to Europe in the same way we consider Native Americans or Indians indigenous to the Americas.

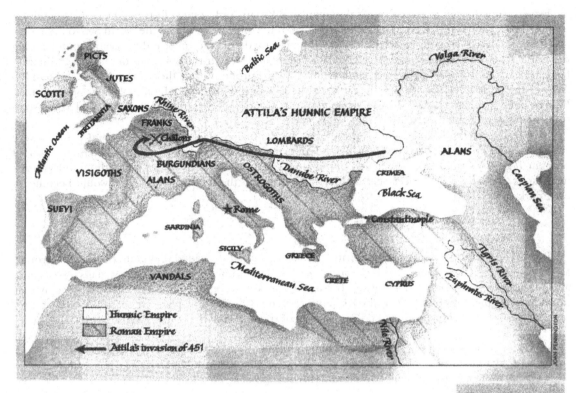

Fig. 7
Another view of Attila's Empire—here also showing Denmark as part of Hunnish territory. The Huns (depicted in lighter shading) would hold territory as far west as the Rhine and were turned back at Chalons, in France, in a tremendous battle by combined Germanic and Roman troops. Note also Jutes and Saxons occupying England—probably fleeing there to escape onrushing Hunnish armies.

Fleeing before the Huns, Germanic tribes put a strain on the faltering Roman Empire, which fought some invaders and sought accommodating alliances with others against the common threat from the East.

The Blacks of Britain and continental Europe were representative of a once vast black-skinned population, which at one time overspread the whole continent—who, by the onset of the Dark Ages (i.e., 500 AD), were relegated primarily to the northern and western extremities of the continent, as mentioned earlier. The northern groups, inhabiting Scandinavia and Baltic regions extending into Finland and Russia, were largely unaffected by Roman expansion in western Europe. Although Scandinavian precursors—Cimbri (or Kymry), Teutons and Ambrones—were eventually defeated by Roman legions (102 BC) and driven back to the north, the Romans had not pursued their re—treating armies, and their numbers and courageousness were replenished enough so that they could halt a Roman invasion of Germany at the Rhine in 133 AD.

Even during the centuries of Rome's dominance of Britain and western Europe, the seafaring culture of these black- and dark-skinned Europeans dominated northern waters from the North Sea to the Baltic, and they often fought amongst each other for influence and dominance in Scandinavia and lands fringing the Baltic from northern Germany to Estonia and Finland—which today is considered a Scandinavian land but was not directly involved in attacks in western Europe during the Viking Age (i.e., 800-1100 AD). As the period of the Dark Ages began to settle over Europe after the demise of the western Roman Empire, the inhabitants of Scandinavia began to yearn for more of what the world offered and would soon venture out to seek their fortunes.

By the time of the Viking raids of the 8th and 9th centuries, black- and dark-skinned peoples were still prominent in much of western Europe and all over northern Europe so that Friedrich Hertz could state, in *Race and Civilization*, "the actual population of Europe is the result of some thousand years of migrations and crossings of races" (118). And at the onset of the 9th century, Europe would become an even darker continent.

*   *   *   *   *

Regarding the Norse invaders of the British Isles, Irish annalists divided them into two distinct groups, as mentioned by Gwyn Jones, in *A History of the Vikings*: "White Foreigners, Norwegians (*Finn-gaill*), and Black Foreigners, Danes (*Dubh-gaill*), but it was a lesson no one heeded; nor do we know why they distinguished them by color" (76-77). In a footnote, Jones—in the only place he discusses race—points out that the Welsh chroniclers made no distinctions of color, stating that to Welsh historians:

> The Danes coming in by way of England and the Norwegtians by way of Ireland were pretty well all black: Black Gentiles (*y Kenedloed Duon*), Black Norsemen (*y Normanyeit Duon*), Black Host, Pagans, Devils, and the like. (op. cit. 77)

The question of the Irish distinction between Norwegians and Danes will be discussed further on. The reader will note, however, that the Danes—in the statement above and in future statements that will be presented—are emphatically styled *black* by historians who do comment on the race of the Norsemen. And while Irish historians refer to Norwegians as Finn-gaill, or White Foreigners (and we are speaking of annalists of the Viking period, not modern-day historians), this conclusion might not have been a unanimous one, since Rosalind Mitchison, in *A History of Scotland*, states that "[t]he '*black gentiles*', as the *Irish called them*, sailed down the west coast of Scotland . . . and all the islands were pillaged by 'this valiant, wrathful and purely pagan people'" (*my emphasis*, 9). So, apparently some Irish historians of the day styled both Danes *and* Norwegians black-skinned.

After incursions in Iona, which was burned in 802 and 806, when the monks were massacred, Norsemen ruled the northern half of Ireland, presumably Norwegians in this instance—although my use of the term Vikings, Norse or Norsemen will refer to Danes, Swedes and Norwegians. Danish Vikings were raiding England and the Frankish coast (northwest Germany), annexing the Frisian Islands. In the mid-9th century Danes were invading and settling areas of southeast England and, according to Agnes Mure MacKenzie, in *The Foundations of Scotland*, "in 841 they had formed a settlement on the lower Seine [in or near Paris]" (75), as they extended their exploits into France.

Master ship-builders of the age, Norsemen came as armed colonists to the British Isles in their beautiful and efficient long-ships, which normally contained a crew of forty. Some of their ships could hold twice as many men, whose age ranged from 16 to 60, all fighters. Ship-building must have been extensive all over Scandinavia and, in Denmark at least, the population must have been considerable, for the *Anglo-Saxon Chronicle* states in an entry for 850-1: "[H]eathen men [Danes] settled over winter in Thanet. And the same year came three hundred fifty ships to the mouth of the Thames and stormed Canterbury and London" (Helm, P.H. 52).

Afterward the Danes moved north to Northumbria to solidify their holdings there after quisling ruler, Egbert, had been overthrown. When Mercia finally fell to the Danes, Wessex, in the south was the only independent state remaining in what would become England (i.e., 874 AD). Wessex was assaulted by the Danes in 876 and, by 878, the Danes pretty much dominated the whole of England under the *Danelaw*, under which Danish customs and laws prevailed throughout Danish-controlled areas—at least half of the future England.

The Danelaw did not bring about any resettling or evacuation of the English people who, by now, seem to have been predominantly Caucasian—albeit a mixed race of ancient Black Celtic, Roman and more recently arrived Angle and Saxon stock from German lands, presumably white-skinned. In fact, the English living under the Danelaw began to adopt Danish customs, attitudes and clothing, and a multitude of Danish words were incorporated into the English language of the time—generally termed *Old English*.

Since English is primarily a Germanic language, it is probable that the English language ushered in by the Angles and the Norse or Old Norse spoken in Scandinavia was mutually intelligible to both groups as well as to the Picts who, as has been said, came originally from Germany long before Norsemen, Angles and Romans arrived in the British Isles. Dutch and Saxon derive from the same Germanic root, and some have attached Irish to it, which may not be completely accurate. I cannot provide examples of Old Norse and Old English for the reader's consideration; however, if one looks at Middle English, exemplified by the works of Chaucer (1343-1400), whose most famous work is *Canterbury Tales,* one would see that Middle English sounds almost German and is sprinkled with German-like words and phrases. Here is just the briefest sample from the General Prologue of *Canterbury Tales:*

> Oure counseil was nat longe for to seeche;
> Us thoughte it was nat worth to make it wis,
> And graunted him withouten more avis,
> and bade him saye his voirdit as him leste.

The verse seems almost comprehensible, but the actual pronunciation of the words is not as simple as one might think at first glance. Now, try to fathom what the English language sounded like 500 years prior to Chaucer's Middle English—the English spoken during the Norse invasions.

If, as is reasonable to suppose, an overarching German, Germanic or Old Norse tongue was widely spoken throughout Germany and Scandinavia, the Picts, who originated in Germany and/or Scandinavia would have been familiar with it; the Angles and Saxons who supposedly arrived from Jutland would have brought essentially the same language to Britain when they arrived several centuries before the Norsemen; and the Norsemen—by all accounts, Germanic—would have understood and spoken pretty much the same basic language, taking into account various loan words and infusions of words derived from other languages (i.e., Latin words retained from Romanized Britain, and later, French words incorporated into English after the Norman invasion).

However, Viking Age Norsemen or Scandinavians are credited with infecting the English spoken in the British Isles with numerous words during and after the period of the Danelaw—words we are quite familiar with like: *law, by-law, outlaw, riding, husband, happy, ill, loose, skin, ugly, brink, thrift, trust, window, crawl, lift, scare,* and numerous others. More will be discussed regarding language in a much later chapter, especially whether *Indo-European* is an accurate or suitable term for the origin of European languages.

The reader is reminded (and will be reminded again), that the Danes of the Viking Age are styled *black*, black-skinned people—not dirty people, crude people, wild people or bad people. By *black*, I do not necessarily mean *African* people possessing Negroid traits. However, we should not reject the probability that men and women of African or Egyptian descent made up a sizeable percentage of the Norsemen who dominated not only the British Isles but Europe, in general, during the Dark Ages, or the first half of the Middle Ages. As we shall shortly see (keeping our earlier discussion of Greater Ethiopia in mind), the Asia of yesteryear could also have been called the Dark Continent, as Africa was once popularly referred to. And we shall also see that yesteryear was not that long ago.

In volume I of *Anacalypsis*, Godfrey Higgins notes that Herodotus "says . . . that there were two Ethiopian nations, one in India, the other in Egypt. He derived this information from the Egyptian priests . . ." (54). Higgins cites others—Philostratus, Eustathius, Homer, and his contemporaries, Dr. Shuckford, a Mr. Maurice and others, both ancient and contemporary—attesting to a great black nation east of the Euphrates and the Indus being related to the western Ethiopians and Egyptians. Higgins feels the only question is whether Egypt borrowed from India or India from Egypt, which is not paramount to our current discussion. Higgins cites one Mr. Wilson who states that it cannot "be reasonably doubted, that a race of Negroes formerly had power and preeminence in India" (57).

In an article entitled "African Presence in Early Asia," contained in a book of the same title (ed. Ivan Van Sertima), author James Brunson asserts: "Anthropological finds dating from the Upper Paleolithic through the Mesolithic periods (20,000 BC-8,000 BC) substantiate the existence of "Negroid" types in China" (120). Brunson cites Sterling Means, Te-K'un Cheng, Anta Diop and Kwang-chih Chang, among others, to substantiate this. Brunson asserts that this black or African element is what initially moved China toward civilization and that even earlier remains of Negroid types, dating from 50,000 to 10,000 BC, have been found. These early fossil remains (i.e., 50,000 BC) would directly link these remote Chinese inhabitants to Australoids and Australian Aborigines, whom modern DNA geneticists have affirmed were the earliest human migrants out of Africa.

Fairly recent research has extended Aborigine occupation of Australia to at least 62,000 years, which would mean that this earliest human migration would have begun not later than 100,000 years ago or earlier, calling into question the theory that the earliest human beings, presumably Grimaldis, reached Europe only 40,000 years ago. The Grimaldi entrance into Europe had to have been at least 100,000 years ago, if not earlier. The gravesite at Lake Mungo in southeastern Australia was dated at 62,000 years in 1998; yet, considering this new information, Eurocentric scientists revised the date for man's entrance into Europe only a mere 5,000 years—from 40,000 years to 45,000 years ago.

Be that as it may, offshoots of these earliest Asian migrants (Grimaldi-Australoids) would have settled in areas traversed by the vanguard groups, spawning the earliest modern human habitations of Asia. From these earliest offshoots arose the earliest settlements in Asia, out of which these black *African* migrants spread still further, eventually reaching Japan. They were the earliest Papuan peoples whom we designate *Melanesians*. The reader is reminded that in these remote times and for long millennia afterward, all human beings were, in essence, *black Africans*, with Negroid features, the earliest of whom, Australoid, and Grimaldi, were essentially the same type of humans often referred to as *Negritos*—short, pygmy-like peoples, most probably no taller than 5'3". Those of China are likened to Australian Aborigines who have been designated the *shoulder ax culture*, whose type extended from Szechwan and Yunnan (western China) to India and eastward to Korea and Japan (Brunson 121).

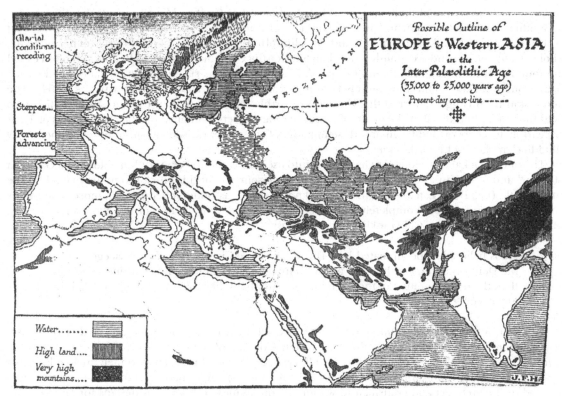

Fig. 8

Extent of the Wurm glacial 35,000 to 25,000 years ago. Note that Iberian Peninsule and Italy and Sicily are attached to North Africa by land bridges and that the Mediterranean is divided into two large lakes. Grimaldi man had been in Europe for at least 15,000 years and had entered Asia much earlier.

Brunson cites Armand De Quatrefages, author of *The Pygmies,* as stating:

> The Negro type . . . in southern Asia . . . was the sole occupant for an infinite period of time . . . Invasions or infiltrations of various yellow and white races have separated the Negro populations which formerly occupied a continuous area . . . . (123)

These earliest Negroid or Grimaldi-Australoid inhabitants of Asia and China endured for many millennia; they were not transitory and did not "vanish." We have already heard from historian J.A. Rogers in regard to more recent accounts of the remnants of the Negroids or Grimaldi-Ausstraloids of China, and Brunson asserts that even during the Chin Dynasty (221-206 BC):

> Negritos whom the Chinese call "Black Dwarfs" are reported in the mountainous districts south of Yangtze . . . Some emigrated, but others remained and were assimilated by the dominant southern Mongolian stock, as witness to kinky hair and swarthy skin . . . . (121)

In his *Celtic Druids*, published seven years before *Anacalypsis*, Godfrey Higgins asserts that the worship of Buddha is extremely ancient and, in statues and other iconography, was from earliest times represented as "black as jet," with kinky hair, flat face and thick lips (162). The worship of this black icon pervaded the whole of ancient Asia and is certainly older than Siddhartha Gautama (c. 563-483 BC), who is often called the founder of Buddhism. In *Anacalypsis, vol. I*, Higgins mentions sixteen different names of Buddha (citing one Mr. Faber) and that "he was known at different times and in different places" (154). The impression from Higgins' work is that there were earthly representatives of the ancient god chosen to hold the title of Buddha after the death of a previous earthly representative (as the Dalai Lamas of Tibet are earthly teachers of Buddhism and disseminators of the ancient wisdom) whose title became simply "Buddha" in place of his birth name.

The title Dalai Lama is reputed to have come into use during the 15th century, but Siddhartha Gautama of the 6th and 5th centuries BC was an early earthly representative of this office two millennia before the current title (i.e., Dalai Lama) was introduced, known simply as Buddha because he, more than others before or after him, more completely embodied the attributes and wisdom of this most ancient deity, whose early representative Col Franklin describes thusly:

> He is believed to be animated by a Divine Spirit, and is regarded as the vicegerent of the Deity on earth, and by some as the Deity incarnate, and death is nothing more . . . than the transmigration of the spirit into another body, like that of the Bull God Apis in Egypt. (op. cit. 232)

However, historian Albert Churchward, whom we will hear more from later, asserts that Buddhism originated in Egypt—Buddha being "the representative of Ptah of the Egyptians" (*The Origin & Evolution of Religion* 331). According to Churchward, Buddha is a corruption of Ptah, an extremely ancient Egyptian god who, according to historian James Breasted, in *A History of Egypt*, "had been from the remotest ages the god of the architect and craftsman to whom he communicated plans and designs for architectural works and the products of the industrial arts" (356).

Eurocentric Western scholars have not given us all the details of ancient civilizations and rarely elaborate on the religious beliefs of Scythian peoples who sent waves of black-skinned Asian humanity westward into Europe before and after Caucasians began to dominate it. Attila is said to have killed his brother, Bleda, in 443 AD, becoming sole king or Khan of the Black Huns, who nearly devastated the Balkans, part of the Eastern Roman Empire, before moving into western Europe, where he would eventually suffer his only defeat at the Battle of Chalons (or at Orleans, the precise battlefield still in question).

Western scholars focus on the military exploits of the fearsome Huns and other Scythian peoples, but did any of the peoples designated Scythians worship Buddha and carry the precepts of the faith with them into Europe? Western scholars do not offer much commentary in this regard, while Higgins informs us that—

> Attila, the Scythian and the Hun, and a Khan of Tartary . . . professed to be the owner of the sword God Acinaces, a kind of Palladium [guard, protector, shield], which entitled him to the sovereignty of the universe. (*Anac., vol. I* 631)

Despite killing his brother, Bleda, it is obvious that Attila was revered by his followers, thousands of whom (but not all) accompanied his body back to his homeland after his death in 453 AD. According to Higgins, Attila was 124 years-old at his death, and many scholars assert that his actual burial site is unknown because the people who buried him were all killed so that no one could reveal it. Higgins also connects him to Scandinavia, noting that "[i]t is probable that he was held out to be a renewed incarnation of Odin" (op. cit.).

The map of Europe during the period of Hunnish invasions of the 4th and 5th centuries is confusing, as are the actual races of Gothic peoples whom—because they are said to have been "Germanic"—we assume were Caucasians like the Germans we know of today. Whatever the case, which we will revisit later, the Huns of this epoch were "very dark, almost black," and we have to assume that racial intermingling was fairly rampant throughout Europe since, as we know, women are always a large part of the conquerors' spoils of war.

Before moving on, it should be noted that Attila "called his capital in the West the City of Buda, Buddha, Babylonia, and Susa" (op. cit.), undoubtedly the location of present day Budapest in Hungary—a territory of the Huns to which historical atlases have attached the name *Kingdom of the Gepids* or the Gepid Kingdom (so-called because of a "Germanic" tribe called Gepidae (who could *not* have been in power during Attila's reign) said to have been crushed by Roman legions around 269 AD. A steady influx of Scythic peoples entered the territory for nearly two centuries afterward, including the Black Huns of Bleda and Attila. It is not until after Attila's death that the Gepidae resurface, uniting with other Germanic tribes to drive out the Huns in 454. What Budapest was called before Attila named his western capital Buda or Buddha is either lost or hidden by Eurocentric scholars (the *Encyclopedia Brittanica* says the name came about in 1873, mentioning nothing about Attila and the Huns). However, if Higgins is correct regarding the name Buda or Buddha being bestowed by Attila, there would seem to be more that needs to be learned about Attila's Divine intentions as well as his belief that he was entitled to the "sovereignty of the universe."

Higgins, as well as Gerald Massey, whom we will hear from later, cites the worship of Buddha as the source of the monotheistic religions we know today as Islam, Judaism and Christianity. But each author has a different view as to where the worship of Buddha originated—Higgins declaring Asia or India as the source; Massey asserting that ancient Egypt was most responsible for bringing religion, religious iconography and esoteric wisdom into Europe. Outside of origins, their delineation of black-skinned humanity's civilizing effect, dominance and profound influence upon Europe are quite similar. But to hopefully simplify matters, we will consider Higgins' theories first, then, in later chapters, consider Massey's views.

According to Higgins, the teachers of the ancient religion of Buddhism were the Druids, whom we mostly hear of in connection to the British Isles. They were the priests whom the Romans found in both Gaul (France) and Britain when they invaded these territories, regarding whom Higgins asserts: "The Druid of the Celtae answered in every respect to the Magus [i.e., Magi] of the Persians . . . Pliny confirms this and says, 'the Gauls call their Magi, Druids'" (*Celtic Druids* 95). The Celtae Higgins refers to are the early or Black Celts earlier discussed, inhabiting Britain under various tribal names, and related to the Gauls, inhabiting the territory which would later be called France.

Like the Celtae or Black Celts of Britain, the Gauls were part of that older, pre-Caucasian world of western Europe that the new Romans set out to conquer after destroying the Etruscan and Carthaginian civilizations. Being disseminators of an ancient wisdom long extant in western Europe, Celtic Druids or priests were hunted down by Roman authorities in Gaul and Britain—of which more will be said later.

Much of the information presented so far was extant from the early 20th century back to the early 19th, so I have not presented information which was unknown to later historians of the 20th century. We have looked at extremely remote migrations out of Africa, Greater Ethiopia, early civilizations of India, China, Mesopotamia, and the outward spread of humanity to Indonesia, the isles of the western Pacific and the earliest civilizations in and around the Mediterranean—all of which will be revisted in later chapters.

Our look at the Iceman strongly confirms (perhaps not to everyone's satisfaction) that black-skinned people were still present in Europe 5,000 years ago; they would have a continuing presence on the continent into historical times and beyond as Picts (likened to Germans and Scandinavians), Celtic Britons (early or Black Celts, including the Welsh), Ligurians, Basques and Iberians (*Iberian*, seemingly a generic term to which most of the former could be classed under)—all essentially Africoid peoples (Asian, to Higgins) according to historians who discuss race. And we have briefly discussed Aegean peoples, like those occupying the Greek Isles, Crete and Mycenae prior to the arrival of mostly white-skinned Greeks

(Hellenes) c. 1500 BC, and the Etruscans of Italy, who may have been dark-skinned Asians, a blend of Afro-Asiatics, or simply indigenous Africoids, having the "countenances of Negroes." As difficult as it may be for some readers to imagine, the evidence makes it clear that black- and dark-skinned peoples predominated in Europe—from the Mediterranean to Scandinavia—from remote into historic times.

Fig. 9
Korean prisoners captured during the "First Korean War" in about 1868. Note their near black complexions—evidence that Asia was once a caudron of black-skinned humanity.

*   *   *   *   *

Cheik Anta Diop, quoted earlier, asserts that the present Chinese type developed about 17,000 years ago, but these must still have been essentially black- or dark-skinned, retaining their pigmentation for long millennia afterwards. The photos below (see Figs. 10a and 10b) were taken just over 100 years ago. Note the very dark-skinned Chinese Boxer captives and other dark-skinned Chinese. Most southern areas of Asia—Burma (Myanmar), Cambodia, Southeast Asia in general—had similarly pigmented populations, not to forget the predominantly black-skinned populations of Borneo, New Guinea, Solomon Islands and the western Pacific.

The striking photo of captured Koreans in Fig. 9, above, was taken about 1870 when the United States sent gunboats up the Taedong River on a mission to "open up" Korea (then called Choson) to trade with the West in what author Eric Niderost calls the First Korean War ("Fighting the Tiger," *Military Heritage*, Aug. 2002: 30-39, 90). The captured Koreans in Fig. 9 are clearly black-skinned, standing (one kneeling) in bright sunshine in the typical attire and hair-style of the period (i.e., mid-19th century), although their attire might be the military uniform of the common soldier. Niderost calls the Korean soldier of the mid-19th century "an anachronism, a product of an inward-looking society that had been effectively isolated from the outside world for almost 300 years . . . wearing traditional white garb as a 'uniform'" (op. cit. 34).

Fig. 10 A. Dark-skinned Japanese troops fighting in a European alliance during the Boxer Rebellion, c. 1900.

Fig. 10 B. Captured Chinese Boxers await their fates. Note that many are black in complexion.

Some readers may observe the photos in Figs. 9 and 10 and still deny the blackness of the subjects in them, especially the Koreans, who are not representative of Koreans seen today. But photographs don't lie, and if the subjects depicted are not black or extremely dark-skinned, then what complexion are they? No, we don't see Chinese, Koreans or Japanese as dark today, but they certainly existed a mere century or so ago, as the photographs attest. What lightened the general complexions of the majority of these peoples in such a short time might be touched upon later. The question for the present is: If these peoples were so dark-skinned only a century to a century-and-a-half ago, how dark were they 500 years ago? A thousand? Two thousand? Five thousand? Does the reader now have any doubt that a great black nation existed in Asia in ancient times as Higgins and other historians have asserted? Is there any doubt that Mongoloid peoples, like the Hiong-nou, Huns of Attila's time, and the Mongols of Genghis Khan—who spread into Europe from roughly 350-1350 AD—were similarly, or even more, black-skinned than the subjects in the relatively recent photos above?

Higgins, as well, connects a number of other tribes or peoples out of the black Asian cauldron who migrated westward into Europe. He asserts, for instance that the Arabians originally came from India, connecting them with Turkic peoples linguistically and culturally (*Anac., vol. I* 420). He asserts that Persians, ancient Hebrews, Phoenicians, Thracians, Ionians, Scythians, Etruscans, among others, were all related through religion, language, customs and race. Gerald Massey, whom we will hear from later, looks to most ancient Egypt as the origin of the above peoples, and we should not forget that Africa was the origin of *all* the earliest peoples who ventured eastwards into Asia in the remotest of times. All the peoples that we call Asians had long inhabited that continent, where they differentiated physically, re-interbred in some cases, then began west—and southwesterly migrations toward Europe and the Middle East in a quest for living space outside of the black Asian cauldron which had become crowded by increasingly contentious tribes—in essence, backtracking over territory their distant ancestors had trodden to reach Asian destinations.

Although Eurocentric scholars, especially those of the early 20th century, wrote tome after tome inflating the populations and accomplishments of the white or Caucasian race, the works they produced seem now but a reaction to what was probably already known to them regarding the far more ancient civilizations Caucasians encountered when they felt powerful enough to move southward and westward out of the hinterlands I refer to as the Great White Forest. When Eurocentric historians wrote of Caucasian or Aryan achievements and civilization after the onset of the 20th century, they had the works of Higgins, Sergi, Massey and Sir William Jones at hand. They had abundant scholarly evidence in the mid-19th century showing that the earliest civilizations, the foundations of their own civilization, had flowed out of that Proto-negroid belt of mankind mentioned earlier, and that the bearers of the knowledge, sciences and religions brought into Europe were black-skinned when they arrived.

Rather than present an honest picture of European history, they chose to subvert this knowledge, insinuating whiteness into the Indians, Sumerians, Babylonians and, of course, ancient Egyptians—a practice they have yet to abstain from. The advent of motion pictures, from the early 20th century to the present, greatly aided their whitening or whitewashing of history—Biblical films promoting the notion that Egyptians were white-skinned, along with Jesus, Moses and all the peoples inhabiting Middle Eastern lands in ancient times. So, in the minds of the mass of Americans and Europeans, black-and dark-skinned people played no part in the ancient world, and the Blacks who *are* seen in some of these films are depicted as subservient—slaves or servants who are seen briefly but almost never heard. A later chapter will discuss about a dozen films that do present elements of truth by their inclusion of black characters in them, but they represent only a fraction of the films in which Blacks might have been prominently represented in if the filmmakers and producers were motivated by truth and accuracy.

Individual Caucasian tribes might have ventured east- and westward out of the Great White Forest prior to c. 2000 BC, but there is no verifiable evidence that the barbaric masses of them did so. Only after 2000 BC, or roughly 4,000 years ago, did masses of Caucasians or Aryans begin to descend east—, south—, and westward into coveted areas of more advanced cultures and civilizations, generally wreaking havoc and rapine when they arrived. It is generally believed that Aryans descended upon northern India and northern Mesopotamia around 1700 BC, Central and northeastern parts of Asia shortly afterward, the Balkans, Greece and Aegean areas not before 1500 BC, wreaking especial destruction in these areas, as has been noted.

It is only after Caucasian invasions into these areas as conquerors, and the ensuing racial intermingling that occurred, that the complexions of the inhabitants in the abovementioned areas began to lighten—although the general populations remained dark-skinned. But it is the influx of Caucasians into these areas that dispose Eurocentric historians to allege a Caucasian pedigree to the populations of Mycenae, Mesopotamia, India, Arabia, and warrior peoples who arose in the general area of Mesopotamia—like the Hittites, Babylonians, Assyrians and Hyksos. Of the abovementioned peoples, only the Greeks would make the most successful transition into a predominantly Caucasian or Caucasian-appearing people—a process that would take a millennium or more before light- or white-skinned people would prevail there. Yet, even today, many Greek complexions—like the complexions of Spaniards and southern Italians—betray extensive racial interbreeding with the original black-skinned inhabitants of the country.

What is certain is that an earlier, predominantly black- and dark-skinned population under the general nomenclatures of Iberians or Basques, overspread western Europe from the Mediterranean to Scandinavia as late as 2000 BPE and would gradually be supplanted by a later-arriving Caucasoid population. The reader is again encouraged to think of the territory comprising he United States 500 years ago. A dozen

Native American tribes occupied what is now the Greater New York City area. Maybe the reader is familiar with New York City, or has visited it and walked through the Times Square area marveling at the bright lights and excitement to be found there. In *Gotham*, authors Edwin G. Burrows and Mike Wallace tell us:

> By the time Europeans appeared on the scene, a mere five hundred years ago, what is now New York City had as many as fifteen thousand inhabitants [Native Americans] . . . with perhaps another thirty to fifty thousand in the adjacent parts of New Jersey, Connecticut, Westchester County, and Long Island. (5)

And regarding the world famous Times Square area, Evan T. Pritchard, author of *Native New Yorkers*, remarks that Broadway, where it intersects with Seventh Avenue "was one of the most tranquil and peaceful spots . . . suitable for contemplation and undisturbed rest for the wandering trader" (93).

Gawking at the bright lights, large computer-like screens on buildings, weaving through endless pedestrian traffic, lingering on the streets in the area long after Broadway shows have closed and most New Yorkers have set their alarms and gone to sleep, almost no one gives a thought to the fact that a mere 500 years ago a different race of people occupied the whole area—this whole land. These people are almost never seen today and, if they are, they are not recognized as descendants of the original inhabitant of the territory we call the United States.

The same concept can be applied to Europe. Just as a few clusters of Whites on the east coast of what would become the U.S. burgeoned into a violent, consuming stream of avaricious usurpers, dispossessing and practically annihilating the native peoples they found here, a similar wave of aggressive Whites would transform the faces of western Europe from dark to white from 1500 BC onward. However, even a millennium ago this transformation was not complete. There were still areas of dark-skinned people on the continent—the most numerous and significant of which inhabited Scandinavia. And history would not forget them.

CHAPTER 5

AFRO-ASIATIC REALMS—PART II

A subject that challenges age old beliefs, reinforced by centuries of repetition, is not often welcomed or considered objectively on its merits. Discussing black Vikings exclusively, without offering the reader some preparation, would still leave unanswered questions, doubts—which is why I've proceeded deliberately, hopefully providing the reader with a fresh reappraisal of European history. It is essential to consider transmigrations of other peoples or races into Europe so that the reader can fully comprehend how black-skinned races occupied Scandinavia and other northern areas of the continent in order to challenge the age old model of blue-eyed, blond Vikings and demonstrate—employing evidence from reputable sources, most of whom are overlooked today—that the Norsemen who made Europe tremble throughout the first half of the Middle Ages were actually a race of black- and dark-skinned people dominating the northern region of the continent only a thousand years ago.

The average reader's reluctance to accept such a notion is understandable, given the numerous body of historical works testifying to the enduring whiteness of Europe, so it will be necessary to revisit some areas, some tribes, some peoples of Europe to reemphasize the presence of Blacks and other dark-skinned races who resided there, while presenting additional information on these to offer more than mere repetition.

The whole of 5th century Europe is rather complicated and I won't pretend to understand all the events and movements of peoples that took place. It was a century of tribes under various names moving helter-skelter about the continent. Contingents of the later wave of Huns would take up residence in Dacia and give military support to Rome against other Hunnish groups, like Goths and Visigoths. The map of Europe during this period is absolutely confusing, and historical accounts differ as to alliances between Hunnish peoples, Hunnish alliances to Rome and to particular Roman leaders, as well as the reasons certain peoples or tribes migrated from one area to another.

The Vandals—who do not seem to be located near Italy and most of the concentrated action, but somewhere in central Germany—unbelievably migrate westward into Gaul, continue south into Iberia (Spain), cross into North Africa, then travel east to Carthage (i.e., modern Tunis) along the coast—all this distance *in a 30-year period!* Although one source I consulted and a documentary I recorded state that the Vandals made an agreement with an emperor of Rome to assist him from Africa against Hunnish inroads in Italy, Roger Collins, in *Early Medieval Europe 300-1000*, states: "A Vandal fleet sailed from Africa, and descended upon an undefended Rome [435 AD], giving the city a second sack, and perhaps a more thorough one than that of 410" (85).

So, while a historical atlas of Europe during the 5th century seems to illustrate presumably white tribes fleeing in disorder and confusion throughout western Europe, we at least now have the understanding that the Huns of Attila, Vandals, Goths, Alans and Suevi (not previously mentioned) were similarly black- and dark-skinned peoples. The assaults on Rome and its various territories take place from about 400-460 AD. Historians single out Huns (without noting their race) as the primary invaders, probably in concert with Gothic or Germanic tribes, although these latter had been sent reeling about western Europe by the massive Hunnish invasion. So, if Goths were—like Vandals, Alans, Visigoths, Attila's Huns and other Hunnish tribes—black- and dark-skinned (whether Asiatic or descendants of ancient Africoids, like the Scandinavians seem to have been) might not the swift Vandal departure for North Africa have been part of a planned flanking maneuver to assault the Western Roman Empire? Why would a people (historians usually assert that the Vandals numbered 80,000 souls, including women and children) seemingly race from central Europe, sail across the Gibraltar Strait to Africa, and purposefully scurry along the north African coast to Tunisia—the ancient domain of Carthage—and set about assaulting Rome (435 AD) almost upon their arrival? Some pieces of this puzzle are missing. Could the Hunnish, Gothic and Vandal assaults on Rome have been much broader and more purposeful in scope than we have been informed of?

The reader should also consult a historical atlas and note that the Kingdom of Attila includes a sizeable portion of Russia, northeast Germany, *southern Sweden and all of Denmark*. As of this writing, I have not discovered any direct references to a Hunnish invasion of Denmark and Sweden, yet the half dozen historical atlases I have consulted depict these territories as part of the Kingdom of Attila. A map presented in Richard Gordon's article ("Stopping Attila: The Battle of Chalons") shows that southeastern Eng-land and all of Ireland are part of the Visigothic kingdom in the mid-5th century, although I have not sought out any historical documentation offering details of this occupation.

During this same period (5th and 6th century), the Jutes, Angles and Saxons depart Jutland (Denmark) for Britain. One might assume these were Caucasian peoples fleeing the onslaught of the Huns into the Jutland Peninsula. Most historians do not make reference to Hunnish incursions into Jutland to explain the seemingly sudden departure of these tribes for Britain, so who were they, really? Historical records seem to indicate that the Jutland Peninsula had been occupied by black-skinned people since at least 2000 BC (Cimbri/Kymry), and certainly from 200 BC onwards. There are no references to *Jutes* (presumably, people of Jutland) or *Angles* on atlases prior to the 5th century, when they invaded what would become England.

The *Saxons* who, along with Jutes and Angles, invaded England, have a traceable history in Baltic regions of northern Germany but are not directly connected to the ancient Saxons—Saca, Sacae or Sacya—much earlier arrivals in Britain, who, according to Higgins, worshipped Buddha. The Saxons who entered Britain with Jutes and Angles will henceforth be referred to herein as *new* or *later* Saxons. The three groups suddenly appear on historical atlases in the mid-5th century, but of what race or races were they? And could Jutes and Angles have actually been Hunnish peoples designated these names to obscure a *Hunnish* invasion of Britain? To put it frankly, there does not appear to have been any room for a multitude of Whites in Jutland before and up to the 5th century AD.

And if these presumably white Jutes, Angles and Saxons were powerful enough to invade the future England, why did they not defend their supposed homelands on the Jutland Peninsula before having to suddenly depart? Instead, they suddenly appear magically in the mid-5th century at the very same time Attila and his Huns are storming into Gaul toward Paris—Jutes and Angles having not been mentioned in historical records before this time.

Although the works of Western historians smoothly outline the events of European history and seem to be in general agreement about the years certain rulers came to power and the years particular events occurred, they are not always in total accord. What Western historians *do* seem to be in total accord on is eliminating the presence of black- and dark-skinned people from the history of Europe, white-washing it to have us believe that Blacks have never played a role in its development. The Blacks of Britain and northern Europe in historical times are representative of a wider black-skinned population, which at one time overspread the whole continent, most of whom, by the onset of the 3rd century AD, had begun to be pushed to the northern and western extremities of the continent, as mentioned earlier.

I did not intend this work to be a chronological discourse on the Vikings, but I have gotten slightly ahead of myself, and we need to backtrack just a bit to get a clearer picture of the peoples occupying northern Europe just prior to the onset of the Viking Age. As well, we will have to briefly return to Greece and Asia in this chapter to build upon what was earlier presented and strengthen previous assertions regarding ancient British and Norse origins, although some readers might feel they have read enough to to fathom what may follow. I am thinking of my harshest critics in this regard, those who still doubt the evidence presented thus far and feel they need more convincing proof before accepting the notion of black Norsemen and other Blacks so recently occupying northern Europe. So I ask for the reader's further indulgence before we turn our full attention to the Vikings.

While Eurocentric scholars situate Caucasoids in Europe much earlier than 2,000 BC, Higgins, Massey, Sergi and Churchward, strangely, hardly mention them. And although many Eurocentric scholars cite Scandinavia as a cauldron of Caucasian peoples, including the people who became known as Vikings, B.F. De Costa, in *The Pre-Columbian Discovery of America by the Northmen*, states what has already been suggested in part in this work:

> The Northmen were descendants of a race that in early times migrated from Asia and traveled toward the north, settling down in what is now the kingdom of Denmark. From thence they overran Norway and Sweden, and afterward colonized Iceland and Greenland. (19)

While De Costa's book, published in 1890, is rather small (186 pages) in comparison to other works on the Vikings, it provides much of information on Norse characters and exploits to North America long prior to Columbus. One of the characters De Costa mentions is Thorhall the Hunter, who is mentioned in several sagas. He is described as a valuable aide to Eric the Red, and De Costa states: "This Thorhall was a man of immense size and great strength, and dark complexion and taciturn . . ." (121). Asiatics, or Mongoloids are not generally known for their height—a point that will be reemphasized later. Author Don Luke describes Thorhall as being a "mentor and closest companion of Eric the Red" (*African* 228). And author Frederick J. Pohl, in *Atlantic Crossings Before Columbus*, says of Thorhall:

> [H]e had long been with Erik and served him as huntsman in summer and steward in winter; he was a large man, and strong, black and like a giant, silent and foul-mouthed in his speech . . . [H]e was well acquainted with uninhabited parts. (136-7)

Thorhall the Hunter (or Huntsman) was also the guide of other Norse leaders and explorers. He is always spoken of as knowing uncharted areas of the ocean as well as often being truculent and mean-spirited, abandoning them when it suited his fancy.

Author Don Luke likens Thorhall the Hunter (also Huntsman) to a strong, tall black African, asserting that Africans were an important part of Viking populations. Of course, this does not fit the popular histories of the Northmen: Africans are not cold-weather people; Africans were never in Europe; Africans were never sea-going and certainly were not navigators. How could they have been? The extent of their shipbuilding abilities were dugout canoes, which don't have ocean-travel capabilities—or so we have been lead to believe.

These falsehoods, and far more negative ones, have been in circulation for several centuries, disseminated, of course, by Eurocentric writers after white Europeans had gained enough power to subjugate and destroy dark-skinned cultures, civilizations and any written records these may have possessed. Then Europeans wrote their own history, often claiming the achievements of dark-skinned people as their own, in works presented in an all-knowing fashion, which always omitted dark-skinned protagonists.

An analysis of the information extant makes it evident that northern Germany seems to have been the historic melting pot or convergence area of Africoids and Asiatic peoples for millennia. We also need to realize that northern Europe had long been inhabited by black-skinned people—from the very ancient

Egyptian megalith builders to the Germanic Picts, Goths, Scandinavians and Germans of western Europe, to the Lapps, ancient Finns, Balts, Ugrians, Bulgars and Slavs extending east into Russia. Nearly all these peoples (and others under various names) were settled and in place before the arrival of any significant Caucasoid populations—although more easterly tribes had already begun intermingling with Caucasoids streaming out of the Great White Forest.

The popular histories are generally selective in discussing Europe, Western scholars invariably beginning their discourses of the continent and its peoples through the eyes of the Greeks and the civilizations known to them at the time of Hellenic invasions of Thrace and the Greek mainland and isles. Only a rare Western scholar offers any indication that barbaric Greek invaders entered a realm dominated by black- and dark-skinned, highly civilized peoples known by various names like Mycenaeans, Pelasgians and Arkadians, among others. For instance, in *Black Athena vol. 1*, Martin Bernal states:

> There is little doubt about the presence of Egyptian and Semitic religious influences throughout Northern Greece and Thrace [birthplace of Alexander the Great] . . . . It is clear that Dorian kings continued to be proud of their Egypto-Hyksos ancestry well into Hellenistic times. (82)

Many of the peoples inhabiting various parts of the Greek mainland and isles, though known under a number of names, were ethnically similar but rendered different by Western scholars' penchant for separating tribes and peoples and giving the impression that each was different and unrelated—except for all being supposedly Caucasian. Even related peoples have squabbles and fight each other over territory, trade, or real or imagined slights. Native American tribes often contended with each other over such matters and, while their specific origin-myths may not have been the same, most of them were racially similar, and it was to their detriment that their various peoples could not come together for the benefit of all once Europeans arrived.

Three millennia before the epoch of the European conquest of North America, the peoples of what is referred to as the Aegean civilization were faced with a relatively similar series of events: barbaric invaders, Caucasoids, were descending into the Aegean world; the longer-established peoples in the area were engaged in age-old disputes over territory and dominance, although the cultures of most were of Egyptian origin or influence; and some Aegean tribes formed alliances with the Hellenic invaders to wage warfare against others they shared cultural, religious and ethnic affinities with, resulting in the eventual destruction of what is commonly referred to as Archaic Civilization, to which the Mycenaean and Minoan civilizations belonged. Western scholars have, as in other areas of European history, presented us with names and nomenclatures bereft of clear faces and ethnic data, leaving us with the assumption that *all* the contending peoples were Caucasian, while Bernal demonstrates that Egyptian—black Egyptian—culture suffused the whole Aegean civilization prior to the arrival of the Hellenes, informing us, for instance, that "[I]n the mid-5th century [BC] the 18th Dynasty established a powerful empire in the Levant, and received tribute from the Aegean" (21). He speaks of the *Heraklids* who, besides claiming descent from Herakles [Hercules], viewed Egyptians and Phoenicians as their royal ancestors. To confirm the Heraklids' claim to royal descent, Bernal states:

> There is no doubt that the descendants of these conquerors, the Dorian kings of Classical and Hellenistic times, believed themselves to be descended from Egyptians and Phoenicians. (op. cit.)

Egyptian influence—and Egyptian peoples—would continue to influence Aegean culture long after the arrival of the presumably Caucasian Hellenes, and a later chapter will even show that the Spartans were primarily black-skinned Egyptians (or Ethiopians or other Africans) and that such peoples were prominent in the Trojan War. Homer's *Iliad*, which many of us read in middle or high school (in an abridged version, perhaps) mentions Blacks participating in the Trojan War, clearly indicating that some prominent personages (like Agamemnon) were *black-skinned* Greeks or Africans, something we'll return to much later.

For now, let us understand that, although in decline by about 1,200 BC, Egypt (with Ethiopians, Nubians and Cushites) had long been the reigning super-power of the Ages, dominating the Aegean and Medierranean worlds from the Near East (and beyond) to Iberia. But they had spread even beyond the Pillars of Hercules (i.e., Gibraltar Strait) long before this—probably during the Late Paleolithic—establishing colonies in the British Isles and western Europe all the way to Scandinavia, erecting megalithic structures in all the areas they must have populated with many thousands—people Eurocentric historians have called Mediterraneans and "dark whites" to obscure their origin. Our previously mentioned Iceman is a sudden, stark, disturbing, in the flesh representative of these people and has tongue-tied Western scientists who originated the system of racial classification. They will not even dare to call the Iceman a *dark white*, a term that once prompted the eminent W.E.B. Du Bois to quip: "We cannot, if we are sane, divide the world into whites, yellows, and blacks and then call blacks whites" (qtd. in Luke, *African Presence* 239).

Even in the 5th century BC, during the period Herodotus was compiling his history of the region, it cannot be asserted that the Greeks were a white-skinned people, although Eurocentric historians have long promoted this presumption. Western historians have written Blacks out of the entire region with their colorless recounting of Greek history, leaving us to conclude that black-skinned people were never there. They have continuously insisted that Egyptians were Caucasian so that even when proof is offered that they were black- and dark-skinned, the admirer of the architecturally immaculate Great Pyramid and the still astounding Abu Simbel, Temple of Dendera, and Great Sphinx finds it impossible to fathom that black people erected them—some, long before Hellenic Greece was in her infancy.

Some Eurocentric scholars have maintained that this megalithic culture began in the north of Europe and spread southward, convenient for them because it obviates a northward movement of populations from North Africa, the Iberian Peninsula and the Mediterranean. A few, like Higgins (although I do not consider him typically Eurocentric), claim that Asiatic peoples were the builders of megaliths, coming mainly from the areas of Mesopotamia and Asia Minor. But if this were so, why would these people have outrightly bypassed so much territory—the Balkans, central Europe and most of Italy—to reach the far west of the continent before erecting megaliths? Let's be logical.

In *The Sphinx and the Megaliths,* author John Ivimy discounts the theory that primitive people living in Britain could have been responsible for raising huge stones, and states:

> [T]he stones were erected by men who had a very considerable knowledge of geometry and astronomy . . . . We postulate . . . that a colony of highly civilized people came to Britain from Egypt and established themselves . . . . *Egypt was the only civilized country in existence within reasonable reach of Britain at the time Stonehenge was founded.* (*my emphasis* 70)

While Ivimy mentions a *colony* of highly civilized Egyptians coming into Britain, it had to have been more like a *flood* of black-skinned humanity, since it would have taken a significant multitude of people to erect the hundreds of megalithic structures in Britain, and even more to erect those littering Ireland. So there had to be thousands—hundreds of thousands—of people engaged in megalith-building over the period of the megalithic age and hundreds of thousands more in continental Europe erecting the thousands of megalith monuments in Germany, France, Iberia and Scandinavia. They were more than colonists; they had to have been settlers, denizens, inhabitants of Europe who should rightly be considered aboriginals—*black Europeans who occupied western Europe millennia before the first Caucasians arrived in those areas.*

So they would have come as settlers, immigrants, pioneers, arriving over many centuries with their wives, children, personal belongings, necessary equipment and implements, and they would have built numerous towns in the areas of the megaliths and wherever they settled—probably intermingling to an extent with even earlier settled Grimaldi and Australoid peoples. Many of these towns would have had dwellings built of fitted stones and rocks in snug hillsides with hearths, sleeping and storage areas and passageways connecting each family unit. One of these small towns (or villages) was recently unearthed in the Orkneys (which have their megaliths, too) in very good condition, but the documentary discussing it, of course, gives the impression that ancient Caucasoids had erected it by merely not associating it with the megalithic culture or mentioning the race of the people who probably built it.

However much Eurocentric historians promote the ancientness and superiority of Caucasian people over all the dark-skinned populations who have ever lived on earth, they have yet to present us with archeological evidence in any region of Europe or Asia that can be positively attributed to an advanced *Caucasian* civilization. This is why these historians are so determined to inject Caucasians into nearly every ancient civilization—Egyptian, Sumerian, Indian, Aegean, Hittite, Babylonian, Persian and Phoenician, all located in the ancient territory of Greater Ethiopia and the "protonegroid belt of mankind . . . across the ancient world" (Thomas 339). And regarding the megalith-builders of the Mediterranean and Europe, Ivimy states regarding Egyptians:

> There was no other developed civilization of any kind within reasonable reach of the British Isles, *nor was there any other culture in the world* that had yet learned the arts of quarrying and transporting by land and water huge blocks of stone, cutting and tooling them to shape, and erecting them one on top of the other. (*my emphasis* 83)

Lest the reader misunderstand, we are not speaking here of the people that presently occupy Egypt today who are mostly of Arab descent. Arabs began sending hordes of people into Egypt around the middle of the 7th century AD, who spread the religion of Islam and intermingled with the predominantly black-skinned population to produce the type of people one sees in Egypt and North Africa today. The Egyptians along the Mediterranean coast were considerably lighter-skinned due to long intermingling with light- or white-skinned Greeks from the time of Alexander's invasion and onward. We are speaking of most ancient Egypt in regard to the megalithic culture, an Egypt which, prior to 3,700 years ago, had been essentially untouched by outsiders. These were predominantly black-skinned people with mixtures of Nubians, Cushites, Pygmies, Ethiopians and, perhaps, original black Arabs when Egypt and all the Mediterranean lands west to Iberia were the western lands of Greater Ethiopia, which also included a wide expanse of land extending eastward to the Indus and beyond, all inhabited by culturally and racially similar peoples. And if ancient Egypt was reaching its zenith 5,000 or more years ago, megalithic culture in Europe would have been in existence for at least 2,000 years, and our 5,300-year-old Alpine Iceman would have been contemporary with both.

In 1993 or 1994 an African-American ex-professor of mine, Dr. Amos Wilson, told me he had an article for me when I stopped in at his printing office in the South Bronx (New York City) one evening. We had become fast buddies after I took a Psychology course with him. Stacks of his dozen published books filled the shelves of one wall. He knew I was researching black Vikings. Fishing around the drawer of a file cabinet, he extracted a copy he had made of an article from the *New York Times* entitled "A Geneticist Maps Ancient Migrations," by Louise Levathes (27 July 1993). Sadly, Dr. Wilson would pass on only a year or two later—a young 53—but I remain indebted to him for giving me the article and showing concern for what I was doing.

The article concerned the work of Italian geneticist Dr. Luigi Cavalli-Sforza, then at Stanford University, who had made a study of DNA samples from people living in different parts of the world in order to genetically chart man's origins and movements around the earth. Dr. Cavalli-Sforza confirmed that Homo sapiens spread around the earth beginning 100,000 years ago after leaving Africa and that they had reached every continent by 60,000 years ago. He found that people from the Middle East moved into Europe sometime after 10,000 years ago, claiming that the Basques are their sole direct survivors.

Ms. Levathes' article provides many interesting insights, which we can only touch on here. What most interested me was Dr. Cavalli-Sforza's assertion that:

> . . . Europeans [today's Europeans] are a mixed population that emerged only about 30,000 years ago and appears to have *65 percent Asian ancestry and 35 percent African ancestry* (with an error rate of plus or minus 8 percent.) (*my emphasis*, op. cit.)

A genetic map based on Dr. Cavalli-Sforza's study was presented in the article, and it purports to show the most and least genetically similar populations. This genetic map clearly implies that Africans and Europeans are extremely close genetically. The claim that 35 percent of Europeans show indications of African ancestry confirms quite a lot about what has and will continue to be presented in this work. Europeans' genetic relationship to Africans is quite intriguing.

A curious statement in the article is that "Australian aboriginals, though they appear to look more like Africans, are genetically closer to Chinese" (op. cit.). These are Ms. Levathes' words, but it is like saying that the pyramids of Egypt look like those of Meso-America, or that Daddy looks like Junior. Aren't the Australian Aborigines far older than the Chinese, whom Diop asserts developed c. 17,000 years ago? There *were* no Chinese when the earliest migrants out of Africa, the Australoid Aboriginals, or Grimaldis trekked eastward, reaching Australia at least 62,000 years ago.

At the time this article was published Dr. Cavalli-Sforza was working on a book of his studies. Published in 1994, the book, *The History and Geography of Human Genes* (Princeton University Press, by Cavalli-Sforza, Paulo Menozzi and Alberto Piazza), is extremely technical (even the abridged version I have) and wearisome to read. However, it seems to complicate what seemed simpler in Ms. Levathes' article. The genetic map in the book (Fig. 20) has been altered from the one appearing in Ms. Levathes' article in regard to African and European genetic connections; however, even the altered map suits our purpose here, but there seems to be an effort to lessen the genetic impact of Africans in the rest of the world. Two later chapters will discuss the findings and assertions made in *The History and Geography of Human Genes*.

While most historians believe man has been sailing the Mediterranean for at least 7,000 years, seafaring, as discussed earlier, was a much older occupation, and Egyptians were early masters of shipbuilding and sea travel. So if the huge stones employed in megalith-building were ferried to the territories they were erected in, ancient Egyptians had to have constructed ships strong enough to carry them, had to have the ingenuity to load and unload them, had to have enough space on those ships to contain them, had to have the ability to navigate them to their intended destinations, had to have the ingenuity to transport them many miles overland to their places of construction—with a large enough fleet to manage such operations expeditiously. We have to assume that some ships never reached their intended destinations because of sea storms or adverse weather and that over the centuries improvements were made in ship construction and maneuverability. We have to envision generation after generation of rugged men and women adapting to a sometimes harsh environment and learning about both the sea and the lands they called home. If such industriousness was extant from Iberia to Denmark and southern Sweden, should the reader be surprised that several millennia afterward a seagoing culture existed in Scandinavia (and along all the western waterways from Iberia to Sweden) and that later Vikings and Norsemen constructed the most seaworthy ships in the world when they rose to prominence? But we have been programmed to believe that Blacks—even Egyptians—were incapable of such industry, and scholars would rather attribute ancient seamanship in the area to others, especially the Phoenicians, who were much later arrivals on the world scene than ancient Egyptians.

If Euroentric historians had admitted that Egyptians or Africans built seaworthy ships, even a child looking at a map of the Mediterranean and the lands that surround it would see that it would be extremely easy for Africans to cross the narrow Strait of Gibraltar, a mere 15 miles or less, to reach Europe.

"Couldn't they do it, Daddy? It's not that far."

"Well, no, son. They didn't know how to navigate by the stars, didn't know east from west, north from south."

"So they never tried it? Couldn't they see Spain just across the water".

"No, son. For thousands of years they just stood on he beach watching the waves go in and out, waiting for white people like us to come and show them how to do it."

If Western historians admitted that thousands of years ago Africans were capable of sea travel, they could not possibly have written Blacks out of Europe as effectively as they have. They had to dispel any African ability to reach Europe—even by the fabled ancient Egyptians—to foist this deception on the world, a world far older, perhaps, than they dare to admit. In *Signs and Symbols of Primordial Man*, Churchward discusses the types of human beings who emerged out of Africa "and then spread all over the world, taking with him, at various epochs, all the knowledge . . . with which he left" (489). He writes of the *Stellar Mythos* people out of Egypt who laid out the constellations and associated them with gods and goddesses whom we still read about today when we read the mythologies of the Greeks, Egyptians, Indians and Sumerians. All of these gods and goddesses originated in Egypt untold millennia before anyone heard of a Greek. According to Churchward, the cult of Stellar Mythos people lasted for *258,270 years*, and:

> It was these people who built the Great Pyramid and temples in Central and South America, and other parts of the world, where we now find the remains of their former greatness . . . . They came from Egypt. (489-90)

It would seem that the antiquity of the Great Pyramid, Sphinx and other ancient Egyptian monuments merit serious reassessment if Churchward is correct. More such commentary will be briefly mentioned later, but the limitations of this work preclude any reassessment (except by implication) of the ages of Egyptian monuments and architectural wonders. It is foolish to entertain the belief that black men—Egyptians and other Africans—did not possess ship-building and seafaring capabilities during and prior to the Megalithic age discussed above.

The post-glacial penetration of Europe by African and Africoid peoples reached other northern regions of the continent. A number of historians and anthropologists, like G. Sergi, Diop, Friedrich Hertz and Churchward attest to undeniable evidence of Neolithic and ancient (as well as historical) Negroid remains in the Balkans, Germany, Baltic regions and Russia. Churchward, for instance, informs us that, "The skulls and physical types of these [human remains] in North Africa have so many characteristics similar to the Finns (a northern people)" . . . (136).

The Finns (or the ancestors of people who would become known as Finns) early occupy a wide expanse of territory east of the Baltic Sea, often classed as Mongoloids, whom most associate with Huns. Although the Finns of the Viking Age are not generally classed as Scandinavians, it is probable that Finns were also represented in Viking fleets, many living in Scandinavia and intermingling with Norse peoples. And according to Gibbon and many others, the language of the black-skinned Hungarians who ravaged the Balkans as Huns, Magyars and Turks "bears a close and clear affinity to the idioms of the Fennic [i.e., Finnic] race, of an obsolete and savage race, which formerly occupied the northern regions of Asia and Europe" (Gibbon vol. 2, 338).

The penchant of Eurocentric historians to divide peoples into separate, faceless, colorless groups has limited our ability to see connections between one people and another. When it comes to Europe, we are shown how presumably white Europeans spread from Europe to the Near East, to North America, to Australia and other areas they have colonized. Whatever particular country of Europe the colonizers hailed from, we are never allowed to lose sight of the fact that they were part of the Caucasian, Aryan, or white division of mankind—presumably a superior race of people. When Eurocentric historians and scientists discuss the migrations of black-skinned peoples out of Africa and Egypt into Asia, however (I leave out Europe here because they never admit Africans entered it), these black-skinned people quickly lose their African identity becoming, suddenly, a multitude of *Asiatic* peoples—Semites, Arabians, Mesopotamians, Indians, Scythians, Medes, and so on—immediately upon departing Africa! Their Africanness, their connectedness, is instantly expunged by Western historians, obscuring the obvious fact that all the migrants out of the continent were at one time racially akin and black- or dark-skinned Negroids, who remained so for millennia after their departure. Only a few historians, like the aforementioned Churchward, have commented on the racial similarities between the Finns and African peoples, verifying that Africans, in their ancient migrations, journeyed over the whole earth, including areas of northern Europe.

*   *   *   *   *

After the new-Roman usurpation and eventual destruction of Etruria and the Etruscans, they set their sights on the *Carthaginians* of North Africa, a city-state we have to assume was at least as old as Etruria. Both nations were in existence about the middle of the 9th century BC (most Eurocentric historians assert that the Etruscan Empire began in 750 BC, but this is debatable). The royalty of both nations wore royal vestments of a particular purple color and had significant commerce with each other over several centuries. We earlier discussed the advanced engineering capabilities of the Etruscans, but little is known about their considerable naval prowess. According to Werner Keller:

> It was as seafaring people that the Etruscans made their appearance in Italy . . . Quite early they must have built a merchant navy for shipping their imports and exports, and also have maintained a powerful fleet of warships for the defense of their harbors, coasts, and trading empire. (67)

In the mid-6th century BC, Carthage and Etruria made a "great alliance" to fend off the growing power of the Greeks, whom we must assume were largely white-skinned by this time, having gained racial ascendancy over the disintegrating Aegean civilization. Greeks called *Phocaeans*, coming from Ionia, had established a settlement protected by warships in Massilia (modern Marseilles) in 600 BC and had defeated a Carthaginian fleet, threatening Carthaginian commerce with Liguria (reduced to southern Gaul). The Phocaeans were eventually defeated by the combined naval might of the Carthaginians and Etruscans, and their alliance would become closer after this. And we have to assume that intermarriage was common between the two nations over the centuries of their alliance.

Most writers acknowledge the naval power of the Carthaginians, although they tend to stress that Carthaginians were *Phoenicians* hoping, I am certain, to drape an Asian cast over them in our minds. The same veil is draped over the Etruscans to dispel any notion that a portion of them, if not most, may have had African or Egyptian ancestry.

Mentioned earlier was that Mr. Franklin likened Etruscan countenances to Negroes, but his fuller statement is: "the ancient Etruscans had the countenances of Negroes, the same as the images of Buddha in India" (qtd. in Higgins *Anac., vol 1*, 166). And regarding Etruscan naval power, Keller informs us:

> Ancient writers depict the Etruscans as bold and awe-inspiring seafarers. Legends, episodes, and incidents of derring-do gathered about them. To the Greeks they were pirates whose audacious raids and pillaging expeditions were feared throughout the Mediterranean. (67)

Three centuries later, new-Romans (Etruscans, remember, began Rome) brought down the Etruscan empire, destroying her fabulous cities while slaying untold numbers of its inhabitants throughout its considerable territory.

The Roman Empire would endure for nearly a thousand years, but had emerged into a Europe that was still largely dominated by Africoid peoples whose commercial network extended from North Africa and the western Mediterranean to the British Isles, through western Europe into Germany, and through Germany to the Baltic and Scandinavia, along roads formerly utilized by the Etruscans. And it was through the Etruscans—teachers and civilizers of the white inhabitants of southern Italy who would eventually become the new Romans—that early Romans learned of this vigorous world of commerce. In Etruria, fertile soil allowed agriculture to support a large population, but iron and copper could also be found and was exploited. As the new Romans insinuated themselves into Etruscan society, peacefully at first and adopting Etruscans culture, they soon began to covet Etruscan wealth and territory when they realized how extensive their trade routes were and the profits and power that could be realized by appropriating the natural or manufactured resources not only of Etruria, but those of her trading partners as well—gold, iron and silver mines in Iberia; tin mines and woolen goods in Britain; pottery, grain, silver and iron mines in Gaul; pottery, olive oil, glass and amber in Germany—and understanding that more amber could be obtained from Scandinavian sources along the Baltic. These are the commodities the new Romans desired for themselves, and the Etruscans were eventually destroyed when Romans gained enough knowledge of the sources of these various commodities and the trade routes to reach them.

During the 3rd century BC, the first of three wars between Carthage and Rome would be fought. For whatever reason, the sophistic term *Punic Wars* has been applied to them. I am unable to locate the source of the term *Punic*, although it seems related to Phoenicians in some way—but is used to refer to *Carthaginians, Carthage,* or to artifacts not directly connected to Phoenicia or the Levant. The three sources I have on Carthage and the Punic Wars don't offer an explanation of the term. And my fat *Webster's Twentieth Century Dictionary* relates Punic to Carthage, Carthaginians and, under a second Punic, the West Semitic language of ancient Carthage. It seems *Punic* denotes *Carthaginian*. So, why don't historians simply apply the term *Carthaginian Wars* in regard to their battles with Rome instead of Punic Wars?

The Levant and Phoenicia were invaded by a number of peoples—the Philistines, who carved out territory in the area now known as Gaza, the Hittites, and the Persians. We must assume that inter-racial mixing occurred and that Phoenicians were not unaffected. They were primarily merchants and traders, not ordinarily a martial people, and intermingled and intermarried with their more powerful invaders to maintain their influence and mercantile hegemony in the area. However, they eventually lost much of their power and independence, especially to the Assyrians, during the first half of the 7th century BC.

Carthage, meanwhile, gained in stature and military might. Its connection to Tyre (the Phoenician capital city) and the Phoenician homeland had remained strong through several centuries; however, says Serge Lancel, in *Carthage, A History,* "the military conquests of the Carthaginians in Sicily and Sardenia, in the second half of the sixth century, then the victory over the Phocaeans in Corsica . . . [allowed] Carthage to form itself *de facto* into an autonomous power" (81).

Over the centuries Carthaginians had intermingled, intermarried and formed alliances with the still black-skinned tribes of North Africa—Numidians, Libyco-Berbers and Mauritanians—and the Carthaginian population, even the mostly Phoenician ruling class, must have exhibited a generally dark-skinned appearance, with the usual variations of complexion. It was primarily the Carthaginians who controlled the Pillars of Hercules to prevent rivals from reaching the Atlantic Ocean. This was especially so after the Etruscans lost their power in Italy. So, black- and dark-skinned Africans—as Carthaginians—were still dominating the Mediterranean, venturing into the Atlantic Ocean and up the western coast of continental Europe on commercial voyages, which took them to the British Isles, western Gaul, northern Germany and Zealand, in Scandinavia. Carthaginians are also reputed to have made numerous voyages to North and Meso-America, and their great navigator Hanno, ". . . with sixty fifty-oar vessels, with about 30,000 men and women on board, together with the necessary victuals and equipment," sailed around the great western bulge of Africa to what is now Cameroon in the 5th century BC" (Lancel 102).

When a significant number of Whites reached westernmost Europe (c. 600-500 BC)—assuming the vanguard of the arriving *new*, or *later* Celts into the area were predominantly Caucasian—the Carthaginians were an old story. While Western historians date the Phoenician establishment of Carthage to 814 BC, many date the establishment of Utica, a Phoenician city-state in the same general area, to about 1100 BC. But both city-states may have been longer established than historians care to admit.

Most Eurocentric scholars insist that the Phoenicians were Caucasian, or white. Despite all the evidence of affinity between Egyptians and Phoenicians—in art, religion, shared deities, military and commercial ties, language and more—L.A. Waddell, in the preface of his *Phoenician Origin of the Britons, Scots and Anglo-Saxons* asserts:

> I have found by indisputable inscriptional and other evidence . . . [the Phoenicians were] *not Semites as hitherto supposed, but were Aryans in Race, Speech and Script* . . . That is to say, they were of the fair and long-haired civilizing "Northern" race. (vi)

In typical Eurocentric fashion of the time, Waddell Caucasianizes the Egyptians and other peoples of the Near East, stating he has found—

> . . . the Lost Origin of the *Aryans*, the fair, long-headed North European race, the traditional ancestors of our forbears of the Brito-Scandinavian race who gave to Europe in prehistoric times its Higher Civilization and civilized Languages. (op. cit. v-vi)

Phoenician Origin of the Britons, Scots and Anglo-Saxons was published in 1924, a dozen years after Churchward's *Signs and Symbols of Primordial Man,* in which Churchward emphatically asserts that Egypt is far more ancient than Western historians have admitted, noting that Greek historian Diodorus Siculus declared:

> . . . the Egyptians claimed to have sent out colonies over the whole world in times of the remotest antiquity. They affirmed that they had not only taught the Babylonians astronomy, but that Belus [same as Baal and Bel] and his subjects were a colony that went out of Egypt. (283)

Without getting overly detailed here, Baal, Bel or Belus was a god-figure also known as Kronos by the Assyrians, whose son, Ninus (identified with Nimrod) is said to be the founder of Babylon. The worship of Belus or Baal overspread the whole of Sumer and Syrio-Palestine, an area which included ancient Phoenicia. The Phoenicians were primarily responsible for the spread of the worship of this god to Britain, western Europe and, possibly, the Americas. And Waddell should not have been unaware of Churchward's work, in which he states, citing Eusebius, Plato and Tacitus:

> . . . the Phoenicians did not claim to be themselves the inventors of the art of writing, but admitted that it was obtained by them from Egypt. Therefore the Egyptians were the inventors of the alphabet. (op. cit. 43)

Waddell's *Phoenician Origin*, though, should not be tossed aside, for it presents a wealth of information on the Phoenicians and insights of the Ancient World that are quite accurate and revelatory. My objection to this work is Waddell's almost maniacal assertion that Phoenicians were "Aryans, [of] the fair, long-headed North European race," which he emphasizes over and over, as if repetition will make it so. The work comes across as almost a personal, angry diatribe against the notion that *black-skinned* Phoenicians could have been partly responsible for bringing civilization into early Europe. And nearly a century before *Phoenician Origins* was published, Higgins, in *Celtic Druids*, emphasizes that "swarms" of black-skinned peoples and tribes departed southern Asia to invade and settle what was to become Europe, stating:

> An original cast had no doubt advanced across the Euphrates, perhaps had been pushed on by fresh swarms until it arrived at the Mediterranean Sea: it there settled, built cities, and formed Phoenicia. (68)

In addition to emphasizing the Asian origin of the Phoenicians, most Western scholars assert that Phoenicians were the navigators on the Egyptian ships that sailed the Mediterranean and voyaged into the Atlantic to the British Isles, Scandinavia and other areas of the world. If Churchward's 258,270-year length of the Stellar Mythos people is accurate (a *Lunar,* then a *Solar Mythos* people followed them), and he believes that Egyptians "sent out colonies over the whole world in times of the remotest antiquity" (Churchward 283), then Egyptians *themselves* must have navigated their own vessels, having charted the constellations and their movements from various parts of the earth, which must have involved establishing the four cardinal points (i.e., north, south, east and west). Ancient Egyptians accomplished these without the assistance of Phoenicians.

The common date for the beginning of the Megalithic Age is 4,000 BC, but this date should probably be put back at least another thousand years. Some Western scholars have even credited the Phoenicians as the erectors of the megaliths, but the earliest date I have come across for their appearance is c. 3,200 BC, and there is scant evidence of megalith building in their presumed homeland in the Levant; they weren't generally builders—though many credit them with building Solomon's Temple. However, they were not in existence during the earlier period of megalith-building, which commenced several millennia before their appearance on the world stage. Moreover, if Phoenicians were numerous enough to send thousands of men strong enough to erect megaliths all over western Europe, why could they not utilize this manpower and ingenuity to solidify, defend or expand their home territory in the Levant? No. They were not the builders of the megaliths. No. The Egyptians did not need them to navigate waters they, Egyptians, had been navigating for millennia.

Higgins and Bernal include the Phoenicians as part of the black- and dark-skinned *Pelasgi* who overran the Greek Isles and much of the Near East, the Phoenicians taking a southerly course to the Levant where they soon take to the sea as merchants and form an alliance with Egypt. Either the Phoenicians were extremely fast learners after arriving in the Levant with no seafaring skills out of Asia, or they began as an originally Egyptian colony who set out for Asia with knowledge of navigation learned in Egypt who retraced their steps back toward Egypt after finding Asia to turbulent to dominate or inhabit. They are acquainted with seamanship and shipbuilding from he moment they emerge in history, leading me to believe that they were more than likely an Egyptian colony. Their precise origin will be further discussed herein, but it is noteworthy that Higgins states that the Pelasgi (i.e., Pelasgians) were from Phoenicia and "the Phoenicians and *Etruscans* were the same people" (*my emphasis, Celtic Druids* 264).

If Phoenicians and Etruscans were the same people, the Etruscan relationship to Carthage becomes even more significant, uniting the ruling classes of both territories to Phoenicia, which most Western scholars have not informed us of. When the new-Romans suppressed, then destroyed Etruria, becoming the new power on the Italian peninsula, they soon afterwards focused their attention on Carthage in order to challenge Carthaginian supremacy in the western Mediterranean, leading to the first of three wars with Carthage, referred to as the *Punic Wars.*

The most famous of these was the second, beginning in 218 BC, when Hannibal crossed into Spain with an army of 90,000 men and forty battle-elephants, trekked across southern Gaul, traversed the Alps and descended into Italy—vanquishing all the armies Rome sent against him. Might his northern descent into Italy have been an attempt to aid and resuscitate the dispossessed Etruscans and enlist them in an assault on Rome? Couldn't Hannibal's ultimate mission have been to demonstrate allegiance to a beleaguered ally that Carthage would need to maintain hegemony in the western Mediterranean? In the popular works on Hannibal and the Punic Wars, only a rare Western scholar has mentioned the Etruscan and Carthaginian kinship. Hannibal's assault on the new Roman Empire is usually spoken of as a war to avenge his father, Hamilcar's defeat by Rome during the First Punic War (264-241 BC), 264 BC being the precise year new-Rome completely took control of the Rome *the Etruscans* had established centuries earlier. So, Hamilcar Barca's assault against Rome might also be seen as an attempt to restore the Etruscan nation to power, but Western historians never seem to consider this. Hopefully, this probability is now apparent to the reader.

Need I mention that Hannibal was a black African, as were the 90,000 (some say 80,000) men he crossed into Spain with in the first leg of his assault on Rome? Along the way the Carthaginians took control of three-fourths of the Iberian Peninsula before crossing the Pyrenees mountain range into Gaul—minus the troops who remained behind to secure Spain. Moving through southern Gaul, Hannibal's army was attacked by several Celtic tribes before his army reached the Alps. To this day, no one can claim for sure which route he took through the Alps to enter northern Italy, but he lost a number of men and elephants along the way—arriving in northern Italy, according to Harold Lamb, author of *Hannibal: One Man Against Rome*, with "12,000 Africans on foot . . . 8,000 Spaniards, and 6,000 horsemen. So 26,000 in all followed Hannibal down a stream . . . into the headwaters of the Po. Perhaps 12,000 had strayed or been lost on the journey from the Pyrenees" (89).

Serge Lancel (*Carthage, A History*) gives identical figures, noting that Hannibal had lost nearly all his elephants after his first encounter with Roman troops. Although Hannibal attracted Gauls (i.e., Celts) and several Italic tribes to his cause, he did not receive the response he expected from the demoralized Etruscans, who knew they could expect severe reprisals if Hannibal's venture failed.

Although Hannibal never lost a battle on Italian soil in the sixteen years he maneuvered throughout the peninsula, he was constrained to abandon Italy in 203 BC to defend Carthage from a Roman assault. Hannibal suffered his first defeat at Zama, Carthage, in 202 BC, then fled Cathage for the eastern Mediterreanean where he continued to try to enlist forces to fight against Rome, which was extending her military power toward Greece and Asia Minor. Continually pursued by Roman troops wherever he sought refuge, Hannibal took his own life in Bithynia (northern Asia Minor) in 183 BC. After the Third Punic War in 146 BC, Carthage was completely burned to the ground by the victorious Romans who afterwards spread salt over the entire area so that nothing would ever again grow in the soil of the vanquished empire. Rome became the reigning power in the west, and her military might would continue to grow. In another century, Julius Caesar would proclaim himself a god and set Roman attention on northern Europe and Egypt.

The eclipse of Etruria and Carthage close the final curtain on the Archaic world, whose final act had begun with their almost simultaneous establishment around the 9th century BC, if not earlier. The Second Punic War, in which Hannibal nearly destroyed Rome, can be looked upon as the climax of this final act, Cheikh Anta Diop, in *The African Origin of Civilization*, noting:

> It can be said that, with his [i.e., Hannibal's] defeat, the supremacy of the Negro or Negroid world ended. Henceforth the torch passed to the European populations of the northern Mediterranean . . . From then on the northern Mediterranean dominated the southern Mediterranean. (119)

The Phoenician ruling elite had carried eastern influences out of Egypt and the Near East into the western Mediterranean and points beyond the Pillars of Hercules. Egyptian (and to a lesser extent, Phoenician) influences would still suffuse western Europe, the British Isles and Scandinavia—evidence that well into historical times, black- and dark-skinned peoples had inhabited and dominated western Europe from the Mediterranean and Iberia, through Britain and Gaul, to Scandinavia and the Baltic in that world before our own.

The rub is that Eurocentric historians and scientists have stamped an Aryan or Caucasian label on nearly every people associated with Europe and branded "mysterious" any people whose art-works, religious rites, racial depictions and artifacts do not fit the Aryan mold. In an article entitled "Preserving the Eurosupremacist Myth" (*Egypt vs. Greece* 2002), Don Luke, Ph.D., accurately summarizes this labeling process:

> [W]hen an independent non-Indo European presence is discovered in early Europe, the African is automatically eliminated as the possible occupant. And among other

possibilities (which includes anyone else), the most likely candidates are always some non-descript unidentifiable quasi-Caucasoid type which makes its appearance from out of nowhere only to disappear without a trace once the particular episode which required their presence is past. (92)

Looking at the expansion of Rome after Carthage was defeated, one must sometimes wonder what drove Romans—new Romans—to the areas they set out to conquer. The Balkans, Asia Minor, Egypt and the Near East are understandable, being the most fabled areas, remnants of Greater Ethiopia, and the gateway to the Orient and wealth. But why Gaul, Spain, Germany and Britain—presumably not as wealthy, less fabled and, in the case of Germany and Britain, having a colder climate? What could Rome have been seeking that had any value? Or was their objective simply naked aggression, as the general histories seem to imply? The emphasis in standard histories always seems to be on Roman legions, warfare for the sake of conquest, territorial expansion. Why weren't the Romans content to remain in Italy and its nearby environs?

It was not until I was well into this humble work you are reading that an answer became obvious: the Romans invaded and sought to conquer the very territories which the Phoenico-Etruscans and Carthaginians had formerly dominated; the land and sea routes of the Etruscans to the Baltic and North Seas; the Phoenico-Carthaginian trade routes to Britain and the western coast of continental Europe. In these areas were to be obtained tin, iron, lead, wool, textiles, glass, pottery, salt, gold, silver and amber, all valuable commodities formerly monopolized by Carthaginians and Etruscans, whom the Romans learned of *from* them. The Etruscans had a network of roads extending throughout Gaul to Northern Germany and the Baltic where they had access to amber from Scandinavia, although they don't seem to have had direct ties to Scandinavian tribes.

It would have been impossible for the Romans to undertake their conquest of the west without auxiliaries of foreign troops; the Italian Peninsula alone could not have supplied enough manpower for the task. As areas were conquered, Numidians (North Africans), Iberians, Phrygians, Greeks and others were added to the ranks of Roman legions, as well as to the population of Rome. Rome was not the great white empire that writers and films would have us believe. Racial intermingling had always occurred on the peninsula. One of Rome's greatest generals was Septimus Severus, who was born in Carthage and considered African. There were several black, or mulatto, Roman emperors, generals and senators, and later there would be at least three black African popes. But the majority of the Roman people and leadership were Caucasian, militaristic and driven by a desire to possess all the known world's commerce and treasures, a desire that would also take them to Egypt and the Holy Land.

It was the ascendancy of Rome—*new*-Rome—that contributed most to the shift in racial demographics in western Europe and began the decline of its dark-skinned populations. By the time Rome invaded Spain, Gaul, Germany and Britain, the populations of these territories had already been considerably lightened by several centuries of new-Celtic occupation—earlier black Celtic and Iberian tribes having been steadily pushed to the western extremities of continental Europe, Britain and Ireland. But even predominantly Caucasian Celtic tribes could not have been purely white-skinned; centuries of intermingling with captive women of the black- and dark-skinned tribes they had encountered in their western migrations were visible in their populations—which must have exhibited darkish complexions on people who, except for complexion, had physically Caucasian features.

The Roman invasions of Gaul, Germany and Britain, and the killing of untold numbers of men of the black- and dark-skinned tribes still present in these territories would aid Europe's lightening process—eventually absorbing the negritude which had formerly been predominant—as the Caucasian gene-pool increased. The same lightening process would take place in eastern Europe, the Balkans, Asia Minor and the Levant when Roman armies moved into these areas, while future invasions of black-skinned Asians like Huns, Magyars, Moors and Mongols would inhibit it.

*   *   *   *   *

In his assessment (citing the *Cambridge Dictionary* of 1693) of the Danes and related northern peoples in and around Scandinavia at the onset of the Dark Ages (i.e., c. 500 AD), David MacRitchie factors in the Black Huns of Attila, significant numbers of whom must have remained to rejuvenate the Cimbric/Danish populations in and around the Jutland Peninsula (Denmark). The Huns of Attila had exacted tribute from the Eastern (Roman) Empire, sacked seventy towns in southern Russia, and taken thousands of slaves. Although Attila's forces were repulsed at the Battle of Chalons in 451, an extensive territory stretching from the eastern border of Gaul (i.e., France) to the China Sea was effectively dominated by Black Huns. As well, the Jutland Peninsula (Denmark) and southern Sweden were included in this Hunnish empire, where significant numbers of Huns would remain after Attila's death in 453. It has already been stressed that women have always been a portion of the spoils extracted by conquerors, and in *The Age of Faith*, Will Durant makes it clear that "[t]he captured women were added to the wives of the captors, and so began generations of blood mixture that left traces of Mongol features as far west as Bavaria" (39).

Black Huns who entered Scandinavia replenished the population of black-skinned humanity that had long existed there—Cimbri, Danes, Swedes, along with remnants of ancient Egyptians, Carthaginians, Etruscans and Phoenicians. Concerning this mixture of Scandinavian peoples who would re-emerge as Norsemen and Vikings three centuries later, MacRitchie states:

> The Huns were "of a dark complexion," and so also were the Cimbri . . . Both were plainly of a warlike and nomadic disposition . . . If this be the case, then the comely, fair-skinned people now inhabiting Denmark are out of the question [as being Vikings], as having nothing in common with the Dani of "vast bodies and dreadful looks." (*Britons, vol. 1* 112)

When Rome fell, its light would continue to flicker in western Europe. Roman legions, though, had ceased to march and had been withdrawn from Britain and Iberia in an ultimately futile effort to defend the Western Empire from the onrush of Hunnish and Gothic invaders who brought it down around 480 AD. The Eastern Roman Empire, whose capital was Constantinople, would continue to flourish as the *Byzantine Empire* for many centuries, with only limited influence in the affairs of western Europe.

By the onset of the 6th century, Europe was settling into what historians have termed the *Dark Ages*. The ascendancy of European civilization—*white* European civilization—diminished with the demise of Rome. Learning had come to a standstill, and writing was almost non-existent except in Ireland where monks continued to record the history of the British Isles and the bits of information they could gather about events taking place on the continent. The Romans, though, had managed to plant the seeds of Roman Christianity in Britain and Gaul, but converts were few. Most Europeans—black, white or other—were devotees of so-called *pagan* religions acquired from the Africoid and Asiatic peoples formerly in possession of the entire continent; even the Romans had worshipped pagan religions before Christianity took tentative root. Roman roads and bridges (originally Etruscan roads and bridges) fell into decay; trade and societal organization lapsed; and barbarism reigned throughout the continent as petty chieftains rose and fell, fighting over territories offering fertile farmlands, natural resources they could exploit, or living space.

Relatively little precise information is known about Scandinavia during the early period of the Dark Ages except that it was not directly affected by events in Europe further to the south—although its inhabitants would have known of a major event like the fall of Rome. Uninvolved with the conflicts and turmoil in the south, and only moderately influenced by Roman civilization, Scandinavia was not bereft of organization or vision, unlike most of western Europe. However, the various Scandinavian tribes throughout the realm contended amongst each other for territory. Picts, who are known primarily as ancient inhabitants of Britain and Alban (Scotland), may have still occupied areas of northern Germany, which evidence indicates they anciently occupied. MacRitchie quotes one Mr. Martin as stating: "[I]t is generally acknowledged that the Picts were originally German, and particularly from that part of it bordering upon the Baltic Sea" (*Britons, vol.1*, 110). And MacRitchie, himself, opines:

> Therefore, it becomes evident that some race of Scandinavians must have been Black
> Huns also, with physical characteristics approaching those of the Pictish Moors, either
> in the Australoid or in the Mongoloid direction. (op. cit.)

In *Celtic Scotland*, W.F. Skene calls the Picts a tribe out of Scythia. And MacRitchie notes that Bede "included among the 'Scythians' the ancient inhabitants of Norway, Sweden, and Denmark, the Daci, Getae, and other nations" (*Britons, vol. 1*, 29).

There are lesser known tribes in the mix, like the *Americans*, who settled the western coast of Gaul and had trade relations with black Celts in Britain. And there are strong indications that all the above-mentioned peoples were racially similar and spoke a similar language. According to Prudence Jones and Nigel Pennick, authors of *A History of Pagan Europe*, Tacitus "reported the existence of the mysterious Aestii on the *eastern shore* of the Baltic, who spoke a language *akin to British*, and . . . worshipped the mother of the gods" (*my emphasis* 165).

European tribes and peoples mentioned by Eurocentric historians are generally obscured by a myriad of names and the failure of those historians to discuss racial, cultural or linguistic connections. Among artifacts found in Sweden are Etruscan bronzes, indicating that Scandinavians, for all their purported barbarism, sought and traded for items of civilization like finely crafted goblets, bronze belt hooks and gold jewelry—often studded with amber obtained from the north—fashioned by Etruscan craftsmen. The Roman invasion of Gaul and Germany, then, must have been undertaken to appropriate Etruscan trade routes and the commodities and resources of the north—a lively, seaborne commercial consortium which extended from the eastern shores of the Baltic to the British Isles and had been unreachable to Rome while the Etruscans and Carthaginians remained in power.

The Romans coveted this northern realm of predominantly black- and dark-skinned inhabitants, and they disrupted affairs in Gaul and Britain for more than four centuries in hopes of making headway to it. But their invasions of northern territories to control this consortium was a mission they would only partially realize. In Albion, or Britain, the fierce attacks by the Picts, later in concert with Scots, prevented the Romans from conquering the whole island. But Britain would forever be changed and Roman influences would remain despite the departure of her legions.

So we have at last made our way to the far north of Europe and Scandinavia where, at the onset of the Dark Ages, there existed an extensive world of related peoples that Eurocentric historians have never told us about—a mixture of black- and dark-skinned peoples whose tribes, especially those in Denmark, included descendants of Attila's Black Huns. I have cited eminent *European* historians, like MacRitchie, who asserts that Huns, Vandals, Goths and Alans were racially akin and "all . . . in effect, *Picti*" (*Britons, vol. 1*, 34) And Higgins affirms that Goths, Scythians, Celtae and Cimbri "were all the *same*, using the same language . . . with the small differences which would inevitably arise in . . . time, and under their migratory . . . habits of life and circumstance" (*Druids* 100).

Because Western historians have written extensively on Greek and Roman personages and a multitude of films have been made depicting them and what life was like in ancient Rome and Greece, we can more easily visualize a Greek or Roman warrior, statesman, emperor, or woman of leisure—harlot or queen—resplendent in what we have been shown to be the flowing attire of the time, in addition to busts, full-body sculptures and images on pottery depicting aspects of societal activities. Contrast these with what artifacts and particulars we have of northern peoples: few films, which are not well made; no identifiable busts, but helmets, swords, shields, axes, chain mail, tattered clothing and a few coins. The people are quite faceless, except we have been told incessantly that they were white, Aryan, Teutonic, *Nordic*. But the evidence demonstrates that most of these northern peoples—especially those of ancient Scandinavia—were not white, and if they were Nordic, then they were *black* Nordics.

Their being racially and linguistically akin did not preclude sometimes violent conflicts, even inter-tribal ones which would continue into the Viking Age. Though these northern peoples may still be generally faceless to us, we at least have attached a complexion to them—a complexion not based on assumption, but on the words of preeminent historians and anthropologists. As we proceed, we will read more conclusive statements from ancient and more modern historians. The Anglo-Saxon historian Bede (672-735) is one of the enduring sources on the peoples of Dark Age Europe, and according to Peter Hunter Blair, in *The World of Bede*:

> Bede himself knew that *Germania* was a country inhabited by a great many different peoples who were still observing pagan rites, and in addition to the Angles and Saxons then living in Britain, he names Frisians, Rugians, Danes, Huns, [and] Old Saxons . . . . (23-24)

These are some of the peoples and tribes comprising northern Germany during the early period of the Dark Ages, and the evidence presented here illustrates that Germany had long been inhabited by such peoples who, except perhaps for new or *later*-Angles and Saxons, were primarily black- and dark-skinned.

There may have been areas in Germany where Caucasian types were predominant; if so, they had not become powerful enough to repel the onslaught of Black Huns who had so recently dominated all of Germany and had "left traces of Mongol features as far west as Bavaria" in the south of the country. And up to the onset of the Dark Ages, none of the historians so far cited, with the lone exception of L.A. Waddell, has offered definitive, verifiable accounts of any sizeable contingents of Caucasian or white people in Germany, Gaul, Britain or Scandinavia. This writer concedes that the new-Celts were predominantly Caucasian, along with the Saxons; the Angles who invaded Britain might also have been so. But 6th century western Europe, according to the historians cited here-in (most of them white) seems overrun with black- and dark-skinned people—particularly northern Europe.

Two centuries ago, Eurocentric scientists and historians began publishing works—both scientific and historical—promoting the superiority of white Europeans in order to justify the enslavement of Africans in the New World, and engendering a general debasement of people of color worldwide. Germany began to be promoted as the country most representative of the superior Caucasian or *Nordic* race, its people the quintessence of Aryan perfection and intelligence. However, the reader has been presented with information that casts doubt on an eternal *Nordic* or Caucasian homeland in Germany, and has seen evidence that black- and dark-skinned people occupied it into historical times. And before departing the area of Germany for Scandinavia, the reader should consider the following comment from Professor Sergi in *The Mediterranean Race*, which should clarify what might not have been made clear enough above:

> For some time past I have reached the conclusion that the so-called Reihengraber type of the Germans and the Viking type of the Scandinavians, being identical in character with the *Mediterranean and Hamitic* types, had the s*ame African origin . . . separate branches of the same stock.* (*my emphasis* 252)

From what has been presented in this chapter, it is questionable where new-Saxons, as well as where Adolph Hitler's "Aryan" Germans fit into the picture of Germany only 1,500 years ago, and by now, the reader should envision a far different picture of Europe than popular histories have consistently presented. While some readers may be dismayed over what has been presented, at least some information must appeal to their logic and sense of reason. The reader is encouraged to reread the popular histories he or she may be familiar with to determine whether their authors offer proofs of their assertions that Norsemen of the Viking Age were blond, blue-eyed Nordics, or whether they rely on *presumption* and unceasing *repetition*. Eurocentric authors' insistence on the whiteness of the Vikings, and ancient Europeans in general, has almost bordered on schizophrenia—like a long, low-pitched continuous note blown on a tuba; or the lusty, monotonal blast of a ship's foghorn, discouraging anyone from attempting to speak or even *think* before the note ends. Only, it never ends.

Important areas of Europe—Greece, Iberia, Italy, Gaul, Germany and the Mediterranean—have, I think, been sufficiently covered to establish that black- and dark-skinned peoples were preponderant everywhere in western Europe until fairly recent historical times. We have focused some attention on Egypt, the Near East and Asia regarding its various peoples and will revisit Asia and look at the Americas further along, especially the Viking migration to North America. Along the way we will hopefully come to realize that humanity is not comprised of the independent racial identities Eurocentric historians and scientists have grouped us into, with Caucasians somehow an exclusive classification. Nearly all of us are products of millennia of interracial and genetic blendings and only differ in the nationalities, racial groups, cultures and religious affiliations we have associated ourselves with.

Our descent into the Viking world of the Early Middle Ages will not necessarily be chronological or concern itself with a detailed succession of the kings or chieftains who rose and fell throughout the period, though some of these will, of course, be highlighted. My primary purpose is to demonstrate that the Viking *peoples*—for we have seen that various tribes came to abide in the territories known as Scandinavia—were predominantly black-skinned and that they had a farther-reaching impact on Europe than we have been told. The Norse migration to Iceland and North America some 500 years before Columbus will be discussed as fully as possible, as well as the reluctance of historians to regard them as the *European* discoverers of America.

CHAPTER 6

TRUE MYTH

The Tuatha de Danaan, descendants of the goddess Danan or Danae, were a people said to have fled Greece and sailed to Albion or Britain. Mentioned in mythological texts, they are most often discussed in regard to the early history of Ireland and said to have been uncommonly skilled and god-like. In addition to their connection to the goddess Danae, mythological tales trace the Tuatha de Danaan to Danaos, an Egyptian leader who arrived in Argos (in Greece) where he soon after becomes king. According to the myth, he arrives in Argos with a fleet of ships, a large army and his fifty daughters. The period of his arrival in Argos is said to have been c. 1721 to 1511 BC.

When his brother, Aigyptos, learns of Danaos' ascension to king, he went to Greece with his own fleet and demanded that his fifty sons be allowed to marry Danaos' fifty daughters—their cousins. Another version has Aigyptos proposing the marriages *while in Egypt* and Danaos sailing to Argos to avoid the mass nuptials. Danaos reluctantly agrees to the marriages but gives each of his daughters daggers, ordering them to kill their bridegrooms in their sleep. This they each did, except Hypermnestra, Danaos' oldest daughter, who does not honor her father's order. Her husband, Lynkeos (Lynceus), becomes king after Danaos' reign, with Danaos being remembered as a fine and able ruler. Perseus and Herakles are two of the "Greek" heroes produced from this dynasty. (There is a variation of this story with Rameses—probably Rameses I—being the brother of Danaos—whose Egyptian name was Harmais—and the aforementioned events taking place in *Egypt.*)

If the abovementioned period for Danaos and the Tuatha de Danaan is accurate, it demonstrates that Egyptians of the time were numerous and still sending out colonists to various parts of the world—in this case, Greece and its isles where they still seem to have dominated and influenced. The marriage of Danaos' fifty daughters to his brother Aigyptos' fifty sons may imply internal conflict and jealousies among Egyptians in their quest for and acquisition of various territories—conflicts that may have resulted in national wars as various powerful chieftains sought more power and influence. The period for the arrival of the Tuatha de Dannan would have been prior to the arrival of the barbaric, Caucasian Hellenes, who would largely destroy the predominating Aegean or Egyptian civilization, which may have led to the exodus of the Tuatha de Danaan and other tribes from the area.

I do not in any way claim expertise in Egyptian or Greek mythology and will simply discuss the origin of the Tuatha de Danaan as the legends of Ireland present them—as descendants of the goddess Danae and their being a divine race who were defeated after arriving in Ireland by the longer-settled Firbolgs and who "retired into the hills and mounds" of the island. In *Ancient Egypt, The Light of the World vol. 2*, Gerald Massey regards the Tuatha de Danaan as heavenly beings and cites Giraldus (*Topographia Hibernia*) as stating that learned men believed the Tuatha "were of the number of the exiles driven out of heaven" (635).

Dates for most mythological events are impossible to determine, and many of the most ancient myths were merely human renderings of astrological events or movements of constellations. Some, however, possibly derived from actual occurrences, or else described the exploits of actual personages, which over time were rendered into symbolic patterns so that they could be more easily remembered and passed down to succeeding generations orally. As writing advanced and myths were recorded, the actual meanings of myths that illiterate peoples understood were eventually lost over long generations and in some instances resulted in two or more versions of the same myth because the writers of the myth interpreted the details according to their own understanding and perceptions extant in the generation in which they happened to be living in. So the same tale or myth written down by two different recorders may have two spellings of the names of the same characters, different names for two characters, two different locations for where the event took place, two outcomes, even, at the end of the tale, though the events leading up to a particular mythological event may be similar, even identical.

We have looked at the spread of the megalith-building culture, which overspread most of the British Isles, Sardinia, Corsica, Iberia, Gaul (France), northern Germany, Sicily, Italy and southern Scandinavia. While most historians claim ignorance to their purpose and the people responsible for erecting them, the reader has been presented with statements from eminent scholars asserting that only the ancient Egyptians had the ability to erect such monuments. Egypt, or the northeastern quadrant of Africa, was the origin for all later civilizations, sending colonists to most areas of the earth who planted seeds of civilization extending through Asia and the Pacific—even to the Americas. The reader, I'm sure, knows of the pyramids of Meso-America, which many have compared to those of Egypt. There are a number of pyramidal structures that were discovered in the mid-1940s in the Shensi Province of China, which the Chinese government has so far prevented archeologists from examining. So, remote Egyptian colonists, it must be inferred, certainly spread their civilization around the earth. And although the names and achievements of these colonists are long lost to us, the Tuatha de Danaan (children, or tribe of Danaan or Danae), meanwhile, are remembered in Greece, Ireland and other areas of Europe and Asia.

Information regarding the Tuatha de Danaan is generally not found in contemporary or popular histories. Many historians, if they do mention them, consign them to myth and, admittedly, an accurate date for their prominence is conjecture. They are far less known than other rarely defined major peoples like the Merovingians, Etruscans and Elamites, and only a rare historian lifts them out of the fog that shrouds them to offer us any verifiable particulars of their actual existence.

In *The Story of the Irish Race*, Seumus MacManus identifies a number of peoples or tribes coming to Ireland–all shrouded in historical mist and myth, with no discernible time frame. All of them arrive from Egypt (which might be interpreted as a general reference to North Africa). According to MacManus, the Gaedhal or Gaels were originally out of Scythia; yet they also passed through the same territories as the tribes which had preceded them–Egypt, Crete and Iberia or Spain–before arriving in Ireland. MacManus calls the Tuatha de Danaan and the later arriving *Milesians* (for some reason regarded as the founders of modern Ireland) *Egyptians*. Outside of the earliest true humans (i.e., Grimaldi man) into Europe over landbridges connecting Africa with Europe, the migration routes of all the earliest named tribes into Ireland do not seem to vary at all from that of the later arriving Milesians, regarding whom MacManus states:

> They came to Ireland through Egypt, Crete, and Spain. They were called Gaedhal (Gael) because their remote ancestor, in the days of Moses, was Gaodhal Glas . . . . Niul, a grandson of Gaodhal . . . married Pharoah's daughter Scota . . . and the Irish Scoti or Scots are the descendants of Niul and Scota. (8)

McManus relates that their leader, when they departed Spain (Iberia) for Ireland was Miled or Milesius, who also married a Pharoah's daughter named Scota. This new influx of Egyptians (whom we have to assume were black-skinned, although McManus doesn't state this) were called Milesians and are considered to be the founding race of Ireland, although the De Danaan, Firbolgs, *Fomorians* (whom McManus calls "African sea-rovers") and others reportedly preceded them. McManus, however, makes no mention of skin complexion, contributing to the nebulous assumption that these earliest colonizers (except, of course, the African sea-rovers) were white, even the Egyptians themselves. The reader should know better by now. All these early Irish peoples, including the Irish *Scoti* who would much later depart for northern Albion and give the name of *Scotland* to that present territory, were black- and dark-skinned *Africans*, possibly Egyptians, streaming throughout of the Mediterranean basin to inhabit all of western Europe.

As regards to a time frame for their arrival in western Europe, we might look to Martin Bernal who, in *Black Athena, vol. 1,* states: "I want . . . to put Danaos' landing in Greece near the beginning of the Hyksos period, at around 1720 BC" (20), associating them with the Egyptian 18th Dynasty, the Hyksos' expulsion from Egypt and the time Greek legends assert that Danaos came to Argos. McManus offers no information about when the De Danaan arrived in Ireland, but Egyptian mariners had plied the Mediterranean for several millennia before this time (let us not forget the megalith builders) and it should not be unrealistic to believe that the De Danaan had made it to the British Isles (and probably other areas of western Europe) within the next century or so—doing so at least a millennium before any significant number of Caucasians (i.e., new Celts) had arrived.

The time periods for the arrival of early Egyptian and North African migrants in Britain and western Europe is indeterminate, so I will not attempt to assign any, although we know for certain that the black- and dark-skinned Irish Scoti moved into what would become Scotland in the late 4th and 5th centuries AD, intermingling with the longer settled black Germanic Pictish tribes, jointly engaging in battles against Roman troops, and eventually becoming dominant in the whole territory. While Godfrey Higgins asserts that the Druids or priests were of Eastern or Asiatic origin, Albert Churchward declares that ancient Druids "were undoubtedly descendants of the ancient Egyptian priests" who came to the British Isles (197). The Tuatha de Danaan had a Druidical order, but as to whether this order was the *first* Druidical order in Europe or whether earlier Egyptian settlers in the British Isles included Druids, I have not investigated.

Because the Tuatha de Danaan are called "heavenly" or a "divine race," it is easy to perceive them as existing only in the realm of myth. We associate Heaven and Divine with religion and mysticism because we cannot conceive of ordinary men possessing attributes warranting such veneration. But there was a world—perhaps several worlds—before our present one that has been glimpsed only through mythologies that we have lost the ability to interpret with any accuracy. We have come to believe that no human beings before us and our time could possibly have attained the knowledge that we have and to be so highly regarded. Although the Tuatha de Danaan are not mentioned in most popular histories and may be considered a mythological race by those that do discuss them, it seems that they actually existed, whatever their precise time frame. And along with what is mentioned regarding the Tuatha de Danaan above, Albert Churchward (*Signs and Symbols of Primordial Man*), has this to say:

> The Tuatha-de-Dananns, who came to Ireland, were *of the same race* and spoke the *same language* as the Fir-Bolgs and the Fomorians, *possessed ships, knew the art of navigation,* had *a compass or magnetic needle, worked in metals,* had a large army, thoroughly organized, and *a body of surgeons*; had a "Bardic or Druid class of priests." (*my emphasis* 197)

So, it seems entirely probable that the term *Dane* is derived from the Tuatha de Danaan (or Danaan) and that they are, or became, the <u>*Dani*</u>—who were also known as Cimbri, Cimbrians, or Cimmarians of Denmark (*Dan*-mark).

Mentioned earlier was John Phillip Cohane's *The Key*, which offers a number of *Don/Dan* place-names applied to rivers throughout Asia and Europe (even Africa, which we did not mention in this regard). Cohane's reference to the Tuatha de Danaan's ancestor Danaus (Danaos) is at variance with those who believe they were descendants of the goddess Danan or Danae, which is less important to us than the fact that the Tuatha de Danaan were actual people originating in Egypt, who in remote times journeyed to Crete, Greece, Iberia, Ireland, Britain and Scandinavia—or at least Denmark—which probably received its name from their occupation of it, the river-name Dan, perhaps, being a reference to their seamanship on rivers and in large bodies of water. They may have even been related to the ancient megalith-builders of Europe, and could have been considered a heavenly race because they were "uncommonly skilled in the few arts of the time" (McManus 5).

They were considered magicians and were immortalized in legends not only in Ireland, where they are most heard of, but on the continent of Europe. They supposedly maintained alliances with Greece down to the time of Alexander. In Ireland, though, they were considered gods, or at least god-like. According to Donald Mackenzie, in *Ancient Man in Britain*, there is no evidence of the De Danaan in Scotland, but he mentions that a group of Welsh gods called "the children of Don" resemble the De Danaan of Ireland, stating: "The Irish Danaan god Nuada has been identified with the British Nudd whose children formed the group of "the children of Nudd" (203).

There were at least two invasions of Germany by Britons, according to L.A.Waddell, one about 970 BC by the sons of Ebraucus, who conquered Germany and settled there (186). A second invasion by Britons led to an occupation of Denmark before the 5th century BC. Waddell cites the *British Chronicles* for this second invasion and states that the Anglo-Saxons (of northern Germany) were a branch of the British Phoenicians or Britons, and cites language affinities for this assertion (187). Although he does not mention the De Danaan per se, the dates of these invasions—especially the first—occur within the period of De Danaan lore in Ireland, Wales and Britain.

It is quite probable that De Danaan or Danaid lore was extended into Germany and Denmark during this period, and that the invaders of Germany and Jutland were actually the Tuatha de Danaan who, as mentioned above, were driven out of Ireland by the Firbolgs. These De Danaan or Danaids—from the time they departed Egypt for Greece (where they were called Danoi), and Greece for Iberia, Britain and Ireland—are always styled *black* by historians who mention color or race. In *Egypt vs. Greece and the American Academy*, Don Luke states:

> Both brothers, Danaos and Egyptos [Aigyptos], and the Danaids are explicitly described
> as being "black." It is not certain that the *early* Danes of Scandinavia were Danaids. But
> that the early Danes were black like the Danaids is clear. (100)

In *The Heroic Legends of Denmark* (294), Axel Olrik claims that a personage named Dan was the first king of what would later be *Dan*mark, and speaks of "races" of men residing in Scandinavia—but never elaborates on what differentiates these races one from another. It is not clear what constitutes *race*. He makes no mention of skin color that I have come across—no mention of phenotype, skull shapes or physiognomy. So what does he mean by race? He is certainly not alone in this omission, a generally common oversight by Eurocentric historians who rarely employ any mention of race when discussing people we (and they) have been led to assume are Caucasian or white.

The term _Dane_ in all likelihood derives from De Danaan, Danaid or Tuatha de Danaan who arrived in Scandinavia in their fleets when they were driven out of Ireland, becoming another of the racially congeneric *tribes* or *peoples* inhabiting the area, sharing language, customs and religious practices. Churchward asserts that "the Tuatha, or tribes . . . brought the *Ancient Solar wisdom out of Lower Egypt . . .* [and] *were genuine Egyptians*" (199). So it would seem that the Tuatha de Danaan were one of other tribes or *Tuatha* bringing Solar cult (i.e., sun worship) wisdom to various areas of the earth, a system which replaced the Stellar wisdom which had long prevailed. And, further, Churchward states:

> There can be no reasonable doubt that some of the Egyptian priests emigrated to Ireland
> and the British Isles and brought their religion with them, and here, in the British Isles,
> they founded and built temples . . . . (244)

I have not investigated whether these temples and religious rites were brought wholly to Scandinavia, but it is probable that some aspects of De Danaan religious worship must have been. However, aside from religious worship, the De Danaan would have certainly brought their considerable navigational, metal-working and military talents to Scandinavia, along with surgical knowledge and a Bardic tradition that would have made them superior to other peoples living in the area. The "king" Dan, whom Olrik claims the Danes and *Dan*mark were named for, may be a composite reference to the superior De Danaan, or Danae, being transmutated into myth because of their legendary renown among the Cimbric peoples and others.

Through much of the early portion of his *A History of the Vikings*, Gwyn Jones avoids elaborating on race. But he warms up, mentioning on page 44 that the Danes were of the same stock as the Swedes, that the above-mentioned, and perhaps actual, King Dan had a brother named Angul, and that this was the origin of the name Angles, the northern Germanic people who would invade England, and that "a collection of peoples bearing the name Dani were dominant in geographical Denmark and Skane soon after the beginning of the sixth century" (45). However, if a Danish king called Dan *did* exist and was leader of the superior black-skinned Dani, or De Danaan, originally out of Egypt, it would be most reasonable to presume that his brother, Angul, as well as Angul's followers, would have been black-skinned also—meaning the invasion of England by Angul and his followers would have been an invasion of chiefly *black*, not white Germanics, who are referred to as *Angles*.

Noted earlier was that on page 76, Jones notes that Irish historians distinguished between White (Norwegian) Foreigners and Black (Danish) Foreigners, who incessantly invaded the British Isles. And on page 77, as noted earlier, he states (in a footnote, which I feel bears repeating):

> The Welsh chroniclers . . . made no such clear distinction. The Danes coming in by way of England and the Norwegians by way of Ireland were pretty well all black: Black Gentiles . . . Black Norsemen . . . Black Host, Pagans, Devils, and the like. (77)

A dozen or more years ago while flipping channels on my TV, I caught Mr. Jones at the end of an interview where he backed off from this bold assertion saying, as I recall, that he "regretted" making the claim. But it is highly suspect when a historian would make such a comment long after his work was published unless some kind of pressure constrained him to do so. Just as I would seize on his comment more than two decades later and investigate further, he, and perhaps the Eurocentric Brotherhood of Academia, must have been aware that other non-white scholars had done so, as well, and felt he must atone for his "error." Even so, I commend him for venturing to go forward with his initial publication in 1968, which can still be obtained, unaltered, in any decent bookstore or library. But pressure and conscience is the fate of an honest historian working in a field dominated by a Eurocentric mindset, for which the following comment from Don Luke is apropos:

> Far too many Eurocentric scholars have attempted to maintain the axiom of the superiority of European culture over that of all others . . . Consequently, when an independent non-Indo-European presence is discovered in Early Europe, the African is automatically eliminated as the possible occupant. (*Egypt* 92-93)

Although Gwyn Jones' comment on the Welsh making no distinction between the blackness of Norwegians and Danes was contained in a footnote, and no further mention was made of the complexions of these peoples in the remainder of this work, the comment was a violation of the Eurocentric old-boy covenant which Caucasian authors in Europe and America have always felt constrained to honor. Rather than admit an African presence, they would rather assign an Asian origin, even claiming that such Asians, themselves, were *Indo-European*—a term that has come to imply Caucasian, and will be looked at in a later chapter.

The evidence presented demonstrates that the early Scandinavians were, like most inhabitants of western Europe, primarily and phenotypically of African stock—at the very least, Afro-Asiatic. This would include the earliest inhabitants of Britain, Gaul (France), Italy, Iberia, Germany and areas abutting the

Adriatic and Aegean Seas. Asian elements would arrive afterwards, the largest influx into Scandinavia being the Black Huns of the 5th century under Attila—who are, probably, the heathen Aesir of Norse legends. Whether Eurocentrists, out-and-out racists, or DNA scientists like it or not, Europe has always been more accessible from Africa than from Asia; and whether the Danes derived their nomenclature from the Danaids, De Danaan or a king called Dan, enough evidence has been presented to demonstrate that they were a black-skinned race (or races) of chiefly Egyptian origin who, according to Olrik, "are seen to be one of the great powers of that time, known from the year 500 [AD] in Greece, Italy, and France" (31). Olrik (without, of course, mentioning complexion) alludes to the "great extent of the Danish realm," noting their appellations of "Spear-Danes," "North-Danes," and "Sea-Danes" (23-24), proving that they must have been a maritime nation before 500 AD and—tracing their migrations from Egypt, Greece, Iberia, Britain and Scandinavia—were renowned as a seafaring people.

This is not to diminish the maritime peoples mentioned earlier—Etruscans, Picts, Fomorians, Albans and *Amoricans,* who occupied Italy, Britain and Gaul, respectively, whom some have assigned to Iberian stock (except for the Etruscans). When Phoenicians and Carthaginians ventured to Britain, Gaul and Scandinavia, they would have traded, fought against and intermingled with all of these peoples—all of whom were part of an older world in existence before the earliest barbaric Caucasians entered western Europe in any significant numbers. This assemblage of black-skinned Africoid humanity constituted the earliest socio-economic, mercantilistic, industrial complex known in all of Europe—a world already in existence at the time Hellenistic Greece was born. Some of the peoples, like the De Danaan and the Phoenicians, maintained ties to Egypt and perhaps Greece, connections that would begin to be disrupted as Hellenistic Greece began to coalesce and set her sights farther afield.

The enterprising of these ancient *black* Europeans and cultures encompassed the whole of Europe, from the Mediterranean to the Baltic, and included relations of varying degree to Egypt, North Africa, the Hebrides and Orkneys as well as the Near East. Most of the history of this old world and these peoples is lost or hidden, but there are several Irish and Welsh sources offering insights into this ancient period that have not been consulted for this work but which are alluded to by some of the sources which have.

The source for Jones' "pretty well all black" statement was *Old Norse Relations With Wales,* by B.G. Charles, who cites Welsh sources that refer to all invading Norsemen as "'y Normanyeit duon' (the black Normans) . . . 'Nordmani' (Northmen) . . . and 'dub gint' (the black heathen)'" (ix). Charles' work does not allude to the old world civilization mentioned just above, but Jones' comment is derived from this older source, and he was justified in attempting to inject a little known kernel of truth into his work. So his expression of regret—a quarter-century after the publication of *A History of the Vikings* (1968) could only have been an unnecessary concession to the Eurocentric Brotherhood of Academia for revealing contents behind a door closed many decades ago. Information pertaining to black Norsemen is by no means abundant; for every source mentioning black Vikings or Norsemen, forty or fifty can be found asserting that they were white. These are the sources most accessible and have given the world the impression (and always without an iota of actual proof) that the Vikings were blond-haired, blue-eyed Whites.

The territory of Germany seems to have been the convergence point between Africans and Asians from ancient to historical times, their cultures melding, resulting in the mythologies that have come down to us from northern Europe—Odin, Thor, Aesir, Black Dwarfs, magic, Asgard (the home of Norse gods), among others. Some of these will be mentioned as needed. My primary focus is the obscured history and impact of black- and dark-skinned peoples and events in Dark and Middle Ages Europe, and of these peoples, the Vikings or Norsemen would emerge as the most fearsome, adventurous and influential.

*   *   *   *   *

Most people today cannot explain the precise meanings of mythological tales to any respectable degree, separating what is symbolic from what may be rooted in fact. *Mythology* can be subdivided into a dozen forms or categories. However, my comments regarding myth in this chapter are only applied to the most elementary function of mythology: rendering actual events into allegory, which we are inclined to interpret as fantasies because we no longer understand the symbolism or connectors that we assume more ancient people in a mostly illiterate world understood. So, it would seem that people closest to a particular actual event, personage or location presented in a given myth would have had a clearer understanding of its meaning (even if symbolic) than we moderns do.

However, there is one particular mythological tale, *The Golden Fleece*, which seems to contain decipherable elements, rendering it, in effect, a *true myth*. Reading the tale alone, exclusively, without benefit of other information, would most likely not allow a reader to encompass the meaning I believe it holds. I have not consulted any works on the meaning of mythology to validate what I present below, but historical information I have come across in my personal studies made this tale—if one purpose of mythology is to render cogency to a natural or actual event—quite clear to me, and I beg the reader's indulgence as I delineate my interpretation of the aforementioned tale.

Briefly, *The Golden Fleece* concerns Jason and the Argonauts—Argonauts being his crew of Greek heroes who set off for the fabled land of Colchis, said to be at the end of the world—to obtain the magical Golden Fleece. On their journey, they encounter many difficulties: they are side-tracked on Lemnos, an island of women, who delay them with food, wine and their bodies; they encounter Harpies who torment a seer, or wise man, they seek information from regarding directions; and they battle fire-breathing bulls when they arrive in Colchis, where king Aeetes refuses to give them the Fleece, or golden sheep's hide, they have come to obtain. With the help of Medea—along with divine assistance from the goddess Hera—Jason steals the Fleece and returns to Greece. There are other versions of the tale with Jason and his crew battling other creatures, like Talos, the bronze giant. Certainly this tale was cogent to the ancient Greeks (and other peoples who heard it) living closer to the time who would have understood its meaning, though for us it is mythology—compelling, visceral, frightening, fantastic. But can a truthful explanation be discerned from this tale?

A dozen years ago I taped a <u>Terra X</u> documentary called "The Golden Fleece" on a PBS television station that attempted to ascertain the veracity of *The Golden Fleece* tale. The country of Georgia, at the eastern end of the Black Sea and formerly part of the U.S.S.R., is located precisely in the heartland of what was once ancient Colchis, although Colchis extended farther north along the Black Sea coast and further southwest into present-day northern Armenia. The documentary showed modern-day Georgians obtaining gold particles from mountain streams, catching these particles in tightly woven mesh nets. So, gold must have actually been present, even abundant, in ancient Colchis.

In *The Histories*, Herodotus states emphatically that the Colchians were *black*, like Egyptians and Ethiopians and had woolly hair, and he believed that the Colchians were originally a colony of Egyptians (134). Ancient Egyptians were master workmen in gold. Gold must have been quite plentiful in ancient Colchis if it can still be extracted from rivers and running streams today. The nets used to extract gold from the streams are made of interwoven lamb's wool, so finely wrought as to snare the minutest gold particles. The tale of the Fleece, then, would seem to have a basis in fact and probably signifies Greek efforts to acquire either gold or this unique "gold mining" method and the opposition they faced in doing so—the Colchians being reluctant to reveal their secret process.

Although Herodotus (c. 490-420 BC) is called the father of history for his descriptive recording of history and for actually visiting many of the areas he wrote about, he has always had detractors. I once brought him up in an ESL (English as a Second Language) class I was teaching at a school in midtown Manhattan a few years ago. A young Russian man commented that Herodotus was "unreliable," although he did not specify why; the reader may have heard the same comment from a history professor, or has read such a comment about Herodotus. However, in 1913, a Russian naturalist published an article in a Tbilisi newspaper called *Kavkaz*, revealing that there were black people living in Georgia. In a book titled *Russia and the Negro*, Allison Blakely states that V.P. Vradii's article and subsequent letters to the paper revealed that:

Negroes resided in what is now the small state of Abkhazia and in parts of what was until fairly recently the Georgian Soviet Socialist Republic [now <u>Georgia</u>], an area which became fully a part of the Russian Empire . . . [in] the 1870s" (6).

Vradii visited the seaport town of Batumi in 1912 and discovered twenty to thirty Blacks living there. Another writer, F. Elius, visited the area and reported in an article in *Argus* magazine during the same year that there were two hundred Blacks in the Batumi province. Soon World War I began, and interest in these newly discovered Blacks waned, not to resurface until 1923 when journalist and explorer Zinaida Richter "visited an entire village of Negroes near Sukhumi" (op. cit. 8).

Fig. 11
Early 20th early photograph of individuals of black or Negroid inhabitants of Abkhazia in area that was once part of the ancient Colchis.

These "Caucasian Negroes" (*Caucasian,* because they lived in the Caucasus Mountains range) lived in mountainous regions that often isolated one province or town from another so that even neighboring provinces might not be familiar with the language spoken in the next province over. The Russian Empire was, for the most part, unaware of the existence of these Blacks who "were at times referred to as Arabs, Lazs, or Adzhars by the local people around Batumi" (op. cit.). There had been intermarriage between white Georgians and these Blacks, and Blakely notes that "Vradii . . . [found] some were black with pronounced Negroid features, and others looked more like the lighter-complexioned Adzhars . . . were Moslems and spoke only the Abkhazian language" (op. cit.). Some were also Roman Catholic, and most were farmers, respected by their white-skinned neighbors. Blakely also notes:

> The Negroes of Abkhazia, along with the other subject peoples of Transcaucasia and Central Asia, were pressed into the tsar's "native division" during the final desperate phase of World War I. (9)

If these Caucasian blacks had any written history, it is not mentioned, but many of them said their ancestors had lived in the area for centuries. Blakely discusses Herodotus' connection of Colchians with Egyptians and Ethiopians and, as earlier touched upon, the possibility that Colchians were remnants of Egyptian ruler Sesostris' conquering army which had subdued much of Asia. After an 1881 archeological congress in Tbilisi (then called Tiflis), a collection of classical writings was produced which concluded, among other findings regarding the Caucasus region, "that the Laz people of Abkhazia had formerly been called Colchians . . . [citing] a number of Greek writers, including Procopius, to support this contention" (op. cit. 10).

There is probably much more to "The Golden Fleece" tale than the myth implies, or that we moderns have been able to interpret. In *Georgia in Antiquity,* David Braund tells us:

> The land of Colchis is presented as a land of special danger and riches . . . . The name of Colchis evoked magic and especially witchcraft, particularly as practiced in the family of Aeetes . . . This was the homeland of the "root-cutters": magic was something else that Colchis had in common with Egypt. (21)

Braund suggests that the Greeks valued Colchis for reasons other than gold, noting that "gold is only found in any quantity from the fifth century BC: before the seventh century there is almost nothing" (24). Iron ore, silver and copper were also abundant in Colchis, and Braund believes these are what the Greeks initially sought there.

Perhaps the Laz people are truly the descendants of the Colchians. Blakely opines that the majority of Blacks may have been "Numidian mercenaries from the Sudan serving in the Turkish army in the late 19th century" who deserted, remaining in the area they had raided (79). In 1925 a young African-American Communist visited a village near Sukhumi, which had at least 800 families of black Caucasians. Under Stalin (who was born in Georgia) in the 1930s, most of these Caucasian Blacks were relocated to other areas of the Soviet Union against their will, although some did remain. But if some said they had lived in the Caucasus region for hundreds of years, I am inclined to believe that their presence in the area extended even farther back and that Herodotus's assertion that the Colchians occupying the territory in the mid-5th century BC were black like Egyptians is undoubtedly factual. And just as black-skinned Europeans were eventually absorbed into the dominant white population, Colchians, through intermingling and intermarriage, were absorbed over time by the influx of predominantly lighter-skinned inhabitants into the area of Georgia that Blacks were once predominant in. We also must consider the probability that since Herodotus' time, many Colchians over the centuries were involved in the military conflicts in the region, emigrated to other areas, until only pockets of them remained to be "discovered" in the early part of the 20th century—most, still identifiably black-skinned and Negroid in appearance.

Most importantly, we have keys to understanding "The Golden Fleece" tale: black-skinned Colchians; gold, or valuable ores and metals; traditional nets made of finely interwoven *lamb's* wool (i.e., fleece), made in the same fashion as in ancient times and still in use today; the understanding that Greece was expanding her influence; magic and witchcraft (see Braund's comment, above), that may account for the seductive women (Medea, being witchcraft, personified, although she is moved to assist Jason in obtaining the fleece); and certainly the dangers presented by fire-breathing bulls and other perils, representative of Colchian anger and resistance to Greek incursions through warfare and terrible visions induced through magic.

In the matter of *this* mythological tale, there are enough elements to discern a plausible meaning: Expanding Greeks looking to increase their wealth are willing to sail to the end of the earth to obtain a secret that will bring this about. The journey is fraught with setbacks, to say nothing of Colchian resistance and unwillingness to reveal their secret wisdom which, doing so, might lead to their demise. Colchis was the land of root-cutters, magic and spells whose origins were found among the ancient Egyptians and other African peoples.

While we today regard magic as folly—a magician pulling a rabbit out of a hat, or pulling a stream of scarves from his sleeve—the magic implied here was much more ominous and deadly. A practitioner of this brand of magic might cause boulders on a hill to rain down on an enemy, induce a violent sea storm to sink an enemy vessel, or involve shape-shifting—a practitioner turning him or herself into an animal to evade or attack an enemy. It was this type of magic that the Greeks feared and which the Colchians—descendants of Egyptians and Ethiopians—possessed. Later we will see that this very real dark art had practitioners among the Norsemen of Scandinavia.

Not being at all well-versed in mythologies, I will not attempt to decipher any more of them here. The True Myth of the title of this work is meant to convey the elementary definition of myth: *the actuality of something long considered fanciful or mythic.* Half-way through completing an initial 65-page research paper on black Vikings, I found this oxymoron appropriate in regard to the so-called Dark Ages in Europe—something that will become more clear below and in the next chapter or two. What I hope to demonstrate regarding "The Golden Fleece" tale outlined above is that the tale is rife with elements that can be seen as truthful—forgetting the back-story regarding Jason's decision to acquire the fleece and the irony of his death by a chunk of the Argo falling on his head.

The mythologist might approach the tale entirely differently, perhaps employing his knowledge of astrology, or explaining the myth in association with particular gods and goddesses in vogue at the time a myth evolved. He might compare several versions of the same myth to arrive at a higher meaning, which still may baffle a reader seeking the *meaning* of the myth that can be understood in human terms. When I read mythologies, I try to discern whether gods, goddesses and personages mentioned were *real*; did they really produce offspring with humans?; were Hercules, Cronus, Lamia and other personages actual people; what does Persephone's being taken underground by Hades signify?—things like that. The few writings or criticism I have read of mythologies never answer these concerns to any satisfactory degree, so I don't generally pursue mythology.

I approach the tale of "The Golden Fleece" as a historian might, associating actual historical events—if I discover any that seem to relate to a particular myth—with the fanciful occurrences in the story. For me, what I outline above seems entirely reasonable. The circumstances (most of them) contained in the myth, then, can be applied to actual matters of fact. So in this sense, we can say that "The Golden Fleece" tale is a *true myth*. My use of this oxymoron in the title of this work can as well be applied to Europe during the Middle Ages—and, perhaps, even more precisely to the early portion of the Middle Ages known as the Dark Ages, which will be discussed presently.

*   *   *   *   *

Western historians write of the Europe after the fall of the Western Roman Empire as being suffused in an enveloping gloom which they have termed *The Dark Ages.* They write of the period as if a pervading murkiness descended over the continent after 500 AD. It is doubtful that the people inhabiting Europe at the time—black or white—felt this way; they were too concerned with reordering their lives after the order that Rome brought to Europe (not that it was in any way as widespread as historians would have us believe) fell away; they were concerned with feeding their families and going without supplies they once obtained regularly. What little reading, writing, entertainment and Christian religious pursuits they had begun to engage in became less important than merely surviving and holding onto their farms or villages against unchecked marauders who cropped up with the absence of the authority and general civility that the Romans had established. Life had especially changed for the increasing Caucasian population of Europe, but living essentially in restricted territories, it is doubtful they realized how widely this debilitation had overspread the continent to consider it a dark age.

It would be later historians who attached this label to the period, Western historians who came to view the Western Roman Empire as a civilizing, Aryan monolith, the epitome of white European power, organization and superiority. Rome was most responsible for *Caucasian* ascendancy in Europe, shifting the balance of power toward the steadily increasing white or lightening populaces and away from the Afro-Asiatic population which had previously dominated the continent. I don't mean to imply that the Romans realized the Caucasianizing process they had set in motion, but Eurocentric historians looking at Greek and Roman history must have, which may be why they designated the period after Rome's demise as the Dark Ages. The period was an interruption of Caucasian ascendancy on the continent, which Rome had set in motion with the destruction of Etruria, Carthage, and conquests in Iberia, Gaul, half of Britain and part of Germany—areas where black- and dark-skinned people still predominated even after the opening of the Christian Era (CE).

After the fall of Rome, an all-pervading gloom seems to engulf our view of the age, a gloominess passed down to us by Western writers. They describe a dark, *gothic* period where "there were few places where men could write, and little encouragement to write at all" (Wells, vol. 1 443). While varying views of the Dark Ages are presented by writers—some of whom view the age as the incubation period of the future Renaissance in Europe—most write of the period as an age of barbarism and gloom in which, states John Davies, author of *A History of Wales:*

> [T]he economy was stone-dead and the trade, the industries, the cities and the extensive literacy which had been dependent on it had vanished. With them vanished the ethos which had sprung from the Greeks and which had been spread by the Romans. (44)

We will see later that Rome was not totally vanquished, that her appetite for world domination underwent a transformation in which her legions of sword-wielding warriors became cadres of robe-clad disseminators of a religious doctrine that ultimately accomplished what the efforts of her military machine could not.

The onset of the 6th century in Europe is one of particular murkiness. An atlas of the period shows a number of peoples occupying the western sector of the continent, peoples whose identities and racial makeup are almost never defined—Thuringians, Burgundians, Lombards, Alamans, and another mysterious tribe of people called Merovingians. The Merovingians are another people seen through mist and gloom, but they became kings of the early Franks and are invariably called Germanic. Better known is the Merovingian king Clovis who, originally pagan, converted to Catholicism around 500 AD. This Frankish dynasty is considered "the first race of kings of what is now France," according to author Jim Marrs in *Rule by Secrecy* (326). Although Marrs is not ordinarily known as a historian—mostly concerned with uncovering sinister governmental and international plots—he nevertheless offers more detailed information on the Merovingians than I have been able to find in many historical works.

Marrs claims that the first ruler of the Merovingians was a man named Francio, a descendant of the Biblical Noah, who gathered his people and migrated to Europe from the ancient city of Troy in Asia Minor where, as we know, a great war was once fought. According to Marrs: "They named their settlement Troyes after their hometown. Paris was named for the Greek [sic] hero Paris whose elopement with Helen to Troy precipitated the Trojan War" [Paris was a *Trojan* hero] (op. cit.). In Gaul, Meroveus became king and Childeric I, his son, succeeded him. King Clovis I was Meroveus' grandson.

Marrs does not describe the physical appearance of the Merovingians, nor does he say in what numbers they came, but coming from Asia Minor at this time, I can only assume that the Merovingians were another infusion of dark-skinned Asiatic people into western Europe who must have intermingled with the dark- and black-skinned Germanic Goths, Huns and Caucasians in the region. I used to wonder why atlases show the territory occupied by the Merovingians or early Franks as *Austrasia*, but Marrs' explaination of Merovingian origins clarifies this. Consulting my very fat *Webster's New Twentieth Century Dictionary*, I found that the prefix <u>aust</u> means *south*—not east, as I had always believed; <u>austral</u>, means southern, <u>auster</u>, southward—the prefix <u>aust</u> being Latin. So Australia, the continent, seems appropriately named, being south of the equator. And *Australasia* refers to southern Asia or that general portion of the world. The scientific world calls the ancient inhabitants of Australia and Asians related to them *Australoids,* and we know them to have been black-skinned peoples. In an earlier chapter, we also noted that there were skeletal remains of Australoids in western Europe, probably related to Grimaldi man, Negroids. And if we look a little further, it may be that the Ostrogoths, whom we have been told were an *eastern* branch of Goths, should properly be called *Austro*goths, and connote this with how a nomenclature like Austrasia could turn up in western Europe in the 6th century or thereabouts. The reader may also want to consider the country of Austria, which once covered a larger territory, and may have once been included as a branch of more ancient Austrasia—a designation more than likely attached to the area by later historians for some as yet unknown reason.

Of course, Western historians omit any mention of Merovingian origins; they merely have them appear from out of nowhere, call them Germanic and leave us to believe they were a Caucasian people. In fact, Fr. Funck-Brentano, in *A History of Gaul,* says that the Franks of the period had fair or red hair and "generally had green eyes" (220), an obvious attempt to Caucasianize them. So, Jim Marrs' assertion that the Merovingians migrated to Europe from Troy in Asia Minor (i.e., Turkey) offers us new insight, and his assertion that the cities of Troyes and Paris (in present-day France, and within one hundred miles of each other) were named for Troy in ancient Ilium and Prince Paris—who was Trojan, not Greek—strikes this writer as quite credible.

In the writings of Western historians, the fires of western Europe blaze again with the rise of the Carolingians, Charles Martel, the Franks, Charlemagne and the formation of the Frankish Kingdoms in the 8th and 9th centuries. The establishment of the Frankish kingdoms began a significant, presumably Caucasian-ruled order in France and Germany (i.e., West Frankish Kingdom and the East Frankish Kingdom, or greater Germany) that would become allied with the popes of Rome and which would evolve into the Holy Roman Empire during Charlemagne's reign. The *Encyclopedia Britannica* notes that *Holy Roman Empire* was a "convention adopted by modern historians; it was never officially used" (vol. 6 21). In any case, its alliance with the Papal States did most to restore Rome's diminished authority and provide Rome with a powerful military arm with which to again bring Europe under its influence.

The Viking Age begins to unfold toward the end of the 8th century, but Western historians do not speak of them with the same fiery enthusiasm as they do Charlemagne and his presumably Caucasian Frankish Kingdom. The fires of the Norsemen are fires of destruction, black smoke, death and rapine. Europe cowers before these new usurpers, who are generally termed heathen and barbarian, and seem to have no regard for established society and civilized comportment. So, another black period descends over western Europe, spreading darkness west and southward, threatening the very existence of the idea of Europe as an entity. The Vikings, Northmen or Norsemen are not written of as if they were considered a part of mainstream Europe and always—even to modern historians—considered invaders, with their strange gods, heathen sacrifices and a predilection for vandalism and savagery. Prior to their emergence and the inception of the kingdom of Charlemagne and the Franks, there are relatively scant accounts of affairs in western Europe for the first three centuries of the Dark Ages. Davies captures the essence of how historians regard this period when he states: "With the long sunset came an age of myth and fantasy almost devoid of historical certainties" (44).

The early centuries of the Dark Ages (c. 500-800 AD) is presented as if it were a wholly mythical epoch. Even the later-written Norse or Icelandic sagas were seen as myths until the 19th century. They were more advanced than any medieval writing of the age, were complex, moving, controlled and visceral, striking readers as extremely realistic and exciting. It was long believed that they could only be fiction. Then 19th century scholars began to see many connections to actual personages and real historical events that took place during the centuries prior to their being written. The sagas are now considered more reality than myth, and in these tales there are personages who are described as black- and dark-skinned, like the previously mentioned Thorhall the Hunter and many others who will be outlined in ensuing chapters. Perhaps this is one of the reasons Western scholars chose to regard the sagas as myths for so long. Blacks were not supposed to have ever been in Europe, and certainly not in Scandinavia; such a possibility was unacceptable to the Eurocentric Brotherhood of Academia. References to black in the sagas and other literary works really meant *bad, wicked, villainous,* they proclaimed, and our high school and college instructors passed along these falsehoods to us whenever a personage in British, Norse or European literature in a medieval work was referred to as black. This method of misrepresentation has been so effective that the idea of black-skinned, especially Negroid-looking people ever inhabiting Europe seems preposterous to the average person.

Western historians generally do not write of the Vikings as if they were the common, white-skinned inhabitants of a supposedly Caucasian continent even though they invariably described Norsemen as blond-haired and blue-eyed. Norsemen are presented as if they evoked the same terror as the Huns of Attila, the Mongols of Genghis Khan or the Moors who overran Spain and other areas of Europe. Hunnish, Norse, Moorish and Mongol invasions of Europe (although the Norse can be said to be indigenous to the continent in comparison to the other abovementioned groups) all fall within the period of the *Dark* and *Middle Ages,* an age that would span a millennium (i.e., 500-1500 AD). This long age is also referred to as the *Medieval* period, another murky term that seems to denote unfathomable darkness, and Western historians transformed supposedly white men into "black" men—evil men—whose deeds and penchant for villainy relegated them to the lowest order of mankind—savage, lusty, innately cruel devils. What Caucasian Europeans were ever described in such a fashion by Western scholars?

If the Germanic Goths were white, why do we associate the term *gothic* with blackness, murkiness and evil—the term conjuring images of black-robed men or dark, mythological beings whose likenesses are never clearly delineated? Goths, whose ranks, we have seen, also included Vandals, Alans, Avars and Huns, were inhabiting large sectors of Europe, but there are only scant references regarding their actual civilization or established European homelands—although Western historians have generally associated them with "Germanic"—presumably white—peoples. The reader has already seen that, although they were Germanic, they were not the white-skinned people we have been lead to believe they were.

The dominant impression conveyed by Western writers remarking on the "medieval" period is abject gloom and dejection throughout western Europe which, along with the rise of Charlemagne and the Franks, abated for several centuries before the advent of the Vikings. However, the Vikings are written of as being almost otherworldly and *un-*European. The flames of the Viking Age did not brighten the Europe of Western writers; they deepen the suffering, extend the darkness, instill a sense of doom in the psyches of the inhabitants—white inhabitants—of Europe. It is not surprising that the more learned Europeans of the time were anticipating the end of the world in 1000 AD.

But, there *was* activity in Europe, especially northern Europe, where Norsemen—those mostly indigenous descendants of Old World Africans and black Asians—had begun to stir, sailing out from their homelands in Denmark and other areas of Scandinavia to descend upon the coastal areas of northern Europe, presaging larger, more organized future assaults. However, there are mentions of Danish expeditions to the Rhine in about 516 AD.; France in 565 (Olrik 30, 32); and Deira, on the east coast of England, in 595 AD (Davies 61). There were Danes in Frisia (i.e., the Netherlands and islands off its coast), Sweden and Estonia long before the official onset of the Viking Age. The epic poem *Beowulf* is thought to have been written around 500 AD or soon after and, if it is mostly historic as some aver, it illustrates some of the activity taking place in the north of Europe and demonstrates that there were kings, realms and alliances among the tribes occupying northern territories. If *Beowulf* is not historical but mythical, it nevertheless offers a realistic depiction of Scandinavia during the early period of the Dark Ages—the ruggedness of the terrain, the way people gathered together and socialized, built rude, sturdy wooden structures to live in, and demonstrates that seafaring was certainly common. My assessment is that it is composed of both fact and mythology and that—although it is called a poem—it can be considered an original precursor of the European novel, which would not be equaled for a millennium or more. *Beowulf* is an intricately written tale from an age whose historic certainties can only be pieced together from spare fragments of factual information and the mythology that Western scholars have shrouded the period in.

Two Europes existed during the Dark Ages. One Europe dreaded a looming dark shadow draping the continent and threatening its future. This could only have been the perception of the growing population of Europeans who looked upon themselves as the inheritors of the Greco-Roman legacy; or else it is the perception of later Eurocentric historians looking back upon an epoch realizing that the survival of Greco-Roman Europe was tenuous, as was the survival of a Caucasian humanity they had come to view as different, "white," more civilized and deserving than the dark-skinned barbarians rampaging through European territories. For it seems the other Europe, Northern Europe, Norse Europe, did not suffer the same dread. I have yet to encounter any writings indicating that Norsemen or Vikings feared the Dark Ages.

During the earliest centuries of the Dark Ages, Norse power was beginning to expand, and even though their above-mentioned forays to the Rhine and into France ultimately met with defeat, they were being perceived as a growing menace on the continent and in the British Isles. They *were* the dread, and it may well be that the term *Dark Ages* was the creation of Western historians who realized how demoralizing the period became for the Caucasian population of Europe, who had adopted the rudiments of early Christianity and envisioned Europe as a long-sought white homeland rid of the unalike black-skinned inhabitants who formerly possessed most of it.

Despite the silence of Eurocentric historians on the matter, black men and women had always occupied Europe and were still present in significant numbers at the onset of the Dark Ages, mostly in its northern and western extremities. Fifteen-hundred years ago, the greatest concentration of European Blacks seems to have been in Denmark, with Scotland a close second. If they were concentrated in Denmark, they must have been in Norway and southern Sweden as well, as Danes and Cimbri had long colonized these territories and Sweden and Denmark had been part of Attila's vast Black Hunnish empire. But there were still considerable numbers of black- and dark-skinned peoples in Iberia, Ireland, Russia, Estonia and western France—then known as Aqutania—with numbers of them still in Germany and areas of eastern and central Europe.

In the early centuries of the Dark Ages the Danes grow in prominence, although most English-language historians begin Danish Viking history in the late 8th century when Danes begin their incursions in the British Isles. Their cunning and savagery is often highlighted, while other aspects of their lives and culture are overlooked or never discussed. Speaking of the unknown composer of *Beowulf* and his depiction of the Danes, Axel Olrik states:

> It is not, however the warlike aspect . . . of the Danes that impresses . . . but rather the peaceful and splendid life of the royal hall: the magnificent structure of the palace Heorot . . . [W]e see noble lines of chieftains, richly adorned . . . [and] precious drinking vessels intended to imitate exactly the correct Roman way of serving wine . . . showing the Danes of that period as the most highly civilized race in the North. (40-41)

Beowulf also demonstrates that Danes honored their pledges of allegiance to allies, that they honored oaths for past kindnesses shown to a relative, and the protagonist, Beowulf, is shown to have genuine concern for the welfare of his men, treating their wounds and single-handedly battling the monstrous Grendl as many of his cadre lay injured or dead. He stands out as an example of a true, brave and compassionate leader.

In the northern realms of Europe, and particularly in Scandinavia, are diminuutive people who are referred to as Black Dwarfs or Elves. They are mentioned in a number of Norse sagas, though their existence has been mostly relegated to myth. However, there is strong evidence that they were more than mythological, that they were men (and there must have been women) who were highly valued for their knowledge of working metals to the highest degree, possessed the ability to craft special items like jewelry and amulets, and for their considerable knowledge of magic. In fact, they were thought to possess supernatural powers and were frequently sought out by Norse peoples to aid them through prophecy and magic.

They are a pygmy-like race of beings, whose "realm is known as *Svartalheim*, the black community" (Luke, *African Presence* 230). Looking at Black Dwarfs or Elves as actual people, historian Don Luke and others liken them to Negritos, those diminutive earliest humans who once populated the whole earth and were our first homo sapiens ancestors. The Pygmies of central Africa (also called *Twa*) are thought to be the truest modern representation of them. As well, the *Lapps* of northernmost Scandinavia and Asia—although appearing light- to ruddy-skinned today—are thought to be remnants of Negritos, as are the *Ainu*, the most ancient inhabitants of Japan (Rogers, vol. 1 71). These diminutive, Negroid peoples are known to have inhabited most areas of the earth, their remains being unearthed from Spain (Iberia) to Siberia, south Asia and North America.

Speaking of the considerable talents of the Black Dwarfs of the sagas, David MacRitchie states, in *Testimony of Tradition:*

> In one aspect, the dwarf races appear as possessed of a higher culture than the race or races who were physically their superiors. They forge swords of "magic" temper, and armour of proof, beautiful-wrought goblets of gold and silver, silver-mounted bridles, garments of silk, and personal ornaments of precious metals and precious stones, are all associated with them. (156)

As for dwarf magic, which MacRitchie and others have associated with the "Chaldean Magi," MacRitchie notes:

> They are deeply versed in "magic," and this renders them the teachers of the taller races, in religion, and in many forms of knowledge. In short, it is only in physical stature that they are below the latter people; in everything else they are above them. (op. cit.)

Black Dwarfs, according to myth, were banished to *Svart-alfa-heim*, situated underground and, supposedly, they could only emerge at night. In *Myths of the Norsemen*, H.A. Guerber notes that "[t]hey were called Dwarfs, Trolls, Gnomes, or Kobolds, and spent all their time and energy in exploring the secret recesses of the earth. They collected gold, silver, and precious stones . . ." (10-11).

Light Elves are also spoken of in the legends of Scandinavia, but their identity is uncertain. Some historians consider them, as well, members of the Negrito people. Don Luke contends that "the skin tone of the Twa ranges from dark brown or 'black' to yellow so the Light Elves could refer to the Lapps of northern Scandinavia . . . ." (*African Presence* 230). But Black Dwarves are more highly valued, and Luke gives an indication of how valued they were compared to Light Elves:

> It is the black Dwarves who inhabit the underground caves and work the mines, who forged Thor's magic hammer, Miolnir. It is the master craftsman, Dvalin, a Black Dwarf who fashions the enchanted spear, Gungnir, for All-father Odin. When the evil Loki faces a certain punishment from Thor for his evil deeds, it is to the Black Dwarves, not the Light Elves, that he goes for help and advice. (*African Presence* 231)

Don Luke cites MacRitchie, who speaks of the "well known prophetic or 'supernatural' power of the dwarf races" (op. cit. 230), and suggests that these short races are possibly connected to Grimaldi man who overspread Europe 40,000 years ago. Luke feels that the dwarf races of Scandinavia had an African origin, and also connects Scandinavian dwarfs with the diminutive and black-skinned *Skraelings* that Erik the Red found in Greenland. Other Vikings encountered them along the coasts of Newfoundland and Northern Canada (op. cit. 230).

The limitations of this paper do not allow for further examination of Black Dwarves and Elves, except to note that they are mentioned in the legends of many cultures around the world. Luke, and a number of other researchers, "argue that the Twa, Lapp, Ainu and Eskimos are all variations of the same original Africoid stock . . . reflecting varying degrees of mixture and environmental adaptation" (op. cit. 230). Black Dwarves and Elves became the Gnomes, Trolls and Fairies of nursery tales; the Wee Folk and Leprechauns of Irish folktales. Such beings—or parodies of them—have been included in a number of films (usually fantasy films) over many years, and in a later chapter a widely known popular film featuring beings reminiscent of Black Dwarves will be discussed.

Another event of ominous import for European Whites with Greco-Roman aspirations was the Moorish invasion of Europe in 711 AD. The invasion was primarily an African one, as North African converts to the rapidly spreading religion of Islam overran the entire Iberian Peninsula (i.e., Spain/Portugal) and continued their European incursion into Gaul—not yet called France. They vanquished the Visigothic Kingdom which had ruled Iberia for at least two centuries, but were repulsed, with heavy losses in Gaul by Franks under the command of Charles Martel—grandfather of Charlemagne—at the Battle of Poitiers (also called the Battle of Tours) in Aquitania in 732 AD. Defeated in Gaul, the Moors retreated to Iberia (Spain), some to southern France. The Moors would dominate Iberia for centuries making it, essentially, an extension of Africa in Europe up to the Pyrennes bordering France. While most Western historians imply that the Moorish invasion of Spain was an Arab invasion, most Arabs arrived as contingents and sometimes leaders of Moorish armies, but there were far fewer numbers of them than of Africans.

Western historians have converted this African invasion into an Arab one in order to lessen the spectre of black Africans dominating this *southern* sector of Europe. Despite the references in historical works and films to Moors as *Arabs,* John G. Jackson, in *Introduction to African Civilizations,* assures us, in this regard: "The conquest of Spain was an African conquest. They were Mohammadan Africans, not Arabs, who laid low the Gothic kingdom of Spain" (175)

Although the Arabs of this time were much darker-skinned than the Arabs of today, Western scholars prefer to admit to presumably light-skinned Arabs dominating Europe rather than black-skinned Africans, while also stressing that North Africans are lighter-skinned than sub-Saharan Africans—going so far (which we will see in a later chapter) as to claim that North Africans are essentially Caucasians! The religion of Islam had exploded out of the Arabian Peninsula upon the death of Prophet Muhammad in 632 AD, and in less than 200 years its Arab adherents had spread its influence from Spain to India and as far north as northern present-day Kazakhstan, above the Aral Sea.

Rome quaked, and the Byzantine Empire, which had grown out of the Eastern Roman Empire, felt itself directly threatened, with Islamic territories right outside its eastern borders. However, the Christian Byzantine Empire was at the height of its power and influence and would remain intact for many centuries more. In the west, Rome, under the aegis of the Byzantine Empire since its downfall, sought furiously to convert as many Europeans (and, I would surmise, Caucasian Europeans) as it could to Christianity and bring them under the rule of the Roman Church. In *Man, God, and Civilization,* John G. Jackson remarks that during the Dark Ages, "[t]he Church not only perpetuated slavery, but created it where it had never existed under Roman Law," and notes that there are recorded cases of Church officials foully abusing their slaves, mutilating them and sometimes starving them to death (261). And Jackson goes on to state:

> The story of the Dark Ages in Europe presents a chronicle of horrors almost without parallel in human history; and the saddest part of it is the story of the conversion of Europe to Christianity. (op. cit.)

But Europeans—light and mixed-race Europeans, whose descendants would become Whites—who were not slaves often experienced the same horrors and abuses from desperate Church officials intent on recruiting as many souls as possible under Roman overlordship to combat the spread of Islam on the continent. The darkness of the Church of Rome and its conversion methods contributed to the general bleakness of the period.

There should no longer be any doubt in the reader's mind that black- and dark-skinned peoples inhabited areas of Europe at the onset of the Dark Ages and that when the Viking Age began (c. 800-1100 AD), black-skinned people predominated in the territories comprising Scandinavia. The expansion of Whites on the continent was stalled, their future uncertain, and the invasion of the continent by the Moors must have conjured images of Hannibal and a second coming of Carthage in the minds of those who recorded and remembered history. Blacks under various tribal names were still present in the British Isles and on the fringes of continental western Europe, with significant numbers of them remaining in Germany, Baltic regions, like Estonia and Finland, and portions of Russia.

Western historians have effectively expurgated them from European history, injecting their works on Europe with a plethora of faceless, colorless tribes and peoples they leave us to conclude were Caucasian. Except for the rise of the Frankish Empire, practically the whole period of the Dark Ages (i.e., 500-800 AD) is presented to us as a netherworld of myth. The black- and dark-skinned peoples we have discussed were converted to Whites—declared so outright, or else by the omission of any information which would show them to have been other than the fair-skinned Europeans we know inhabit the continent today.

The Norsemen must be added to this list of unrecognized black- and dark-skinned peoples, unrecognized because Eurocentric historians almost unanimously converted them to white men—blond, blue-eyed *Nordics*, although there is scant evidence for such an assertion. While Western historians have insisted Norsemen were tall, bearded, savage Whites, their depredations throughout the Viking Age are deemed horrendous, amoral, and villainous—a certain ogre-like blackness enshrouding the very thought of Vikings, who worshipped their black god, Thor, and often attacked villages after nightfall. So in the general histories written of these people, their purported whiteness is overshadowed by a veneer of darkness and "they appeared to mainstream Europe like uncanny visitors from another world" (Jones and Pennick 132). We only get to approach them somewhat, see them as men, when they begin to settle in eastern and central England and treat with Alfred (the Great) who battles them to preserve the England abandoned by the Romans, or in their dealings with King Charles the Simple in northern France where they acquire the territory named after them—Normandy. However, they yet remain faceless and fairly mythological because Eurocentric historians refuse to add color to their faces and allow us to get a clear picture of the kind of men they really were: actual black- and dark-skinned men who would in no way be considered akin to present-day Caucasians.

During the Dark Ages, black- and dark-skinned people remained prominent in many areas of Europe, which is surely why MacRitchie states that the whole period of the Dark Ages was "*dark* in a double sense" (*Britons* 137). Even a millennium ago, in the midst of the Middle Ages, it cannot be said that Europe was populated exclusively by white-skinned people. Historians present the Dark Ages to us almost bereft of actual men and factual events, projecting images of bleakness and mist overspreading the whole continent; opaque, black-robed, presumably Caucasian men appearing out of foggy shadowlands, moving about on nefarious missions.

In the 6th century, Norsemen began to stir in Scandinavia, beginning to steer their dragon ships in the direction of the British Isles and France. These *Northmen* are peoples Eurocentric writers have always insisted were white, blond and blue-eyed, asserting that such people were typical in the northern climes of Europe. The reader has already been presented with evidence that this assertion is false, that Scandinavia had long been occupied by black-skinned people. The authors cited in this regard *make no mention* of Caucasians of any significance being present there during the long period we have discussed—the Megalithic age to the eve of the Viking Age. While Western historians overwhelmingly insist that Norsemen were Caucasian, white, *Nordic* or, according to Waddell, *Aryan*, they invariably write of them as being outsiders, invaders, barbarians, inhuman, heathen and *black* in regard to their bloodlust. They—though presumably white, blond blue-eyed, the quintessence of Caucasian purity—are not considered part of the European family and are discussed with the same vituperation that Moors, Huns and Mongols are.

While the period of the Dark Ages is so named because the aggressiveness and dynamism of Caucasian, Greco-Roman aspiring Europe was stagnant, spent and decaying, it was also dark because it was inhabited by *actual* black- and dark-skinned peoples Eurocentric historians have chosen not to clearly depict or identify. The age was not dark for them; any notable exploits and vitality in Europe was effectuated by them. Therefore, it is a myth that the age is called "Dark" *solely* because learning, commerce, industry, the love of the arts and the advancement of Roman culture had stagnated; it is so-called because very real black- and dark-skinned peoples—peoples Western historians have edited out of their works—still abounded in Europe, retaking the reins of initiative that the expansion of the Roman Empire had usurped from them over several centuries.

The most fearsome, and perhaps most numerous, of these black-skinned peoples were the very real Black Norsemen—peoples Western historians have expurgated from history by insisting that the Vikings were fair and blond. The evidence presented so far, with evidence still to come, demonstrates that these Blacks were real—a *true myth* of the Dark Ages that were "*dark* in a double sense." Seafaring was intrinsic to these men of the far North as well as a warrior disposition. And, while the art of shipbuilding had long diminished in the rest of the continent, they would produce the sturdiest, sleekest, fastest ships ever constructed up to that time. Despite a general paucity of information regarding b*lack* Vikings, enough evidence has already been presented showing that northern Europe, particularly the territories of Scandinavia, was primarily inhabited by black-skinned peoples, and the reader will shortly realize that evidence of black Norsemen or Vikings is not new or unknown and should no longer be overlooked.

CHAPTER 7

NORTHERN SUNRISE

By most accounts, Denmark was inhabited by the "royal race" of Norsemen whose legendary kings were the Skjoldungs, called Scyldings in *Beowulf*. This royal race was descended from Skjold who, in the *Ynglinga Saga,* is the son of Odinn (Odin).

Whether Dan, supposedly a legendary king for whom *Dan*-mark was named was accepted by all Danes during his reign is uncertain, as is the specific time he supposedly lived—which we must assume is sometime before 500 AD. As discussed in the previous chapter, Jutland probably acquired the name Danmark because of its occupation by the De Danaan, or Tuatha de Danaan, who anciently occupied it after they were expelled from the British Isles.

Essentially of Egyptian origin, they would have come into contact with descendants of earlier Africoids and Egyptians whose ancestors had long before erected the megalithic tombs and other structures throughout western Europe, as well as Africoid Picts, Teutones and Cimbric peoples who had overspread much of Germany and the British Isles. Arriving in Jutland with an advanced culture, their fleets and significant numbers of people, it would not have been difficult for the De Danaan to become a dominant force there, powerful enough to become the ruling elite. Over the centuries (L.A. Waddell dates their arrival in Jutland in the 10th century BC) they would intermingle with peoples residing in Scandinavia as well as with later arriving dark-skinned Scythic peoples coming in from Asia and—if Waddell's date for their arrival is correct—challenge the expanding Roman Empire in Pannonia late in the 2nd century BC as Cimbri, discussed earlier. Over the centuries newer people emerged in Scandinavia—Teutones, Ambrones and Getae, who more than likely were the *Goths,* who are first noticed in Sweden and northern Germany. However, by the 7th century the Danes or Dani, also known as Cimbri, became most prominent as the royal race who dominated not only Denmark but southern Norway and Sweden as well.

It should also be understood that other races were present in Scandinavia, like the previously-mentioned Lapps, who overspread the more northerly regions of Scandinavia, and the Sitones of central and northern Sweden, a Finnic people by most accounts, related to the Finns across the Baltic in Finland, a dark, shortish people who many connect to Inuit or Eskimo peoples who Western anthropologists class as Ugritic or Mongoloid. Other scientists connect the early Finns to Africoids, and not without reason, and this connection will be looked at further on. Finns were also a seafaring people, some of whom may have been contingents of Viking raiders, although there is not a lot of information as to whether they had ship-building capabilities. They sometimes intermarried with Norsemen and are mentioned in the Norse sagas as being practitioners of *magic.*

Sometime around the year 700 AD, Vikings invaded the Shetland Islands and within a decade established a stronghold in the Orkneys, building fortifications, securing the best ports, and setting up farming communities which did not portend much success. These Vikings are said to have been *Norwegians,* but they did not come to these islands in large numbers until the end of the 8th century when the land was more suitable for farming. Their takeover of these islands seems to have been to set up a base for further raids to the south—Scotland and eventually Ireland.

Though many equate Norse with Norwegian, Norse is generally applied to the language and to the people inhabiting Scandinavia during the first half of the Middle Ages. Implicit in the term Norse is <u>north</u>, and in Norsemen, *Northmen,* by which these Scandinavian invaders were regarded by the peoples of the British Isles. They were racially similar, spoke the same language, had similar customs, physiognomy and religious beliefs—considered *pagan,* which must have evolved from a blending of Egyptian and Asiatic belief systems. They also had the same predilection for raiding and rapine. The Danes are often cited as particularly barbarous, and ancient chroniclers called them <u>black</u> as historical works of the period attest.

The Shetlands, notably the islands of Fetlar and Unst, were anciently occupied by people similar to Finns who were aboriginals inhabiting northern Scandinavia and territories stretching eastward into northern Asia. These Finns were a short, dark-complexioned people who overspread the Arctic regions from Europe into eastern Asia. Such people were occupying the Shetlands when the Norse arrived, and most are presumed to have been killed or taken into slavery. Most historians aver that the Norse invaders were Norwegians. The Norse called the aboriginal people of northern Scandinavia *Finns,* but we need to understand that in more ancient times Finns were not confined to the country we know today as Finland. According to Farley Mowat, author of *The Farfarers,* such people continued to inhabit the islands of Unst and Fetlar after the Norse invasion of the Shetlands, and he informs us:

> Shetlanders used the same name [i.e., <u>Finns</u>] for these s*mall-statured, dark-skinned strangers* [i.e., <u>Norsemen</u>] that their ancestors had given to the people who preceded the Norse in Shetland. (*my emphasis* 110)

In chapter 5 it was noted that there was an affinity between Finnic and North African skull types, and there was Gibbon's testimony of "a close and clear affinity" between the idioms of the Black Hungarians and the old Finnic race, which modern linguists confirm, classifying the Finnish and Hungarian languages as Finno-Ugric.

Fifteen- or sixteen-hundred years ago when Black Huns were storming into Europe, the racial connection between these two peoples (i.e., Finns and Hungarians) would have been obvious; they looked like—and perhaps were—the same people, branches of them moving north and northwest to the Baltic and Scandinavia, others moving southwest into eastern Europe from an original central Asian homeland. The question for us is how long they had been migrating into northern Europe, and were the Finns in Scandinavia and the Shetlands the result of an early migration into northern Europe, or a branch of the Hunnish surge into the continent during the 4th and 5th centuries. In any event, 7th century Shetlanders called the dark-skinned, short-statured Norse invaders *Finns,* who actually began raiding the islands and those of the Orkneys around 681 AD. Mowat's reference to these Norsemen is the earliest mention of Norwegian Vikings I have so far come across, and their short stature signifies that they were a predominantly Asiatic type of people. The Finnic cranial affinity with ancient North Africans bespeaks an older connection with that continent dating back to remote migrations of Africans, or a *type* of African, out of the Mother Continent to that part of Asia where so-called Mongoloid people would emerge.

The Orkneys were low-lying and more fertile than the Shetlands, occupied by people known as Peti and Papae. Mowat cites a Norwegian historian who states that the Peti "were scarcely taller than Pygmies," and Peti spearmen were repulsed by the raiding Norsemen who destroyed them, securing the islands for themselves (op. cit. 111). If the Peti were Pygmy-like in height, then the "small-statured, dark-skinned" Norwegian strangers, short of stature themselves, must have been primarily Finns who at the time made up the greater population of Norway.

According to Mowat, Vikings were raiding Scotland by 681, but they were repulsed in their efforts to subdue it. The black Picts and Scots remained dominant in Alba, as ancient Scotland was known, and we know that they were fierce fighters, themselves, having repulsed Roman attempts to subdue all of Alban, the largest British island. Early in the 8th century Oengus mac Fergus came to power in Alba (c. 729) and tried to organize the country to resist Viking incursions. Rosalind Mitchison, author of *A History of Scotland,* has Oengus mac Fergus, whom she calls the "Pictish King Oengus" (Oengus probably the same as <u>Angus</u>), ruling the Scots in 741 and enjoying a long reign (5). It is doubtful that Mac Fergus ruled for as long as Mitchison seems to indicate, for Mowat mentions Irish annals stating that a fleet of 150 Pictish vessels were lost off Cape Wrath (off the northwest coast of Scotland) in 729 and that Pictish naval power wanes after this date. He quotes Archibald Lewis as stating:

> We hear nothing more of the Pictish fleet which had been active off the coasts of Scotland and about Orkney . . . . Now it was the mariners from Western Norway who began probing south, doing so with little opposition. (112)

Mowat states that Mac Fergus' reign lasted until 761, and that before the end of the 8th century, "Vikings were rampaging almost unchallenged through the west" (113).

Just prior to this, Mac Fergus, the Pictish king, "was desperately engaged in land battles against Scotti [Scots] in the west and Britons in the south," being finally defeated by the Scotti in 750" (113). In 756 the Picts were militarily crushed by the north Britons, losing possession of their Hebridean Islands territories and, within a few decades, most of Pictland (i.e., Alba or Scotland).

The Scotti, or Scots, originally from Ireland, subdued most of Alba, giving their name to it, and the reader is reminded that all the peoples being spoken of here were primarily black-skinned—Picts, Scotti and Britons. While the term *Briton* is generally applied to the Welsh in the southwest, there were Britons occupying central and northern England, and the Welsh may have been allied (if not related) to some of them—peoples more anciently known as Celts, or Black Celts who occupied most of Alban when the Romans invaded. The Picts and Scots would intermarry over the ensuing century until Pictland, over which the Picts retained nominal control of, was completely conquered by Kenneth mac Alpin, known as King of the Scots, in 843.

By this time, Vikings had been raiding areas of Britain for a half-century. The first recorded raid on what would become England took place in 793 when Danish Vikings attacked Lindisfarne, looting and destroying the church there, called "God's Church." It was earlier mentioned that Irish chroniclers made a distinction between white, Norwegian invaders and black, Danish Vikings, while the Welsh—whose territory was partly occupied by Romans and assailed by presumably light- or white-skinned Saxons which lightened their population—called both groups of these invaders black. Still, some Irish accounts, as noted earlier by Rosalind Mitchison, referred to Norwegian invaders as "*black gentiles*" (9).

Iona was burned and devastated in 802 and again in 806 when the monks were massacred by Viking raiders. Iona was a great religious center connected, according to Higgins, to Iona in Greece and the Ionians, originally black-skinned, who migrated to the island many centuries before. At the time of the Viking invasions, it was ruled by Scots, a territory of Scottic Dal Riada, but the Norse, whether Norwegian or Danish, seemed hell-bent on obliterating anything that had to do with Christianity.

Although many historians have followed the Irish chroniclers' example of dividing Norwegians and Danish Vikings into white and black, respectively, the historians who *do* comment on the race of these peoples invariably describe them as black-skinned, including Swedish Vikings, who had less to do with raids on Britain and France, concentrating their raids on areas around the Baltic and Russia. The 7th century historian Jordanes—while remarking on how notable Swedes were for being taller than other men—states, as cited by Gwyn Jones, that the Danes were "*of the same race as the Swedes*" (*my emphasis*, Vikings 26). If Norwegians and Danes were black-skinned, as Welsh historians and some Irish chroniclers insist (according to Mitchison), and if the Danes were of the same race as the Swedes, as Jordanes avers, then the Norsemen of the Dark Ages were predominantly black-skinned peoples inhabiting and dominating Scandinavia in relatively recent historical times—with Danes invariably called b*lack-skinned*—not just dark—by those who discuss the race of Viking peoples.

There is a strong suggestion that the term <u>Dane</u>, itself came to *imply* "black," or *meant* <u>a black man speaking the Danish tongue</u>, at the very least. The reader has already seen quite enough evidence that black-skinned people occupied the Jutland Peninsula and its environs from prehistoric times. There is nothing to indicate that there was any alteration of this fact over the ensuing centuries, since the Danes were called "black gentiles," "black strangers," or "dubh gaill" (black foreigners) throughout the British Isles during the whole of the Viking Age (i.e., 800-1100 AD). And David MacRitchie punctuates this fact when he states:

> There can be no question about it. The designation given by the common peoples of one race to another is almost invariably founded upon some physical feature, and the most natural distinction is that of color where the races differ in complexion . . . . Therefore, when the white races of Britain styled the Danes "Black heathen," they simply made use of the most natural term that would occur to them. (*Britons* vol. *1* 114)

Regarding Norsemen being called *black heathen,* MacRitchie makes a point of noting: "It was not only in Scotland that the Danes received this name, but throughout the British Islands" (op. cit.).

In *The Pre-Columbian Discovery of America,* B.F. De Costa, commenting briefly on the colonization of Iceland c. 860, states that the discovery of Iceland had been made known to Norsemen "by a <u>*Dane of Swedish descent*</u> named Gardar" (*my emphasis,* 119).

And since we know that the Danes of this period were black, De Costa's comment infers that Swedes were the same (as stated by Jordanes, above), and perhaps that the term <u>Dane</u> *implied* black.

The first recorded reference to <u>Danmark</u> was in 908, more than a century after Norse invasions of the British Isles began, indicating, as well, that Dan or Dane was originally applied to a *people* and only later attached to the country from which they derived. Danes were clearly discernible because of their complexions, and since the name *Dan*mark was not in vogue in 860 when Iceland was discovered, its being discovered by "a <u>Dane</u> of Swedish descent" is tantamount to saying it was discovered by "a black man from Sweden." De Costa does not mention the complexion of this Northman, but does state that they [Northmen] "were descendants of a race that in early times migrated from Asia . . . settling down in . . . Denmark" (op. cit.). However, De Costa does not equate Danes with the typical European we are familiar with today.

While Irish chroniclers, for whatever reason, referred to Norwegians as *Finn gaill,* supposedly white foreigners, evidence has been presented above that the early Norwegians who invaded the Shetland and Orkney Islands around the opening of the 8th century were short-statured and dark-skinned, a fact that there is no reason to believe would have been altered a century later when Norwegians began foraying into Ireland, although possible intermingling with Danes and Swedes may have produced taller people over three or four generations. Gwyn Jones informs us:

> The leading families of Scandinavia were much intermarried for sound business reasons . . . . [T]here was a leaven of Danes in Norway and Sweden, Norwegians in Sweden and Denmark, Swedes in Denmark and Norway, ruling, serving, fighting . . . mating and marrying, seeking or losing the world's good . . . . (*Vikings* 75)

The 9th century saw a significant increase in Viking activity. After the looting, burning and massacre of the monks in Iona in 806, Vikings intensified their raids on England and the rest of the British Isles. Notes Agnes Mure Mackenzie in *The Foundations of Scotland:*

> In 824 the invaders [in this instance, Danes] sacked Bangor, in 825 Moville, and Iona again . . . By 834 they held the whole North of Ireland [probably Norwegians] . . . In 838 they were back in the South of England . . . . (74-75)

Primarily Danish Vikings were also raiding coastal and inland areas of France. Ms. Mackenzie has them forming a settlement on the lower Seine in 841, which must have been around the time that Rouen was attacked, for Gwyn Jones states:

> In 841 it was the turn of Rouen, when Asgeir appeared from nowhere off the mouth of the Seine, headed upriver, sacked and burned the town, took a quick tribute of destruction and money from the town, and had his ships . . . away before the . . . defenders could lay hand on him. (*Vikings* 210)

There was also conflict among the three nations for possession of various islands and territories in and around Scandinavia, and in the British Isles open warfare would break out between Norwegians and Danes in Ireland from 850-853. Norwegians eventually prevailed there (around Dublin), but Danes would form small settlements farther south in the country.

The revelation of black-skinned people occupying Scandinavia in fairly recent historical times must be shocking to many readers; however, this information, presented primarily by *white* or European historians, has been extant for quite some time. David MacRitchie's monumental *Ancient and Modern Britons,* a positively profound work, was published in 1884 and was pretty much unavailable until 1985 when it was republished. Nearly half of the first volume is devoted to black- and dark-skinned occupants of Europe, especially black Vikings, showing that this information has been known for quite some time and was simply ignored throughout most of the 20th century while a less-than-honest image of Vikings and Europe was promoted by Western historians.

At the time that Viking raids were intensifying in the British Isles there was general turmoil in the rest of western Europe. Among the Frankish and Germanic states there was much in-fighting. During the early 9th century Charlemagne conquered Germanic Saxons, made an alliance with Slavonic communities, and attempted to control all trade from the Baltic to the west coast of the continent, an area that had long been the realm of Denmark, "which had enjoyed prosperity for *more than two thousand years* by virtue of her position on two European trade routes" (*my emphasis,* Jones, *Vikings* 99). To curtail growing conflict with the Frankish Kingdom, Danes constructed the <u>Danevirke</u>—a system of earthworks in the south of the Jutland Peninsula—erected as a defensive barrier against attack from the south, built over a period of several centuries (c.810-1160 AD).

Charlemagne sent his son Charles on an expedition to attack the Danes, but Charles thought better, diverting his troops toward the Baltic and a lesser adventure.

Charlemagne never directly challenged the Danes, Jones stating in this regard: "It is clear that Charlemagne had no thought of conquering the Danes" (*Vikings* 101). There is more intrigue to these events which took place around 810, but it is not essential to our main discourse. After Charlemagne's death in 814, conflict ensued in the territory he had unified through kingship, and a resurgent Christianity had spread widely in the Frankish Kingdom. There were several attempts to introduce this new, unwanted religion to the Danes, which they fiercely resisted.

Norsemen were called heathen, pagan, and lived according to the strange dictates of their gods—Thor, Freyr, Woden or Odin, and Freyja, whom they called upon often when preparing for raids or larger ventures of conquest. Norse kings or warriors often had dreams while contemplating some adventure, dreams which warned them of treachery or promised them success. There is no evidence of any religious book they abided by, and it is unclear whether their marriages—which seemed easy to effect—involved any religious rites—though they probably did. It is even doubtful that *all* Norsemen, whether Danes, Swedes or Norwegians, were conversant with all the aspects of their religion, which is mostly unknown to us. What *is* known is that Norsemen abhorred Christianity and that Christian churches were frequently looted of their treasures and burned to the ground when Vikings attacked a town.

Nevertheless, Rome was determined to convert the heathen north to Christianity.

From the onset of the 9th century missions and missionaries were sent north by Roman popes. Charlemagne had much success consolidating most of his realm under the Christian banner, and his son, Louis the Pious, had some success in converting a few individual Norsemen to the faith. Even more successful, though with much difficulty, was Anskar (also Ansgar), born in Austrasia, who converted an exiled Danish king, Harold, to the faith around 823. Anskar went with Harold to Denmark in an attempt to gain converts. They were driven out, and Anskar would attempt to find converts among the Swedes several years later. In 831 Anskar was made archbishop of Hamburg and given the mission of converting all the northern peoples—Swedes, Danes, Slavs, and others. But when Louis the Pious died in 840, his three sons battled over the empire, and the realm fell into complete disarray. The Danes were pleased by this turn of events and, states Jones:

> They at once intensified their attacks south, and among other depredations carried out the sack of Hamburg in 845 with a fleet reputedly of *six hundred ships*. (*my emphasis*, *Vikings* 107)

Anskar escaped with a few sacred relics, "but church, school, and library were destroyed with the rest of the city" (op. cit.). Anskar would next attempt a mission to Denmark in 849, and there would be many more missions to convert the north by others over the next three centuries. One has to wonder why there was such an urgency by the seat of Christendom in Rome to convert the northern regions, especially the inhabitants of Denmark, who exhibited an abhorrence to the faith. More will be considered later regarding this question.

Back in the British Isles, Vikings were increasing their raids, especially in England. The *Anglo-Saxon Chronicle* tells of a great host of Danes coming to Cornwall in 838, uniting with the Britons (Black Celts) there to fight against Egbert, king of Wessex. The Vikings and Britons were eventually repulsed. In 840 Danes, along with men of Dorset, took possession of Portland. In fact, Danes raided both the southern and eastern portions of England continuously from about 800 to 850 and onwards, their raids and the results too numerous to detail here. Alfred, Aethelwulf, Aethelberht and other petty kings and rulers of various territories, did their utmost to fend off the surging waves of Norse invaders who were attacking all over what would become Great Britain.

About 870 or 871 there was a great battle in Reading and another at Ashdown, where the Danes won the victory after much slaughter on both sides. In 871 or 872 the Danes went to London where they took winter quarters and afterwards began to settle in the places where they had won victories.

*   *   *   *   *

Most historical sources assert that Rolfe the Ganger's, or Rollo's, invasion of northern France took place in 911; however, the *Anglo-Saxon Chronicle* lists his invasion as taking place in 876. Many accounts aver that Rollo, Rolfe or Hrolf the Ganger was a Dane, while others insist he was Norwegian. Regarding Hrolf's nationality, Gwyn Jones states:

> We cannot say for certain whether Rollo was a Norwegian or a Dane . . . . But Norman historical tradition is unaware of any such Norwegian Hrolf . . . . On the scene of action itself Rollo was considered to be a Dane. (*Vikings* 229).

While the issue of Hrolf the Ganger's nationality may seem unimportant on the surface, it entails a wider significance when one considers that Western scholars have generally adopted the ancient Irish historians' convention of dividing Norse invaders into White (Norwegian) Foreigners and Black (Danish) Foreigners (or *Strangers*). Western historians are more comfortable with a Norwegian (presumably white) leader and his army invading France than a Danish (definitely black) leader doing so. It upholds the supposed purity of Europe that they have endeavored to maintain in the minds of readers, alleviating any disturbing thought of racial intermingling between black men and white women. But the reader must understand by now that racial intermingling had always taken place in Europe, and 9th and 10th century France would be no exception. Whether Rollo was a Norwegian or a Dane, Jones informs us, "the nationality of the leader is less important than that of his army, which there is every reason to believe was predominantly Danish" (op. cit., 229-230), which is to say that Rollo's army was primarily composed of black-skinned men.

While the earliest Danish incursions in France were undertaken for plunder—the Danes raided, sacked or burned Rouen, Nantes, Bordeaux, Toulouse, Angers, Tours, Orleans and Paris from 843 to the 860s—Rollo was granted a vast territory in the north to which the name *Normandy* was given. Rollo was appointed Duke of Normandy by King Charles the Simple and promised to defend the territory for France; so the same Dubh Ghenti, or black gentiles, dominating England and other areas in the British Isles were legitimately established in part of the West Frankish Kingdom, and Normandy would remain autonomous.

For one or two generations the Danes of Normandy continued to speak their native tongue, but afterwards adopted French. Acquiring the French tongue would not have taken long since Norsemen took French wives and had numerous progeny. The French had become a predominantly white-skinned people by this time, but numerous dark- or tawny-skinned Frenchmen and women still inhabited the region of Aquitaine in the west and southwest, and Brittany in the northwest. Gwyn Jones informs us: "The [Norse] invaders brought very few women of their own with them . . . so intermarriage . . . between Danes and French must have been common from the beginning" (*Vikings* 230-231). Normandy became an area of widespread racial mixing where brown and tawny faces must have been in evidence for several centuries. Rollo and the bulk of Danish Vikings also converted to Christianity, that formerly hated religion, further distancing Normandy from her Scandinavian homeland.

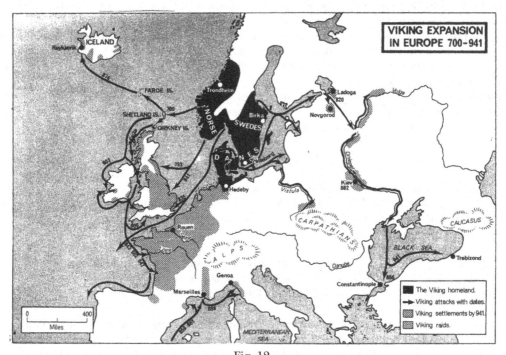

Fig. 12
Blackened territory indicates the Viking homelands. Shaded areas depict Viking settlement in England and France as well as areas of Viking raids.

During the same period that Danes were raiding France and settling Normandy (i.e., mid-9th to early 10th centuries), they raided areas of Muslim Iberia (Spain/Portugal, which was then called the *Spanish Caliphate*) and ventured into the Mediterranean and Ligurian Seas where they raided areas in North Africa, southern France (Burgundy, not part of Charles the Simple's French holdings), and plundered Pisa in 860 along with other areas of northeastern Italy—including Luna, which they mistook for Rome. Two centuries later Norsemen would carve out a kingdom in southern Italy and Sicily.

Primarily Norwegian Vikings began their assaults on Ireland at the onset of the 9th century when, as noted by Holger Arbman in *The Vikings*, who cites the *Annals of Ulster*: "The Ocean poured torrents of foreigners over Erin, so that not a harbour of landing, fort or stronghold, was without fleets of Scandinavians and pirates" (68).

Arbman goes on to say that in 836 two separate fleets of 60 ships raided all over Meath and that Vikings established a colony in Dublin the same year. Then "[I]n 850 the Black Strangers [Danish Vikings] arrived, and harried Dublin" (69). Jones notes regarding the Danish arrival: "The Irish preferred the newcomers to the old, but with a plague on both their houses" (*Vikings* 207). In 852 the Norwegians attacked the Danish fleet situated in Carlingford, to the north, and a great three day battle ensued. According to Arbman, 5,000 Norwegians were killed, only a handful surviving, and:

> . . . the triumphant Danes, honouring a promise given to the Irish high-king's messengers
> on the battlefield, surrendered a large chest of gold and silver to St. Patrick, "for the
> Danes had at least a kind of piety . . ." (69)

In 853 the Norwegians reentered Ireland "with a royal fleet under the command of Olaf (Amlaibh), son of the king of Norway (Lochlann), though which son of what king is hard to determine" (Jones, *Vikings* 207). This Olaf is often referred to as Olaf the White, but Jones discusses the difficulty of the precise identification of this individual in a footnote on the page. At any rate, Olaf or Amlaibh worked out an agreement between the feuding Viking factions and became the ruler of Dublin. Danes who could not abide by Norwegian rule left for England to press their attacks in that part of the British Isles.

Many Norsemen are identified by color names, and it is reasonable to assume that Olaf the White was, if not actually Caucasian, a very light-skinned black man, since both Danes and Norwegians at this time were predominantly black- and dark-skinned. Olaf's lightness or white complexion may have been the result of his being bi-racial, which I believe is most probable. His light skin could not have been typical of Norwegians of the time and would have been his most distinguishing feature. His esteem might have derived form his being married to Aud the Deep-minded, daughter of a powerful chieftain known as Ketil Flatnose, sometimes called Caitill Finn, or Ketil the White, by Irish historians. But Rosalind Mitchison, like Gwyn Jones, Welsh chroniclers, David Macritchie and other sources, states emphatically that both Danes and Norwegians were "black gentiles," as has been noted in this chapter and previously.

MacRitchie has more to say regarding Ketil Flatnose. Mentioning that he was called Caitill Finn and Caitill the White, MacRitchie asserts that this personage being called Flatnose "point[s] to the possession of Ugrian blood" (*Britons* 119), which would connect him to Black Huns. MacRitchie says that the precise meaning of Finn is difficult to determine, while acknowledging Irish historians' use of the term to imply *white*. But he is hesitant to embrace this application fully, feeling the term, if I interpret him accurately, may be more correctly associated with Finns, proper, the Asiatic race of people of the Ugrian or Mongoloid type who, as earlier noted, occupied the more northerly regions of Norway and Sweden and whom the Shetland islanders likened the 8th century Norwegians to. So Ketil Flatnose may have actually been a Finn or strongly resembled a typical Finn of the time, whom we know had dark complexions. And since Finns predominated in the territory known as *Finnmark*—the northern areas of Norway, Sweden and the Finnic homeland across the Gulf of Bothnia, it is certainly probable that Finns made up a percentage of Viking fleets, whether Danish, Norwegian or Swedish—although Finns seem to have had more intercourse with Swedish Vikings.

So, Caitill Finn's, or Ketil Flatnose's moniker—*Finn*—probably had more to do with his actually being a swarthy Finn, or resembling one, than with his being white-skinned, as early Irish historians, and Western scholars following their lead, have endeavored to imply. His daughter, Aud the Deep-minded, also known as Aud Ketilsdottir the Deep-minded, would more than likely have been swarthy-skinned also. Olaf the White might also have been all or part Finn, a light-skinned black man or, indeed, white. Norsemen respected bravery in battle and Olaf may have distinguished himself in such a way. As well, Norse chieftains often adopted the sons of their subjects, granting them earldoms or other positions of leadership when they came of age, and Whites would become more common in Scandinavia as Norsemen were in the habit of taking slaves and concubines back to their homelands from places they raided.

The whole period of the Dark Ages (500-1100), especially the Viking Age (800-1100), was a period of considerable racial intermingling in Europe since the women of the vanquished were always part of the spoils of the victor. Although intermarriage took place between Norsemen and the women of the defeated—Irish, English, German, Slavic, Italian, French, etc.,—Gwyn Jones, in *The Norse Atlantic Saga*, informs us:

> In addition there must have been a great deal of concubinage, for the Norsemen abroad
> (and for that matter at home) were notoriously addicted to the use of women. (49)

A son of Olaf the White and Aud the Deep-minded was named Thorstein the Red, his color name, no doubt, evidence of mixed racial parentage. While Olaf may have actually been white, the vast number of interracial couplings in the age when Norsemen dominated Europe would have been between black-skinned men and white-, tawny-, brown-, or lightish-skinned women—since a general intermingling of races in Europe had been taking place for at least two millennia and most Whites—actual Whites (or *pure* Whites, if you like)—were in no way genetically unblemished by other races.

Thorstein the Red would, himself, become a chieftain, setting off to raid many areas of Scotland and becoming ruler of half the country after making peace with the Scots. The Scots (or Scotti, still essentially black- and dark-skinned at this time) broke their agreement with Thorstein, and he was killed in Caithness about 875.

In Britain and the north of Europe, the stirring of peoples out of Scandinavia had begun. It was a smoke filled sunrise of promise, riches, new territory and adventure for ascendant Norsemen. For Caucasian, Christianized Europe it was an ominous rumble, presaging dread, uncertainty and perhaps doom. At first Norsemen came as pirates and plunderers, content to loot whatever valuables they could easily obtain from castles, churches or homes, committing rapes and carrying off into slavery those unfortunates who could not escape their onslaughts quickly enough. By the middle of the 9th century, primarily Danish Norsemen began to settle in the areas they plundered in England—Northumbria, East Anglia, Derby, Nottingham, the Five Boroughs of Stamford, as well as areas of Wales.

Primarily Norwegian Vikings carved out territories in Ireland and Scotland and harried the coasts of Wales; in the east, primarily Swedish Vikings along with Norwegians—but initially spear-headed by Danes—probed the vast territory across the Baltic Sea which would come to be called Russia, a name derived from *Rus,* which the natives whose towns were attacked called these invaders—invaders who began settling in them and establishing trading outposts.

In the mid-9th century, England was not the England we know today but was comprised of the territories of Wessex and Kent in the south of the main British island where Alfred—later to be called Alfred the Great—would lead a war against the ever-encroaching black gentiles, winning battles here and there, losing others, and fleeing to fight another day. At the Treaty of Wedmere in 878, he came to terms with Guthrum, leader of the Danish forces threatening Wessex. The treaty's terms had Guthrum withdraw his forces from Wessex and accept baptism, allowing Christianity to exist without prejudice in his domain.

Guthrum and the Danes would maintain sovereignty over the eastern half of England which would be subject to Danish laws and customs, becoming known as *The Danelaw*. Alfred was compelled to accept this, although he would harbor thoughts of bringing the territory under English rule.

The map in Fig. 12 illustrates the domination of western Europe by Black Norsemen. The shaded area in England approximates he extent of The Danelaw. West of Rouen lies the Danish possession of northern France, which came to be known as Normandy, and the map shows that Norsemen intensively raided northwestern Germany, the Netherlands, Belgium, and the whole of western France. What is not shown is that nearly the whole of the Iberian Peninsula was still under Moorish (African) occupation, which would continue for many centuries more. And it must be assumed that racial intermingling—miscegenation, if you like—was extensive, with black- and dark-skinned men the primary instigators. With the exceptions of Scandinavia, Scotland, much of northern Ireland and, perhaps westernmost France, Whites had come to overspread most territories of western Europe by the onset of the 9th century. But most of these were not without admixtures of the peoples they had encountered—as conquerors or as subjects—in their three-millennia westward migration from the Great White Forest. They were not a homogeneous race, as Western scientists, scholars and DNA researchers would like us to believe; there were different groups of them with different physical appearances, hair textures and colors, complexions, skull shapes, hirsuteness, languages and customs. Their singlemost identifiable trait was their lack of pigmentation or general whiteness, effectuated by that original mutated gene-core responsible for the production of melanin which had strengthened during the isolation of that original large albinoid population in the Great White Forest over many millennia. The gene responsible for dark pigmentation had become stultified, made negligible by the mutated, non-melanin-producing gene having grown powerful enough to dominate melanin-producing ones.

In their westward migration many Caucasoids intermingled with black- and dark-skinned peoples, and dark- or brown-skinned offspring resulted. But the re-intermingling of these within the dominant Caucasian mass "bred-out" the darker elements over a half-dozen or more generations, and the general population remained essentially Caucasian or white in appearance. These Caucasian groups saw themselves as distinctly different from darker-skinned races and resolved to retain that distinction, which lead to the psychological "reaction formation" and hatred that Dr. Frances Welsing's earlier analysis outlined (see Chapter 2). Some of this will be revisited later, but the reader should understand that Caucasian feelings of distinction, group loyalty and abhorrence toward darker-skinned human beings were generally entrenched in the temperaments of most European Whites by the 9th century, especially Christianized Whites with Greco-Roman sentiments and aspirations—although the sense of superiority intrinsic in Whites over the last several centuries might not yet have developed.

Midway through the 9th century, primarily African Moors were in possession of Iberia, North Africa was becoming increasingly Islamic, and Arabs, who had introduced this great religion to the world, migrated into Egypt and North Africa in larger numbers, settling among and intermingling with black African, Berber and other mixed-race populations there. Many Arabs were part of the Moorish occupation of Iberia (Spain/Portugal), as were Sephardic Jews, out of northeast Africa and the Holy Land, and the three groups—Moors, Arabs and Jews (chiefly black- and dark-skinned Jews)—civilized the country, bringing highly developed art, architecture, science, medicine, agricultural innovations, animal husbandry, manufacturing, industry, music and advanced mathematics—algebra and geometry, previously unknown in Europe—to the continent. Moors, Jews and Arabs established the first universities of any kind in Europe, which would directly lead to the educational advancement of the continent and the European Renaissance of the 15th and 16th centuries.

However, Rome viewed Islam and the presence of the Moors in Spain and southern areas of Europe as a threat to the power and influence of The Church, and the Moorish, Arab and growing Turkish presence in the Mediterranean was an increasing disturbance to the Byzantine Empire. Islamicized Turks (often called *Saracens*, but this term was as well applied to Moors) were menacing Byzantium and would chip away at her eastern frontier until the Ottoman Empire overran all of Asia Minor in the 15th century. The 9th century, though, was the darkest period of the Dark Ages for Rome and the Caucasian populations of Europe; along with the Moors in Iberia, a dark, northern sunrise was taking place, with black-skinned Norsemen stepping up their raids in the British Isles and the northwestern portion of the continent, beginning to settle in England, France and, within a century, areas of Russia. But it was only the beginning. The situation would become much bleaker, graver, darker for Rome and Caucasian Europe.

CHAPTER 8

DARK SHORES, DARK GODS

Although most histories that discuss The Danelaw trace its beginnings to the Treaty of Wedmere in 878, the period in which its full effect was felt was a decade later after another treaty between Alfred and Guthrum in 886 established its southern boundary. Gwyn Jones asserts that its political independence lasted only about fifty years, however, "its separate, i.e., Scandinavian, quality was recognized not only by Alfred and his English successors, but by the laws of Knut in the early eleventh century and by the Norman lawgivers after the [Norman] Conquest" (421). So, for at least two centuries, at least half of what would become the England that we know was effectively under Danish control which would be extended to at least the onset of the 12th century under different Norse and *Norman* rulers—those French-speaking Norsemen from Normandy who invaded England under William (the Conqueror) in 1066.

Non-Norse (or Norman) England, and Scotland in the north, was still a mish-mash of warring ethnicities who had been migrating and co-mingling in the Isles since before the time of Roman occupation—Britons, Silures, Maetae, Caledonians, Scots, Picts, Iceni, Welsh—dark-skinned tribes, who had lost most of their original territories and influence to Romans, Saxons, Belgae, and other Caucasian invaders (perhaps Angles), who had forced the darker-skinned races ever westward in the Isles (and southward, in the case of many early Britons who fled across the Channel to the northwestern tip of France where they are known to us as *Bretons,* in the area we know today as Brittany) a century or two before Norse invasions began. Alfred would form alliances with many of these dispossessed peoples in his efforts to stem the Norse tide during the 9th century.

Many of these peoples had been coerced into giving up their old gods and accepting Christianity, the religion of their Aryan overlords, who were fortified by their connections to Rome and sought to Christianize all of Britain in order to forestall a complete takeover by the heathen Danish invaders. Much the same was occurring in Ireland whose black- and dark-skinned inhabitants were akin to those in Britain and Wales—Black Celtic descendants of the ancient Neolithic race which had formerly overspead all of Europe out of which Basques, Iberians, "the 'small swarthy Welshman,' the 'small dark highlander,' and the 'Black Celts to the west of the Shannon,' . . . [and] the typical inhabitants of Aquitania and Brittany" all emerged (MacRitchie 12).

The Black Celts of Ireland fled or were driven across the Shannon River in western Ireland where their descendants could be found or could be discerned even a millennium afterward. Their location in the western portion of the Emerald Isle attests to their having been—as in the case of Britons in the western portions of Britain's main island—invaded by white-skinned peoples (probably Saxons) entering Ireland from the east or southeast just as had been the case in England. The Scotti who, as mentioned earlier, had arrived from Egypt, fled north crossing the North Channel into Scotland, while many of their relatives and countrymen would linger in Northern Ireland for many more centuries.

Western historians have almost never presented an accurate account of black civilizations in Europe for which the rise of white European civilization is indebted.

Significant in this were the achievements by the Moors occupying Iberia, which Western historians invariably attribute to Arabs to obfuscate the black African presence there. So, along with what was mentioned in the last chapter, a few more contributions deserve mention. Speaking of the Moors, John G. Jackson, author of *An Introduction to African Civilizations,* observes:

> They, for instance, introduced the silk industry into Spain. In the field of agriculture they . . . introduced rice, sugar cane, dates, ginger, cotton, lemons and strawberries into the country. (175)

But these, above, were in addition to building irrigations systems with water flowing through lead pipes through the mountains of Cordova, introducing brass and iron industries, public schools, and the first real universities in Europe, "while in Christian Europe 99 percent of the people were illiterate and even kings could neither read nor write" (op. cit. 176).

In fact, there was never a time when the Iberian Peninsula was without a significant African or Africoid population. In *Sex and Race vol. 1,* J. A. Rogers points out that "[t]he oldest skulls found in the peninsula are Negroid," which of course, has been mentioned by Sergi and others. But Rogers says, further, that "the original Negro type persists," and mentions the statement from Napoleon that "Africa begins at the Pyrenees" made just over two centuries ago (op. cit. 151).

In *Egyptian Romany,* in which he discusses the actual Egyptian origin of the Gypsies or Gitanos of Spain, historian Moustafa Gadalla discusses how Western scholars have evaded attributing Africans and Egyptians (Gitano) with their many accomplishments on the Iberian Peninsula, stating:

> Certain "chosen" groups (Phoenicians, Romans, Arabs, etc.) are credited with many things, such as introducing highly productive farming techniques, numerous settlements, crafts, organizational government, arts, etc. into the Iberian Peninsula. Yet none of these groups have a history of such "talents" in their home countries . . . because one cannot teach/contribute what one has never known and practiced in their home country. (55)

The *re*invasion of the Iberian Peninsula by Moors in 711 AD and afterwards extended and built upon earlier African innovations that had been interrupted primarily by the Roman conquest during the Punic Wars against Carthage.

With black- and dark-skinned men once more dominant in the Mediterranean and southwestern territories of Europe (again commanding the Pillars of Hercules) and black-skinned Danes and other Norsemen dominating the northern lands from the eastern shores of the Baltic to the British Isles, we can understand more plainly why MacRitchie declared the Dark Ages "*dark* in a double sense" (*Britons* 137). By the close of the 9th century the Danes had annexed half or more of what would become England; Norwegians held territories in Ireland, Scotland and most of the islands between them; Danes had carved out a sizeable territory in northern France (Normandy) but still rampaged throughout the west of the country; and mainly Swedish Vikings (called Rus or Rhos as well as *Varangians*) had established a number of settlements in the future Russia and dominated the eastern Baltic, completely occupying the coasts of Finland, Latvia and Estonia. During the late 9th century, mainly Norwegian Vikings—by most accounts, but surely a good portion of Danes—had begun migrating to Iceland which had been discovered in 860 by Gardar, "a *Dane* of Swedish descent" (*my emphasis*, De Costa 19).

Considering the often bloody conflicts that arose between Norwegians and Danes in Ireland during the 9th century, it is unlikely that Danes would have stood idly by and allowed Norwegians to wholly settle Iceland—an island territory that a Dane had discovered. Danes, remember, were considered the royal race of the emergent Scandinavian nations and from Denmark had early on colonized southern Norway and Sweden, so that the term *Dane* could have been applied to almost *any* Norse inhabitant of the three Viking nations—*Dane*, as earlier mentioned, perhaps implying *black*, or a black man. We have looked at how Western scholars have continually obscured the black presence in Europe, and the reader is reminded of the distinction Irish historians made between Norwegian and Danish Vikings, designating them White and Black Foreigners, respectively. So it would not be surprising that calling the settlers of Iceland Norwegians is a further attempt at obfuscating the presence of Blacks or Black Norsemen, in this case, in Iceland and North America, which Norsemen would soon begin probing. However, even if this is so, the reader has been presented with evidence that Norwegian Norsemen were black-and dark-skinned, and more evidence regarding this will be offered when some of the settlers in Iceland are discussed in ensuing chapters.

The state of affairs in Europe did not bode well for those Europeans of lighter hue in whose hearts burned the dream of a continent of white-skinned inhabitants, those who longed to complete the vision of the early Romans who first attempted this seemingly impossible undertaking. The organization, inventiveness and formidable legions of the Western Roman Empire were a distant memory now, and western Europe seemed on the verge of being overwhelmed by the hordes of black- and dark-skinned men now rampaging throughout most of the continent.

It seems that Norsemen lacked the time or inclination to record their exploits. The most cogent, detailed histories regarding Norsemen come from British sources—Irish, English, Scottish or Welsh—and those sources, fairly unanimously, describe the Norsemen of this period, particularly the Danes, as black-skinned. What Scandinavian writings we have come to us in the form of sagas—most written from one to three centuries after the events they describe took place. The historical accuracy of the sagas might be considered debatable; the years that particular events took place, when kings ascended to power, when particular territories were invaded, or when areas were discovered are often omitted. But historians who have intensively matched events in the sagas with dependable historical writings of other nations have found that events in the sagas are generally accurate and coincidental with those recorded histories—though the sagas sometimes do take liberties that approach the supernatural for dramatic effect.

But we are primarily concerned with the race of the Norsemen of the Viking Age, and in Welsh author B.G. Charles' *Old Norse Relations With Wales,* the historian explains "the early historians made a conscious attempt to distinguish the Danes from the Norwegians" (5) and, although Charles discourses on Norwegians pre-dating Danes in Ireland and battling Danes for dominance of the isle, he discusses several Danish invasions during the mid-9th century, like the one led by Horm (also Gorm), "a chieftain of no small standing in Ireland," who came with his Dubh-Ghenti," "black gentiles," or "black hosts" to Ireland (5, 6). And despite the "conscious attempt" by chroniclers, especially early Irish chroniclers, to depict Norwegians and Danes as racially dissimilar, there is no logical reason to entertain this assertion.

It has been remarked upon that black-skinned Egyptian megalith builders were among the earliest settlers of Denmark and Sweden; black-skinned Cimbri occupied Denmark and were also called Dani, and were probably descendants of the Tuatha de Danaan; that these Cimbri spread into Norway and Sweden; that the early Vikings out of Norway were short-statured and dark-skinned like Finns; that other Irish historians (as indicated by Mitchison) called both Danes and Norwegians "black gentiles'; and that Danes, Norwegians and Swedes (who resembled Danes) freely intermarried with each other with numbers of each group residing in each Scandinavian territory. None of the authors whose works have been cited herein in regard to Norsemen being black-skinned have made any claim to Whites being among their general numbers, and this writer will no longer entertain the issue—except to assume that a Norse personage with a color name "the White" was either Caucasian or a very light-skinned black man.

It should be considered that Eurocentric historians, from the early Middle Ages to the present, regard the Danes, Swedes and Norwegians of this period as *other than European* in their works. Both early and later historians decry their un-Christian beliefs, calling them heathen, alien, pagan, practically inhuman in their descriptions. The impression of the early annalists is that these Norse peoples could never be part of the great, white European family. Although *later* Celts (white-skinned invaders of western Europe and

Britain) are frequently called *barbarian*, they are not described with the vitriol and abject repugnance that is fairly typical in descriptions of the Norsemen by presumably white, Eurocentric chroniclers.

These dubh-gaill, Dubh-Ghenti, and black strangers out of Scandinavia are spoken of by early historians as if hey are outside the human family, very much like the Black Huns of Attila's epoch, the hordes of Genghis Khan and Gibbon's Black Hungarians are described. Most of these negative references emanate from ecclesiastical writers, people of the Christian Church who had, to whatever degree, accepted the precepts of Christianity as the determinant of rightness for all men, the barometer of civilized behavior and actions. Deviations from this Roman-inspired, reconstructed, reinvented form of religion were unacceptable to the Christian clergy and were considered paganistic, idolatrous, although Christianity's origins emanated from so-called pagan beliefs. At the very time the Norse were being vilified as heathen and inhuman, many thousands of Britons all over the Isles—and many thousands over western and northwestern Europe—still practiced older religious rites not too dissimilar to that practiced by the Norse peoples.

Of the sources utilized by this writer, Godfrey Higgins' *Celtic Druids* most easily explains the connections between the religion of ancient Asia—which he contends was ancient Buddhism—and its earliest manifestations in Europe and Western Asia where it underwent alterations over many centuries from its original form. Although this religion was preserved and spread by Druid Priests (black Asians to Higgins, black Egyptians to Massey and Churchward) through northern Europe and the British Isles, changes inevitably ensued owing to divergence of language, and territorial and tribal diffusion. Higgins' *Anacalypsis* is another trove of revelation where, for instance, he shows that <u>*Aesar*</u> was a term denoting <u>*God*</u> in the Etruscan language and how <u>*Caesar*</u>—not Julius' adopted surname—was an application of *godliness* to Julius Caesar and Roman emperors who followed him. Higgins explains that in the language of the Goths, "As, Aes, Aesus, is the name of Odin," connecting these in the plural to Asar and <u>*Aesir*</u> (*Anac. Vol. 1* 610), a term designating Asian or eastern in the Norse sagas, or else a *people* coming from the east. And "Odin," says Higgins, "will not be denied to be the same as Woden," the origin of our English <u>Wo-den's-day</u>, or *Wednesday* (op. cit.). The reader may want to consult the abovementioned works for a detailed analysis of religious connections between the ancient East and West and traceable linguistic affinities. These few connections are mentioned here to demonstrate that there is a recognizable, east to west religious affinity that was still apparent in so-called paganistic religions in Asia and Europe during the early Middle Ages.

Of the Norse gods, we hear mostly of Thor, who ruled thunder, lightening and the air; Odin (Odinn, Woden, Wodan), responsible for war, giving strength to men against their enemies; and Frey (Fricco), the granter of pleasure and peace to mortals (Jones, *Vikings* 326). There were sacred places and groves where each of these gods were venerated, Uppsala, for instance, being the chief town of worship for Frey. Thor and Odin were more generally venerated and called upon during the Viking Age as Norsemen sought success in their efforts of conquest and pillage. Sacrifice, often blood sacrifice, was a necessary rite in the worship of these gods.

There were other gods of lesser stature in the Norse panoply, however, this work is not intended to detail them or their periods of prominence. Very little is known of actual Norse religious beliefs; even Higgins, who provides very detailed information on northern European connections with eastern gods does not provide this. If we want to know something about Islam, Buddhism, Christianity or Judaism, we can consult an encyclopedia and get some idea of their belief systems and basic tenets. Not so with Norse beliefs. We merely read of gods and goddesses called upon for one purpose or another without symmetry, order, or synthesis. There is no name for the religion the Norse practiced, though it is certain it sustained them, was palpable, and delivered what they desired more often than not.

They abhorred Christianity, which had absorbed or adopted many pagan elements from the 'old religion," including the "eating of the flesh" of Catholicism. Significant schisms had taken place since the days of that great universal Afro-Asiatic religion of Greater Ethiopia emanating from Egypt and Ethiopia, which had spread to India and beyond, and reentering Western Asia and Europe in greatly altered forms. Diversifying humanity had lost the early connections with the ancient East and, coming forward in time, the newly Christianized West came to consider their adulterated version of religion superior to all others, and those who practiced older faiths heathenistic or pagan. Thus were the Norse so considered when they began their depredations in the British Isles and northern Europe.

Fig. 13
Short statue or
carving of the
Norse god Thor.

Besides their domination of the British Isles, north and northwestern France, and the whole eastern Baltic coastline, primarily Danes (by then called *Normans*) plundered areas of Italy and would establish the Norman Kingdom of southern Italy in the 11th century, which included all of Sicily. Danes joined Swedish Vikings in raiding areas of what would become Russia and from there established contact with Greece, then part of the Byzantine Empire, having discovered a route to the Orient by way of the Volga River early in the 9th century. These Rus and Varangians plied all the major rivers—the Don, Dneiper, Dniester, and Dvina which carried them into the Orient and Black and Caspian Seas where they established trading settlements in territories largely inhabited by Slavonic peoples. The Rus traded in furs, ivory, swords, amber, and slaves. Danish and Swedish Viking fleets became a common sight on the rivers of this vast Eurasian territory as they sought the goods of the Orient—silver and gold, brooches, pots, hairpins, jewelry, Roman weights and measures, glass beakers, and silver and bronze eating and drinking vessels. Masses of coinage also flowed back north out of which came Scandinavian <u>ore</u>, and better-quality woolens, Chinese silks, Indian spices and Persian glass, also brought into Norse homelands.

But the acquisition of slaves became a major objective of Norse forays and trade in the area of Russia. Russia began with the establishment by Swedish and Danish Vikings of Novgorod late in the 10th century when Vladimar (Vladimir) came to power there in 972 "and in 980 became Grand Duke (Great Prince) of Kiev and all of Russia" (Jones, *Vikings* 131). On the eastern fringes of Russia, east of the Dnieper in southern Russia was the territory of the Khazars (also Chazars), a warlike Turkic people who must have been largely racially mixed, because there is mention of black Khazars and white Khazars occupying the same territory, which spread eastward to the Caspian Sea. Khazars also exploited and enslaved Slavonic peoples within their territory, and during the 9th and 10th centuries were in the process of converting to Judaism, a course begun about 740 when Khazar King Bulan converted to the new faith. The conversion of the Khazars to Judaism occurred over a century-and-a-half and is the origin of the Ashkenazi, or European branch of Jews who later spread into Ukraine, Poland, Germany and central and eastern Europe. When the Norse came into contact with them during the 9th and 10th centuries, the Khazars had established their capital in Itil, a fortress-town overlooking the Volga.

Other peoples Norsemen encountered were the Bulgars—a people also composed of black and white branches—who had migrated southward into a territory west of the Black Sea, and Asiatic Finns occupying a large territory twice the size of present-day Finland, including the area surrounding Lake Ladoga, northeast of St. Petersburg.

Although Norsemen fought skirmishes with all these peoples they, more importantly, worked out trade agreements and treaties with them and "the Swedes were eventually assimilated to the Finns and Slavs among whom they had lived so long" (Jones, *Vikings* 251). Slavs, though, were still subject to being enslaved with thousands, male and female, being transported to Scandinavian lands. Intermarriage and intermingling occurred between Norse and Slavs in Russia, and intermarriage between the Norse and Slavonic royalty only increased Norse assimilation in the territory, as the following comment from Prudence Jones and Nigel Pennick attests:

> The Vikings retained close contact with their Scandinavian homeland, and although they intermarried with the indigenous ruling families, the latter and their peoples remained essentially Slavic. (185)

I have not come across any references to the Slavs being other than Caucasian or white-skinned, although the area they inhabited in Russia was long prone to migrations, incursions or outright invasions by dark-skinned peoples—Turks, Huns and other peoples out of Tartary. If Slavs were essentially Caucasian, it is safe to say they were admixed with the races who are known to have crossed or settled in adjacent territories or within the Slavonic realm. As well, the factor most responsible for the lightening of the black-skinned races of Scandinavia may be the thousands of Slavs carried into slavery, intermarriage and concubinage in Scandinavian lands over two or more centuries.

There were different branches of Slavs loosely organized over a large territory who frequently fought amongst themselves for living space and dominance. Their primary weapons were bows and spears, but they lacked the organization to unite and stave off depredations by invaders like the abovementioned Turks, Huns and Khazars. But there were other invaders like the Alans (an aggressive Hunnish or Mongolian people), Bulgars and the Norse, who began infiltrating the vast Slavonic territory in the mid-10th century or earlier. The Norse, however, became a stabilizing force for the Slavs and began a cooperative relationship with the various tribes that would eventually fortify the region, which became the nucleus of Russia.

The Slavs were divided into at least a dozen major tribes—the Polyanians, the Radimichians, the Vyatichians, the Severians, and the Wends, to name a few. Some, like the Polyanians, were generally peaceful, respecting ancestral customs of marriage and family. Other tribes are said to have been bestial and aggressive, seizing young women for marriage or for purely lustful purposes. Along with the Ossi (Osilians), Finni and the Aestii (Estonians), who were probably dark-skinned Slavs occupying the territory east of the Baltic, the Wends (Venedi) were the westernmost branch of the Slavic peoples settled in areas of what would be modern-day Poland and Germany. The Wends were a somewhat nomadic branch of

Slavs, generally aggressive, although they did practice agriculture. But history sees them as raiders, for the most part, moving from one area to another plundering any lands and people they could.

Their constant moving about gives us our English word "wend," meaning to meander from place to place, or make one's way somewhere in a leisurely fashion. My feeling is that these western branches of Slavonic peoples—the Ossi, Finni, Aestii, or Estonians, and Wends—were black- or dark-skinned Slavs with Ugrian affinities, since MacRitchie earlier asserted that Ugrian type people were inhabiting Estonia and areas of the eastern Baltic well into the 11th century. Eastern Slavs, as far as can be ascertained, were Caucasian with a large percentage of blonds and light-eyed members. Their territory fell within the general territory of the Great White Forest where Caucasians germinated many millennia before. As there were black and white Bulgars, Khazars and Hunnish peoples, there were probably black and white-skinned Slavonian branches—*Slavic* being merely a linguistic designation, not a racial one, although the term is often used as a racial application.

Slavic speaking peoples were composed of various ethnic admixtures just as the people called *Germanics* were—which might be said of almost any people. Of the Slavs occupying Russia during the 9th and 10th centuries, Will Durant states, in *The Age of Faith:*

> Periodically overrun by nomad hordes, often enslaved, always oppressed and poor, they [Slavs] grew patient and strong through endless hardships; and the fertility of their women overcame the high mortality born of famine, disease and chronic war. (445)

The Hunnish invasion four to five centuries earlier had greatly impacted the Slavic populations in what would become Russia, driving many of these westward where, according to Durant, "they became the Wends, Poles, Czechs, Vlachs, and Slovaks of later history" (op. cit.). Some Slavs even fled south into Greece, infusing them with a considerable dose of Slavic blood, and those who remained in their Russian homeland must have been greatly infused with the blood of Huns.

The Wends (often described as Germanic) may have been the earliest Slavic tribe to move west, long prior to the arrival of Attila's Huns, for they are mentioned by Ptolemy, the 2nd century Greek geographer, as living on the eastern Baltic shore (Jones & Pennick 165). L.A. Waddell, however, connects the Wends to an extensive population of people called *Vans*, whose various tribal groups stretched from India in the east to Iberia in Europe. It seems probable that *Van* is another designation for *Iberian*, since the territories they inhabited seem to be precisely the same and, according to Waddell, they left their ethnic name in:

> . . . a more or less continuous chain from Lake Van [eastern Turkey] westward, through Asia Minor to the Dardanelles and Bosphorus . . . along the Danube to Vienna and Austrian Galatia to Fin-land and the Southern shores of the Baltic and westwards to Iberia . . . Gaul, and thence to the British Isles. (*Phoenician Origin* 100)

Like the ancient Iberians, the Vans (out of which derives *Bans, Fens,* the *Pani* of Vedic tales, *Fins, Vanii and Wends,* owing to dialect) are described as "dark or black-complexioned" and, according to Waddell:

> They were presumably of the smallish-statured, dark, long-headed "Dravidian" tribes of Indo-Persia, akin to the Iberian type, and represented by the present-day nomadic Yuruk and Gipsy tribes of Van. (99-100)

Whether to consider this vast population of people Vans or Iberians depends on what angle one perceives them from—the Asiatic, European or African view. Much earlier we spoke of man's dispersal out of Africa and the existence of Greater Ethiopia, with racially similar peoples from Africa to India, which should also be factored into the above equation. Most noteworthy is that we are speaking of racially similar people under different nomenclatures—Wends sometimes called Slavic, more often called Germanic, depending on the historian. In any case, we have seen that they belonged to a widespread, ancient racial group extending over two continents, related to other groups who remained "dark or black-complexioned" into the Dark and Middle Ages.

In the mid-9th century Wendish territory lay just south and southeast of Denmark (Holstein) and part of Charlemagnes's Empire, along the lands abutting the southern Baltic and eastward to the Vistula in present-day Poland. The Danes had had some intercourse with the Slavic Wends since at least the beginning of the 9th century, and both groups detested the Germans of Charlemagne's realm. The Germans considered the Wends "animals to be hunted and slaves to be sold" (Jones, *Vikings* 127), but the Danes found them useful and some intermarriage occurred between Vikings and Wends, perhaps the most notable being King Harald Fairhair's marriage to a Wendish princess in 965.

Numerous tribes appear in eastern and northeastern Europe at the onset of the Christian Era, many of them out of Asia and Eurasia. The Slavic nucleus was Eurasia where, over the millennia, man lost his black pigmentation as various peoples encountered each other in the Great White Forest area where albinoids were once dominant in a vast area. Intermingling among these various peoples lead to a lightening process of the general populaces, and the colder climate with less direct sunlight resulted in more fair-skinned and fair-haired individuals over the centuries of crossbreeding. This is why, in historical times, we hear of Black Khazars and White Khazars, Black Tartars and White Tartars, Black Bulgars and White Bulgars, and so on, although Western scholars have offered other explanations for these designations. In my own travels (in the U.S.) I have personally encountered blond, dark-skinned Poles having typically Caucasian features, and I would expect to see a lot more in Poland and other Eastern European countries. Of the peoples occupying Eastern Europe, the Bulgars, for instance, originally inhabited a territory in the far north of Russia and, asserts Durant:

> The Bulgars, originally a mixture of Hun, Ugrian, and Turkish blood, had formed part of the Hun empire in Russia. After Attila's death one branch established a kingdom—"Old Bulgaria"—along the Volga around the modern Kazan . . . In the fifth century another branch migrated southwest to the valley of the Don; one tribe of these, the Utigurs, crossed the Danube (679), founded a second Bulgarian kingdom . . . enslaved the Slavs there, adopted their language and institutions, and were ultimately absorbed into the Slavic stock. (443)

Of the Magyars, who will be revisited later, Durant states that they, "like the Bulgars, were probably derived from . . . Ugri or Igurs . . . who wandered on the western confines of China; they too had . . . a strong infusion of Hun and Turkish blood" (op. cit. 444). So, while these people appear Caucasian or white today, there is no denying that these white peoples of Eastern Europe, including Russians and Slavs, are mixed with black- and dark-skinned peoples, most having lost the outward traces of their dark-skinned ancestors. The same can be said of the modern white population of Western Europe. While Durant, like other Western historians, does not specifically call some of abovementioned peoples (Huns, Ugrians or Ugri Bulgars) black- and dark-skinned, the reader has already been presented with evidence of this reality by Higgins, MacRitchie and Waddell, and if we follow Durant's recitation, Slavs and Wends should be classed among them, for Durant states: "by the sixth century the Elbe was the *ethnic . . . frontier* between the Slavic and the Western world" (*my emphasis* op. cit. 510).

Assuming that the territory of 9th and 10th century Germany was occupied by predominantly white-skinned Germans (remember, the territory was earlier occupied by black-skinned Picts, Cimbri, Teutones and Goths), the Elbe, sixty or so miles west of Berlin, was the dividing line between predominantly white-skinned western Europe and an eastern Europe occupied by darker-skinned peoples, according to Durant's analysis.

Durant calls the Wends "Slavic Wends," placing them in that mix of peoples of predominantly Ugrian blood and characteristics, and all the abovementioned peoples inhabiting the eastern Baltic into Russia in the period under discussion support the earlier comment from MacRitchie that: "In Livonia [Lithuania], in Esthonia, and in three-fourths of European Russia the Ugrians were, even in the 11th century, the preponderating population" (9).

Slavic is classified by most linguists as belonging to the Indo-European branch of languages, as most European languages are said to belong. Regarding the Slavic language, the *Encyclopedia Britannica* states:

> The literary languages within the Slavic branch of Indo-European may be divided into three geographical zones: East Slavic, West Slavic, and South Slavic, of which zones Russian, Polish, and Serbo-Croatian are respective examples. (*Micropedia, vol. 7* 147)

The term Indo-European is, itself, illusory and deceptive. While most European languages are classified as belonging to this main branch, which includes sub-branches like the Romance languages (French, Italian, Spanish, etc.), a Spanish or French speaker would not be understood by a Pole or Russian, nor would an Italian or Portuguese speaker understand a Greek or German speaker. The supposed affinity of these so-called Indo-European languages is just not apparent.

What if a linguist had come up with the term Sino-American, implying that all Native American languages (originally more than 200) were akin to Chinese? Or how about Egypto-Asian, implying that all Asiatic languages were connected to Egypt (which would not seem outlandish) and then made their way into Europe. Would Egypto-Asian or Egypto-European be an acceptable term for the profusion of languages spoken throughout Asia and Europe over the millennia down to today? And would Eurocentrists be comfortable with the implication that the languages spoken in Europe had their origins in Africa (which does seem plausible)? Probably not. So, some Eurocentric philologists found Sanskritic elements in the words of a dozen European languages and devised a theory that Aryans (presumably white-skinned) invaded India four millennia ago, subjugated it, civilized it, imposed their Aryan language, and in the imposition or exchange of language Sanskrit evolved and was carried into Europe. And because of Arya-Indian intermingling, according to the Eurocentric hypothesis, Indians are a Caucasian race and and all European languages (except for Basque, Hungarian, and Finnish) emanated from India as Asiatic peoples migrated to Europe over several millennia.

In *Underworld, The Mysterious Origins of Civilization,* author Graham Hancock explains how the theory of an Aryan invasion of India has been disparaged in the last decade, citing Gregory Possehl as stating:

> In the end there is no reason to believe today that there ever was an Aryan race that spoke Indo-European languages and was possessed of a coherent . . . set of Aryan or Indo-European cultural features. (99)

Hancock goes on to state, regarding the ancient, ruined Indus Valley cities of Harappa and Mohenjodaro:

> [T]hese sophisticated, centrally planned cities were much older than the supposed 1500 BC date for the Aryan invasion of India and . . . belonged to a previously unidentified high civilization of remote antiquity, perhaps almost as old . . . as Sumer or Egypt . . ." (op. cit. 98)

Yes, there are Sanskritic elements to be found in some European languages (Hancock mentions German, Norwegian, Latin, English and Greek in this regard); but my question is: Why settle on India if there is evidence of a "previously unidentified high civilization of remote antiquity" that Harappan civilization was connected to? This civilization of remote antiquity could only have been that of Greater Ethiopia, which ancient India was a part of, sharing a common culture, belief system and language. So, why stop with India if there is evidence that Sanskrit or some other widely spoken Indian language derived from an even older language—which may prove to be the root of all languages?

There will be more language considerations in this regard in a later chapter. The digression here is meant to question the classification of European languages as Indo-European when many Europeans languages are mutually unintelligible to one another, some having relatively few affinitive words. I do not believe philologists have explored the subject as thoroughly as they could and use the term Indo-European as a way of expanding Aryan, Caucasian or white predominance into Asia—in the same way that Eurocentric historians have labeled obviously non-white peoples Caucasian.

At some point Slavic, whatever its derivatives, became dominant in a wide expanse of southern Russia while Slavs, generally, "lived in caves or mud huts; hunted, herded, fished, and tended bees . . . and slowly resigned themselves to settled tillage" (Durant 445).

This was their general condition when Vikings came eastward into Russia in the 10th century. While some Slavic tribes may have been dark-skinned—having admixtures of Hunnish, Tartar, Khazar and Turkic blood, as did Bulgars—I am inclined to believe that the majority of those living between the Vistula and Dnieper were, in the main, an essentially light- to near-white-skinned people "hunted even into hardly accessible marshes and forests, brutally captured and callously sold" (op. cit.). And the Vikings were prominent in both capturing and trading for thousands of Slavs when they established the city of Novgorod in 862 (considered the birth of modern Russia) and set up trading posts in numerous towns along the territory's major rivers in the vast territory they called Garthariki or Gardaric. In another century Kiev would be established as a major city of the Rus or Rhos—so-called by the Slavic inhabitants of Russia because of their darkish or reddish complexions. But the reader has been presented with evidence that the Danes were predominantly black-skinned and the likelihood that the term *Dane*, itself, implied black or a black man. And while Western historians insist that primarily Swedish Vikings invaded eastern Baltic areas and the territory that would come to be known as Russia, Gwyn Jones informs us: "The Norsemen in Kiev in 1018, despite their unquestioned Swedish origin, were described by Thietmar of Merseburg as being for the most part *Danes*" (*my emphasis, Vikings* 76)—therefore, decidedly black-skinned men.

Norse gods and religion were added to the various religious beliefs and practices of the inhabitants of Garthariki, all of which the Fathers of the Church in Rome classified as pagan. From the once uniform, civilizing beliefs and practices that once characterized ancient Greater Ethiopia—emanating from an original system out of Egypt and Ethiopia, or the northeastern quadrant of Africa—a number of varied religious beliefs arose, generated by disruptive wars and great migrations on the Asian continent over several millennia. The earliest religions, and certainly that of Greater Ethiopia, venerated women and royal lines of descent were matrilineal. This was certainly true in ancient Egypt as well as in Indus Valley civilization among the Harappans. The veneration of women was evident among the earliest European cultures, from the earliest Black Celtic tribes of Britain to the ancient Africoid cultures of central Europe who sculpted the "Venuses" which have been unearthed at sites as far away as Siberia. The veneration of women pervades all the cultures of the ancient world, and beyond India could be found in Australia, the isles of the Pacific and in the Americas, where most Native Americans—regardless of tribe—referred to the earth as the Great Spirit and thought of it as a feminine configuration, or as the Great Mother, as did other early societies. Even early Norse ancestors—the Picts, De Danaan and Cimbri—had a matrilineal society and traced descent from the mother.

This worldwide matrilineal culture would be disrupted with the emergence of so-called Indo-Europeans or Caucasoids who began emigrating out of the Great White Forest about 4000 BC—the Aryan hordes who invaded civilized Afro-Asiatic societies bringing a patrilineal or male-oriented ethos, which has come to dominate most societies of the world down to the present. According to Wayne B. Chandler, author of *Ancient Future:*

The Indo-Europeans who went West became the Greeks, Slavs, Germans, Celts, Thracians, Balts, and Illyrians. Those who invaded the eastern areas became the Anatolians, Phrygians, Armenians, Indo-Iranians, and Tocharians . . . forcing their way into Mesopotamia, Canaan, and finally Northwest India . . . areas [which] had for millennia been major centers of civilization for people of African descent. (117)

Their violent descent upon the peoples of the Near East and the resultant intermingling with them brought about the rise of societies we have become familiar with in history like the Hittites, Assyrians and Parthians, although these racially mixed peoples would remain essentially dark-skinned despite their being labeled Caucasians by Western historians. More ominously, according to Chandler, "[t]hey carried with them a propensity for extreme aggression and violence as never before witnessed in our epoch" (op. cit. 116-117).

Chandler asserts that the Caucasian or Indo-European mindset was "diametrically opposed" to the philosophical mores of the invaded Afro-Asiatic civilizations and lists the resultant destructive ideologies that still plague the world today: "(1) warfare or extreme and aberrant aggression; (2) racism and segregation by color; (3) the subjugation, disdain, inferiority, and impurity of women; and (4) absence of respect and understanding of the planet and its ecosystems" (118). As well, older gods and goddesses gave way to newer ones, or their names and attributes would be changed even within the same territories as newer invaders rose to power over the centuries—masculine gods becoming ever more dominant, subjugating the Feminine Principle or Great Mother concept nearly everywhere, over time.

Despite the Aryan or Indo-European invasions of light- or white-skinned peoples, these gods and goddesses would continue to be conceived as black—Buddha, Krishna, Kali and others in India; Diana (Artemis), Dionysus, Hera and many others in Western mythology—even in Hellenic Greece and Rome when those civilizations rose to prominence. The dispersion of Indo-Europeans into Asia and Europe could not displace the long entrenched gods and belief systems of Greater Ethiopia; the northern, male dominated belief systems of invading Caucasian peoples were absorbed into the older systems and new gods, or altered names for older gods and goddesses, emerged—many of these carried back to the north or into the west through migration or invasion where they experienced additional alteration. Even after the Egyptian Akhenaten began spreading the one, universal God concept about 1370 BC (extant in ancient Egypt long before him), which would eventually make its way to Europe and the Near East, the multitude of gods and goddesses suffusing Europe and Western Asia would continue to be revered. A fuller explanation of the above would require a lengthy essay—perhaps even a book. But a more detailed analysis cannot be pursued here. There are essentially three or four points I would like the reader to bear in mind: (1) the Caucasians or Indo-Europeans who poured out of the Great White Forest introduced a patrilineal or male-oriented ethos into the civilized world, which is still with us; (2) these light- or white-skinned invaders were largely absorbed into the black-skinned populaces they invaded, generally lightening the complexions of the inhabitants but not eradicating their genetic Afro-Asiatic connections or their dark complexions; (3) just as white-skinned Indo-Europeans were absorbed by the dominant black-skinned populations, Indo-European gods were absorbed into the older belief systems, and the emergent gods and goddesses—despite name alterations and functions—were still conceived as black- and dark-skinned, even when they reached western and northern Europe and areas of Asia; (4) these black- and dark-skinned gods and goddesses would continue to be worshipped in their blackness all over a whitened Europe even after the advent of Christianity and the promotion of a white-skinned image of Jesus Christ. But this would arise much later.

During the Dark Ages, how bleak the situation in Europe must have looked to the Fathers of the Church in Rome. At the close of the 9th century Moors still dominated most of Spain and the western Mediterranean; Norsemen dominated most of Britain, northern France, territories bordering the Baltic Sea, and Russia, effectively dominating all of Northern Europe. They were also infiltrating the Byzantine Empire where they became known as Varangians, and mainly Danish Norsemen were entering the

Mediterranean through the Strait of Gibraltar (formerly the Pillars of Hercules) assailing areas of Moorish Spain, southern France and the Italian Peninsula itself where, as mentioned above, they would establish the Norman Kingdom of South Italy in the mid-11th century, which would include the cities of Naples, Capua and Salerno and whose northern border was only 50 miles south of Rome.

These Norsemen or *Normans,* as they would come to be known in continental Europe after their conquest and acquisition of Normandy two centuries earlier, became Christians. At the close of the 9th century Norsemen, as mentioned, were regarded as heathen, pagan, bloodthirsty barbarians. Their gods and goddesses, like those of most non-Christian European and Eurasian peoples like the Slavs, were alien, fearsome and black. It had evolved out of elements of West Asian and northern belief systems just spoken of, which had coalesced with the once predominant Egyptian belief systems extant in Scandinavia, as Gwyn Jones informs us when he states:

> The beliefs of the Hindus, Persians, Egyptians, Greeks, Romans, and Celts have all yielded striking comparisons [to each other], and the Norse Gods display significant resemblances to members of other pantheons . . . . Male and female alike, they were representative of an earlier religion in the north, whom the Aesir figuratively overcame in battle, but failed to destroy or drive out. (*Vikings* 319, 321)

Extremely confident that their gods and goddesses supported them, Norsemen had fearlessly embarked on a mission of conquest, which took them to nearly every area of Europe they could reach by sea, up any river that could accommodate their black dragon ships. But they were not averse to disembarking and trekking many miles inland to raid towns promising irresistible booty or which boasted large churches known to contain a hoard of gold and silver—goblets, plates, candelabra, bells, crosses, chalices, statues, jewelry and Bishops' mitres. Afterwards, the churches were usually burned to the ground.

So, in the 9th century Vikings had begun to settle many of the areas they had plundered—England, Ireland, the Orkney Islands, France, Russia, the eastern Baltic coast—as many Norsemen were farmers and husbandrymen and sought arable lands for these endeavors. Sweden and Denmark offered suitable land, but Denmark—long the seat of Viking royalty—was becoming overcrowded, and Sweden was thickly wooded with forests, and large tracts of arable land were becoming difficult to obtain with the increase in population. Arable land in Norway was limited to the south and western coastline, and the growing population began to move northward where farming space was more limited than in the south.

Danes abandoning Denmark for Norway heightened tensions there, and "wars and counter-wars, native jealousies and foreign aggression would all too frequently set Norwegians at each other's throats" (op. cit. 96)—bloody battles often erupting between rival chieftains and the followers in their realms over land. It was not until the mid-9th century that Norway was first recognized as a nation when Halfdan the Black, a mere 18-years-old, acquired the territory of Agdir and the eastern half of Vestfold, then began campaigns of conquest against kings of other nearby territories, becoming the "first king of a united Norway" (Luke, *African Presence* 228).

However, we should not regard Norway's "unification" as permanent or in any way similar to our modern concept of a nation; there would be more fractious conflicts, bloody encounters and avaricious rulers over the next two centuries as there would be in Denmark and, to a lesser extent, Sweden. To Greco-Roman-minded Europe, all Norsemen were a dark menace looming over the continent, although the Byzantine Empire found them useful in ongoing skirmishes with Saracens, and a Varangian Guard protected the emperor and his palace. But Rome, or rather the Fathers of the Church in Rome, had designs on western Europe and wanted to break free from the overlordship of Byzantium, whose aegis they had been under since the demise of the Western Roman Empire four centuries earlier. If Norsemen could completely unite under an intelligent, far-sighted ruler, stimulated by the dark, pagan gods that propelled them to their near domination of most of western Europe, The Church's vision of reconquering

Europe and placing it under the vassalage of Rome would be thwarted. Rome could no longer physically subdue the continent with well-armed legions, so the Fathers of the Church contrived to disarm the Norse menace with psychological cunning. Knowing how abhorrent the Christian religion was to the Norse, The Church Fathers increased their missions of conversion to areas of Scandinavia, specifically targeting Norse kings and chieftains of influence, and they importuned Christian monarchs—especially in Britain—to make conversion to the hated faith a prerequisite to any peace treaty.

CHAPTER 9

THE MAKINGS OF EMPIRE

When they encountered their intended victims or met rival armies on a battlefield in larger confrontations, many Norsemen were clad in *mail* or *chain-mail*, which rendered them less vulnerable to injury. They wore mail-shirts, a meshed steel garment, adding ten pounds or more of weight to the wearers but allowing them more fluidity of movement than cumbersome plate-armor. This garment had sleeves and often an attached hood covering the head, ears and neck. Prior to the 10th century mail-shirts were waist-length, but they were extended to the thighs or knees beginning in the 10th century, and the tightly-woven iron or steel ringlets could protect the wearer from most chopping or slicing sword-thrusts. Only a direct thrust from a sword or spear, delivered straight on and force—fully point-first, had a chance of penetrating the mesh and seriously injuring the wearer. Along with the mail-shirt, the Viking warrior wore a steel helmet and carried a round shield of which there were varied types, usually wood with iron plating, or a "bossed" exterior with raised iron knobs or mounds to increase impenetrability.

Viking swords are legendary, far surpassing any produced in Europe during the early Middle Ages. Often long, heavy and ornamented, they were the most durable blades ever produced on a mass scale during their time. Some swords were intricately made, and two or three different steels were used in the blades—elongated and twisted together, "very similar to that involved in the production of a stick of patterned candy," states Holger Arbman, author of *The Vikings* (20). These elongated rods were fused together, a pattern called *damascening*, which Scandinavian sword-smiths perfected but whose actual origin was more than likely ancient Damascus (Syria), where the first attempts at such a process were made. Damascus steel, though, became more famous in the 12th century—just *after* the Viking Age—but there is probably a connection since, as Varangians, Norsemen had been a presence the Byzantine Empire since the 9th century and some may have ventured into the area of Syria on commercial expeditions. In any case, Scandinavian sword-smiths continued to experiment with the damascening process and came up with many successful variations, becoming proficient in constructing swords of both soft iron and steel which served them better in very cold climates as opposed to the warmer weather conditions of the Near East.

Quite possibly, though, their ability to construct superior swords was of an indigenous nature, the result of generations of trial and error. We earlier touched on the Black Dwarves who still inhabited areas of Scandinavia and had a long tradition of proficiency in working metals, and we should not forget that the peopling of Scandinavia also involved an east-to-west migration of groups out of Asia like the Black Huns of Attila and earlier migrants who might have come from northern India and areas of the Near East who brought their skills, icons, lore and cultural practices along with them into a territory that would one day become part of a continent called Europe.

Norse shipbuilding seems to have taken place all over Scandinavia and was not the product of one or two centers where Danes, Norwegians and Swedes all went to have ships built and outfitted. Where in more ancient times Egyptians, Phocaens, Greeks and Carthaginians may have contracted Phoenicians to construct sailing vessels out of their native cedars, Norsemen of the three principal Scandinavian countries developed the ability to construct water-tight, seaworthy ships around the middle of the 8th century.

Most dragon ships, the sleek vessels that took Norsemen on raiding missions by sea or upriver, could be navigated by sail or oar according to need and weather conditions. They had rudders hung off the starboard side and a row of round shields rimming the vessel along the bulwark on either side. War vessels were usually 60 to 90 feet in length and could accommodate 40 to 60 men. Some war vessels were longer and could accommodate 80 men. But Vikings had different kinds of ships, like the *knorr,* which was wider and of shorter length, ideal for transporting cargo, livestock and families, and many ships of this type must have been utilized in transporting families to Iceland when Norsemen began moving there. For a description of the construction of a typical Norse vessel, see Gwyn Jones' account in *A History of the Vikings,* pp. 186-189. Oak seems to have been the principal wood used in Viking ships, with pine being used for masts, oars and lashings. And each Scandinavian nation was able to churn out great numbers of ships with fleets of 100 to 200 vessels being common during an invasion.

The makings of empire existed in the Scandinavia of the 10th century. Nearly all of northern Europe had fallen to the Norsemen or were under Norse influence—the British Isles, northern and western France, eastern Baltic territories which included Estonia, Latvia, Lithuania, Prussia (later part of Poland), Russia, and, a century later, southern Italy and Sicily. Territories which had not succumbed to the Northmen suffered Norse raids and cringed at the possibility that they could be invaded at any time by these dark, impetuous, seaborne warriors. Poland, Moorish Iberia and Germany did not suffer meaningful Norse incursions, although Danish Vikings often raided deeply into northern areas of the East Frankish Kingdom and harried Iberian coastal areas. By the mid-10th century all of Europe—even though most inhabitants were illiterate—knew of the Norsemen, even if some areas of the neophyte continent had not directly encountered them.

*   *   *   *   *

For nearly a century Norsemen in increasing numbers had been journeying westward to Iceland which, as has been remarked upon, was discovered by Gardar Svavarson, "a Dane of Swedish descent," around 860. The island was first called Gardar's Island, and it should not be of much import whether Gardar—who was also known as Gardar the Swede—was a Dane or a Swede since both peoples were physically and racially akin and much intermarried. And, again, the peoples of Scandinavia may have all been Dani and, as we have been informed, black-skinned—rather than people from a given territory. Fur—ther, Gardar the Swede had a son called Uni the Dane who became a representative of Harald Fairhair, the first king of a united Norway. King Harald would send Uni the Dane to Iceland to subject the island to King Harald's rule in the early 10th century.

A pirate called Nadodd arrived in Iceland in 864 and named the place *Snowland,* and one source even deems him the island's discoverer. But more sources credit Gardar Svavarson as Iceland's discoverer and the first to navigate the island. It is also fairly cer—tain that Iceland was already inhabited when Gardar the Swede arrived. The inhabitants are said to have been Irish monks, Christians, who may have emigrated there a century or more before Gardar's arrival. When and why they went to Iceland can only be conjectured, but the consensus of opinion is that these monks departed Ireland because of persecution. It is almost certain that these monks were not the Irish we know today, though most historians never go beyond noting that they were Irish. The monks that the Vikings found on Iceland had to have been members of the black- and dark-skinned Celtic Irish, whose nominally Christianized members were hunted down and driven to the west of Ireland by invading Caucasians, probably new Saxons, for secretly continuing their old "pagan" rites. These and other Germanic invaders had also impelled the Scotti to leave the north of Ireland and eventually settle in Scotland, where they eventually took pos—session of that territory from the Picts.

Of the Irish monks in Iceland, B.F. De Costa cites Ari Frode, compiler of *Landanama Book,* who states "[the] Christian people whom the Northmen called papas . . . afterward went away, because they would not be here among heathens; and left behind them Irish books, and bells, and crosiers, from which it could be seen that they were Irishmen" (22). De Costa also refers to these Christian inhabitants as "monks or *Culdees,* who had come hither from Ireland" (*my emphasis* 23)—Culdee connecting them to Godfrey Higgins' black nation of Asia and the Chaldeans of Mesopotamia, multitudes of whom migrated westward to Europe and the British Isles in very ancient times. In *Celtic Druids,* Higgins states, "The Culdees of the British Isles were, in many other respects besides their names, similar to the Chaldees of Assyria" (193), which would mean that they were the same as the Druids, high teachers of a more ancient religion, whose influence in the British Isles was significantly disrupted by the Roman occupation.

Persecution by the Romans, who hunted down and killed those they found, and further persecution by newly invading Saxons and Angles impelled these monks or priests to seek an unblemished territory in which to practice their ancient faith. Those who remained in Ireland were compelled to adopt the Christian faith, although many would practice their old religion in secret. They were of the *ancient* black Irish, and the present Irish are called such for the simple reason that they adopted the ancient alphabet, books, teachings and language of the Black Celts and Culdees, or Druids, whom their more recent ancestors helped to subdue and drive away. But the new invaders, or new Irish, never fully embraced the essence of the old religion because their warrior mentality prevented them from doing so and, having become nominally Christian themselves, they generally abhorred what was considered a pagan faith. However, some of the more learned of the new invaders—or their displaced or racially mixed offspring—did become adepts of the old faith—upholding its traditions and ceremonies—and probably made up a portion of the Celi Dei of Iceland. Those who somehow escaped punishment in Ireland are responsible for elements of the Old Religion surviving into modern times.

The papas, or black Celtic monks who fled Ireland for Iceland in the 7th and 8th centuries are called Christians, but the application of Christianity to them was more than likely a contrivance of later Irish chroniclers. If they were, indeed, Christians, why did they feel the need to flee Ireland, which they had long inhabited, for a desolate, frigid, uninhabited island six-hundred miles or so north of Ireland in the North Atlantic? While there is some evidence that ancient humans had arrived in Iceland in some unknown epoch, there is no sure evidence of people living in Iceland when the Culdees, papas or Irish monks reached it.

Farley Mowat, in *The Farfarers,* mentions that papa or *papar,* "was probably a generic Norse term meaning the followers of White Christ" (342), but it may have simply been a term denoting a monk or priest, just as Papa, today, is an endearing title for the popes of Rome. It is also probable that Celtic monks or Culdees had been compelled to accept the white-skinned Christ on pain of death before leaving Ireland and held on to this image after their departure. It is doubtful that images of the white Christ were extant at the time of their departure from Ireland; although an early image of a white Christ may have begun to be promoted by Rome during this period. Most evidence indicates that the Madonna and Child were worshipped as *black* in many areas of Europe until fairly recent modern times—a tradition which continues in Poland to this day. But it is very probable that images of a white Madonna and Child were in an early stage of development by the late 9th century when Vikings began venturing to Iceland.

Deeming these early Icelandic émigrés *Irish* leads the average reader to envision present-day Irish, the Irish of red hair, white skin and bellicose natures. Western historians are contented that we accept the less-than-honest renderings of history they have presented that we have inculcated unquestioningly. But the ancestors of these Irish who fled to Iceland had been part of an earlier world, that pre-Roman world of western Europe where Egyptians, Picts, Iberians, Phoenicians, Carthaginians, Culdees, Etruscans and various Black Celtic tribes interacted, traded, warred and intermingled. Higgins asserts that the early Irish—Black Celts under various tribal names—migrated west from the heart of Asia and were the source of the Druidic teachings that had suffused most of Eur—ope and the British Isles (Churchward proclaims an *Egyptian* origin for the Druids, to be discussed in a later chapter). And regarding the Irish alphabet,

Higgins asserts: "the sys—tem of letters of . . . the Hebrews, the Greeks, and the Irish Celts, must have been original—ly the same" (*Druids* 16). And although Higgins does not spend a lot of time on it, he does link Phoenician and Arabic primary letters to the Irish [Black] Celtic system of letters as well (op. cit.). And while there is no verifiable record of Iceland being occupied prior to the arrival of the Irish monks, Barry Fell, in *Saga America,* makes a case for earlier settlement of North America by Carthaginians, Libyans, Iberians and others in even earlier times (op. cit., 3-11), and it would certainly have been possible that some of these peoples sojourned in Iceland.

Eurocentric historians have restricted our perceptions regarding the navigational abilities of ancient peoples, and we cannot readily envision ancient mariners making Atlantic Ocean crossings from Africa and Europe to western destinations and returning safely. But the Irish monks who went to Iceland must have known of its existence (or the existence of a land to the west) before setting off, and over at least a century-and-a-half a number of voyages must have been made in knorrs—small, sturdy watercraft able to hold about twenty people—from Ireland to Iceland by monks seeking to escape persecution or death in Ireland.

In Scandinavia, meanwhile, living and farming space was becoming scarce. The expanding populations in Denmark and the habitable areas of Norway are the reasons most often cited for Viking settlement in Britain and France during the 9th century and afterward. Some Norsemen began to leave Norway and Denmark because they had prices on their heads for violating laws or angering a powerful king or petty chieftain. There were many of these in Scandinavia [i.e., petty rulers], and conflicts between rival kings or chieftains were common. Adversaries were sometimes brothers, fathers and sons—or widows bent on exacting revenge against the slayers of husbands or sons. While the primary impetus for the westward migration of Norsemen to Iceland may have been land—a place to farm, raise families without fear of conflict or revenge killings—another may have been the avarice of powerful kings, notably King Harald Fairhair of Norway, who had begun to consolidate his power, often confiscating lands as punishment for crimes. Far-flung Norse raids on other territories had offered a glimpse of how more settled people lived, and many desired to escape the warrior life extant in Scandinavia, longing for a life of pastoral complacence more akin to the lives of the unfortunates whose lives they had brutally interrupted or destroyed on foreign shores.

The pastoral life of farming and husbandry was really not a new occupation for Norsemen. Their early encroachments westward to the Shetlands, Ireland and Alban were land-grabbing excursions for the purpose of setting up farming communities. The Norse were not one-dimensional people; a large percentage of Norsemen—whether Norwegians, Danes or Swedes—had always engaged in farming in Scandinavia or in the lands they ravaged and annexed. And so, in the late 9th and early 10th centuries, hundreds of Norsemen and their families began emigrating to Iceland, whose climate was not much different from southern Scandinavia or northern Britain, a climate those who study such matters unanimously affirm was, on average, five to ten degrees warmer than today. In the habitable areas of Iceland there was plentiful grass, timber, blueberries and arable land where corn was grown by the earliest generations of Norse. Gwyn Jones notes that "[the] lakes and rivers were filled with trout and salmon, the surrounding seas with fish and seals and whales, and the coasts and islands bred innumerable seafowl" (*Vikings* 277). To men and women used to the harsher climate of northern Europe, Iceland must have seemed a veritable paradise—twice the size of Denmark, with only a negligible remnant of earlier settlers who offered no resistance to the new immigrants. It was also far enough away from the Scandinavian homelands to offer fugitive Norsemen a safe haven from arrest or worse at the behest of a disaffected ruler or countryman back home.

Perhaps the most famous fugitive from justice was Erik, or Eirik Thorvaldsson, the Red, commonly known as Erik the Red. A Norwegian, Erik fled the country when he was charged with manslaughter. He sailed to Iceland around 982 but supposedly ran afoul of fledgling Icelandic laws for killings there. Banned from Iceland for three years, he sailed westward to seek and explore a new island that had been rumored to exist after a Norwegian named Gunnbjorn, blown off-course in a storm, claimed to have sighted it. Eirik, sailing west along the 65th parallel and then southwest, landed at the southern tip of Greenland which, after several weeks of exploration, seemed uninhabited. Among Eirik's crewmen was Thorhall the Huntsman, or Hunter, mentioned earlier, who had been with him for years. Thorhall is described, remember, as "a large man, and strong, black and like a giant" (Pohl 136-7); "a large man, dark and coarse-featured" (*The Sagas of the Icelanders* 666); and "a large dark champion" (Arbman 115). Thorhall also "had a wide knowledge of the uninhabited regions [of the ocean]" (*Sagas of the Icelanders* 666), although he is said to have been silent, foul-mouthed and unpopular with most people.

Eirik had an additional two ships with him, all three ships making a total of about 140 men. They rounded the southern tip of Greenland and sailed up the western coastline, setting up a Western Settlement in addition to the Eastern Settlement which they had set up at the southern landing point. Eirik staked out land claims for himself and some of his men. While Eirik remained in Greenland, one of his ships returned to Iceland with glowing reports of this vast new territory, called *Greenland* by Eirik. Naming this rugged land Greenland—although there were mountains and glaciers in the center of it—was done to make the land seem more appealing and induce settlers to venture there, which some began to do within a couple of years.

Sailing west off the coast of Greenland into what is now the Labrador Sea—whether for exploration or on fishing expeditions—it would not have taken long for Norsemen, or Greenlanders, to realize there was more land to be found. So, about the year 1000, a son of Eirik, Leif, known as Leif Eiriksson, voyaged west and southwestward, landing on the mainland of North America in a wide expanse of territory known today as Labrador. One area of it he named Markland, another Vinland or Wineland, an area whose exact location is still disputed but whom many believe is the northern appendage of Newfoundland—the easternmost extremity of present-day Canada. Leif's crew, however, did not find these new lands uninhabited. It is not clear whether they encountered natives of the land during their initial landing, but they must have noticed signs of habitation since, it is said, Leif wintered in Vinland. The explorers returned to Greenland the following summer praising Vinland's climate, grapes, abundant fish and timber. Leif had grown tired of exploring and, since Eirik the Red had died, Leif chose to assume his father's responsibilities and remain close to his own family. His brother, Thorvald, decided he would spearhead another discovery expedition to Vinland. It was on this expedition that Norsemen encountered Native Americans for the first time. All the circumstances are not known, but it is said that the Norsemen instigated hostilities and Thorvald was killed by an arrow. His crew returned to a base further north to spend the winter, and in the spring returned to Greenland with the news of Thorvald's death.

Thorfinn Karlsefni made the next significant voyage to Vinland, his crew taking livestock with the intention of a prolonged stay, some taking their wives. Karlsefni's expedition was comprised of three ships and 160 men. There is disagreement in the sagas as to his exact route. He perhaps landed on Baffin Island, which he named Helluland, then he sailed south to Markland. Gwyn Jones points out the differences in *Eirik's Saga* and *Graenlendinga Saga* (*Vikings* 301-3) as to Karlsefni's voyage, neither of which I will support or defend. But Karlsefni does end up in Vinland where the Norsemen encountered hostilities with the native population—called *Skraelings* by the Greenlanders.

At first they traded with these people who, most accounts say, were short, dark-skinned, and ill-tempered, with "ugly hair." During a trading encounter the Skraelings offered animal pelts for red cloth, and bartering was peacefully undertaken, although the Norsemen refused to trade or sell swords or spears. The next encounter with Skraelings was violent and an indecisive battle ensued with several losses of life on both sides. Karlsefni and his crew spent three winters in Vinland, the Norsemen finally realizing that their position there would remain tenuous and stress-filled, with hostilities cropping up every so often with the native inhabitants. So Karlsefni and his crew returned to Greenland, and early Norse attempts at colonization on the North American mainland ended about the year 1020, by most accounts.

*   *   *   *   *

There is another chapter to this tale of early exploration and colonization, which will be remarked upon further on. But it would be unrealistic to conclude that the documented accounts of Norse exploration of North America, sagas or otherwise, were the only ones. If nothing else, the Norse people were adventurous and enterprising, and they were quick to exploit any suggestion that an untapped, unexplored region might promise wealth, profit or advantage. It would not be unreasonable to think that other Norsemen, unrecorded and unknown to us now, ventured into areas of the North American wilderness to seek fortunes. Author Barry Fell (though he makes no mention of *black* Norsemen), citing coins and other artifacts found in burial mounds, opines that a succession of voyages must have followed Leif Eiriksson's and that they ranged "southward . . . along the New England coast, then farther southward around Florida to the mouth of the Mississippi, and then up the Mississippi river . . . into Oklahoma" (*Saga* 310, 321).

Fell, though, like many before and after him, promulgates the assumption that Norsemen were Caucasian and mixed themselves with Native Americans creating "blue-eyed Indians" and "fair-haired corpses" supposedly found by Pilgrims. I have yet to go on any archeological digs, and I have not read all of Mr. Fell's works, but my personal library has more than six-dozen books on Native Americans, a half-dozen on the Indians of New England, and I have never read any such thing in any of them. And, although I have read that the Mandans of the upper Missouri River in North Dakota were lighter-skinned than other tribes, I have never read anything authenticated regarding blue-eyed or fair-haired Mandans. I have seen some photographs of Mandans, and they look quite dark-skinned, so perhaps the renowned George Catlin worked a few wonders with his paint-brush in his depictions of the Mandans and other tribes when he portrayed them as light-skinned.

As to who the Skraelings were, there seem to be two, perhaps three possibilities.

They could have been typical Native Americans, dark-skinned, dark-eyed, with straight hair and aggressive natures. It is possible that they may have been Inuit or Eskimo people who were recent migrants to northeastern North America, if general timetables of their migration from Asia to North America are to be believed. The Inuit were also dark-skinned with straight or curly hair, and they are now considered a branch of Native Americans who, for whatever reasons, chose to live in more northerly climes. A map from Gwyn Jones' *A History of the Vikings* (below) shows Inuit and Native Americans living in close proximity to each other in Labrador and Newfoundland at the time of Leif Eiriksson's voyages to the area, about 1000. The map, as well, illustrates that some Indians lived farther north than Inuit or Eskimos, so Eiriksson and Karlsefni could have encountered members of either peoples if, indeed, there was any notable difference between the two at the time.

The third possibility is that the Skraelings were remnants of an even older people—diminutive Blacks, Pygmies or Negritos who had once overspread the whole earth in extremely remote times. Other terms were used by Norsemen to describe these short, black-skinned people, but *skraeling* was the term most commonly applied to them.

Author Don Luke (*African Presence*) likens them to Twa and Black or Dark Elves mentioned in Scandinavian mythologies which, if North American skraelings were related to the diminutive northern European Dark Elves, would mean that Norsemen were not totally unfamiliar with these people. However, there could have been differences in the aggressiveness of each group since one, the European, had been in touch with advanced civilization and had had contact with different peoples over several centuries while the other, the North American, presumably had not.

What seems certain is that Norsemen were outnumbered by the native populations they encountered on North American shores. There were no prosperous cities for them to target and raid, and there was a wide sea separating them from timely reinforcements in manpower from British and Scandinavian bases. There were no shipbuilding centers where they could build, refit or repair ships. Events in Europe were too tumultuous for Scandinavian countries to devote more effort into keeping Iceland or Greenland supplied with necessary provisions and assistance. Many, if not most, of Iceland's inhabitants were disaffected peoples—Norwegians, Danes, Albans, Norse-Irish—fleeing the constraints of Norse rulers, like Harald Fairhair and lesser chieftains, who might claim Icelandic or Greenland territories in return for any assistance. King Harald Fairhair had already made nominal claims on the newly settled territories and, from Norway, was seeking every opportunity to confiscate estates as punishment for crimes. Even chieftains had abandoned Norway when Harald united the territory and became its first officially recognized king (his father, Halfdan the Black, had primarily unified the territory of Vestfold, not the expanded territory of Norway). So, as James Enterline states in *Viking America*, "Iceland was . . . set up as a free state completely independent of Norway, and it soon developed the first democratic parliament in the world" (4).

In the earliest days of settlement in Iceland, migrants acquired land according to first-comers' right, after which homes and parcels of land would be granted to faithful followers, sons, or other relatives. The first settlers were mostly heathen, and temples were erected for the worship of Thor. Less often, temples were built for Tyr, Odinn, Balder and Njord. Most often the wealthiest, most authoritative men took charge of religious rites, acquiring the title of *godi* (i.e., godly one), a secular priest. Although the title of godi could be bestowed by appointment, or shared by agreement, the wealthiest Norsemen were the *godar* until after 930 when the *althing* was created. Initially the althing, or national assembly, was still controlled by the godar. A president was elected to a three-year term, which was renewable, and a constitution was drawn up. Iceland was divided into North, South, East, and West Quarters and there were assemblies for judging lawsuits and disputes, granting pardons and issuing punishments. There were reforms and reorganizations to the althing to make just laws for all free men, though it continued to be administered by the island's most authoritative, affluent men into the 11th century.

*   *   *   *   *

Before returning to Scandinavia and the landscape of 10th century Europe, however, there is an appendage to this initial glimpse of the Viking movement west to Iceland and North America. In an article entitled "The Mysterious Black Vikings: The Rediscovery of a Lost Tribe," writer Axtol Greizer discusses a 1997 article in *Scientific Historian* entitled "The Black Vikings: Myth or Reality?" by Dr. Hector Andre-Jones. In the *Scientific Historian* article, Dr. Andre-Jones discusses Aben Arou, the illegitimate child of a Senegalese prince and an Egyptian noblewoman, who had a quite adventurous life. Sent off to Rome with thirty Senegalese guards and a dozen Egyptian tutors, Aben Arou and his entourage went along on a campaign to northern Europe and the British Isles with Roman general Barnabus Maximus. Dr. Andre-Jones writes that while General Maximus and his legions returned to Rome, Aben Arou and his entourage were captured by Norsemen and enslaved. Andre-Jones believes Aben Arou's entire crew was consigned to oarsman duties on a ship that went to Greenland in 982 during the great island's initial Norse colonization. Aben Arou would have been 20 years-old at this time, and his ship was part of a large fleet commanded by Rolf Tollefson. Most of the ships in this fleet were lost in a storm which blew them off course. The surviving vessels beached somewhere on the shores of northern Maine, an area that was inhabited by Native Americans of the Maliseet tribe.

Andre-Jones cites the work of anthropologist Bjarni Herjulfsson, whose theory, based on diggings and artifacts found in the area, is that the Viking survivors were assimilated into the Maliseet tribe—Aben Arou, his Senegalese guards, Egyptian tutors, and the actual Norse Vikings making up the bulk of the retinue. The artifacts Herjulfsson cites include part of the prow of a Viking ship, and a considerable number of tablets on which linguists have deciphered "Norse symbols, Latin alphabetical characters, Egyptian hieroglyphics and early Senegalese 'picture words'" (*Viking Heritage in Maine*).

The Maliseets soon discovered that Aben Arou was extremely knowledgeable and had held high stature in his former life, almost from birth. Among the Maliseets he soon rose to a high position in tribal councils, eventually becoming a chief of the tribe. His status as chief allowed him to have many wives—Maliseet women as well as Egyptian and Viking females. One of the women he married was Rolf Tollefson's widow, Olga Sorensdotter, who had flaming red hair and bore at least a dozen of the many children Aben Arou fathered. The Maliseets prospered in the area for many more centuries, a tribe whose racial composition of Native American, Senegalese, Egyptian and Norse must have produced extremely handsome male and female individuals.

Many centuries later, in 1607, the explorer Henry Hudson held a council with the Maliseets and described the chief of the tribe as having an "unusual bronze complexion," standing a "head and a half above other men," possessing "hair the colour of the breast of a robin" (op. cit.). The chief was called Ah-ben-Ah, but was called by later English colonists Red Lion and, according to Herjulfsson, was a descendant of Aben Arou and Olga Sorensdotter.

While the above-mentioned Dr. Andre-Jones' article, highlighted in Axtol Greizer's "The Mysterious Black Vikings: The Rediscovery of a Lost Tribe" (American Features Syndicate, Ltd., Chicago, Illinois), assimilates Aben Arou and his African retinue into the Viking company, it does not assert that the Viking contingent was black-skinned, and mentioning the "flaming red hair" of Olga Sorensdotter lends credence to the belief that the Vikings were white-skinned, since most of us associate blond and red hair with Caucasians. But we have come too far to fall back into oft-stated, unsubstantiated Eurocentric assertions regarding the race of the Vikings during this period. And we know that Vikings took women as wives and concubines from every part of their subjugated territories during the Viking Age—French, English, Irish, Slavic and Greek women. So Olga Sorensdotter's flaming red hair should not alter what we have learned about the complexions of Norse peoples.

The Maliseets were related to the Micmac tribe as well as to the Abnaki, all part of a large Algonquian confederacy that stretched into Canada. The Micmacs are probably the best known of the Maine tribes, and it is likely the Maliseets, the least known of these tribes, are confused with them by historians remarking on the above-mentioned Egyptian hieroglyphs found on artifacts and inscribed tablets discovered all over the area once inhabited by the Maliseets, whose descendants still occupy parts of their former homeland. While "The Rediscovery of a Lost Tribe" is a fairly recent article (published in 2000) and Aben Arou a new historical figure, the reference to Egyptian hieroglyphs connected with a Native American tribe is not. In *America B.C.*, published in 1976, Barry Fell discusses the striking similarity between the Micmac writing system first noticed by French colonists in Maine and Egyptian hieroglyphic writing, stating that "someone familiar with the Egyptian hieroglyphic system had contrived the Micmac writing" (253), and concluding that "the Micmac writing system (and also part of their language) is derived from ancient Egyptian" (257). Athough much of *America B.C.* is concerned with ancient peoples like Egyptians, Phoenicians and Romans who may also have landed and settled in parts of North America, Fell accurately asserts that the Micmacs and related Algonquian members are not descendants from ancient Egyptian settlers, stating:

> However, a limited but recognizable Egyptian vocabulary is present, suggestive of contacts with Egyptian or Libyan speakers from whom these words could have been acquired as loan elements, at the same time as the writing system was acquired. (260).

The Maliseets, close neighbors of the Micmacs, are not mentioned in Mr. Fell's work and are only occasionally mentioned in others, perhaps because their numbers were smaller or because European settlers simply grouped them with Micmacs, a larger tribe with which they had most contact. In any case, we have a substantiation of the information presented in "The Rediscovery of a Lost Tribe," which also mentions "numerous raids by rival tribes upon the Maliseet" in which members of the tribe were often kidnapped—more than 100 in one raid. Several kidnapped Maliseet tribesmen managed to escape captivity and return to Maine, saying that they had been taken far away to a village called Sanasopet, later identified as being in southeastern Virginia.

Assuming the Maliseets had generally peaceful relations with their Algonquian brethren, it would have been normal that some African and Norse individuals or their descendants were passed along to neighboring tribes like the Micmacs and Abnaki or Wabanaki, spreading the Egyptian hieroglyphic writing system, as well as Latin and Senegalese characters, among these—perhaps even into Great Lakes regions and Canada, leaving future historians and anthropologists to speculate over their possible origins.

Aben Arou, "a great black warrior . . . wise in the ways of the Gods . . . educated in most of the arts and sciences of the day" (Greizer), seems to have remained with the Maliseets, producing an untold number of progeny and descendants, one of whom, named Red Lion, "[with] hair the colour of the breast of a robin . . . [and] an unusual bronze complexion," would meet with Henry Hudson many centuries later.

*   *   *   *   *

In Russia, Norsemen had established settlements to control their expanding commercial empire, with fresh hordes of warriors from Ireland, Scotland, England, France, Iceland and Germany coming in to support their efforts there. So, although Western historians attribute the Norse establishment of Russia to Swedish Vikings, Danish and Norwegian Vikings were equally involved. Several great rivers connected the Baltic and Black Seas, and noted historian Will Durant states:

> Moslem merchants came up from Baghdad and Byzantium and traded spices, wines, silks, and gems for furs, amber, honey, wax, and slaves; hence the great number of Islamic and Byzantine coins found along these rivers, and even in Scandinavia . . . . [T]owns like Novgorod, Smolensk, Chernigov, Kiev, and Rostov flourished through Scandinavian, Slavic, Moslem, and Byzantine trade. (448)

This expansion of commerce and domination took place during the mid- to late-9th century and would lead to the establishment of Russia a century later under Scandinavian rulers. Durant further informs us:

> Oleg, Igor and the able Princess Olga (Igor's widow), and her warrior son Sviatoslav (962-72) widened the Kievan realm until it embraced nearly all the eastern Slavonic tribes, and the towns of Polotsk, Smolensk, Chernigov, and Rostov. (op. cit.)

Durant considers the above-mentioned rulers—Oleg, Igor and Princess Olga—the true founders of the vast territory that would come to be known as Russia.

From 860 to 1043 there were a half-dozen expeditions out of Kiev to capture Constantinople, which failed. But tenuous truces were made and, as mentioned, Varangians were employed by the Byzantine Empire as mercenaries and palace guards. By taking Constantinople, Norsemen had hoped to secure territory that would link their expanding realm to the eastern Mediterranean where they could join forces with their mainly Danish brethren entering the Mediterranean through the Gibraltar Strait for attacks on southern France and Italy. Had they done so, the Norse would have been able to effectively encircle Europe and perhaps invade the Italian peninsula in an effort to bring down Rome.

The situation was that dire for Greco-Roman-minded Europe, engulfed in an eastwest conflict of a religious nature. After the Western Roman Empire was brought down at the end of the 5th century, the Eastern Roman Empire remained intact and eventually became known as the Byzantine Empire (from Byzantium, an earlier name of Constantinople), with a divergent Christian philosophy than that of Rome. Flourishing after the demise of the Western Roman Empire, Byzantine Christianity became dominant, and Roman or Latin Christianity was constrained to function under its supervision for a time. However, as a resurgent Roman Church regained influence and won converts in western Europe, especially with the addition of Charlemagne's Frankish Empire to its fold, the Latin Church would again assert its independence and compete with the Byzantine Church for the conversion of pagan souls in Europe—especially among the Slavs. So, during the late-9th and early 10th centuries, according to Durant:

> Moravia, Bohemia, and Slovakia (these constituting the Czechoslovakia of today), and later Hungary and Poland, were won to the Latin Church and rite; while Bulgaria, Serbia,

and Russia accepted the Slavonic liturgy and alphabet, gave their allegiance to the Greek
Church, and took their culture from Byzantium. (535-6)

The conversions of various Slavic peoples did not take place all at once, nor should their conversions
imply that each and every Slav was immediately won over to one or the other Christian rite.

The Latin and Greek Churches invariably achieved conversions by converting kings or powerful
leaders who were expected to use their power or office to convert their subjects. So, for the most part, the
conversion of European peoples to Christianity would take place in piecemeal fashion—tribe by tribe,
group by group, territory by territory.

The Slavs, and other European peoples, for example, would remain largely pagan into the 13th century.
In the 10th century, despite nominal gains, both the Roman and Greek Churches faced, to varying degrees,
the same threat: an expanding Islamic Empire from Spain to the Near East—bordering the Byzantine
Empire itself, from the eastern end of the Black Sea to the Mediterranean; and the expanding Viking
menace in northern Europe from the British Isles in the east to Russia—with a southern incursion that
had already insinuated itself into Byzaantium.

By the mid-10th century the ingredients for a powerful Norse empire were in place. What was lacking
was a powerful leader with foresight who might have united the often fractious internecine conflicts
between the three principal Norse countries and organized them into a unified entity and poised them
for an organized assault on Europe—particularly Rome and the Roman Church which, itself, was reeling
from internal conflict and moral degradation (see Durant, pp. 536-541). Norse smiths were able to weave
flexible mail-shirts that were nearly impenetrable, durable helmets, fearsome battle-axes and the most
superior swords of the age, which could be forged for particular weather conditions. Each Scandinavian
country had imported thousands of slaves whose male members were sometimes utilized as auxiliaries in
battle. Norsemen of the three principal Scandinavian countries were proficient in building the fastest,
most stream-lined ships of the age—some much longer than 100 feet, though most ranged from 60-80
feet—and Viking chieftains could easily muster 200 or more vessels for an attack on their adversaries.

Far too often, however, a chieftain's adversary was another Viking chieftain, as Norsemen often
contended with each other for territories within the Scandinavian realm.

There were especially bitter rivalries between Norwegian and Danish chieftains and petty kings over
territory, which would continue until the Danish King Canute (also Knut) became the ruler of Denmark
and England (1018) and added Norway to his territory ten years later—the acquisition of which produced
the Kingdom of Canute (1028-35). The whole southern portion of Sweden became Danish territory at
this time, however, King Canute seriously entertained the thought of adding the rest of Sweden, or most
of present-day Sweden to his kingdom.

But King Canute's arrival on the historical scene was way too late; the time for a true Norse empire
in Europe was lost, had long passed, and the opportunity would never arise again. Had Canute—or a
king with the determination of Canute—arisen in the early part of the 10th century and somehow unified
the contending Norse factions, offering them a vision of a Europe under their domination, perhaps
the quest for true empire—on the order of the old Roman Empire—might have succeeded. Although
Norsemen were known more for their prowess as sea-raiders who attacked coastal areas, they did venture
overland to do battle if their needs demanded it. And while they were not known as tactical fighters and
for employing the troop formations that the Roman Empire made famous in its heyday, their members
were often fearless individual fighters whose ferocity made up for their generally smaller numbers. A
number of them were known as *berserksgangr* or *berserkers,* taking such pleasure in battle that they fought
in an unconscious frenzy without mail-shirts, howling like animals, collapsing from exhaustion when
the battle was over. They would often prepare for battle by praying to their personal god, performing
rites of magic, sometimes stripping naked except for sword, shield and spear, and often did not suffer
serious wounds. But often their heroic efforts—like those of their kinsmen—were against Viking rivals in
territorial disputes, fighting for one king against another.

No European sovereign or nation seriously contemplated an assault on Denmark, the seat of the Viking nations; not Charlemagne nor any of the rulers of the East or West Frankish Empires who followed him; not any of the kings of the Holy Roman Empire; not the kings of England who, from the time of Alfred the Great, had to endure the Danelaw and new influxes of Danish settlers. But the Fathers of the Church in Rome had discovered a secret weapon through trial and error and began to employ it more assiduously after a few successful results. They were encouraged when it worked in Normandy, so they employed it in England, and it seemed to be starting to take hold there. And so they targeted Denmark, believing that a strike at the Viking heartland was the ideal place to unleash this most promising weapon.

The Roman Church had continuously sent missions to Scandinavia seeking converts to Christianity, a faith so abhorrent to Norsemen that early missionaries were lucky to leave the north alive. But in 960, for whatever reason, King Harald Bluetooth formally accepted the Christian faith and set about to convert all of Denmark to the hated religion. Pagan worship, of course, did not disappear all at once. In most of Scandinavia, as well as in Iceland after Christianity was imposed there in 1000, the old gods would continue to be worshipped in secret by many for two or more centuries.

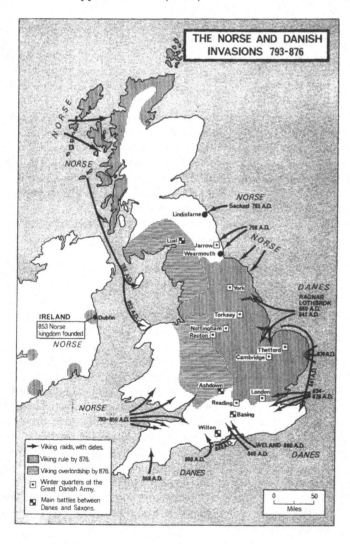

Fig. 14
Norwegian and Danish settlement in future England. Large, central darkened area approximates territory of the Danelaw which would be imposed by 878—The latter part of the 9th century.

Although the Danelaw prevailed in England for a century (until the last quarter of the 10th century), the practice of having Viking chieftains convert to Christianity to cement any truces or territorial agreements had been in place since Alfred (the Great), king of Wessex, had required Danish chieftain Guthrum to accept baptism as a precondition to any truce at the treaty of Wedmore in 878. The custom, of course, was instigated and en—couraged by the Roman Church, and often brought about dissention, sometimes rebellion, among Norse chieftains and their followers. Gradually, however, most Norsemen in Eng—land and Ireland grudgingly allowed themselves to be baptized.

So, the conversion of Danes to Christianity imposed on them by King Harald Bluetooth might not have been as difficult as later conversions of Norse peoples since, as Gwyn Jones notes:

> . . . by this time there must have been many Christians in Denmark, especially in the marts and havens, partly through the influx of traders and travelers, partly as a result of the missions from Hamburg-Bremen, partly by virtue of the Christianized Danes of the Danelaw with their substantial influence on the Danish homeland. (*Vikings* 126)

It is doubtful, though, that all Danes in Denmark immediately embraced the new faith unquestioningly, without rancor or even open hostility. But their king had established the precedent, as would future kings, and Denmark became part of the Greco-Roman-aspir-ing European family during the reign of Harald Bluetooth.

When Hakon the Good, son of Harald Fairhair, took power in southwestern Norway in the 940s, he was already a Christian. He was the foster son of Athelstan, king of England, having been raised in Athelstan's court. Foster-parentage was common among Scandinavian royalty, who by mutual agreement, allowed a son or sons to be reared in the courts of English or other Scandinavian kings' courts as bonds of alliance. The practice was also prevalent among non-royals—Norse sons being given to be raised by uncles or friends, and growing to maturity in their households.

Hakon came to Norway wanting to introduce Christianity, as his father had attempted, "[b]ut once he found the new religion obnoxious to the great majority of his subjects he promptly embraced the old" (Jones, *Vikings* 119). Later, Hakon would engage in battles with the Danes who had territorial claims in Norway and would be mortally wounded in a battle against them. Norway would not become predominantly Christian until the early 11th century through the efforts of St. Olaf (Olaf the Stout) who, despite later achieving the status of saint, employed uncompromising methods to convert pagan Norwegians to the new faith: Speaking of St. Olaf's conversion methods, Gwyn Jones states: "[H]e executed the recalcitrant, blinded or maimed them, drove them from their homes, cast down their images and marred their sacred places" (op. cit. 377). He would die in battle in 1030, suffering defeat at the hands of his own kinsmen fighting for an independent Norway. More will be said regarding St. Olaf in a later chapter.

Sweden was the last of the three Viking nations to adopt the Christian faith. King Olaf Skottkonung accepted baptism in 1008 but did not impose Christianity on his countrymen. It was not until the 12th century—a hundred years after Olaf Skottkunung became a Christian—that the pagan shrines in Uppsala were razed and most Swedes reluctantly accepted the hated religion. Most people in the Western world today are "born" Christian—baptized into the faith in infancy—and grow up hearing Bible tales that remain in their minds until adulthood, only a relatively few stepping outside of what they were taught to study other religious philosophies or convert to other religions.

It surprises us that anyone would reject the Christian doctrines we are familiar with today, that anyone would find Christian teachings abhorrent. Yet, most Norsemen did (along with other European peoples), and only converted to the faith because it was imposed on them by kings or powerful chieftains. They preferred to retain their own so-called pagan faiths: gods and goddesses they understood, who answered their needs; who granted them fine harvests, fertility and victories in battle; who granted them a place in Valhalla for their bravery; blessed them with numerous sons and daughters, lands and valuables, things they could see and touch; gods who kept them attuned to natural forces, proffered dreams and portents of good or evil, which always came to pass. The Norse religion, in essence, was generally not very different from the beliefs of so-called "primitive" peoples—for instance, peoples more familiar to us like Australian Aborigines and Native Americans—beliefs that had sustained mankind for many thousands of years.

Proponents of Christianity came to regard such belief systems as pagan, even though much of the Christian doctrine was siphoned from so-called pagan beliefs. But the Norse peoples, who esteemed bravery, who were taught at a very early age to be courageous even in the face of overwhelming odds, who slew and were not afraid to be slain in battle, were imposed upon to accept a faith whose primary representative was a man who had disliked fighting and had allowed himself to be humiliated, whipped, and marched to a hill bearing a cross heavier than he was, upon which he was nailed and crucified—without the least show of resistance.

And why were the Fathers of the Church in Rome so determined to convert the Norse peoples to Christianity? Why had Rome sent mission after mission to Britain and Scandinavia for two centuries (in Denmark, from c. 700 AD onward), invariably targeting Viking chieftains and kings who, at least in the beginning, showed disdain toward the faith as well as to Chrisstian missionaries? Does the reader believe the Roman effort was humanitarian? Were the Roman Fathers concerned with saving Viking souls? Did they say to themselves: *"Those poor, benighted Norsemen are in need of salvation. We must do what we can to save them so that they may enter God's kingdom when they die. Let us tell them that they need to accept Jesus Christ so that they may enter Heaven."*? Does the reader actually believe saving Norse souls was the motivating factor in the centuries-long drive to effect Norse conversion to Christianity?

I think the reader has read enough to understand that saving Norse souls was surely not a consideration of the Church Fathers in Rome: The reason was to save the Roman Church and the influence it sought in Europe to escape obliteration. Christianity has always been presented to us as something good, unstained by bloodshed, interested only in salvation and love. This has not always been the case, and research into the origin of Christianity will bear this out. The sources employed in this work do not offer a reason for Norse conversion to the faith, nor can I. But early on I asked that the reader use common sense and logic and remind him to do so now. My comments regarding Christianity are from a historical perspective; it is in no way my intent to denigrate the religion, its beliefs, or to disparage Christian believers. But *historically*, looking at the evidence, I can say (as many others have) that the Fathers of the Church sought power and influence over the continent of Europe and it was imperative that they defuse the power and spirit of Norse peoples. Despite the Church's strong ties with the Christianized East Frankish Kingdom (i.e., Germany), which would later combine with other territories to form the Holy Roman Empire, they could not do this militarily. So the Norse peoples were attacked with a new weapon, a new form of warfare that did not involve direct confrontation, battlefield formations, physical weapons or the shedding of blood. The Norse peo-ples were attacked psychologically, chieftain by chieftain, area by area, over a protracted period, which sowed seeds of dissention between chieftains and their followers, kings and their subjects; among allies and among families. The imposition of Christianity on the masses by their leaders ultimately unhinged the Norse peoples from a belief system that had long sustained them, empowered them, and driven them to the brink of conquering most of Europe.

Most histories write of the Norse conversion to Christianity as incidental, without articulating why this occurred; what motivated Norse leaders to jeopardize relations with their subjects by demanding they convert; what the Fathers of the Church in Rome promised. The impression given is that conversion was simply *right*; paganism was wrong, passé, and it was time for Europe to accept its Christian destiny. With what has been presented, the reader should be able to see beyond this simplistic assumption, which Viking historians never get around to elucidating. Author Eric Oxenstierna (*The World of the Norsemen*) calls the conflicting struggle among the Norse between the Old Religion and Christianity "the most momentous happening of the Viking age" (148)—without, however, discussing its larger ramifications.

We have seen the extent of the Norse conquest, expansion and influence over western and northern Europe; their domination of the vast territory of Russia; their entry into the Mediterranean and assaults on areas of Spain, southern France and Italy; their incursions into the Byzantine Empire and areas of Greece where, according to Edward Gibbon: "the Normans spread themselves by sea, and over the provinces . . . and the venerable age of Athens, Thebes, and Corinth, was violated by rapine and cruelty" (363). By this time most Norse were Christian, and it was *Christianized* Normans who plundered and ruined these cities and others in Greece.

Generally speaking, the conversion to Christianity dampened the rage and aggressiveness of the Norsemen and obliged them to look to the Roman Church for guidance and approbation. I did not consult any source to arrive at this conclusion; the reader need only look at the result of the machinations of the Fathers of the Church, just as I have. Norse expansionist ambitions in Europe came to a virtual halt; the resources and military potential of their western Atlantic colonies in Iceland and Greenland were practically ignored; and the internecine conflicts over territory and inheritances continued in the Viking homelands of Scandinavia.

Although conversion to the hated faith reduced the threat of Norse expeditions of naked expansion, fostering a desire to settle and adopt the ways of the peoples whose lands they had once despoiled, Viking raids did not cease altogether. In the mid-11th century, Robert Guiscard and his Norman army invaded southern Italy, wresting it from Byzantine rule and establishing the Norman Kingdom, which included southern Italy and Sicily (also known as the Kingdom of Sicily). And in 1066, William, Duke of Normandy (William the Conqueror) invaded England with a Norman host, establishing the England that we know today (more will be said about the Norman Conquest later).

Rome, however, had finally accomplished by artifice what she had dared not—could not—attempt by force of arms: Rome had effectively subdued the churning Norse cauldron by replacing their trusted, fathomable Norse gods and goddesses with a mysterious, unfathomable one. Norse rulers and their converted followers turned to the popes of Rome for guidance—precisely what the Fathers of the Church had long desired. The Church Fathers in Rome sought power for themselves—and a Europe under their unquestioned control. They could now include a considerable number of fierce Viking fighters—men they had once feared, and who were still regarded as heathen and outside the human family—to their Holy Roman army in a quest to convert the remainder of pagan Europe to Christianity and mount a Crusade (in 1096) to the Holy Land to wrest Jerusalem from the Muslim Saracens (i.e., Turks, Arabs, Africans), whom they called *Infidels*. The Roman Church was *never* interested in saving Norse souls. The reader cannot honestly believe this.

Chapter 10

NOTABLE NORSE KINGS AND CHIEFTAINS

After two centuries of absorbing the historiography presented by Eurocentric historians, most people have been indoctrinated with the supposed superiority of Europeans in all matters of learning, civilization, warfare, science and human development. The attendant assumption is that Europeans—white Europeans—are, and always have been the preeminent "race" on the planet. European and American historians have been able inject Caucasians into civilizations far older and dynamic than the Greece that emerged after Hellenic invasions by merely assigning the black- and dark-skinned erectors of these civilizations to the Caucasian family. They have succeeded in this because the last five centuries of disruption and ruin suffered by nations and territories invaded or colonized by Europeans have relegated education, scholarship and writing secondary to organizing and rebuilding the commerce, governmental organization, economic recovery and history of subjected nations. The study of their own long lost cultures, writing and related pursuits are luxuries few of them can afford.

So, most of the black- and dark-skinned progeny of ruined nations must adapt to modern realities, travel to Western nations to study and master English, French, German or some other European language, to do well in universities abroad. While Nursing, Economics or Architecture may be fairly universal in application, studies in Literature, Anthropology and History will often subject students to Western or Eurocentric views or conclusions, which most people have inculcated over the last five centuries and which a historian or researcher must contend with if he or she writes anything counter to long held beliefs and assumptions—precisely what this writer has set out to do.

The reader who may have completely doubted the premise of this work has, I think, been presented with a great deal of evidence demonstrating that Europe has been the abode of numerous black- and dark-skinned inhabitants—not only in remote times, but even from the Christian Era into the early Middle Ages. It should no longer be doubted that the Norsemen of the Dark and Middle Ages were predominantly black- and dark-skinned. By "dark-skinned," I do not mean <u>tanned</u>, as some might be inclined to interpret it. And I am not referring to Whites who, because of *atavism*—the interaction of recessive genes—are darker-skinned than their siblings or other members of their societies. There are notable white people who are (or were) dark-skinned. Look carefully at photographs or at films of President John F. Kennedy—in color, or black and white—and you can easily notice that his complexion was darker than his siblings, his wife, his parents or other Whites. He also had thick, coarse hair. Newspaper and magazine articles often called him "tanned," or suggested that his complexion was the result of pills he took for a medical condition. But if we understand that Ireland, where Kennedy's descendants were from, was historically inhabited by black-skinned people (Milesians Firbolgs, Formorians, Tuatha de Danaan, Scots, who have been mentioned) even into the Middle Ages, it should not surprise the reader that individuals darker-skinned than other family members, or the general white populace, are fairly commonplace.

The American actor George Hamilton is another example of this fairly common circumstance. Writers have spoken of his "perpetual tan," and movie critic Leonard Maltin mentions "his impossibly deep tan" in *Leonard Maltin's Movie Encyclopedia* (366). Although Hamilton was born in the U.S., his lineage can probably be traced to somewhere in the British Isles. There are a dozen other celebrities and personalities I could mention, which I won't. But the reader has already learned a few things regarding the history of the British Isles. The same holds true, however, for the rest of Europe.

So, in regard to "dark-skinned" Scandinavians or Norsemen, I am speaking of people whose immediate ancestors—parents, grandparents, and so on—passed along to them a significant degree of melanin—taking into account admixtures of white-skinned individuals, as well—producing individuals of tawny, reddish-brown, brown and dark-brown skin. Black-skinned Norsemen, as the Danes of the Dark Ages are universally referred to by those who mention complexion, connote unmixed individuals or—since we know that race-mixing has always occurred—people with a negligible admixture of white- or lighter-skinned descendants. This implies that black-skinned women had to have been prominent and made up a sizeable proportion of women in Scandinavia—from the Egyptians and Africoids who earlier over—spread western and northern Europe, to those accompanying men who migrated to northern Germany and Jutland in early migrations from the Near East and other areas of Asia. There was a comingling of the newer arrivals with earlier-settled Africoid or Egyptian peoples who thoroughly over—spread the western portion of continental Europe, as has been shown.

The Etruscans of pre-new-Roman central and northern Italy were certainly involved in this nexus of ancient European peoples. We know that they were a dark, perhaps black-skinned people, with the "countenances of Negroes," according to at least one scholar. And historian Werner Keller makes clear that:

> Long before Rome existed, they [Etruscans] had already established an empire on Italian soil, with big cities, industry, arts and crafts, and *world-wide trade*. But of all this the general public has been told almost nothing. (*emphasis mine*, xiv)

The general public has also not been informed of how extensively Etruscan trade and influence may have extended, or if Etruscans were actually akin to other black northern European tribes and whether these relationships might have extended to the British Isles.

The general public, as well, has been told almost nothing of the older, pre-Aryan European world which new-Romans destroyed. Etruscans had a written language and probably documented their history, which might have included valuable information regarding the pre-new-Roman world, perhaps discoursed on their precise origins, religion, territory, the origins of contemporary peoples of that older world of similarly dark—skinned humanity. Their writings might have mentioned trade routes to *eastern* Europe, the Black Sea, the Near East and Asia, since most historians assert they migrated from those areas. They might have had knowledge of the Great Flood, ancient European wars, cosmogonical data. Godfrey Higgins states that "[t]he ancient Etruscans were thought by many to be a colony which escaped from Egypt when the Shepard kings conquered that country. The identity of the worship of ancient Etruria and Egypt makes this not unlikely" (*Anac. vol. 2*, 67).

What we know of the Etruscans is derived chiefly from the *remnants* of their civilization, since their historical records were deliberately obliterated by the new-Romans. If their territory did not extend beyond the Italian peninsula, their influence certainly did, and it is known that they had relations with the pre-Viking Age peoples of Scandinavia. Western historians restrict their extensive commercial ventures to land routes, but Etruscans, we now know, also had fleets and could have reached Scandinavia by sea, sailing through the Pillars of Hercules to the north—an accomplishment bestowed upon their Phoenicians kinsmen and no one else. If Etruscans were actually related to Egyptians, then shipbuilding would have been a common vocation, and their ships might have been similar to those of the early Scandinavian peoples, who were descendants of megalith-building Egyptians and other Africoids who had settled northern and western Europe in remote times.

Western historians never seem to make clear whether sails were employed 6,000 or 7,000 years ago. But if we are speaking of ancient Egyptians who had already built the Great Sphinx, had begun building pyramids and other monuments, had learned the movements of constellations, understood geophysics, developed the higher mathematics which are emphatically evident in the Great Pyramid of Gizeh—built at least 5,000 years ago despite the insistence of Western scholars and Egyptologists that it is less ancient than this (Massey asserts it is far more ancient than 5,000 years)—does the reader believe that the advantage of a sail to catch the wind and improve the speed of a ship or boat did not occur to them five-, six- or seven-thousand years ago when they were crossing the Mediterranean, sailing beyond the Pillars of Hercules into the Atlantic, or setting off eastward into the Indian Ocean for India and other areas of southern and eastern Asia? In *A Book of the Beginnings, vol. 1,* Gerald Massey makes it clear that:

> Ship-building yards were extant [in Egypt] and are shown to be busy in the time of the pyramid builders . . . It is the height of absurdity or the profoundest ignorance to suppose they did not build ships and launch navies. (22-23)

Massey, the reader may recall, suggests an extremely more ancient date for the Great Pyramid at Gizeh, which will be discussed in a later chapter. The point for now is that the ancient Egyptians who settled western Europe and Scandinavia must have engaged in ship-building, which their descendants—having diverged into separate tribes under varying names—continued and improved upon into historical times. This could account for the durability and seaworthiness of later Viking dragon-ships and their obvious resemblance to ancient Egyptian vessels.

We have looked at evidence demonstrating that Scandinavia was inhabited primarily by black- and dark-skinned populations at least into the 11th century and probably into the 12th. Common sense dictates the inhabitants of the area would remain at least dark-skinned for a century or two afterwards so that Snorri Sturluson could write, in the 13th century, "There are giants and dwarfs; there are *black men* and many kinds of strange tribes" in Svithjoth, or Sweden (*my emphasis, Heimskringla* 6). Using the present tense, Sturluson mentions black-skinned people inhabiting a territory western scholars are loathe to admit to—northern Europe (i.e., Russia, Sweden) in the 13th century. The reader has been presented with statements from primarily British sources attesting to the black complexions of the Britons who had long occupied the British Isles—descendants of Egyptians, Iberians and other Africoids who generally occupied western Europe from remote times; the black complexions of the Danes who invaded England throughout the 9th and 10th centuries; and we should not forget that Welsh historians "draw no clear distinction between two different groups of migrants"—supposedly white Norwegians and black Danes—referring to Norwegians and Danes as *black foreigners, black Normans, black heathens,* among other terms (Charles ix).

Fig. 15
Author Don Lake calls 10th century Danish stone motif: "A dark-skinned, wooly-haired, prominent individual." Note what might be an Asiatic or Afro-Asiatic appearance— a phenotype unlike any Caucasian. The Danes of period are invariably called black.

So, it is time to look at some of the notable personages from the sagas and historical accounts concerning the period. The brief biographies in this and proceding chapters—some, more extensive than others—will not adhere to chronological order or lines of succession, except where family ties can be easily discerned, offering more evidence of black Viking personages. For most of these personages, the evidence of their blackness is derived chiefly from their "color names" and from written assertions in historical ac—counts or the sagas that individuals were black- or dark-skinned—though some names might *not* indicate skin color. Besides "color names" like *the Black* or *the Red*—or assertions that particular individuals were dark-skinned—there is another designation that denotes a black or dark complexion: the term *grim,* which is affixed to numerous Viking names, like *Thorgrim* or *Grimhild.* This term will be explained in more detail further on when individuals with this particular affixation to their names are mentioned.

*   *   *   *   *

The kings and chieftains that follow lived from the 9th to 12th centuries—the general span of the Viking Age. It has already been established that black-skinned peoples occupied Scandinavia (as well as Germany and the British Isles) prior to the Viking Age, but *certain* information regarding chieftains and kings prior to the Viking Age is scant or nonexistent. So, we will begin with the chieftains for which *certain* evidence exists—although information regarding the first personage—Gorm the Old, an early Danish king—is not precise, or mostly lacking. The same is true of Danish kings prior to Gorm the Old. Will Durant claims that an early Danish chieftain, "Dan Mikillati, gave his name to Denmark—Dan's march or province" (502). In *The Heroic Legends of Denmark,* Axel Olrik mentions a king called Dan as the origin of the name Denmark (294), although he gives no surname. Other historians, like Gwyn Jones assert that the name Denmark (*Dan*-mark, Denimarca) was not in use until the onset of the 10th century, or about 908 (*Vikings* 114). So, while historians offer varying dates for the life and reign of Gorm the Old, as will be seen below, even less is known about Danish kings before his time; therefore he remains to many the first certifiable Danish king of note.

Gorm the Old (also Horm)

A Danish king, Gorm the Old lived during the 10th century and seems to be the first king who thought of unifying Denmark. He would not achieve this in his lifetime, but his son, Harold Gormsson (also known as Harold Bluetooth), would get credit for this achievement. His wife was named Thyri, of whom little information is known. The precise years of Gorm's birth and death are not generally agreed upon, varying according to the source. Will Durant lists his life-span as 860-935. Other sources list Gorm's death as 945, while others contend that Gorm died in 955—Harold Bluetooth becoming king after either of those years, or in 960, although Bluetooth's reign is usually given as 945-985. Another source asserts that Gorm died in 958. And Gwyn Jones states that "Gorm was dead by 950 at the latest" (*Vikings* 118).

It would be fruitless to pursue the matter further and best to conclude that such a personage did exist—the earliest mention of a truly revered king in the most royal territory of Scandinavia. But, to add one more bit of confusion, Henry Loyn, in *The Vikings in Britain,* discussing Welsh resistance to Viking attempts to settle in Anglesey, states that Rhodri Mawr, prince of Gwynedd, "defeated and killed the Danish leader Gorm in what seems to have been a campaign of more than usual importance in *855"* (*my emphasis,* 37). Whether this is another Gorm or Gorm the Old is not made clear in the text; but apparently must be an earlier Gorm, since both are listed in Loyn's index. We will leave this matter here.

All indications are that Gorm was a great warrior-chieftain who unified a large portion of the Danish mainland and islands during a turbulent reign. Although Gorm was largely successful in bringing the districts of Denmark under his control, he still had to withstand and repel incursions by Danish Vikings who had no qualms about raiding their own homelands and rejecting anyone who presumed authority over them. Perhaps the most notable point regarding Gorm the Old is that besides being the father of Harold Bluetooth, he was the grandfather of Svein Haroldsson Fork-beard, another king of Denmark, as well as the great-grandfather of Canute Sveinsson the Great, who would become King of Denmark and England in the early part of the 11th century.

Halfdan the Black (Gudrodarson)

Halfdan the Black lived during the 9th century. His father was Gudrod the Hunting King, his mother, Asa, whose father was the king of Adgir. Asa's father refused to give his daughter to Gudrod, Halfdan's father, in marriage, so Gudrod killed her father and brother and took her. Halfdan was the product of their marriage. Gudrod was killed by a spear when Halfdan was a year-old. Gudrod had one son by a previous marriage, Olaf Geirstada-Alf, who was twenty years older than his half-brother, Halfdan, and succeeded Gudrod as king of the small territories his father had held. When he was 18 years-old, Halfdan acquired the territory of Agdir and the eastern half of Vestfold, then began campaigns of conquest against kings of other nearby territories in Norway. He is described as "warlike, acquisitive, intelligent and powerful" (Jones, *Vikings* 86).

Halfdan the Black married Ragnhild, and they had a son who was named Harold, after Ragnhild's father, King Harold Goldenbeard of Sogn. *The Saga of Halfdan the Black* tells of battles of acquisition by Halfdan that cannot be included here, but he consolidated territories in southern Norway. When he was 40 years-old, he perished as he and a band of his men crossed a lake that was frozen over. It was spring and the ice covering the lake was not as solid as it seemed. Horses and men broke through and Halfdan drowned. He was so revered that men of influence from territories under Halfdan's overlordship came and prayed and asked that his body be interred in their lands. The saga says that his body was severed, including his head, and buried in mounds in four territories. These mounds are called the Mounds of Halfdan.

King Harald Fairhair (Halfdansson)

Harald Fairhair succeeded his father, Halfdan the Black, as ruler of the kingdom his father had established. The year of Harald's birth is disputed, tradition claiming c. 850, while a noted historian opines 865-870. Many dates in Norse history are not consistent, one source to another, a circumstance that cannot be rectified in this work. Since Harald was 10 years-old when his father died (c. 860, according to tradition), his maternal uncle Guthorm oversaw matters of the governance of Harald's territory as commander of the army.

Many chieftains made assaults on the territory Halfdan the Black's son had acquired. Guthorm defended the territory against these would-be usurpers and, if we are to believe the sagas, 10 or 11 year-old Harald accompanied Guthorm and his army into battle. Harold and Guthorm soon bring central Norway into their realm after more battles.

No particular years are specified for these battles, but the implication is that Harald was still quite young, perhaps no more than 13. According to Gwyn Jones, "Harold was strong-willed and energetic, with a need and desire for riches; but he had sense and judgement, too" (*Vikings* 91).

According to *The Saga of Harald Fairhair*, Harald sent messengers to bring a maiden named Gytha to him for marriage, as she had great beauty. Gytha refused his proposal but later sent word that she would become his wife only if he would conquer all Norway and become a sovereign king. Harald's messengers proposed kidnapping the maiden, but he demurred. She supposedly awakened in Harald something he had not considered before: becoming ruler of all Norway. It is at this time that Harald vows not to cut or enhance his hair by combing. He is—after the conquest of Norway—nicknamed *Fairhair* after either trimming or combing out his hair. Ordinarily, one would think the sobriquet Fairhair implied *blond* hair, as this writer did, assuming Harald had a black father and a white and blonde-haired mother in Ragnhild, whose father was nicknamed Goldenbeard. My thinking was that if Scandinavians were supposedly white and mostly fair-haired, why would Harald's fair or blond hair be notable at all? If he were dark-skinned with blond hair, that might be something that stood out to the average black- or dark-skinned Scandinavian at the time.

Modern-day anthropologists found it unusual that a percentage of black-skinned Australian Aborigines were blond-haired a century and more ago when most of them were unmixed with Europeans. A majority of Aborigine children retained their blond hair until they were six or seven years-old, then their hair darkened to red or black. But interbreeding between fair-haired Whites and naturally dark- or black-haired Blacks does produce offspring with intermediate hair coloring between the two extremes—and could have been the case with Harald who in other sagas is referred to as Harald Tangle-hair (which may simply be the translator's choice of terminology) before he unified Norway—with no indication of blondness.

More battles are fought—at Orka Dale, Trondheim, Sokskel and Vermaland. In all cases farmers of the districts were required to pay taxes to Harald; fallen chieftains either swore allegiance to Harald or were killed—if they were not killed in battle; newly won districts were incorporated into Harald's realm. The Battle of Havsfjord is mentioned as the greatest battle Harald ever fought. This battle took place in an area called Rogaland in southwestern Norway. Several enemy kings fell in what was primarily a sea battle close to shore with heavy losses on both sides. But Harald and his fleet emerged victoriously in the last battle

Harald fought in Norway. After this battle "many of the nobility fled King Harald as outlaws and went on viking (i.e., pirating) expeditions to the west" (Sturluson, *Heimskringla* 76).

King Harald Fairhair is considered the first king of Norway, or of a united Norway. There is no clear year given for this achievement, but 872 is the traditionally accepted year. Snorri Sturluson states that after Harald's conquest at Havsfjord, he sent for Gytha and had several sons with her. But he marries several other women and has many sons and daughters (op. cit. 76-7). Of his sons, the most notable were Halfdan the Black and Halfdan the White, twins born by Asa before he married Gytha; Eirik Bloodyaxe, by Ragnhild the Powerful, daughter of a king Eirik in Jutland (Denmark); and Hakon the Good, who was born in Harald's old age. Whether Harald's wives were legal wives is open to question. In the early part of his kingship Harald was still "heathen," living by traditional standards, which included concubinage. He is said to have fathered anywhere from nine to twenty sons by several mothers and was in his eighties when he died.

After uniting Norway and having married Gytha, young King Harald traveled with his retinue to Uppland where he became acquainted with a Finn named Svasi. Svasi invited the king to his home where the king encountered Svasi's daughter, Snoefrith, and was immediately smitten by the beautiful woman who poured him a drink. A burning like fire consumed Harald and he wanted to sleep with the girl that night. Svasi declared that the king could not do this except with consent and in lawful marriage. The king acquiesced and "betrothed himself to Snoefrith, and loved her so madly that he neglected his kingdom and all his duties" (Sturluson 80).

Harald and Snoefrith had four sons after which Snoefrith died, though *The Saga of Harald Fairhair* does not indicate how or why. However, according to the saga, "her color changed in no-wise, so she was as *ruddy* [i.e., dark] as when she was alive" (*my emphasis*, op. cit.). Earlier mentioned was that the Norwegian invaders of the Shetlands were dark-skinned and likened to Finns, and Snoefrith's stated complexion exemplifies this. I have also mentioned my reasoning that *ruddy* and the attachment "the Red" indicate <u>brown</u>, or a brown-skinned individual, which seems reasonable since there was extensive racial intermixing in Scandinavia throughout the Viking Age—yet there are no individuals in the sagas referred to as "the Brown." The early Finns were akin to Inuit or Eskimo peoples, and may have included Lapps. They inhabited an extensive territory called Finnmark, which spread from northern Russia to northern Sweden and Norway. Present-day Finland was merely the central portion of this expansive territory thoroughly inhabited by dark-skinned people.

At any rate, according to the saga, Harald remained by Snoefrith's side for three years hoping that Snoefrith would come back to life (the Finns were known to possess strong magical powers), and it was only after Thorleif the Wise raised up her body so Harald could smell the stench of death that the king returned to his senses. The saga states that Harald became "clear of the deception of the Finnish woman" and drove away the sons he had had with her—although I am not clear what this "deception" refers to. There is also the curious comment that these sons made to Harald—stating they wished they had "better lineage on their mother's side" (op. cit. 81)—whereupon Harald reembraced his sons by Snoefrith and they were given territories like the sons of his other wives had received.

King Harald was unrelenting in his pursuit of dominance over all of Norway, and this consumption of territory and the attendant demotion or slaying of the chieftains of formerly independent districts led to the exodus of thousands. Chieftains, their families, slaves and followers left Norway for the Hebrides, British Isles, Denmark and other locales. Most, perhaps, most sailed for the recently discovered Iceland, "which was . . . set up as a free state completely independent of Norway" (Enterline 4). Many exiles from Norway who had fled King Harald's tyranny for the Hebrides, Shetlands and Orkneys began journeying back to Norway on raiding expeditions. In response, King Harald set up naval patrols and eventually "sailed with his fleet to the Atlantic islands, and put all he caught to the sword in Shetland, Orkney and the Hebrides" (Jones, *Vikings* 90). These events took place after 874, according to traditional dating, but all of Harald's western expeditions, including incursions into Scotland, cannot be accurately delineated.

The tyranny of King Harold in Norway may, indeed, have contributed to numbers of people leaving the territory, but many historians blame this outpouring on a general desire for open land and farming space. It seemed to be in the very nature of Norsemen to be independent masters of their own districts, within families, or under chieftains who did not overburden them. Overpopulation in Denmark is often cited as the chief reason Danes began leaving Jutland for the British Isles and France from the mid-9th century onward.

Although Norway is at least three times the size of Denmark, a mountainous spine runs through it from north to south and most people settled along the western and southern coastal areas, the only areas amenable to farming and commerce. So, Norway may have, indeed, become overcrowded, spurring many inhabitants to look westward for more hospitable and less densely populated homesteads. But even if overcrowding was the chief cause of an exodus to the west, Harald's usurpation of formerly independent districts, his assigning of loyal Jarls and later his sons over them, levying taxes in those areas, and demanding ships and men to man them at his behest, must have made living in Norway more and more unbearable. Speaking of many who deserted Norway for Iceland, Gwyn Jones states:

> They resented the loss of their titles, saw no reason why they should hold their estates of the king, regarded taxes as robbery and oaths of allegiance as the diminution of a free man's dignity. (*Saga* 47)

Fig. 16
Part of a round Gold bracteate
or small disc of jewelry. Note the
Negroid visages of the faces on this
bracteate from Viking Age Sweden.

As more men and their families made ready to depart for Iceland, a fee was levied on those who would leave—with women exempted from paying the levy. Other Norsemen departed the Atlantic islands—the Shetlands, Scotland, especially Ireland—for the promising new territory that offered independence from Harald's despotism.

By most accounts, the early settlers of Iceland were heathen, worshiping the old gods—Thor, Odin, Frigg, Freyja—and they had erected monuments to them. Christians were no doubt among the early settlers, Norsemen having intermarried with Irish, Scots and Britons who had accepted the faith. But their numbers were small, and nearly a century would pass before Christianity would grow to become a larger issue in Iceland, becoming the official religion about the year 1000.

Although King Harald's fleets harried the western or Atlantic islands to bring their chieftains under his rule, the Norse who controlled large areas of Ireland and, to a lesser degree, Scotland, had attained too much power and would have presented a formidable challenge if Harald had tried to subdue them. They remained autonomous and had formed alliances with native kings and chieftains—especially through intermarriage—even though most of the native populations resented their overlordship. And if Harald had any designs on Iceland, they are not evident in the sources. He would have had to outfit at least two hundred ships with, perhaps 8,000 fighting men and spend several months away from a still-restless Norway, most of whose population generally resented him. He might not have had enough loyal followers to hold together his kingdom until he returned.

Harald continued to secure his hold on Norway, appointing his sons over various districts, sending other sons to be raised at the courts of other kings, even while they were in pre-pubescence. Two of his sons, Halfdan the Black and Sigroth, were raised at the court of Sigurth, earl of Trondheim; Rognvald was sent to Hathaland; Hakon, later to be called Hakon the Good, was sent to be raised at the court of King Aethelstan, king of England, with whom Harald had an alliance. All of Harald's progeny cannot be profiled here, and the reader can easily surmise that his daughters—and females in general—were of negligible importance. Daughters of kings and chieftains were often given in marriage to other kings and nobles for alliance purposes, and chroniclers give less attention to most of them and their fates. Often their chief contribution in life, judging by the writers of the sagas, is being the mother of a king or warrior of note.

It was King Harald's wish that his son Eirik Bloodaxe succeed him as king of Norway. Around 930 Harald, at least 80 years-old, by most accounts, installed Eirik in his high seat and gave him power over all of Norway. Eirik's succession, however, did not please several of Harald's other sons—most notably, Halfdan the Black. Skirmishing for more territory and influence ensued. King Harald, who had been physically enfeebled over the last several years of his life, died about 933, heathen to the end. He was buried in a mound by the Karmt Sound at Haugar, with a slab placed over him and loose stones strewn around the gravesite. Upon his death, Norway fell into a period of turmoil as other sons of his fought each other for rulership of the land.

Harald Bluetooth (Harald Blatonn; Harald Gormsson)

Harald Bluetooth succeeded his father Gorm the Old as king of Denmark around 950, but as noted above, dates for Gorm's death and Harald's succession differ among chroniclers. He formally became a Christian c. 960 and is credited with making Denmark a Christian country. As king, he was involved in intrigues to gain power in Norway and Sweden, even involving relatives of his, schemes too complicated to delineate here. But in one intrigue, from *The Saga of Olaf Tryggvason*, he plots with a duplicitous Earl Hakon to seize power in Norway by having his nephew, Gold-Harald—who had asked Bluetooth for joint rulership of Denmark—kill King Graycloak of Norway. But because Earl Hakon mentioned to Bluetooth that Gold-Harald had no compunction about killing King Harald for his share of Denmark, Bluetooth overlooks Earl Hakon's killing of his nephew Gold-Harald after Gold-Harald kills the Norwegian king, Harald Graycloak. King Harald Bluetooth awards Earl Hakon territories in Norway after Hakon's promise to remain loyal to him.

The reader, however, might find *The Saga of Olaf Tryggvason* somewhat difficult to follow with all the <u>Haralds</u> it mentions and its curt, shifting style. Still, it is manageable enough, and does indicate the inter-Scandinavian intrigues, shifting loyalties, quests for power and general turmoil of the period. There was also an invasion by Germans into Holstein under Otto II—Frisians, Wends, Saxons, Franks—after Danish incursions there. Danes, along with Norwegian allies, were repelled and, according to Jones, "it was under German pressure that king Harald now took steps to evangelize Norway" (*Vikings* 128). Denmark was already Christianaized, but Norwegians under heathen Earl Hakon Sigurdarson (the same Hakon who plotted with Harald Bluetooth in the deaths of King Harald Graycloak and Gold-Harald) remained fiercely resistant to the faith, and the alliance between King Harald Bluetooth and Earl Hakon was severed.

A decade later (983) Danish forces, led by Harald's son, Svein Forkbeard, drove the Germans out of Holstein at the same time King Mistivoj of Wendland, father-in-law of Harald Bluetooth, burned Hamburg and assisted Svein in Holstein—after which Har—ald became ruler of all Denmark. However, Harald had become unpopular among a large number of Danes because of his monarchical power and landholding policies and "various great lords found their ancient rights in land threatened and in some cases diminished" (op. cit. 129). And although Denmark was nominally a Christian nation, a large proportion of Danes remembered that the Church of Denmark had been established by pressure from Germany and that it acquiesced to German interests. The Danish populace resented Bluetooth for not resisting German pressure and for insisting that Danes convert to the faith. Gwyn Jones mentions that Harald Bluetooth had also lost face with Norway—a nation even more resistant to Christianity than Denmark—and with jarl (Earl) Hakon.

Svein Forkbeard demanded a share of Denmark from Harald Bluetooth, but the father would not divide his territory into two realms or give Forkbeard any part of the dominion. According to *The Saga of Olaf Tryggvason*, Svein gathered a large fleet which attacked his father's fleet at Seeland (Zealand; modern Sjeeland—the island upon which Copenhagen is situated) but was driven off when more ships arrived to aid Harald.

However, Harald was mortally wounded in the sea battle, dying within a few days.

Afterward, Svein Forkbeard becomes king of Denmark. Svein would rule Denmark until 1014, becoming a king of England shortly before his death.

Most notable, though, is that Svein Forkbeard was the father of Canute Sveinsson, whose accomplishments would far surpass those of his father and make him the most revered Norse king of the Viking Age.

Canute Sveinsson (Knut, Cnut; Canute the Great; King Canute I)

As with many Norse personages of the age, there is no precise date of birth for King Canute, a Dane, who is widely considered the most dynamic European ruler of the early Middle Ages. He is certainly regarded as the greatest of the Norse kings. One source speculates that he was born in 995. His father, Svein Forkbeard, conquered most of England during his reign. Nearly two-thirds of England had remained under the Danelaw since the last quarter of the 9th century—period when the Danes were overwhelmingly heathen. Svein Forkbeard's father, Harald Bluetooth, had accepted Christianity about 960, so Svein and the Danes of his time had also become nominally Christian, although heathenism lingered in both England and Denmark.

In the territory of the Danelaw in England, Danish Vikings accepted the repugnant faith out of expedience rather than a sincere love of The Christ. As they hoped to enhance their standing among their subjects, Danish chieftains converted to make relations between themselves and their English charges more amenable in regard to trade, marriage, alliances and general intercourse. However, as historian Henry Loyn observes: "Conversion did not necessarily involve savage rejection of all the attributes of the old religion; paganism lingered on in out-of-the-way places, tolerated and ineffective" (52).

For Harald Bluetooth and Svein Forkbeard, accepting Christianity was a way of endearing Denmark to the ever-widening power of the popes of Rome whose influence had overspread most of western Europe—the British Isles, France, Italy, Germany—and was expanding in Iberia. In northern Iberia (i.e., Spain), Christians had begun an effort to drive back the Islamic and primarily African Moors who had conquered the whole peninsula two-and-a-half centuries before, an effort that would take more than six centuries.

The primarily German or Germanic Holy Roman Empire (a term, the reader will recall, was applied centuries later by Western historians and was not in vogue at the time) had expanded its territory into central Europe to become the most powerful bulwark of the Christian Church, and conflicts with the German Duchy of Saxony had been increasing since the last half of the 10th century. In England, resistance to the Danelaw continued throughout most of the 10th century, and the Viking hold on the country was being seriously challenged. In the spring of 1013 Svein Forkbeard invaded England, bringing Canute with him and placing him in charge of the fleet left at Sandwich while he ven—tured north to Gainsborough, where he was recognized as king by Northumbria and the Five Boroughs before marching south to secure other districts. Ethelred, the English king based in London, continued his resistance to Danish domination. With his Danish Viking ally, Thorkell the Tall, who had sworn allegiance to Ethelred hoping to himself gain prominance in England, Ethelred fought skirmishes in southern England against the onrushing Danes under Svein. Ethelred and his family finally fled to Normandy. In five months Svein had become the ruler of all England and is considered one of the leading Viking kings. During his reign he had taken Hedeby from the Germans, strengthened Danish influence in Wendland and Norway, and become the undisputed king of England. But a month-and-a-half after becoming master of England, he died at the age of 55, in February, 1014.

The young Canute, no more than 18 or 19 years-old, lacked political and military experience, however, Svein's men extended their allegiance to him. Despite Svein's accomplishment, the English were not totally subdued. They invited Ethelred to return from Normandy, and he promptly set about raising an army to repel the Danes. Canute and his fleet embarked for Denmark where Harald, his elder brother, was king, succeeding Svein. With the help of Harald and Eirik of Hladir, a Norwegian ruling a portion of Norway by Danish permission and who was also a son-in-law of Svein, Canute gained considerable knowledge state and military affairs. Then, strangely, Thorkell the Tall abandoned the returned king Ethelred and sailed to Denmark with nine ships, offering allegiance to Canute.

In the summer of 1015 Canute's powerful fleet sailed to England. He defeated English armies in Wessex and Warwickshire, effectively taking half of the country. Then he moved north to York and won Northumbria, putting it under Eirik of Hladir.

Afterwards, Canute's fleet sailed for London where his troops were vigorously opposed by the army of King Edmund (who had become king upon the death of his father, Ethelred). Edmund drove the Danes back in London and at Oxford, slaying all the Danes he could. Then at Ashington, in Essex, Edmund and his army were soundly defeated, especially after Eadric and his men fled the battlefield, and Jones notes: "All the flower of the English nation" were destroyed in this Danish victory (*Vikings* 371). King Edmund (Ironside) fled to Gloucestershire, and Canute pursued him there. An agreement was accomplished there without fighting; Edmund could continue control of Wessex, but Canute would have control of the rest of the country. Perhaps it was in respect for a valiant youth near his own age that Canute and his forces did not press on until the total annihilation of Edmund and his beleaguered army. Allowing Edmund to rule the substantial territory of Wessex in southernmost England would surely lead to future conflict; however, Edmund died in November of 1015 at the age of 22, and all of England accepted Canute as its king, even though he was younger than King Edmund had been.

Canute divided England, maintaining Wessex under his control. Eirik Hladir was awarded Northumbria, and Thorkell the Tall was given East Anglia. Eadric Streona was given Mercia, but he was later murdered and Mercia was given to Eirik Hladir, who would die in 1023. In 1017, Canuate married Emma, widow of Ethelred and, although the English Aelgifu of Northampton was already his consort, Canute's children by

Emma would be destined for the English throne—taking precedence over Emma's sons by Ethelred and any children Canute had by Aelgifu.

Canaute's brother Harald, king of Denmark, died in 1018-19, and Canute returned to Denmark to succeed Harald as king there. The untrustworthy Thorkell the Tall remained in England, but one of his sons was given territory in Denmark. Thorkell died in 1023 eliciting no grief from Canute. Norway was nominally under the overlordship of Denmark, but there was some resistance to Danish authority in many districts. Olaf Haraldsson, later to be called Saint Olaf, came to power in Norway and challenged Denmark's claim to the country. Canaute spent most of his time in England, considering it his most important possession. His chief aide, Eirik Hladir, was often with him and away from Norway where he wielded much influence. Olaf Haraldsson defeated pro-Danish forces in the south of Norway in 1015 and declared himself king of that country.

Olaf (later to become Saint Olaf) was born in 995 and began his viking (pirating) escapades at the age of 12. He was not tall, but of medium height, and he possessed great strength. Snorri Sturluson describes his appearance thusly: "His hair was of light chestnut color and his face, broad, of light complexion, and *ruddy*" (*my emphasis, Heimskringla* 243). He was skilled in the use of weapons, especially hurling spears. By all accounts, he was an able, effective ruler. He was baptized while in Normandy in 1013 and is most renowned for bringing Chris—tianity to all of Norway. As touched upon earlier, his methods to effect conversion were often ruthless and extreme—blinding or maiming the recalcitrant, and driving them from their lands. He had more trouble organizing a state church for Norway, but eventually succeeded in doing this. "But one thing is clear," states Gwyn Jones. "[B]y the time he died Norway was a Christian country, and no relapse into heathendom was possible" (*Vikings* 378).

He is said to have brought Norway into the expanding European family, "the fuller European civilization of the time" (op. cit. 377). But he had a mean streak, which was exhibited when the Swedish king, seeking to claim Norwegian territory, sent tax-gatherers to several Norwegian districts. Olaf had them hanged and let the twelve bodies hang from a ridge so ravens could tear the flesh off their bodies for sport and as a warning to the Swedish king. However, several years later, c. 1025 or 1026, Olaf formed an anti-Danish alliance with King Onund-Jakob of Sweden.

When Olaf and Onund-Jakob began to harry Zealand and Skane, Canute returned to Denmark with a fleet and organized a second fleet of Danes and set off for Zealand, prompting Olaf's fleet to depart for Skane where it joined the Swedish fleet. Both fleets then ceased attacks, taking defensive positions at the mouth of Helga-a, Holy River, on the Baltic side of Skane. Canute's fleet met them there and a battle was fought. By most accounts the battle was indecisive, though some say that one side or the other won a victory. In the immediate aftermath, the Swedish fleet headed for home with only minor casualties. Olaf, not wanting to risk being attacked in the Oresund (The Sound; the channel between Zealand and Sweden), abandoned his ships and returned overland to Norway. Canute returned to Denmark, his reputation and standing intact.

In 1028 Canute assembled a powerful fleet that sailed up the western coastline of Noway to the Trondheim area. He was unopposed, as Olaf could not gather enough men to aid him, and former allies in battle deserted him. Canute, on the other hand, was hailed wherever he put ashore and soon after was accepted as Norway's king. He even gained some influence in Sweden in 1030. His official empire included all of England and Wessex, the Earldom of Orkney, which included the northern part of Scotland (al—though most of Scotland and Wales remained independent), all of Denmark, all of Norway, and the southern end of Sweden (with influence farther north)—which was incor—porated into Denmark. Canute gave the kingship of Denmark to his son Hordacanute (also Hordaknut), and Norway was given to his son Svein by his English wife, Aelgifu, who accompanied her son to Norway where she would be an unpopular queen. Both sons would encounter difficulties holding together the kingdom Canute had established.

Canute died in 1035, having strung together a kingdom whose territory spanned the North Sea and did bring about a relative stability to northern Europe. The brazen, far-flung, violent pillaging raids of two-and-a-half centuries had diminished, and Canute's journey to Rome in 1026 for the coronation of Emperor Conrad II brought him the blessing of the pope. Although pockets of the old religion continued to endure in the four nations Canute had made his, Scandinavia was effectively Christianized, earning acceptance into an expanding Europe.

Some historians refer to Canute's realm as an empire, others call it a kingdom. The latter seems most appropriate since the term empire implies something more enduring. There is also the implication of control in empire, of a central government with the ability to rein in or subdue any dissident parts of the realm, punish any offender under laws understood and accepted by all its inhabitants. We need not mention the Roman or Persian empires that were much longer-lived; even the empire of Alexander cannot be included with the former because it lacked cohesion, universally accepted laws of governance, a pacified populace, as well as longevity. The empire of Canute, like Alexander's, did not last more than a decade, and opposition to his rule never totally ceased. The Kingdom of Canute is a more accurate appellation for the territories this Danish monarch brought under his control and, although fighting, rebellions and fratricides resumed upon his death, the breadth of Europe was expanded to the far north into an area that had previously been considered alien and unapproachable.

Olaf Haraldsson (Olaf the Stout; Saint Olaf)

Birth information on Olaf Haraldsson was given in the biography of Canute Sveinsson, above. In his early years, he was known as Olaf the Stout, presumably because he was somewhat portly. He was born a pagan, was a Viking warrior at the age of 12, and was a descendant of Harald Fairhair. While still a young boy, he was called "king" by his crew because of his connection to the family of Norwegian king Harald Fairhair. He had an extremely adventurous early career, raiding and fighting in battles from Scandinavia to France and Spain. About 1011 or 1012, Olaf (born in 995) allied himself to English king Aethelred II, fighting against the Danes who had driven him out of England and France. Repulsed by Danish forces in England, Olaf eventually went to France and was baptized a Christian in 1013. Returning to Norway in 1015, he fought for and conquered territory held by Danish forces. All of his battles and adventures cannot be recounted here, but after his return to Norway he was proclaimed king and resolutely undertook the task of converting Norway to Christianity.

Saint Olaf's Saga, describes Olaf as having hair of a light chestnut color, a broad face, and having a light complexion, which is ruddy. As earlier touched upon, the color b<u>rown</u> does not seem to have come into vogue during the Viking Age—or even by saga writer Snorri Sturluson's time (i.e., the 13th century). Norse color-name attachments were *the Black, the Red, the White* and sometimes *the Tawny, the Red* certainly indicating a brown-skinned individual—whatever shade of brown he might have been. There are no *the Brown* appellations that I have come across. Olaf's above description indicates that he could have been referred to as *the Red* or *the Tawny* if *the Stout* had not been so early attached to his name. The description of his face and stature reminds one of the dark-skinned Norwegians who arrived in the Shetlands at the close of the 7th century. Olaf was also a descendant of the royal Ynglings, originally from Denmark, who early spread into Norway, the isles of the Kattegat Strait and Sweden, and who were black-skinned, as the reader has been presented with abundant evidence of.

Even as Norsemen were expanding into other areas of Europe, rivalries between the rulers of Denmark, Sweden and Norway never abated for very long, never long enough for them to put aside ancient rivalries and realize that, with unity, they could effectively rule nearly all of Europe. Initially at odds with King Olaf of Sweden, Olaf of Norway and the Swedish king reconciled their differences, viewing the expansion of the empire of King Canute as a threat to both their realms. Olaf married the Swedish king's daughter, Astrid and, states Gwyn Jones, "[c]ommon interest and fear of the Danes brought about an alliance of Norway and Sweden" (*Vikings* 379). King Olaf of Sweden died in 1022, and Olaf of Norway made a compact with his son Onund (sharing the kingship of Sweden with his brother Olaf Skottkonung) to invade Denmark. This impelled King Canute to return, in person, to Denmark (1025-1026) at the head of a large fleet which drove Olaf's invading fleet out of the Kattegat Strait and forced Olaf to flee to Sweden and then Russia, where he began making preparations for another invasion of Denmark.

Although the inhabitants of Norway longed to be free of foreign rule (i.e., the Danish king Canute), many others had accepted Canute's overlordship. When Olaf returned to Norway in 1030 with a force of 3,600 men, "made up of Norwegians from his own southeastern part of Norway, Swedes, and an assortment of unidentifiable riff-raff, many of them heathens" (op. cit. 383), he was opposed by a force of 14,400 men, most of whom were Norwegians opposed to his return. At Stiklarstadir, north of Trondheim on the western coast of Norway, Olaf's forces were defeated and Olaf was killed in the land battle. Norway was now securely part of the Kingdom of Canute. King Canute would die five years later in 1035, and his "empire" would soon after begin to disintegrate.

Legends would grow about the holiness of King Olaf, "of the maimed or blind or dead made whole by his blood" (op. cit. 385). A cult worshiping his legend and his miracles arose and spread throughout northern Europe and Russia, and he would soon after be declared a true saint. His greatest accomplishment was transforming Norway into a Christian country, a feat the Fathers of the Church in Rome must have been abundantly pleased about. The Church's grand stratagem had ultimately proved effective, forestalling the expansion of predominantly black-skinned Norsemen into other areas of Europe, which may eventually have threatened he existence of the Church of Rome itself.

What Norse kings hoped to procure from allegiance to the pope in Rome, what they were promised in return—other than acceptance into a Church-dominated amalgam of ever-changing European principalities which would one day coalesce into a monolithic continental entity—is a question that cannot be answered with absolute accuracy. On the other hand, when Norse chieftains and kings who had converted to Christianity began insisting that their recalcitrant followers convert, dissension ensued in the Viking ranks; numerous Vikings fled their homelands for the new settlements in Iceland and Greenland; and as Norsemen in Europe grudgingly submitted to the insistent demands of their great kings, Norse assaults into new areas of Europe practically ceased. The artifice of the Fathers of the Church brought about the abandonment of Thor, Odin, Freyia and Frigg for a less tangible god whose visage was comprehended through increasingly whitened renderings of Jesus Christ and Mother Mary; and the fact that these had been borrowed and re-worked from the far more ancient Egyptian Isis and Horus had already been forgotten—or totally unknown by the masses of Christianized Europe.

One might view the Norse conversion to Christianity and the forsaking of their old gods as a positive advance toward civilization, an emergence from heathenism, blood sacrifice and benightedness. One might, as white historians generally do, regard the Vikings as barbaric, irreverent, warlike and in dire need of redemption, which conversion to Christianity ultimately brought them. Whatever one's feelings, and however much one may view Christianity or the Catholicism of this early period as the true religion, the forced and widely undesired conversion to Christianity was psychologically detrimental to the Norse peoples. Their old gods and old religion made Norsemen who they were, allowed them a clear interpretation of their world; made them itinerant beings unbound by any laws but their own, fearful of no gods but those whose guidance had enriched them wherever they raided or journeyed; and whose omens, seen in nature, in the clouds or in dreams, had often came to pass. When Norsemen were wrenched from what was tangible to them and thrust into an intangible spirituality, a mental limbo arose which sapped them of their former power and dynamism.

Does this scenario sound familiar to the reader?

*   *   *   *   *

By the onset of the 11th century, the Fathers of the Church were exultant, observing the effect their psychological artifice had had on these once powerful black-skinned Europeans they had never considered part of their vision of Europe. Their insidious mas—ter plan had succeeded beyond their trepidatious expectations, and its effectiveness would be duly noted for future Church designs. *The Norsemen were, in effect, the first black-skinned people psychologically assailed with the weapon of Christianity—a white-skinned Jesus at its head denoting a white-skinned God.* The success of this psychological assault against the Norsemen is the primary reason white Europeans would thereafter employ the same stratagem to disunite, confuse, subdue, divide, conquer or destroy every black- or dark-skinned people they came into contact with in other parts of the world. Every single one.

If the reader cannot fathom this now, he or she will be given ample proof further on. An entire book could be written to illustrate how Europeans used Christianity to undermine dark-skinned nations and peoples, the effects of which are still evident today.

Along with the introduction of Christianity by Europeans to black- and dark-skinned people came superior weapons, division, murder, slavery, licentiousness, loss of freedom, territory, and sometimes genocide. No one should be offended by these remarks, for even a cursory glance at the history of Africa and the Americas over the last five-hundred years will validate them. The Norsemen were too powerful, too fearless, and too numerous to suffer the fates of West Africans, (sub-Saharan Africans, in general), Native Americans and Australian Aborigines. Like these peoples would in the future, Norsemen lost the underpinnings of their own faith and the intrepid, irreverent spirit that once made white Europeans tremble and flee at the sight of their dragon-ships skulking off-shore or slinking upriver.

The names of the above-mentioned Norse kings and the names of Norsemen to follow in the next two chapters may cause the reader to drift back to an assumption that the individuals being spoken of are Caucasian, or white personages—so-called *Nordics*. Western historians have presented them as such for so long, and more than 90 percent of books written on the Vikings proclaim this view. A miniscule percentage of Viking books mention race, but these are often unknown to the average reader or else difficult to locate—most readers not venturing beyond the popular books in bookstores. Although I have endeavored to accurately identify certain European races as black- or dark-skinned, several have been problematic primarily because Eurocentric historians (and our knowledge that modern Europeans are white-skinned) have always implied their whiteness. If the reader finds him—or herself drifting back to familiar, long-entrenched visions of white, "Nordic" Vikings and other European peoples mentioned in this work, the following quote from David MacRitchie's *Accounts of the Gypsies of India* should be instructive, tying in peoples who have been mentioned:

> The early Saxons and Danes . . . are understood to have been "Goths," and to have painted and tattooed their skins. Now, these people are spoken of as *nigrae gentes, dubh galls* or *black heathen,* in our early records; and at a later time, as "Saracens," this last being a common appellation of "Moors" and gypsies . . . . The result . . . of a few glances at the recognized "Goths" of Europe, is not contradictory to the theory "that the Jauts are related to the ancient Getae or Goths." (89-90)

The above-mentioned Jauts MacRitchie refers to are a people of supposedly Indian origin who came to be known as *Gypsies*, a people who will be discussed in some detail further on. For now, understand that MacRitchie links old Saxons, Danes, Moors, Goths and Saracens, calling them essentially the same people known under different names—all of whom were dubh galls (black strangers), nigrae gentes (black people), and black heathen in early historical records.

Historians and anthropologists of the last major race to attain civilization—acquiring it from the black- and dark-skinned civilizations which preceded them in Africa, Asia *and* Europe, and who, after their emergence, were confined to Europe until Columbus' voyages opened the floodgates to the rest of the world for them—tout Caucasians as the preeminent civilizers of the world. For maximum effect, the presence of black- and dark-skinned people in Europe was erased, or else, black-skinned people were declared to have been white, blond and blue-eyed to remove any indication that Blacks ever resided in Europe, ever played a part in events that changed or affected European civilization. The Black Norsemen of early Middle Ages Europe were transformed into fierce white men by Western historians to expurgate the stigma of black men dominating the continent only a millennium ago. *Who* decided to transform the Vikings into white, blue-eyed, blond-haired "Nordics," and when that decision was made, I cannot say and have not investigated. But such a decision was made and has been adhered to by the vast majority of Eurocentric historians to this day.

If the term *revisionist* comes to mind in regard to this work, I submit that it should rightly be applied to those historians and writers who deliberately ignored early historical works referring to Norsemen, especially Danes, as "Dubh Gaill," "dubh Gennti," "gentiles Nigri," "y Normanyeit duon," and "dieifyl du"—Black Foreigners, black gentiles, the black host, black Normans, black devils—in English, Welsh and Irish historical accounts. These same historians and writers, as well, overlook physical descriptions of Viking personages in the sagas, falsely attributing color-names to hair color, body painting or the dark-colored coats-of-mail they often wore. Twentieth and 21st century authors could have found a mass of information on Vikings in MacRitchie's *Ancient and Modern Britons* (published in 1884), but this monumental work describes them as black-skinned, which does not fit the Eurocentric matrix and it continues to be overlooked. That being said, let us move on to other Norse personages from the sagas whose color-names, and in some cases, physical descriptions, indicate their probable complexions.

CHAPTER 11

NOTABLE BLACK NORSEMEN FROM THE SAGAS

Having looked at some of the early kings involved with the beginnings of Norway and Denmark (those of Sweden are less known and were not focused on), let us now look at a number of personages mentioned in the sagas whose names indicate that they were black- or dark-skinned. Like the kings and chieftains in the previous chapter, they must remain, for the most part, faceless. They have not been immortalized in serious films (only a half-dozen or so Viking movies have been made by American and British companies, and Vikings were portrayed as white); there are no busts or statuary of famous Viking kings like those of early Roman or Greek emperors and statesmen (the reader can easily visualize sandal- and toga-clad Greeks or Romans) and centuries of the white-washing of history has rendered it difficult to imagine black men manning ships, dictating laws, running white people out of towns and villages—not to mention slaying and enslaving them, and having their way with captured or subjugated white women. However, this is what the Dubh Gaill, dubh Gennti and gentiles nigri were doing—just over 900 years ago in Europe (i.e., from c. 700-1100 A.D.), despite the reticence and omissions of Western historians.

The biographies that follow present individuals whose names are referred to as "color names" by David MacRitchie; individuals who may not have had color names, but are described as black- and dark-skinned in the sagas or in historical accounts; personages who were the offspring of persons with color names, or offspring of persons described as black- or dark-skinned whose parent or parents were *not* known by a color name. One of these latter was Aud the Deep-minded (Aud Ketilsdottir) whose father, Ketil Flatnose (Caitill Finn), was mentioned in an earlier chapter and is described by MacRitchie as black-skinned and probably of the Ugrian race. We have to assume his daughter, Aud, was also black- or dark-skinned even if her mother, Yngvild, was a white woman (which is unascertained)—though she probably was not.

Some of the biographies will be very brief, others longer and more detailed. Some personages have been mentioned earlier, but most will be names of persons not previously mentioned. Attention has not been given to chronological or alphabetical order, and related or incidental information will be presented—in some cases expanding on previously mentioned points.

If the reader has not caught on to it yet, many Norse offspring were bestowed with names identifying them with their *fathers* so that people would know what family line they came from. So, for instance, Ketil Flatnose's daughter, Aud, was called Aud Ketilsdottir—*the Deep-minded* being affixed to her name when she became an adult, or when she exhibited a particular talent. Eirik (Thorvaldsson) the Red's son, Leif became Leif Eiriksson. Norse peoples did not carry family names down generation to generation as we are in the habit of doing today. Their naming system was anciently developed, tribal, and served them adequately when Norse groups moved together as related and extended family members and relatives through marriage who maintained ties and bonds of friendship. These groups, of course, would expand as their associated Norse family groups expanded, often added to by the servants many families had as well as the slaves they owned, worked their farmsteads and in some cases became accepted as family members.

The notoriety of significant Norsemen—known for a special talent, bravery or fighting skill, or for honesty—or chieftains would spread to neighboring territories, or become known throughout the realm, and a person meeting his son or daughter would know who the father was and what family he or she derived from. So, the Norse naming system was appropriate in its day—a time when the world was smaller.

Ottar the Black

A poet, probably Norwegian, who was a fixture in the court of King Olaf Haraldsson (St. Olaf) of Norway. He wrote poetry (or merely recited poetry) depicting Harald's exploits over many years.

Gizur the Black

A contemporary of Ottar the black, above, who was also in the court of King Olaf. He is called a "skald"—an Old Norse term for poet. Both Gizur and Ottar the Black were in the court of King Olaf at the same time. Gizur the Black also served as intercessor to the king.

Thorfinn the Black of Snos

In 12th century Norway Thorfinn the Black of Snos was an ally of King Eystein while various chieftains fought over rulership of the country. Thorfinn led a troop of Viking fighters which aided the new king in subduing the Trondheim and Uppland districts.

Atli

There is not much information in *Heimskringla* about this person except that he was the father of Barth the Black. In the 11th century a Wendish army invaded Denmark (c. 1043). King Magnus defeated the Wends but had many wounded men. King Magnus picked out twelve men who had the softest palms and said they should bandage the wounded. Although none of them had experience of this sort:

> . . . they all became most excellent physicians. There were two Icelanders among them,
> Thorkel Geirason . . . and Atli, the father of Barth the Black in Selar Dale, and from
> them are descended many physicians in later times. (Sturluson, *Heimskringla* 563)

I have, however, not found much more information on Barth the Black.

Several more Atlis are mentioned in *Heimskringla*, the most notable being the legendary Atli, king of the Huns—or Attila, mentioned earlier. Atli was a common name during the Viking Age, although I have not yet discovered a written source placing Attila the Hun in Scandinavia. As mentioned earlier, Denmark and other areas of Scandinavia were part of Attila's expansive empire in the mid-5th century, so numerous Huns must have gone there and remained; perhaps Attila, himself, resided there at some point.

Atli—*Attila*—became a fairly common name in Scandinavia. There are five mentioned in *Heimskringla*, and several more in sagas not included in *Heimskringla*. The histories written about the Huns of the mid-5th century concern themselves with the Hunnish attacks on the Roman Empire, the Balkans, Germany, France and Italy. Hunnish incursions into more northerly regions of Europe are only hinted at. But why would historical atlases show Denmark and other areas of Scandinavia as part of Attila's empire if Huns did not invade or reside in them? And then there is the question of why so many Norsemen in the sagas were called Atli—the Norse name for Attila.

What is missing—what I have not yet found—are written records detailing when and how the events leading to the Hunnish acquisition of Scandinavian lands took place. Although it is widely known that Attila's European empire spread from the Urals to the Rhine, historical atlases also show the southern half of Sweden included in it. Could Attila's territory have been more expansive than we have been informed? For now, consider a comment from Otto J. Maenchen-Helfin's *The World of the Huns,* which hints at Hunnish activity in the far north:

> Mommsen [a historian] thought that the islands in the ocean over which Attila was said to rule were the British Isles, Thompson [another historian] thinks of Bornholm in the Baltic Sea . . . . (125)

Bornholm is an island about 25 miles or so to the southeast of southern Sweden currently belonging to Denmark. And the fact that the sagas include at least a dozen Atlis tells us that a sizeable portion of information regarding the Huns in Scandinavia and the far north has yet to be discovered or else remains hidden by Western historians.

Bjorn Buna (Grimsson)

Son of Grim of Sogn, who was a *hersir* (i.e., a local leader whose rank was hereditary). Notably. he was the father of Ketil Flatnose.

Ketil Flatnose (Caitill Finn)

Discussed in an earlier chapter, Ketil Flatnose was a hersir from Raumarike (i.e., Norway). He married Yngvild, who bore him two sons, Bjorn and Helgi and three daughters—Aud the Deep-minded, Thorunn Hyrna and Jorunn Manivitsbrekka. When Harald Fairhair became king of Norway, many Norwegians fled Norway for the Orkneys, the Hebrides (island groups off the northern and western coasts of Scotland) and Iceland.

King Harald Fairhair chose Ketil Flatnose as the leader of an army that was sent west to extend Harald's control to those island groups. At first, Ketil refused, but then he lead the force to the west when Harald insisted.

Flatnose became ruler of the Hebrides, forming alliances with the most influential leaders in those isles. *The Saga of the People of Eyri* informs us:

> He [Flatnose] sent his army back east to Norway, and when they returned to King Harald they announced that Ketil Flat-nose was the leader of the Hebrides but that they were not certain whether he had extended Harald's realm into the Western Isles. When the king heard this, he confiscated Ketil's estates in Norway. (74)

Years later, Ketil's son, Bjorn Ketilsson, journeyed to Norway to take back his and his father's estates from Harald's appointed agents. The saga is unclear about how successful Bjorn was.

When Bjorn returned to the Hebrides, Ketil had died, but his brother and a sister allowed him to stay at their estate. But, says the saga:

> Bjorn became aware that they [his siblings] now practiced a different religion, and he found it degrading that they had rejected the traditional faith their ancestors had revered . . . [W]hen they discovered that he was not receptive to his family's ideas, they named him Bjorn the Easterner and took a dim view of his reluctance to settle there. (op. cit. 77)

After staying two years in the Hebrides, Bjorn the Easterner emigrated to Iceland.

Though Ketil Flatnose was sent to the Hebrides to quell a revolt against King Harald's rule, some historical accounts have him subduing these islands on his own.

He was of noble descent and attained both power and wealth while in the Hebrides. As discussed earlier, he more than likely was black-skinned and seems to have possessed an Ugrian (i.e., black Mongoloid or Australoid) appearance (see MacRitchie, *Ancient and Modern Britons, vol. 1,* 119).

If Ketil Flatnose was black-skinned, we do not need to rely on DNA to understand that his offspring—Aud, Bjorn, Helgi, Thorunn Hyrna and Jorunn—were also black- or dark-skinned, whatever the racial makeup of their mother, Yngvild (whose name hints that she was related to the royal race of Danes—the Ynglings—who were Blacks).

Helgi Ketilsson (Bjolan)

A son of Ketil Flatnose, brother of Aud the Deep-minded. Emigrated to Iceland and was there to welcome his sister, Aud, when she sailed there from the Orkneys.

Bjorn Ketilsson (Bjorn the Easterner)

Another son of Ketil Flatnose, brother of Helgi and of Aud the Deep-minded. From the Hebrides, he embarked on a mission to recover his father's estates in Norway after they are confiscated by King Harald Fairhair (see biography of Ketil Flatnose, above). Bjorn Ketilsson emigrated to Iceland from Norway or the Hebrides and is called the first of the Icelandic settlers to die (*Saga of the People of Eyri* 78).

Aud Ketilsdottir (Aud the Deep-minded; Unn the Deep-Minded

Aud the Deep-minded was a daughter of Ketil Flatnose, who was a hersir in Norway and became a more powerful hersir in the Hebrides. As in the case of most women in the Viking world, there is no early history of Aud. She is heard of when she is taken to wife by Olaf the White, of Norwegian extraction, who conquered Dublin after many expeditions around Britain. He declared himself king of Dublin and fought battles with Danish Vikings to keep Dublin under Norwegian control.

Aud the Deep-minded and Olaf the White had a son who was named Thorstein the Red (if Olaf the White was indeed Caucasian, *the Red* attached to Thorstein's name would indicate he was the product of mixed-race parentage, having a brown, light-brown, or reddish-brown complexion—Aud being black- or dark-skinned). Olaf the White, according to MacRitchie, also married another woman, a daughter of Norse chieftain Kenneth MacAlpin, and produced a child or two with her. Several years later, Olaf was killed in battle, and Aud and son, Thorstein the Red, went to the Hebrides, her father's old territory. There, Thorstein married and had children. He became a warrior-king and conquered half of Scotland, having made alliances with several Scottish tribes. Later, the Scots betrayed him, and he died in battle—the fate of most warrior-chieftains during the period.

After Aud learned of her son's death, she had her family and companions secretly build a knorr (sometimes knarr) in the forest. A knorr was a merchant ship, shorter and bulkier than the usual longships of the day. It had a single, large square sail for propulsion and had a deep draft. Knorrs were generally 45-50 feet in length, sturdy and ideal for beach landings. When the knorr was finished, Aud, her family members and companions sailed to the Orkneys, where one of her daughters, Groa (perhaps Aud had remarried), was married to Earl Thorfinn the Skull-splitter. Afterwards, Aud sailed to Iceland where she claimed a large territory and settled in Hvamm. She was accompanied by some family members and men who had been prisoners of Vikings, called bondsmen.

She allotted farm sites to most of these and became a matron of influence on the fledgling island-nation. Having been baptized a Christian, she had crosses erected on Krossholar Hill, and she was buried, when she died, below high-water mark so that she would have to lie in unconsecrated earth "like her heathen neighbors" (Jones, *Vikings* 277). Her death occurred during ongoing conflict in Iceland between Christianity and the Old Religion, of which more will be said further on.

Although there is not a lot of information about Aud Ketillsdottir the Deep-minded, the reader will not easily find a Viking woman more written about during the age. She was certainly proud and resilient;

daughter of a chieftain, who married a warrior-chieftain, and produced a warrior-chieftain in Thorstein the Red. When Thorstein was killed, she would not be content to live under the rule of some other warlord or under Harald Fairhair's despotic rule. In middle age, she carved out a new life for herself, setting sail for a newly discovered land that did not promise much except freedom from tyranny for her, her family and companions.

Earl Thorfinn (Thorfinn Sigurdarson)

David MacRitchie describes Earl Thorfinn as a "notable Black Dane . . . the most distinguished of all the earls in the islands" (*Britons* 117). He was a mere five years-old when King Malcolm of the Scots gave him the title of earl and the territory of Caithness to rule. He was 14 when he began warring against the territories of other princes, his greatest achievement being the defeat of the army of Kali Hundason, who was king of the Scots.

Earl Thorfinn's career is one of the most dynamic and turbulent of the Viking Age. His rulershsps of Caithness and the Orkneys was frought with battles, enmity between himself and relatives—like his brother, Earl Einar, and his nephew, Rognvald Brusason—and intrigues involving King Olaf of Norway. At times he was impelled to cede part of his territory to one or another of his relatives who had made a pact with King Olaf, and he had a tenuous relationship with King Magnus who succeeded Olaf as king of Norway. Earl Thorfinn's exploits are too numerous to delineate here but can be found in *Orkneyinga Saga*. When he did have to cede some part of his territory, it was never for very long; he would muster troops from Scotland (being on good terms with the Scottish king), the Hebrides or the Orkneys, despite the odds sometimes seeming to be against him, and regain what he had lost.

When his nephew, Rognvald, made a pact with King Magnus of Norway to secure his share of the Orkneys bequeathed to him by his father, Brusi, he sailed back to the Orkneys in mid-winter after leaving Norway and learned that Thorfinn and a small force of his men were wintering in Mainland, the largest Orkney island. Thorfinn and his group suspected nothing until their attackers had blocked every door of the house. Most of his men were asleep but Thorfinn was still drinking. Smelling smoke, Thorfinn roused his men and told them to ask who was responsible. They were told it was Rognvald.

Thorfinn's men ran for their weapons, but there was no way to unblock the doors to get outside. Rognvald yelled out he would allow the women and slaves out but that Thorfinn and his men would remain inside to die. Womenfolk and slaves were helped outside through the smoke. The house was burning fast. Somehow, Earl Thorfinn broke out through a wooden wall and carried out his wife, Ingibjorg in his arms. The pitch-dark night and smoke allowed him to escape from the house undetected by Rognvald's men. He found a small boat and rowed off to Caithness that same night. The farmhouse burned to ashes as did those trapped inside, and everyone thought that Thorfinn had died as well.

Afterwards, Rognvald sent envoys to the Hebrides and Caithness claiming all the territory Earl Thorfinn had ruled. Thorfinn, meanwhile, was in Caithness living secretly with friends in several places. Just before Christmas, Rognvald and his men were feasting on Stronsay Island. He had put all of the Orkneys under his authority and, with no more worries about Earl Thorfinn, their feast was particularly jubilant. After a while they heard wood being heaped in front of the door and discovered they had been surrounded by Earl Thorfinn and his men. The house was set on fire, and Thorfinn said everyone could leave except Rognvald's men. When most of the women and servants had been let out, a man wearing a long nightshirt appeared in the doorway. The man suddenly vaulted over the woodpile past the circle of Thorfinn's men and ran into the night.

Thorfinn said that Rognvald was the only man able to execute such a feat and ordered his men to split into several groups and apprehend him. Rognvald was found among rocks by the shore. The men who found him were reluctant to slay him, so Thorkel the Fosterer stepped forward to do the deed, having sworn to do anything to aid Earl Thorfinn.

Thorfinn and his men killed all of Rognvald's companions, and Thorfinn claimed all of Orkney and the territories Rognvald had usurped. His territories included all of Orkney, all of the Hebrides, nine

Scottish earldoms, and a large portion of Ireland when he died in 1064 or 1065. So the events in the life of Earl Thorfinn were part of the turbulent 11th century, although precise dates for these events are difficult to pin down. Before his death, Earl Thorfinn visited, and received a warm welcome from Harold, another king of Norway, King Svein of Denmark, and Emperor Henry of Saxony, before traveling to Rome where he received an audience and absolution from the Pope. After this, he returned to Orkney and had a church built, Christchurch at Birsay, where was buried.

Thorhall the Hunter (or Huntsman)

As earlier mentioned, Thorhall the Hunter was a navigator familiar with "unchartered [uncharted] and uninhabitable parts" of the northern seas (Luke, *African Presence* 228). As noted previously, he was "a large men, and strong, black, and like a giant, silent and foul-mouthed in his speech" (MacRitchie, *Britons* 117). For many years he was a trusted companion of Erik the Red, accompanying Erik on summer hunting expeditions. Around the onset of the 11th century, he served aboard Thorvard's ship which carried Northmen to the coasts of Iceland, Greenland, and Helluland, which was the Norse name for Baffin Island. This would put Thorhall and Norsemen in North America, proper, and Viking artifacts have been found on Baffin and way north of there on Ellesmere Island (off northwesternmost Greenlandand across the Nares Strait) and islands west of it.

Later, on an expedition with Thorfinn Karlsefni, Thorhall disappeared but was found several days later on the edge of a cliff, "staring skywards, with his mouth, nostrils and eyes wide open, scratching and pinching himself and mumbling something" *The Sagas of Icelanders: Eirik the Red's Saga* 667).

MacRitchie quotes the *West Highland Tales (vol. III,* 280), which refers to Thorhall as "a bad Christian," and his disappearance and his being found staring skywards, eyes agape, as noted above, may have been some sort of personnel pilgrimage to assuage his guilt over converting to Christianity. This was during the period when Norsemen in Scandinavia and Iceland were converting to this strange religion—many doing so against their will. About 1000, Christianity became the official religion of Iceland and, perhaps while putting in there for provisions or to pass the winter until the waters were navigable, Thorhall had been compelled to convert.

Karlsefni's staunch crew were starving, finding little food or game in the place they had debarked. After Thorhall rejoined them, they found a beached whale and began boiling parts they had carved up. Thorhall then made a speech, saying:

> "Didn't Old Redbeard [Erik] prove to be more help than your Christ? This was my payment for the poem I composed about Thor, my guardian, who's seldom disappointed me." (*Sagas* 668).

Thorhall clearly retains faith in the old gods and religion. After his speech no one wanted to eat whale meat and threw the meat off a cliff, deciding to trust in God's mercy. Shortly, weather conditions improved so that they could fish and obtain supplies.

Afterwards, the crew split up because Karlsefni and Thorhall wanted to sail in different directions from where they were. The crew split up, with Thorhall taking nine men with him on his ship. The two ships set off together, Karlsefni's ship following Thorhall's for a time. Then Thorhall's ship turned west [east?] but ran into storms and was blown off its intended course to the shores of Ireland. There, it is said, they were beaten and then enslaved. There is not much more information about Thorhall the Hunter, except that he died in Ireland.

Fig. 17

An obviously black-skinned Norse individual from Sweden battling or befriending what looks to be a bear. Note curly hair of man and Afro-Asiatic appearance. He holds an axe in one hand and is touching what looks like a carved ornamental implement with the other.

Thorstein the Black the Wise (Thorstein Surt; Hallsteinsson)

In *The Greenlanders Saga* (he is also mentioned in *Eirik the Red's Saga*), Thorstein the Black is most noted for aiding Thorstein Eiriksson (son of Eirik the Red) and his wife, Gudrid, who washed ashore on Greenland after terrible storms and didn't know where they were. Thorstein the Black invited them to stay with him and his wife for the winter, which was just beginning. Thorstein Eiriksson agreed to this, but soon some kind of sickness began overtaking some Greenlanders, including Thorstein the Black's wife, Grimhild, who died. Soon afterward, Thorstein Eiriksson was stricken and died from the sickness, which must have been some kind of contagion. The saga insinuates some kind of attraction between Thorstein the Black, described as "a large, strong men," and Gudrid, "a woman of striking appearance," although no physical relationship is spoken of. Thorstein continues to help the widow, who later marries Thorfinn Karlsefni.

Thorstein the Black

This Thorstein the Black is mentioned in *The Saga of the People of Laxardal*, a territory in northwestern Iceland. Described as "a big, strong man," he went on many merchant voyages and participated in fighting to avenge the death of a comrade.

Illugi the Black

Illugi the Black was a wealthy landowner in Iceland, well respected and fair-minded. He had many children, but the most notable was Gunnlaug, the focus of *The Saga of Gunnlaug Serpent-Tongue*. The saga is primarily concerned with Gunnlaug's efforts to marry an extremely beautiful girl named Helga the Fair, to whom he becomes betrothed after some difficulty with her father. His well-respected father, Illugi the Black, influences the father to accept his son's marriage to Helga (whose long, golden hair could cover her entire body) if Gunnlaug returns from his overseas exploits within three-years-time. While Gunnlaug is abroad, he has a falling-out with a former friend named Hrafn, in Norway. Hrafn returns to Iceland and asks Helga's father for her hand, knowing that she is betrothed to Gunnlaug. Illugi and Thorstein Egilsson, Helga's father, meet to reaffirm their earlier agreement that if gunnlaug does not return within three years the betrothal agreement would be broken and other suitors could ask for Helga's hand.

Gunnlaug returns to Iceland in a little bit more than three years, right about the time that Hrafn weds Helga—who really loved Gunnlaug. Helga feels that Hrafn has tricked her, and their relationship sours. From time to time she sees Gunnlaug at feasts or other events, and those who watched her saw love for him still in her eyes. Hrafn and Gunnlaug agree to fight a duel. Hrafn was given first-thrust and rent Gunnlaug's shield, injuring him slightly. Relatives on both sides rushed in to discontinue the duel, but both men were still angry and determined to duel another day. Next day the Law council permanently abolished dueling in Iceland, and the abbreviated contest is said to be the last duel to take place in the country. So the combatants decide to go to Norway to duel.

In an area called Gleipnisvellir they came together, Gunnlaug having one companion with him, Hrafn having two. Both sides began fighting. Gunnlaug slew both of Hrafn's companions, while Hrafn killed Thorkel the Black, Gunnlaug's kinsman. Then the two men fought, going at each other unmercifully. Gunnlaug hacked off one of Hrafn's legs and Hrafn fell back against a tree stump without going down. He said he would continue the fight if Gunnlaug brought him a drink of water, which Gunnlaug foolishly did. Fetching water from a nearby brook with his helmet, he took it to Hrafn, who reached for the helmet with his left hand but struck at Gunnlaug with the sword in his right hand, causing a horrible wound to his head. Both men seriously wounded, Gunnlaug finished off Hrafn, but Gunnlaug died three days later of his wound.

Illugi the Black had a dream in which Gunnlaug appeared to him, covered in blood, and told him how Hrafn had tricked him during their duel. Gunnlaug's death had to be avenged. The following spring Hermund Illugason (one of Gunnlaug's brothers) rode a horse out to a merchant ship owned by a man named Hrafn, a nephew of Onund, the slain Hrafn's father. Skipper Hrafn was on shosre almost ready to leave, but Hermund rode right up to him, thrust his spear through him, and rode away, avenging his brother's treacherous death.

Sometime later, Helga married a man named Thorkel Hallkelson, although she really had no love for him. While they had many children, she never forgot Gunnlaug. She would eventually die of a terrible illness that struck her family, her life giving out as she clutched a beautiful cloak Gunnlaug had given to her many years before when he returned from abroad.

Thorgrim Kjallaksson

Mentioned in *Eyrbyggja Saga*, Thorgrim Kjallaksson was a settler in Iceland. He was married to a woman named Thorhild and they had three sons—Brand, Arngrim and Vermund. Thorgrim became involved in a serious dispute with Illugi the Black in regard to a marriage settlement due Ingibjord, Illugi the Black's wife. The matter was to be settled at an assembly headed by Snorri Godi, but several days of severe storms prevented Thorgrim and his kinsmen from attending. Proceedings went on in his absence and the assembly upheld, Illugi's claim.

When Thorgrim Kjallaksson and his retinue arrived afterwards, Thorgrim was incensed at the assembly's decision and would not abide by it. A skirmish ensued and several men on either side were killed. The two sides (Illugi had 120 men, Thorgrim, presumably, an equal number) were separated and Snorri Godi (*godi*, meaning a judge or leader) negotiated a truce between the two sides.

Arngrim (Killer-Styr) Thorgrimsson

The second son of Thorgrim Kjallaksson (above). *Eyrbyggja Saga* describes Arngrim thusly: "He was swarthy and had a big nose and coarse features. His hair was red—dish-blond, and he early became bald on the forehead above the temples." Arngrim is said to have been, "a very overbearing and unjust man," coming to be called Styr (meaning "battle, turmoil"), so that he received the nickname "Slaying-Styr," or *Killer Styr*, because of his penchant for slaying men. Killer Styr would become a friend of Eirik the Red, who had settled in Iceland to avoid punishment for killings in Norway. Eirik would subsequently leave Iceland over killings there and settle in Greenland, from where his son, Leif (Eiriksson) would set out about the year 1000 AD to establish a short-lived colony on the mainland of North America in Newfoundland.

In Iceland, a landholder named Vigfus enlists one of his slaves, Svart the Strong, to slay Snorri godi—promising Svart the Strong his freedom for doing so. Vigfus tells Svart to go to Snorri godi's residence at Helgafell and conceal himself in the loft above the front entrance. When Snorri goes out to relieve himself, Svart is to fall upon him and stab Snorri in the back so hard that the sword comes out of his belly. Svart should then get up on the roof, jump down and escape into the darkness.

Svart did as he was instructed, concealing himself unnoticed by Snorri or his men. But Snorri, followed by several of his men, got to the door before Svart could lunge upon him; Svart stabbed the man walking behind Snorri instead before he fell to the floor. He was grabbed by Snorri who wanted to know who put him up to the deed. Svart revealed what Vigfus and he had planned, adding that Vigfus was out burning charcoal in the woods outside his residence. Snorri rounded up six of his men and went to where Vigfus and several of his People were burning charcoal. They had not been detected, and Snorri killed Vigfus, Sparing his servants.

Thorgerd, the widow of the slain Vigfus, went to Styr, or Killer-Styr, asking him to take up her cause for the prosecution of Vigfus' killers. But Styr felt bound an agreement he had made with Snorri godi not to oppose him in any disputes. Although Killer-Styr had been on good terms with Vigfus, he felt honor-bound to his oath. Styr advised the widow to appeal to his brother Vermund, which Thorgerd did. More than any of his kinsman, Vigfus had had the utmost confidence in Vermund. Vermund asks the widow to enlist the aid of Arnkel, another kinsmen of Vigfus, and the following spring a suit was brought against Snorri at the Thorsness Assembly, Arnkel putting forth his argument with great vigor.

Snorri was found culpable in Vigfus' killing, and fines were assessed. With the shaking of hands, Snorri agreed to the arbitration and paid the fines. Since a mutual agreement had been reached, the assembly was concluded to the satisfaction of the parties involved.

Somewhat earlier, while on a visit to Norway, Vermund was visited by the then ruler of Norway, Earl Hakon Sigurdarson, who gave Vermund two brothers, Halli and Leiknir. They are described as Swedes, and "were men of such great size and strength that there was no one their equal at that time in Norway and far a wide elsewhere" (*Eyrbyggja Saga* 45). The brothers were berserkers, and in that state, "they did not behave like human beings but went about like mad dogs and feared neither fire nor iron" (op. cit.), becoming extremely violent if anyone irked them, although they could be peaceable if not antagonized. Vermund thought the two brothers would be valuable to him as bodyguards—especially since he felt that his brother, Killer-Styr, was encroaching on his property in Iceland, dealing with him as unfairly as he often dealt with others.

Earl Hakon suggested that Vermund ask the brothers whether they would be willing to make the trip to Iceland. The brothers agreed to go, warning Vermund that he should grant them whatever they wished, else they would become angry. Vermund agrees to the bargain, returning to Iceland with the hulking berserkers. Soon after their return Halli tells Vermund that he would like to marry. Vermund did not believe any woman from a respectable family would marry a berserker and was evasive in his response. Sensing this, the brothers became rebellious, and Vermund began to regret that he had brought them to Iceland.

In the fall, Vermund invited Arnkel godi and people of Eyr, as well as his brother, Styr to a great feast he prepared. After the feast, vermund offered the brothers to Arnkel, who declined the offer, suggesting Vermund give the berserkers to Killer-Styr, believing Styr to be suited to handling them. So, when Styr was in the process of leaving the feast, Vermund went to him proposing that they end their bitter differences and proposing that he take the berserkers in order to strengthen his position, adding that no one would start a fight with him having such fearsome men among his followers. Styr agrees that Halli and Leiknir would be assets, but he had heard bad reports about them. However, Styr agrees to the bargain and departs with the berserkers, although the brothers resented being pawned off and treated like thralls. But they felt they would rather follow Styr than his brother, Vermund, and departed with Styr, assisting Styr with killing a rival—Thorbjorn Kjalki—that very night, although it was Styr who actually killed Thorbjorn.

Soon after the brothers took up residence with Styr, Halli began conversing with Asdis, Styr's daughter, an accomplished, precocious young woman. After Styr learned they had been talking to each other, he asked Halli not to beguile his daughter or cause him any disgrace. Halli responds intelligently, telling Styr that it is no disgrace if he talks with his daughter and that he does not intend to bring shame upon Styr. But he has been smitten by Asdis and requests that Styr and he become fast friends, and asks for Asdis' hand in marriage. After speaking to Styr about the advantages that would come with he and his brother attached to Styr's family, Halli warns: "But if you will not grant me this request, that will put an end to our friendship; and then each of us will proceed as suits him best. And then it will not do you any good to complain about my talking with Asdis"—adding that their friendship depended on Styr's response.

The next morning, Styr went to see Snorri godi, and they talked all day atop a high hill. When Styr returned home, Halli asked him if he had considered what they had spoken of the day before. Styr reminded Halli that he had no possessions, asking him how he could make up for this lack. Halli replied that he would do what he could, whereupon Styr tells him that he could earn the marriage by doing great deeds, like men of old. He instructs Halli to clear a pathway over a lava field to another district, then build a boundary wall between his property and that of his brother, Vermund's. Then he should build a sheep enclosure, and after doing all of that, he could have Asdis in marriage. Halli agrees to do all this if he can afterwards have Asdis in marriage.

Halli sets about his given tasks along with his brother, Leiknir. They cleared a pathway over the lava field, built the boundary wall, and then the sheep enclosure—activities which must have taken several days. While they were engaged in this labor, Styr dug a bath into the ground at his residence with a window where water could be poured in from the outside. Under the window was an oven where water could be boiled and poured into the bath room, which could become very hot. Styr also spread a raw ox hide spread before the entrance.

When the brothers were nearly done with their final task of building the sheep enclosure, Asdis, dressed in her best finery, walked past them. The saga says: "When Halli and his companion accosted her, she did not answer." Then both Halli and his brother each recite a verse praising her beauty and finery, suggesting (to this writer) that they seduced or raped the young woman (op. cit. 55-56). Directly after Leiknir's verse spoken to Asdis, the saga continues: "After that they parted. The berserkers went home that evening and were very tired, as is the nature of men who go berserk, that all their strength leaves them once their rage ebbs.

Styr greets them upon their return inviting them to use the bath he had dug out and rest when they were done. Once they were in the bath, Styr closed the overhead trapdoor, piling heavy rocks upon it. Then he had water poured into the bath, the room becoming so hot the berserkers could not endure it, running for the door. Halli broke through the trapdoor and jumped out, but slipped and fell on the ox hide. Styr gave him a death blow—probably cutting off his head. Then Leiknir emerged through the trap-door, whereupon Styr thrust a spear through him, Leiknir falling back into the bath where he died.

Afterwards, Snorri godi rode out to Styr's farmstead and they again talked alone all day. The result of their discussion was that Asdis became betrothed to Snorri godi, and the couple married the following autumn. Both men benefited from the marriage, gaining more prestige and numerous followers.

$$*\qquad*\qquad*\qquad*\qquad*$$

Following are more Norsemen whose names or family ties indicate their racial makeup, but of whom not much is written or known:

Giermund Hjorsson Dark-skin

Yr Giermundardottir (Dark-skin)
Daughter of Giermund Hjorsson Dark-skin (above-named). She is noted for marrying a man named Ketil Steam.

Vigdis
Daughter of Illugi the Black.

Thorkel the Black
In *The Saga of Gunnlaug Serpent-Tongue* (in *the Sagas of the Icelanders*), Thorkel the Black is described as a member of Illugi the Black's household as well as a close relative of Illugi.

Gest Thorhallsson
Son of Thorhall the Hunter.

Osk Thorstein's-daughter (Thorsteinsdottir)
Daughter of Thorstein the Black the Wise (Surt) above, who befriended Thorstein Eiriksson and aided his widow.

Gudrid Thorstein's-daughter (Thorsteinsdottir)
Another daughter of Thorstein the Black the Wise (Surt), sister of Osk and Olof Thorstein's-daughter.

Solveig
Solveig was the sister of the second Thorstein he Black mentioned above. She was married to a strong man named Helgi who became a warrior and was generous in his dealings with his kinsmen. However, Helgi would be killed in battle while on a mission with Halldor and Thorstein the Black to settle a feud with rivals in Iceland. Helgi and Solveig had at least two sons who received compensation for their father's slaying. Helgi's surname was Hardbeinsson, and one of his sons, Hardbein Helgason. There is no further mention of Solveig.

Bjorn the Black (a berserker)
Mentioned in *Gisli Sursson's Saga*, Bjorn the Black is a berserk (of the fierce fighting men who deliberately forced their beings into an animalistic frenzy making them impervious to blows from weapons), who went

around challenging men to fight. He challenged a man named Ari to fight him or to hand over his wife and farm. Ari fought him and was killed. Rather than allow shame to fall on Ari's family, his brother, Gisli, fought Bjorn the Black and slew him, then married his dead brother's wife. Soon after, his father died and he inherited great wealth.

But for the fight with Bjorn the Black, Gisli had borrowed a sword called *Grasida* from Kol, a slave of his dead brother and his wife. After Bjorn was slain and Gisli gained his brother's widow and wealth, he offered Kol money rather than return the sword, Grasida. Kol thereupon attacked Gisli and wounded him seriously. Gisli, in turn, landed a blow with Grasida that cracked Kol's skull, and both men died.

Thorarin Thorolfsson the Black

An Icelandic settler who is described, in *The Saga of the People of Eyri*, as "a big strong man, ugly and taciturn" (89). Thorarin Thorolfsson the Black is said to have been very impartial in his dealings with men and "his enemies said his disposition was as much a woman's" (op. cit.). He was married and probably had children, but is mentioned in the saga for joining a small troop of men to defend his honor after he was accused of stealing horses. The whole tale won't be recounted here, except to say that during an ensuing fight Thorarin killed a farmhand and later his chief accuser, dispelling any beliefs that he had a woman's disposition or was in any way cowardly.

Thorbjorn the Black

A poet of Earl Rognvald Brusason of Orkney, nephew of Earl Thorfinn Sigudarson, mentioned above. Thorbjorn the Black travels to the south with Rognvald and is involved in disputes with Norwegians in the Mediterranean as well as a sea-battle with Saracens. Thorbjorn dies in Acre and is buried there.

Ottar Moddansson the Black

Mentioned in *Orkneyinga Saga* as the Earl of Thurso. He is the brother of a woman named Frakokk, who is mentioned just below.

Frakokk

Sister of Ottar Moddansson the Black, who was Earl of Thurso, the Orkneys (mentioned above). She was married to Ljot the Renegade, about whom there is not much information. Frakokk had three daughters and at least five sons. She was born in Scotland but went to Orkney after Ljot the Renegade died. Frakokk and Helga, her sister, had much input in the government of Earl Harald of Orkney, who was he nephew. Her sister, Helga,. had been the concubine of Earl Hakon of the Orkneys, and Earl Harald was Helga's son. Earl Paul Hakonarson was Harald's brother, and the brothers ruled the Orkneys together (it is indicated that both Harald and Paul were the sons of Helga).

Frakokk and Helga contributed to the ongoing strife in the Orkneys, causing people to choose sides and form factions. Earl Harald and a confederate killed Thorkell the Fosterer. Brother, Earl Paul, was outraged, as Thorkell had been an ally of his. Both brothers gathered their forces, but friends of both intervened to produce a settlement that would avoid bloodshed. Sigurd the Fake-Deacon, the confederate who had aided Earl Harald in the killing of Thorkell, was banished from the islands, along with all others responsible. Harald paid compensation for Thorkell's death, and it was decided by the friends of both brothers that the brothers should respect their bonds of kinships and spend time together during major festivals, like Christmas.

Sometime later, a Christmas feast was being organized at Harald's estate where Frakokk and Helga were staying, helping with preparations. The women had just completed needlework on a beautiful white garment, stitched with gold thread. When Harald came into the room and saw the garment, he asked who it was for. When Frakokk told him it was meant for his brother, Paul, Earl Harald asked them why they so carefully made clothes for Paul and never took such great pains for him. When he took up the garment and unfolded it, intending to put it on, his mother (Helga) snatched it from him and told him not to be envious of his brother. Harald snatched it back, whereupon the women pulled off their bonnets, tears coming from their eyes, and snatched handfuls of their hair. They screamed that his life would be at risk if he put the garment on. Harald ignored their remonstrations and put the garment on; his skin began to crawl and quiver, and he felt agonizing pain. He immediately went to bed, but soon afterwards he died.

Earl Paul became ruler of all the Orkneys, but he realized that the fine garment—the "death cloak"—had been meant for him. He banished Frakaokk and Helga from the Orkneys, and the sisters went to Scotland to stay at Frakokk's estates in Sutherland. While there, Frakokk became involved in other intrigues, most notably as an ally to Earl Rognvald who was awarded the whole of the Orkneys to rule by King Harald of Norway. The Orkneys were still ruled by her nephew, Earl Paul, but Frakokk agreed to raised ships and an army to help Rognvald fight Paula for possession of the islands. After some delays, Frakokk raised a small army and a dozen ships and set out from the Hebrides to join forces with Rognvald. Olvir Thorljotssson, Frakokk's grandson, led the coterie of vessels. Olvir and his ships were driven off. A few days later Earl Paul's fleet killed many men guarding Rognvald's fleet while the fleet was docked. Rognvald wasn't on board and could mount no response.

Some time later, Earl Paul is surprised and captured while at a feast. He is blinded, put in prison, and killed through the machinations of his sister, Margaret; he disappears from the saga (*Orkneyinga Saga*). When Paul doesn't return to his men, inquiries are made, and suspicion falls on Frakokk and Olvir. Rognvald becomes the ruler of the Orkneys, and the people submitted to him. Frakokk and Olvir come under suspicion, as well, for the burning of Olaf Hrolfsson, who had been given authority in Caithness, having been an ally of Earl Paul. Olaf's son, Svein Asleifarson asks Earl Rognvald for ships and men so that he can take revenge on Frakokk and Olvir. He is given two ships and men. He sails to Sutherland, and makes his way to Helmsdale, Frakokk's estate. Olvir escapes, but Svein's men loot everything they can carry, then set fire to the house, burning everyone inside, including Frakokk, who vanishes from the saga along with Olvir.

Frakokk is one of a handful of Norse women who are mentioned in the sagas for something more than giving birth to a particular ruler or warrior chieftain. She was certainly a woman who practiced the Old Religion and was conversant with sorcery and the spells or magic endemic to it. The fullest account of Frakokk is found in *Orkneyinga Saga,* which notes that she was of royal blood and wielded considerable influence on events in Sutherland, the Hebrides and the Orkneys during her time, even being sought out as an ally in her old age by men of influence.

Hopefully, the reader has noted the relationships between some of the individuals mentioned above—fathers, sons, daughters, and so on. If the fathers or other close relatives were black-skinned as their color-names indicate, it follows that their offspring were the same, or at least partially so (brown, red, light-skinned, etc.), whether the mothers of some may not have had color-names or were white-skinned, which must have been the case in many instances. However difficult it may be for some to conceive of, Blacks were dominant in northern Europe a mere millennium ago and had been for a very long time—whether Africoid, Asian, or Afro-Asian—as the evidence presented in this work shows. While perusing the sagas, the reader may also note that there is no indication of racism as we understand it today, none of the attendant virulence often associated with it—at least on the part of Scandinavians—although it is obvious that varying racial types had been co-mingling there, and in other areas of Europe, for centuries up to, and including, the Viking Age (i.e., 800-1100)—the latter part of the so-called Dark Ages.

By the onset of the 11th century, the number of white-skinned people in Scandinavian lands must have been expanding, mostly due to their importation as slaves, servants and concubines. Obviously, black- and dark-skinned people still predominated, as Norse invaders of Britain continued to be styled *black* by historians of the period. But with no new major influx of black-skinned people into northern Europe since the time of the Black Hunnish expansion into Europe, the general population of Scandinavia must have begun to lighten in complexion due to inter-racial marriage and concubinage with the thousands of Slavic,

German, Greek, French and English women being brought in. Many black Danes and Norwegians had married white-skinned English and Irish women to strengthen relations with kings and petty chieftains, and the offspring of these unions were bequeathed territories in Denmark and Norway, which often included royal titles and connections to extended families in both countries, as well as in England, Ireland, the Orkneys, Hebrides and, to a lesser degree, Sweden—more involved in Russia, the Balkans and Eastern Europe. Over the generations of increasing intermixing, the proportion of truly black-skinned women must have declined as racially mixed offspring multiplied, matured, married and produced offspring of their own. There are no written sources that detail these matters.

Considering what we know of the Vikings' usage of women, some Norsemen marrying several wives or producing children with concubines, it is only common sense that racial intermingling brought about a general lightening of the Scandinavian population, although it remained essentially black- and dark-skinned. There had to have been a considerable percentage of mixed-race people inhabiting the northern territories of Europe over the centuries of Norse domination, many of whom ruled as chieftains, kings, queens, princes and jarls, while there were still those who chose to maintain their claim to royal blood by continuing to mate with women whose skin was as black as their own. But such individuals had become a smaller portion of the population, perhaps fading with the demise of the Old Religion.

CHAPTER 12

MORE NOTABLE BLACK NORSEMEN

Along with the color names attached to Norse individuals, there are two other commonly used color attachments or indicators denoting probable blackness or dark skin. Most have heard that *schwartz* means <u>black</u> in German, as do its variations in other Germanic languages: it is *svart* in Norwegian; *svart* in Swedish; *zwart* in Dutch; *svaerte* in Danish; and *schwarze* in Yiddish. In German, Dutch and Yiddish, the <u>*w*</u> is pronounced like a <u>*v*</u>, and the words are pronounced slightly differently in each language. But all mean <u>black</u> in their respective languages, or can mean a black person.

In the sagas, there are several individuals with the name Svart, who will be discussed below, along with others. Mentioned earlier was a territory or realm called *Svartalheim,* meaning the black town or the black community, where Black Dwarfs reside. They are mentioned in several sagas, but are more often seen as characters in tales that are considered myths and therefore presented as mythological beings. In *Myths of the Norsemen*, H.A. Guerber comments on Black Dwarfs in Scandinavian tales, stating:

> Those which were dark, treacherous, and cunning by nature were banished to Svart-alfa-heim, the home of the black dwarfs, situated underground, whence they were never allowed to come forth during the day, under penalty of being turned into stone. They were called Dwarfs, Trolls, Gnomes, or Kobolds, and spent all their time and energy in exploring the secret recesses of the earth. They collected gold, silver, and precious stones . . . . (10-11)

Light Elves, according to Guerber, "were fair, good, and useful, the gods called [them] Fairies and Elves, and they sent them to dwell in the airy realm of Alf-heim (home of the light-elves), situated between heaven and earth . . ." (op. cit. 11). There is an obvious indication to black as evil and light (or white) denoting good; *when* these Norse tales were written down must also be considered. More than likely, they were put to paper after the so-called heathen period—probably influenced by writers who had accepted Christianity. So, it is likely that Light Elves were a purely mythological creation. But there *is* some basis for Black Dwarfs being actual people or beings—although most writers have rel—egated them to the realm of myth, as well.

In Norse tales, however, the gods find the Black Dwarfs far more useful, and it is to the Black Dwarfs that they go for special weapons or magic to aid them in missions or battles with giants or other gods. Black Dwarfs, not Light Elves, aid Odin and Frey, fashion a beautiful necklace for Freya, and make long, golden hair for Sif, Thor's wife. They also aid mortals in the sagas, mainly fashioning swords with special power and durability. It was earlier implied that black Dwarfs were remnants of earlier peoples—diminutive Grimaldi—or early pygmoid-type remnants of Egyptian peoples who once overspread the earth, with the knowledge of magic, metal-working and cosmogony, who also had the ability to locate areas of intense energy in the earth. Descendants of these earlier peoples were most likely still inhabiting Scandinavia during (as well as prior to) the Viking Age—the source for the many tales of Black Dwarfs, Trolls and magical beings in British, German and Scandinavian mythology. In these mythologies they are almost always associated with the underground, and they are styled *black*.

There must be a cogent reason that Black Dwarfs or diminutive black people have come down to us in the folklore of northern Europe—depicted in short tales in countries supposedly always inhabited by white, or so-called *Nordic* peoples. The reader, however, has already been presented with evidence of diminutive black peoples in Europe—Egyptoid or Africoid—in remote times. Our very ancient Iceman is one such example of this type. Waves of taller, more robust Africoids would arrive—like Black Celts, crowding out the earlier arrivals—perhaps killing many of them off, until only pockets of them remained in areas they had once predominated in. But those who remained into historical times, those whom Norsemen had occasion to interact with because of their superior talents; those very real beings who were skilled in the arts of magic and were included and passed down in the lore of Scandinavia for generations, were transformed into the myths—*true myths*—that are still with us.

However, we must proceed with our look at notable black Norsemen, and I will leave off this discussion of black Dwarfs with a comment—called "A Conjecture,"—from H.A. Guerber from *Myths of the Norsemen:*

> Some writers have ventured a conjecture that the dwarfs so often mentioned in the ancient sagas and fairy-tales were real beings, probably the Phoenician miners, who, working the coal, iron, copper, gold, and tin mines of England, Norway, Sweden, etc., took advantage of the simplicity and credulity of the early inhabitants to make them believe that they belonged to a supernatural race and always dwelt underground, in a region which was called Svart-alfa-heim, or the home of the black elves. (145)

Guerber would be more correct if he said *Egyptians*, rather than Phoenicians in the above statement, since Egyptians long predated the Phoenicians in Britain and Scandinavia and were the erectors of the megalithic structures found all over western and northern Europe. Most European historians—as we have discussed—have attached Phoenicians to the Caucasian race, *never* referring to them as black-skinned (which they probably were). Svartalheim, or Svart-alfa-heim, however, means the *black* town, the *black* community, or home of the Blacks, and Phoenicians (according to Western writers) would not seem at all to fit this description. The important point moving forward is that *Schwarz, zwart, svart* and *svaerte* denote <u>black</u> in the abovementioned Germanic (supposedly Indo-European) languages, and individuals named Svart in several sagas will be outlined below, along with others.

Mentioned in the previous chapter was that another word indicating black or blackness is the term *grim*, which often appears as part of an individual's first or last name, as in Grimolf or Grimhilde. *Grim* is also common as a masculine first name, as in Grim the Hairy or Grim Thorsteinsson. We use the word <u>grim</u> today to mean dire, bad, gloomy, dark, ugly or solemn. David MacRitchie, however, asserts that *grim* once signified *black*, mentioning that the Black Douglasses, a royal family of medieval Scotland, were referred to as such (i.e., *black*) because of their complexions (*Britons* 221). He says further that:

> The chief associations of the word, then, were blackness, ugliness, and surliness; and its history in this country [i.e., Britain] seems clearly to prove its connection with one division or another of the "black foreigners [Danes]." The wall that Antoninus built . . . to keep back the Scoto-Pictish Moors, is popularly known as the *Grimes'* Dyke. (op. cit. 222)

(The Scoto-Pictish Moors MacRitchie refers to were the black-skinned populaces north of the firths of Forth and Clyde that staved off the Romans in their attempt to conquer Britain.) MacRitchie cites historians who also state that <u>grim</u> meant "morose, dark, gloomy," and that the word has Danish roots (op.

cit.). His primary point is that grim was a term used to describe all these people of similar complexions and that the term originally implied black, mentioning also that a son of "the good Sir James," of the Black Douglass clan, was "surnamed '*the Grim*'" (op. cit. 221).

Also note that the adjective *skall* means *skin*, in modern Norwegian, and I presume it meant the same in Old Norse during the Viking Age. So, when *skall* is combined with *grim*, we can presume the resultant meaning to be black-skin. One of he individuals we will be looking at in this chapter is Skalla-Grim Kveldulfsson of Iceland and some of his family line, originating in Norway, which can be found in *Egil's Saga*. As in the previous chapter, we are discussing names which indicate that the bearers were black- or dark-skinned; some relatives of these individuals who must have been the same; and other individuals whose names may not imply color or race but who are described as black- or dark-skinned. Other Norsemen littering the sagas who do not have color names or color indicators in their names more than likely were predominantly black-skinned, but not having enough information on them, the meanings or translations of their names, nor a working knowledge of Old Norse or any Scandinavian language, I will not include them. But the reader has been presented with statements from historians of the time, or from more modern day historians quoting them, that the Norsemen of the Viking Age were essentially black-skinned—and these historians make no mention of fair-skinned, blond-haired, blue-eyed Vikings, though an occasional "the White" color name, or women with long blond or red hair are mentioned (I grant, however, that some Whites did become Vikings; and we've already mentioned the taking of foreign women into Scandinavia, which over time contributed to the general lightening of the population).

The reader should now be familiar with the Norse practice of adding -*son* or -*dottir* (for son and daughter) to the surname of offspring, which was attached to the first name of the father. So, as mentioned, Ketil Flatnose's daughter, Aud, was called Aud the Deep-minded *Ketilsdottir;* Harald Fairhair's son, Eirik, was called Eirik *Haraldsson*, later becoming known as Eirik Bloodyaxe. This sort of naming seems to have emanated from a time when Vikings were ruled by chieftains ruling districts or provinces small enough to comfortably defend—before the idea of kingship and controlling large territories came into vogue. The population within the district or province was relatively small and most people knew each other. Even the provincial chieftain knew most of the families within the province. When this naming system began is not clear but might be a very ancient practice. It gives the impression of a more localized or communal world where everyone knew each other, knew children and relatives of people in neighboring towns, and distinguished people by physical characteristics and name associations before their world became larger. As offspring often shared the same first name—Harald, Eirik, Grimhild or Thorgeir—a surname which included the father's first name was an effective way of identifying people and the particular families they belonged to in this much smaller world. Norsemen would retain this communal practice and feeling and transport it across the Atlantic when they emigrated to Iceland.

Svart

This Svart, in *The Saga of the People of Vatnsdal,* is described as an assassin from the Hebrides, who comes to Iceland. He was a strong man who was unpopular and had few friends. A man offers Svart hospitality and soon requests that Svart avenge certain wrongs that a man named Ingolf of Vatnsdal has beset him with. Svart replies that he should be successful because he had experience in raiding and often was the only man to escape in raids. As Svart's ship had been badly damaged, Ottar, his benefactor, promised Svart winter quarters and help repairing his ship if Svart would cut off Ingolf's hand or foot, or kill a man named Gudbrand if he could not get to Ingolf. But Svart would have to find lodging for himself if he could not complete the task.

Svart journeyed to Ingolf's home and, finding him outside, asked Ingolf for some men to help him search for horses to help him carry his wares. When Ingolf told him that not many men were around at that time, Svart asked Ingolf to accompany him to direct him to the next farm. Ingolf did, but became suspicious when Svart continually walked behind him, since he was wearing his weapons. Ingolf refused to take Svart further, telling him that he looked untrustworthy. He told Svart to leave his territory, and he set off back home.

Svart arrived at Gudbrand's home with the same sad tale of having lost his horses. Gudbrand went along with him, found horses and, along with his visitor returned to his home, allowing Svart to stay. When Gudbrand met with Ingolf later, Ingolf expressed misgivings about the stranger, "because this fellow looks like a hired killer to me . . . Something tells me that he is evil." However, Svart stayed the winter and into the spring. Late in the spring as Gudbrand, his wife and Svart were moving Gudbrand's household to another location, Svart thrust his spear into Gudbrand. Gudbrand drew his sword and slashed Svart in his torso. Both men died, and when Ingolf heard the news from Gudbrand's wife, he brought a lawsuit against Ottar for plotting to kill him and his brother, Gudbrand. In the end, both men were compensated and eventually reconciled.

Svart

This Svart is described as a slave in *Egil's Saga* and was among a group of slaves who set fire to a landowner's farmstead and stole cattle. He was later pursued and killed by the owner and his men.

Svart

In *Gisli Sursson's Saga,* this Svart is a slave belonging to Ingjald. Gisli, the saga's protagonist, has been hiding out at Ingjald's house after killing the brother of Bork, Ingjald's landlord. While out fishing with Ingjald, Gisli sees a ship approaching and suspects it is manned by Bork and his men, who have learned that Gisli was still alive from a spy who had spent time at Ingjald's home. Svart and a woman named Bothiod, also a slave of Ingjald, were fishing in another boat nearby. Gisli quickly devises a plan to fool the pursuing Bork: he exchanges clothes with Svart and tells Ingjald to row to nearby land with Svart so that Bork's men will believe that Svart is he. This they do. Gisli would pretend to be Ingjald's oafish son, Helgi. He entangles himself in the tackle and hung himself overboard. When Bork's ship came upon them, Bothild told Bork and his men that Ing—jald rowed to land, but that she didn't know anything about Gisli. Meanwhile, Gisli, dressed in Svart's clothes and acting like an imbecile, amused Bork's men. Bork and his crew surmised that it had been Gisli in the boat with Ingjald and sailed off after it, buying time for Gisli, who rows off for a distant shore with Bothild. But Bork and his men have discovered the ruse and are closing on them. When Gisli and Bothild reach shore, Gisli gives her two rings for Ingjald and his wife, telling Bothild to tell them to give her and Svart freedom. There is nothing more said regarding Svart.

Grim

There are a dozen Grims in *The Sagas of Icelanders*: one, simply called Grim. There is a Grim Bardason; Grim Eidsson; Grim Heggsson; Grim Svertingsson (possibly *Svart-*ingsson?), mentioned in *Egil's Saga,* who is described as "wealthy and of good family" (*Icelanders* 149) and becomes a Lawspeaker; Grim Ingjaldsson; Grim Thorsteinsson (Egilsson), and several other Grims.

There is also Grima, wife of Korkel, who "practise[d] strong magic rites, and was stoned to death with her husband (*The Saga of the People of Laxardal*); Grimhild, wife of Thorstein the Black (*The Saga of the Greenlanders*), "a very large woman, with the strength of a man," (*Icelanders* 644), who dies of a curious illness; and there is a Grimar Grimsson, a Grimolf and a Grim Grimolfsson (*Egil's Saga,* in *Icelanders* 47) who owned property in Iceland and had towns named after them. (The above statements are from sagas included within *The Sagas of Icelanders.*)

To touch upon each of the abovementioned in biographies would be a bit too tedious at this point. Hopefully, however, the reader has noted the number of individuals named Grim—with male and female equivalents—from the sagas and realizes the frequency of names which indicate the probable complexions of their bearers.

Kveldulf (Ulf) Bjalfason

Originally named Ulf (the Norse word for <u>wolf</u>, which in modern Norwegian is u<u>lv</u>), Kveldulf is said to have been so large and strong that no one was a match for him. He was the son of Bjalfi and Hallbera, who was the daughter of Ulf the Fearless. He married the beautiful daughter of his companion Kari, whose name was Salbjorg. In Iceland he was a fairly wealthy farmer who was very clever. He woke up early to inspect his farmlands and gave people advice if they needed it. Towards evening, though, he grew solemn and bad-tempered, and always went to bed early. People thought he was a *shape-shifter,* a man (or woman) believed to possess the ability to assume animal form while asleep or in a trance. Native American lore contains stories of individuals who had the power to shape-shift and, along with their practice of using color names and bestowing names based on an individual's physical features, seems to exhibit a curious affinity—possibly congeneric—to the Norse manner of giving personal names. Because Ulf was thought to possess shape-shifting abilities, he began to be called Kveldulf—*Night Wolf.*

Kveldulf and Salbjorg had two sons—Thorolf, who was "attractive and highly accomplished," and Grim, who was "*swarthy* and ugly, *resembling his father* in both *appearance* and character" (*my emphasis, Icelanders* 8). In *Egil's Saga,* "Grim was a dark and ugly man, like his father in appearance and disposition" (1).

From the above, the reader should be able to discern that Bjalfi and Kveldulf were black-skinned—Bjalfi being so, even though his name is not a color name. The wives of these individuals were, as well, probably black-skinned, although the saga implies that Grim's older brother, Thorolf, "was handsome . . . like his mother's people, cheerful, generous . . ." (op. cit.), giving one the impression that she was fair or white-skinned—which should not suggest that black-skinned people were bereft of such attributes. But Grim is unquestionably swarthy or black, like his father, Kveldulf, whose father, Bjalfi (and perhaps both *his* parents) was also black.

Kveldulf and his family were Norwegians, living during the reign of Harald Fairhair (c. 848-931). King Harald was consolidating his territory and sent messengers asking Kveldulf to come and meet with him because he'd heard that Kveldulf was a distinguished man. Kveldulf was promised great favors from the king but told the messengers that he was too old to be fighting on warships. He told them he would stay at home and no longer serve kings. The messengers suggested Grim visit the king in his father's place, that he was a large man who looked like a good fighter. Grim told them: "I do not wish to be made a nobleman while my father lives. He shall be my chief while he lives" (*Egil's Saga* 5).

When Harald heard the messengers' report he was offended. A king's aide named Olvir then visited Kveldulf telling him of Harald's generosity toward distinguished men who befriended him. Kveldulf had a strong feeling that his family would receive ill fortune from Harald, and he still refused to meet him. But he agreed to allow Thorolf to go in his place, assuring that he, Kveldulf, would be a friend to the king.

When Thorolf returned from a voyage, Kveldulf told him about the visit from the king's messengers and Olvir and what had been the result of the meeting with Olvir.

Kveldulf had a premonition that the association with Harald would lead to Thorolf's death at the hand of the king, but Thorolf had a different feeling and agreed to go to Harald in his father's place. Despite Kveldulf's misgivings, he allowed Thorolf to go, warning him not to fight men who were stronger than himself.

Of Kveldulf's early exploits before his marriage to Salbjorg, there is not much information. Although he is described as stern, uncommunicative, and probably a shape-shifter—which conjures dark and other-worldly evil, he manages to impress the reader of *Egil's Saga* as a father with deep concern for his offspring. Most sagas do not contain the unquestioning love of a father for his sons that this saga exhibits. While Viking fathers in other sagas often have no advice for their sons, resent their sons, or care about them only insofar as carrying on the bloodline, Kveldulf seems to truly cherish Thorolf the way we imagine a good modern-day father would. They have a civil conversation over Thorolf's impending journey to King Harald; Kveldulf worries that Thorolf might be overly rash and battle someone he should avoid; and believes that Grim, who most takes after him, would be better able to handle himself in Harald's court or in a fight. Kveldulf goes down to Thorolf's ship with him and embraces him before he departs.

Thorolf Kveld-Ulfsson

Thorolf Kveld-Ulfsson, son of Kvellulf, and older brother of Grim, journeys to King Harald's realm and becomes a respected man in Harald's court after swearing allegiance to the king. (All the preceding events take place in Norway.) Thorolf went with King Harald and fought in Harald's greatest victory, the battle in Havsfjord in Rogaland. It was after this battle, Harald's last, that Harald gained control of all Norway.

Thorolf found great favor with the king and was made a nobleman. A man named Bard died from wounds suffered in the battle of Havefjord. He had been given trading rights with the Lapps, which provided him with a source of considerable income. Before he died he, with the permission of King Harald, bequeathed all his land and money to Thorolf. In addition, he gave him his wife and the care of his young son. Thorolf also received the trading rights with the Lapps from Bard. Thorolf completely accepted Bard's bequests, marrying his widow, Sigrid, who knew that he was an outstanding man.

Thorolf prospered. Then the sons of a woman named Hildirid visited him, stating that they were due a portion of the property that their father, Bjorgolf, had owned. They explained their position to Thorolf: Bjorgolf, a widower with a son named Brynjolf, had married their mother, Hildirid, when he was very old. His son, Brunjolf, who lived with his father, was against the marriage and resented Hildirid living in the house. But he could do nothing. The sons, Harek and Hroerek, were born. Shortly afterward, old Bjorgolf died. Soon after the old man's burial, Brynjolf sent Hildirid and her sons—his half-brothers—away. Hildirid went to her father's house and her sons were raised there. Bard received the inheritance, including the Lapp trading enterprise, as he was the son of Brynjolf—Bard Brynjolfsson. Now Thorolf had been bequeathed property which Harek and Hroerik believed rightfully they should have been given.

Thorolf replied to them that he had heard bard refer to them as "bastards," inferring that Hildirid had not been legally married to Bjorgolf. The sons said they could bring witnesses to back their claim, and that they had spoken to Bard regarding their grievance but had been rebuffed. Thorolf became irritable, asking: "Why should I think you legitimate, when I've heard that your mother was taken by force, and brought back as loot?" The sons promised that they wouldn't keep silent about their loss, and the discussion was broken off.

During the summer some months later, Thorolf organized a feast for King Harald at his estate. Many of Thorolf's men were present as were many distinguished guests.

During the feast King Harald was seen by some to become angry; he was perturbed by the large number of Thorolf's men who were present. However, he remained at Thorolf's estate three days. When he was ready to depart, Thorolf made him a gift of a dragon ship he had had built and assured Harald that the only reason he had so many men with him was to do the king honor. Harald was very pleased and the men parted amicably.

Afterwards, the sons of Hildirid invited the king to their house for a feast, which the king accepted. Once there, the brothers insinuated that Harald's life might be in danger, that Harald was fortunate that no attempt on his life had been made at Thorolf's feast. King Harald was told that Thorolf had made plans to kill him, which was why so many of Thorolf's men were present at his estate. Harek and Hroerek convinced Harald that they were truthful, offering their allegiance and reminding the king that their father, Bjorgolf, had handled his duties of royal administrator well for many years. Having the king's ear, they later induced the king to believe that Thorolf was not giving him the full share of the Lapp tribute and, in a later conversation with Thorolf, told Thorolf that the king would not again accept his hospitality. And then Harald took from Thorolf the administration of Halogaland and awarded it to Hildirid's sons.

Soon King Harald completely turned against Thorolf and set out to kill him, burning down the house that Thorolf and his men were occupying. As the men ran out, they were cut down by King Harald's men. When Thorolf ran out to escape the flames, he ran at the king's bodyguard who surrounded Harald. He was injured by sword and spear, and Harald, himself struck the death blow, Thorolf falling at his feet. Kveldulf was very distressed when he heard about the death of Thorolf and took to his bed. He and Grim (now referred to as Skalla-Grim—i.e., Black Skin in *Egil's Saga*) want to avenge Thorolf's death. Later they are visited by Olvir Hnufa, the king's representative, and from him learn the details of Thorolf's demise. Olvir suggests that if they go to visit the king (which Harald has sent Olvir to persuade them to do) they would be compensated for Thorolf's death. Kveldulf refuses to go because of his age. Olvir asks Grim (Skalla-Grim) if he would go, and Grim promises to go when he is ready. He tells Olvir when he thinks he will be ready, and Olvir hurries back to see King Harald and tell him the news.

Skalla-Grim (Grim) Kveld-ulfsson

The son of Kveldulf, brother of Thorolf Kveld-Ulfsson, Skalla-Grim Kveld-Ulfsson, became a powerful chieftain like his father in 10th century Norway. While there he establishes himself as a brave fighter (it is said he is a berserker), a fair-minded man, and a man prone to be taciturn at times, like his father, Kveldulf.

After his brother Thorolf's death, he gathered twelve of the strongest men of his household together for his visit to King Harald to ask for compensation. Many of these were said to have been shape-changers (i.e., shape-shifters). After a short journey in a rowing-boat, they trekked overland to the estate where King Harald was feasting. The man who announced their presence outside the house informed the king's representative, Olvir, that they looked like giants. Olvir came outside and Skalla-grim asked to speak with the king.

Rather than offering recompense for Thorolf, Harald told Skalla-Grim to join him in service and that if Skalla-Grim pleased him he might give him the recompense he sought. As diplomatically as he could, Skalla-Grim refused to become one of the king's men. The king turned red with anger, saying nothing more, and Olvir turned and told Skalla-Grim and his men to leave at once, warning him to be on guard against the king and his troops. Harald sent men after them with orders to kill grim. But Grim and hiss men had reached the lake and their boat and were on their way back to their territory to tell Kveldulf what had transpired.

Kveldulf was glad that Skalla-grim had not been submissive to the king, but they both concluded that they could no longer remain in Norway. They provisioned two cargo ships the following spring, each carrying thirty men along with women and children, and sailed to the Solund Islands off the coast of western Norway. During the summer they spied a ship in harbor there that had once belonged to Thorolf, now captained by Hall—vard, one of the king's men. They attacked this ship at night, Kveldulf going berserk, and killed fifty men. From a few unimportant survivors they learned that the king had sent Hallvard to collect the sons of one of his men who had died and to bring the boys to him so they could be raised at his court. The two boys had died in the fight from drowning. Skalla-grim gave he survivors a message of vengeance to deliver to the king. Then Grim loaded the cargo of one of his ships onto the larger one they had captured and sank the abandoned ship.

There were several shape-changers and berserks among Skalla-Grim's men. While they were caught up in their fury they were so strong that nothing could hurt them. But when the fury subsided they were much weaker than usual. This happened to Kveldulf, who became extremely weak when his fury ebbed, he had to take to his bed as the men in their two ships set off for Iceland. Kveldulf's fatigue became worse, and he gave instructions to the men on his ship to put his body in a coffin and set it adrift; if the coffin drifted to Iceland, Skalla-Grim was to build his house close to where it came to shore. The coffin drifted ashore and Skalla-Grim built his first house near the place as the men on Kveldulf's ship told Skalla-Grim his father had instructed him to do. The men of the two ships unloaded their cargo at a place they named Knarrarnes, and Skalla-Grim went about exploring the land. He claimed a large area and allotted several of his men land within it. Iceland had yet to be fully settled, and almost no one lived in the area where Skalla-Grim and his men landed.

Skalla-Grim and his wife Bera, it is said, lost their first children; then Bera gave birth to a son who was named Thorolf, daughters Seaun and Thorun, then another son, whom they named Egil. Thorolf was like his deceased uncle, Thorolf, in appearance and abilities; Egil took after his father, "very ugly . . .

and black-haired," according to *Egil's Saga* (45), but surely dark- or black-skinned, like his father and grandfather, is implied.

It is probable that Thorolf (like his uncle and namesake) was dark-skinned, as well—perhaps lighter-skinned or red-complexioned (i.e., brown) who, compared to men the complexion of his father, could be considered fair-skinned in a predominantly black- or dark-skinned populace. Or his being "fair" or fair-skinned could be an affectation of later times; the saga was written three centuries after the events described when Scandinavia was overwhelmingly Christian and images of a white Jesus common. The general population of Scandinavia might have been brown- to tawny-skinned by this time (i.e., the 14th century), and even Snorri Sturluson may have been influenced to inject more whiteness (or less blackness) into his works. Neither Thorolf, however, is ever referred to as fair-haired or blue-eyed in the saga; they are simply called cheerful, generous, handsome and ambitious.

Back in Norway, King Harald Fairhair confiscated the lands that Skalla-Grim owned as well as the lands of some of the men who had accompanied him to Iceland. In his pursuit of more lands and riches, Harald impelled many Norwegians to flee the country. One of these was Bjorn the Freeholder or Brynjolfsson, although the reason he in—voked Harald's ire is unclear. King Harald ordered that he be killed on sight, and this message was spread all the way to the Hebrides. Bjorn, failing to get the permission of Thorir Hroaldsson to wed his beautiful, young sister, Thora, stole the girl and left Norway. Eventually reaching Iceland, Bjorn's ships came ashore at Borgarfjord, Skalla-Grim's territory. Some men there told Bjorn that the nearby farm was called Borg and that the farmer was Skalla-Grim, whom Bjorn had heard of.

When Bjorn told Grim that his father was Brynjolf, whom Skalla-Grim knew well, Skalla-Grim offered Bjorn any assistance he needed. Skalla-grim was pleased to learn that Thora was Bjorn's wife, for her brother, Thorir was Skalla-Grim's foster-brother. Skalla-Grim invited both of them to his house along with their men.

Some months later when more ships arrived in Iceland from Norway, Grim discovered that Bjorn had taken and married Thora without her brother's permission. Skalla-Grim was extremely angry that Bjorn had come to him having done such a thing. Grim's son, Thorolf interceded and calmed his father down. Then Thora gave birth to a daughter, who was named Asgerd, and Bjorn and his men stayed at Skalla-Grim's farm over the winter.

Thorolf and Bjorn became very close, and in the spring Thorolf proposed that Skalla-Grim send men to Norway to make peace with Thorir and atone for what Bjorn had done. Skalla-Grim thought well of Thorolf's suggestion and the journey was made the following summer. Atonement was offered by Brynjolf (Bjorn's father) for Bjorn's deed and, after Skalla-Grim's messengers spent the winter in Norway, they returned with the news of Brynjolf's acceptance of terms for Bjorn from Thorir.

Much has been written of the Viking penchant for heathen practices, violence, bouts of drunkenness and licentious behavior, but the account of Bjorn's misdeed, Skalla-Grim's angry reaction, and the atonement for Bjorn demonstrate that Norsemen did observe moralistic codes of behavior and compensation for wrongs or violations of established practices. Although so-called heathenism, or the Old Religion, was still fairly widespread in Scandinavia and Iceland during the 10th century when the events described in *Egil's Saga* take place, the gathering of free men at things or less formal gatherings adequately settled most disputes, lawsuits or land disputes. There was scarcely a country or realm in Europe that handled legal matters as equitably. Powerful men, though, like King Harald, made their own rules, or decided which decrees they would abide by—favoring parties loyal to them or to whom they had family ties.

In Iceland, Skalla-grim tended to his farm and watched his children grow. Like his father, he was known as a generous man who sometimes had bouts of dark moods or sudden bursts of emotion. It is evident, though, that he was concerned with the welfare of his children and was fair in his dealings with men.

Thorolf Skalla-Grimsson and Egil Skalla-Grimsson

Thorolf Skalla-Grimsson, first-born son of Skalla-Grim, lived c. 900-937 and, as noted above, was called handsome, cheerful and gifted. As a young man he decided to go to Norway with Bjorn the Freeholder in Bjorn's quest to seek atonement for kidnapping Thora when her brother, Thorir, did not consent to Thora's marriage to Bjorn. While there, Thorolf befriends Eirik Bloodyaxe, favored son of King Harald Fairhair. Bjorn persuades Thorolf to give Prince Eirik his finely-made ship as a token of friendship, feeling the gesture would assuage King Harald's rancor toward Thorolf's father, Skalla-Grim. After receiving the gift from Thorolf, Eirik spoke to his father about Thorolf and King Harald promised peace between himself and Thorolf stipulating, though, that Thorolf should never come to see him.

Soon afterwards, Eirik Bloodyaxe assusmed much of his father's power in Nor—way and prepared to go on an expedition to Bjarmaland—a territory east of present-day Finland bordering the White Sea, in northern Russia. Thorolf and selected men accompany him. A great battle is fought against the inhabitants of Bjarmaland, and Thorolf, "by then bigger and stronger than anyone, being like his father" (*Egils Saga* 53), took part in this battle on the Dvina River aiding Eirik in the victory.

Egil Skalla-Grimsson exhibited a mean temper and an independent nature almost from the time he could walk. He was also seen as a poet, composing his first verses by the time he was five or younger. Born about 910, he was a decade younger than his brother, Thorolf, and was destined to be even bigger and more powerful in strength. It is said that at 12 years-old, "he was so tall that there was scarcely anyone so big or so gifted with strength that Egil could not beat" in wrestling games (op. cit. 57).

At around the same age, Egil wanted to go abroad with Thorolf; Skalla-Grim thought he would be unmanageable and told him to talk to Thorolf, who told Egil that if their father thought he was unfit, then he would not take him to foreign ports. "Then, maybe neither of us will go," Egil retorted and, that night during a gale, cut the ropes holding the ships at dock so that they drifted out into the fjord. Some men near the shore rescued the ships, intervened between an angry Thorolf and his willful younger brother, and Egil was taken along on the journey.

In Norway, Thorolf goes to visit King Eirik, giving him a finely made sail, and then goes to stay with Thorir, Skalla-aGrim's foster brother. Thorolf and Egil still had a straiained relationship, but Thorir had a son, Arinbjorn, to whom Egil became attached.

Arinbjorn was a few years older than Egil, but they liked each other and became almost inseparable. Thorolf marries Asgerd, the daughter of Bjorn the Freeholder and, it seems, the brothers separated for a while, Egil going off with Olvir, the king's man, and joining a feast at the home of Bard where the king and his wife were also present.

Egil runs Bard through with his sword after he discovers that Queen Gunnhild and Bard put poison in his beer, attempting to kill him over an insult levied at Bard. Egil flees and the king's men are sent after him. Egil escapes by swimming to a nearby island. When the king's men arrive in a small boat to search the island, Egil kills several of them, takes their boat, and rows all night and the next day until he reaches the home of Thorir, who had just returned with Thorolf after Thorolf's marriage to Asgerd. Olvir had also returned and told them the circumstances of Bard's death at the hand of Egil. Thorir then went off to visit the king in Egil's behalf and paid compensation for the men Egil had killed. But King Eirik was extremely angry and warned that Egil should not remain in his kingdom much longer.

After spending the winter with Thorir, Thorolf and Egil sailed into the Baltic on viking raids and fought frequent battles. Off on an inland expedition, Egil and twelve companions are surrounded and captured by Kurlanders, bound, and locked in a room.

Egil frees himself and then his companions, as well as three Danish men the Kurlanders had captured the year before. They stole a chestful of treasure and silver and broke out of the house without their captors being aware. They fled to the woods, but Egil returned to block the doors of the house with timber and set it ablaze. All inside died.

Egil and his companions returned to their ship with the treasure, where they saw Thorolf and his crew who were greatly relieved that Egil and his men were alive. The men of both ships then set off for Denmark, plundering towns and trading-ships as they went. The freed Danish prisoners, a father and his sons, were well acquainted with the Danish coastline and towns ripe for plunder, and the expedition was very fruitful for the Norse Icelanders.

The brothers continued raiding expeditions, raiding in Denmark, Frisia, Germany, Flanders and the Baltic, before sailing to England where young King Aethelstan had succeeded his father, Edward (son of Alfred the Great), as king of England. Aethelstan needed help in putting down insurgency in several districts, and Thorolf offered the king assistance. The king asked the brothers to be *provisionally* baptized, which they assented to (they could keep their own faith). And so, Thorolf and Egil participated in the shaping of English history, fighting battles that aided King Aethelstan in retaining control of his realm. But in a great battle against the Scots, Thorolf was slain by Earl Adils and men with him. Egil had been leading another troop of fighters, but when he learned of Thorolf's death he fought his way through the men struggling with each other in battle, felling enemy troops in his path until he found Earl Adils and slew him. The troops around the earl retreated when their leader fell, but Egil and his men chased after them and killed all they caught up to. Returning to Thorolf's corpse, Egil composed a verse:

> Flame-hearted Thorolf, fear's
> foe, Earl-killer, who so
> dared danger in Odin's
> dark wars is dead at last.
> Here, by Vina's bank, my
> brother lies under earth. This
> now's become death-bitter.
> But grief's best laid to rest.
>
> I filled the English field
> full of corpses. We fought
> savagely and sure, our
> standard tall at my back.
> I attacked Adils with blue
> Adder, young Olaf stormed
> our troops, and Hring fought, too.
> To-day the ravens gorge.

A precise chronology of events is difficult if not impossible concerning the sagas, and *Egil's Saga* flows so engagingly that one has to pause here and there to consider time sequences, or consult other sources to pin down when certain events may have actually occurred. The battle in which Thorolf lost his life must have taken place in 937, as that is the accepted year of Thorolf's death; but only seven sections earlier, a 12 year-old Egil undertakes a journey with his older brother (i.e., 922). So, presumably fifteen years have passed in a few pages of *Egil's Saga*, meaning that when his brother is killed Egil is a grown man of 27, if he was born in 910. He has established himself as a valiant, fearsome fighter. Returning to Norway, he marries his brother's widow, Asgerd—who has a daughter, Thordis, by Thorolf—and they have five children together, two daughters and three sons. We have already considered Egil's complexion, that he was black, or very dark-skinned, like his father and grandfather. There is a further description of Egil in the saga for the reader to consider:

Egil's features were strongly marked; a broad forehead, heavy brows, *a nose not long but very wide, lips broad and full,* the chin unusually broad . . . a thick neck and shoulders broader than most men have, harsh-looking and fierce when he was angry. He was . . . taller than anyone else, with *thick wolfgrey hair,* and he soon became bald . . . . Egil had black eyes and dark brows. (my emphasis, op. cit. 84)

Mentioned earlier was the probability that the Norse were a mixture of black-skinned Asians and Africans who met and intermingled in the expanse of territory comprising Germany from ancient times to the period under discussion. Of course there were admixtures of other types—probably Near Eastern and Caucasian types. But the above description of Egil strongly hints of a person of African ancestry, and in no way does it bring to mind a fair-skinned, blond Caucasian with aquiline features—not even a dark-haired one. (Egil's description brings to this writer's mind a person who might have resembled former American heavyweight boxing champions Sonny Liston and a young George Foreman; or ex-football great and actor Jim Brown—but a black or much darker-skinned man than the latter two.)

Egil returns to Iceland after hearing of the death of his father, Skalla-grim (c. 946). Hakon, another son of Harald Fairhair, and foster-son of Aethelstan, assumed the kingship of Norway when his brother, Eirik Bloodyaxe, fled Hakon's march to Trondheim. Arinbjorn, friend of Egil, was also Eirik's foster-brother and fled with Eirik to the Orkneys and Scotland.

After establishing himself, ex-king Eirik forayed into England, impelling King Aethelstan to gather troops and march against him. A treaty was established whereby the king of England gave Eirik control of Northumbria to guard against Scot and Irish raids against his kingdom. Ex-Queen Gunnhild's hatred of Egil continued, and she worked spells so that he would never know peace in Iceland. After burying his father and brooding over the winter, Egil sailed to England where he found that Eirik and Gunnhild were in residence in York. Egil rides to York to speak with Eirik and, through Arinbjorn, is invited inside to commiserate with Eirik. The ex-king is not moved by Egil's act of contriteness, and Gunnhild orders Egil to be taken out and killed. But Egil is allowed to leave and shortly afterwards visits King Aethelstan and tells him of his plans to visit Norway and attempt to retrieve some property (land) Eirik had taken which had belonged to his father when Skalla-Grim departed Norway.

After several skirmishes, Egil retrieved the property as well as property his wife, Asgerd, should have inherited from her father. Those matters resolved, Egil went raiding with Arinbjorn in Germany and Frisia. Returning to Norway, he was staying at the home of a man named Thorfinn whose daughter, Helga, was abed and had been ill for a very long time. Thorfinn told Egil that runes had been carved for her by a nearby farmer's son, but the girl had become sicker. Egil had he girl removed from her bed and found a whale-bone with runes carved into it. He read them, then threw the bone into the fire. He carved new runes (the saga does not say on what material, but these were runes containing magic properties) and put them under Helga's pillow. When she was placed back into bed, she woke from her deep sleep and, although still weak, said that she felt much better, to the relief of her parents.

In fighting, Egil is almost a one-man army, killing four men here, eight there, and in one vicious skirmish, eleven or twelve men who attacked him all at once. Although he is not called a berserker, he certainly must have inherited this trait (if such a thing could be passed along genetically) or learned this ability from his father and grandfather. Egil never suffered any serious wounds and, like his father before him, and did seem to enter into a berserker frenzy when fighting several men simultaneously. In answer to a young poet in Iceland who asked Egil about his most severe test, Egil composed this verse:

> Once I fought eight on my
> own. Eleven men, twice.
> We left the dead to wolves. I
> was the one man to kill.
> But they were bitter fights.

Battering swords on shields
we marred and split metal.
My sword flickered flame-red.

Back in Iceland, Egil composes poetry, including an especially long one praising his old friend Arinbjorn, who would die soon afterwards in Norway. There is no hint of Egil's age when he returns to Iceland, but he remained there until his death at about 80 years-old in 990, going blind in his last years.

Although two of Egil's sons, Gunnar and Bodvar (whose death in a storm was very painful for Egil) did not marry or produce (as far as is known) any offspring, his daughters did. Thordis, Asgerd's daughter with Thorolf, married a man called Grim Svertingsson, whose name indicates that he was probably dark-skinned. Of the descendants of Skalla-Grim's line, *Egil's Saga* concludes:

> For a long time in that family the men continued to be strong and good fighters, some of them men of wisdom. The big difference is that into that family the finest-looking men in Iceland have been born . . . but most of the Myramen [men of Myrar, area where Skalla-Grim settled in Iceland] were extremely ugly. (171)

Thorstein Egilsson was baptized a Christian when the majority of Icelanders began accepting the religion at the close of the 10th century, and it is said that many poets and men of distinction are descended from him. As well, Snorri Sturluson, author of *Egil's Saga* and many others, is said to be a descendant of Egil Skalla-Grimsson.

Hopefully, the reader has noted that many of the individuals outlined in this and the previous chapter were *Norwegians,* many of whom settled in Iceland. Perhaps the still-skeptical reader is thinking that these black-skinned Norsemen were in the minority, that white-skinned Norsemen must have constituted the vast majority of Norse peoples in Scandinavia; therefore, appellations like "the White,"—as opposed to more numerous color names like "the Black" and "the Red"—were unnecessary. At first, this might seem like a valid assumption. But would the reader also accept the idea that a *minority* of black-skinned people dominated an expansive territory in which they were vastly outnumbered by white-skinned Scandinavians? That these *minority* black-skinned people ordered majority white-skinned Scandinavians into ships and led them in raids against other white-skinned people in England, France, Germany, Ireland, Russia and Italy? That these *minority* Blacks asked for and were granted, without rancor, the hands of the majority Whites' daughters in marriage—even daughters of royal lineage? That these activities continued for three or more centuries without a major rebellion to drive this black *minority* out of Scandinavia?

The most reeasonable and logical conclusion—which has been mentioned and which the reader has been presented with evidence for—is that these black- and dark-skinned warrior peoples were the majority—the *vast* majority—population in Scandinavia and had been for a very long time—influxes of other black- and dark-skinned migrants to the area adding to their numbers, as has been mentioned. This numerical domination in northern Europe continued into the 12th century, and perhaps at least a century longer. Included in later numbers of Scandinavians were many thousands of mixed-race Norsemen—products of centuries of intermingling between black-skinned Danes, Norwegians and Swedes with black-skinned Asians, like the Black Huns, and captive Caucasian women brought to Scandinavia for marriage and concubinage.

A fair number of Caucasian men and boys must also have been brought to Scandinavia as slaves, captured in raids into various territories. Numerous dark-skinned, Mongoloid Finns were part of the mix, as the ancient territory once called Finnmark included northern Sweden and Norway. People from areas bordering the Baltic, like Estonia and Wendland, admixed with Slavic, Turkic and Hunnish peoples, were also part of the mix. As has been discussed, northern Europe, extending into Russia, was home to a multitude of black- and dark-skinned peoples under various tribal names into the 11th century.

The sagas make no mention of racial animosity in Scandinavia during the period of the early Middle Ages indicating, as some have averred, that the racism we understand today is a recent aberration in human history, engendered during the slave trade in the 16th century. The white vs. black racism that so pollutes our planet today could not have existed in Scandinavia during the Viking Age since the Norse population was predominantly black and became more racially diverse with the influx, amalgamation and intermingling of the abovementioned peoples. As far as is known, black-skinned Scandinavians harbored no racial animus toward white-skinned peoples, per se, and discrimination because of skin color was a non-issue—although, at least early on, it seems they were concerned with maintaining royal bloodlines, and the most royal blood was Danish, the Danes being indisputably black-skinned, as has been noted. To the Norse, people were people—whether for plunder or pleasure, slaying or slavery, knavery or knowledge. And there are no recorded incidences of the genocidal slaughter of masses of white-skinned people to achieve territorial ambitions.

As has been glimpsed in several of the extended biographies above, strangers were often invited to eat and lodge at the homes of farmers or landholders—the only pay being the gift of a jacket, weapon, help with some task, or the promise of future friendship or aid. And, probably, any Caucasians in the north were more tolerant of racial differences than those in the south of Europe and the British Isles. Living in a more harsh environment, with killer cold and deep snowfalls in the winter, people would be more understanding of others' need for shelter, food and warmth, whatever a person's race—as long as the needy person was not a savage. In such an environment, a man cherished good neighbors and valued those who could help repair a roof caved in by heavy snow, sell him a ram to replace one that had died, bring him supplies from a place too far for him to reach himself, or provide him with a woman, even one of another race—despite any language difference—to perform expected wifely duties. One might also be amenable to marrying off his daughter to someone of another race, which would offer her something more in life and lessen the burden of feeding the rest of his family.

Our modern comforts and complacency hardly allows us to imagine the lives our ancestors lived even a century ago—let alone a millennium. Only a century ago in the United States, half the population lived by farming, but even average persons living in cities weren't much better off. Let us exclude the wealthy and imagine the lives of average people in the United States, Europe, Africa and Asia a century ago: Of course the modern playthings of the last two decades or so weren't in existence—computers, cellphones, CDs, DVDs and such. But a century ago there were hardly any cars or telephones, and passenger airplanes were two decades in the future. There were no TVs, radios, supermarkets, refrigerators, vacuum cleaners, electric typewriters; there was no electricity in homes, packaged, ready-cut meat, traffic lights, sound in movies, or record players. There were no department stores, paved streets; instant food, vaccines against polio, influenza, chicken pox and a dozen other diseases; no air conditioning, powered lawn-mowers, or pasteurized milk, and hardly a bathroom inside an apartment or home.

Do we contemplate how life must have been for our recent ancestors—grandparents, great-grand-parents in a place like Paris or New York City? How people may have trekked across New York City's Brooklyn Bridge to go to work every single day and recrossed it at night to return home? Do we think about how women and girls sewed dresses, repaired torn pants, darned socks and spent part of most days scrubbing clothes on a washboard in a washtub? Can we imagine how people spent their nights in those pre-radio days, tossing coals in a stove to keep the apartment warm; children reading library books or doing homework by the glow of kerosene lamps? How much warmer an apartment must have seemed with the company of a few friends or neighbors who happened by.

That was only a century ago in the modern industrial world—a mere one-hundred years. Two-hundred, three-hundred years ago, peoples' lives were much bleaker—at least to us moderns. Surely people in those days did not consider themselves bereft of the basic needs of their day, or considered themselves backward. Average people labored or farmed, repaired their homes, harvested, went to the ports when ships came in, seeking fresh supplies or news from abroad. They sold their produce in town, went to church, had many children, lived as honestly as they could, looked after their parents, went off to war when called upon, loved, and dreamed of a better life.

A millennium ago in Scandinavia, life was, perhaps, abundantly more bleak, although average temperatures were actually up to 10 degrees warmer than today. It was customary that guests were invited to stay for days, even months, at one's home, to feed strangers and offer them lodging—especially in winter. In Viking movies, there are often scenes of Norsemen in a great hall, carousing and boastful, drinking great quantities of beer or mead, making merry with females, drunkenly challenging one another in axe-throwing contests or other feats of strength and prowess.

Perhaps some of this may be accurate, but the sagas almost never describe such scenes. However, Norsemen gathered in a great hall or a home to drink and socialize was not uncommon. At such gatherings, the sagas describe business being discussed—plans for the spring, sailing ventures, raising a crew, a pending invasion or fight, who to beware of, what a chieftain's plans were, who a son or daughter should wed. We can glean some of these from some of the above biographies in this and the previous chapter. Gatherings such as these, hosting and feeding relatives or parties on a mission, drinking large quantities of intoxicating beverages helped the night pass—especially during winter months.

Norsemen were quite social, generally fair-minded and moral, adhering to standards of proper conduct regarding marriage (of course, married women were expected to remain chaste—and most did—while men often had concubines and had children with them), oaths of loyalty, and respecting another man's home and property. Rebuke would follow the breaking of traditional practices; grievances or lawsuits would be filed, and a *thing* would often be held to settle the matter. If the thing (public gathering of landholders) could not resolve a dispute, then a duel, violence or killing might follow.

The *althing* was developed in Iceland, and Gwyn Jones describes the althing as "unquestionably an assembly for law of all free men who chose or were appointed to attend it" (*Vikings* 283), although the *godar* (presiding justices) were often the largest landholders or the most influential men. Still, things and althings were the first public courts developed in Europe, and were eventually spread to England and France by the Danes. These public courts or hearings would develop into the jurisprudence we practice today—considering modifications and improvements over the centuries, of course—with variations from country to country. But, imperfect as things and althings may have been, they originated with the Norsemen, Black Vikings, whose domination and influence in Europe would be felt beyond the Viking Age.

In the Scandinavia of a millennium ago, racism was not a factor. Danes, Swedes and Norwegians generally co-existed on amicable terms—intermarrying and moving easily between their respective countries because the vast majority of them were racially akin. Relations in the British Isles were another matter. The fact that Norsemen, especially Danes who poured into England during the 9th century, were referred to as "'gentiles nigri' (the black heathen), 'y llu du' (the black host) . . . 'y Normanyeit' (the black Normans) . . . [and] 'dub gint' (the black heathen, cf. 'dubh Gennti' of the Irish Chron—icles)'"—see *Old Norse Relations With Wales,* ix), reveals that racial hostility was prevalent among the fair-skinned English and Irish inhabitants of Britain (whose black-skinned Britons were in decline by the and of the Viking Age). In Scotland, though, black- and brown-skinned people remained prominent, but fair-skinned English, often coming as Norse auxiliaries in battles against the Scots, were pushing into the country and settling. There are no indications that Norsemen held racial animosity toward any of the peoples they plundered or enslaved, although their penchant for enslaving Slavs can be interpreted as a kind of racism, in itself. But Britons, fair-skinned Britons, had displayed a virulent antagonism toward Norsemen (Danes, in this case) since the 9th century when King Alfred marshaled all the forces he could muster to oppose them.

It is only natural for a people to want to expel an invading force from their territory, but Alfred's zeal seemed to go beyond that, was uncompromising. It was a consuming, seething hatred against Danish invaders, a hatred that was ingested by other fair-skinned Britons. Although treaties were agreed upon and alliances formed between Norsemen and future English and Irish sovereigns, the Viking period seems to betoken the dawn of modern racial hatred, the racism exhibited by Whites toward people of color all over the world. Understand that I do not mean to accuse each and every white person of embracing this mindset; it is meant in a collective sense, and we need only to look historically at the expansion of white Europeans into the Americas, Africa, India, and Australia, for starters, to see what destruction was brought upon the natives in these places. I am convinced that the modern disease of racism arose primarily in Britain a millennium or more ago, the product of abject abhorrence for the Black Norsemen who ravaged and settled the British Isles.

These were *black* Scandinavians, Norsemen, Vikings, *Nordics* who have been rendered white through repeated assertions by Eurocentric historians in an ongoing effort to portray Europe as the eternal homeland of Caucasians—and as a continent never sullied by black-skinned men. And, sadly, DNA science is now being used to buttress the falseness and incompleteness of European history that Eurocentrists have been feeding the world for the last three centuries or so, which will be discussed a bit further on.

Any commentary about black- or dark-skinned inhabitants in Europe has been simply ignored or denied—or else excused to infer some other meaning other than the most plausible. So, Western historians have asserted that Vikings who were designated "black" by historians of the time were so labeled because they had black hair or because of their evil deeds; so, black, as in "the black strangers," meant the *evil* strangers, and so on. In *The Story of the Irish Race*, Seumas MacManus discusses the Irish chroniclers' distinguishing supposedly white Norwegian Vikings from Danish ones by stating:

> This was not due to the color of the hair or complexion, for the overwhelming mass of the foreigners, whether Norwegians or Danes, must have been all fair and ruddy. (271)

Typical of Eurocentric writers, MacManus does snot explain or offer valid rationale as to *why* these foreigners "*must have been*" fair or white-skinned. Explaining the Irish distinction, he states, regarding the Danes being styled black:

> It is to be found only in the fact that the Danes were clad in body armor . . . dark metal coats of mail, helmets and visors . . . As they were the first mail-clad warriors the Irish had ever seen, it is no wonder if they seemed to be "dark blue" or "blue-green," as they called them. (op. cit.)

The armor explanation may seem plausible to some—juveniles, unimaginative people, or those who want to cling to the image of an eternally Caucasian Europe. As fundamentally a part-time writer, I consider myself ill-equipped to dispute a writer of MacManus' stature or the stature of any of the sources cited in this work. But the reader must look critically at what is presented to him—in *any* work or treatise—and question salient remarks an author alleges are factual, including the remarks of *this* author.

Are we to believe that the Irish never saw these warriors *unhelmeted*? That Danish Vikings wore armor but Norwegian Vikings did not? That a Viking of either country did not lift his vizor to speak or eat or sleep? Did the Irish, over a two or three century span, never pull off the helmet of a fallen Dane and see that he was white inside his black body armor (if Norsemen *must have been* all fair and ruddy, as supposed)? And if one Irishman had not discovered that these "blue-green" men were actually white men in helmets and visors, would not another Irishman have revealed it to him or to other Irishmen? Fair-skinned Britons and Welsh described the mainly Danish Vikings invading England and Wales in the same way, and the reader has seen by now that Norwegians were not different in any way in regard to complexion. And to be styled "blue-green" or "dark blue" further tells us that these invaders were *very* black when they began invading the British Isles.

The reader will recall that Hrolf the Ganger or Rollo (also known as Gongu-Hrolfr), who invaded northern France in the early 10th century or before (the 911 date often given for his invasion is disputed), came with an invading force of what must have been "dark blue" Danes who carved out the territory called Normandy, intermarrying with West Frankish (French) women, losing their Danish language after two generations, and producing racially mixed children throughout the territory.

So, a century-and-a-half or more later when Duke William of Normandy (great-, great-, great-,great-, great-grandson of Rollo) landed an invasion fleet of Normans in southeastern England, he and his Normans by that time had probably lost much of the blackness their forebears possessed but still must have included complexions ranging from black to tawny, or even near-white. With Duke William's invasion fleet were Bretons, also of mixed stock (former black Britons who departed southern England for northern France during the Anglo-Saxon invasions of the 5th century) who, having intermingled with Gauls as well as West Franks, must have had similarly dark- to light-skinned complexions.

Duke William landed in England with a great deal of luck or providence: Harald Hardradi of Norway also claimed the throne of England; he and William had planned a coordinated attack, Harald from Norway, William from Normandy. Harald's fleet was detected, impelling King Harald of England to make a forced march to meet him. King Harald of England's army defeated Harald Hardradi's army at Stamford Bridge near York, but in doing so, King Harald had left fortified positions in the southeast of England where his army waited all summer for an expected attack by William of Normandy. With King Harald two-hundred miles north, Duke William's forces landed unopposed near Hastings, in the southeast. Their assault on England had been delayed for more than a week because they had awaited a southerly wind to get them to the English shores. In the meantime, Harald Hardradi's earlier arrival—and the belief that no fleet would attempt to reach England in the fall—were factors in King Harald uprooting his army and moving north to face a sure menace.

The invading Normans had time to rest their men as well as gather food and horses from nearby towns for the expected return of King Harald. That came less than a week later, and another great battle was fought at Hastings. The Battle of Hastings was hard-fought, 8,000 Normans and their allies against 9,000-10,000 English. The numbers of men are estimates, but the battle could have gone either way, it was so evenly matched. Toward sundown the battle still raged, and most chroniclers say the English lost an opportunity to drive back the Normans because they failed to charge forward when the Norman ranks were in disorder. King Harald stayed in the background and was not seen in the midst of the fighting like William, who rode back and forth exhorting his men, taking an active part in the battle—having three horses killed under him in the process. A Norman archer, aiming high, shot an arrow into King Harald's eye. Seeing this, several Normans rode to where the injured king lay writhing in abject pain and cut him to pieces. it was then that the English began retreating, disappearing into the forest as night descended on the battlefield.

It took William another five years to subdue all of England. He was not popular because he took the land and property of Englishmen and awarded it to the men—Normans and French—that he had promised spoils of war for accompanying him on his mission. In *1066, The Year of the Conquest,* David Howarth states that 200,000 Normans and Frenchmen settled in England over the next two decades, "while three hundred thousand English people, one in five of the native population, were killed in William's ravages or starved by the seizure of their farm stock and their land (198). King William confiscated church treasures, taxed and oppressed the poor, took land away from its rightful owners and mistreated "revered and respected figures in English life, who were deprived of of—fice, reduced to penury, thrown at his whim into dungeons, chained and manacled, blinded and castrated" (op. cit. 199).

While the Vikings in Iceland and Scandinavia seemed to have exhausted their penchant for rapine, thievery and mayhem, settling into more pastoral lives respecting the rule of law, William's conquest of England was a throwback to the savagery of a bygone era that England and Europe had not yet forgotten. Most of the Danes and Norwegians who had settled in England, Scotland, Ireland and Wales had intermarried with the native populations of those countries, and descendants of Danes in England—considering themselves Englishmen, some slaughtered at the Battle of Hastings—were no doubt among the victims of King William's twisted wrath when he became king of England.

England—and Europe, in general—was not and never had been the exclusive dominion of white-skinned people, as Western historians have ever asserted and continue to suggest—now through DNA science. Should we discount the assertions of historians like MacRitchie, Higgins, Churchward, B.G. Charles, Sergi, Roland Dixon and others who have written of the presence of Blacks living in and dominating Scandinavia, the British Isles, Germany and other areas of Europe? Were these respected historians and anthropologists lying?

The Eurocentric elite, for whatever reason, had to (has to) keep Europe white, inviolate, purely Caucasian so that all other theories of race, evolution and superiority could be upheld without argument. So we have been told: the ancient Etruscans of Italy were a "mysterious" people, origin unknown; the language of the Basques of the Pyrennes region is an "anomaly" in an otherwise Indo-European speaking continent; Herodotus' *Histories* "has flaws," so perhaps his assertion that the Colchians were black and woolly-haired like the Egyptians was erroneous; the Moors who overran Iberia (Spain and Portugal) in the 8th century were *Arabs*, not Africans; Our Lady of Czestochowa (i.e., The Black Madonna of Czestochowa) is called *black* because soot has darkened her image over the centuries, not because she was originally painted as black; ancient Egyptians, Ethiopians, Indians, and the peoples of the Near East were, and are, of the Caucasian branch of races; *Nordics*, like Scandinavians, are, and always were, white-skinned, blond-haired and blue-eyed. Blacks have never inhabited Europe.

In the case of the latter—Scandinavians—we now know that these *Nordics* were black-skinned, that they settled Iceland, established several settlements in Greenland, explored Markland (Labrador) and Newfoundland (North America, proper), and ventured into the Gulf of St. Lawrence and, probably, other areas of what is now the United States. Norse artifacts have been found along the Hudson Strait to the north of Markland and at Godard Point in the Bay of Fundy in northern Maine. There are Norse cairns or mounds in southwest Greenland, and long-ship rivets were found on Ellesmere Island—northern-most North America whose northern half lies within the Arctic Circle—north of Baffin Bay, demonstrating that Norsemen actively explored parts of North America, proper. There was also interaction, however tenuous, with the natives of the continent, including skirmishes with Skraelings and Native Americans in Newfoundland, Greenland and elsewhere and, reportedly, significant intermingling between Vikings and Native Americans in Maine.

If these Scandinavians were blond, white-skinned, blue-eyed Nordics—the crème de la crème of Caucasians—who dominated Europe, terrorized the British Isles, became Christians by 1000 A.D., developed a system of laws to govern themselves which they carried to Iceland, why are they not given credit for "discovering" America over Christopher Columbus—who arrived 500 years later?

CHAPTER 13

COLUMBUS—AND CONQUERORS
OF PARADISE

All of us in the western hemisphere know the story, learned it in the first or second grade of elementary school: Christopher Columbus discovered America in 1492.

He came here in three ships, the Nina, the Pinta and the Santa Maria, and found people here whom he called Indians because he thought he had landed on an island off the coast of India or China. Columbus' "discovery" is honored annually with parades and celebrations, and Italians and Italian-Americans have taken pride over the years in Columbus' accomplishment.

However, even a cursory examination of voyagers to the Americas demonstrates that other men and groups of seafarers preceded Columbus to American shores—preceded even the Vikings, who arrived here five centuries earlier than he did. We have already touched on Irish monks or priests (Celi Dei) that Norsemen found in Iceland upon their arrival, and the Skraelings that Norsemen encountered and skirmished with in Newfoundland. However, visitors to the Americas have been numerous, beginning thousands of years ago.

The most obvious arrivals were the earliest Native Americans—later to become known as Indians—who most historians believe trekked over the land-bridge connecting northeasternmost Asia with Alaska for upwards of 30,000 years—until about 11,500 years ago when the Great Ice Age (Wurm glacial) ended. Such a migration of Asians to North America would have taken many hundreds of years, perhaps a millennium or two, just for the vanguard group (or their direct descendants) to arrive—each generation ad—vancing further than the previous one until the original vanguard group (or groups) ad—vanced into North and Central America all the way to the tip of South America. This widely accepted theory, though, fails to answer the question *why* descendants of the van—guard group continued to move so far?

If vanguard groups of these first peoples into North America arrived via the landbridge during an ice age—a journey which may even have taken *several* millennia—they would certainly have been people who were adapted to cold weather, having lived in the frigid zone of northeast Asia for many centuries before migrating to Beringia (the landbridge). After a millennium or two in northeastern Asia, they would have lived in the glacial vastness of Beringia, Alaska and western Canada perhaps several more millennia before migrating to the relatively milder climate of the future western United States. Why would such cold-weather people continue trekking south—through Mexico and Central America into South America, all of which, even then, would have had hot climates? Yet, this migration theory of the peopling of the Americas is the most prevalent.

Harold S. Gladwin, in *Men Out of Asia*, asserts that there were five major waves of migrants to North America from Asia. The first wave were Australoids, who became the earliest inhabitants of central and southeast Asia, displacing earlier Pygmy-like populations who had spread into the area. These first true men (Australoids) to leave Africa trekked east and southeastwards, peopling Australia, and then in all directions—traversing Beringia between 25,000-15,000 B.C. They then migrated down the western coast of the future United States through Mexico to the northern and eastern coastal regions of South America. Gladwin calls a second migration of Asians *Proto Negroids*, who "drifted eastward through India to southeastern Asia and thence through Indonesia and Melanesia to Australia . . . through central Polynesia as far as Easter Island" (op. cit. 94). This second major migration out of Asia to North America took place, according to Gladwin, between 15,000 and 2,500 B.C., and should also confirm for the reader earlier statements from Godfrey Higgins and others that central Asia was a cauldron of black-skinned peoples—some of whom, like Australoids, had already entered Europe. Other than in classification, there were probably no significant racial or physical differences between the two groups of migrants other than height—both types originating in Africa.

These proto-Negroids moved into the southwestern area of the United States, running into Australoids who had spread from the west coast of California to the Gulf of Mexico and northern Texas, and south into Mexico. The proto-Negroids became the so-called Folsom Man of New Mexico and went on to occupy the central portion of the U.S. There is evidence of interbreeding between second-wave proto-Negroids and first-wave Australoids, resulting in the people called Basket Makers—who spread into the Mississippi Valley and almost to the east coast of the continent.

Moving forward in time, there is also evidence that Chinese mariners set out eastward across the Pacific to reach the Americas. In 499 A.D. a Chinese Buddhist monk returned to China to report on a forty-year sojourn in *Fu-Sang*, a land 7,000 miles east of China. This monk, Hui-Shen (also Hoei-Shin), had taken a northeasterly route, sailing past the Aleutian chain of islands to Alaska and eventually southeast along western North America, noting the customs of the tribes of inhabitants he encountered. His story was written down, but parts of it, like his description of a Kingdom of Women who took serpents as husbands, seemed quite fantastic. Hui-Shen's account, most notably presented in *Fusang*, by Charles G. Leland, was examined by western scholars, many of whom doubted the voyage actually reached the west coast of North America. But a majority of scholars believe the account to be true, presenting us with a Chinese claimant to the discovery of America more than a thousand years before Columbus.

The Phoenicians are believed by some to have reached the Americas at least two millennia before Columbus. In *They All Discovered America*, Charles M. Boland informs us that "[i]n the sixth century B.C., they circumnavigated Africa, thus anticipating Vasco da Gama by a good 2,000 years" (23). This voyage was lead by Hanno, who departed from the Phoenician-established city of Gades (modern Cadiz, on the south coast of Spain) with sixty "fifty-oar vessels" with about 30,000 men, women and necessary foodstuffs and equipment. Phoenicians had established Carthage by 814 B.C., but a number of scholars believe Carthage was much older, perhaps being established prior to 1,000 B.C. From their cities in southern Iberia and the northern coast of Africa, the Phoenicians controlled the Pillars of Hercules and set sail westward, reaching the Azores and areas of the Americas—North and South. And lest we forget, it is very likely that Phoenician fleets were manned by significant numbers of Egyptians and north Africans—or that Egyptians, rather than Phoenicians, were the actual mariners.

There is evidence that Punic (i.e., Phoenician-Carthaginian) ships reached New England as long as 2,000 years ago. There are Native American pictographs on a stone at Assawompsett, Massachusetts, depicting a ship, and a partially hewed out Doric column in a rock in Guilford, Connecticut, and evidence of a Phoenician colony in North Salem, Massachusetts (Boland 32-34). There is evidence that Carthaginians sought iron in the Susquehanna Valley in Pennsylvania, establishing a colony there (op. cit. 40).

Inscriptions thought to be Phoenician have been uncovered in Brazil and other areas of South America. And Phoenicians (Carthaginians?) may have visited Iceland in the 5th century B.C. (op. cit. 26). It is unknown who the first Phoenician or Carthaginian to reach the Americas was, but we have in them yet another contender for the "discovery" of America.

Other contenders are rumored—especially people out of Asian and south Asian points who island-hopped across the Pacific Ocean before reaching areas of California, Mexico, Peru and other parts of South America—*children of the sun*—whose origins author W.J. Perry traces back to ancient Egypt. In *The Children of the Sun,* Perry skillfully connects archaic Egypt with archaic India and an eastward movement of these related peoples who, in still very ancient times, migrated through Indonesia to Oceania, Polynesia and the Americas, spreading culture, religion and architectural skills (i.e., (Teotihuacan, in Mexico; Tiahuanaco, in Peru) that many have compared to ancient Egypt. Perry asserts that these Children of the Sun assumed rulership over the populations of the territories traveled to, and asserts: "from Egypt to the ends of the Pacific, the archaic civilization was apparently ruled over by the Children of the Sun, incarnate gods . . . . Thus the Maya kings were probably Children of the Sun" (op. cit. 140-141).

These ancient builders of civilizations came to the future United States, as well, and were surely the innovators of the *Moundbuilder* societies sprinkled along either side of the Missouri and Mississippi Rivers. Perry claims that the Natchez tribe of southern Louisiana "had ruling over them, at the time of the arrival of the Spaniards, the Children of the Sun . . . . descended from immigrants from a country in the direction of Mexico" (op. cit.). Perry also attributes (as we have discussed) the megalithic monuments of western Europe to these Children of the Sun, who moved into Europe before the First Dynasty in ancient Egypt. He states, as well:

> Wherever it is possible to examine the ruling classes of the archaic civilization, it is found that they were what are termed gods, that they had the attributes of gods, and that they usually called themselves the Children of the Sun. This is the case in Egypt, Sumaria [Sumer], India, Indonesia, Micronesia, Melanesia, Polynesia, and America—that is, from one end of the region to the other. (op. cit.)

Mr. Perry's work is a detailed explanation of the spread of ancient Egyptian civilization radiating eastward out of Egypt. Although he does not use the term, he makes the case for there being a Greater Ethiopia—the term I used early on in this work to describe the land and people from Egypt to India in very ancient times. And unlike Eurocentric historians, Perry does not attempt to Aryanize, or whiten, these ancient peoples who took civilization around the earth, including the Americas, many millennia before Columbus.

*   *   *   *   *

Returning to more recent times and the men who dared to sail westward from European shores, we know that men of Scandinavian origin explored and settled Iceland, Greenland and parts of North America, proper, leaving evidence—in addition to more permanent settlements in Iceland and Greenland—that a small settlement was built at L'Anse aux Meadows on the northern end of Newfoundland, and that they ventured into the Gulf of St. Lawrence and trekked through Massachusetts, leaving artifacts here and there for future archeologists to stumble upon.

Then there is the tale, related earlier, of Aben Arou, the African nobleman, whose crew was captured by Norsemen and taken to Greenland with the fleet of Rolf Tollefson in 982. Blown off course in a storm, Arou's ship and several others landed in northern Maine and were taken in by the Native American Maliseet tribe. Arou later became chief of the tribe, had many wives and produced numerous offspring. There are also indications, perhaps more conjecture than factual, that Norsemen penetrated more deeply into North America—the ultimate fates of them unknown—some of which was touched upon earlier.

So, considering the last millennium or a little more, there is no doubt that Norsemen reached and settled in North America, proper. Maps indicate that Greenland is included in North America, as is the western portion of Iceland. Most believe that Norse settlements in Greenland were active until at least the 16th century—or for about 500 years—before Norsemen either departed or met some other fate. Some believe that the descendants of Norsemen "went native" and amalgamated with the Inuit people, probably something that went on during the entire period of Norse settlement there. Soon after Norse settlement, both Iceland and Greenland maintained ties to Scandinavia, but Greenland may have seemed too distant and primitive for Norway and Denmark to invest in. Certainly Greenlanders maintained trading ties to Iceland and sailed there for manufactured goods they, themselves, could not easily produce—furs, hides, white bear furs and rope. But for corn, European garments and wrought weapons, they had to depend on Norway and more than likely obtained these necessities through middlemen in Iceland.

Greenland did have a promising beginning, and to get an idea of how promising things seemed, we turn to Gwyn Jones, who states:

> The colonization of Greenland began with perhaps 450 souls, almost all of them Icelanders, and eventually the population would number 3,000 . . . . A decade or so later men had pushed on north as far as the modern Godthab, and there by the *fourteenth century* the Western Settlement would come to number ninety farms and four churches. (*my emphasis, Vikings* 293)

So it would seem that Greenland *did* prosper for quite some time despite its relative remoteness (the Western Settlement being the most remote), and Vikings are thought to have survived at least until 1500. In 1492 "a letter of Pope Alexander VI speaks of the church (cathedral) at Gardar and the grim condition of the Greenlanders, short of food, beleaguered by ice" (op. cit. 310). The fate of the Greenlanders can only be speculated upon, and Jones offers his on page 311 in the abovementioned work.

It is unknown exactly how long the small settlement at L'Anse aux Meadows remained intact, but its ruins remained to bear witness to the Vikings having been there. And New England is dotted with Norse inscriptions, cairns, coins and ship parts pointing to a Norse presence there, however fragmentary. There is also strong evidence, at least in one instance, that the Norse mingled their blood with Native Americans when Aben Arou and the Norsemen with him were taken in by the Maliseets of Maine—undeniable evidence that Europeans out of Scandinavia landed on the mainland of North America at least 500 years before Columbus made his initial voyage of "discovery." Why haven't our history books credited these earlier Europeans with the discovery of America?

Understand that when we speak of the discovery of America, we are speaking of the discovery of America *by Europeans* since, as discussed above, America was visited and settled by numerous people emanating from northern and southern Asia—overland as well as by sail and/or oar across the Pacific, island by island until men reached parts of either continent. Discoveries of human remains in California and southern Chile in the last two decades have extended human habitation in the Americas back to at least 40,000 years, and it could well be that the date for Gladwin's Australoid migration (*Men Out of Asia* was published in 1947) occurred at least that long ago, if not earlier. And while it is probable that, in addition to circumnavigating Africa in the 6th century B.C., Phoenicians, Carthaginians and probably Egyptians crossed the Atlantic to North and South America much earlier, their exploits are glossed over, marginalized by Eurocentric historians. So, we will look at Christopher Columbus' achievement to possibly ascertain why he is given credit for the *European* discovery of America.

First, we have come to understand over the last two or three decades that Columbus was a man of mystery. Doubt has been cast regarding his supposed birth in Genoa, Italy. Was he Italian? Spanish? Portuguese? In addition to Christopher Columbus, his name has been rendered Cristobal and Cristoforo Colombo. It seems that he wrote letters and log entries in *Spanish* and had a poor grasp of the Italian language, and never wrote in it. He supposedly had humble beginnings, yet was able to marry a woman of noble Portuguese background. He was said to have attended a university, but there are no re—cords to support such a claim. And he first sought backing for his American expedition from Portugal and, his request being rejected, ultimately appealed to the king and queen of Spain who, after much debate, agreed to finance his adventure.

Columbus was born, by most accounts, in 1451 during the last stages of the *Reconquista* and the expulsion of Moors, Arabs and Jews from Spain—unless they converted to Christianity. Having once been overlords of the entire Iberian Peninsula, by the time of Columbus' birth, the Moors only held sway in the Kingdom of Granada in the south of the country. By 1492 the expulsion of the Moors and Jews (Sephardic Jews) was being completed, and only those who had converted to the Christian faith—called *Conversos*—remained in Spain. Historian Salvador de Madariaga, quoted in *Lost Tribes and Promised Lands*, by Ronald Sanders, theorizes that Columbus' forebears "were a family of New Christians, most likely descended from Catalan Jews converted by the pogroms of 1391 who had subsequently migrated to Italy" (75). The family could have continued speaking Spanish after moving to Italy, never becoming fluent speakers or writers of the language. However, there are no birth records showing Columbus was born there, and Madariaga's theory—although sounding reasonable—can only be taken as conjecture until other facts along this line are uncovered.

It is doubtful that in 1492 most people, even Europeans, believed the earth was flat. Columbus surely did not believe this and certainly must have learned of the existence of a great continent to the west across the Atlantic from Icelanders when he visited Iceland in 1477 on a trade-ship. He had to have heard of Greenland, roughly 200 miles west of Iceland, and of the great landmass 500 miles southwest of its southern tip. Most of the exports from Greenland, especially wood for roof beams and ship-building, came from the forests of Markland. The Icelanders also informed him that the weather had grown colder over the last few generations and that extremely icy seas prevented Greenlanders from making voyages to Iceland. Columbus also spoke to several Spanish mariners who had been blown off course in storms and had sighted land far off in the west. So, when he and his three ships set off from Spain on August 3, 1492, he took a south—westerly course, certain he would reach land.

On October 12, 1492, his ships landed on an island that he named San Salvador, claiming it in the name of Spain. The island was one of several hundred in the Bahamas, but Columbus assumed he had reached some outer islands of India (or China, or Tartary) and called the extremely friendly natives who greeted him *Indians*. Those shallow, clear blue waters must have convinced him that he was somewhere off the great continent of Asia. Exploring further, he passed other islands of varying size in the Bahamas chain and stumbled upon Cuba, asking the natives he found there about gold and getting the impression that a khan ruled the large island. He found no gold but did find tobacco. Turning about (and losing a possible chance to sight the southern tip of Florida), Columbus sailed southeast along the coastline of Cuba and found the island of modern Haiti and the Dominican Republic, which he named *Hispaniola*, meeting more friendly native people and marveling at the exquisite beauty of this large island. He returned to Spain with samples of the produce of these islands and a number of captured natives as gifts for Queen Isabella and King Ferdinand of Spain.

In three subsequent voyages with larger fleets, Columbus discovered Puerto Rico, Guadalupe, Jamaica, Honduras, Panama, Trinidad (names, of course, bestowed by the Spaniards), and several islands of the Lesser Antilles. By now Columbus and the Spaniards had a serious case of gold fever, having come across natives wearing gold earrings and nose-rings. In some cases, gold-wearing Indians were ordered to stand in line, and Spaniards ripped these adornments right off the body parts they were attached to. These beautiful native peoples were unceremoniously put to the task of bringing more gold to the increasingly aggressive Spaniards and forced to produce other valuables like silver, tobacco and pearls. These avaricious men forced young boys to dive all day without food or rest to bring up oysters containing the precious glowing pearls encased within them. All the while, priests that had been brought along on the voyages were extolling the virtues of Jesus Christ and the salvation offered by accepting Christianity to the increasingly brutalized and enslaved natives. Those who rebelled against the harsh treatment imposed by the Spanish were killed or tortured—and many rebelled.

Subsequent Spanish adventurers continued what the Spaniards arriving with Columbus had begun, contributing to the near genocide of the native populations of the Caribbean. Bartolome de Las Casas (1474-1566) visited Hispaniola with his father in 1502, a decade after Columbus' arrival in the Caribbean.

Eight years later he returned to the Caribbean as a priest and found that the natives inhabiting many islands had suffered horrific slaughter at the hands of the Spaniards. In *A Short Account of the Destruction of the Indies*, De Las Casas records, regarding Puerto Rico and Jamaica:

> Here [in Puerto Rico and Jamaica] they [Spaniards] perpetrated the same outrages . . . devising yet further refinements of cruelty, murdering the native people, burning and roasting them alive, throwing them to wild dogs . . . oppressing, tormenting and plaguing them with toil down the mines . . . killing off these poor innocents to such an effect that . . . fewer than two hundred survive on each of the two islands. (26)

De Las Casas is saying that of a total of at least 600,000 or more natives on each island, by 1509, when he returned to them, only about 200 natives remained on each. His estimates may not be entirely accurate; in Jamaica, for instance, hundreds of Indians surely escaped into the mountains, and Puerto Rico had its share of hilly terrain where hundreds could have taken refuge. But the disappearance of souls on either island must have been alarming for De Las Casas to put forth such a claim.

I will not spend a lot of time here but would like the reader, if he has not looked into what the Spanish wrought upon discovering these beautiful lands, to get a sense of what Columbus' "discovery" engendered in this hemisphere. Writing in regard to HispanIola, De Las Casas states regarding the behavior of the Spanish there:

> They forced their way into native settlements, slaughtering everyone they found there, including small children, old men, pregnant women, and even women who had just given birth . . . . Some they chose to keep alive and simply cut their wrists, leaving their hands dangling. (op. cit. 15)

The same sorts of atrocities—and worse—occurred wherever the Spanish went in the Americas, and the priests who came along with them continued to preach the importance of accepting Christ as Savior to those who remained alive. Soon, however, even those who accepted this new and alien faith would die tragically at the hands of the barbaric Spaniards. From the Caribbean to Mexico and Peru, Native Americans were enslaved and forced to do the bidding of their oppressors on pain of death or mutilation. In two or three decades the Spanish had decimated most of the inhabitants of these areas, necessitating the importation of Africans so that the exploitation of the lands could continue. And it was primarily these imported Africans—who were spiritually broken and abused much the same as the Native Americans were—that are mostly responsible, over time, for replenishing the populations of the nearly depopulated Caribbean.

If the reader needs a fairly accurate visual picture of the period of African slavery in the Americas, European competition among each other for dominance, slave revolts and the abject conditions Blacks endured, he might go out and find a 1969 film called "Burn!" starring the late Marlon Brando as a British mercenary sent to incite a slave rebellion against the Portuguese on a Portuguese-controlled island. Another film worth viewing, stunningly filmed, is "The Mission," starring Robert De Niro, released in 1986. A less known but memorable film is "Royal Hunt of the Sun," 1969, with the late Robert Shaw as Pizzaro, attempting to extort gold from the natives of Peru.

No film, however, can make one feel, to the full, to the marrow, the horror, abasement, hopelessness and agony that Native Americans had to endure for the rest of their lives under the harsh Spanish yoke of slavery, rapine and murder. Enslaved Africans experienced much of the same misery and were also compelled to accept Christ by priests who consorted with their oppressors, and their condition never seemed to improve—though they faired better than Native Americans, who were shorn from paradise. African runaways were often tracked down by vicious dogs, which had developed a taste for human flesh; victims were often partially eaten after an excruciating death. Some recaptured runaways—fleeing

Spanish, Portuguese or English masters—often had feet or hands lopped off as punishment, while others were broken on the wheel, hanged, or had their bodies rent in two by the downward slice of a heavy sword. Numerous rebellions were put down, but many slaves *did* manage to escape, sometimes finding refuge with bands of escaped Indians living precariously in the denser, less accessible parts of the land.

In Brazil, colonized by the Portuguese, and on many Caribbean islands—most notably in Jamaica—enslaved Africans escaped from plantations, farms and smaller households, fleeing to mountainous or fairly inaccessible areas and banding together in m*aroon* communities. At first, these communities were primarily comprised of adults who fought off attempts by European colonizers to recapture them—some communities more effectively than others. In the Spanish colonies these communities were called *palenques*; in Portuguese colonies, *quilombos* or *mocambos*. In the English colonies they were called maroons, and Franklin W. Knight, in *The Caribbean*, informs us:

> The word "maroon" was first used to describe the range cattle that had gone wild after the first attempts at Spanish colonization on the island of Hispaniola. Then the Spanish transferred the term to the escaped Indian slaves, and finally to their African successors. In any case, *marronage*—the flight from servitude—became an intrinsic dimension of American slavery, enduring as long as the institution of slavery itself. (69)

Knight points out that "one of the most successful of the Jamaican Maroon leaders was a formidable lady called Nanny" (70), and that some communities went on raids for the purpose of capturing women (presumably Indian women, as African women were later arrivals) to increase their numbers, and that other communities practiced "the enforced sharing of women" (71).

Constant vigilance was a preoccupation in these communities, and although many of them initially suffered from malnutrition, starvation and disease, their existence—and resistance to attempts to destroy them—threatened the order and control of their European colonizers. Specially trained dogs were employed in Jamaica and Cuba to locate and recapture Maroons, but, states Knight:

> Notwithstanding the hazards, Maroon communities recruited and trained enough manpower to defy local authorities, wage successful wars, and secure their own peace treaties, as did the Jamaican Maroons in 1739 and 1795 . . . or a modus vivendi with the local communities . . . as did the Maroons in le Maniel in southern Saint-Dominque. (72)

Columbus never set foot on the mainland of North America—America, *proper*. Though it is often said that the Spanish came to the Indies in peace, that peace evaporated as soon as Columbus and his companions smelled tobacco, saw gold, and got a sense of the riches that could be obtained by possessing the startlingly beautiful islands he "discovered." Spanish aggression was heightened when they saw how peaceable the natives were, how giving, how innocent—and how they lacked any weapons that might pose a threat to them.

Perhaps the aggressiveness and hostility toward the natives was forged in the vicious struggle to wrest Iberia from the Moors who had dominated the Iberian Peninsula for 700 years which, along with white renderings of Jesus and Mary, must have instilled a racial hatred for black skin in the expanding Caucasian population of Spain. An attendant mantra that Whites must always rule Blacks also had developed—not only in Spain, but throughout whitening Europe—and the black- and bronze-skinned, black-haired natives of the Caribbean were unimportant, disposable objects to the Spanish and other European adventurers—people undeserving of the beautiful lands they lived upon and the riches that abounded within and beneath them—lands and riches the Creator had seen fit to place them in. (After nearly 800 years of Moorish domination which ended in 1492, it is doubtful that Spaniards were *white* in the same way that we view Germans or Englishmen as white today. Even today the Spanish are considered *dark* by northern Europeans, so common sense should dictate that immediately after the expulsion of Moors, most Spaniards would have exhibited signs of racial intermixture, though they may have been white-skinned compared to the natives of the Americas.)

An added impetus to this assumed superiority the Spanish felt came from the Catholic church. Although the worship of the Black Madonna and Child was still present in areas of Europe during the 16th century, more paintings and sculptures of these icons were appearing as white and replacing black ones in cathedrals and houses of worship, consciously strengthening the myth of white superiority and privilege in the minds of Christian Whites. The standard of perfection had become whiteness of flesh under the banner of Christianity. White-skinned people now dominated Europe, and actual black-skinned people were no longer seen by the greater mass of Europeans who (although the racial ancestry of most would reveal Egyptian, Carthaginian, Britonnic, black Nordic, Etruscan, African and Hunnish forebears) could not recollect Blacks ever having lived there.

Blacks, however, never completely left Europe, and many more were brought into Europe as slaves and servants by the countries who began colonizing areas of Africa, the Caribbean and the Americas—Portugal, Spain, France, the Netherlands and England. We know that Africans were brought into the Americas and made slaves, but many who were brought into European countries did not suffer the same dehumanizing fates. Many young black African boys were purchased by noble families, becoming "favorites" of duchesses, princesses and other noblewomen. These received fine clothes, were often bedecked in jewelry, and spent hours playing with and entertaining their benefactresses, riding in fine coaches with them to social affairs. These favorites were coddled, doted upon and sometimes slept in the beds of their mistresses. When they got older and too big to cavort with their mistresses, they were made servants in the house or castle and, in many cases, married women of social standing, the marriages arranged by their appreciative benefactresses. Historian J.A. Rogers, whose works demonstrated extensive research regarding the presence of Africans in Europe, focuses primarily on black males, and vigorously states, in *Nature Knows No color Line,* that a "source of considerable Negro strain in the white stock were the black pages who were common in the families of the nobility and the rich throughout Europe as far north as Russia . . . They usually married into white families . . . ." (130). Less documented are African females brought into European homes or castles, so I will not venture to speculate on their fates, although human nature being what it is, I would assume white-skinned males—royal or otherwise—sampled the fruits of these otherworldly creatures. Brown-skinned babies were born, and these grew up to also pro-create.

Nature Knows No Color Line presents illustrations of coats-of-arms of noble families with Blacks in them, coats-of-arms from Britain, Spain, France, Italy, Germany and Central Europe. Rogers lists family surnames whose nomenclatures express blackness or a black origin. We have looked at Svart and Schwartz, but *Moor* became a widespread designation for a black man all over Europe and from it we get surnames such as: Moore, Morrison, Murray, and Muir in Britain; Maure, Moret, Moreau in France; Mohr, Mohrenstecher, Morhbach in Germany; Moro, Moretti, Morello in Italy, and so on, just to offer a few of the multitude of names with black indicators or roots. In old Rome, *Niger* was a common surname for a black man, and a number of Romans had this name, including Pescennius Niger, who was proclaimed emperor in 193 A.D. but reigned for only a year or two. And regarding the Moors of Spain who lost their power in 1492 but continued to linger in Spain, Edward Scobie informs us, in *African Presence in Early Europe:* "In 1619 they were finally driven across Africa and over the Pyrenees into France. Many journeyed into Holland, Belgium and Germany" (191). These were not only men, but families, so we must assume that wives and daughters were among the emigrés to these territories.

Blacks were not imported into Europe in the numbers they were imported into the Americas, were not as brutalized, dehumanized or subjected to the rigors of plantation life prevalent, as well, on larger plantations on colonized Caribbean islands. The Africans brought into Europe appear to have been utilized mostly by European nobility and in the confines of castles and estates so that the masses of the European populaces almost never saw them and, when they did, stared in utter amazement at these sable-skinned men and women wondering where they had come from and how they had arrived in the country.

Other Blacks who were gawked at in wonder were the Gypsies, who suddenly appeared encamped outside of towns, or prancing along the main street of a city in a surreal caravan of horse-drawn wagons with colorfully attired men and women flanking each side of the train. Although the Gypsies (a derogation of the term *Egyptian*) seen today are light-brown, olive-toned or white in complexion, with various colors and textures of hair, they were unequivocally described as *black-skinned* when they first began to appear in countries and principalities all over Europe from the 15th century onward. Males and females had jet-black, curly hair, which, on women, often flowed down to their waists. In *Ancient and Modern Britons*, David MacRitchie cites an author who states:

> Late in 1417 there came to Luneburg [Germany] a band of 300 wanderers, "black as Tartars and calling themselves *Secani*".... Next comes a long notice of a troop of fully 100 lean, black, hideous Egyptians in the *Chronicle di Bologna* [Italy] (July 18, 1422) .... (140)

While most historians promote an eastern origin for Gypsies, this writer does not consider the issue satisfactorily established. However, they appeared in Europe at a time when Blacks were no longer prominent on the continent and were long persecuted and killed because of their perceived alienness. Along with the Jews exterminated in Hitler's Germany, it is estimated that at least 500,000 to 800,000 Gypsies met the same fate there. Much more will be said regarding the Gypsies of Europe in later chapters of this work.

*   *   *   *   *

In addition to never landing on the mainland of North America, Columbus did not seem to have time to establish anything that could be considered a town, so absorbed was he in finding gold and fame. There is almost no talk of the Spanish establishing anything resembling a town until 1508 when Ponce de Leon established the town of San Juan in Puerto Rico. But how much of a town could it have been? Certainly it had a church and several barracks for soldiers, a handful of priests, sailors and land developers to sleep in. Perhaps a fort and some kind of trading house were also erected. But who utilized them? The "towns" erected on other islands ravaged by the Spaniards could not have been much different and, except for the towns of the natives which the Spanish unmercifully burned to the ground, the islands were completely undeveloped and were certainly not places one would bring his wife and children to. These would arrive much later after the heat of gold fever subsided in these vicious men who felt no remorse for the horrors they had brought upon the kind-hearted native survivors they had found in these verdant paradises.

Who attended the churches in these defiled Edens except some of the very conquerers of paradise who, even after attending them, returned to their same destructive behavior the very next day? Native converts to Christianity? Yes, of course these attended—the bedraggled, dispirited remnants of a once cheerful people. But how many of these could have attended a church when, if we are to believe De Las Casas, only 200 native souls—and these, most likely native women—remained in Puerto Rico and Jamaica?

As the years of African slavery descended upon the Caribbean, Africans, too, would become Christians (as would most of the remaining Native Americans in Mexico, Central America and Peru)—the only difference being that they had not had their lands stolen from them in the Caribbean. Europeans would begin killing them and steadily encroaching on their homelands in Africa, and if slaves could have somehow returned to Africa, they would have found the same desolation and rapine there—much of it instigated by black African tribal henchmen of the European powers.

Besides the Spanish, the tormentors of Native Americans and Africans were the French, English, Dutch and Portuguese, who all competed with each other for territory on the two recently discovered American continents. African slaves, a significant number of whom had probably been Muslims back home, were also told they had to accept Jesus Christ as their savior if they wanted to improve their lot and, seeing no other way out except death, most of them and their descendants eventually would do so—in the Americas as well as in Africa.

Today the descendants of those African slaves and Native Americans, who managed to survive brutal oppression and murder, continue to cling to the religion forced upon their ancestors by men who demonstrated an inhuman disregard for the lives of people of color everywhere. They are Catholic, Protestant, Anglican, Methodist, Seventh-Day Adventists, Jehovah Witnesses, Pentecostal—*Christians*, not realizing that Christianity was imposed on their ancestors on pain of death, or knowing anything about the belief systems their 16th century ancestors practiced and thrived within before being colonized, enslaved and killed by men who were only nominally Christian; men who were almost always absolved of their sins by Christian priests who knew the wrongs they had perpetrated against innocent human beings. The modern-day descendants of African slaves and Native Americans (largely intermixed with Spanish, European, African, East Indian and Chinese blood in Mexico and Central and South America) continue to wait, hope and pray for deliverance from deprivation, fear and oppression—just as their ancestors did—while the ancestors of the colonizers and enslavers continue to live in comparative luxury, ease and opportunity throughout the Western World.

If there were any established courts in the early days of the colonies the Spanish established, they don't seem to have been effective. Any courts would surely not have brought justice to Native Americans or Africans. The Spanish were constantly involved in slave raids, killing without compunction any Indian or African who resisted, or attempted to flee his oppression. Such people had no rights to property, possessions, or their lives after the Spaniards and other Europeans arrived in the New World.

In the colonies there seemed always to be dissention among the Spanish over land, loot or command. These were the issues debated in the courts of the Spaniards. There was no discernible order in Puerto Rico, Cuba or Hispaniola in the second decade of the 16th century and, says Franklin Knight, author of *The Caribbean*:

> Cities in the Indies were mere glorified villages of crude huts and ubiquitous squalor . . . .
> Moreover the settlers rapidly learned to spurn agriculture and value only precious metals . . . destroying cattle, forests, and local Indians with callous abandon . . . (33)

And because of the fractious relationships between the Spaniards which often lead to internecine warfare and killings, a plenipotentiary (diplomat) sent to Hispaniola in 1500 took Columbus and his two brothers back to Spain in manacles and chains. Columbus' arrest and brief imprisonment is not fully comprehensible and will not be remarked upon here. What matters is that despite the destruction his landing in the hemisphere wrought, the negative effects of which continue to this day, he is lauded by the Western world as a great historical personage who transformed the world with his implausible sea adventure to the unknown West.

Questionable is whether this transformation was a positive one. Unquestionable, however, is that the Vikings arrived in and explored the *mainland* of North America more than 500 years prior to Columbus' landing in the Caribbean and, in at least one recorded case, intermingled—presumably peacefully—with Native Americans (the Maliseets of Maine). There is evidence that Vikings trod the soil of New England at least as far south as Massachusetts and established a settlement in Newfoundland, where it meets with the easternmost end of the Canadian mainland—an area the Vikings named Markland. From L'Anse aux Meadows they certainly explored further field, surely Prince Edward Island, Nova Scotia and easternmost Quebec, which they called Vinland. From the Eastern and Western Settlements in Greenland there is evidence they sailed as far north as northwestern Greenland and set foot on Ellesmere Island, both at the north end of Baffin Bay, about 80 degrees North Latitude—the area Commander Peary set off from on his several quests to reach the North Pole in the early 20th century—where several cairns, thought to be Norse, have been found.

Norsemen made regular hunting and trading voyages to the area trading, one would presume, with the Inuit (Eskimos), the only other people who would be living in the area, more than 400 miles north of the Arctic Circle. The Inuit the Norse traded with in those northern regions may have been a different Inuit group from the Inuits—called Skraelings—that Norsemen initially encountered and skirmished with when they first arrived in Greenland. Those earlier Inuit, or Skraelings, with "ugly hair" could have been members of the *Dorset* culture who occupied those northern regions from c. 1000 B.C. to 1100 A.D. The sagas describe them as *black* and living in holes in the ground (*igloos*, perhaps?) like the Black Dwarfs of Scandinavia. Their description reminds one of the Pygmy or Negrito people who were the first humans to spread around the earth before taller, modern humans made their appearance and did the same.

The Thule-Inuit people moved into Canada about 800 A.D., overrunning territory the Dorset people had previously occupied, and as the Dorset moved further east to out—pace them, they viewed the newly-arrived Norsemen as a threat to their shrinking territory. The newly-arrived Thule-Inuit could have found that trade with the Norsemen was advantageous; for polar bear or musk-ox hides, they may have received a few metal implements, a few hundred feet of sturdy rope, a small ax with a metal head and blade. And there is no evidence that Vikings killed Native Americans wantonly for territory or treasure. In fact, they may have acquired Inuit wives, although no solid evidence of this possibility has been established with certainty in Greenland.

The Vikings seemed to have undergone a transformation in the New World. The most feared fighters and raiders of their age in all of Europe, they seemed content in their pursuit of a more pastoral existence. The earliest settlers in Iceland secured large tracts of land, mostly engaging in farming and animal husbandry. In the earliest days, disputes and duels, as we know, flared up over land and the stealing of livestock or property, until dueling was outlawed in the early decades of the 11th century in Iceland. Althings were established by the onset of the 11th century where Norsemen could take disputes that would avoid the fighting and bloodshed that had always occurred in Norway, Denmark and the British Isles. Blood, though, was shed at times in those early years and, as we saw with Egil Skalla-Grimsson, sometimes Norsemen returned to Norway to claim lands they previously owned or which they felt rightfully belonged to family members. Norsemen who were declared outlaws by King Harald Fairhair found it expedient to flee to Iceland where they could escape the tyrant's influence. Men who, in those early years, committed crimes in Iceland—like Eirik the Red—often went to Greenland because they had departed for Iceland with many who had not paid King Harald's tax levy and would have been subject to punishment, fines or worse upon returning to Norway or any territory in Britain under Harald's sway. So, Grenlanders established two main settlements—the Eastern and Western Settlements, as well as an althing, to settle disputes among Norsemen there.

Although the Old Religion is thought to have survived longer in Greenland than in Iceland, Christianity became (c. 1000) the recognized or official religion, and Catholic priests would arrive in Greenland soon after its establishment in 999. Leif Eiriksson, in fact, was ordered by King Olaf of Norway to take a priest back to Greenland with him after he returned to Norway to tell of Greenland's discovery. As well, the then Pope of Rome was made aware of Greenland's discovery by King Olaf, thereby extending the Church's influence from Norway and Europe westward across the Atlantic to Norway's colonies. *So, both Iceland and Greenland were known to exist by Rome and other European principalities nearly five hundred years before Columbus' first voyage!* Greenland's first bishop arrived there in 1112 and, according to James Enterline:

> By then the Church was so well aware of the existence of new land discovered west of Greenland [North America] that . . . Bishop Eirik Gnupsson, upon his visit to the Greenland parish, sailed on from there expressly to visit Vinland. (175-176)

Leif Eiriksson is credited with discovering Vinland (America, proper) in 1000 A.D., and it is probable that a priest was along on the voyage, though it is not known whether a church was established there. As for Greenland (part of North America), Enterline notes that it was forced to pay taxes to the Church, and asserts:

> In this pre-Columbian period seventeen churches were erected on the west coast facing America across the Davis Straits, and in addition . . . [an] Episcopal residence . . . [and] two monasteries . . . (176)

Being less accessible than Iceland and having a smaller population, Greenland's development was generally slower and less attended to by Norway and the Church. One problem that cropped up was marriage between relatives, which came to the attention of Pope Alexander III, who was asked to consider that it was difficult for Greenlanders to sail to places where they could find brides. Iceland was a twelve-day journey (from Greenland), and Ireland a longer trip. The Pope consented to allow marriages as close as the fifth generation where the standard was that those separated by seven generations could marry. This seems peculiar, since the same sort of marriages were occurring in Europe, with even less of a distance between relatives, and would continue to occur down to fairly modern times. In *Royal Babylon*, for instance, author Karl Shaw informs us that: "Emperor Ferdinand I's [of Spain, 1016-1065] parents were first cousins" (78), and that "[b]y the beginning of World War I, the major royal families of Europe . . . were all intimately related to each other by blood or by marriage" (67-68), which has been pointed out by other chroniclers.

What is most relevant is that Catholic priests and houses of worship were established early on in Iceland and Greenland. The popes of Rome knew of their existence *from the beginning* and also knew of land west of them five centuries before Columbus. Whatever altruistic sentiments intrinsic in Catholicism five centuries later does not seem to have taken root until long after colonized native populations of American and Caribbean colonies were practically decimated. Whatever Catholicism was in the hearts of the Spanish conquerors of paradise did not quell their deceit, greed or butchery. Ponce de Leon landed in Florida in 1513 not realizing he had found the mainland of North America. More Spaniards followed—Pizarro, Cortez, Balboa—committing the same butcheries encased within their Catholic hearts that neither priests, Spain, nor the popes of Rome were able to quell.

Norse laws and religious practices, as far as is known, did not abuse Native American peoples and were fair in comparison to what the Spanish and other European adventurers brought to the New World. There is evidence that Norse trade with the Inuit, or the Thule-Inuit, was continuous in Greenland and its environs and that the two groups be-came rather dependent on each other—the Inuit receiving steel harpoon heads, saws, rope and iron blades; the Norse getting soapstone products, in addition to hides, whalebone and ivory in return.

Iceland, of course, continues to exist and prosper. They have always had a wool industry and produce their own milk and meat. Of course, fishing is a primary industry there, and they manufacture aluminum, textiles and ferro-silicon. Its population is called homogeneous, but, according to the *Encyclopedia Britannica*: "Historians differ as to t*heir exact origin and ethnic composition* but agree that between 60 and 80 percent were of *Nordic* stock, mostly from Norway. The remainder, from Scotland and Ireland, was largely of Celtic stock" (*emphasis mine, Micropedia, vol. 6*, 233). *Ethnic* does not refer to nationality so much as racial, tribal, genetic or phylogenetic background, and the reader has already been presented with ethnic evidence in regard to "Nordics" of the Viking Age, including those from Norway.

Greenland prospered for a time but was not as fortunate as Iceland. There is, however, evidence demonstrating that the Norse colonies there survived for several centuries, at least until 1500, with a few scholars believing the Norse lingered there until 1600. So, in regard to Greenland, are not five centuries of Norse occupation long enough to warrant a citation for *discovery*?

Fig. 18

Author Barry Fell speculates that Vikings explored the eastern coastline of North America, probably reaching the Mississippi River and points inland. In Canada, Viking artifacts have been discovered in both Baffin and Hudson Bays. There is also evidence that they reached the Bering Strait and the Pacific Ocean.

Even if Norsemen had remained only six months, leaving a few artifacts to affirm their presence, they were still there and, I believe, should receive due recognition. Most students in the United States—from elementary school through college—would answer John Glenn if they were asked who the first American into space was. Even older Americans, born after his February, 1962 flight would give the same answer. John Glenn is still living, makes several appearances each year, and the media attention he receives when he does gives people the impression that he was the first American into outer space—even that he was the *first* person into space, ever.

Even though only a half century has elapsed since manned space flight began, very few Americans know that Alan B. Shepard was the first American to travel into space (May 5, 1961; a *sub-orbital* flight). John Glenn made the first *orbital* flight into space. And, perhaps almost no present-day students or persons of middle-age are aware that the U.S.S.R.'s Yuri Gagarin was the *first* man who was launched into space (an *orbital* flight, April 12, 1961), nearly a month before Alan B. Shephard. Because Glenn orbited the earth and Shepard merely went up and came back down, should Shephard's accomplishment be overlooked by Americans? He was the first American launched into space, though the media never seem to remind us of this.

In the same way, Western historians have elevated Columbus to legend, despite knowing that Vikings preceded him to America by five centuries—and knowing the genocidal effects on native populations his coming engendered. Ronald Sanders accurately notes that Columbus has been deified by historians and notes that one biographer likens him to the Messiah (80). In contrast, the Norse achievement is diminished, practically unmentioned. Why?

We spoke earlier about the white European predilection for usurping the history and accomplishments of others and claiming them as their own. Over the last two centuries or so, Western historians have insinuated Caucasians into ancient Egypt, Sumer, India, Crete, asserting that the black- and dark-skinned people of these civilizations were actually white or Aryan—whitening as well the Phoenicians, Aborigines, early Celts and Teutons—to manufacture a more ancient history for the so called white race. To validate their claim that Whites have always occupied Europe, and to justify evolutionary concepts that a cold climate necessitates humans having little or no melanin, that they need to be white-skinned to better survive, it was compulsory to claim that Scandinavians were *Nordics*—presumably blond-haired, blue-eyed and white-skinned—and that Nordics, and Europeans in general, had always been white-skinned. And so, we in the western hemisphere, inundated over several centuries with Eurocentric scholarship concerning the history of the world and the movement of peoples, have relied on the integrity of historians who may not have been entirely honest and free of racist designs in their assessments and declarations contained in their works.

Except for China's ancient civilization, Eurocentric historians have insinuated Whites into the cultures of practically every other ancient civilization that ever existed.

Another exception to this practice would be the Native American cultures of North and South America, although historians make reference to light-skinned tribes, or North American tribes with numerous light- or white-skinned members, having blue eyes and various hair colors, suggesting a supposed admixture with Vikings or Phoenicians. Such statements also reinforce Western declarations that Vikings and Phoenicians were *white-skinned*, imbedding two arrows with one shot into readers' minds.

Several authors, including at least one Native American one, claim that Chief Crazy Horse, of the dark- to black-skinned Oglala Sioux, was light-skinned with light-colored hair. In *Crazy Horse*, Native American author Mari Sandoz states that 12 year-old Crazy Horse was "quiet, serious, very light-skinned for an Indian, with hair so soft and pale that he was called Curly or the Light-Haired Boy" (viii). Sandoz' book was published in 1942, just over 50 years after the last Indian "battle"—the massacre of Indians by U.S. soldiers at Wounded Knee. The remaining Indians in U.S. territory were recovering from their near genocide in the 19th century when all their land was taken by the expanding United States and most remaining tribes were relegated to reservations, often distant from their original territories. Most were living in deprivation, still depending on government allotments for their existence, which didn't noticeably improve their condition. Sandoz may have felt constrained to lighten the image of this famed warrior so that her book could be published—although it is not impossible for black- or dark-skinned people to have light or blond hair in their youth (remember Aborigine children). There is not one photograph or illustration in the 400-page book. But others who have written about the Oglala chief have offered a similar description of him. But later writers on the Oglala chief have repeated her description of him.

Fig. 19

It is claimed that no photograph of Chief Crazy Horse exists. The army major who took
this photo alleged it to be him. Even if it is not Crazy Horse, the Indian in this photo is
quite black.

It is widely claimed that no official photograph of Chief Crazy Horse exists, but this assertion is
probably untrue. Chief Crazy Horse was a "hostile," a proud chief who repeatedly refused to lead his
tribe onto the reservation U.S. government officials had designated for them. He was a significant force
in the decimation of General Custer's command at the Little Big Horn in 1876 and became the most
wanted Indian fugitive after that great battle. His people starving, bedraggled and tired of fleeing bands
of soldiers, Crazy Horse finally brought his people near to Fort Robinson and the Spotted Tail Agency
in northwest Nebraska intending to negotiate the surrender of his people. Soldiers captured him at the
agency and brought him to Fort Robinson. It is unclear whether he was stabbed with a bayonet that night
or the following night, but the photograph in Fig. 19 is purported to be him, although it is unclear where
it was taken.

It is said that Crazy Horse attended at least one council regarding the dispensation of Indian lands. Newspapermen and photographers were often installed at U.S. Army forts, hanging around for days or weeks when councils were held or when significant events took place. Does it seem credible that no news photographer ever photographed Crazy Horse at the one council he attended or when he—the most wanted Indian on the plains—was finally captured and secured in a cell, or even in death? If the man in the photograph (Fig. 19) *is* Crazy Horse, one might understand the reluctance of some to admit that he was ever photographed. The man is clearly black-skinned as were many of the Sioux seen in photographs of the period. If the man in the photo is *not* Chief Crazy Horse, but some other Native American, his complexion aptly demonstrates that entering North America through Beringia many millennia ago, after living in ice age weather conditions for millennia in northeastern Asia, did not impede the production of melanin in Native Americans.

If the reader scrutinizes indoor photographs of Native Americans taken from the early 1850s onward, he or she can discern that extra flash powder must have been used to make the subjects in these portraits appear lighter in complexion. However, it is easily noticeable that most were considerably dark-skinned, especially in photographs taken outdoors in natural sunlight.

We are told by Eurocentric historians that Native American peoples had traditions that white-skinned men, long before Columbus' adventure, had visited them and said they would return. It is often stated that when the Spanish came to Mexico the Aztecs received them warmly because they believed them to be the returning gods of their traditions, and the Vikings—"white-skinned, bearded men"—are often cited as their early visitors. The same story is told regarding the Native American Incas of Peru and western South America. Although Phoenicians and Irish have been suggested as early visitors, the Vikings are the most mentioned in North America, and perhaps they were—with only the complexions being changed to jibe with Eurocentric historical assertions. For, if the Vikings or Norsemen were white, blond-haired, blue-eyed, Catholic and, considering the Eurocentric penchant for inserting Whites in the most ancient civilizations, why is Columbus bestowed with the discovery of America over them? Wouldn't Eurocentric historians jump at a certifiable earlier date of discovery?

The answer should be clear by now, and the reader need only review the evidence presented in previous chapters. The Norsemen of the Viking Age were primarily black- and dark-skinned and atypical of the Europeans we are familiar with today—described as such by the presumably white-skinned people who saw them. It would be redundant at this point to revisit how chroniclers at the time described them. And while Irish chroniclers made a distinction between Norwegian and Danish Vikings, calling Norwegians Finn-gaill or White Foreigners, other Irish historians, including Seumas MacManus—who often seems reluctant to reveal the extent of black-skinned people in Ireland—assert that they were black, as well. Regarding this desire to promote a white Norwegian element in Ireland, three points should be understood before moving on to the next chapter. Point one is that the distinction is a deliberate falsehood so as to lighten the impact of the invasion of the British Isles by black-skinned men (notwithstanding the original black-skinned Celtic inhabitants of the island). Point two is to lighten Scandinavia and lessen the specter of envisioning so large a black-skinned population in the far north of a Europe Western scholars have always insisted was inhabited solely by white-skinned people. (The Danes are emphatically declared *black-skinned* by all the early chroniclers who have described the Norse invaders of the British Isles, so lightening them would be a daunting task and too obvious a falsification.) Point three is that some historians, Rosalind Mitchison, MacRitchie, and even Seumas MacManus (however indirectly) *have* asserted that the Norwegians who invaded Ireland were, indeed, black-skinned, but most modern historians on the Vikings completely ignore racial considerations. So our mental images of Vikings, gathered from books, movies, comic strips, TV commercials, oft-repeated declarations, and the knowledge that Europe is overwhelmingly white today, promote in our minds the belief that the Vikings or Norsemen were indisputably Caucasian—the ultimate Caucasians: tall, broad, blond, blue-eyed and white.

Further, the reader has been presented with a number of *Norwegian* Vikings from the actual sagas who are described as black-skinned. Many of these emigrated to the Orkneys, Iceland and Greenland where they tried to establish a new, less stressful existence. They were no longer seeking riches, plunder or fame, perhaps having seen the value in pursuing the quieter vocations of the people they had once ravished and despoiled. Europe had become too crowded, and monarchs too powerful and avaricious for Vikings to continue their old occupations. But when they arrived in Iceland and North America, they brought along something they could not discard by a change of habit, could not abandon like their farmlands in Scandinavia, could not vanquish with the mighty thrust of a trusted sword as they had vanquished so many of their victims. Most of them brought—because there was no way they could not—their black, brown and tawny complexions to Iceland and the shores of North America.

The Eurocentric predilection for inserting Caucasians into the earliest civilizations has produced a less than honest picture of history—in particular, European history. In the process, Western historians have falsely elevated the achievements of Whites to the detriment of the black and brown producers of the earliest civilizations, denying black- and dark-skinned people today the opportunity to take pride in the achievements of people like themselves because such people have been knowingly purged from Western history. As mentioned several times, such people are either never identified as Blacks, or they have been transformed into Whites by Western historians—the Vikings, an example of the latter.

Again, the question is posed: If the Vikings or Norsemen of Scandinavia were white, blond, blue-eyed Nordics, why have Western historians been so reluctant to credit them outright with the European discovery of America—especially if they could claim an earlier date for Caucasian achievement in seamanship and exploration?

In the areas of seamanship and exploration, Western historians have whitened the ancient Egyptians, Cretans, Greeks and Phoenicians so that we envision any ancient fleets—like those who plied the Mediterranean, or sailed to Troy to recover Helen—to have been exclusively Caucasian. The Phoenicians have been whitened to the extent that a Caucasian drape has been cast over the Carthaginians, the ancient miners of the British Isles, Phoenicians, who might have arrived in the Americas, and North Africa in general, casting doubt on the maritime abilities of the ancient Egyptians, who supposedly *hired* Phoenicians to navigate their ships. The histories of Western writers give the impression that only *white* Europeans had the ability to undertake significant maritime voyages and exhibit—according to Charles S. Finch III, author of *The Star of Deep Beginnings*—

> . . . a pronounced tendency to ignore or minimize the possibility or significance of the transoceanic voyages of *all* non-Europeans. The message clearly is that, prior to the Iberian voyages of the 15th century, *no* other people (with the possible exception of the Vikings) had ventured across the Atlantic *or* the Pacific. (203)

But while Western historians admit to trans-Atlantic crossings by the Norsemen—who *did* establish colonies in North America, most notably in Greenland—they somehow remain strangely reluctant to claim a European discovery of America five centuries before Columbus. The reader has already been presented with the only logical reason for their reluctance over the last several chapters. The Norsemen who migrated to Iceland and North America did not physically resemble the present European type. They were considered alien and *un*-European by their contemporaries as well as by later historians who sought to promote the view that Europe had always been the domain of the present European type (those we refer to as Caucasians)—a superior race of people who were (and *are*) solely responsible for bringing civilization to the world and were the world's primary civilizers and explorers.

The Vikings, however, did not match the present European type; the reader has already been presented with sufficient evidence of this reality. Evidence that the Vikings or Norsemen were predominantly black-skinned is not abundant, but there is enough extant to perceive the reluctance of Western historians to credit them with so significant an achievement as the European discovery of America. The post-Roman, superior European paradigm does not allow for black-skinned people undertaking trans-oceanic voyages of discovery; in fact, all trans-oceanic voyages by non-white people have been rendered unofficial or unsubstantiated in the writings of Western historians.

The Norse achievement, however, could not be easily discarded: they had ongoing relationships for centuries with their countries of origin in Scandinavia; the Roman Church knew of the existence of the Iceland and Greenland colonies and sent bishops to them over the centuries; and Iceland has continued to thrive into modern times, its settlement known to have been begun by Scandinavian peoples—whom Europeans at the time considered generally barbaric and alien to Europe. To reconcile the incongruity of black-skinned, alien people living in northern Europe, dominating most of the continent for several centuries, then crossing the North Atlantic to establish themselves, however tenuously, on a huge continent that almost no Europeans had known existed, Vikings were transformed into blond, blue-eyed white men—*Nordics*—by Western writers so as to conform to the desired, modern, superior European paradigm that infests the Western world.

Columbus' "discovery," in effect, brought the Middle Ages to a close, just as the European Renaissance was unfolding. Demographically, Europe had finally become what one could call a predominantly white continent. The Moors had effectively been driven from Spain; the Mongol invasion into Russia and eastern Europe had finally spent itself; and the dark menace of the Viking North was a distant memory, two or three centuries old. There remained a growing threat to Europe to the southeast from the Muslim Ottoman Turks who had expanded into the Balkans and would threaten to consume Austria and Poland, but the "discovery" of the two huge continents across the Atlantic presaged the modern world—a world that would now be dominated by a whitened Europe.

The most seaworthy European nations, having gained the wherewithal to travel greater distances from the continent, began maritime ventures to establish outposts that promised greater wealth: west, and southwest to the Americas, where immense tracts of land would be claimed; south, to Africa, where they would find the manpower to clear the land and work the plantations they were establishing in the Americas—engendering the African Slave Trade; east, to India and the Spice Islands, an area that had formerly been inaccessible except through Saracen middlemen. The superior weapons Europeans had developed enabled them to protect their interests and turn outposts into colonies—some of which would expand and endure for centuries.

By the 19th century, much of the black- and dark-skinned world had fallen under European colonial domination or influence, their civilizations and cultures suppressed, disrupted, in some instances, irretrievably destroyed. Ensuing histories written by Europeans would depict Europe as having always been a continent of Whites, espousing the notion that white Europeans were superior to the black and brown peoples whose territories they had colonized and that European subjugation had even improved the lives of these peoples. In histories written about Europe, dark invaders of the continent were lightened as much as possible—Arabized, regarding the Moorish invasion of Spain; Asianized almost everywhere else. Asians, no doubt, made up the largest contingent of more historically recent invaders. But Western historians have persuaded us that such Asians were of the "yellow," or Chinese type, not the *black-skinned* Asians Higgins, Gibbon and MacRitchie speak of—often obscured in nomenclatures like Scythians, Ugrians and Sarmatians, among others.

Since Western historians have long presented Europe as a continent eternally inhabited by Whites, *not* mentioning the race of a particular invading group renders it *white* in readers' minds. Coupled with scientific assertions that only people with white skin could have survived in northern climes with less direct sunlight, it has been made easier to promote the belief that the Vikings—living in northern Europe—were a blond, blue-eyed race of people. Native Americans, the majority of whose ancestors must have spent millennia in frigid northeast Asia prior to spending several more millennia in frigid Beringia and Canada before migrating into present U.S. territory—the majority still black- and dark-skinned when Europeans encountered them—are never factored into this cold climate theory. Nor are later arriving Inuit or Eskimo peoples (related to Native Americans) who long inhabited Arctic Asian regions, and still retain enough melanin to render them dark-skinned.

The Vikings, however, became white by *transformation*. I have not researched *when* they were transformed into Caucasians by Western historians, but there is no doubt that they were, and continue to be depicted as such—evident in comic strips, like the long running "Prince Valiant," movies, television commercials and films.

Except for spurious assertions by some Irish annalists that Norwegian Vikings were Finn-gaill, which supposedly meant White Foreigners, nearly all the histories of the Viking Age refer to Vikings—whether from Norway or Denmark—as Dubh-gaill (Black Foreigners), Black Gentiles, (gentiles nigri), black heathen, black devils and the black host, as has been discussed. These appellations included Vikings out of Norway, and the reader has been presented with a list of Norwegian personages from the sagas bearing color names indicating black or dark complexions, or who are described as swarthy or dark-skinned. So, sometime after white Europeans became dominant on the continent, ventured to distant locales, began the African Slave Trade, colonized many African and Asian territories inhabited by dark-skinned people, and began writing their histories of Europe and the world, they knowingly ignored earlier historical accounts of *black* Vikings or Norsemen, converting them into Whites—by declaration and repetition.

If the Norsemen were white Europeans, as most writers assert, it remains confounding that even Eurocentric historians do not credit them with America's discovery. Instead, Western historians often make comments similar to the following by C.W. Ceram, who states, in *The First American:*

> [W]e can only say that the landings of the Vikings in America, interesting as they are from many points of view, d*id not change Western man's view of the world or have any effect on his economic patterns.* That was accomplished by Columbus . . . by the Spaniards who were destined to conquer the North American continent . . . . (*my emphasis,* 54)

Although the Vikings of Iceland and Greenland did maintain and engage in trade, religious affiliation (i.e., Christian conversion) and, to a lesser degree, political ties with their homelands and with merchants in Ireland and Britain, their commerce did not extend to the whole of Europe, rendering such activities, one would presume from Ceram's comment above, negligible.

There is no record of Vikings conquering the wilderness or the indigenous tribes on the mainland to create a sizeable territory of their own—presumably another prerequisite for legitimate discovery since, historically, white Europeans invaded and occupied the lands of others for territorial and economic gain. If conquest and the acquisition of territory are prerequisites for discovery, then these supposedly blond, blue-eyed Nordics fail to meet the Eurocentric standard. Columbus and the Spaniards that followed in his wake apparently did—laying claim to verdant Caribbean islands and parts of continents; purloining gold, tobacco, silver, pearls and whatever other commodities they found profitable; kidnapping, raping, enslaving and killing the native inhabitants in every territory they intruded upon, which led to the near genocide of Native Americans in the Caribbean, Mexico and Peru—the total number of Native American deaths estimated in the millions. All of this before the English and French arrived in the Americas to continue the general practices of usurpation, enslavement and death—though not on as grand a scale as the Spanish.

To be sure, long festering European racism had reared its ugly head. This racism toward all people of color did not begin five centuries ago, as some historians allege. It had been germinating in Europe for centuries: in the zeal with which the Romans waged war against, and eventually destroyed, the Etruscans and Carthaginians, culminating in the conquests of Spain, Gaul and Britain in order to destroy entirely the black world and the commerce that had long dominated western Europe; in the frantic Roman efforts to arrest incursions by Black Huns and related peoples into the continent; in the way that white Britons referred to invading Norsemen as "black heathen," "black devils" and "black pagans," exhibiting an inordinate distaste for their complexions as well as their humanity; in the Crusades to the Holy Land to wrest Jerusalem from Saracen "infidels"; climaxed by now-Christianized Spain's vicious, century-long campaign to finally oust the Moors from the Iberian Peninsula.

The racism we understand today did not suddenly begin five centuries ago. Rather, it was five centuries ago that white Europeans realized they had the power to contend more formidably with previously stronger enemies and set out to impose their new-found military and naval strength chiefly on people of color in Africa, the Americas and Asia. Their successes in these territories fed their growing sense of superiority—white superiority. But to insure that this doctrine of superiority would be passed along to future generations (white as well as black) it could never be revealed that Europe was ever occupied by other than white-skinned people. Such a revelation would tarnish the mystique of white superiority.

European historians began producing works that expunged dark-skinned people from Europe—especially those whose ancestry could be traced to Africa. Allowing that Europeans—Scandinavians—found the shores of North America five centuries prior to Columbus would add luster to the image of the superior European; mentioning that b*lack* Scandinavians had achieved this feat would not. And so Eurocentric historians converted black Norsemen into Whites in their historical works without, however, crediting Scandinavians *positively* with the discovery of America. The reason for this oversight should by now be abundantly clear.

CHAPTER 14

OF FILM, FACT, AND FANTASY

There was a time when movies—*film*—had the power to reach the often unexplored regions of our minds. I am speaking in a general sense, and I refer to the better quality films, although films of lesser stature—even B-movies—sometimes had the same effect. When filmmaking was new, some silent movies even had such power, a number of them still considered landmarks in filmmaking history. When "talkies" emerged after 1927 (the first "talkies" appeared in 1927, but most films with sound were made from 1929 on) a film's ability to impact viewers was heightened, especially when supervised by producers and directors, European or American, who were not afraid to experiment, startle or explore realities of human character and relationships not attempted in film before.

In some of the better films, there was more honesty; one could sense the desire of filmmakers to challenge viewers' mores, jolt them with a characters' decisions, invade viewers' psyches in ways that had not been attempted before. Most modern films attempt this with action, special effects and preposterous story-lines—producers most concerned with how much profit a film can make. Of course, there are different genres of film, but I speak here primarily of dramas and the less fantastic ones. In the past, even if a film fell short of viewers' or critics' expectations, they would still come away feeling that the filmmakers were sincere in their efforts to present reality.

In a general sense, the better films of the '30s, '40s, '50s through about 1980 possess those qualities—vibrancy, honesty, revelation. If they were successful on all levels—whatever the genre—they were sometimes deemed "great." But even if they did not attain the level of greatness, the viewer's psyche or emotions were so assaulted that he or she would walk out of a theater feeling he had seen something so striking that he or she would think about the film until falling asleep that night; even the next day scenes from the film would surge up in his or her consciousness, flitting about his or her mind at work, on the subway, or walking down a street. In a general sense, many older films had that kind of impact.

Generally, films today do not come close to equaling films made before, say, 1980. Younger people, of course, would disagree with me here, but older folks and film aficionados understand what I mean—folks who recall the impressionable films and actors of the '30s, '40s and '50s; the impact of Orson Welles' "Citizen Kane" and several of his other films; the *film noir* period of the '40s and '50s; the explosive impact a young Marlon Brando made on film, on acting and the psyche; American and European films of the '60s and '70s that probed human feelings and situations formerly taboo or superficially treated in earlier films—especially situations involving sex and unfaithfulness.

Only rarely does a remake of an older film equal the original; only a handful have (and I'm not speaking of necessarily great films here) that I can think of, among them: "Invasion of the Body Snatchers" (1978), original, same title, 1956; "Farewell, My Lovely" (1975), original, "Murder My Sweet," 1944; "Lolita" (1997), original, same title, 1962; "King Kong" (2005), original, same title, 1933. The reader, and film critics, might add several more. In the case of the 2005 remake of "King Kong," which I grudgingly include, it is primarily the special effects that put it on a par with the original. However, most of the dozens of remakes of older films should never have been attempted.

The driving force behind most movies today is the money they will bring in at the box-office. The special touches that producers and directors of bygone days injected are rarely seen in films today. Thinking about a film after one leaves the theater is a rare occurrence; there is almost nothing to think about or remember. In older days one left the theater having learned something—something about love, inter-racial relationships, South Pacific sunsets, struggles to survive in a tumultuous era, people in other lands. Many included understated elements of truth—efforts by the filmmakers to inject what I will call *extra-reality* into films which, on the surface, may have struck the viewer as an anomaly—if the viewer even caught the inserted extra-reality ingredient. Certainly the extra-reality ingredients in films were the conscious choices of filmmakers, just as each element of a superior literary work is deliberately inserted and necessary to the plot, however minor. A few filmmakers have been skillful enough to weave allegory into a film, often without the viewer realizing it. The viewer may miss the allegory completely on a conscious level, but something will tug at the unconscious region of his or her mind, and it may even take a third, tenth or twentieth viewing of a film before he or she discerns the allegory and says: "Ohhh! Now I get it!" I had this experience with one of the films I discuss below.

Following are a dozen mostly American films in which I will briefly highlight truths, racial themes or aspects that I believe their filmmakers injected in an effort to be honest, insert reality or present an allegorical theme. The films below are not necessarily great films, though several are so considered. Except to refamiliarize myself with the plot of one film, I have not consulted any written works or documentaries, or spoken to any filmmakers or critics regarding any of the films I mention. I *did* see a piece of a documentary on the "Star Wars" series, but the documentary's commentary did not touch upon what I have to say regarding the first two films in the series. This excursion into film is not unwarranted; the films commented upon relate to themes that have been discussed throughout this work. In a few instances, more factual information will be offered, expanding on previous commentary. The views expressed are mine, and while some of the comments may be less compelling than others (or the reader may not find them compelling at all), I trust the reader will find some value in this digression. The reader has probably seen several of the films that follow but is encouraged to view them again to check the accuracy (or inaccuracy) of my comments. I will be as brief as possible, beginning with Viking films, which have never been cinematically successful or particularly memorable.

$$*\quad*\quad*\quad*\quad*$$

THE VIKINGS (1958)

At the beginning of this film, starring Kirk Douglas and Tony Curtis, we witness a Viking raid somewhere in England. Of course, all the Vikings are white men, and they have come at night, consistent with true accounts of their raids. One Viking leader invades the tent of an English lady, seizes her, and it is obvious that the woman will be raped as the scene ends. Two months pass in which King Edwin dies without an heir. We then find that the raped woman was his wife, the queen. Edwin's cousin, Aella, has illegally become king, but then we find out that the queen is pregnant with the child of Ragnar (played by Ernest Borgnine), the Viking who raped her. The matter is kept quiet by a bishop who has learned the truth from the queen, and the child is sent to Italy when it is born.

Twenty years later the queen has died, Aella is still king, and he is about to take a Welsh princess as his bride. The child who was sent away twenty years earlier reappears; he has been captured and is a slave. A fellow slave is with him, a black man whom we assume has been a long-time companion of the white slave, the adult son (Curtis) of Ragnar and the deceased queen. He has reappeared in Scandinavia (we are never told which Scandinavian country) after Einar (Douglas) has attacked and captured an English ship from which he abducts Morgana, the intended bride of King Aella. Eric (Curtis), who does not know he is the still-living Ragnar's son and the half-brother of the egotistical Einar, rescues Morgana from the lustful advances of Einar and, with his faithful black companion and the princess's maidservant, escapes Scandinavia in a boat and goes to England.

A vengeful Einar vows to kill the slave who took away the woman he wanted and was responsible for Ragnar's death. It was believed that Ragnar died pursuing the boat carrying Morgana, but Ragnar had been pulled aboard the boat by Eric after the pursuing Viking ships crashed on a rock in heavy fog, and Ragnar was also taken to England where he dies by the hand of King Aella (this particular story element is fact based).

The movie was an action film with the usual Viking clichés—sword-fighting, drunken revelry, revenge—which, perhaps could have been better. The point I want to emphasize is the presence of the black man who is seen throughout most of the film. It is mentioned early on that he was deaf and dumb, so he doesn't utter a word but is, nevertheless, present almost to the end of the picture. Later, when Einar and Eric return to England to rescue Morgana, the black man is seen with a kind of compass—a fish-shaped metal apparatus hung from a small chain—guiding the direction of the Viking ships on their route. The presence of the black man (called a slave) on the ship and the inclusion of the scene showing him guiding the ships has to be an homage to Viking navigational prowess—more probably to Thorhall the Hunter who, as has been mentioned, was chief guide to Eirik the Red and other Vikings.

Ohh. The brothers don't find out about their relationship until the end of the film, but they battle over Morgana and Eric (Tony Curtis) slays Einar and gets the girl (Janet Leigh, to whom he was actually married to at the time; they are the parents of actress Jamie Lee Curtis).

THE NORSEMEN (1978)

This is a forgettable film, which I saw once and had no interest in seeing again. It stars Lee Majors, who had gained television fame as "The Six-Million Dollar Man." I had to check a movie guide on this one, and can say that it concerns an 11th century Viking who comes to North America to find his father who had been captured by Native Americans. The one thing I most recall about this film is that there was also a black man along for the ride (ex-football player, turned actor, Bubba Smith). I don't recall this Black having any lines, either, and he was also supposed to have been a slave. I believe this film and the one above are two of only three American Viking films made up to 1978. Significantly, both include black men on Viking ships when they did not have to—certainly a nod to Norsemen, who were truly black.

THE LONG SHIPS (1964)

In this film, a ne'er-do-well Viking (Richard Widmark) goes on a quest to capture a ten-foot-tall solid gold bell that would bring him riches and pay off a debt his father owes to the king of the country (never named). He raises a crew, steals a ship and sails for Spain to find the giant bell whose deafening toll he once heard in a violent storm before his ship broke apart on rocks in an earlier quest to acquire it.

It is understood that the bell is somewhere near the Pillars of Hercules (Strait of Gibraltar), but on this second voyage to secure the bell, his ship runs aground and he and his crew (along with the Viking king's daughter, whom he had kidnapped) are captured by Moors, the leader of whom is portrayed by Sidney Poitier, who has seen the Viking leader (Widmark) before.

There is a lot of action—palace intrigues, harems, homosexual eunuchs, battles—in this film which mires it in a comic-book matrix that the few plausible scenes cannot pull it out of. But it may be the most interesting of the three Viking films mentioned here. There are no black Vikings in this one, but black-skinned Sidney Poitier as the Moorish leader was a bold decision in 1964, something Hollywood (this film was British-made) had not ever contemplated. Moors in those days—as in 1961's "El Cid"—were always presented as *Arabs*. In 1966's "Othello," Sir Laurence Olivier played the title-role in blackface'; and he was darkened up—and given an Arab visage—in "Khartoum," also 1966, as the Mahdi, fighting against the British in the Sudan.

THE FALL OF THE ROMAN EMPIRE (1964)

A better-than-average spectacle detailing the deterioration of the Roman Empire due to fragmenting personal relationships, deception and conflicts over power. It stars Sophia Loren, James Mason and Alec Guinness. Shortly after the beginning of the film the Roman elite are honoring the legions that have brought Rome victory in a recent war. One legion or division is a Numidian (black African) cavalry mounted on steeds. Films about Rome up to that time, and since, rarely show even one black face. Historian J.A. Rogers states that Rome had no color distinctions and that, "Some of the most illustrious Romans bore the surname 'Niger' . . . as [did] Pescennius Niger, one of their greatest emperors" (86). As the film progresses, there are several scenes where individual Blacks can be seen in Roman attire as soldiers or guards, their faces partially obscured by helmets. The viewer has to look carefully to spot them, but they are in evidence through most of the film.

THE SCARLET EMPRESS (1934)

A really good film starring Marlene Dietrich as Catherine the Great, with Sam Jaffe (five years before his portrayal of the title character in "Gunga Din") as the imbecilic Czar Peter she is forced to marry. Watch closely whenever Peter enters. He is always accompanied by two dwarfish black attendants. They look middle-aged, stand about five feet tall, and are dressed in fine coats. They walk Czar Peter's Great Danes or carry his toys. J.A. Rogers notes that Roland Dixon, in *The Racial History of Man*, states "the early Negro type could be discerned in Eastern Russia as late as the Middle Ages" (174), and that Schuyler, in *Life of Peter the Great*, states:

> Negroes were in esteem . . . Volynsky sent from Astrakan a couple to Catherine in order
> to ingratiate himself with her and Peter had several, one of whom was Abram or Ibrahim
> Hannibal. (op. cit.)

Abraham Hannibal, born in Africa, was kidnapped and sold into slavery in Turkey. He was later taken to Russia where he showed talent in mathematics, engineering and military strategy. Czar Peter appointed him to tutor Crown Prince Peter (later Peter II) in mathematics, and eventually black-skinned Abraham Hannibal became commander-in-chief of the Russian army.

The film, of course, does not present Abraham Hannibal, but does indicate the presence of Blacks in Russia in the persons of Czar Peter's black attendants. It is certain director Josef von Sternberg sought a more realistic depiction of Russia during this period than viewers were used to seeing in films, although the film may not have been historically accurate on all levels. Most of it, though, is truly fascinating to watch.

THE THIEF OF BAGDAD (1940)

This remake of the 1924 silent film, which starred Douglas Fairbanks, Sr., certainly ranks as one of the best ever fantasy films. Starring Indian-born Sabu as the thief, the film is replete with magical ingredients—a flying carpet, a life-sized toy horse that comes to life and flies, a huge genie, evil spells, and a beautiful, six-armed dancing enchantress, who kills with her embrace.

This film was a super production when it was released in 1940 in beautiful color (although the lead actor, John Justin was bland) and must have had the impact that "Star Wars" had in 1977. Most significant, however, was the number of Blacks seen in the film. They are seen primarily as palace guards at a time when Blacks rarely appeared in Hollywood films (this was a British-made film). One black woman appears as a character in the film—a maidservant who sings to the ravishingly beautiful lead actress (June Duprez), and another stands out briefly as a Bagdad resident. The viewer gets the impression that Blacks were prominent in this Oriental land (which they once truly were).

As discussed earlier, the whole of Mesopotamia and adjoining territories, were once inhabited by black-skinned people—part of Greater Ethiopia. Many historians have attested to this, but here I will only offer a passage from J.A. Rogers' *Sex and Race*, quoting one J.P. Dieulafoy, who wanted to—

> . . . attempt to show to what distant antiquity belongs the establishment of the Negritos upon he left bank of the Tigris and the elements constituting the Susian monarchy . . . . Towards 2300 B.C., the plains of the Tigris and Anzan-Susinka were ruled by a dynasty of Negro kings. (58)

The Blacks in the film are not seen as rulers, only as protectors of the palace, sword-wielding, turban-clad guards. But they were given a prominence not seen in films before 1940—or after, come to think of it. And African-American actor Rex Ingram's turn as a giant, flying genie with a booming voice lent another powerful black image to the film. Although three directors are listed for the film, the producer was Hungarian-born Alexander Korda, who produced a number of significant British films, like "The Private Life of Henry the Eighth," "Rembrandt" and "Fire Over England."

JASON AND THE ARGONAUTS (1963)

The Greek Jason and his crew of heroes, which includes Hercules, sail to Colchis to obtain the Golden Fleece. The film, of course, is derived from the Greek myth (discussed in chapter 6) and depicts Jason's travails as he sails toward Colchis, including a battle with a giant bronze warrior named Talos, who comes to life on the Isle of Bronze after Hercules steals a large gold pin from the huge vault upon which Talos kneels.

Nearing Colchis, the crew rescues blind Phineus from the Harpies that plague him, and navigate a narrow passage of water between high cliffs that begin to crumble and cascade into the strait. A sea god, perhaps Neptune, rises out of the water and holds back the falling rocks, allowing the Argo to pass through the channel without being crushed. Once through, they rescue a woman whose ship was wrecked by the cascading rocks. She informs Jason that her name is Medea. So, with Medea aboard, they sail to Colchis, where she departs from them. The film does not follow every detail of the mythical tale, but is entertaining throughout.

The scene the viewer should watch carefully is when Jason goes to the palace of King Aeetes. Women are dancing seductively, with Medea the lead dancer. But her skin has been darkened so that she appears to be bronze-toned or Negroid—not the white-skinned woman Jason's crew pulled out of the sea. Jason does not recognize her at first. And pay special attention to the entrance of King Aeetes. As he enters, he is flanked by at least four light-skinned black men who are his guards. This is easy to miss the first time one sees this film. I missed it as a teen in 1963 (as probably most viewers did) and the first time I viewed it as an adult when I bought the VHS. The reader will probably have to hit the pause button on his or her VCR or DVD to verify this, but will be able to note this extra-reality insertion.

King Aeetes is obviously white in the film, but he has very black, curly hair down to his shoulders. The insertion of these dark elements in this scene is obviously an admission to the blackness or Africanness of the Colchians that Herodotus remarked upon in his *Histories*. And while the film takes liberties with the actual myth (which also has variations, as discussed earlier), the inclusion of Blacks was a daring decision by the film's British producers who, nevertheless, made these insertions as imperceptibly as possible.

KING KONG (1933)

By 1977 I had seen this movie maybe thirty times since I first saw it in a theater when I was 8 years-old. I watched it nearly every time it aired on TV, mostly anticipating King Kong's first appearance, breaking through the trees to snatch Ann Darrow (Fay Wray). On Thanksgiving Day, 1977, it was coming on again, and it suddenly struck me that "King Kong" had been aired every Thanksgiving Day for the last ten years or more. Why? I asked myself.

I decided I would watch it afresh and listen more carefully. I'd heard the dialogue before, but Carl Denham's (Robert Armstrong) line, "I tell you Skipper, there's something no white man has ever seen!" as they sailed towards Kong's Island made me pay even closer attention.

When the group lands on Kong's Island, Denham asks: "What'd I tell you about that wall, Skipper?" referring to a high wall that cuts off the inhabited peninsula from the interior of the island. The captain responds: "It's colossal! It might almost be *Egyptian!*"

When Denham—a big-game hunter, filmmaker and leader of the expedition, had first mentioned the wall on the way to the island, he'd said it was "a wall built so long ago that *the people who built it have slipped back, forgotten the higher civilization that built it!*" When the captain made the comment, "It might almost be Egyptian!" the meaning of the film became clearer to me than ever.

Denham's remark that the people who built the wall had "slipped back, forgotten the higher civilization that built it," and the reference to *Egyptian*, correlates to ancient Egypt and its architectural wonders; it is a subtle admission that black Africans were the builders of structures like the Pyramid at Gizeh and Great Sphinx, at the same time noting that they had lost the knowledge of how they had built them, evidenced by the lowly condition of their contemporary societies. In the first half of the 20th century Eurocentric historians made every effort to assign the building of these great structures of ancient Egypt to Asians or Whites. However, a smaller group of white historians had always insisted that black Africans were responsible for them, and it seems that the filmmakers were obviously in accord with these.

Kong is offered Ann by the natives, who have kidnapped her from the ship as a sacrifice to the god of the island—represented by Kong. It seems to be a rite performed annually to appease this god. Kong takes her to his lair, killing a dozen of the pursuing crewmembers along the way. Safely back in his lair, Kong begins to slowly peel off Ann's clothes, sniffing the tattered garments (one minute of film edited out just before the film's 1933 release and reinserted in 1976) as he does so. She is rescued by Jack Driscoll (Bruce Cabot), the two making an unbelievably long plunge into a dark lake to escape. They run through the jungle until they reach the native village inside the wall, with Kong in close pursuit.

The white men, captain and crew, have command of the village now and direct the natives to help them defend the huge doors in the wall against a vengeful Kong, who bursts through the wall's giant doors, killing everyone he can in an effort to retrieve his sacrificial bride. Kong is felled by gas bombs the white intruders have brought along. As an unconscious Kong lies sprawled on the beach, Denham yells to the crewmen to get anchor-chains to build a raft to float Kong to the ship: "Why, the whole world will pay to see this!" The captain says dryly: "No chains will ever hold that," to which Denham retorts (and these lines are very prophetic): "We'll give him more than chains! He's always been *king* of his world! But we'll teach him *fear!* We're millionaires, boys! I'll share it with all of you!"

You know the rest of the story: Kong is taken to New York City and unveiled in a large theater in chains, looking almost like a huge Christ figure on a cross. He escapes, and recaptures Ann; wreaks havoc in New York City, destroys part of the now dismantled Third Avenue El in the process. He climbs to the top of the Empire State Building and is shot down by several airplanes. Ann Darrow never falls in love with the greatest ape, as she does in the special-effects-driven 2005 remake, which does not capture the mood and mystery that the black-and-white 1933 film casts.

Denham's rants accurately reflect the feelings of Europeans or Whites in regard to Africans and their enslavement. He calls for chains to secure his powerful black cargo. When the skipper doubts that chains would hold this powerful creature, Denham's retort is, ". . . we'll teach him *fear!*" precisely what enslaving Whites had to do to effect the enslavement of Blacks—otherwise, it could not have been accomplished. And Denham's pronouncement that Kong had "always been *king* of his world," accurately captures how Europeans had regarded Africa and Africans: Africa had once been impregnable, a dark, unknown, foreboding continent inhabited by powerful black men who had once spread the light of civilization and reigned over most of the ancient world—kings, in effect, who had "slipped back, forgotten the higher civilization that built it." Denham's declaration: "We're millionaires, boys! I'll share it with all of you!"

reflects the enormous profits Europeans expected to make from their capture and enslavement of this fearsome being once they taught him fear and put him to work for their advantage.

What an allegory of the Black Man, Africans, being brought to America! This was the haunting subtext that continued to draw me to the original "King Kong" over and over—something I could never put my finger on until that Thanksgiving day in 1977, although I had always seen Kong as representative of a black man. Now the *whole*, underlying meaning of the film became clear to me. I have not researched reviews of the film at the time of its release in 1933. Some reviewer might have seen the allegory and written an article outlining it. I don't know.

The film must have made a stupendous impact on viewers—released only five or six years after sound was added to films. White men sail to a place they know nothing about that a powerful being, more powerful than anything they can imagine, is supreme ruler of. In their zeal to uncover the mysteries the island holds, they disrupt the normal activities of the natives, tempting them with a white woman, arriving with superior arms, quickly eliminating native leadership. They capture Kong—god or Supreme Being of the island—and take him away so they can make millions off of him in America.

While each and every detail may not correspond precisely to Africans being brought to the Americas— the white woman, for instance, can represent new and alluring ideas, products like guns, garments or whiskey, items that Africans had never seen and desired to possess—the allegory should be apparent to the reader by now. Kong, the Supreme Being of the island, is the spirit or unconquered essence of Africa; he (or it) is alien, mysterious, omnipotent. He is representative of the millions of strong black men who were taken out of Africa and enslaved, and Denham's remarks, after Kong has been felled by a gas bomb and is lying on the shore, accurately summarizes the feelings of the European slave-raiders that have echoed for five centuries: "He's always been king of his world! But we'll teach him *fear!*"—precisely what European and American enslavers had to instill in the Africans they brought to the Americas in order to contain them.

While the subjugation and enslavement of Blacks by colonial powers in Africa brought economic power to Europe, it was black slave labor—the work, sweat and suffering these enslaved Africans endured, without pay—that made America rich and elevated her above the other nations of the world. We've heard that African slaves served as the engines of agriculture in the southern United States, working the cotton and tobacco plantations, but their contribution to the economic development and enrichment of colonial America and then the United States went beyond this. In *How Europe Underdeveloped Africa,* author Walter Rodney states:

> [I]n New England, trade with Africa, Europe, and the West Indies in slaves and slave-grown products supplied cargo for their [i.e., American colonies] merchant marine, stimulated the growth of their shipbuilding industry, built up their towns and their cities, and enabled them to utilize their forests, fisheries, and soil more effectively . . . . [P]rofits from the slave activities went into the coffers of political parties . . . [and] the African stimulation and black labor played a vital role in extending European control over the present territory of the United States—notably in the South, but including also the "Wild West," where black cowboys were active. (87)

The Thanksgiving Day holiday is not only a celebration of the so-called Pilgrims' feast with Native Americans of the Wampanoag tribe; it is a celebration of all the things that made America a great nation, and these include the African slaves that fundamentally enriched America. This has to be the reason that "King Kong,"—the original 1933 version—was aired every Thanksgiving Day for at least two decades, from the '60s into the '80s.

But much more can be said about this film, having to do with race and the general disregard that Whites exhibited toward Blacks in 1933 America.

Generally, white males have always resented—hated—the idea of black men consorting with white women, found even the thought of it abominable both before and after slavery—in every part of the United States. Many white males still become incensed at seeing a black man consorting with a white woman today—whether the couple are married or not. These feelings are deeply ingrained and are not likely to disappear any time soon. They were far more rampant in 1933, and so in no way would predominantly white audiences accept King Kong being allowed to have a meaningful relationship with Ann Darrow—even if one were somehow possible. It could not happen in America. I'm certain that most viewers saw Kong as more than a huge ape, associating him with black people since he lived among black natives on an unexplored island, quite similar to the way Whites had once regarded sub-Saharan Africa until the need for slave labor drove them to explore areas further inland. Previously, it had truly been a "dark continent" to Europeans.

Ann's incessant screaming was more than a rejection against whatever fate awaited her from Kong: they were screams against all black men, of being touched by them, stared at lasciviously, clutched and handled by them. Ann was young, pretty, white and blond—the quintessential white woman. She could not be handled and abused by a huge, strong, black *ape*—a lingering concept of black men from the days of slavery and a contemporary belief in the minds of most Whites fostered by well-known anthropologists and psychologists of the late 19th and early 20th century, like Carl Jung who once opined that Blacks had one less layer of brain matter than Whites. Others equated Blacks with apes, concluding they were slow-witted, imitative rather than innovative, and not quite human. Most of these beliefs lingered past the mid-20th century (and even continue into the 21st) but were vastly more common in the 1930's.

In 1915 D.W. Griffith's film, "The Birth of a Nation," promoted white racist sentiments, with at least one scene of a lust-consumed black man (a white actor in black-face) chasing a white woman through the woods intending to rape her. This film had a powerful impact in its day. "King Kong" debuted 18 years later, and it might be said that the black ape-white woman relationship in the film was a rehashing of the sentiments espoused in "Birth of a Nation." Hearing Ann Darrow's alternate screams and whimpers, the white hero of the film (Cabot) dares all in his pursuit of Kong, willing to sacrifice his life to rescue her from the black ape's clutches—the same actions white men in the south would have taken had a white woman been abducted by a black man. The mere hint that a black man had insulted or violated a white woman summoned posses of white men to hunt down even *innocent* Blacks, drag them out of their hovels, out of jail cells, off of trains and into the woods to mutilate their bodies, hang them from trees, or publicly hang them in broad daylight before hundreds of onlookers, some with children in tow. Blacks should not consort with white women. Ann's screams, the white hero's relentless pursuit of the black ape who had taken her, the movie "King Kong," itself, is a precise reflection of white America's sentiments at the time.

Film commentators often call "King Kong" a fantasy, considering it another version the children's tale *La Belle et la bete*—"Beauty and the Beast"—which Carl Denham alludes to in the film. But the film is more than a fantasy. Ann Darrow never warms to her lustful captor, screaming whenever Kong reaches for her. In the end, Kong—unloved and pursued—climbs to the top of perhaps the most famous phallic symbol ever constructed: the Empire State Building. This was as far as he could rise above the turmoil and hatred that greeted him in New York City. After the airplanes fire enough bullets to mortally wound him, he lifts up Ann Darrow in a final, tender embrace. Ann does not scream this time, eying him with just a hint of respect, perhaps admiration.

Then Kong gently lays her down before tumbling down to the street. Jack Driscoll then emerges from inside the dome of the roof to embrace Ann at the top of a man-made white world, buildings far below them stretching to the horizon.

Despite its age, "King Kong" is widely regarded as one of the greatest American films ever made—still in the top 100 greatest films of all time. Call it a fantasy or an adventure film, if you like. But the allegory of Africans being captured and brought to America to make money for their captors, along with the other aspects discussed above, is unmistakable. I have to believe that the producers of this film clearly understood the ingredients they were weaving into it. The mood, power and menace of the film is still evident to someone who views it seriously. The new film (forget the 1976, Dino De Laurentiis-produced version) has truly spectacular special effects and shows an almost humanized Kong in an amusing scene as he watches Ann Darrow (Naomi Watts) cavort near the edge of a cliff as she tries to figure out a way to escape. The 1933 King Kong is somewhat humanized, but his humanization is accomplished with human-like gestures—checking the jaw of a tyrannosaurus he has just killed to see if it was dead; breaking a branch off a tree and tossing it behind him as if trying to cover his tracks—but he never betrays his ferociousness or feral instincts.

And while the original "King Kong" is a great film as it is, it is greater still—b*rilliant*—for the allegory it effectively embodies.

THE WICKER MAN (1973)

Considered a horror film when it was initially released, this film offers the astute viewer some insight into aspects of the *Old Religion,* or so-called *paganism,* which once suffused the whole of Europe before the conquest of Christianity. In a modern-day setting, a Scottish police inspector receives a mysterious letter regarding the disappearance of a young girl on Summerisle, an actual island off the west coast of England in the Irish Sea.

The inspector, Sergeant Howie (Edward Woodward), is a fervent Christian and part-time minister who soon discovers that the inhabitants of the island do not share his Christian faith and, in fact, seem to abhor Christianity. In the pub at night they sing sexually suggestive folk songs, and their adolescents are encouraged to be sexually active. On his first night on the island, Sgt. Howie hears lovemaking between a youth and an older woman in the room adjoining his in the pub or inn. When he ventures outside, he sees several pairs of youths engaged in sex in a field. And no one he speaks to seems to know of any young girl who has disappeared on the small island.

When he meets Lord Summerisle (Christopher Lee), leader of the island, he receives confirmation that the island's inhabitants are indeed pagans. When Sgt. Howie attempts to leave the island, he finds that his small sea-plane has been damaged. There are preparations underway for an annual festival. Howie goes about looking for information regarding Rowan, the missing girl, and finds her mother and sister who say that she is not dead but has been transformed into a hare. Howie sees children dancing around a maypole (a phallic symbol) as a man sings a sexually-laden folk-song; he sees umbilical cords of babies hanging from trees near a cemetery, and naked, teenaged girls dancing around and leaping over a fire in broad daylight in the countryside.

On the day of the festival, he enters houses in search of the girl. Island people are not at home, and Sgt. Howie sees some of them in costumes as he goes from place to place. He knocks out a reveler inside his house and dresses in the man's costume so he can infiltrate a group of costumed revelers, marching with them to a rocky area over-looking the sea. Then he catches sight of the missing girl, who flees into a cave. He pursues her and follows her to what she insists will be a place of safety. As they emerge from another entrance to the cave, the islanders are waiting for him. Then the girl runs to Lord Summerisle's side and asks: "Did I do it right?" Yes, he tells her. He goes on to explain to Sgt. Howie that the island's well-being depends on its crops, which had failed the year before. A sacrifice was needed, a human sacrifice, to insure a good harvest this year.

And now Howie—who has donned the costume of the Fool—was to meet the *Wicker Man.* Howie is subdued and marched to a 50-foot tall wooden structure in the form of a man. He is placed into a compartment within the structure and it is set afire while the islanders—dressed in costumes for the occasion—encircle the structure, singing and dancing gaily. The scene of Howie's sacrificial demise is still a shocking, harrowing sight as he screams, "*JESUS! JESUS!*" as the flames begin licking at his feet and soon consume him. The reader will find this particular sacrifice and information about pagan rites in James Frazer's *The Golden Bough* (pp. 650-658). The book details pagan practices that took place in various areas of Europe to the time of the book's publication (1944).

While it is not certain what beliefs and particular practices the Norse religion entailed, the film reveals that the pagan practices of the people on Summerisle performed without the slightest guilt, were wholly natural to them. This was what was so shocking to Sergeant Howie and to critics and movie-goers in 1973.

Although no Blacks are seen in the film, there are hints of association and references to Blacks in the chocolate men confections and large sun-cakes the islanders prepare for their big festival. And, for whatever it is worth, notice the dark-skinned, curly haired man sitting in the church at the beginning of the film. We have discussed black Picts, Scots, and Celts as ancient inhabitants of Scotland and Britain. The man sitting on the church pew is much darker than the other attendees and, I'm certain, is there as a testament to the formerly black-skinned inhabitants of the British Isles who practiced the Old Religion—although the dark-skinned man is now in a Christian church.

QUEST FOR FIRE (1981)

This film is set in Europe 80,000 years ago and concerns a tribe of Europeans living precariously in an environment rife with danger: saber-toothed lions, wolves, woolly mammoths, and tribes of sub-human sapiens. In their cold environment, they have become familiar with the benefits of fire—for warmth, cooking meat, and protection from wild animals. But they have not yet learned to produce fire themselves. They acquire it from wherever they can get it—lightning-struck trees or grass, or stealing it from other sapiens. They have fashioned a bone-constructed implement for preserving fire, draped over with a piece of animal hide to keep the living flame from being blown out, and an elder is entrusted with carrying it around.

After this human tribe is attacked by a tribe of hairy sub-humans, and then chased by vicious wolves, the Europeans flee to a small island in a marsh. They shiver from the cold, their animal-skin garments no protection from the wind. They spot the fire-bearer across the marsh with the hide-covered fire-holder. They excitedly rant and howl as the fire-bearer wades through the marsh-water toward the small island. They are obviously anticipating the warmth they will soon feel. Some members wade into the water to grab the fire-holder from the old man to receive it sooner, but the man who takes it loses his balance and stumbles into the water. The flame is doused as the fire-keeping device falls into the water.

The tribe members compel the one who dropped the fire-holder to go find a new fire. So, he and his two brothers set off into the wilderness to do so, a tall, blond brother (Everett McGill) leading the trio. In their travels they spy smoke and make their way to the source. Drawing closer, they see a small group of fearsome-looking humanoids, different from the sub-human sapiens who attacked their tribe earlier. The humanoids were eating, gathered around a good-burning fire. The brothers also spy two females of a different tribe—and of human type—trussed in some bushes nearby. One has had an arm cut off, and the brothers realize the fearsome-looking humanoids are cannibals when they see one member pull the girl's arm from out of the fire and begin to snack on it.

One of the brothers diverts the tribe's attention with shouts, while the blond brother manages to steal a burning log in the confusion and starts to flee with it. But he is attacked and bitten in the groin by the leader of the humanoids. He manages to pick up a stone and crush the creature's skull, before making off with a few burning branches.

Reunited in concealing bushes some distance away, the brothers are enjoying the warmth from the fire-holder they have relit when the uninjured girl, who escaped her captors in the confusion, approaches them cautiously. She soothes the blond brother's injury and, reluctantly is allowed to stay with the brothers. It is clear that the girl (Rae Dawn Chong) is dark-skinned, despite her body being covered in a muddy substance. Her body is, nevertheless, slim and appealing.

The brothers have a very primitive language, but hers is more advanced. She also laughs a lot, something the brothers seem perplexed about; laughter does not come easy to them or the members of their tribe. A few days later, she sees a flock of birds high in the sky and excitedly points at their southward course. She urges the brothers to follow her. The brothers, however, continue their trek northward, wanting to return to their destitute tribesmen. They awake the next morning to find that the girl has departed. They continue their trek, but the next day the blond brother, who has fallen in love with the girl, misses her. He turns southward to the dismay of his brothers, who reluctantly follow him—demonstrating that these ancient white men had no notion of love.

The brothers are seen crossing a narrow stream which, I believe, represents the Mediterranean, nearly devoid of water, as it must have been during the great ice age. Having moved far ahead of his brothers, the blond brother spies the girl's tribe. The tribe members are dark-skinned and mud-covered like the girl—apparently a tribal practice. They live in huts made of animal skins, wear jewelry, laugh a lot, have an advanced spear-flinging weapon or slingshot arrow, and are obviously an infinitely more advanced tribe than the one the blond and his brothers come from. They also know the secret of making fire. The blond brother is captured by the tribe and rolled in mud so that he can resemble other members of the tribe.

A few days later, a member of the tribe—quite obviously a black, African-looking man—sits the blond brother in a cave and squats on the ground himself. He begins compacting grasses into a small mud-cake, which he puts on the ground. Then he puts a foot-long stick of wood vertically into the middle of the mud-cake and begins rubbing it rapidly between his palms. The blond brother watches him, unaware of what the man is doing. Then he sees a small stream of smoke emanate from the mud-cake as the man rubs the stick more rapidly. The blond brother perks up, staring intently now as smoke continues to drift upward. When the black man puts a few small twigs over the mud-cake, a small fire ignites and grows when the man adds larger twigs to the flame. The expression on the blond European's face is one of total wonderment and awe. He seems on the verge of tears at the miracle he is witnessing.

Reunited with his brothers who have abducted him from the village—along with the girl, who has followed them—the group begins trekking north back to Europe. We get no indication of how long they have been away or how far they have traveled, but when they return the white tribe is still without fire, still languishing in the cold on the small island in the marsh. The blond brother regales the tribe with tales of their adventures and then tells them that he knows the secret of making fire. When he attempts to create a fire in the way he was shown in the cave, he fails. The girl takes over, and the tribe watches in utter amazement as she easily produces a fire.

"Quest for Fire" is a wonderful, intriguing film without a big-budget look because it isn't a big-budget picture. But it is allegorical in that it shows that, as has been discussed in this book, Europeans received knowledge and civilization from the south, from Africa and black-skinned people. We can assume that the lives of the film's white European tribe were greatly improved from fire and the talents of the black girl who has come into their midst with a more advanced language, knowledge of jewelry-making, medicinal herbs, shelter construction, and the ability to bring humor and laughter to these formerly humorless people.

A larger budget might have benefited this film—if the producers adhered to the basic plot without trying to make it spectacular. As it is, it is unpretentious, honest, and does offer a vivid glimpse of the mundane lives and typical hardships people living in Europe may have had to face—particularly if they lacked fire. The film does not tug at our emotions; but it does have funny moments and scenes that will strike the viewer as absolutely realistic. The allegory of Europeans receiving civilization from advanced black-skinned people is understated but becomes clearer in the final third of the film. If the reader has not seen "Quest for Fire," he or she should take the time to watch this unsung gem of a film.

STAR WARS (1977)

When it debuted in 1977, "Star Wars" became the ultimate in science fantasy films up to that time (except, perhaps, for "2001: A Space Odyssey"), with a slew of characters that made their way into millions of peoples' imaginations, spawning a dozen children's toys based on them—Han Solo (Harrison Ford), Princess Leia (Carrie Fisher), light-sabers, Wookies, and the evil Darth Vader (David Prowse, whose voice was provided by unbilled African-American actor James Earl Jones). These characters, along with C-3PO and R2-D2 robot toys were on every child's wish-list, along with Yoda, a character in the second film in the first series, "The Empire Strikes Back." My first reaction to the film was that it was a popcorn-bubble gum, sci-fi flick geared toward impressionable youth. However, it broke all existing box-office records and a good number of adults, young and old, made up viewing audiences.

The main character is Luke Skywalker (Mark Hamill), who seeks revenge on The Empire when his aunt and uncle are killed. Luke had purchased a robot (R2-D2) that The Empire was searching for because it contained a plea from Princess Leia to Obi Wan Kenobi (Alec Guinness) for help. Obi Wan Kenobi was a once powerful, but aged, Jedi Knight who had fought against The Empire, whose forces had been destroyed and dispersed in an earlier battle in the Empire's quest for control of the universe. Luke Skywalker is not at home when some of the Empire's troops kill his aunt and uncle—whose brother happens to be Darth Vader, once part of the Resistance, who had been won over to the Dark Side and was now commander of The Empire's extensive forces, which include a moon-sized Death Star that has destroyed whole planets.

The film has dazzling special effects, spectacular battles, comedic moments, and does tug at one's emotions. There is an ever-present symbology of good vs. evil, evil personified by the black-helmeted and entirely black-clad Darth Vader whose deep voice (supplied by James Earl Jones) exudes power and menace. I do not intend to discuss the plot of this film—but the characters that intrigued me the most on a subconscious level.

These were the *Jawas*. At the time, I couldn't put my finger on what piqued my interest in them. But something about the Jawas wracked at my brain, and I wouldn't discover—consciously discover—what it was until fifteen years later when I began initial research on the Vikings.

The Jawas are the dwarf-like creatures in hooded, dark robes seen in the first part of the film. Their faces are unseen except for two gold, glowing eyes, giving the impression that they are black-skinned or, at least, were intended to convey that impression. I thought of the fairy tales I had read or seen in Disney cartoons—"Snow White and the Seven Dwarfs"; the troll that lived under a bridge, maybe. I just couldn't place the Jawas, but they seemed familiar to me. In 1991 or 1992 when I wrote a 65-page research paper (never published) on Black Vikings, I could directly associate the Jawas in the film with the black dwarfs in Norse sagas and tales; however, it is difficult to explain why the Jawas intrigued me so much prior to my beginning research in this area.

The Jawas in the film are reminiscent of the Black Dwarves or Black Elves of the sagas and Norse tales, diminutive peoples whose "realm is known as *Svartalheim,* the black community´ (Luke 230), earlier mentioned. Black Dwarfs are often likened to the Negritos who once populated the earth, and the Pygmies of central Africa are thought to be the truest modern representation of them. The Lapps of northern Scandinavia and Asia are thought by many to be remnants of Negritos, as are the Ainu, the most ancient inhabitants of Japan (Rogers 71). And so, several minutes into "Star Wars," the viewer is reminded of these mythical Black Dwarfs in the persons of the Jawas, who man a huge, six-storey high, tank-like, mobile metal factory and specialize in repairing and selling robots, metalwork, and other mechanical intricacies.

Black Dwarfs were associated with magic, and in the Norse tale "The Lady of the Vanir," Freyia, a lovely goddess, goes to Svartalfheim (i.e., Svartalheim) to watch the Black Dwarfs at work and obtains a beautiful necklace from them, having to kiss the four dwarves she observes in order to obtain it. "The Six Gifts" tells how the evil Loki goes to the Black Dwarfs to have them fashion Gungnir, a spear that would always hit its target, and how Thor sought them out to fashion Miolnir, a mighty hammer (see Barbara Leonie Picard's *Tales of the Norse Gods and Heroes*). As for dwarf magic, another mention of an earlier comment from David MacRitchie, associating Black Dwarfs with "Chaldean Magi," is apropos:

> They are deeply versed in "magic," and this renders them the teachers of the taller races, in religion, and in many forms of knowledge. In short, it is only in physical stature that they are below the latter people; in everything else they are above them. (*Testimony* 156)

And so, several minutes into "Star Wars," the astute viewer (*most* viewers probably felt the same nagging sensation in the back of their minds as I did) is reminded of these mythical Black Dwarfs in the persons of the Jawas, who are hard bargainers and know the value of their craftsmanship—an aspect of the Black Dwarf character evident in Norse tales. I cannot say if the producers or director George Lucas styled the Jawas after the Black Dwarfs, whose mention in the sagas and tales must have some basis in fact. A connection to them was not at all mentioned in the "Star Wars" documentary I saw a couple of years ago. But the parallels between Jawas and the Black Dwarfs of northern Europe—who seem always to be associated with metalwork and magic—are certainly striking.

The black-clad Darth Vader is the supreme field-marshal of The Empire, on a mission to capture and eliminate all members of the Rebel Alliance—Luke Skywalker, Princess Leia, Obi Wan Kenobi and those who follow them—so that The Empire can rule the known universe. His black, metallic helmet has a built-in visor that conceals his eyes; he has a deep timorous voice; he is a master of the Force, which he learned to use as a young Jedi Knight—before he chose to embrace the Dark Side. He can summon his mental powers to strangle someone from a distance and move or repel objects. When I first saw the film, I wondered why James Earl Jones, still a relatively youthful man, did not play the actual character. More about this below.

The climax of the film is a Rebel assault on the Death Star, the moon-sized nerve center of The Empire. Luke Skywalker, the young hero of the film, manages to fire a missile that blows up the Death Star, and Vader is last seen spinning off into space in his partially destroyed jet fighter. The movie was a smash-hit, and almost no one (except for the producers and director) imagined that there would be a sequel.

THE EMPIRE STRIKES BACK (1980)

The sequel to "Star Wars," "The Empire Strikes Back," came in 1980 and was a bigger smash-hit and, in my opinion, is the best of the original three-film trilogy (another three-film trilogy began in 1989, serving as "prequels" to the original three). The Empire has repaired the Death Star and attacks the Rebel Alliance forces on a snow-covered planet at the beginning of the film. The Alliance is routed and evacuates their base. Luke Skywalker flies a two-man rocket-jet away from the base, carrying the robot R2-D2 along with him.

Luke is traveling to a planet to learn the ways of a Jedi Knight from Yoda, a grand-master Jedi Knight who also taught Luke's father the power of the Force. In the original film, Obi Wan Kenobi told Luke that his father had been a powerful Jedi Knight and that Darth Vader had killed his father. Yoda is first seen as a doddering, diminutive gnome, standing only about 3 ½ feet tall. Luke has no idea that this little creature is the Jedi master that he has come seeking until the voice of the deceased Obi Wan Kenobi, speaking to Yoda (which Luke also hears), confirms this fact for Luke. Luke gets further confirmation when Yoda, using his mental powers, raises Luke's rocket-jet out of a murky pond, lifts it above the water, then guides it above the water's surface and deposits it on the bank.

"I don't believe it!" Luke says, incredulously.

"*That*," says Yoda dryly, "is why you fail."

Although Yoda is even more diminutive than the above-mentioned Black Dwarfs who, on average, were 4 ½ to 5 ½ feet tall, his presence is also reminiscent of the power of these earliest—probably African—humans who were deeply versed in "magic . . . and in many forms of knowledge." There is more talk about Luke's father, and there is a dream sequence, probably induced by Yoda, in which Darth Vader appears and advances toward Luke, and they battle with light-sabers. Afterwards, Luke senses that his friends are in danger and leaves the planet to rescue them.

The climax of the film is a light-saber battle between Luke and Vader where Luke, who has acquired the ability to use the Force, holds his own until Vader turns up his Force-fed intensity and slices off one of Luke's hands. As Luke clings to a walkway spanning a deep chasm, Vader says, in his timorous voice:

"Obi Wan never told you what happened to your father."

"He told me enough!" Luke retorts. "He told me you *killed* him!"

"No," Vader responds. "*I* am your father!"

"No . . . No . . . That's not true! That's *impossible!*"

"Search your feelings. You *know* it to be true!" says Vader.

"Noooo . . . !" Luke screams.

He looks down and allows himself to drop into the chasm, then is fortuitously rescued by Han Solo and Princess Leia, who have arrived in Solo's space rocket.

I saw this movie with my then young children in a packed theater. A quite audible gasp issued from the crowd as Vader revealed the dark secret of Luke's parentage. A buzz of voices continued until the next scene, and viewers seemed just as aghast as Skywalker at this startling revelation.

Oh, it was only a movie, the reader might say. Only science-fantasy. But the astute reader, any astute observer of art, knows that many films or works of art are often imbedded with symbolism. The writer of a novel, the producer or director of a film, has a purpose for each character, each scene, so that what is presented to the reader or viewer will resonate on a deeper level of his or her consciousness. Darth Vader's revelation does that. In the first two films of the "Star Wars" series he symbolizes evil; he is black, a black-clad man with a deep, foreboding black man's voice who is the supreme commander of the evil Empire.

Yes, it is only a movie, science-fantasy. But the film evoked strong emotions in viewers, and Vader's brash disclosure, and Skywalker's reaction, went beyond mere plot and drama, registering on both a conscious and unconscious level—especially with white viewers. It is more than Luke discovering that this *evil* man is his father; Vader's revelation is tantamount to scientists and historians revealing to white people that their ancestors were black or had African origins; that the black-skinned people they have learned to despise were the people from whom they spawned, that black blood—in a sense—courses through their bodies beneath their white exterior, whatever they look like today.

"NOOOOOOOOO!"

A handful of respected *European* anthropologists and historians have claimed this for two centuries or more. Dr. Louis Leakey's excavations in East Africa during the 1930s offered proof of the earlier assertions that modern man originated in Africa. In the late 1980s and afterwards DNA research confirmed this emphatically. However, even today many, if not most, Whites are loathe to accept that their ancestors originated in Africa, or appease their psyches by choosing to believe that, if their ancestors *did* emerge from Africa, they were somehow not black-skinned, but white. But what should be obvious by now is that even some of their more *recent* forebears in Europe were black-skinned, and that Blacks—whether of African or Asiatic origin—were the progenitors of many white Europeans, even those in royal families.

Because the movie is American-made and its hero white, Skywalker's father could *not* be a black man; despite the multitude of strange looking beings and people seen in the film, a union between a possibly black human man and a white human woman to produce a white-looking human Luke Skywalker would not have been acceptable to American audiences, although it would certainly be in the realm of possibility "A long time ago, in a galaxy far far away"—the opening line of the film. Therefore, James Earl Jones could only lend his powerful, reverberant and memorable *voice* to the character of Darth Vader. In the third film of the first "Star Wars" series, "Return of the Jedi," Vader is revealed to be a white man (David Prowse) after he is mortally wounded and his black helmet and visor are removed. Up until that time, Darth Vader effectively *functions* as a black man—an entirely black-clad man who is remorselessly evil. In Western thought—especially in the areas of literature, religion, film, and society in general—*black* has undeniably been equated with *evil*, with Satan, and death. I should not have to explain how, in the Euro-Western world, innate evil has been ascribed—particularly through Christian doctrine—to Blacks and people of color, in general, dehumanizing them, which is why Whites—European or American—have had no compunction about oppressing and slaughtering black Africans, Native Americans, Aborigines, Viet-Namese and, more recently, Iraqis and Afghanis, while attaching derogatory names to them.

Vader, however, is not oppressed; obviously, he has earned his position as commander, ruling thousands of totally white-clad troops (whose white faces can be seen through their clear visors, and reveal one or two black troopers), and throughout the first film seems to be the ruler of The Empire. In "The Empire Strikes Back," we see that he has superiors, a Council that issues him directives (one might think of Othello), who do not always approve of his methods. Nevertheless, he is highly regarded, much like a black man in the Western world who has proven his capabilities in a white-dominated world (one might think of Colin Powell or President Obama) and is accorded due respect—even the command of predominantly white troopers. Vader's character, though, is an obvious synthesis of black with evil. This is not in any way to imply that the filmmakers' decision in this regard had a malicious or racist intent; the black-as-evil theme lent an additional element of power to Darth Vader's character (heightened by Jones' forceful, all-powerful voice) that an actor, who could have been seen as white through a clear visor might not have generated. It was a splendid choice by the producers and director. But African-American actor James Earl Jones could not physically play the role of Luke Skywalker's father.

Many Whites, including knowledgeable Eurocentric historians and scientists, are still endeavoring to sidestep evidence that modern man evolved in and emerged out of Africa, still exploring counter-theories, still screaming "NOOOOO!" to the evidence that black-skinned people out of Africa are the progenitors of all the peoples of the earth (notwithstanding interbreeding with Neanderthals, who might also have originally been black and emerged from Africa as well) and that the ancestors of people they have come to loathe (mainly because of racial conditioning)—who are, in essence, their ancestors, as well—were responsible for the world's earliest civilizations as well as the white European civilization that has dominated the world for the last millennium or less.

I do not mean to imply that *all* Whites embrace racist feelings, but most seem to, and historically have collectively oppressed, subjugated and wantonly slaughtered the darker peoples of the earth. The films discussed above represent efforts by filmmakers of conscience to inject—consciously (and unconsciously, perhaps)—truthful elements regarding Blacks into their works. There may be more such films, but on the whole such films make up a tiny percentage of the many thousands produced by white filmmakers. Similarly, in the fields of science and history the percentage of honest, conscientious Whites are dwarfed by the number of Eurocentric ones whose works are more popular and more widely promoted in bookstores, schools and universities. These echo the accepted conclusions of earlier Eurocentrists—those who usurped the history and achievements of Africans and other dark-skinned peoples and civilizations and attributed them to Caucasians; those who obscured the black- and dark-skinned races that once predominated in Europe by not revealing racial particulars; those whose writings promote the superiority of Caucasians or white-skinned people over all non-Whites.

When DNA (deoxyribonucleic acid), the material in the chromosomes that carry genetic information in humans and animal species, was isolated about three decades ago it was, of course a scientific breakthrough which promised to allow scientists to improve upon older techniques of tracing human differentiation through the ages of our existence on earth. But even this relatively new science seems to have been infected by the same sort of racism that has infested previous Eurocentric scientific and historical conclusions.

The following chapter will begin an assessment of the findings of several DNA scientists, demonstrating, hopefully, that white European and American scholars cannot seem to divorce themselves from the racist sentiments that continue to pervade their works.

CHAPTER 15

THE DNA FACTOR—PART I:
SAME OLD STORY

In studying the emergence of man prior to the discovery of DNA (deoxyribonucleic acid), scientists—archeologists, anthropologists, biologists, and so on—relied on body build, skull formation, facial traits, cranium capacity, skin color and bone length and structure to determine where individuals—or the remains of individuals—fit into the scheme of human evolution and how they should be classified in regard to race. DNA research would rectify erroneous assumptions made by scientists and historians over the last two centuries regarding the migration of peoples, be a more accurate process than carbon-14 dating, and finally pin down the actual origin of homo sapiens sapiens, or modern humans, which scientists and historians over the last two centuries had claimed originated in various parts of the world, excepting Antarctica and the Americas.

The more accurate conclusions determined that modern man originated in Asia or Africa, with most Eurocentric historians asserting the former continent well into the 20th century—although precisely where in Asia was still open to debate. But even in the late 18th century—while the African slave trade continued unabated—a few bold historians saw Africa as the birthplace of modern man. But even Dr. Louis Leakey's unearthing of the then oldest human remains in the Olduvai Gorge during the 1930s and afterwards didn't alter the "Africa, no" opinion of the Eurocentric world body of historians enough for them to look seriously at Africa. This would not happen until the mid- to late-1960s, and one of the prime reasons was the publication of Robert Ardrey's *African Genesis* in 1961. The book was written in layman's language and highlighted the work of scientists who had labored to demonstrate the ancientness of man in Africa—Charles Darwin, Raymond Dart, Dr. Leakey—and informed the reader of the violence in our heritage and the reasons we developed the traits we possess. It also made the tongue-twister *Australopithicus* an essential nomenclature in the study of man and his predecessors. Ardrey was not a scientist or historian when he wrote the book; I believe he was an actor and director who had an interest in the debate over man's origin and decided to research a subject which fascinated him. The book's opening lines were direct and assured:

> Not in innocence, and not in Asia, was mankind born. The home of our fathers was that African highland reaching north from the Cape [i.e., South Africa] to the Lakes of the Nile. (9)

The book dispelled the notion of Asia as the birthplace of modern man, presenting the evidence of modern man's evolution in Africa in clear and fathomable language. I read the book in 1968 or '69, and it seems that more attention began to be paid to Africa as man's birthplace from this period on.

African-American historians rose up from the tumult of the Civil Rights struggle in the United States at that time adding even more information on the ancientness and ingenuity of African peoples. The ancient Egyptians and Ethiopians were declared once and for all to have been black people, and the world body of historians would surely reassess their opinions on the subject with the plethora of new information being revealed. But some refused to accept what seemed to be a solid case.

Even biologist Allan C. Wilson's 1987 DNA research project tracing all human beings to a black woman in Africa was derided by many who felt that *African-Americans* should not have been included in the study! Of the 189 samples of DNA Wilson obtained from people all over the world, critics felt that African-Americans had intermixed with Whites for so long that their genes were almost worthless for such an experiment.

Mentioned in an earlier chapter, Louise Levathes *New York Times* article, "A Geneticist Maps Ancient Migrations" (27 July 1993), detailed Dr. Luigi Luca Cavalli-Sforza's research in the tracing of man's migration out of Africa. It was mentioned in the article that Dr. Cavalli-Sforza, with two other geneticists, was preparing a soon to be published book entitled *The History and Geography of Human Genes*, in which DNA samples were collected from more than 400 targeted populations around the world. *The History and Geography of Human Genes* (HGHG) was published in 1994 in unabridged and abridged editions. I purchased the abridged edition several years ago, and most of my comments on the DNA factor in human migration and evolution below are in response to the findings put forward in the abridged version.

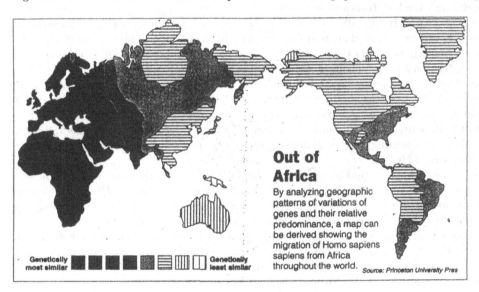

Out of Africa

By analyzing geographic patterns of variations of genes and their relative predominance, a map can be derived showing the migration of Homo sapiens sapiens from Africa throughout the world. *Source: Princeton University Pres*

Genetically most similar ■ ■ ■ ▓ ▤ ▥ ▢ Genetically least similar

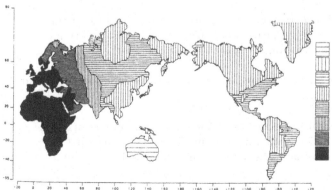

Fig. 20
Above map appeared in Louise Levethes' 1993 New York Times article discussing Dr. Cavalli-Sforza's work, showing the closeness and extent of genetically similar people in Africa and Europe. In History and Geography of Human Genes (1994) same map has been dramatically altered to lessen the genetic extent of African and European populations.

In Ms. Levathes' *New York Times* article, a map (see Fig.20) of geographic patterns was featured illustrating patterns of gene variation on all the continents (except Antarctica). On the left side of the map were the landmasses of Africa, Europe and Asia.

A small graphic in the lower portion has small, vari-patterned boxes, some shaded, illustrating areas of genetically most similar and dissimilar populations. From the shading of the continents Africa, Arabia, Asia Minor and the territory east to the border of India, and almost all of Europe have he same dark shade, meaning, one would presume, that the populations of those areas are most similar in relation to populations in other areas.

When I was given the article around 1995 by a former professor of mine, Dr. Amos Wilson (no relation to biologist Allan C. Wilson), I was enthusiastic. Dr. Wilson knew I had recently written a research paper on black Vikings that I was still revising and researching for a possible book. *The History and Geography of Human Genes* (HGHG) had already been published, but I did not know this. Busy with teaching several English courses and working several other part-time jobs, I had forgotten about the forthcoming publication of HGHG, and it didn't come to mind again until I was one hundred pages into a first draft of this book. When I obtained HGHG more than a decade after its publication, I looked forward to locating this geographical map in the book along with more information on the European connection with Africa. When I found the map, I was disappointed; the map was altered, revised, reworked from the map that had appeared in Ms. Levathes' *New York Times* article.

If you compare Fig. 20a. with Fig. 20b., you will see the maps are identical, but the representative patterns have been altered. Some shaded areas in Fig. 20a. have been changed to lined areas in Fig. 20b., but the boundaries between genetic types are unchanged—except in Europe, whose genetic boundaries have been reworked. Eastern Europe has been eliminated as being closely related genetically to Africa or western Europe. Most of Scandinavia has been altered, as has southern Arabia and eastern Asia Minor and the territory east to India. Only the southern end of Scandinavia shows a close genetic relationship to western Europe and Africa. Every other genetic boundary, including those in Australia and the Americas, remains the same in both maps. Why is the only alteration in Europe (along with smaller alterations in Asia Minor and Arabia)? Did startling new evidence emerge in the span of a year between the Levathes article and the publication of HGHG?

I was dismayed by the technical language contained in HGHG. The language may be palatable to a geneticist or biologist, but it is not layman-friendly. So in my discourse regarding HGHG I will dispense with the technical jargon and graphics as much as possible. There is enough layman-friendly language for me to make the points I need to make regarding the authors' assertions and conclusions.

Regarding this book, I strongly believe its authors must have been persuaded by some Eurocentric entity to revise or alter their findings so as to correspond to a particular theory on migration that has lately been promoted in books and documentaries having to do with DNA and the evolution of man in different areas of the earth. For instance, in her 1993 article, Ms. Levathes writes:

> [T]he new studies have . . . indicated that Europeans are a mixed population that emerged only about 30,000 years ago and appears to have 65 percent Asian ancestry and 35 percent African ancestry (with an error rate of plus or minus 8 percent). (C9)

In HGHG there is no mention of percentages in the section in which Fig. 20b. appears, and the language in the section goes something like this:

> The correlations between a PC and the 82 genes express the relative importance of each gene in determining the PC (134). The first synthetic map (fig. 2.11.1) shows that the poles of the first PC are Africa and Australia, which are the maximum and the minimum respectively. (135)

PC stands for principle-component, and the interested reader may peruse the section or the entire book to decipher what is being said. The language of the book, in general, is quite beyond a layman's comprehension. Reading it is tedious and enervating. I had anticipated something more fathomable, but perhaps the book was not intended for a general audience.

The book does conclude that modern man developed in and migrated out of Africa, stating:

> Support for an African origin . . . comes from the existence of earlier archaic specimens
> that seem to be in the direct line of descent to modern humans and that have not so far
> been found in the Middle East. (op. cit. 64)

As other recent studies have asserted, Cavalli-Sforza, Paulo Menozzi and Alberto Piazza trace modern man's first migrations out of northeastern Africa to Arabia, Mesopotamia and Asia Minor. The latter area is significant because recent studies assert that Europe was peopled from Asia Minor, a point I will return to shortly. The earliest migration of modern man out of Africa had to be the group of humans who trekked through southern Asia and India to reach Australia, now thought to have been populated for at least 62,000 years.

Albert Churchward calls the first humans out of Africa *Pygmies*, who eventually occupied most areas of the earth before taller humans evolved. Whether the early Australoids were of this Pygmy race is a question that would take more time and effort than is planned here, but it is certainly probable that the earliest people to populate southern Asia and Australia were of this type and that the Pygmies, Grimaldi men and Negritos were essentially the same and represent the earliest modern humans. Millions of short-statured people are still found in southern Asia—from southern India through Indonesia, Malaysia, the Philippines, and further east to many islands in the western Pacific. So, the earliest Australians could certainly have been Pygmy-like in stature, as the Aborigines of 150-200 years ago were (before their near genocide by British settlers), though significantly taller than present-day African Pygmies.

Some positive things have come out of DNA research that are undeniable. Man has been effectively traced by to his origins, although there are still scientists who are uncomfortable with the findings and seek ways to discredit his African genesis. In criminal matters, DNA samples can be obtained from evidence that is several decades old and older and used to determine whether an imprisoned person was indeed the perpetrator of a crime. In the United States, roughly five-dozen prisoners have been freed based on DNA evidence that was not available at the time they were tried and convicted of violent crimes. DNA technology has also allowed authorities to apprehend people who were never prosecuted for old crimes because no evidence had been found years before when the technology did not exist. DNA technology can determine for certain whether a man is the biological father in paternity suits, or whether someone is a blood relative or descendant of another person. Such technology is also useful in studying the evolution of animals, insects—even the origin and progression of viruses, which may eventually lead to cures for harmful diseases.

But in the areas of man's origins, his emergence out of Africa, migrations to different areas of the world and physiognomic mutations or alterations into distinct "races," Eurocentric DNA scientists—and those who present us with their findings, like the authors of *The History and Geography of Human Genes* (HGHG) and others—seem to reassert the same general concepts earlier Eurocenric historians, scholars and scientists have given us over the last two centuries. This chapter will focus on several concepts seemingly confirmed by modern DNA research which regurgitate Eurocentric notions of migrations around the earth—but especially the migration of man into Europe. Other areas to be touched upon may sound redundant—the injection of Caucasians or Aryans into other peoples not generally thought of as Caucasian, and the downplaying of "race" intended, this writer believes, to confuse readers rather than increase their ability to coherently decipher information obtained through DNA technology.

Who benefits more from this confusion than the race of people who have dominated the world over the last five centuries? It can be argued that European or white domination of the world has been in effect far longer: a millennium, 2000 years, 3,000, 6,000; some believe that Whites have dominated the earth forever. But for certain, we need not go back more than 500 years or so when Columbus' voyages allowed white Europeans to escape the confines of Europe and ignite the European mind to investigate what other areas of the world they could exploit. We in the Western hemisphere—including, unfortunately, the continent of Africa—have absorbed the history of the world as narrated by Eurocentric Whites over the last several centuries and now can only stand by passively as today's DNA masters use the dynamic technology to reinforce the half-truths and disinformation most of us have inculcated.

Most Western historians (and DNA researchers confirm) that man migrated out of Africa by way of Arabia and the Fertile Crescent (the area comprising the lower Nile Valley; Middle East, or The Levant; and Mesopotamia, the area of the Tigris and Euphrates Rivers, (i.e., modern Iraq). That first supposedly small group set off eastward, eventually reaching Australia. Along the way, numbers of them, presumably (and this writer has no problem with this theory), remained in Mesopotamia, India, Southeast Asia and probably southern China, while later migrants continued on to Australia and points beyond. But how long did these migrations take? Those who stopped and settled in areas along the route—Mesopotamia, India, et al—became the first anatomically modern humans (a.m.h.) in those areas where, perhaps, earlier progenitors of man—Homo Erectus, Neanderthal—may still have been living. But eventually a.m.h. came to predominate in the areas they settled.

Other migrations ensued, perhaps taking a more northeasterly route into Asia, so that central Asia became populated. Still later, the Western scholars assert, groups out of Africa took a northwesterly route to inhabit Asia Minor (i.e., Turkey) from where man eventually entered Europe. This migration theory was touted by the more honest, pre-DNA historians, many of whom had only recently—and reluctantly—accepted the probability that man emerged from Africa. Current DNA research supports this theory: Asia was the next continent after Africa to be inhabited by a.m.h. (anatomically modern humans), followed by Asia Minor (i.e., Turkey; West Asia), eventually leading to human occupation of Europe, say, 40,000-50-000 years ago.

Wurm glacial ice sheets still covered northern Europe and Asia during this epoch and would not fully recede until about 10,000-12,000 years ago, so man's access to the northern latitudes was barred until that time. Cavalli-Sforza, Menozzi and Piazza state in HGHG:

> An ancient population of West Asia, sandwiched between those of Africa and East Asia before the expansion of a.m.h. to Europe, may have become genetically intermediate between the groups. (92)

It is not clear what period the authors are speaking of here, but it seems to be prior to 10,000 BPE (before the present era) and 40,000 BPE. By East Asia they can only mean Mesopotamia and, perhaps the area around the Caucasus Mountains between the Black and Caspian Seas, but Arabia might be included. West Asia implies Asia Minor, or Turkey. This is not an expansive area: A line drawn from Cairo to Tehran would measure roughly 1,000 miles; from Cairo to Istanbul, less than that. But the authors (and the pre-DNA Eurocentric historians before them) are implying that mankind has already undergone some kind of mutational alteration in this relatively limited area that made the West Asian group *racially* (though the authors do not use this word here) divergent. "An ancient population of West Asia, sandwiched between those of Africa and East Asia" implies that West Asians (i.e., living in Asia Minor, or Turkey) had somehow changed markedly from their nearby African ancestors and that an "admixture between the two [now divergent] groups" resulted in a different race of people in West Asia.

The authors, of course, don't refer to skin color or race, but what color could these early people have been other than black? They were black-skinned when they left Africa and migrated to the Asian subcontinent; black-skinned when they moved into central Asia, Arabia, the Caucasus region and Asia

Minor. It seems that any admixture of Africans and East or West Asians—a mere thousand miles from Cairo—would still have resulted in black-skinned people. The authors, like the pre-DNA historians before them, imply that West Asians had somehow differentiated, became somehow racially unlike other nearby peoples—peoples who might never have ceased migrating out of Africa to these areas! The earlier migrants, who had undergone a seemingly abrupt genetic alteration within this thousand mile radius, intermingle with later migrants out of Africa to produce people "genetically intermediate" between these now divergent groups of West Asians and Africans. Or are the authors of HGHG saying that the intermingling of East Asians (i.e., Mesopotamians and Arabians) with black Africans—still within a 1,000 mile radius from Cairo—somehow produced "genetically intermediate" people in West Asia? How and when would East Asians—in this 1,000 mile radius—have differentiated from Africans, whose migrants were *still* moving into East Asia? It is also unclear how West Asia could be "sandwiched" between Africa and East Asia. Consult a map. The statement just doesn't make sense.

Also confusing is the authors' statement that, "In more recent times, modern Europeans also received an important genetic contribution from the Middle East at the time of farmers' expansions (9000-5000 years ago) . . . ." (op. cit.). Were people somehow *already* inhabiting Europe, or were West Asians (who must have already *had* Middle Eastern blood through intermixing, as discussed above) the a.m.h. migrants into Europe?

I trust the reader can discern the confusion in the statements as well as the authors' effort to create racial differences between people occupying a relatively small area—people who must have looked essentially the same for many thousands of years.

By 9,000 or 10,000 BPE there may have been physiognomic alterations among humans in the region under discussion, but there is no logical reason to believe people in the area exhibited drastic alterations in skin, eye or hair color or general appearance. We have to assume that man had reached most parts of Asia by about 30,000 years BPE, probably much earlier since the small groups of humans who dropped out of the original Australia-bound vanguard of humanity multiplied in Mesopotamia, India and southeast Asia and expanded farther afield from these areas. So, human occupation in these areas would logically be older than the human occupation of Australia (i.e., 62,000 years).

How long did the journey from Africa to Australia take? Did the original vanguard follow the coastline of the Indian Ocean non-stop, directly to Australia which, presumably, they did not know existed? Or would the vanguard have stopped and settled, say, in Mesopotamia, reproduce for several generations, or a millennium—their offspring continuing the eastward journey, say, into India, stopping to settle and reproduce for several millennia there before *their* offspring pushed further eastward again, and so on, so that the journey to Australia took many, many millennia.

Why would people rush to a continent they did not know existed as, generation after generation, they must have continued moving eastward through lush surrounding lands, built small settlements, found fresh, plentiful water, abundant game, and fertile soil? The peopling of Australia was the culmination of an extremely long migration, and perhaps a thousand years may have passed before some unknown condition impelled a group that had settled an area along the way to again trek eastward—perhaps seeking the location of the sunrise. After settling in India, future generations pushed into Southeast Asia, the islands of Indonesia, and a vanguard of *their* offspring—now proficient in constructing sturdy boats—eventually reached Australia and settled parts of it before *their* children or great-, great-, great-, great-grandchildren set out for New Zealand and islands of the Pacific Ocean rife with vegetation, fish, fertile soils and agreeable climates. And this outline is the *short* version of the Australian migration.

In the meantime, other vanguard groups of a.m.h. set off out of Africa taking a northeasterly route and, by the same slow process, peopled central Asia and western China. Glacial ice still covered the northern landmass of Europe and Asia 40,000 to 50,000 years ago, so humans could not have found many habitable living areas north of the Caucasus Range and, presumably, did not venture very far north before 15,000 years ago when glacial ice had receded considerably.

The most widely accepted theory is that humans entered Europe from West Asia (Asia Minor or Turkey) by c. 30,000 years BPE, which the authors of HGHG say their research supports. If so, would their physical appearance have been any different from the human populations within the 1,000 mile radius of Cairo—the general area of the Cradle of Civilization? Mankind, it would seem, would still have been essentially black-skinned within that area, even 12,000 years ago, since the area possessed the same general climate and, in those pre-agricultural days, most humankind lived a hunting and gathering existence. But the authors of HGHG, like the vast body of modern scholars, would have us believe that there were dynamic racial changes between Africans and East Asians (i.e., Mesopotamians) and that their interbreeding produced a hybrid population in West Asia dramatically divergent from the two populations that produced it—and that it was this new type of human who moved into Europe 30,000 years BPE whom we are encouraged to believe were *Caucasian*.

Further, the authors of HGHG mention a "separation date of African and non-African populations" (87). If all humans originated in Africa and spread around he world from there, how could there at the same time be *non-Africans*—especially since the authors seem to be talking of a date beyond 100,000 years BPE when a.m.h. began their migrations out of the Mother Continent? Playing with words in this manner is meant to create a distance between Africa and human beings in other parts of the earth, and if the reader buys into this wordplay it is easier for him or her to swallow a statement like the following:

> Therefore, Melanesians are closer to the Chinese and Caucasoid groups, and the root is located between the two African populations on one side, with the three non-African populations on the other. (op. cit. 90)

Again, I am dispensing with the technical language, abbreviations and various charts or graphs included in HGHG and sticking with what is clear language and what the authors conclude with the evidence they present. The authors split the human family into groups, creating a distance between these groups and the African tree which sprouted them because they desire to imply in the end that Caucasoids or Whites are, ultimately, extremely distinct from the black mass of humanity from which they sprang. In brief, they are implying that Whites or Caucasians evolved from ostensibly yellow-skinned Asians rather than black-skinned Africans.

The problem is that those earliest Asians were black- and brown-skinned and remained so into historical times—even much of the Chinese and Korean populations, as noted in an earlier chapter. And although they try, Cavalli-Sforza et al cannot fully escape Africa. Considering the origin of Europeans, they state:

> We tested the hypothesis of the origin of Europeans by admixture by trying various admixture hypotheses (between African ancestors and ancestors of Melanesians, of Chinese, or both) . . . The only hypothesis compatible with the data is that there was an admixture between African ancestors and Chinese ancestors. (92)

The authors cite another study, which "showed that Europeans and Asians are significantly closer . . . than Europeans and Africans" (op. cit.). Of course, different types of Asians would eventually evolve, exhibiting changes in hair texture and eye alterations in the case of Mesopotamians, Indians, Chinese and Southeast Asians, who eventually emerged out of an original black African or Negroid type. However, these genotypic alterations would develop much later, and may have evolved in Africa—arriving later in areas of Asia as fresher waves of African migrants moved into areas of the Asian continent. Nevertheless, the authors of HGHG conclude the section by stating that—

> . . . the European population underwent substantial hybridization about 30 kya [30,000 years ago] . . . In general, it reflects the geographic intermediacy between East Asia and Africa of European ancestors, who probably originated in West Asia. (93)

Several authors presented earlier have already been cited attesting to "a black belt of mankind . . . across the ancient world from Africa to Malaya" (see Chapter 1) and, although DNA research confirms this, Eurocentric scholars and DNA pioneers, like the authors of HGHG, insist on separating these earliest migrants from their African roots, and further confound matters by declaring some groups "non-African" which, as during pre-DNA times, includes even the earliest migrants out of Africa—those who settled in Mesopotamian and southern Asian areas like India, Southeast Asia and on the continent of Australia (i.e., Aborigines). Like pre-DNA Eurocentric scholars, the authors of HGHG divide and segregate even closely related *African* peoples (for Africa is where the earliest Asian migrants derived from) by supposedly genetic findings, stating, for instance:

> [T]he information available on individual groups in Ethiopia and North Africa is . . . sufficient to show that they are all separate from sub-Saharan Africans and that North Africans and East Africans (Ethiopians and neighbors) are all *clearly separate.* (*my emphasis,* 174)

It is not clear what specific period the authors are focusing on in this instance, but I suspect they are speaking of relatively recent prehistoric times, perhaps the Neolithic. It is certain that over long millennia different "types" of humans evolved *within* the African cauldron to occupy a specific territory of that continent, while some migrated northward or eastward into Arabia, the Near East (what Charles S. Finch III calls Africa's Northeast Extension), or followed the routes of more ancient African migrants into south Asia (Iraq, Iran) or India. Different hair textures, physiognomies and variations in pigmentation may have developed (light-brown, dark-brown, reddish-brown, as the Egyptians are said to have been), but these migrants were essentially black-skinned *African* peoples and *Negroid*—since there were no other pre-existing human types out of which they *could* have evolved within Africa. Eurocentric historians and scientists, however, like the authors of HGHG, are quick to pronounce these waves of African migrants into Asia *non-African* as soon as they reach destinations outside of Africa, as has been shown—often citing amorphous evidence to classify them somehow *Caucasian.* And where there is no evidence of Caucasoids, the authors of HGHG simply create some and then present this information as *factual.*

We have lived under the authority of Eurocentric scholarship for several hundred years and have become used to accepting whatever conclusions this august European Brotherhood of Academia has produced, lacking the wherewithal to counter its supposedly factual assertions. Relatively few non-Whites have been able to publish works refuting the findings of Eurocentric scholarship; major publishing houses in the U.S. generally reject their work or, if they do agree to publish the work of a non-white or African-American historian, the work is not enthusiastically promoted like the works of white authors. The non-white author has to turn to smaller publishing houses or else self-publish and, in most cases, his work does not reach the widest possible audience. As well, few non-whites obtain the necessary funding to travel to different parts of the world in order to produce documentaries or finance archeological expeditions, or research subjects of interest to them. For non-Whites, funds and backing are difficult or impossible to obtain, and most of us in the Western world know the sad reason for this: the stench of anti-black racism that suffuses the Western world, a disease that is particularly rampant in the United States despite efforts by many over the years to eradicate it.

Any interpretation of history or historical events in the Western world is essentially Eurocentric, and the masters of the various media have continually used them to promote white superiority, European superiority—in pre-DNA days and in the present—and DNA scientists appear to be validating what pre-DNA historians and scientists have always asserted—now with ostensibly the authority of DNA technology, which we have been programmed to believe is trustworthy and irrefutable. Eurocentric scholars, as ever, continue to take liberties with the truth because there is no effective counterforce to keep them honest, and the works of non-white scholars and scientists lack exposure to wide audiences, confined, for the most part, to Black Studies courses in colleges and universities and rarely used by white professors teaching standard history or anthropology courses.

So, it has been quite easy for Eurocentric scholars to manipulate history to their advantage and uphold the pretense of European superiority. And, as mentioned above, where no Caucasoids exist, they create them—even in Africa. For instance, the authors of HGHG state:

> The presence of Caucasoids in northern Africa is attested to by the archeological information. Caucasoids arrived in the western part of North Africa from the Iberian peninsula at an early time, perhaps 20 kya [i.e., 20,000 years] or more. (193)

Like pre-DNA Eurocentric historians before them, the authors plant Caucasoids—presumably white people—in North Africa for their ulterior purpose of injecting themselves into the oldest civilizations and take credit for any achievements those civilizations produced. Injecting Caucasians into various African groups, the authors of HGHG state, for instance:

> In the Neolithic period, the northern and central part of the Sahara was probably populated by Caucasoids and the central and southern part by Negroid peoples. (op. cit.)

Surely the authors of HGHG are counting on our knowledge of the present distribution of North African peoples to validate this assertion. Today, and for 1,300 years, North Africa has been dominated by Arab peoples, many of whom have light-brown and near-white complexions. An equal number of these Arabs are black-skinned but identify more with Arabs than black Africans. News footage regarding the current problems in the Sudan show the Arab rulers of the country to be black-skinned like the general population. In Algeria and Libya Arabs are light-skinned. In the central and southern parts of these countries black- or dark-skinned Arabs predominate, and in Mali and Niger there is evidence of extensive intermingling, with much of the population exhibiting the same range of complexional variation as African-Americans—due to the interbreeding of black-skinned native populations with Arabs who entered those areas 1,300 years ago, when the religion of Islam was spread to these territories by Arabs out of Arabia.

Twenty-thousand years ago there were no Caucasoids occupying North Africa, and there was no significant influx of Caucasoids into North Africa until Alexander's army invaded Egypt in the 4th century BC. In fact, 20,000 years ago there may not have been *any* actual Caucasians in existence. Where would this new type of human have emanated from? The authors of HGHG allege that Caucasoids resulted from a mixture of Africans and East Asians, as discussed above. But, no matter how one tries to spin this, these earliest peoples—those who stopped off in Mesopotamia, south Asia, India, Southeast Asia and probably China—were black-skinned and essentially Negroid, as skeletal remains have borne out. They were still black-skinned when Alexander's Greek and Macedonian armies encountered them in the 4th century BC; when the Romans expanded their empire to North Africa, Egypt and Mesopotamia from the 1st century BC to the 2nd century AD; and when more modern Europeans arrived in India and Australia during the 18th century—though these populations (except for Australians)—were, by then, generally lighter in complexion due to intermixture with intervening invasions by northern peoples over many centuries—all of which cannot be enumerated now.

*   *   *   *   *

The authors of HGHG never explain how the *earliest* East Asians become so light-skinned that a mixture between them and black-skinned North Africans produced Caucasoids 30,000 years ago (or how these supposed Caucasoids multiplied and somehow came to overspread all of North Africa!). I assume these East Asians were Mesopotamians, however, the authors seem to imply these East Asians were of the *Chinese* type. If this were the case, how would the interbreeding of black Africans and Chinese have produced the *Caucasians* who supposedly emerged in West Asia? The distance between Egypt and western China is roughly 4,000 miles. Did large numbers of Chinese backtrack through India and Mesopotamia to return to North Africa to intermingle with their ancestors? Or did large numbers of Africans trek to western China, cavort with numerous women and return through India and Mesopotamia into West Asia with their impregnated women to begin a new life there—their women miraculously giving birth to Caucasian, or white, offspring?

The *African + Chinese= Caucasoid* scenario doesn't hold up for three reasons: (1.) there is far too much distance between the two groups for direct interbreeding to have occurred; (2.) 30,000 years ago, if man had indeed entered what is now western China by that time, how would he have been other than black-skinned?; (3.) even if the Chinese had somehow lightened to the same general complexion that they are today, the offspring of an unmixed African and a Chinese person would in no way result in an even *lighter-skinned* offspring! And how many instances have there been of masses of people returning to a place they migrated out of? Is there evidence, for instance, of the earliest migrants to North America returning en masse over the Bering landbridge to reenter northeast Asia after living in North America for several millennia? Is there evidence of masses of people who anciently reached Australia backtracking to the Indian subcontinent millennia later?

As pre-DNA Eurocentric scholars did, the authors of HGHG insinuate Caucasoids into nearly every ancient civilization—Ethiopian, Egyptian, Indian, Arabian, Persian, Australian—which has already been mentioned but is worth mentioning again to illustrate how modern DNA masters are using the technology to corroborate earlier Eurocentric falsehoods. Any group showing a tendency to lighter skin is said to possess Caucasoid admixture, then the *entire* people is often deemed to be Caucasian; this, despite the fact that no one has actually located a Caucasian homeland other than *possibly* West Asia (Turkey), an area that puts Caucasoids in the general vicinity of mass migrations out of Africa and the general area of the Cradle of Civilization. That is not to say that *some* Caucasians did not eventually develop there, but that occurrence must have taken place much later than 30,000 years ago because the earliest people living in that 1,000 mile radius from Cairo could not have been notably racially divergent.

The authors of HGHG then theorize that Caucasoid West Asians migrated in all directions out of Asia Minor and that a significant number moved westward into southern Europe, presumably occupying the Balkans, France, Italy and Iberia (Spain/Portugal) at the western end of the continent. They then allege, and present supposed DNA evidence, that these Caucasoids returned to Africa via the Pillars of Hercules (Gibraltar Strait) to completely occupy the northern part of the continent all the way eastward to Libya and Egypt and southward to the mid-Sahara. Then they go on to state:

> Today the continent [i.e., Africa] is inhabited by two major *aboriginal* groups, *Caucasoids* in the north almost down to the *southern* border of the Sahara, and Negroids in subSaharan Africa. In the east, however, and especially in Ethiopia and Somalia, people have lighter skin and are considered Negroid by some, Caucasoid by others. (*my emphasis*, 167)

This declaration is saying that all the inhabitants of Western Sahara, Mauritania, Algeria, Libya, Egypt, and half or more of the inhabitants of Mali, Niger, Chad, Sudan, and all of Ethiopia were, in the main, *Caucasoid*—essentially white! I presume this would also include the populaces of Morocco and Tunisia, as well.

The above statement would be ludicrous if it weren't so pompous and insulting.

Considering the behavior of *actual* Caucasoids or European Whites toward the people of these countries—the savagery brought to them by the invasions of Alexander's Greeks, Julius Caesar's Romans, and the rapine by Europeans over the last five centuries through slavery, colonialism, land-theft, exploitation, usurpation of natural resources, and generally inhumane treatment—calling North Africans Caucasoids is hypocritical and blasphemous. Frankly, it is like urinating on a man one has robbed and beaten into unconsciousness—a man lying face-down in the mud who can in no way fight back. Beginning in March,

2003, *actual* Caucasoids began the bombing and devastation of Iraq, an ancient country inhabited by "Caucasoids," and are presently threatening to invade Iran (ancient Persia), another nation inhabited by supposed "Caucasoids," because *actual* Caucasoids are against Iranian "Caucasoids" having nuclear energy like other Caucasian nations as well as some non-Caucasian ones.

Declaring North Africans Caucasoids, with supposed DNA evidence to support this, validates the claim of Eurocentric scholars of old that North Africa and southern Europe were inhabited by "dark *whites*," hoping to dispel any notion that black Africans were ever near enough to Europe to set foot on the continent. "Caucasoid" North Africans, presumably, would have prevented any attempt by black Africans to attempt to approach Europe. The problem for Western historians and scientists is that North Africans were black-skinned 100,000 years ago, 50,000 years ago, 20,000 years ago, and remained pre-dominantly so until Greek, Roman and Arab invasions brought about a general lightening of North African populations over roughly a thousand-year period—from the 4th century BC to the 8th century AD. Black-skinned people—Arab, non-Arab, or other—are still numerous in all the countries of North Africa, descendants of the black-skinned peoples—not Caucasoids—who once dominated the whole of North Africa. And there is nothing in any of the writings of Greek or Roman historians stating that the people inhabiting North Africa, from Mauritania to Egypt, were anything but black-skinned when Greece and, later, Rome launched invasions into the continent.

Not surprisingly, the Negroid Grimaldi skeletons found in a cave in Menton, France, (near the border of Italy) in 1901 are not mentioned in HGHG (at least in the abridged version). DNA technology can supposedly extract genetic information from archaic human and animal remains, but I have not heard of any DNA investigation of these ancient Grimaldi remains as of this writing, though I am certain that such testing will find them older than their presently estimated 40,000 years. In his article entitled "The First Invaders," author Legrand Clegg II discusses how modern scientists point to Cro-Magnons as the earliest humans in Europe and "write and teach history as if there is no evidence to the contrary" (*African Presence* 30). The DNA scientists and writers of HGHG are obviously adding the weight of modern science to this long-accepted assertion with their avowal that the earliest humans entered Europe 30,000 years BPE and that these were Caucasoids who had developed in West Asia. But the spectre of the Grimaldi skeletons found at Menton looms heavily over the debate. And, although Cro Magnon skeletons were found within the same cave at Menton, the "Cro Magnon skeletons were found on the upper two levels and Grimaldi skeletons lay at the lower level" (op. cit. 24).

By declaring the ancient inhabitants of North Africa Caucasoids, Eurocentric historians and scientists effected a crowning stratagem, which DNA researchers, like the authors of HGHG have seemingly confirmed. And perhaps readers of HGHG or similar works are confident that the new science has, indeed, set the record of modern man in order. If so, then the grand stratagem has achieved its objective, and Eurocentric scholars can congratulate themselves for demonstrating once again that particular characteristic they have shown over and over: that they are masters of *deceit*. For, to convince people that the earliest North African populations were Caucasoid is to put blinders on them as one does a horse pulling a carriage. The blinders insure that peoples' vision is restricted, blind to what is to their left or right. They look at what Eurocentric scholars have trained them to see—Africa's front door, the main road out of the Mother Continent where, within a thousand miles of it, humans in short order transformed into non-African Caucasoids who became the Aryan civilizers of the ancient world.

The blinders then direct our focus on a Caucasoid dispersal out of Asia Minor and westward through Europe to Iberia, where they *reenter* Africa to become the "dark whites" or "Brunet people" we have long heard of. The crowning stratagem enacted by Eurocentric historians effectively closed Africa's *back* door out of the continent—the narrow Strait of Gibraltar where Europe practically kisses North Africa at the southern tip of Spain. And all the reader need do is consult an atlas to see this stark reality that a six-year-old would not miss. The purpose of Eurocentric historians has always been to choke off any suggestion that black Africans migrated northward into Europe by way of the Strait of Gibraltar—which might have been Africa's *earliest* route into Europe.

The 40,000 year-old Grimaldi skeletons are the oldest human remains found in Europe *so far,* which does not preclude African homo sapiens entering Europe even earlier. Let us not forget that 40,000 years ago the earth was in the grip of the Wurm ice age (which peaked 40,000 to 50,000 years ago), and the northern half of Europe and a large expanse of northern Asia were covered by glacial ice, which lowered sea levels everywhere. Landbridges connected Africa to Iberia, and to Italy by way of Sicily, and these landbridges existed for many millennia, effectively splitting the Mediterranean Sea into two gigantic lakes (see Fig. 8). For millennia Africans entered Europe on foot—into Sicily, Italy, Iberia and France—and, when the glacial ice began to recede, trekked into Britain and Scandinavia. Most, if not all of Europe was inhabited by black-skinned African peoples from remotest times, who occupied the continent long before *actual* Caucasoids even *developed.* Eurocentric historians and DNA researchers simply ignore statements from more honest pre-DNA historians, like Roland B. Dixon, who states "the Mediterranean type spread into Spain *from Africa*" (*my emphasis* 154), and that in early times a Proto-Australoid type of mankind was dominant in France, and that "[this] Proto-Australoid type was also in Spain the dominant factor" (op. cit., 152-153).

Dixon, relying on skull types and cranial measurements, the chief indicators of race employed in his time, shows that proto-Australoid and proto-Negroid peoples were in every area of Europe in remote times and were still in evidence when Mongoloids and Caucasoids entered the continent. All these peoples eventually intermingled, and there is scant reason to believe that Caucasoid ancestors of present-day Europeans are the product of some pure central core that remained untouched by other races. Even pro-Aryanist historian L.A. Waddell, who claims the Phoenicians were a Caucasoid, and presumably white-skinned people, cannot escape injecting elements of truth into his work when he states:

> [W]hile philologists and popular writers . . . assume that the "Celts" were Aryans in race . . . scientific anthropologists and classic historians have proved that the "Celts" of history were the *non-Aryan, round-headed, darkish, small-statured race of south Germany and Switzerland,* and that "*Celts*" properly so-called are *"totally lacking in the British Isles."* (*some, my emphasis,* 127-128)

Unlike Eurocentric, pre-DNA historians of his day (i.e., early 1900s), Waddell unwittingly corroborates the assessments of Higgins, Churchward and other historians that the Celts of Europe and the British Isles, those I referr to as *early Celts,* were short, black- or dark-skinned peoples, whom Churchward and others assert were of Egyptian origin. As discussed in an earlier chapter, Godfrey Higgins asserted they were black Asiatics, stressing that "the Celtae, the Scythians, and the [early] Saxons, were all tribes of the same people" (*Anacalypsis* 273).

There is an interesting and instructive comment from American scientist and diplomat Benjamin Franklin in Scott L. Malcomson's *One Drop of Blood: The American Misadventure of Race.* In the mid-18th century, discussing the issue of slavery—whether the African slave trade should continue; the rights slaves (chiefly African) should *not* have; and the possible *bastardization* of the Anglo-American society by newly arriving *European* peoples—Franklin claimed that black slaves had already "blacken'd half *America,*" and went on to state:

> Why should Pennsylvania, founded by the English, become a colony of Aliens, who will shortly be so numerous as to *Germanize* us instead of our Anglifying them . . . [?] The number of purely white people in the world is proportionally very small. All Africa is black or tawny. Asia chiefly tawny. America (exclusive of the new comers) wholly so. *And in Europe, the Spaniards, Italians, French, Russians and Swedes are generally of what we call a swarthy complexion; as are the Germans also, the Saxons only excepted, who with the English make the principal body of white people on the face of the earth.* (*my emphasis,* 177)

Franklin's comment was a reflection of the extreme degree of race-consciousness in English (or *Anglo*) colonial America prior to the 19th century, a society that feared even the slightest racial contamination by European immigrants whom we consider *white* today. The darkness of the Spaniards and Italians has already been discussed. But note the Europeans Franklin considered *swarthy* as well: the French, Swedes, Russians, and most Germans—for the most part, *northern* Europeans.

I have not explored how conversant Franklin was with history or anthropology, but it is certain that he was one of the most knowledgeable men of his day. However, he, like most English-oriented Americans of his time, was deeply infected with racism as, apparently most Englishmen must have been, believing that only German *Saxons* and the English were *pure* Whites who had seemingly, miraculously, avoided the slightest intermingling with darker races in Europe and in the British Isles. But Franklin's belief that Frenchmen, Swedes, Germans and Russians were swarthy races is testament to Europe once having been predominantly inhabited by black- and dark-skinned people, a fact that Eurocentric historians and DNA researchers are continually endeavoring to conceal.

Perhaps DNA technology *can* definitively provide answers to age-old debates regarding early humans, but attaining an acceptable consensus requires—in addition to archeological remains, artifacts, geological considerations and DNA findings—sincerity, integrity and open-mindedness on the part of the scientists and scholars exploring the matter. Just as European and American scholars have been the predominant disseminators of history over the last two or three centuries, DNA scientists are predominantly European and white American, which calls into question their motives, openness and honesty—especially if their findings support pre-DNA assertions which, in many cases, were already questionable, if not totally spurious. In our present world, dominated for the last five centuries by people who seemed bent on destroying any non-white civilization they came into contact with—a practice which is still glaringly evident—the findings of DNA scientists, like the authors of HGHG, need to be seriously contemplated.

Modern Eurocentric scientists and scholars have compartmentalized genetics into minute, dialectic, scientific justifications purporting to explain differences in man's racial make-up, admixtures which produced them and the way natural selection or environment brought about mutational alterations to enhance the survivability of these types in the environments they found themselves in. In regard to skin color, the possession, or lack of, vitamin D in the body has lately been touted as the primary factor determining the complexion of the inhabitants of a given area. So, as a general rule, according to vitamin D proponents, sub-Saharan Africans are black-skinned because the rays of the sun hit the earth most directly at the equator. The sun's rays bombard the earth with UVR (ultra-violet radiation) which breaks down important biomolecules in the skin. To prevent the total breakdown of chemical compounds necessary for reproduction, melanin is produced to counter harmful UVR and also retard the production of vitamin D in the body. The vitamin D from the sun's rays ensures that individuals receive enough of the vitamin from the tropical environment they live in. Conversely, according to Nina G. Jablonski, author of *Skin:*

> As we move out of the tropics into the middle latitudes, from about 25 degrees to 50 degrees, there is not enough UVR to produce vitamin D in the skin of a lightly pigmented person . . . . In latitudes above about 50 degrees, in the far north, levels of UVR are much lower . . . . [T]he farther north you go, the harder it is for you to make vitamin D in your skin. (81)

According to Jablonski and proponents of the theory, people living in the far north need lighter skin to be able to absorb as much UVR (she also mentions UVB) as possible from the sun's less intense rays. So, skin pigmentation is lighter the further people are from the tropical heat of equatorial areas.

Jablonski cites a study of South African schoolchildren, a dark-skinned group and an albino group. The darkly pigmented children had much lower vitamin D levels and needed to take supplements of vitamin D to maintain normal physiological functions. The author also stresses: "At high latitudes, it is almost impossible for dark-skinned people to produce vitamin D during most of the year" (op. cit.). The reasoning regarding vitamin D's connection with pigmentation seems plausible, but Jablonski's analysis does not suggest a time factor. If a group of black-skinned people migrated to northern Europe, how long would the process of depigmentation take? Centuries? Millennia? Or could the process unfold quickly, as the authors of HGHG suggest when they state:

> *Natural selection* is the automatic choice of "fitter" types, which can eventually make . . . a single mutant, the most common in a population, provided it is advantageous to the individuals carrying it. (111)

Cavalli-Sforza et al don't suggest a time frame either, but their hypothesis is plausible, as well. We are speaking, basically, of skin pigmentation here, which does not explain eye color, hair texture or color, changes in bone structure (for instance, cheek bones becoming more, or less, prominent), or the thinning of lips, factors we often cite in regard to racial differences in humans.

While Cavalli-Sforza et al divide Africans into a number of groupings and then declare some of these Caucasoids, they discuss Europeans differently (the same as pre-DNA scientists)—country by country—calling small groups who don't fit the general norms of the nations they are living in *outliers*—mentioning Lapps, Sardinians, Icelanders and Basques specifically. They place more emphasis on linguistic aspects of Europeans of specific nations, stressing that the vast majority of Europeans speak "Indo-European" languages while emphasizing their *Eurasianness*. They provide mostly unintelligible charts and graphs, which are not layman-friendly, while discussing admixtures, alleles, single-gene studies, mtDNA, polymorphisms, and so forth in the process. Where I had initially anticipated acquiring and reading this book after reading Louise Levathes' 1993 *New York Times* article, my reading of HGHG sputtered and ground to a halt at the two-thirds point. The alarm bells had begun to ring when the authors first used the term *non-African* on page 87. I asked myself: If the roots and trunk of the human tree was African, how can the branches jutting off that tree be non-African? If Africans migrated out of the continent black-skinned and spread to the farthest regions of the earth, they still must have been black-skinned, like the original inhabitants of Australia and all those who stopped off at points *between* the two continents—like the original inhabitants of central Asia must have been, some of whom continued migrating north—eastward and eventually into North America; like the original inhabitants of West Asia and Europe whose skeletal remains bear mute witness to their *black* African origins, despite declarations that these somehow quickly lost their Africanness and became non-African Caucasoids.

Then these Caucasoids spread in all directions, according to Cavalli-Sforza et al, even returning to Africa, via Iberia (Spain), to become the original inhabitants of North Africa The authors then go about connecting nearly all people outside of sub-Saharan Africa to Caucasoids, including even Native Americans! After initially affirming that modern man originated in and migrated out of Africa, these authors proceed to obfuscate or dismiss the Africanness in all human beings outside of the continent and imply that most of mankind is Caucasoid! Somehow the final human type or extract from the African trunk came to predominate over the original, which had spawned all modern humans! This final extract of mankind developed in an area that is yet to be accurately determined, then went into all the areas of older black-skinned humanity, intermingling enough so that the authors of HGHG declare nearly the entire populations of Asia and Europe—which remained predominantly black- and dark-skinned well into historical times—*Caucasoid*, allowing the reader to continue to believe that Caucasians were responsible for the achievements of the world's earliest, most dynamic and advanced civilizations!—the same as pre-DNA, Eurocentric historians and scientists did.

Chapter 16

THE DNA FACTOR: LOST IN TRANSMISSION

Considering all the inventions and innovations that came about during the 20th century which absolutely improved our lives, one would tend to believe that at this point in our existence on earth a breakthrough like DNA technology could only benefit us more positively. We would, at last, be able to unlock the mystery of our origins: correct the confused or erroneous assumptions of the past; finally validate what historians have long told us of our emergence and dispersion around the earth; accurately assign racial types to the builders of various past civilizations, culminating in today's modern Western civilization; racially trace the emergence of the various cultures out of which particular civilizations may have emerged; or the races who developed cultures and cultural practices that have endured the thrust of civilization and continue an independent existence, albeit tenuous or threatened with extinction.

Cavalli-Sforza et al present their findings and conclusions with the weight of ostensibly irrefutable proof, as DNA scientists have long touted the science offers.

However, the work of these scientists comes off as a codification of the assertions of pre-DNA Eurocenric scholars who began the practice of usurping the achievements of the black-skinned originators of civilization, validating assertions that white Europeans were responsible for them. Bold historians like Churchward, Higgins, MacRitchie, Sergi and several others, who defied convention and wrote of black-skinned men and women occupying most areas of the earth, including Europe, at a time when doing so was highly unpopular, are simply forgotten, ignored or dismissed. This writer must reject the conclusions of Cavalli-Sforza et al, as their supposedly objective findings often defy common sense and logic—as outlined in the previous chapter.

Some, of course, will be satisfied with their findings; however, in the authors of HGHG, we witness Eurocentric extremism to the highest degree in that their conclusions mirror the spurious declarations of Eurocentric scholars and scientists before them. I am unable to argue with their supposed DNA findings since I lack training in this field. I assume there are some non-white college students pursuing training in this area. I have met one, a young man from Madagascar, pursuing a degree in DNA science. But many more non-white students are needed to one day independently conduct research in the area of man's history and migrations and counter the spurious findings presented in HGHG and similar works. As things stand now, it is a field dominated by Caucasians, just as the fields of history and science have been for centuries, and a non-white counterweight of individuals (who are proud of their origins, and who do not secretly desire to be Caucasian or be accepted by them) is necessary to bring objectivity and balance into it.

Despite their convoluted assertion that various non-white people around the earth are actually Caucasoids in their physical makeup, the authors of HGHG do not pinpoint a Caucasian homeland. We know the homeland of black- and brown-skinned Africans, the black- and tawny-skinned Mongoloids; we know the origin, or the most likely origin, of Native Americans, who entered North and South America in extremely archaic times (though many probably arrived after crossing the Pacific Ocean, and perhaps the Atlantic, as well); and we know that Australians (Aborigines) occupied that continent in extremely remote times. We also know that black-skinned Africans, or Africoids, were the earliest inhabitants of Europe (i.e., Grimaldis, Australoids) at least 40,000 years ago, if not earlier. So, in what area was the Caucasoid homeland? How and where did Caucasoids develop? And what did they do, build, or create while they were there?

If their homeland was somewhere in Europe, what ancient structures offer evidence of their germination and development there? What unearthed cities, archeological ruins, significant artifacts? The authors of HGHG offer nothing definitive. Regarding the origin of Caucasoids, they state:

> The ancestors of modern Caucasoids and modern East Indians (let us call them Eurasians) developed either in northeastern Africa, or in West Asia or southeastern Europe from an originally African source during the period between 100 and 50 kya. (253)

What they conclude is mere speculation: "Either here, or here, or here." Though there is an admission that Caucasoids are tied to Africa, the authors say, *"(let us call them Eurasians),"* to distance them from Africa and blackness—from Original Man. They propose an extremely long span of time ("between 100 and 50 kya") for Caucasian development, so that their emergence conveniently corresponds with the period most scientists and historians believe modern man was migrating out of Africa to other areas of the earth.

Continuing their discussion on the location of the Caucasian homeland, the authors next state:

> *There was a wide area, difficult to locate in the absence of archeological evidence,* in which cultural maturation took place until about 50 kya. One speculates that it *might have been in West Asia* [Turkey]. (*my emphasis,* op. cit.)

Does the above sound definitive?—not to mention that there is an *"absence of archeological evidence"* to validate their claim.

The authors of HGHG leave all options open and in the next paragraph, speculate on a supposed Caucasoid migration out of wherever their homeland might have been, stating: "It may have originated from East Africa (going across the Red Sea) or from the speculative West Asian area of maturation" (op. cit.). More speculation, despite all their charts with supposedly factual DNA evidence, as well as a lack of archeological evidence. Then, to support everything they asserted earlier, they throw the kitchen sink:

> Whether or not it partially hybridized with local descendants of early archaic H. sapiens or H. erectus, *the Eurasian moity* [each of the two parts] *was ready for an expansion,* perhaps *about 50-40 kya, and expanded in all directions: north and then east, occupying northeastern Asia, the Arctic, and America; west toward West Asia and Europe; and southeast, where it may have mixed with the descendants of the southern branch of the African migration.* (*my emphasis,* op. cit.)

After initially stating that Caucasoids developed 30,000 years ago in West Asia, they lengthen the existence of Caucasoids to 40,000-50,000 years ago, the same period that Grimaldi man (long classified as Negroid, and whom the authors never mention) was entering Europe.

No *specific* homeland is cited for Caucasoids; no evidence that ancient Caucasoids erected any significant architectural monuments, cities; had anything that could be called a civilization. Even pre-DNA scholars never seemed to locate a *verifiable* area of maturation, all the while claiming Europe or Eurasia as the eternal domain of Caucasoids. The authors of HGHG attach Caucasoids to nearly all other early societies, just as pre-DNA historians did while beating their chests and declaring to the world: "We were the primary authors and shapers of civilization!" In the end, all the authors of HGHG do is offer speculation, render their conclusions fallacious, self-serving and blatantly dishonest. The reader who has not been mesmerized and confused by their charts, technical terms and deceptive language is still left asking: In what specific area was the Caucasoid homeland located? What did they do, build, or create there? What ancient structures, archeological ruins or significant artifacts offer evidence of their independent existence there?

To evade these questions, Cavalli-Sforza et al, like pre-DNA historians before them, attach Caucasoids to peoples with verifiable homelands, archeological ruins, buried cities, standing stones and various other artifacts, then declare these peoples *Caucasian,* even though many of these peoples remain black- and brown-skinned to this day and do not resemble present-day Europeans, or *actual* Caucasoids. The mere fact that Caucasoids invaded a particular area inhabited by black- and brown-skinned peoples and intermingled with them is quite enough for Eurocentric scholars to declare the *invaded* people Caucasoid, as they have with Indians and peoples of Mesopotamia and the Near East—many of whom have come to embrace the whiteness Eurocentric scholars have bestowed upon them. But this deceptive practice by Eurocentric historians and scientists has been employed chiefly to convolve a more ancient history for modern white Europeans, *actual* Caucasoids.

During the long ago epoch discussed above, only black-skinned people were coming out of Africa, and those who ventured to West Asia, East Asia and Australia had, as well, to have been black-skinned. So, how did East Asians lighten up? Are the authors implying Chinese when they speak of East Asians? Indic or Mesopotamian peoples? The authors never explain how such people became light-skinned enough to produce a Caucasian or white race when they supposedly backtracked westward toward Africa and interbred with black- and brown-skinned Africans to somehow produce a *Caucasian* race in West Asia (i.e., Turkey).

For the origin of Caucasoids, I honestly believe we need to return to the Great White Forest we visited in Chapter 2. Caucasians—white-skinned people—could not have evolved from the interbreeding of black-skinned Africans and black- and brown-complexioned Chinese or Indians. Such a theory is a biological impossibility, which does not require a degree in DNA science to comprehend. What was suggested in Chapter 2 seems far more reasonable: Some genetic factor caused black-skinned people to lose melanin and produce offspring in whom melanin production was thwarted, resulting in albinism or albino-ism in them over a protracted period of time. Perhaps certain vitamin deficiencies had something to do with this—possibly brought on by an as yet unknown natural disaster like a huge meteor crashing to earth and setting off catastrophic volcanic eruptions that filled the atmosphere with suffocating ash and sulfuric gases for an unknown period of time, which contaminated water and vegetation, negatively affecting all animal life over a widespread area. While this is speculative, many scientists believe that a giant meteor crashing to earth is responsible for the demise of dinosaurs sixty to seventy-million years ago, engendering mutations and new forms of animal life. It is believed that such catastrophic events have occurred many times in our planet's history.

Some such event could have disturbed man's genetic makeup to where one third to half of children were born with an inability to produce melanin, and it is plausible to presume that those afflicted were banished from their societies because of this abnormality. They would have been treated in the same manner that history shows lepers were treated.

According to biologists, and even Cavalli-Sforza et al, if a chemical imbalance interferes with the hormonal stimulus needed to produce pigment cells in the embryonic development of humans, albinism in the newborn will be the result, even if both parents have jet-black complexions. And this anomaly in human genes can be inherited. While the authors of HGHG do not spend a lot of time discussing albinism, they do offer telling statements, like that, "[t]ransmission error in the reproduction of DNA is called m*utation,*" and "[m]utation in the dividing cell of an organism . . . may lead to alteration of part of the organism, but is not transmitted to the descendants unless it occurs in *germinal* cells, or *gametes* . . . *dedicated* to the production of individuals of the next generation, and mutations occurring in them can be passed on to progeny and thus have evolutionary consequences" (5).

Just as in the animal, marine and insect realms, mutations occur as a way of ensuring the survival of a specie in its environment, or a suddenly altered environment it finds itself in. Although albinism may not be precisely the same as mutation in technical terms, the difference between the two is minor in the way they occur, and a significant outbreak of albinism in black-skinned migrants out of Africa after moving into unfamiliar environments—in combination with wetter, cooler climates, less UVR, or a catastrophic geological event—could have led to the emergence of what Cavalli-Sforza et al call a "fitter" type, which developed into a mutation in the affected populations. A mutation is a relatively rapid alteration, a *revolutionary* change in a specie to enhance its survival in an altered environment.

The long promoted assertion that Caucasoids lost pigmentation due to living in a harsh, cold, snow-driven environment for long millennia means, essentially, that the Caucasoid emergence out of originally black-skinned humanity was due to mutation, occurring over an unknown period of time—lightening the pigmentation of northern peoples to allow them to absorb more UVR so as to enhance their ability to survive the harshness of their frigid environment. However, this long-asserted theory is defective.

In his 1947 book, *Men Out of Asia*, Harold S. Gladwin states that Australoids began arriving in North America as long ago as 25,000 years—a date that must now be pushed back to at least 40,000 years in light of skeletal remains found in California dated to 37,000 years old and more recent discoveries in South America, believed to be much older. This means that the North and South American migrants were roughly contemorary with the Australoids inhabiting Europe (Grimaldi man), Asia and Australia, and that the American migrants were branches of Asian Australoids who had, presumably, expanded within Asia far to the northeast where numbers of them eventually crossed over Beringia (the landbridge connecting northeast Asia to Alaska) to enter North America. As discussed earlier, this migration did not take place in a year, ten years, a hundred years, or even a millennium. We must assume that northeast Asia had a sizeable population which must have been inhabiting the area for several millennia before some of them decided to leave a now overcrowded area, flee an aggressive tribe, or follow game animals over the ice age landbridge—some migrants eventually settling in the northwestern coastal areas of North America—modern-day Alaska and northwestern Canada.

Reaching and finally settling these northwestern areas would have taken hundreds of years, if not a millennium or two, as generation after generation followed the coastline until the area of California was reached. Radiocarbon dating of an ancient campsite in Monte Verde, Chile, reveals that it was occupied by 12,700 BC. Robert M. Schoch (*Voyages of the Pyramid Buildeers*), commenting on Stone Age migrations, and noting that Monte Verde is 9,000 miles south of Beringia, offers readers a sense of how arduous a migration down the west coast of North America into Mexico and South America would have been:

> There is simply no way that Stone Age hunters crossing even in the first wave of Asian migrants could have covered such a distance in but one millennium, *unless they were traveling at lightning speed*—perhaps . . . following the coastline in small boats. Anthropologists generally agree that it would take 7,000 years for progressive waves of land-bound immigrants to travel that far . . . a calculation that pushes their entry into the New World to 20,000 to 19,000 B.C. (87)

Schoch cites a number of impediments to such a journey—expanding glaciers, mountains, forests and climactic zones ranging from frigid to sweltering.

Schoch also mentions another campsite, this one called Toca do Boquierao da Pedra Furada, in northeastern Brazil, which radiocarbon dating puts at 50,000 to 30,000 BC; he opines that if ensuing research on this site supports this date, "then humans have been in the New World about three times longer than we thought possible . . ." (op. cit. 89).

Later migrations out of Asia into North and South America took place—that of Folsom Man, who was Negroid, and Mongoloids, who were also black-skinned, like their counterparts in Asia—in the same generational manner, and by boat when the landbridge disappeared under water. The point of all this is that if the ancestors of Native Americans—coming to North America 30,000-40-000 years ago (if not earlier) while Wurm glacial ice still covered much of the northern territories of the continent, or coming by sea at later times—maintained their extremely dark (in some cases, black) pigmentation until a century ago (see Fig. 19), then *cold weather conditions, alone, cannot explain the loss of pigmentation in Caucasoids*—even over many millennia. It is true that the 250 or more Native American tribes in North America when Europeans arrived had varying complexions—some reported as near white, like the Menomenees, Zuni and Mandans. But I speak here of the earliest Native migrants to North America who were generally black- or very dark-skinned Australoids and Mongoloids who emanated out of that "great nation of blacks [who] formerly possessed the dominion of Asia," that Godfrey Higgins speaks of (*Anac. vol. 1* 52).

The same can be said of the black-skinned, Africoid Grimaldi (Australoid) populations of Europe who ventured into that continent. Eurocentric historians (and the authors of HGHG) want to lighten the African migrants into Europe coming by way of The Levant; so they insert them in West Asia (i.e., Turkey); Caucasianize them by having dark- or black-skinned Chinese or Indians return to the Near East to interbreed with black- and brown-skinned Africans; then have this suddenly *Caucasian* race spread into Europe. The authors have these sudden Caucasians high-tail it all the way west to Iberia; cross the Strait of Gibraltar; spread throughout North Africa and back eastward to Egypt. Then to preclude any notion of black Africans being anywhere near Europe, they launch an additional assertion—having the ancestors of Caucasoids *develop* in northeastern Africa (see above) and boldly claim the original inhabitants of *all* North Africa *Caucasian*!

The truth is that the earliest migrants into West Asia and eastern Europe were the same varied types of Africans who had moved eastward through southern Asia to India and beyond. Why would they have looked any differently? They arrived with varying shades of black and brown skin with their Australoid and Negroid physiognomy long before their African origins were obscured by names like Alpines, Beaker Folk, Dasyus, Cushites, Semites, Chaldeans, Hindu Kush, Capsian, Combe-Capelle, Aurignacians and others.

While an eastern migration out of the Mother Continent may have preceded a western one by several millennia, we cannot overlook migrations into Europe over the Iberian and Sicilian landbridges after the African population (*black* Africans) expanded to the western and northern areas of North Africa when the Sahara was fertile, rife with vegetation and streams. Precisely *when* these western migrations began is not clear, but 40,000 or more years ago seems reasonable since the Grimaldi skeletons unearthed in Menton are estimated to be at least that age. It is almost certain Grimaldi man entered Europe from the *west*, over the Iberian and Sicilian landbridges, and Cheikh Anta Diop asserts, "there is no other variety of *Homo sapiens* that precedes the Grimaldi Negroid in Europe or Asia" (*Civilization* 15), noting that they were the authors of Aurignacian culture in Europe. Diop goes on to state:

> The Grimaldi Negroids have left their numerous traces all over Europe and Asia, from the Iberian Peninsula to Lake Baykal in Siberia, passing through France, Austria, the Crimea, and the Basin of Don . . . . Negroids survived everywhere in Europe until the Neolithic period: Spain, Portugal, Belgium, the Balkans . . . [and] the Arabian Peninsula . . . . (op. cit. 54, 15)

Grimaldis entered Europe and Asia during the Wurm ice age when average temperatures were colder than they are today but prior to the height of the ice age. (Scientists differ about when the height of the Wurm glacial occurred, with estimates ranging from 20,000-50,000 years ago. Schoch and many others believe the height of the Wurm glaciation to be 20,000 years ago.) Yet, Grimaldi Negroids did not "die out" or lose their pigmentation, surviving in Europe and Asia, into the Neolithic period, noted by Diop and made undeniably clear by the discovery of the previously discussed Iceman—whom the authors of HGHG do not mention in their work.

These Grimaldi populations remaining essentially black- and dark-skinned does not preclude outbreaks of albinism in the continents they inhabited, with afflicted individuals being cast out of the societies of the Normals, which could explain the white- and near-white-skinned tribes of North and South American Indians. While the reader may consider my comments regarding a massive outbreak of albinism speculative, far more erudite historians and researchers have forcefully asserted this theory—Dr. Frances Cress Welsing (see Chapter 2), Charles S. Finch, and Cheikh Anta Diop, to name a few; not to forget that German philosopher Arthur Schopenhauer (1788-1860) stated: "There is no such thing as a white race . . . but every white man is a faded or bleached one." (qtd. in Rogers 29). However, such a theory sounds considerably more plausible than the oft touted frigid weather concept which (considering my comments above on Native American migrants from northeast Asia into North America retaining their pigmentation) seems less probable, the only questions being *how* and *why* this massive outbreak of albinism took place.

While Cavalli-Sforza et al assert that humans entered Europe from North Africa through the Iberian Peninsula (*one* of their theories), they assert these were Cro Magnons—presumably Caucasian—and consistently distance black Africans from other races and populations that notable non-Eurocentric scholars and anthropologists have directly connected them to. Here is a sampling of supposedly DNA-based assertions that the authors of HGHG make:

- "Europeans and Asians are *significantly* closer to each other than to Africans." (70);
- "Europeans (and other Caucasoids) have an intermediate position between Africans and the rest of the world: Asians + Americans and Oceanians" (71);
- "The separation of Berbers from other Africans is certainly no cause for surprise, as North Africans have long been considered Caucasoid" (77);
- "[T]he data show a considerable separation between Africans and all non-Africans, in good agreement with all other data" (89);
- "Melanesians are closer to the Chinese and Caucasoid groups, and the root is located between the two African populations on one side, with the three non-African populations on the other" (90).

There are more similarly convoluted statements presented by the authors of HGHG as a way of distancing practically all peoples from black Africans (whom they confine to sub-Saharan Africa) after initially citing Africa as the birthplace of *all* modern humans. As was the general practice of pre-DNA Eurocentric historians before them, the authors of HGHG classify *any* Africans who set foot out of the continent *non-Africans*, ostensibly Caucasoid, shoot other racial groups off a non-African branch, then assert that the off-shoots are genetically closer to Caucasians than to Africans—despite the obvious similarity of the offshoots, phenotypically and in physiognomy, to black and brown Africans! In the process, they establish *Caucasoids* as a major genetic group rivaling the very African trunk Caucasoids, *themselves*, developed from! I trust the reader sees the sophistry in this logic.

As for albinism, which Cavalli-Sforza et all don't seem to consider as the chief factor in the development of Caucasoids, both they and Charles S. Finch concur that "both parents must carry the *same* class of albino gene, though they themselves do *not* have to be albinos" (Finch, *African Presence* 20). Finch also opines that a population of *H. sapiens* surviving the last glaciation in Eurasia was primarily a group of albinoids better adapted to more frigid northern climactic conditions, their dark-skinned relatives, perhaps dying out. My feeling is that these albinoids were essentially pushed out and abandoned, not allowed to remain among the Normals—which I consider more reasonable than their black-skinned relatives simply dying out, since a colder climate is not a prerequisite for loss of melanin, as I trust was made clear above. Blacks could, and *did*, survive in frigid areas of the earth for millennia—melanin intact.

Humankind originated in *darkest, sub-Saharan* Africa and spread in millennia-long migrations to nearly every part of the earth—including Europe, which Eurocentric historians and scientists continue to try to deny. These earliest migrants arrived black-skinned and remained so as they trekked across landbridges into Europe—through Iberia and Italy, into France, Germany, and probably Switzerland and Austria, areas whose climactic conditions were less harsh than northeastern Asia. As Wurm glacial ice retreated, Britain and Scandinavia were reached, and settlements would have sprung up. Various periods have been proposed for the emergence of Caucasoids, like 35,000 years ago for Cro Magnon man. However, it is not universally accepted that Cro Magnon developed 35,000 years ago, or that he was other than black-skinned, since some scholars have referred to Cro Magnon *Negroids* and have mentioned osteopathic similarities between Cro Magnon and Grimaldi skeletons (see Chapter 2). Diop asserts that Caucasoids did not develop until 20,000 years ago and that "immunological data have confirmed the hypothesis of a recent separation of Blacks and Whites, Negroids and Caucasoids" (*Civilization* 35).

Perhaps more attention should be given to the loathing that developed in Caucasoids—*actual* Caucasoids, not the Indians, Aborigines and other peoples so classified—towards black- and dark-skinned humanity. Wherefore the hatred—especially toward people possessing really black or dark skin? Dr. Frances Cress Welsing's theory regarding the hatred displayed by Whites toward all people of color—Blacks, in particular—may seem to be a stretch to some, but how else can one explain the hatred that Whites, collectively, have exhibited toward people of color around the world since Caucasoid humanity gained ascendancy? Her straightforward explanation about how feelings of alienation, rejection and anger in albino populations (see Chapter 2) resulted in a mental illness in *actual* Caucasoids seems quite reasonable and—while present-day Caucasians will probably not admit to being other than positive and free of prejudice—their historical treatment of Blacks and people of color since their ascendancy confirms this. When confronted with various examples in history demonstrating hatred toward Blacks and people of color, they cannot seem to see things the way people of color see them; or they will explain this seeming hatred away as something that ultimately brought about economic benefit; or, when racism is discussed, or they are reminded of the horrors of American slavery, many simply retort: "*My* ancestors never had slaves." They never can see it, don't get it (or don't admit that they do). Presently, they decry the loss of *American* lives in the on-going, so-called *wars* in Iraq and Afghanistan, but the deaths of hundreds of thousands of Iraqis, thousands of Afghanis and the upheavals and disruption of lives in those countries does not register. And the collective illness continues unchecked, unacknowledged, and will surely be passed down to yet another white American generation.

When barbarous Greeks or Hellenes invaded the territory that would be named after them, they encountered a wondrous civilization, an Egyptian-influenced Aegean or Mycenaean civilization where the goddess Isis was venerated, known as Semiramis in the Mesopotamian portion of Greater Ethiopia. While these earliest Greeks laid waste to Mycenaean civilization, they yet embraced the pantheon of gods and goddesses worshipped by this ancient civilization, black-skinned Isis or Semiramis the most revered—the black Mother Goddess who would be later transformed into the Black Madonna and eventually, Mary, when Christianity emerged.

Of course, this fact is largely unremarked upon by Eurocentric scholars, as is the fact that a large statue of the Black Madonna and Child is, even today, the most revered icon in the Vatican in Rome. The adoration of the Black Madonna by white Europeans is a conscious expression of a subconscious memory of black women who long ago aided, nursed and taught them through a long period of distress, rejection and privation. The mental torture experienced by the earliest rejected albino populations cannot be ascertained through DNA research and, if it could, it is doubtful Eurocentric scholars and scientists would spend much time expounding on the suffering of these earliest Caucasoids. The scholars would rather have us believe that Caucasoids developed fully competent, powerful, conversant with civilization, and that they brought civilization to the black- and brown-skinned masses of North Africa, Mesopotamia and India, people who had domesticated those areas many millennia before Caucasoids arrived; people who had domesticated animals, cultivated crops, discovered medicinal plants and herbs, built towns with streets and sewage drainage systems; weaved cotton garments and colorful silken dresses and, in some places, had long been charting the constellations and abiding by the cycles of the sun and moon. Caucasoids, Eurocentric scholars have long declared, brought their civilization to these people; however, they have yet to locate a verifiable homeland of Caucasoids revealing evidence of an exclusively Caucasoid civilization in Europe or in Eurasia. If so-called Caucasians brought civilization to the lands of black- and brown-skinned people, where is the evidence of *their* civilization? And what did they bring to the table in Greece or in Greater Ethiopia?

They brought nothing because it seems they had no civilization of any kind to bring. So Eurocentric historians would transform the ancient Egyptians, Ethiopians, Mesopotamians and Indians into Caucasoids in their writings to give European Whites a more ancient place in history, crediting them with building the civilizations they actually attempted to destroy when they invaded them. The Caucasoid hordes that descended on the settled towns of Greater Ethiopia probably could not verbalize the inexplicable rage they felt toward the mostly peaceable black-skinned inhabitants living comfortably within them; that they were distant relatives was no longer remembered due to the passage of many millennia. What was remembered was that they had never been welcomed into these societies. That was what most fueled their rage when they decided to stampede the towns and precincts of Greater Ethiopia from Greece to the Indus, massacring inhabitants, desecrating monuments that the people held dear, defiling women and girls, eventually becoming the ruling classes of the invaded territories. But while intermingling would eventually lighten a portion of the population, Caucasoids were essentially absorbed by the dominant populations, which did not—except in the writings of Western historians—render the entire populaces Caucasian. The overwhelming majority of these invaded peoples remained black-skinned and, in most cases, the invading Caucasians adopted their pantheon of gods and goddesses.

Now, DNA researchers, like Cavalli-Sforza et al, use the science to codify the invented fictions of pre-DNA Eurocentrists, stripping the negritude from the ancient peoples of Greater Ethiopia, much of Asia, North Africa, the Middle East, and Western Europe by inventing a non-African population in West Asia (Turkey) and asserting that other races are more closely related to these non-Africans than to Africans—the ancestors of *all* humans, which DNA research has emphatically demonstrated. The authors of HGHG employ technical and authoritative language, utilizing indecipherable charts as they discuss gene frequencies and use codes to represent racial elements within certain groups, which only a student of the science might comprehend. There is no way to ascertain whether their charted codes are correct, whether they are universally accepted by DNA scientists, or whether they are honestly representing black peoples within them—which is why I have chosen to present the *written* conclusions and assessments of this stultifying work. But even their written assertions are not always intelligible—like their conclusion that Caucasoids resulted from the intermingling of Africans and Chinese.

Mentioned above is that Diop believes Caucasoids developed 20,000 years ago as Cro Magnon man in Europe. He is convinced that the Chinese developed from a mixture of Caucasoids and Negroids, probably in Eurasia, and that the H. sapiens in China appeared about 17,000 years ago, "the result of an interbreeding of Black and White in a cold climate, perhaps around the end of the Upper Paleolithic period" (*Civilization* 55). This theory sounds much more reasonable than Caucasoids resulting from an intermixture Negroids and Chinese. If the mutant gene which lead to albinism became so rampant and common in albinos that inbreeding among themselves produced typically Caucasoid individuals resulting in a new racial type of typically white-skinned individuals, then the simple biological process of extensive mixing of Negroids and this new white type resulting in a brown or yellow-brown race of people makes sense.

The probability that Albinoids also interbred at some point with Neanderthals should not be dismissed as conjecture. If Albinoids were simply Negroids who had lost the ability to produce melanin, it should follow that the resulting Caucasoid race would have maintained (except for pigmentation) a basic Negroid physiognomy and would be osteologically similar. However, modern Caucasoids tend to have greater bone mass than Negroids, are generally taller, and considerably more hirsute—traits consistent with Neanderthals. So, while Negroid Grimaldis possibly mated with Neanderthals to some degree, Caucasoids *do* exhibit physical traits associated with Neanderthals, insinuating more extensive interbreeding. So, the Albinoid-Neanderthal scenario laid out in Chapter 2 may not be as far-fetched as it may have seemed earlier.

It is also a matter of fact that *actual* Caucasoids feel more comfortable in a colder climate than do Blacks and other people of color, another trait that may be due to being genetically connected to Neanderthals who, in their estimated 250,000 years of existence in Europe and Asia, would have lived during an ongoing major glaciation period and into the Wurm glacial, which was at its height 20,000 years ago. Caucasoids did not go so far as to take up an Eskimo way of life, but seem to have adapted to colder weather and snowy conditions, whereas modern-day Blacks and people of color—unlike their distant Grimaldi ancestors—prefer a warm climate. Descendants of Grimaldis and Australoids—dark-skinned Eskimos or Inuit, Lapps, ancient Finns, ancient Mongoloids and those black-skinned Asians (Negroids, Australoids) who inhabited northeastern Asia for thousands of years before migrating over the Beringia landbridge into North America—adapted to the frigid environments they found themselves in, *retaining their pigmentation.*

Another trait *actual* Caucasoids have exhibited since their emergence was a predilection to exploit, colonize or destroy any non-white population they came into contact with—a practice which continues to this day. Since their descent upon the dark-skinned civilizations of the world roughly 4,000 years ago, Caucasoids have been preoccupied with weaponry and conquest: Alexander subdued Greater Ethiopia; Rome wantonly destroyed the Etruscan civilization, then that of Carthage, extending its conquests to Iberia and Britain, both inhabited by predominantly black- and dark-skinned people; then she conquered Egypt and the Near East, also inhabited by dark-skinned people; Roman popes sanctioned the bloody Crusades to the Holy Land and the Inquisition. Throwing off Moorish domination, the Spanish slaughtered millions of Native Americans in the Caribbean, Mexico and South America; American colonists and the United States would later do the same on a smaller scale; the British killed untold numbers in India while subjugating that country and decimated the Aboriginal population in Australia; the British and French and other European nations carved up chunks of North Africa (not to forget what they did, along with the Portuguese and Spanish in sub-Saharan Africa, in establishing the African slave trade).

The same groups, along with Germans, Portuguese, Dutch and others, subjugated much of Southeast Asia, brought down great China, gobbled up Pacific Island groups, deposed kings, killed resisters, impregnated women and girls wherever they went, referring to the subjugated peoples by degrading epithets—niggers (even in India), duskies, coolies, Beasties, and so on. Though Eurocentric historical and anthropological works assigned many peoples whose territories Europeans colonized to the Caucasian race, in no way did modern Europeans—*actual* Whites—consider them racially akin to themselves, regarding them no differently than white Americans regarded Africans or African-Americans during the period of slavery.

As in the United States well into the 20th century, colonized or subjugated peoples had to step aside to allow Whites to pass in the streets; any native protests were put down and leaders carted off to prison or killed. As in the United States, the severest penalties were administered to any males who violated, were thought to have violated, made eyes at or spoke suggestively to white women in any of the territories subjugated by white colonial powers. Merely being accused by a white woman of any of the above misdeeds, true or untrue, could be a sentence of death for the perpetrator or supposed perpetrator.

Perhaps the most celebrated example in the U.S. of an incident of this sort was the murder of Emmett Louis Till in 1955. Till, a 14 year-old African-American from Chicago visiting relatives in Mississippi, supposedly made a suggestive comment to a white woman in a store. That night he was abducted from his great-uncle's home by a group of white men and brutally murdered. Although the perpetrators of Till's kidnap and murder were discovered and put on trial, they were exonerated by an all-white jury.

A similar incident of this sort took place in Honolulu in 1931. Hawaii was not a state then but a U.S. protectorate, where 20,000 U.S. military personnel, mostly sailors, were stationed. Thalia Massie, a 20 year-old woman from a wealthy family married to Thomas Massie, a young naval officer, was roughed up and sexually abused after leaving a Honolulu nightspot where her husband and a number of navy personnel were celebrating. She claimed four young Hawaiian men were the culprits. The incident outraged navy personnel, especially the naval commander of the island. Ms. Massie gave police the license plate number of the car she was forced into, and the number was traced to a young Hawaiian male who happened to be in town at the time of the incident. It was later discovered that the number was almost identical to another license plate number on a vehicle owned by an American. But a general outrage continued against dark-skinned Hawaiians by American personnel, and one of the four accused Hawaiians was abducted by Thomas Massie, Thalia Massie's well-to-do mother, and another navy man.

He was interrogated, told to confess and, when he didn't, insisting he had nothing to do with the crime, he was shot to death. His abductors went on trial for his murder and were convicted. But in a strange twist of justice, the governor of the island took it upon himself to commute their sentences and free them less than two hours after their conviction. I have not researched it, but more incidents of this kind have occurred in the U.S., Australia, and probably every country subjugated by *actual* Caucasoids. White men are extremely sensitive regarding relationships or intercourse between white women and dark-skinned men, although Eurocentric scholars and DNA researchers insist that Arabs, Indians, Iranians, Polynesians, and other obviously dark-skinned peoples are part of the great Caucasoid family. How absurd and hypocritical.

Whiteness of skin became the highest standard of beauty, purity, intelligence and privilege for the Caucasoid. He came to India and China as a trader—respectful, smiling, seemingly humble—and ended up subduing these nations, holding them with a combination of chicanery, deception and force, which in the case of India endured for more than 300 years. The British eventually controlled the government, spread Christianity, used Indians to help them fight other Indians, installed a British education system, with English as the official language—continuing their grip on this world's second most populous nation until Gandhi's non-cooperation movement culminated in Britain granting India independence in 1947. All this while Eurocentric historians called India's vast populace Aryan, Caucasoid—a practice which the authors of HGHG perpetuate.

Western historians are quick to cite Adolph Hitler's efforts to bring about racial purity in Germany and Europe and the millions of people killed over the dozen years of his reign as the worst of crimes against humanity. Mostly ignored are the millions of human beings—mostly black, brown, red and yellow—that Europeans and Americans, collectively, have killed since Columbus' first voyage ignited their quest for world domination. We cannot spend more time here, but all the interested reader need do is examine the untold deaths suffered by native populations in Africa, the Americas, the Caribbean, Asia, Australia and the isles of the Pacific from the time *actual* Caucasoids set foot into these territories, or into the individual nations within them.

The pattern of Caucasoid aggression and world domination continues to this day with the United States' destruction and subjugation of Iraq, a country illegally invaded in March, 2003, based on a known fallacy that Iraq possessed nuclear weapons, or weapons of mass destruction (WMD). When no such weapons were found, the purpose of the war brought upon this country was then changed to "bringing democracy" to the country and removing a "brutal dictator," Saddam Hussein, president of the nation for a quarter century. Hussein was eventually captured, put on trial (by a U.S.-backed Iraqi court, not an international court) for crimes against his own people, and hanged in December, 2006.

Most thinking people know that the primary reason for the "war" brought to Iraq is that it contains the world's second largest oil reserves after Saudi Arabia and that the United States and its staunchest ally, Britain, want to control this immense natural resource.

Meanwhile, hundreds of thousands of Iraqis have been killed, one source putting the Iraqi death toll at 700,000 (as of the end of 2008). The war—along with the "war" in Afghanistan, begun by the U.S. in 2001—is clearly (to thinking people) a resumption of aggressive Euro-American imperialism, the same aggressive imperialism that sought to "open up" China, Korea and Japan to trade with the West during the 19th century, something these Asian nations did not desire. The Iraqi war has entered its eighth year (the Afghan war its tenth), with no end in the foreseeable future. It is another war by *actual* Caucasoids—with documented incidents of torture, rape, and murder of innocent Iraqis by American forces—against dark-skinned people who have long been classified Aryan and Caucasian by Western scholars and are so designated by he authors of HGHG.

Actual Caucasoids have generally brought about Hitler-like decimations of the black-, brown-, yellow-, and red-skinned inhabitants of territories they went into—whatever the pretense. And although Eurocentric scholars and scientists have averred that North Africans, Arabs, Near Easterners, Indians, various other Asians, Australians and Pacific Islanders are Caucasoid—or closer to Europeans than to Africans—it would be interesting to learn whether the populations of these abused territories are in agreement with the assertions of Western scholars and anthropologists.

While the authors of HGHG may have tried to demonstrate that, in the words of a *Time* magazine reviewer (seen on the back cover of the abridged soft-cover edition of *The History and Geography of Human Genes*), "there is 'no scientific basis' for theories touting the genetic superiority of any one population over another," the work they have produced belies this. Their creation of an ancient "non African" modern human population, and classification of a large portion of the black- and brown-skinned world as Caucasoid is, in itself, polarizing, dishonest and, ultimately, racist. Using indecipherable graphs and charts to somehow arrive at essentially the same conclusions that pre-DNA Eurocentric scholars did; declaring most of the world's population outside of sub-Saharan Africa Caucasoid; asserting that the victims of historic Caucasoid oppression and rapine were themselves essentially Caucasian, is to further oppress them, mocking the very science that was supposed to provide clarity and correction. Although Joseph-Arthur Gobineau's (1816-1882) writings on Aryan superiority over Blacks and other dark-skinned people (*Essay on the Inequality of Human Races,* 1855) have been discredited, Eurocentric Western scholars betray an ongoing acceptance of his racist theories.

On scant or non-existent evidence, Eurocentric historians declared black- and dark-skinned Asians (Sumerians, Babylonians, Indians, Persians, etc.) Aryans, Caucasoids, white people which, by supposed invasions or migrations into Egypt, rendered the ancient Egyptians Caucasoid, as well. In this regard, consider a few words from Ronald Sanders, author of *Lost Tribes and Promised Lands*:

> To medieval Europeans, Egyptians, living just north of Ethiopia, seemed dark-skinned enough, but Persians—coming as they did from a country virtually identified with India and Ethiopia—probably seemed more so. (106)

Even with an admixture of "white blood," the aforementioned Asians remained essentially black- and dark-skinned people that Caucasians would in no way consider "white" today or treat as equals (consider the invasions of Iraq and Afghanistan). And in *The Destruction of Black Civilization*, historian Chancellor Williams exemplifies the contradiction in the way the Eurocentric Brotherhood of Academia has categorized Blacks, stating:

> From their all-powerful "position of strength" they [Eurocentric scholars] continue to rearrange the world as it pleases them, naming and classifying peoples, places and things as they will: In the United States whites known to have any amount of "Negro blood"—no matter how small—are classified as Negroes; in Africa, North Africa in particular, they do the very opposite. Blacks with any amount of "Caucasian blood" are classified as "White." This scheme was rigorously applied in the history of Egypt . . . where even unmixed black pharaohs became "white" and the originally black population was never referred to as Egyptian at all! (39)

In the same way, the abovementioned Asian peoples were classified as Caucasoids, or Whites, and their accomplishments, like those of the ancient Egyptians, were attributed to the Caucasian race.

Rather than demonstrate that there is no "superiority of any one population over another," the authors of HGHG offer supposedly scientific affirmations to erroneous assertions of the past, extending the myth of white superiority by declaring most of the world's population, including Native Americans, non-African and, ostensibly, Caucasian, which reinforces fraudulent Eurocentric declarations that Caucasians were the force behind all the ancient civilizations and the monumental architectural structures connected to them! So, rather than set things aright, the authors of HGHG continue to promote the racism that has always been inherent in the Eurocentric outline of history.

In another work discussing DNA and ancient migrations of modern man, author Steve Olson, in *Mapping Human History*, is more forthright and honest in his assessment of the common origins of the human population. Although he *does* mention *non-Africans* in his work, he does *not* imply a new specie of human, as Cavalli-Sforza et al seem to. He makes it plain that, "[a]ll non-Africans descend from Africans who left the continent within the past 100,000 years" (56). Olson dispenses with charts and hard to decipher graphs, utilizing effective maps to designate the races that emerged in various areas of the world. He mentions the work of Luca Cavalli-Sforza, his background and initial efforts in the field of genetics. While I do not necessarily agree with all areas of Mr. Olson's analysis, his points and tone are at least reasonable and his language layman-friendly.

My critique of *The History and Geography of Human Genes* is not a denigration of Dr. Cavalli-Sforza and his years of concentration in the field of DNA research; it is possible that the resulting work (written with the contributions of Paolo Menozzi and Alberto Piazza)) did not come out the way he intended it to. I have explained my dissatisfaction with it, chiefly that it reflects the ongoing effort by Eurocentric historians and scientists to diminish black- and dark-skinned people—particularly Africans—and their accomplishments and their creation of the world's earliest civilizations—just as the more popular pre-DNA, Eurocentric scholars, as well as modern-day scholars, have always endeavored to do. In regard to DNA science, Steve Olson's words do not betray age-old Eurocentric resistance when he states:

> [T]he message emerging from our DNA is clear. Everyone alive today is either an African or a descendant of Africans. People on different continents do not have distinct evolutionary histories. Modern humans evolved first and then spread out to occupy the world. (38-9)

If DNA research is to be trusted in identifying and classifying ancient peoples and their movements, it is first necessary that researchers can be trusted and that genetic data are accurately and honestly applied. My purpose in this and the previous chapter is to demonstrate that, as with pre-DNA historical assertions, modern DNA research is subject to misapplication and distortion by researchers to fit a desired conclusion. In this regard, the authors of HGHG went to extreme measures to create a non-African branch of humanity, then call nearly all other humans more closely related to this implausibly created Caucasoid branch than to Africans—relegating Blacks to sub-Saharan Africa and obscurity, making no references to Grimaldi Man nor to Blacks or black Africans ever residing anywhere in Europe, which a number of pre-DNA historians—including Europeans—have attested to.

It is necessary to make one more foray into Europe to present more evidence of the presence of Blacks or Africoids there, touch on language, and discuss a few peoples mentioned earlier, like the Ainu of far eastern Asia and the Gypsies of Europe. There will be references to peoples discussed earlier, and while a point here and there may seem redundant at first, fresh information will follow to provide a more complete analysis or, hopefully, clarify any earlier confusion. Then we will return to Scandinavia, Britain and the Norsemen to tie up loose ends and move to the concluding chapters of this work.

CHAPTER 17

A SECRET HISTORY OF EUROPE—PART I

Modern histories on ancient Europe continue the practice of omitting any references to black-skinned people ever having settled or even sojourned on the continent, even in Iberia where Europe and Africa are plainly visible to each other across the Gibraltar Strait. The more popular DNA researches on the migration of modern man attempt to validate Eurocentric historical claims that only Caucasoids have ever occupied the continent and that Africans or black-skinned people never did. This continuing process of denial is an affront to honest scholarship and research and a dismissal of the serious European historians who did not attempt to evade what their research uncovered.

Proponents of what I have referred to as the Eurocentric Brotherhood of Academia have ignored or rejected a mass of information from historians attesting to the presence of Africans—in remote or historic times—who were numerous in Europe. The attitude of the Eurocentric Brotherhood is deftly summarized by historian Chancellor Williams, who states:

> First of all, they are not ignorant of the true history of the Blacks . . . They simply ignore and refused to publish any facts of African history that upset or even tend to upset their racial philosophy that rests so solidly on premises sanctified by time that they no longer need to be openly proclaimed. (37)

We have been so infused with the whiteness of Europeans that mention of *any* ancient European people brings no other than a white-skinned image to mind. Mention of dark- or black-skinned Europeans evokes consternation, anger or derision.

"Preposterous!" might be the reaction of the average person—but solely because he or she has never read such a thing in school or university texts, or in the more popular histories.

It is hoped that the reader has acquired a new-found respect for ignored or less available historical works and the information they contain, and desires a more honest recounting of history. However, some comments in previous chapters were not fully elucidated in order not to retard the pace of this work. So, this chapter will present a bit more evidence on several areas mentioned earlier. Some of this information will directly link Blacks to Scandinavia; discuss language and the probability that the English language is derived from *ancient Egyptian* rather than a supposed Indo-European source; consider the ancientness of Egypt—with a few important details on the mathematical and geodetic properties of the Great Pyramid in order to consider how widespread Egyptian influence may have been long *before* the emergence of the Archaic World.

In *The Racial History of Man*, historian Roland Dixon mentions Proto-Australoid, Mongoloid and Proto-Negroid elements being present in both ancient and current (i.e., early 20th century) European populations. Speaking of skulls unearthed from megalithic graves in Mecklenburg in northern Germany, he states that they were "composed primarily of Proto-Australoid and Proto-Negroid factors" (74-75). Of northern Europe at about the onset of the Iron Age in Europe (c. 1,200 BC), Dixon states:

> In eastern Sweden (Gottland) the former strong factors of Mediterranean and Alpine types have . . . been replaced by Proto-Negroid and Proto-Australoid elements . . . [E]vidence of the expulsion of the peoples of the Mecklenburg region by the westward advance of the "Nordic" tribes, and the settlement of the refugees in Sweden . . . indicate that these same Proto-Australoid and Proto-Negroid elements were also in the majority there. (76)

All the ancient types of modern humans Dixon mentions above were Africoids, Blacks—Mediterraneans and Alpines akin to early Grimaldis, driven away or replaced by incoming Proto-Australoids and Proto Negroids, who were taller and more advanced peoples.

The European Iron Age began about 1,200 BCE, and the "Nordic" tribes Dixon mentions invading Mecklenburg (a territory of northern Germany between the Elbe and Oder Rivers, stretching to the Baltic coast in the north) *might* have been early elements of Caucasoids into northern Europe. It is unclear why Dixon frames *Nordic* in quotes. Possibly it is meant to question the *implication* that the term refers to *Whites* or *Caucasians,* a belief current at the time as well as today. So the quotation marks framing Nordic seem to imply "so-called Nordic," or "supposed Whites." But if these Nordics, whatever their race, expelled Proto-Australoids and Proto-Negroids from Mecklenburg, it would confirm that black-skinned peoples—Proto-Australoids and Proto-Negroids—were predominant in northern areas of Europe through Neolithic times.

The Mecklenburg area, along with Denmark and southern Sweden, was precisely the area out of which the black-skinned Cimbri and Teutons emerged in the 2nd century BC and were known to have inhabited prior to 1,200 BC. In his next paragraph, Dixon says there is no data for Denmark or Sweden from the Iron Age to late medieval times, however, there is no reason to presume that Teutons and Cimbri were no longer there.

As mentioned earlier, the Cimbri and Teutons instigated attacks against the Roman Empire from 113-101 BC, and Goths—probably a general name for Cimbri, Teutons, Ambrones, Geats and racially similar tribes—would emerge from the same general area two centuries later. Danes must have been pushing into the area from the south or west, but if they were Tuatha de Danaan—originally out of Egypt—they are representative of another wave of Africans spreading into Europe. Their arrival in the north lead to an exodus of Goths from Germany and Scandinavia after 150 AD, or else the outpouring was a natural migration of peoples desiring living space coinciding with the arrival of Danes who were, in effect, a related people not yet known by that designation. That the whole region had been anciently occupied by Egyptian peoples (whatever other names they were known by) is certain, since the whole of Denmark, northern Germany, western Poland (Pomerania) and the whole southern Baltic coast inland to Warsaw was a major region of the Bronze Age Megalithic Culture, with some structures dating to 4,000 BC—structures the ancestors of Goths may have erected.

In any case, all the peoples mentioned above were black- and dark-skinned, with the possible exception of the Nordics Dixon frames in quotation marks. If they were a Caucasoid Nordic tribe that settled in Mecklenburg, just southeast of Denmark, their arrival would validate my earlier assertion that the major migrations of Caucasoids into Europe began after 2,000 BC when a general expansion out of the Eurasian Great White Forest commenced—an assertion in accord with Michael Bradley (*The Iceman Inheritance*) who states:

> Eurasian Neanderthal-Caucasoids existed from the end of Wurm I, but their population did not reach a level permitting expansion in force until about 1500 BC . . . and the population had increased sufficiently, so that a "critical mass" of sorts had been reached. (141)

So, I will allow that Dixon's "Nordics" were among the first Caucasoids in Northern Europe, settling within an area in which Blacks still predominated, continually criss-crossed their territory, and might have intermingled with them to some degree.

In *The Mediterranean Race*, published in 1901, Professor Sergi calls the present population of Europe *Eur-African*, stating of this Eur-African population: "[H]aving had its origin in Africa, where it is still represented by many peoples, it has been diffused from prehistoric times in Europe, and has formed the basis of the most primitive population" (258). Roland Dixon's framing of Nordic in quotation marks must, therefore, infer a different race of people from the dominant Proto-Australoid and Proto-Negroid populations diffused throughout northern Europe—a people *referred to* as Nordic, or *so-called* Nordics, a term which in his time (and presently) had come to imply Caucasian, or white. The term was then applied—or *mis*applied—to all Scandinavians, Germans and northern Europeans, and particularly to Norsemen whom we should now understand were not the blue-eyed, blond, white supermen more modern myths and Eurocentric historians have turned them into. An earlier, instructive comment from Professor Sergi is worth repeating here:

> For some time past I have reached the conclusion that the so-called Reihengraber type
> of the Germans and the Viking type of the Scandinavians, being identical in character
> with the *Mediterranean and Hamitic* types, had the same *African origin . . . separate branches
> of the same stock* [i.e., African]. (*my emphasis*, 252)

Much earlier we cited Seumas MacManus mentioning that Ireland or an island off the coast of Ireland, was invaded by "African sea-rovers" called Fomorians who intruded upon people called Firbolgs, who were in possession of Ireland. We also discussed the Tuatha-de-Danaan who came to Britain and afterwards went to Denmark (or else waves of De Danaan reached both territories, with the British branch eventually migrating to Denmark) and become the ancestors of Norsemen who would later terrorize later arriving Caucasian Celtic inhabitants of the British Isles. Albert Churchward offers much more information on these earlier peoples in *Signs and Symbols of Primordial Man* (1912), which surely was not inaccessible to MacManus and other scholars whose works were published a decade or more after it.

Godfrey Higgins' monumental *Anacalypsis* was published in 1836 and, although he wrote that Asia was the source of most of the black-skinned migrants and invaders of Europe, his analyses of the races of western Europe otherwise jibes with Churchward's. Sergi's work was available, as was Gerald Massey's *A Book of the Beginnings*, another monumental work that set the Eurocentric Brotherhood abuzz. This Eurocentric Brotherhood of Academia rejected the mass of information the works of the abovementioned authors contained because they attributed European civilization to black-skinned people and implied that Blacks were numerous on the continent.

Elements of truth may be inserted into Eurocentric historical works, but in regard to Blacks in Europe or Africoid tribes or peoples in particular territories, information is sparse, furtive, or left out entirely. In an earlier chapter, MacManus mentioned how the Firbolgs occupying Ireland were invaded by "African sea-rovers, the Fomorians, who had a . . . stronghold on Tory Island" (2). He does not mention that the Firbolgs were Africoids, themselves, as were other early migrants into Ireland—although he makes a "colorless" reference to tribes arriving from Egypt by way of Iberia or Spain. *Druids* (whom we will hear more about below) were high priests and teachers of ancient Ireland and western Europe, but Eurocentric historians never mention their race or seem to associate them with particular tribes or peoples other than "Celts," falsely linking Caucasian Celts—who did not reach the British Isles until after 600 BC—to the far older Black Celts, whose religious practices had been brought from Egypt. So, an earlier quote from Albert Churchward regarding the Tuatha de Danaan—tying up what is mentioned just above—is worth repeating here. Some words are eliminated from the earlier quote:

> They [Druids] were undoubtedly descendants of the ancient Egyptian priests, who came . . . [to] Ireland and the West of England . . . who brought with them their religious doctrines and taught and practiced them here. *The Tuatha-de-Dananns,* who came to Ireland, *were of the same race and spoke the same language as the Fir-Bolgs and the Fomorians* . . . [and] had a "Bardic or Druid class of priests" . . . *and all came from Egypt.* (*my emphasis,* 197)

Churchward asserts that the Tuatha de Danaan "were genuine Egyptians," and his comments offer the reader a broader view of Ireland and its ancient peoples allowing the reader to realize how populous Africoids were on the island. All of these early Blacks would be called *Cruithnigh* by later invaders of Ireland, home to a series of Africoid invaders and migrants. Later, originally Egyptian Scots rose to prominence and crossed from Ireland into Scotland (mid-4th century AD), disturbing the Picts there, whom historians consider racially akin to Ireland's Cruithnigh.

The first volume of Gerald Massey's *A Book of the Beginnings* details the Egyptian occupation of the British Isles, the myths, symbols and religious practices that were a result of this occupation (which extended through all of western Europe), and the hieroglyphics found on monuments, dolmens, burial stones and ancient temples everywhere in Europe where the Megalithic Culture existed. Massey's focus, however, is on the British Isles, and his most startling revelation is that the English language is actually descended from the *ancient Egyptian* language. He lists roughly 3,000 Egyptian words according to their hieroglyphic *pronunciations* (because hieroglyphics do not contain a dozen of our letters, like the phonetic C, D, J, Q, X and a few others), with equivalent letters introduced by later Egyptologists (see p. 49). A partial list of these hieroglyphics with their English equivalents is presented below.

The similarity of the phonetic hieroglyphics with their English counterparts is striking. Massey believes that philologists deliberately ignored the ancient Egyptian language as the primary source of the languages of Europe preferring, as is the habit of Eurocentric scholars, an Asiatic origin over an African one for any particular having to do with advancements in civilization. Egypt, and the earliest nearby African cultures (i.e., northeastern quadrant) which contributed to it, produced the first and most glorious civilization ever known in the ancient world. As many historians—ancient and more contemporary—have remarked in their own unique phrasing: Egypt was already quite old when other ancient civilizations first began their stirrings. And just as later civilizations from Iberia to India extended out from Egypt, would it not be sensible to seriously investigate whether Egypt also authored the world's original language? Might not ancient Egyptian have been the original language of Greater Ethiopia, and the language out of which Sanskrit, Hebrew and early Chinese arose?

Churchward emphasizes that Egyptian hieroglyphics "were the images of the things represented in life" (216); that "[a]nyone who can write Symbolic Chinese, can . . . travel through China, Japan . . . throughout the whole of Eastern Asia, and with this symbolic language, make himself perfectly understood," without being able to actually speak the languages of these countries (217); and that "[t]he pictorial writings forming the basis of the cuneiform (Babylonian) and Chinese characters is unmistakably only a species of the hieroglyphics" (264).

Professor Sergi also offers commentary regarding the languages of Europe. He asserts that the populations of Europe are a compound of the ancient Eurafrican species with later-arriving Eurasians who brought with them an Aryan or Indo-European speech.

Speaking of Italy, he opines that if its oldest inhabitants were Mediterraneans, their numbers would have included Libyans, Basques, Ligurians, Egyptians, Iberians, as well as people speaking the Pelasgic language, which he asserts the Etruscans did. Considering this, he states at the end of *The Mediterranean Race:*

> [T]he languages which seem to be altogether Aryan have an archaic stratum, of Eurafrican origin, corresponding to the languages otherwise called Hamitic, like Egyptian and Libyan. (315)

Along with Churchward and Massey, Sergi's research refuted the Eurocentric Brotherhood of Academia's claims that European languages were of *Indo-European* origin. It was out of Africa that Original Man germinated and spread out to populate the entire world in continuing waves for untold millennia, and there is scant reason to doubt that these earliest modern humans left the Mother Continent with a single language—or langauges that were closely related—out of which all other languages mutated and evolved.

But the EBA prefers to seek answers to the question of the root of language in areas outside of Africa, preferring to tout India, especially, as the source of European languages. But Gerald Massey informs us, in *A Book of the Beginnings, vol. 1:*

> The founders of philological science have worked without the most fundamental material of all, the Egyptian . . . From lack of the primaries to be found in that language, a vast number of their conclusions are necessarily false, and *their theory of the Indo-European origin of languages and races is . . . the most spurious product of the century.* (*my emphasis,* 137)

This extremely emphatic statement from Massey defied the accepted conventions of his time and, of course, did not endear him to the EBA which, having discredited Charles Darwin's theories on evolution only a decade or two earlier, was in the process of finally incorporating them into the grand Eurocentric outline of human development that would persist into the 20th century. Massey's rejection of the Indo-European origin of languages and his suggestion that Egypt should be investigated as the origin of European languages was ignored. Following is a very short sampling of Egyptian words (pronunciations) with their English equivalents, randomly selected from Massey's *A Book of the Beginnings vol. 1* (49-81), for the reader to consider:

English	Egyptian	English	Egyptian
aak, oak tree	akh, how great, tall	bait, refreshment	ba-t, rations, food
a, one	a, one	bad, (no good)	bat, bad
abode,	abut, abode	bane, poison	ben, no, not
ahoy, sailor's hail	akhekh, fly, on wing	basket woven	a'khet, to weave
an, hair	anti, opposed to	baudy	buta, abominable
are, plural of *to be*	ar, to be (are)	bay-salt, rock salt	baa', earth, stone, salt
attend, (go to)	aten, to hear	beer, brew	per, liquid from grain
bib, for child's neck	beb, a collar	bough	bu, a branch
bramble	bram, wood, acadia	carry	kar, carry, support
cart	kart, to carry	carve	kherp, to form, model
cherry, ruddy	tsheru, red, red wood	count (a title)	kannt, a title
cover	kepher, (Heb.) to cover	crow, cry	kheru, voice, speech
cut, a cut, a go	khet, to cut, go	east	ast, period of time
ell and elbow	al, measure of length	fagot, tie up, bundle	fakat, gathered result
fat, abundance	fat, a load	far	ar, (far), extremity
fount	fent, sign of inundation	ma (Irish) mother	ma, mother
margin	mari, a border, a margin	married	mer-t, attach, attached
matins	mate, sing, praise	May, the month	mai, seed, germ, growth
mer (Eng. Gyp.) to die	mer, to die	mush, mashed	mussh, mud
Nature	Natr, goddess, time, season	navigate, navy	nef, sailor, to sail
North	narutf, name of the north	not	neti, no, not
of	af, born of	ogham, monuments	aukhem, indestructible
ope, open	ap, opener	ought, should	haut, ought, should

pass	bes, pass	past	past, back, behind
patty	ppatie, cake, kind of food	peace	pash or pekh, bringer of peace
quick,	khi-khi, move fast, be quick	race	rekh, race of people
ray, of sunlight	ra, sun, or go quickly	riot	rruit, whirl
routen, put to rout	ruten, attack	Rye (Eng. Gyp.), a lord	Ra, royal, Pharaoh
sabre	sapara, sabre	sack, to be discharged	suakh, cease, stop
sad	saat, grief	scan, scrutinize	skhan, recognize
settle, for resting on	seter, rest	seve, seven	sef, (kh) seven
shod, covered	shet, clothed	shun, to avoid	shen, avert, turn away
thou	tu, thou, you	thunder	tun, to extend, spread
water	uat-ur, water	write	ruit, engrave, figure
yore	ur, old, oldest	young, junior	hun, youth
youth	uth, youth		

Massey notes: "The compiler is, of course, aware that a few of these words may be claimed to have been directly derived from the Latin or Greek, but they are printed here on purpose to raise the question of an independent derivation from a common source." (op. cit., 81)

Although Massey and others debunked the Indo-European theory of the origin of European languages, in vogue for a century or more prior to his abovementioned work, more than a century after its writing (despite the startlingly obvious similarities between ancient Egyptian and several thousand English words that he lists) the Indo-European origin of European languages continues to be expounded.

*   *   *   *   *

In *Signs and Symbols of Primordial Man*, Churchward, asserts that ancient Egyptians migrated to all parts of the earth, taking with them their hieroglyphic symbols found in Ireland, Britain, Mexico and Central America, which are the same as ancient Egyptian hieroglyphs or picture-writing. The Eurocentric Brotherhood would rather not explore language and writing trails that lead back to Egypt and Africa, the origin of civilization; yet, they easily locate *younger* cultural areas *outside* of Egypt and somehow see trails bringing civilization and writing *to* them—like an infant teaching its parent about the cosmos, architecture, and the elements of speaking, reading and writing. This latter hypothesis is still promoted by Eurocentric scholars—touting the Sumerians as the authors of letters and writing—in their demented efforts to diminish black African contributions to civilization. Even though the ancient Sumerians were black and racially related to Egyptians (Sumer is often referred to as a sister of Egypt), Sumer (i.e., Iraq) was in Asia which—because of Eurocentric historical sophistry and the Caucasian veil that has been draped over it—we have come to believe was anciently inhabited by lighter- or tawny-complexioned populations. Eurocentric scholars are more comfortable with presumably lighter-skinned Asians being the authors of language than Africans—especially in regard to European languages.

The Eurocentric Brotherhood (European and American proponents of European or Caucasian historical superiority) has been successful in spreading their false version of history throughout the world because Europeans and Americans have dominated most of it for the last five centuries. Their armies and expansionist policies have destroyed civilizations on four continents, and their prolonged colonization of parts of Asia, while not equaling the damage inflicted upon the Americas, Africa and Australia, nevertheless interfered with the functioning and intellectual aspirations of countries within them. For instance, while the British no longer rule India, India's educational system remains primarily a British system, the language in schools is English, all children learn English at a young age and the history they learn is from a decidedly British or Eurocentric point of view. The same can be said of former colonial African countries like Ghana, Nigeria and Sierra Leone, among others, as well as Caribbean countries like

Jamaica, Barbados and Saint Lucia. If we look at former French colonies like Senegal, Mali, Niger, Haiti or Martinique, the dynamics are the same: the language, French, the historical viewpoint, Eurocentric. It is the same for former Spanish colonies in the Caribbean and South America. Asian nations seem to be the least infected with Eurocentrism, with China perhaps the least acculturated to Western historical concepts. However, a few million Chinese have emigrated to the United States and Canada, and nearly all Chinese children in China begin learning English in grade school.

In the main, countries and territories which were victims of European colonization and imperialism are still not rid of Eurocentic ideas, cultural concepts, perceptions of history, and have not fully recovered from the blight of colonial oppression which often devastated their own cultural knowledge, knowledge which might enable individuals to break free of the Eurocentric residue still engulfing their nations.

According to Massey, Churchward, and a few other modern historians, ancient Egyptians constituted the majority of Africans occupying Europe, which is most obvious in the western half of the continent. According to these historians (who bestow a much earlier date for their arrival than 40,000 years), Egyptians were already civilized, had ancient cultural practices, religious systems and rites, and were conversant in cosmology—all of which they brought to Europe (and other areas of the world they migrated to). That the ancient Egyptians were the *only* ancient people with the ability to move huge stones over long distances to erect menhirs (standing stones), dolmens and much larger megalithic structures—extending from Iberia to Scandinavia and along southern Baltic coastal regions to Poland—has already been touched upon.

In a couple of earlier chapters we discussed Godfrey Higgins' assertion that "a great nation of blacks" out of Asia, whom he calls Cushites, sent periodic waves of humanity into Europe, bringing civilization to the continent. According to Higgins, these Asian Blacks were the erectors of temples in Asia and Sidon (in modern Lebanon) in The Levant and spread to Britain, bringing with them the worship of Buddha, which is more ancient than we have been told. Higgins must be commended for stating that these early Asian migrants were black-skinned during a time when slavery existed in the United States, the dominant European countries were involved in the slave trade and scientists were relegating black people—Africans and African-Americans in particular—to the lowest echelons of human intelligence. Higgins' *Celtic Druids,* published in 1829, mentions very little about Egypt, focusing on Asia as the source of civilization—including the civilization of Egypt. In *Anacalypsis,* published in 1836, Higgins offers some concessions to Egypt with comments like: "whether Egypt was colonized from India or India from Egypt . . ."; and, "the May-day festival and the Maypole of great Britain . . . are the remains of an ancient festival of Egypt and India . . . when these nations . . . celebrated the entrance of the sun into the sign of Taurus . . ." (21, 24)—while still proclaiming an Asian origin for the earliest civilization in Europe.

I have not investigated whether Higgins withheld information about Egypt be-cause of the growing racism of the period, or whether he based his works solely on the information extant at the time. Europeans had only recently begun studying Egypt, and Jean-Francois Champollion had only recently deciphered hieroglyphics, his dictionary of which was not published until 1842, a decade after his death. A half-century after *Anacalypsis* was published and Egyptian hieroglyphics were deciphered, more was learned about Egyptian history and the extent of Egypt's influence, which is clearly evident in the works of Massey, Churchward, James Breasted and others. But Sergi's and, later, Churchward's work, demonstrated the connection between the ancient Egyptians, Asians and early societies around the world—that all early civilizations were established by people who had migrated out of Egypt, taking Egyptian religious beliefs, burial customs, building techniques, science and hieroglyphic writing with them. Higgins, on the one hand, and Massey and Churchward on the other are, essentially, discussing the same ancient peoples, the same transmigrations, the same diffusion of knowledge—the only difference being their points of origin.

The works of Massey and Churchward demonstrate convincingly that Egypt (i.e., the northeast quadrant of Africa) was the cradle of civilization and knowledge, which its waves of migrants carried to all areas of the earth, including Asia and the Americas. They wrote during a period when Egypt's breaths were labored and giving out after two-and-a-half millennia of debilitating invasions. But each labored gasp unearthed some new tomb, some new monument, some buried city, some new evidence of advanced civilization once thought to have been conjecture. With each new revelation, Eurocentric historians and scientists redoubled their efforts to attribute all that the ancient Egyptians had created—writing, science, even the building of the Great Pyramid—to Aryanized Asian invaders, while declaring them Caucasian, and shrewdly insinuating a white veneer over ancient Egypt. Like Egypt, the rest of Africa had been brought low, and any suggestion that black-skinned Africans, Egyptians or otherwise, had played any part in the civilization, settlement or affairs of Europe was simply not open to serious discussion.

However, at this same period during the 19th century, a small number of European historians and scientists connected the dots and presented a more complete picture of man's diffusion out of Egypt to various parts of the world—including Europe—with corroborating data concerning religion, writing, symbols and related traditions to demonstrate:

> In whatever form or under whatever name we study the origin and trace back the religious beliefs, origin of words and symbolism of the people of Asia, we can only arrive at the conclusion that they came out of Egypt . . . Even the present writing of the Chinese and Japanese are only the old Egyptian Hieroglyphics with linear signs added. (Churchward 264)

Regarding the early civilizers of Europe all the way to the British Isles, Massey and Churchward are most notable in declaring them primarily black-skinned Egyptians who overspread the whole continent—including the *Druids* of legend.

In *A Book of the Beginnings vol. 1,* Massey mentions many of the same peoples Higgins does—Scyths (sic), Chaldees, Firbolgs, Cimbri (whom he renders *Kymry*), Keltae, Saxons—and shows, by association of these names and their Egyptian originals, that these peoples all originated in Egypt, Africa. All these peoples cannot be fully discussed, but the interested reader can peruse volume 1, chapter X of the abovementioned work for more details. We will look briefly at the Kymry (Cimbri) since it was from this race that a significant portion of the future Vikings or Norsemen emerged.

According to Massey, the Kymry or Kimmerians (Cimbri or Cimmerians) were Egyptians who long ago overspread northern Europe and the British Isles. Their name derives from *Kam* or *Khem*, an ancient name for Egypt, and *ruui*, which in ancient Egyptian meant *islands*. Kam-ruui, then, could be interpreted as "Egyptians of the isles," although this could also be interpreted as "discoverers of the isles" (Massey 454, 455).

Massey asserts that *Kheb* and Kam were names for Northern Egypt, thus, "In Egypt only can we find the starting-point of both the Kymry and *Kabiri* as one people" (op. cit. 455). Massey mentions a number of related peoples like the Eusks or Euskarians, "supposed to have left remains in the Basque, the Laps (sic), and among the earliest people of Wales and Ireland" (op. cit. 448), and "the Kafruti, Kvm-ruti, or Khebm-ruti, who went out to become the Sabme-ruti of Lapland, and the Kamruti, Kamari, Kamrekh, or Kymraig, or Kymry of Wales" (op. cit. 456).

Massey is unclear as to specific time-frames in his analysis of these archaic Africoid peoples who overspread Europe and the British Isles but must be speaking of the post-glacial period just prior to the Megalithic Age, which would mean 6,000-8000 BPE, or roughly 9,000 years ago, give or take a few centuries. According to Massey, the Picts, whom we discussed earlier, "never existed in the distinct ethnological sense supposed." Instead, Massey asserts:

> The Kymry were the first known people in Scotland; they preceded the Pict, Scot, and Gael . . . [t]he Kymry being the original race that inhabited Scotland, [and] bifurcated into the Picts and Scots. The Picts vanished, and the Scots' name spread over the land. (op. cit. 471)

Additionally, of these earliest peoples who left Egypt and preceded the Keltae to the Isles, Massey states, "The name of the Kymry testifies to the black complexion" (op. cit. 471).

Massey also connects other previously mentioned peoples to ancient Egyptian occupiers of Europe, notably the Finns, Fir-Bolgs (ancient occupiers of Ireland), Teutons, Tuatha de Danaan and Gypsies, all of whom, we must assume, were black-skinned also.

Higgins mentions these same black-skinned peoples migrating to Europe from Asia, and his analysis, on the surface, does seem strong. He does, however, allude to two Ethiopias, an African and an Asiatic one (this writer's Greater Ethiopia) whose seeming division into two separate entities—with Asia as the primary population and civilizing source—was due to the influence of the anti-black, anti-African hatred existing at the time as well as the desire of Eurocentric historians to obfuscate the racial connection between them.

The question of whether an Asian or an African migration would logically have deposited a more massive population in Europe merits further consideration. Look at a map, preferably a physical map, centering on Europe, Asia and North Africa and extending from India in the east to the British Isles in the west. Ask yourself: Who would have the least difficulty reaching the western extremities of Europe? Asians coming from north—western India taking an overland route over mountainous terrain? Or Egyptians, long conversant with watercraft, who could island-hop to Crete and the Greek Isles or more distant territories like Italy or Iberia? Non-Egyptian North Africans could have done the same, the sight of Iberia across a narrow strait, or Sicily on the horizon, too tempting to ignore. Once on the mainland, no area of Europe would be difficult to reach on foot. From Iberia, France and the British Isles would have been relatively easy to sail to; and sailing northeast through the English Channel, depending on the seaworthiness of the vessel, would bring intrepid mariners to Denmark in a week or so.

Migrants from central Asia or northwest India would have had to traverse several mountain ranges in the area of Samarkand and Afghanistan to reach the area of the Caspian Sea, taking them into a vast steppe region if they passed to the north, and more mountain ranges if they passed to the south of the Caspian—with 2,000 miles still left before reaching the British Isles. If they came from central Asia, they would not have been people generally acquainted with the sea and shipbuilding; and if they were, they would have had to sail up the Persian Gulf or the Red Sea and trek through mostly desert-like terrain, transporting their boats overland to reach The Levant and the eastern Mediterranean. Sailing west through the Mediterranean, they would pass many tempting islands on a northern course, the imposing coast of North Africa on a southern course, have to find their way around Italy and Sicily to reach Iberia and, rounding it, eventually reach Britain.

They would run into more mountainous terrain on an overland route from the Caspian, heavily forested terrain if they passed north of the Black Sea. There would be more mountainous terrain and forests in central and western Europe and, when they reached the English Channel, they would have to have learned to construct sturdy boats in order to cross to Britain—if they weren't too exhausted from their arduous 4,000-5000 mile journey from India. This is not to imply that such a journey was not possible. But compare such an undertaking with migrants leaving North Africa—traversing The Levant, trekking through Asia Minor and into eastern Europe, then moving west toward Britain; or crossing from North Africa to Iberia into Europe and constructing boats (or using the same ones they crossed to Iberia in) to cross the English Channel to Britain; or sailing across the Mediterranean to Greece, Italy or any part of southern Europe; or perhaps sailing the length of the Mediterranean around Iberia to reach Britain. Then decide whether Asians or Africans would have had an easier time delivering a significant population into western Europe and Britain. I would bet on Africans. Yet, Eurocentric historians (and I do not mean to single out Higgins) would have us believe the Asian scenario, and to this day continue to write books and produce documentaries in support of it, still insisting that Asians or outsiders were the architects of Egyptian civilization and brought the worship of Buddha to Britain. There is, of course, the probability that Asian groups did journey westward into Europe and the British Isles.

In *Gods of the Cataclysm,* author Hugh Fox mentions the *Nagas,* or Snakes, a people whose name in Sanscrit meant "cobra." Cobra worship dominated the Dravidian society in India and Afghanistan, "the term Naga gradually superseding the other names used in Sanscrit literature for Dravidians" (Fox 30,31). Author Fox cites Jesuit scholar H. Heras' *Studies in Proto-Indo-Mediterranean Culture,* which describes the Nagas, who flourished 3,000-5,000 BC, as "cultural movers, innovators, creators . . . [who] had moved across the globe in prehistoric times . . . westward across the Arabian Sea into the Persian Gulf," and established Sumer (op. cit. 31). According to Fox, Heras asserts that from Mesopotamia the Indic Nagas spread into the Nile Valley, and while Heras does not credit these serpent or Snake People with the construction of the Great Pyramid and other monumental Egyptian structures, he does state that "the Sumerians and Egyptians are dual expressions of a basic Naga stock" (102).

Not only did Heras' Nagas supposedly spread to Iberia and Britain in the west, but into China in the east and then to the Americas, which they reached by crossing both the Atlantic and Pacific Oceans. Fox asserts they were the authors of the *Chavin* culture of coastal Peru and were the erectors of the Central American pyramids, the Temple of Serpents at Teotihuacan outside of Mexico City and other temples with serpent figures adorning them and other pre-Columbian structures. He calls these ancient Indians "preeminently seafarers," one tribe of them, the *Minas,* actually referred to as "fish" (32). Fox asserts that the Norsemen were descendants of these Minas people (246).

There is compelling information in Fox's work and—in regard to Naga people infesting India, eastern Asia, and being responsible for the ancient pyramid structures and complexes in Central and South America—much to consider. Fox does not belabor the point, but these Nagas were certainly black-skinned. Higgins mentions them several times in *Anacalypsis* without much detail. W.J. Perry, however, has much more to say about them in *Children of the Sun,* equating them with the ancient Dravidians, whose branches included peoples called Asuras, Danavas, Daityas, as well as Nagas, who were a more southerly branch of Dravidians. The history of India is quite ancient, extensive, filled with upheavals and religious conflicts that the reader will have to consult W. J. Perry's work to fathom—although his work goes beyond India into Southeast Asia, Indonesia and Pacific Island groups following a cultural heritage that began in Egypt with what he terms *archaic civilization* whose ruling class referred to themselves as Children of the Sun in whatever area they brought their culture to, including the Americas, stating:

> So, from Egypt to the ends of the Pacific, the archaic civilization was apparently ruled over by the Children of the Sun, incarnate gods . . . Thus the Maya kings were probably Children of the Sun . . . . Wherever it is possible to examine the ruling classes of the archaic civilization, it is found that they were what are termed gods, that they had the attributes of gods, and that they usually called themselves the Children of the Sun. This is the case in Egypt, Sumeria, India, Indonesia, Micronesia, Melanesia, Polynesia, and America—that is, from one end of the region to the other. (140-141)

Perry's work confirms the assertion of writers who saw the civilization of Egypt, Mesopotamia and India as the same: Greater Ethiopia—a vast region of genetically similar people with a similar culture, establishing it among the indigenous populations (or else becoming the indigenous populations) of whatever lands they traveled to.

Perry discusses megalithic structures—dolmens, mastabas and more elaborate structures—to be found in all the abovementioned areas, not to mention the massive pyramids of Central America that more than a few archeologists and historians have equated with those of Egypt. As to the ingenuity of the ancient Egyptians, Perry states:

> By asserting that the archaic civilization originated in Egypt, I do not mean that every element was necessarily invented by the Egyptians: I mean that it took shape in Egypt and was propagated thence [i.e., to other areas]. (428)

Indeed, *The Children of the Sun* focuses primarily on the spread of Egyptian culture and religious practices rather than ethnicity, but he does *not* attribute all aspects of the eastern movement of this culture to Naga people, as does Heras and Fox. It seems, if I understand Perry correctly, that "the ancestors of several ruling houses of Dravidian tribes were Nagas . . . [who] formed part of a dual organization of society" (276). The people called Asuras included Danavas, Nagas, Daityas and others—all essentially black-skinned and akin to the Harappans of the Indus Valley, who are generally called Dravidians.

But just as Egyptian religion had a Sun-cult or skyworld, represented by the sun-god Re, it also had an underworld, the god of which was Set. The same divisions and conflicts between the skyworld and the underworld in Egypt arose in Sumeria and India when the religious beliefs of Egypt were carried there—the names of gods changing in each area. According to Perry, the serpent-worshipping Nagas represented the underworld aspect of the Dravidian belief system. When ancient Indians—Harappan, Asuras or Dravidians—spread the archaic civilization eastward and southeastward to Southeast Asia, Indonesia, the Pacific Isles and America, these skyworld and underworld religious aspects were transported also. So, it would seem, on the surface, erroneous to attribute the eastward spread of archaic civilization exclusively to Nagas who, again, were a mere sub-group of a larger population of people called Asuras or Dravidians who were disturbed by war-like Aryan invaders from a territory north of India (c. 2,000-1,500 BC) who considered themselves divine and established *Varna*, a caste system based on color—white skinned people being the most superior; black-skinned Indians occupying lower levels; Indians of jet-black skin at the very bottom. This caste system endured until fairly modern times, with vestiges of it still present.

This brief sketch of India is rudimentary and would probably not agree with more scholarly works in all respects. I present it in order to view the people called Nagas in a clearer light, and so that the reader might understand that "the ancestors of several ruling houses of Dravidian tribes were Nagas" (op. cit. 276). However, crediting Nagas alone with the spread of Archaic Civilization from India to the Americas or westward into Europe may be overstating their achievements. Generally, though, I do not doubt that the spread of Archaic Civilization—having originated in Egypt—flowed outward from India to spread eastward and southeastward into Southeast Asia, Indonesia, the Pacific and the Americas; the spread of civilization out of the northeast quadrant of Africa strongly demonstrates ongoing *eastward* migrations over many millennia. Of course, it is possible that after reaching Mesopotamia and India, migrations westward and northwestward to Europe took place, spreading the worship of Buddha to the continent and eventually Britain. But Europe was, undeniably, more accessible from North Africa—as was pointed out above—and perhaps we should look at Egypt as the source of the earliest Buddhic worship there.

If Nagas or Indic peoples *did* journey west, the extent of their influence seems to have ceased in the area of Mesopotamia, perhaps The Levant, as serpent-like motifs and gargoyles that adorn some ancient edifices testify. Such motifs are lacking west of the Near East and in Europe, and it may be that Nagas never really migrated as far west as some historians allege. Perhaps they were not an entirely distinct Indic people, but primarily, in the words of Wayne B. Chandler, "monoracial groups—the Ethiopian Negrito and the Proto-Australoid . . . [who] produced the people of the Indus Valley civilization" ("The Jewel in the Lotus: The Ethiopian Presence in the Indus Valley Civilization," *African Presence in Early Asia* 83) still inhabiting Mesopotamia and Near East environs when Indus Valley civilization arose.

In discussing the worship of Buddha here, we are not speaking of Siddhartha Gautama of the 6th century BC, who is customarily referred to as Buddha and the originator of the religion. An older Buddha is meant, the ancient god who is anterior to the man credited by most historians as the source of Buddhic worship. Historians who grudgingly admit to a non-Caucasian presence in Europe invariably credit Asians or Indians, like the Nagas, with bringing the worship of Buddha to Britain, but there is compelling evidence that the religion of Buddha was brought to Britain, as well as to India, by ancient Egyptians.

In the more popular and standardized histories of Egypt, Eurocentric historians and Egyptologists divide the history of Egypt into an "Old Kingdom" and a "Middle Kingdom"—pre-Dynastic and Dynastic periods, and have inserted rulers, invasions, scientific achievements, construction dates for monuments and other events neatly within them. Compared with historians who insist on a much older date for ancient Egypt, its sciences and achievements, the dating systems devised by Eurocentric historians and Egyptologists seem to arrive at the most *minimal* time frames, judging nearly the entire span of the history of Egypt, pre-Dynastic and Dynastic, to be no older than around 6,000 years—the Great Pyramid at Gizeh supposedly constructed between about 2,500 BC and 2,800 BC (depending on the historian), with 2,800 BC, or 4,800 years ago, being the maximum estimated date. This is to say that a people who were largely farmers, herdsmen and fishemen along the Nile Valley until 6,000 years ago, suddenly began to study the cosmos; chart the constellations; began building seaworthy vessels that could sail the Mediterranean; developed an accurate calendar; began a Dynastic system of rulership; developed surgical procedures, which included brain surgery; developed mathemetics, geometry, astronomy and advanced metaphysics; and 1,200 years after a number of them gave up their farming and fishing lives, they were able to erect the most stupendous monuments of the Archaic world (and, arguably, of all time), including the Great Pyramid at Gizeh, which they supposedly constructed—according to the standard history—without knowledge of the wheel and without the use of metal tools! These things, Eurocentric scholars allege, were brought to Egypt by supposedly Caucasoid Asiatic invaders.

Before moving on, here are a few particulars on the Great Pyramid of Gizeh from John G. Jackson's *An Introduction to African Civilizations,* in which Jackson quotes from *The History of Herodotus* (p. 125) and from Abbe Thomas Moreaux's *The Mysterious Science of the Pharaohs,* found on pp. 98-99 in Jackson's work. I begin with Jackson's quote from *The History of Herodotus,* with his own comments on Moreaux's work, to follow:

> The Pyramid itself was twenty years in the building. It is a square 800 feet each way . . . [t]he stones of which it is composed are none of them less than 30 feet in length . . . I perfectly well remember that the interpreter who read the writing [inscribed on the pyramid] to me said that the money expended in this way was about 1,600 talents of silver [i.e., one talent equaled 56 lbs of silver; 1,600 talents 89,000 modern pounds of silver]. If . . . a true record, what a vast sum must have been spent on the *iron tools* used in the work. (*my emphasis* 98)

And from Jackson citing Moreaux:

> In this work [*The Mysterious Science of the Pharaohs*] the Abbe argues that the Great Pyramid was used as a vault for the preservation of scientific instruments and of standard weights and measures, rather than a tomb. In place of a sarcophagus there is a granite slab, which evidently served as a standard of measure. The length of this slab is one ten-millionth of the distance of either pole from the center of the Earth. This invariable distance, only recently determined by modern scientists, is the basis of the metric system. The distance from each of the poles to the center of Earth is 3,949.79 miles. From this measurement we are enabled to calculate the circumference of Earth through the poles, which is 24,817.32 miles. Abbe Moreaux is convinced that this fact was known to the Egyptian astronomers six thousand years ago. The Chaldeans [i.e., Sumerians] were able students of astronomy, but their best estimate of the circumference of Earth was twenty-four thousand miles . . . The height of the Great Pyramid is one-billionth of the distance from Earth to the sun, a unit of measure not accurately established in modern times until 1874 . . . [T]he parallel of longitude passing through the pyramid traverses the most land and the least sea of any in the world—a fact which also applies to the parallel of latitude passing through the structure. (99)

I must abbreviate Jackson's summation of Abbe Moreaux's observations to present further comments from astronomer Richard A. Proctor (*Problems of the Pyramids*), whom Jackson also cites:

> The Great Pyramid was used as an astronomical observatory . . . The geometric paths, and thence the true paths of the planets, could be determined very accurately . . . The added lengths of the four sides of the square base bear to the vertical height the same proportion as that of the circumference of a circle to its radius. This involves the mathematical constant [pi] (3.1416), so important in modern mathematics. The length of each side of the square base is equal to 365 ¼ sacred cubits, an equivalence of the length of the year in days. The two diagonals of the base contain 25,824 pyramid inches, a good approximation of the number of years in the precessional cycle. (Jackson 100)

Several significant particulars regarding the Great Pyramid were omitted for the sake of brevity. But the above data from John G. Jackson's work should convey to the reader how uniquely superior this eternal monument was—*is*—as well as the height of knowledge the ancient Egyptians had attained by the time the Great Pyramid was constructed—long before any invasions of Egypt by outsiders.

According to the time frames Eurocentric historians and Egyptologists have assigned for events in Egyptian history, the physics and astronomical, mathematical and geodetical properties evidenced in the Great Pyramid's construction would have been amassed in roughly 1,200 years. As well, ancient Egyptians must have known that the earth was round; known its circumference; knew the time it took for the earth to circle the sun as well as the sun's distance from the earth; and knew the number of years in the precessional cycle or Great Year—actually 25,827 days in a year (how would they have learned this in only 1,200 years?). For a fuller description of the Great Year, see Gerald Massey's *Ancient Egypt: The Light of the World*, vol. 2, pp. 580-582).

There are certainly indications that Egyptian civilization is far older than we have been told, and along with development of the various sciences, metaphysics, and the geodetic, astronomical and mathematical mastery Egyptians had achieved, there was also religious development, evolving out of primeval mists in periods too remote to attach a timetable to. Eurocentric historians and Egyptologists rarely cite the work of Gerald Massey, who discourses on the origins and development of language in Egypt (i.e., Ethiopia and Africa's northeastern quadrant) out of Sign Language and Totemism, and how observations of naturistic phenomena and animals engendered hieroglyphic symbols, Myth, and the long-forgotten, original ritualistic symbolism attached to them. In *Ancient Egypt: The Light of the World*, vol. 1, Massey discusses fully the sources of ancient Egyptian beliefs and their development into Myth, stating:

> Mythology . . . was in a savage or crudely primitive state in the most ancient Egypt, but the Egyptians who continued to repeat the Myths did not remain savages. The same mythical mode of representing nature that was probably extant in Africa 100,000 years ago survives today amongst races who are no longer the producers of the Myths . . . than they are of language itself. Egyptian mythology is the oldest in the world, and it did not begin as an *explanation* of natural phenomena, but as a *representation* by such primitive means as were available at the time. (5)

There is a considerable amount of information in Massey's *Ancient Egypt: The Light of the World*, as there is in his *A Book of the Beginnings*, so I will have to dispense with some background information so as not to digress too far from the above-stated purpose of examining whether Buddhic worship arrived in Europe from Egypt.

We noted earlier that there were a number of black Africoid tribes or peoples who inhabited Ireland—Firbolgs, Fomorians, Tuatha de Danaan, Black Scots and Celts—and as Roman occupation progressed, a number of other tribes emerged, most notably the Maeatae and Caledonii, whose territory extended from the central portion of the main British island, (i.e., just above Wales) to its northern coast, which included all of Scotland. Regarding these large tribes, William F. Skene, in *Celtic Scotland*, states:

> [T]hey retained the custom of painting their bodies, by puncturing with iron the figures of animals on their skin; and when the inhabitants of these northern regions next appear on the scene after the interval of nearly a century, we find the whole aggregate of these tribes bearing the general name of "Picti." (128-9)

The above from Skene demonstrates that the so-called Picts were not merely a single tribe occupying Scotland (prior to the arrival of the Scots from Ireland), but that "the people known to the Romans . . . as the Caledonian Britons, and described by Tacitus as a distinct people under the designation of inhabitants of Caledonia, consisted of fourteen independent tribes . . . [and] the combined nations bore the name of 'Picti'" (129).

While they were often in contention with each other for various territories within Alba (i.e., Scotland), they spoke the same language and probably had the same basic religious practices, although some religious corruptions might have arisen over the centuries. Ireland was inhabited by similar tribes of black-skinned inhabitants, and Skene informs us:

> The Irish equivalent for the name "Picti" was "Cruithnigh;" and we find during this period a people under this name inhabiting a district *on the north of Ireland,* extending along its north-east coast from the river Newry . . . and consisting of the county of Down and the south half of the county of Antrim . . . and its inhabitants were the remains of a Pictish people believed to have once occupied the whole of Ulster [i.e., the general area of present-day Northern Ireland]. (*my emphasis,* 131)

When presumably Caucasoid invaders (new, or later Celts, etc.) began arriving in Britain and Ireland around 500 BC and afterward, the island was still dominated by indigenous Black Celtic tribes who still practiced their old forms of worship—originally Egyptian forms which Druidic priests continued to disseminate until the arrival of Roman Christianity. Some of the earliest Caucasoids more than likely adopted the religious practices they found there and must have intermingled to some degree with the more populous Black Celtic tribes. When later arriving Caucasoids brought Roman Christianity to the island sometime during the 4th century AD, the indigenous Black Celts and their older forms of religion still predominated, and elements of Egyptoid Celtic worship were infused into Christianity by converted Druids to render the new religion more palatable and gain converts, and this Roman-Christianity—a blending of Roman and Pagan worship—would endure until the 6th century when new invaders (*later* Saxons) imposed a fresher form of Christian worship on Britain's inhabitants.

A more detailed history of Ireland is elusive, especially before the 5th century AD and the coming of St. Patrick to the island. While the sources I have consulted are in general agreement regarding rulers of the Isle, they are generally vague as to precise dates of invasions, what specific peoples (Angles? Frisians? Saxons?) invaded, and the races or ethnicities of Ireland's inhabitants at the coming of Christianity there. One author states that the Romans never ventured to Ireland while they were subjugating Britain; another states that pirates from Ireland sailed to Britain to attack Roman outposts in England and Wales; though whether these pirates were Black Celts or later Caucasian Celts is not made clear. In *The Story of the Irish Race,* Seumus MacManus informs the reader:

> Latin inscriptions have been found on the Rhine front showing that the "Primi Scotti" (First Scots) regiments safeguarded the Roman Empire there. The Emperor Diocletian appointed as Commander in Gaul an Irishman of distinguished abilitity. This was Carausius, who had charge of the defence of the maritime parts. (86)

The Scotti or Scots, we have learned, were black-skinned and seemed to dominate much of Ireland. MacManus also states that at various times Irish kings were kings of Britain, as well, and received tribute from British (presumably Black Celtic) inhabitants—though MacManus does not specify what areas of Britain these Irish kings dominated.

MacManus offers no precise dates for this period of Irish (Scottic) influence in Britain but states that Pictish and Irish invasions in Britain intensified after 331 AD. After this date, Rome began to be disturbed by Gothic raids into her empire on the continent, certainly intensified by the earliest incursions of Black Huns into eastern Europe (c. 375 AD), and MacManus tells us:

> And when at length Rome, threatened by the invading hordes nearer home, had to call back from her [British] island outposts legion after legion of her soldiers, and . . . her army in Britain was weakened, the Irish (Scots, as they were always called by the Roman historians) in alliance with the Picts, helped to push south the garrisons that were left and eventually to crowd them off the island. (87)

The reader has been given ample evidence that the earliest inhabitants of Ireland were black-skinned Africoids, and Skene, adding to authors cited earlier in this work, remarks that "an Iberian or Basque population spread over the whole of Britain and Ireland in the neolithic age" (170). Firbolgs, Fomorians, Tuatha de Danaan and others would emerge later, more than likely racially akin, and certainly Africoid; in fact, Skene asserts that the Picts "are represented in the legendary history of Ireland by the Tuatha De Danann and by the Cruithnigh . . . the Irish equivalent of the Latin 'Picti,' and was applied to the Picts of Scotland" (226-7). The Picts, comprised of tribes called Damnonii, Maeatae, Caledonii, Agathirsi and a dozen others, had anciently occupied the British Isles. Skene also asserts that *Pictish* was a Teutonic language, and revisits something briefly touched upon in an earlier chapter when he states:

> Tacitus says that the Caledonians had a German origin. The Picts were the same people as the Caledonians. The Welsh Triads say that the Picts came from Llychlyn, which is *Scandinavia.* (*my emphasis,* 195)

Although Skene attempts to lighten Picts as well as the Tuatha de Danaan, assertions from historians cited earlier regarding the black complexions of these people outweigh his sophistry in this regard. However, he does allow us to see how widely Picts were dispersed when he states:

> The race of the Picts were not, however, confined to Britain. They originally extended over the whole of the north of Ireland, and though eventually confined to the territory on the east of Ulster called Dalnaraidhe, or Dalaradia, they remained there as a separate people under the name of Cruithnigh till a comparatively late period. Down to the beginning of the seventh century they formed, with the Picts of Scotland, one nation. (198)

They may, as well, have maintained communication with kinsmen who remained in their Scandinavian homeland whose tribal names there are now unknown.

In Ireland the Scots seem to have occupied territory south of Ulster and the Newry River and, according to Skene, were Christianized when they crossed the Irish Sea to begin settling Alba (i.e., Pentland, Pictland, the eponymous Scotland) during the mid-to-latter half of the 4th century AD by agreement with Pictish kings and chieftains whom they would later betray and kill off for possession of the entire territory—or so the story goes. *Why* the Scots departed Ireland for Scotland is never made clear.

It is assumed that the earliest Caucasoids to come in the British Isles arrived in the *new* Celtic wave into western Europe 600-500 BC. But near the end of the Roman occupation, fresher waves of Whites, in the persons of Germanic Saxons, Angles and Frisians crossed into Britain from the area of Belgium, the

Netherlands and northwest Germany. Generally, though, the post-Roman entry of Whites into Britain is not clearly elucidated by historians; some historians, even European ones, claim that even these *new* Saxons, as well as Angles, were dark-skinned. My feeling, however, is that they, certainly the *new* Saxons, were Caucasian, or predominantly so: Romans, alone, could not be responsible for the lightening of the English population, although Romans undoubtedly produced a considerable number of offspring over 400 years of occupation. However Romans were not known for being tall—perhaps on average two or three inches taller than Picts and Black Celts, whose women they certainly intermingled with and even married.

Germanic Whites are known to have been taller than Romans, possessing larger frames. It is often asserted that Saxons, in particular, avoided intermingling with non-Whites, so they, presumably, would have exhibited less racial admixture than any remaining Romans, although it is doubtful that new Saxons were wholly white and unmixed. Although the population of central and western Europe and Germany had lightened considerably and could generally be said to be inhabited by Whites or near-Whites, even white Saxons in what is now Germany would have been sharing the country with dwindling but still prominent black- and dark-skinned tribes in pockets of the territory and would have passed close to black-skinned neighbors in northernmost Germany and Scandinavia on their westward movement to the British Isles.

My presumption is that Germanic Saxons, after invading Wales and Cornwall, slaughtering a multitude of Britons (Black Celts) in those territories (mid-5th century), carried their ferocity across the Celtic Sea to Ireland, establishing colonies there where they did the same with Ireland's Pictish inhabitants. As more Whites—Germanic Saxons, Frisians and possibly remnants or descendants of racially mixed Roman Britons (Romans who had remained in the country after the withdrawal of Roman troops)—emigrated to Ireland, Black Celtic and Pictish tribes were forced toward the western and northern extremities of the island. A number of them probably abandoned Ireland by sea to join their cousins who had departed Cornwall and southern England and established settlements in Brittany in northwestern France, while others may have departed by sea to Spain, the Hebrides or Aquitania.

We have been exploring the racial makeup of the peoples of ancient and historical Europe, so specific battles, kings, their domains and successors would be tedious, time consuming and digressive. What is relevant to our purpose is that Britain—as well as the rest of Europe—was anciently the dominion of black-skinned, Africoid peoples under a multitude of tribal names. The religion they observed (allowing for variations and corruptions) was anciently derived from Egypt, taught to them and presided over by a Druidic order of priests over many centuries—perhaps millennia. But just as the Romans had done in the conquest of England, 6th century Germanic invaders (Frisians, Angles and others lumped together under the name *Saxons*) did as they expanded over Britain and Ireland: capture or kill Druidic priests and eradicate vestiges of ancient religious worship still being observed by indigenous black-skinned tribes. States Gerald Massey in *A Book of the Beginnings vol. 1:* "One part of the process in converting the Irish was to take their ancient deities, the devil included, and transform them into Christian saints" (465).

As an example of this transformation, Massey suggests that "the mythical Patrick appears to be identifiable with the god Ptah" (op. cit.), or that Patrick was the name of a *priest* of the ancient Egyptian god Ptah. Further, he explains that the ancient Egyptian word *rekh* meant wise man or priest and that there may have been many Ptah-rekhi, or priests of Ptah, and that "Patrick, or Ptah-rekh is probably . . . a Druidical title" (op. cit.).

This title endured, and comes down to us today in the form of St. Patrick, whom the Irish annually commemorate with parades and festivities—believing that the St. Patrick they celebrate is an actual 5th century personage who brought Christianity to Ireland and Christianized the Picts and Anglo-Saxons. He is also supposed to have driven the *snakes* out of Ireland—an allegorical tale with a deeper meaning. There was an ancient Serpent-Cult in Ireland and Scotland whose societies were matrilineal and who sculpted stones with interlacing serpent effigies. Could these serpent worshippers have been a tribe of the aforementioned Nagas who made their way to Ireland from India, the Near East or Egypt (or represented the underworld of Egyptian worship, which was essentially the same)?

While Massey does not mention Nagas as the authors of serpent effigies, L.A. Waddell (*The Phoenician Origin of Britons Scots & Anglo-Saxons*) briefly discusses these decorative prehistoric designs which "'St. Patrick the Cat' (or Khatti or Scot) banished . . . from Ireland by the Cross, or in other words banished the old Matriarchist Serpent-worship by introducing there the Religion of the Cross in 433 A.D." (106). So, it would seem that the "snakes" St. Patrick banished were *people* who venerated snakes and dragons—black-skinned Asians or Egyptians whose Serpent-cult came to dominate some areas of the British Isles. Whether an actual personage, or a Ptah-rekh (Druid high priest), St. Patrick is immortalized as a Christian priest who upheld the Cross in carrying out the expulsion of the snakes from Ireland. But just as there are a number of symbolic practices in Christianity, and Biblical stories in Christian belief which cannot be reconciled with historical events, the efforts of Ptah-rekhi (Druidical high priests) to expel the Snakes, or modify their religious practices to conform to Christian doctrine has, seemingly, been transformed into myth—a mythical personage we know as St. Patrick.

The Ptah-rekhi who undertook the conversion of the Snakes, Black Celts and other black Britons had first to be converted to the new faith themselves, probably on pain of death; true believers, especially priests and teachers, of any religion would not take conversion to another religion easily. Torture may have been used, with banishment or an agonizing death the only other options. References to St. Patrick as "the Cat" or Khatti would associate him with pre-Christian, black-skinned Egyptians. And if the reader would peruse chapter X of Waddell's *The Phoenician Origin* . . . and chapter X of Massey's *A Book of the Beginnings, vol 1,* he or she would see that these historians concur on many points regarding the ancient peoples and religion of Britain, the only blemish being Waddell's repetitive assertions that Phoenicians were Aryan and his efforts to Aryanize the ancient Egyptians—a common practice of Eurocentric scholars in the 19th and early 20th centuries.

While Waddell does not mention the religion of Buddha being in the Isles, his "Nine Maidens," or "Maiden" stones, found in parts of Ireland and Britain correspond to Massey's "Put circle of the nine gods," from which the sacred title Budd—a form of Ptah (also rendered Putha)—arose and, at some point, morphed into Buddha (*A Book, vol. 1,* 465). In *A History of Egypt,* James Breasted calls Ptah "one of the early and great gods of Egypt . . . the patron of the artisan, the artificer and artist" (60). Massey does not discuss specific beliefs or rites of this ancient Buddhic religion except to assert that it was Egyptian in origin, associated with the worship of the ancient Ptah of Egypt and was brought into Europe and the British Isles by Egyptian people of the Solar Cult.

Mentioned in an earlier chapter was that Buddha (again, not Siddhartha Gautama of the 6th century) was anciently depicted as black-skinned with Negroid features in representations extending deeply into Asia, and the reader is reminded of Higgins' earlier remark that the worship of "this Negro god is found . . . to have been spread over an immense extent of country, even to the remotest parts of Britain" (*Anacalypsis, vol. 1,* 52).

The movement of peoples of the Stellar, Lunar and Solar Cults (in that order) out of Egypt, and whether the ancient megalithic structures of western Europe were erected by Stellar, Lunar or Solar Cult people is beyond the scope of this work. But regarding Europe, L.A. Waddell cites W.J. Perry's conclusion that megaliths found all around the World "are located in the immediate neighborhood of ancient mine workings for tin, copper, lead and gold or in the area of the pearl and amber trade" (*Phoenician Origin* 218), but he seems perturbed that "Mr. Perry . . . does not even suggest the obvious inference that they were Phoenicians, nor even once mentions that name" (op. cit.). No, W.J. Perry was an honest historian who wasn't consumed with denying the achievements of black-skinned Egyptians. And regarding the megalith builders, Perry states in the conclusion of his work:

> The solar symbols suggest at once the Children of the Sun . . . . The facts suggest that ruling groups were gradually spreading across Europe, beginning in Egypt and moving out by way of Crete and Mycenaean Greece. (500)

And Perry *does* mention the Phoenicians, stating that they originated in the Persian Gulf, migrated to the Syrian coast and spread out along the Mediterranean coast to the Atlantic. He adds, however, "The ruling class of these people were Children of the Sun, who practiced mummification and human sacrifice . . . . The Phoenicians admittedly depended largely on Egypt for their culture" (op. cit. 501, 502). And the reader might recall that the Megalithic Age was practically over by the time Phoenicians first appear in the pages of history.

The early, or original, Celts or Keltae were Africoids related to Egyptians, according to Sergi (69) and worshipped the same gods as the Solar Cult Egyptians, one being Beli, or Baal, according to Massey, who adds: "This points to the Keltae coming by land from Egypt to Spain, and thence to Ireland" (*A Book, vol. 1*, 450). Although historical writings have not documented it, fierce battles must have been fought between resident Africoid groups and onrushing Caucasoid Celts in western Europe. As mentioned much earlier, Gaul, stretching from western Germany to Iberia, must have been an area of considerable intermingling as Africoid tribes ceded territory to these barbaric, warrior invaders whose spoils of battle would certainly have included the women of the dispossessed. These later Celts, or Caucasoid Celts, cannot be reconciled with the *early* Celts or Keltae, the Celts of Massey, Higgins and Churchward—the Egyptian or Black Celts connected with ancient Europe and Britain, akin to the Kymry, Kabiri, Ligurians, Iberians, Fomorians, Chaldees, Basques, Firbolgs, Tuatha de Danaan and Druidic priests of the Solar Cult. The only connection to the early Celts is the *presumed connection attached by Eurocentric historians* by giving the name Celts or Keltoi to this first significant wave of Caucasian invaders of Europe in order to insinuate an earlier presence of Caucasoids in western Europe and Britain!

These Celts are Caucasians, Aryans, predominantly white-skinned, and no effort is spared to lodge them in western Europe at the earliest possible date. So, Fr. Funck-Brentano, in *A History of Gaul*, opens his second chapter by stating:

> The Celts came from the north, from those nurseries of the nations—Jutland [Denmark],
> Friesland and the coasts of the Baltic. They were the Normans of the sixth century before
> our era. (27)

We noted earlier that Eurocentric scholars insisted that the Goths came from the same area (i.e., Scandinavia), a supposed breeding ground of people. But Goths are another people that Eurocentric historians have rendered white through their practice of unashamedly attaching whiteness to black- and dark-skinned people to suggest a more ancient history for Whites in Europe or in more ancient civilizations. When we read of the 7th or 8th century Irish who set off for Iceland and North America, we assume them to have been white; when we read of the Roman conquest of Gaul (i.e., France) we assume all Gauls were white and not the predominantly black- and mixed-race tribes that they were—with Africoid or Negroid features still prominent in the inhabitants residing in the west and southwest in what would later be called Aquitania.

As with later, or *new* Celts, Eurocentric historians refashioned the Norse marauders of northern Europe into Caucasians, *Nordics*—tall, blond, blue-eyed, fearless white men. I have not looked into *when* they began promoting this image, but the belief was universally prevalent by the middle of the 19th century and, since Europeans were dominating world affairs by this time, there was no one to counter any claims Eurocentric scholars made. The 19th century saw the consolidation of the Eurocentric Brotherhood of Academia—lead, of course, by England—whose published works refashioned Europe into an ever-white, ever-superior, civilizing continent, expunging any notion in the average person's mind that black-skinned Africans—despite the mere 8-15 mile distance between Morocco and Spain—resided in any part of Europe at any time.

Chapter 18

A SECRET HISTORY OF EUROPE—PART II

The Gypsies of Europe are another race or "mysterious" people whose origin Western scholars find difficult to account for. Long known for their talents in music, metal-working, animal husbandry, entertainment and a number of crafts, it is generally stated that Gypsies "appeared" in western Europe early in the 15th century. Nearly all western scholars have classified them as Aryan members of the Indo-European family and assert that their origin was in northern or northwestern India.

The Gypsies call themselves *Rom*, meaning *man*, and the language they speak is called *Romany*, spoken and understood, supposedly, by all Gypsies in Asia, Europe, North Africa and, presumably, those who now live in both North and South America. Although Romany is not a written language, Western scholars assert that it is "Indo-European,"—that confusing language class that Massey (above) calls "the most spurious product of the century."

Knowing that languages tend to change over centuries or even generations, it is doubtful that the Romany (or Romani) spoken six or seven centuries ago has remained unaltered. Indeed, Angus Fraser, in *The Gypsies*, asserts that there are at least 60 dialects in Europe, alone, "obviously related to each other to an important degree, but often mutually unintelligible" (12). Fraser, as have many Western scholars, connects Romani to Sanskrit out of which Indo-European languages are supposed to have developed and he, like most Western scholars, claims that Gypsies began a westward migration out of India a little over a millennium ago, which brought them into Persia, Armenia, the Byzantine Empire and the Balkans before they arrived in Italy, Switzerland and Germany in the early 15th century.

Often called Saracens, Tartars or Heiden, depending on the area, it is remarkable that most Gypsies claimed they were from *Egypt*, not India. Fraser cites a German man from Lubeck calling the 300-plus Gypsy people who passed through Holstein, Mecklenburg and Pomerania: "very ugly in appearance and black as Tartars" (67), and states that "[t]he chroniclers represent the Gypsies as an outlandish and very dark people" (68). In other accounts, Gypsies are described as very handsome people, especially the women, who often wore colorful skirts, silver earrings and anklets. Often denied quarters within a town, Gypsies invariably encamped on the outskirts, where they would usually attract villagers to the small fairs they set up at which they would display their horsemanship, acrobatics, juggling and musical talents. Gypsy women told fortunes and were adept at inducing village women to part with their money or valuables with readings that promised imminent love or good fortune. Leaving these fairs, visitors often found that their money or valuables had been lifted, as lifting pockets and purses was a common Gypsy practice. Then authorities would order the Gypsies to move on, and Gypsies would set up camp outside another town where the same scenario of events would be repeated—and they would be told to move on yet again.

Gypsy men, however, were extremely skilled in working with metals and earned legitimate recompense repairing pots, making horseshoes, swords and knives, or merely sharpening them and extending their use. Gypsy music must have sounded otherworldly to 15th century western Europeans. Fiddles were the primary instrument—the deep, melodically moody tunes stroking the souls of listeners, transporting them to realms of feeling they had never experienced before. Faster tunes would bring out Gypsy dancing girls who spun and bent and swirled about in a manner never before seen, often to the staccato clicking of castenets held in the palms of the dancers. In 15th and 16th century Europe, Gypsy music was exotic, soul stirring—music that today would be called avant-garde. Later, European classical composers must certainly have been influenced by it, borrowed from it.

Traveling in family clans, or else as several clans related by common trades, Gypsy groups had their dukes and chieftains who treated with officials of a village or city they desired to enter or camp near. During the 15th century Romany people appeared in nearly all European territories; in addition to the countries mentioned above, like Germany, bands of them, usually in groups of 200 to 500 souls, were present in Austria, Italy, Bohemia and Moravia (i.e., Czech Republic, Slovakia), France, Poland and Scandinavia. The uneasy but general acceptance Gypsies usually received in places they suddenly appeared in would soon deteriorate, so that "from the 1470's onwards, the Gypsies were bought off or turned away when they appeared" (Fraser 99). While the Rom would continue to receive grudging acceptance when they turned up over the next century or two—even performing in the courts of kings now and then—harsh ordinances against them were enacted throughout most of Europe and they were persecuted merely for being Gypsies.

While it is universally acknowledged that European Jews suffered persecution, most people do not realize the extent of Gypsy persecution in Europe. In *A History of Pagan Europe,* for instance, Prudence Jones and Nigel Pennick state:

> They were persecuted wherever they went in Europe, often being killed, or sold into slavery. In 1370, forty Gypsy families in Wallachia, Romania, were taken prisoner and given as slaves to the monastery of St. Anthony at Voditza. In 1530 it was a capital offence to be a Gypsy in England, and in 1665 Gypsies were deported from Edinburgh to be slaves in the West Indies. In Romania, they suffered slavery until 1856. (197)

The animosity toward Gypsies was evident in France, where Louis XIV signed a decree in 1682 ordering—

> [Gypsy] men to be sent to the galleys for life; boys not old enough for the galleys to be put into hospices; and women and girls to have their heads shaved and, if they persisted in their vagrant ways, to be scourged and banished from the realm without any need for a trial. (op. cit. 145)

Equally harsh decrees were enacted against Gypsy Rom in most countries and principalities in Europe; in some cases, marriages *between Gypsies* were banned, and Gypsy children under age five could be taken and raised for several years in white European households in the hope that they would abandon their heritage.

Although Angus Fraser places the Rom in Spain, Portugal and, in the 16th century, England, I have so far not mentioned these countries because Gypsies seem to have been present in them far earlier than the 15th century—and may have always lived in them.

Historian Moustafa Gadalla, in fact, declares the Gypsies of Iberia (or Andalusia) descendants of the Egyptians who once overspread the whole peninsula. This, of course, would connect them to the ancient Egyptians who thoroughly inhabited western Europe and the British Isles. They did not "appear" in Iberia in the 15th century as most Western works allege but demonstrate a continuous occupation of the peninsula stretching back at least 5,000 years, according to Gadalla, which would situate them in the Bronze Age when the Egyptians were erecting megalithic structures in most areas of western Europe and exploiting Iberia and Britain for ores that were scarce or non-existent in Egypt.

The Spanish Romany, even today, live in or nearby sites of mines, some having been worked since ancient times. Called *Gitanos* by the Spanish, Gadalla distinguishes them from the Gypsies who appeared in western Europe in the 15th century who, in the main, were nomadic, essentially ragged beggars compared to the Gypsies of Iberia who did not wear ragged clothes, steal or swindle for a living, lived a settled life and practiced an Animistic religion directly connected to the ancient Egyptians—which they have always maintained they are.

The Gitanos, no doubt, are probably related to the Basques racially and linguistically, since the Basques claim Egyptian ancestry and once occupied a larger territory which extended further south and west of their present territory between northern Spain and southwestern France. The Basques, as well, could be related to the now-vanished Ligurians, for according to Sergi:

> The Ligurian stock was very widely diffused; it occupied the south of France, being linked with the Iberians of Spain and mingling with them at the point of junction. (163)

The "point of junction" is the Pyrennees Mountains range and the surrounding territory where the Basques continue to survive and stubbornly maintain their independence from Spain (which they are commonly associated with) and, to a lesser degree, France. The Basque language has been called the oldest ethnic language of Europe, philologists being unable to connect it to their usual branches. Gadalla informs us:

> The Basque tongue cannot be classed with any Indo-European or Semitic tongue, and appears to be of earlier origin. This must bring to mind the very old Ancient Egyptian language, which is also older than (and the source of many of) present-day language families. (182)

The origin of the Basque language is still considered a "mystery" by Eurocentric philologists even though they have long been given major hints to pursue which would lead them to an answer—an answer they are loathe to accept.

Other historians closely link Basques and Iberians, demonstrating that these peoples were, racially, essentially the same. Noting scientists who found no differences between ancient skulls unearthed in separate areas of Britain, W.F. Skene cites one who concludes:

> We have therefore proofs that an Iberian or Basque population spread over the whole of Britain and Ireland in the neolithic age, inhabiting caves, and burying their dead in caves and chambered tombs, just as in the Iberian peninsula also in the neolithic age. (*Celtic Scotland* 170)

And the Iberians had to have been, being essentially Egyptians, racially akin to the aforementioned Black Celts (Keltae), early Celts, and it is only the various nomenclatures attached to ancient Britons by Eurocenric scholars that prevents us from realizing this common ethnicity. Skene provides a little more clarity in this area, stating:

> Of the Celtic race, which succeeded the Iberians in the British Isles . . . the Romans tell us nothing, save that *those in the interior of the country were believed to be indigenous,* and that those on the regions bordering upon the sea which divides Britain from Gaul had passed over from the latter country. (op. cit., *my emphasis*)

Those Celts "in the interior" were Black Celts—Egyptians, Africoids—who had overspread Gaul and western Europe before being driven further west. Willingly or, more probably, unwillingly, they moved to the western area of Gaul (France), those in Britain to its interior, when significant tribes of Caucasoids gained a foothold in these territories after 500 BC, although Blacks would continue to predominate in both countries for several more centuries.

Some of their descendants would become the "Gypsies" who began to be noticed, or remarked upon, in the British Isles at least a century before they appeared or were noticed in continental western Europe, and MacRitchie (*Ancient and Modern Britons, vol 1*) opines that, "Negroes, therefore, must have been known in England in the dark ages" (137). To Gypsies were applied a number of appellations—Ethiopians, Moors, Saracens, Tinkers or Tinklers (implying that they worked metals), Egyptians and Tartars—that would later be applied to Gypsies on the continent. British Gypsies also called themselves Rom or Roma, and their language Romany. Both MacRitchie and Massey attach them directly to the earlier Egyptian populations of Britain, although MacRitchie seems inclined toward an Asiatic or Mongoloid origin. Considering the expansion of Egyptians into Europe and Asia long before the emergence of Caucasoids as a force, all these peoples under their various nomenclatures could have been essentially the same peoples—the forlorn detritus of Greater Ethiopia whose ancestors had once ruled and civilized the known world.

As new territorial configurations emerged, groups of Gypsy peoples gravitated to the districts of expanding towns and principalities, which were sometimes populated by communities of varying ethnic and language groups where inhabitants intermixed and the population of one or another group expanded and increased by culturally absorbing others. Gypsies preferred to live among themselves according to their culture and traditions. When wars flared up, demographic configurations were often altered; another language, culture or religion might become dominant in a principality, the new authorities informing Roma tribes they were no longer welcome in the territory. Disaffected Roma or Gypsy tribes would then migrate to other territories where they might be allowed to settle, as their older world disintegrated and European civilization stumbled forward. But they stayed together, holding on to their language, culture, traditions, religion and trades—dispossessed and living wherever they could for however long newer authorities, kings, or dominant peoples allowed them to, which was often never long.

Today Gypsies live on every continent, although centuries of intermixing—most often undesired—has considerably lightened the complexions of most. Many today are white-skinned and unrecognizable as Gypsies, living settled lives and owning legitimate businesses—as in the United States, where they have some respite from centuries of persecution. An equal number still retain dark- or light-olive complexions, like those of Spain, the Mideast and areas of eastern and central Europe. But for those remaining in Europe, the nightmare has not quite ended.

*   *   *   *   *

Most historians assert that the convergence of Iberians (Egyptians, Basques, Ligurians, Kymry, Black Celts, etc.) and new Celts was generally peaceful and call the populations occupying the British Isles, Iberian Peninsula and western Gaul in the 5th century BC *Celiberians* (or Celt-Iberians). But these new Celts, unlike the earlier Egyptian groups in Britain, were considerably more war-like and barbaric, and it is unlikely these peoples entered Gaul and crossed over to Britain with peaceful intentions. They arrived with crude but fearsome swords, war-chariots and a goodly number of blood-lusting, screaming warriors who had disheartened their opponents on their thousand-year march from the Great White Forest of central and southern Russia to the westernmost edge of the continent.

In the British Isles, the black- and dark-skinned Africoid populations compelled to vacate the territories their ancestors had once dominated, consolidated themselves so as not to invite full-scale invasions into the areas they had retreated into. Some Druids continued to teach the rites of the old faith. Those Druids who were not killed, as mentioned above, were compelled to convert to Christianity, passing Christian teachings on to Black Celtic tribes interlaced with elements of the Old Religion to make Christianity more acceptable to them. But the rites and practices of the Old Religion continued in secret in England, while in Scotland, on islands like Skye and Mull, and on the continent in western Germany, Holland and

Sweden, so-called pagan rites would persist, and Beltane festivals would continue to be celebrated for centuries—even into the 20th century.

Thirteenth century Europe experienced another great wave of black- and dark-skinned Asiatic invaders as the Golden Horde of Genghis Khan swept through Russia into the Balkans, Hungary and Poland. Whether these Mongols invaded areas of Germany as did their descendants, the Black Huns of Attila, is not known for certain, but German Teutonic Knights were mustered to defend the realm, stationing themselves along the Baltic coast in Prussia. A Khan Batto or Batu ravaged most of Poland and Silesia and it is certain that a significant number of Mongols remained in areas of eastern Europe long after the Mongols broke off hostilities after the death of Genghis Khan in 1227.

Discussing a 15th century map of the area of Esthonia (Estonia), Lithunia (Lithuania) and Courland (perhaps Latvia), described by Sir Walter Scott (in Scott's "Letters on Demonology and Witchcraft"), MacRitchie concludes that it [the territories of the above-named countries]—

> represents . . . a furclad, and probably Ugrian people inhabiting the southern and southeastern shores of the Baltic,—this people thoroughly dominated in certain districts by a black, Tartar race,—and in other districts (most likely the western), the rulers and the ruled uniting to repel the forces of the white-skinned Christians of the West . . . And it is clearly from them that the "amazing number" Lithunian [sic] and Courland gipsies are descended (167)

If Gypsies came from the remnants of these people, remarks MacRitchie, "[t]he Gipsies, then . . . were fierce in nature and swarthy of skin, as far back as the conventional limit allows us to see them" (op. cit.).

It was stated much earlier in this work that Jutland (Denmark) and its surrounding environs were a point of convergence for Africoid and Asiatic elements out of which the people who would come to be known as Norsemen and Vikings emanated. Evidence of Asiatic migrations of black-skinned people has been offered, primarily from Higgins, demonstrating that Asia, long before Attila's Black Huns, sent periodic waves of black-skinned humanity westward into Europe. Between the more ancient Egyptian populations who reached northern Europe and Scandinavia and the black-skinned Asiatics who came into the area afterwards, there was a considerable presence of black-skinned peoples inhabiting northern Europe into historical times that most Western historians have refused to acknowledge as such—having long attached nomenclatures like Scythians, Goths, Nordics, along with the inference that all these peoples were basically "Germanic" and, therefore, Whites, in our minds.

*   *   *   *   *

The language or languages spoken in continental Europe and Britain during this early period is beyond the scope of this work; however, Massey asserts that ancient Egyptian was spoken all over the continent, and there is the possibility that incoming Asians were familiar with it or spoke a dialect of it in their own areas of origin. Hebrew, an offshoot or dialect of ancient Egyptian, was widely dispersed in Asia; so many root-words were the same or similar enough to be understood by speakers of either tongue 4,000 years ago. And root-words in dialects of either language would also have facilitated understanding; people could acquire another language by taking the time to learn it or pick it up from living in proximity to people who spoke it. Whatever the case in northern Europe, a world where mining, metal-working, agriculture, trade, common religious worship, seafaring and commerce existed among Afro-Asiatic people at the top of the world, it seems that many black- and dark-skinned folk shared a racial affinity, which prompts MacRitchie to state confidently:

> Thus, the Moors or Saracens, the Danes and other kindred races, and the Gipsies are *virtually the same people under different names.* (*my emphasis,* 141)

This affirmation may strike the reader as a broad generalization; if so, it is due primarily to the efforts of Western historians to associate peoples with specific geographical areas; implying racial differences which they never elucidate; imply that they belonged to some other ethnic group (i.e., insinuating that Moors who invaded and ruled the Iberian Peninsula were *Arabs*); connect them generally to the Aryan branch of mankind; produce films presenting the above peoples with differing racial features, attire and habits; and, of course, in the case of Danes and other Norsemen, depict them as what the evidence presented in this work clearly shows they were not.

The face of what would become the United States began to alter 400 years ago when a few rude settlements along the Atlantic coast, established by Caucasian émigrés from England, expanded into mobs of avaricious, caustic, deceitful, zealots who spread ever-westward, nearly annihilating the dark-skinned, generally peaceful, but out-gunned native populations on their march to the Pacific. Dispossessed Native Americans—in greatly reduced numbers, living on deflated portions of their former territories—are rarely seen by the majority of Americans and are almost unrecognized in American cities across the U.S. Modern Americans almost never think of Native Americans as they drive through still forested areas, expanses of lush farmland or speed to work through urban areas or on super highways at 75 m.p.h.

Native Americans, or American Indians, come to mind when modern Americans see them depicted in movies, when they go to Indian-owned casinos, when they purchase a Jeep Cherokee, or maybe when they sit down to Thanksgiving dinner. Maybe they think of American Indians when they chance upon a newspaper or TV news report of a border dispute between Indians and Whites in some state, or when a Native American Powwow briefly comes to town. But a day or two later, thoughts of Native Americans drift to the back of most modern Americans' minds. The face of the United States has been transformed from red to white and, despite the black, brown, red, yellow and copper tones that comprise modern Americans today, white is what most people around the world today envision when they think of America and Americans.

Beginning about 2,600 years ago, Western Europe began to undergo this same kind of transformation, a transformation that was still underway less than a millennium ago. Even 500 years ago this process was continuing as: Moors and Sephardic Jews were being expelled from Spain; Gypsies were being persecuted in most areas of the continent; and dark-skinned remnants of Celtic tribes in the British Isles, Magyars in Hungary and Balkan territories, dark-skinned descendants of Mongol invaders in Russia and Poland, and dark-skinned Finns and Baltic peoples were, generation after generation, being absorbed into a now dominant and expanding Caucasian race. The absorption of darker peoples and races over the centuries changed the face of Europe from an originally black and brown population into a mixture of browns and whites, then finally into the predominantly white-skinned population of modern times. Driving through Europe today, it is difficult to believe that any darker races of people ever lived there, just as driving through the present United States it would seem unbelievable to someone unfamiliar with U.S. history that just over 500 years ago there were no Whites of any significance living here, and that dark-skinned people predominated everywhere.

Just as the face of the future United States began to change as significant numbers of Whites arrived, driving out and slaughtering Native American populations, the dark face of Europe had been transformed over a longer period of time—although the racism we are familiar with today has not been made apparent in the history that has been passed down to us. However, its vestiges might be seen in the savagery of the centuries'-long Roman invasions of Gaul and Britain, especially against Britain's black-skinned inhabitants, the destruction of their religious shrines, the hunting down and murder of Druids, and the imposition of Roman-Christianity wherever they gained a foothold. One might see elements of racism in the animosity of Germanic Franks toward the black-skinned Cimbri and later Danes, or the way the English—in the persons of Angles, Frisians, Saxons—steadily encroached upon territories of the Black Celts, Welsh and Britons of Cornwall after the departure of the Romans. *The Anglo-Saxon Chronicle* records many of these events without letting on that those being attacked, driven off or killed were Blacks, but I believe the reader is sophisticated enough now to decipher the obvious in the several examples that follow:

Year 465	In this year Hengest and Aesc fought against the Welsh near Wippedesfleot, and there slew twelve Welsh nobles . . .
Year 477	In this year Aelle came to Britain . . . with three ships . . . and there slew many Welsh and drove some to flight into the wood which is called Cymenesora . . .
Year 495	In this year two princes, Cerdicd and Cynric his son, came to Britain with five ships . . . and the same day they fought against the Welsh.
Year 508	In this year Cerdic and Cynric slew a Welsh kiug, whose name was Nazaleod, and five thousand men with him . . .
Year 514	In this year the West Saxons, Stuf and Wihtgar, came to Britain with three ships . . . and fought against the Britons and put them to flight.

As has been repeatedly emphasized, the Welsh and Britons referred to above were essentially racially akin to the Black Celts, whatever other tribal appellations they might have gone by. Invading Germanic Caucasoids freely assailed them, and during the fifty year period above or soon after, probably crossed over to Ireland and harried related Black Celtic tribes there. And just as the Native American tribes who remained free and defiant on the western plains in the 19th century, dispossessed black- and dark-skinned Europeans stubbornly clung to their traditional territories or to territories they had been forced to flee to. While the Germanic Angles, Saxons and related Caucasian people were killing and dispossessing the dark-skinned populations of Britain, they were making use of another weapon that would prove as lethal as any sword: the religion of Christianity or Catholicism. Again, I do not mean to be disrespectful to believers in Christianity; I am not singling out Christianity to compare it with other religions. But in this case, at this time, we must see—as we did earlier—how Christianity was employed to weaken and eventually undermine the dark-skinned races of the British Isles, in the same way that the religion would be employed a millennium later to undermine Native Americans and African peoples. It is in this historical, political sense that I mention Christianity.

If one disallows a people from practicing a religion that they know, that their ancestors knew, that has influenced every aspect of their lives—that reveals the purpose of their being, makes them strong as a people and allows them to know their Creator and their relationship to the earth, to nature—you effectively obliterate their spiritual life, their self-knowledge. When people, on pain of death, are compelled to accept an alien religion and disavow what they have always known, they are cast into a limbo without foundation or purpose.

One might get a sense of this considering the plight of the Native American Suquamish and Duwamish tribes of Washington state. In the 1830s Catholic missionaries converted their leader, Chief Seattle—for whom the city of Seattle, Washington, was named—to the religion, and in an 1853 speech to American settlers and Indians at which the city was established, Chief Seattle eloquently expresses what I have tried to convey above. The following excerpt is from *Indian Oratory*, by W. C. Vanderwerth:

"Your God is not our God! God loves your people and hates mine. He folds his strong protecting arms lovingly about the pale face and leads him by the hand as a father leads his infant son—but he has forsaken His red children—if they really are His. Our God, the Great Spirit, seems also to have forsaken us. Your God makes your people wax strong every day. Soon they will fill all the land. Our people are ebbing away like a rapidly receding tide that will never return. The white man's God cannot love our people or he would protect them. They seem to be orphans who can look nowhere for help . . . If we have a common heavenly father . . . [w]e never saw Him. He gave you laws but had no word for his red children whose teeming multitudes once filled this vast continent as stars fill the firmament." (119)

Chief Seattle, as did his father who greeted the first white settlers in his territory, did his best to maintain friendly relations with Whites who, nevertheless, continued their depredations against all the native tribes they came into contact with. Seattle's lament would have been justified coming from the mouths of any people brought to ruin by Europeans and the religion Europeans—in priestly robes, in armor, or both—foisted upon them, being no less appropriate in the case of the dark-skinned populations of Britain as they were being slain, driven away and compelled to convert to Christianity in the early centuries of the Dark Ages.

As outlined earlier, Christianity was employed to bring about the demise of the formidable Norsemen of Scandinavia and Britain during the latter half of the Dark Ages—the mid-point of the Middle Ages—and Christian Crusades, sanctioned by the Fathers of the Church in Rome, would be launched against so-called Pagan worship in the rest of Europe, which continued into the 16th century when territories around the Baltic were finally subdued and converted to Catholicism. Most readers have heard of the Crusades to the Holy Land, but few know of Christianizing crusades against the Slavs, Finns and Baltic peoples. Time does not allow for a detailed look at these Church-sponsored, lesser-known campaigns. A commonly repeated phrase is that "Islam was spread by the sword." It is certain that there is some truth to this aphorism; however, the history of the spread of Christianity or Catholicism during the period under discussion is no less bloody and was not carried out for altruistic or spiritual concerns. In *The Northern Crusades,* author Eric Christiansen tells us:

> The Northern Crusades were inspired by intermittent local enthusiasm; by appeals from Rome, and by the commission to wage perpetual Holy War which was granted to the Teutonic Knights . . . . From this point of view, the Northern Crusades began as a consequence of the closer involvement of the Baltic world with the civilization of Latin Christendom in the twelfth century. During this period the idea of the Holy War was grafted onto Baltic affairs to meet a need felt by those who wanted to conquer or convert the heathen coastlands . . . . (260-1)

Mentioned earlier was that Estonia and three-fourths of Russia were populated by dark-skinned Ugrian peoples in the 11th century. In the 13th century the Golden Horde of the Mongols invaded Russia, Poland and Hungary, bringing another infusion of dark blood and thousands of dark-skinned offspring into these countries where pagan worship, or so-called heathenism persisted.

From what has been presented in this work, it should by now be obvious to the reader that European Whites are not a homogeneous race—not "pure," as some hygienists, scientists and historians have often insinuated. While the chromosomal mutation causing albinism strengthened in its mutated form, causing offspring to be born lacking melanin or the gene which produces it, even those earliest inhabitants of the Great White Forest remained essentially African, genetically related to the black African ancestors who rejected them, their Africanness evinced for a time in thick curly hair, full lips, recessive darkish skin and other physical features until interbreeding with each other and environmental factors decreased the occurrence of these.

Although the Great White Forest had once been the primary core of Caucasian civilization, migrations away from it by larger numbers of people had expanded Caucasian populations into most of Europe by 1000 AD. The larger Caucasian body centered in Eurasia had certainly absorbed Tartar, Mongolian and Turkic elements; as Caucasoids expanded westward and southwestward, fraught with invasions by other peoples, racial intermingling would add Magyar, Persian, Norse, North African and Hunnish elements to these predominantly Caucasian peoples, who produced off-spring in which various racial features of these racial admixtures could be physically ascertained, until continued inbreeding among the now dominant white, or near-white, population eventually obscured many of these racial characteristics so that they could no longer be easily perceived. Europeans, for the most part, have never been a homogeneous race, and Steve Olson con-firms this when he states: "Viewed over a long enough time period, every European culture is the product of a prodigious mixing of past groups" (*Mapping* 189).

So, while we tend to believe that countries of Germany or France or Russia or China are comprised of ethnically homogeneous populations, the populations of most countries the world over are comprised of the various ethnicities—some large, some smaller—who historically inhabited the particular territory. And Olson makes it clear that "every European country also has pockets of ethnically distinct groups, such as the Roma (also known as Gypsies), which have remained mostly endogamous for many generations. (op. cit., 189). Although Gypsies may have practiced endogamy [i.e., marrying within the tribe or social group], widespread persecution brought about the abduction and rape of numerous Gypsy women in the European countries they inhabited—since European Gypsies today are much lighter complexioned than the Gypsies who began appearing in Europe six or so centuries ago, who were often described as sable-skinned and "black as Tartars."

While most historians trace Gypsy origins to northern India, the earliest Gypsies to appear in Europe claimed they were Egyptian—hence, the appellation *Gypsy*. Their endogamous culture accounts for many of them maintaining their dark complexions into modern times. Many, however, are "olive"-skinned, near-white, or white and cannot be easily identified as Gypsies. Their generally lighter complexions must be due to thousands of Gypsy women, impregnated over the centuries by white Europeans, who returned to their own or other Gypsy tribes or clans and raised their mixed-race offspring as Gypsies. However, that Gypsies all emanated from India remains open to debate. The Indian origin theory does not account for the Gypsies of Britain and Spain who were present, and referred to as Gypsies, in those countries long before Gypsies were noticed in other areas of continental Europe.

It may well be, as Churchward, Massey and other historians mentioned earlier have asserted, that Egyptians and their culture were more widely diffused around the world than Eurocentric historians have let on. In *Egyptian Romany*, Moustafa Gadalla quotes the 1st century BC Sicilian historian Diodorus as noting that ancient Egypt had a population of at least seven million, unsurpassed in its day, and stating: "In general, the Egyptians say that their ancestors sent forth numerous colonies to many parts of the inhabited world by reason of the pre-eminence of their former kings and their excessive population" (57). Besides Iberia, Gadalla locates ancient Egyptians in Greece and notes their influence in Crete, again citing Diodorus as stating that Egyptians "settled what is practically to oldest city of Greece, Argos," and that "certain rulers of Athens were originally Egyptians" (58).

We know from W.J. Perry that Children of the Sun spread Egyptian megalithic culture practically around the world, and though Perry focused primarily on southeast Asia and islands of the Pacific to South America, we know that Egyptians were the erectors of the megaliths, dolmens, menhirs and tumuli found throughout Europe as far north as Britain, its outer islands, Denmark and southern Sweden. No other people had such ingenuity in those remote periods. Whether Egyptians also sent colonies to the southern end of Africa and reached Antarctica from there, or reached the southernmost continent from Tierra del Fuego at the southern end of South America after reaching that continent, may never be known (ancient mummified remains, many thousands of years old have fairly recently been unearthed in that vicinity). But the geodetic particulars of the Great Pyramid—giving an accurate measurement of the earth's circumference; providing a determination of the course of the sun around the celestial sphere; the moon's regular courses around the earth; the courses the planets in our solar system traverse; an accurate measurement of the distance from each pole to the center of the earth; and the multiplication of the height of the Great Pyramid a certain number of times to accurately measure the earth's distance from the sun—indicates that Egyptian colonists were doing far more than erecting megaliths on their migratory wanderings over the planet. More cannot be remarked upon regarding what astronomer Richard A. Proctor states in *Problems of the Pyramids,* (see Jackson 100), but it is something to think deeply about.

Newer peoples and civilizations arose, flourished, and waned. And still newer ones arose, gained ascendancy, grew powerful, and were remembered and recorded in historical works that have come down to us. The history of lesser-known peoples has also passed down to us (and perhaps Gypsies should be somehow attached to these), whose cultures were not powerful enough to withstand the forces of warfare and change set in motion with the Caucasoid expansion into Europe. Perhaps Gypsies—continental European Gypsies—are no other than remnants, survivors, of Egyptoid populations whose territories were once larger—Basques, Greeks or Mycenaeans, Ligurians, Gauls, early Saxons and Persians—to name a few remembered peoples. We should not forget earlier commentary linking Gypsies to Tartars and Picts, and that Gypsies were often referred to as Moors.

When Gypsies began to "appear" in 15th century continental Europe, most Europeans—certainly now predominantly tawny or white—had probably forgotten (or never knew) that black-skinned people had predominated in Scandinavia and northern Europe only three or four centuries earlier. The Black Death of the mid-14th century—which decimated, by some estimates, up to one-third of Europe's inhabitants—would have been more poignantly recalled. The initial plague lasted from 1347-1351, but there were periodic recurrences of the dreaded pestilence until 1400, causing the depopulation of at least 1,000 villages. It is uncertain whether the Black Death killed off a significant number of Gypsies; presumably, it did but if not, if somehow Gypsies were less affected than white European populations (they were known to possess disease-preventing herbs and Gypsy women were conversant with spells and magic), they may suddenly have stood out to recovering European populations who moved into different districts to rebuild villages, dreading the consequences of rebuilding where the soil and air had been contaminated.

Despite the assertions of Western scholars, there is no definitive trail of a Roma migration from India to Western Europe; instead, Gypsies seemed to appear suddenly in continental Europe (i.e., the 15th century)—black-skinned, energetic, healthy, contented, exotic, and satisfied with their way of living, despite the sometimes bedraggled appearance of some clans. If they *had* suffered the same ravages of the Black Death, their faces were absent the expressions of angst and forlornness etched in the faces of white European survivors of the plague. Strange people. And so they were soon feared. However, they may have inhabited Europe all along and were only noticed suddenly because the white populations of most European countries had been drastically reduced by the plague—necessitating the rebuilding of some towns close to forested areas that had not been formerly explored.

When asked "what they were" (race, national affiliation), nearly all Gypsies, no matter the country or district, called themselves *Rom, Roma,* or *Egyptian,* according to many sources. Western historians often refer to early peoples or tribes by the name of the geographical area or district they inhabited—Iberians, because they overspread Iberia; Ligurians, because they dominated an area called Liguria—or else group them with the dominant people of an area because they were racially or culturally akin, or because they spoke a similar language—Angles and Jutes in the (new) Saxon confederation; Dasyus and Nagas assigned to the Asura civilization, and so on, though the lesser groups often had their own impact on history. But in many, if not most, cases the designated nomenclatures were not how the particular peoples, groups or tribes referred to *themselves*. Native American peoples called themselves by their tribal names—Lakota, Cherokee, Abnaki, or Reckgawawanc. Gypsy tribes referred to themselves as Egyptians, although they had tribal or clan designations as well.

As the black-skinned Africoid or Egyptoid populations of the British Isles were harried, hunted and driven out of territories their ancestors had long dominated, they necessarily reformed into unified groups comprised of different clans so as not to invite full-scale invasions into areas they had retreated to. The same dynamics had taken place in continental Europe at an earlier date when aggressive and powerful Caucasoid groups pushed inexorably into western Europe from Eurasia, dispersing the longer-settled, black-skinned Africoid populations—who are generally remembered as Keltae, old Saxons, Picts, Basques,

Iberians and peoples, whom Massey identifies as fundamentally Egyptian Kymry, Kafruti, Khebm-ruti (all of whom were racially akin and only seen as different because of the various nomenclatures attached to them)—from their original territories in Britain. Some of these peoples, like the Kymry, were numerous and would remain powerful; others would be fragmented and disappear as a recognizable entity. Most of these—no longer powerful or numerous enough to reclaim lost territory—would continue to inhabit areas within the territories they once occupied, districts now dominated by more numerous Caucasoids with organized societies able to quickly form armies to secure the territories their ancestors had seized. The Gypsies, it seems—living in the forests between villages and towns of organized white districts, for the most part avoiding contact with them—are probably the remnants of these once predominant but now dispossessed Egyptian peoples.

These Egyptoid peoples would endure Roman invasions into Spain, Gaul, Germany and eastern Europe. They were present in the Europe of the Dark Ages and during the Viking Age—though, of course, not then referred to as Gypsies. Discussing a 15th century map of the area of Esthonia (Estonia), Lithunia (Lithuania) and Courland (i.e., Latvia) described by Sir Walter Scott in "Letters on Demonology and Witchcraft," David MacRitchie concludes that:

> [It] represents . . . a furclad, and probably Ugrian people inhabiting the southern and southeastern shores of the Baltic,—this people thoroughly dominated in certain districts by a black, Tartar race,—and in other districts (most likely the western), the rulers and the ruled uniting to repel the forces of the white-skinned Christians of the West . . . And it is clearly from them that the "amazing number" of Lithunian and Courland gypsies are descended. (*Britons* 167)

If Gypsies came from the remnants of these people, says MacRitchie, "[t]he Gipsies, then . . . were fierce in nature and swarthy of skin, as far back as the conventional limit allows us to see them" (op. cit.).

Earlier mentioned were invasions of Black Huns and, later, Mongols into Russia and Baltic regions, and it must be assumed that these territories saw a great deal of racial mixture among the peoples inhabiting them—including Caucasian tribes continuing to meander west. Northern Europe, from North Sea and Baltic regions into Russia, was a world where mining, metal-working, agriculture, trade, so-called Pagan worship, seafaring and commerce continued to exist among a generally Afro-Asiatic population, and an earlier comment from MacRitchie is worth repeating here: "[T]he Moors or Saracens, the Danes and other kindred races, and the Gipsies are virtually the same people under different names" (*Britons* 141).

Further, MacRitchie, in *Accounts of the Gypsies of India,* published two years after *Ancient and Modern Britons,* likens Gypsies to the ancient Goths and Getae. Most Western histories have Goths emerging out of Scandinavia, primarily Sweden, and have them streaming from there southeast into Europe (1st century AD) where they eventually break off into eastern and western branches—Ostrogoths and Visigoths, respectively. In *Accounts of the Gypsies of India,* MacRitchie alleges an Indian origin for Europe's Gypsies, likening one branch of Indian Gypsies to *Jauts,* who made up a large portion of Indic peoples who inhabited the Punjab and are included in the great Scythian confederation that entered eastern Europe 800-500 BC. The Jauts, according to MacRitchie, moved westward around the northern end of the Caspian where they first come to notice as Getae in the Balkans, a branch of people known as Massagetae (Great Getae) whose main body inhabited Central Asia in what are now Uzbekistan and Turkmenistan in the general area around the modern city of Bukhara.

MacRitchie likens the Jaut and Getae customs to Goths, citing the 6th century AD Gothic historian Jordanes, and notes that these peoples, like "the gypsies of Galloway [in Scotland] up till the close of the last century . . . [stained] . . . their faces with ruddle or haematite," which "was a *Gothic* custom" (*Gypsies* 86). The custom of tattooing the body was a practice of Gothic peoples, and MacRitchie also associates the Picts with Goths. There also seems to be no question that the Goths, Getae and Jauts (Getae, and especially *Jaut,* being perhaps the same as *Goth*—pronounced differently by different people), along with the Picts were black- and dark-skinned:

> . . . because those Picts were compared by Pliny to Ethiopians in complexion, and the poet Claudian calls them "Moors," And certain traders who were wrecked in the Baltic . . . are styled "Indians" by various writers, and are supposed by some to be no other than those "painted Britons," otherwise "Moors" and "Ethiopians." So that if such British "Picts" were also "Goths," they resembled our Goth-descended Jauts in being of dark complexion, and their custom of tattooing connected them with other gypsy tribes. (op. cit. 89)

There is a further connection that MacRitchie notes between the peoples which stretched from Baltic regions into Germany and Scandinavia demonstrating, as the reader has been told, that the aforementioned peoples were the same peoples under different names. These black- and dark-skinned peoples seemingly constitute the preponderant inhabitants of northern Europe even less than two millennia ago when Claudian (c. 370-404), Pliny (61-113) and others set down their observations. To emphatically demonstrate this, MacRitchie continues his commentary on the related peoples mentioned just above, stating:

> The early Saxons and Danes, also, are understood to have been "Goths," and to have painted and tattooed their skins. Now, these people are spoken of as *nigrae gentes, dubh galls,* or *black heathen,* in our early records; and, at a later time, as "Saracens," this last being a common appellation of "Moors" and gypsies. (op. cit.)

The question that remains to be definitively settled is whether Gypsies emanated from India or from Egypt. There seems to be evidence supporting either region. However, the fact remains that most of those in Europe called themselves "Egyptian" when asked of their origin and were likened, by historians who mentioned them, to Ethiopians and Moors. This brings to mind Greater Ethiopia and Higgins' "great nation of blacks . . . [who] . . . formerly possessed the dominion of Asia" (*Anac.* 52) and the likelihood that, as earlier mentioned, all of them exhibited African racial characteristics and physiognomy extending into India, southern China and Indonesia prior to the emergence of Mongoloids and their related racial types.

Most people have heard of the persecution of Gypsy or Roma people in Europe, believing that those of Europe have always lived as wandering vagabonds on the fringes of organized society. This has surely been the case since their "appearance" in continental Europe six centuries ago. And their present, lighter-skinned complexions is evidence that significant numbers of Roma women were surely subjected to rape and gave birth to lighter-skinned offspring. But Gypsies were undoubtedly black-skinned when they were first noticed centuries ago, and a further comment from MacRitchie notes that:

> The tawniest gipsy now in Europe is probably but a half-blood, and most of them are something like Quadroons . . . . In all the older references to the race, they are spoken of as purely black, not tawny. (164)

MacRitchie, as well, asserts that Gypsies were not always the outcast and often despised minstrels and vagrants that 19th century Europeans were familiar with. Long after the Viking Age (i.e., after 1100 AD), during the second half of the Middle Ages, states MacRitchie, "the Gipsies become visible as armed marauders . . . suggesting a time still farther back when they formed a vast Tartar confederation" (165). Even after Gypsy persecution had begun in most European countries, Roma men were known, sometimes revered, as competent fighters. MacRitchie quotes one Mr. Simson, who writes, in *History:*

> In the thirty years' war [i.e., 1618-1648], the Swedes had a body of them in the army; and the Danes had three companies of them at the siege of Hamburg in 1686. They were chiefly employed in flying parties, to burn, plunder, or lay waste the enemy's country. (op. cit. 165)

MacRitchie compares the "fierce and warlike disposition" of Gypsies to Native American tribes, a similarity he calls "most striking" (op. cit. 168).

Striking, as well, are the fates of Europe's Gypsies and Native Americans. Both groups, in their numerous tribes, predominated in their respective continents until racially different Caucasoids, in similarly diverse tribes, began a steady invasion of the territories their ancestors had occupied for millennia—long millennia, in the case of Gypsies whose ancestors emerged out of the earliest Egyptian colonizers of Europe. The tribes of their ancestors have been mentioned throughout this work, though Eurocentric historians never associate Gypsies with them, leading readers to believe that once numerous Basques, Ligurians, Getae, Wends, Kafruti, Scythians, and others all vanished without a trace—without dispossessed, vagabond members continuing to live on in the same general territories they and their ancestors had always lived in, no longer powerful enough to regain their former homelands and stature. In areas where they remained numerous after they "appeared" in Europe—like in northern areas around the Baltic, parts of Russia and Crimea, and in Bohemia and Moravia, sandwiched between modern Germany, Poland, Austria and Hungary—they would be feared throughout the centuries, although they were generally oppressed and their influence and culture endured in those areas up to the end of the 18th century. Overall, though, their general oppression turned most Gypsies into undesirable vagrants; periodic pogroms reduced their numbers; sexual abuse of their women by white European men considerably lightened them over the centuries; and only a rare Western historian connects them to the considerable Egyptian populations—Goths, Kymry, Picts, Danes—which once overspread the whole of northern Europe—Eurocentric historians effectively writing Gypsies and their ancestors out of history through dissociation.

*   *   *   *   *

The dispossession of Native Americans in the U.S. is more recent and more commonly known, although rarely thought about seriously by the average American today. Americans have been taught to view the making of America (i.e., the United States) as a positive and necessary expansion from the Atlantic to the Pacific; an unselfish undertaking that made life better for *all* Americans (all Americans except Native Americans and enslaved African-Americans). When we read American history, we somehow receive the impression that the Puritans, Founding Fathers, earliest immigrants and all the presidents were good people. The unjustness of the Puritans subjecting Native Americans to *their* (i.e., Puritan) laws; confiscating swaths of Indian territory over the theft of two or three cows that strayed onto Indian land; and slaughtering whole villages of Native Americans over the death of a single white man, somehow does not register as frightfully sinister to most Americans. War was brought against Indians who objected to these inequities, and when a particular New England tribe was defeated, its land was confiscated as just recompense for daring to oppose the good Puritans. In this and similarly nefarious ways, New England territories, and eventually larger ones, were taken from its Native American inhabitants.

When the Revolutionary War commenced with the British, most Americans never hear that the Americans, British and the French often had hundreds of Indian auxiliaries fighting with them [the 1992 film, *The Last of The Mohicans* illustrates this]; so, very often, Indians killed Indians for their European benefactors who promised them rewards—probably riches and more lands—if the benefactor won. After the War of 1812, in which Indians participated and died on the British and American sides, the fledgling United States acquired the Northwest Territory and, after the Louisiana Purchase, the expanding United States extended itself far to the west. However, when we look at historical maps depicting these swaths of territory, it somehow does not register that Native American tribes *were still living within them*—many of them having become miserable vagabonds in their own lands, dislodged from their original territories and greatly reduced in number.

More numerous and still powerful Native American tribes still inhabited the territory west of the Mississippi River, unaffected by the tumult and death in the eastern half of the expanding United States. Then in 1838, as other southern Indian tribes had undergone several years earlier, the Cherokee Nation was forcibly moved out of the south in what is known as the Trail of Tears—when thousands of Cherokee people were marched to the Mississippi in the winter and ferried over into "Indian Territory"—an area which would become the state of Oklahoma in 1907. The idea of President Andrew Jackson and influential people in government was to deposit all remaining eastern Indians into Indian Territory and open the south to more white settlement. A goodly number of Cherokees escaped this forced evacuation and remained in their original homeland of Tennessee and the Carolinas, but the South had been effectively cleansed of its Native American population.

The last frontier was the American West where powerful tribes of Sioux, Crow, Cheyenne, Arapahoe, Navajo and Apache still lived the way they always had, knowing what had happened to their brethren in the east—but never imagining that the same fate would befall them. Then some intrepid Americans decided that a railroad from St. Louis to California would link the Atlantic Ocean to the Pacific and make it easier for American settlers to exploit the riches that had been discovered in the West. Never mind that the railroad passed through the heart of territory inhabited by America's remaining free Native Americans; never mind that it would disperse dwindling buffalo herds, which these tribes of Native Americans depended on for their very existence; never mind that it would violate the very concepts of freedom and liberty that the United States espoused for all men in its Bill of Rights. A railroad to the Pacific would be good for America, and if Indians didn't like it, American soldiers would make sure that they did nothing to stop it. And so the Indian Wars of burned villages, broken treaties and near annihilation of Native Americans began, lasting from about 1862 until a little over a century ago when Chief Big Foot and perhaps 350 of his Minneconjou and other Sioux—men women and children—were massacred in the snow by U.S. soldiers at Wounded Knee, South Dakota, at the end of December, 1890.

Unlike the Gypsies, many Native American tribes were allotted reservations, some quite large, which still exist in a number of states—reservations in western states considerably larger than those in the east. Some reservations are situated in areas encompassing original tribal homelands, but they are generally located on lands lacking desirous resources, are often run-down, have U.S. highways running through them, and their schools, homes and facilities are often inadequate. From time to time, states attempt to chip away more land, more rivers or mineral-rich areas from them. Gypsies received no land nor any compensation for territories they were driven from in less organized, more lawless times. Otherwise, their experience in Europe is strikingly similar to the Native American experience in the United States, except that their demise and eventual dissolution as a viable, energetic people took place over a slightly longer period of time.

However, it seems that Gypsies have always been in Europe, were native to Europe, and the reason they suddenly "appeared" in the 15th century is perhaps due more to Eurocentric historians' need to account for a still numerous black-skinned population, as they concocted the All White European storyline that they have offered us. According to this invented storyline, no black-skinned peoples had anciently set foot on European soil and, accordingly, popular histories avoided identifying the races of particular tribes or peoples so that readers would infer that European peoples had always been white. Even Huns and Mongols were not described in racial terms (or else detailed descriptions by older historians were deliberately deleted) so that readers would envision a horde of yellow-skinned Chinese invading Europe from the Asian steppes rather than the black-skinned Huns and Mongols MacRitchie, Higgins and a few others inform us of.

Scandinavians were shamelessly converted to blond, blue-eyed, white-skinned "Nordics," as were Goths, the supposed progenitors of white-skinned, Nordic Saxons and Germans. Historians could not delete earlier historians' assertions that the Vikings were black-skinned, so some medieval revisionists, seeing numerous references to black Danes, decided to Caucasianize the *Norwegian* element of Vikings by calling them *Norsemen,* and insinuating that they were racially different from their kinsmen in Denmark. Sticking to the popular histories, as most people do, most readers would never discover that Danish Vikings were always styled *black* by historians who went beyond customary colorless historical characterizations to discuss race. So the notion that Vikings were white, blue-eyed and blond has continued to prevail.

Balts, Finns, Teutons, Wends and other northern European peoples were assumed to be "Nordic," and, therefore, white. The popular histories intimated that the Scythians, coming from Asia, may have been admixed with *yellow*-skinned, Chinese-like Asians, but a little yellow didn't hurt and would easily fade to white in a reader's mind after intermingling with supposedly white Nordics was mentioned. So, chiefly through omission of racial particulars (and our knowledge that modern Europeans are considered purely Caucasian today), Western historians effectively expunged black-skinned people from Europe.

To include black-skinned Gypsies as part of the European fabric might have engendered a more intense examination of ancient European peoples by spirited and objective researchers. They had to be portrayed as latecomers, intruders into Europe. To account for their remarkably black skin upon first notice, their reputed origin would have to be an area where black-skinned people predominated. Africa, Egypt or Ethiopia was out of the question; questions about a larger presence of Africans or Egyptians in Europe would obviously be raised—something the Eurocentric Brotherhood of Academia did not care to consider. Therefore, an Indian origin was created to explain Gypsies, an oft-repeated supposition which continues to be promoted by most historians despite references to Gypsies in both Britain (especially Scotland) and Iberia two or more centuries before Gypsies "appeared" in continental Europe. As well, there is no verifiable migration route of Gypsies out of the Balkans—where they were known to be numerous—that definitively traces their entry into Moravia, Italy, Germany, France, Poland, Baltic lands, Denmark and the rest of Scandinavia during the 15th century. *Someone* should have seen and noted the movement of significant numbers of Gypsies into these areas. It seems no one did—probably because they were already there. They only "appeared" in western Europe because later Eurocentric Western historians—feeling constrained to account for them—said they did.

I have not sought information on the religious practices of European Gypsies, but their endogamous culture and religion—condemned as pagan by the expanding Christian Church—seems to have been practiced over the long centuries of their dispersion and oppression, although some claim that they adhered to no particular religion. Gypsies, whatever their tribal names in the northern territories they dominated, were surely among the targeted peoples of the Northern Crusades (1200-1562 AD), whose armies, inspired and supported by the Fathers of the Church in Rome, employed warfare, massacre, and torture against the inhabitants of Poland, Russia and Baltic countries to eradicate paganism and establish Christianity in those regions. MacRitchie mentions the prominence of Gypsies in Lithuania and Courland (Latvia), calling them descendants "of those black pagans . . . 'armed with scimitars, and dressed in caftans' . . . to some extent, the posterity of the thirteenth-century Tartars of Gengyz Khan" (*Britons* 171). In the following commentary, MacRitchie describes the revulsion white Europeans held toward these black Euro-peans, and also indicates that Gypsies and people akin to them were quite numerous in Europe even more than a millennium ago:

> [I]n the thirteenth century [i.e., 1200s] we see them regarded as intruders by the Christian chivalry of the West, to whom they were "Saracens," "Moors," "devils," "heathen," and "pagans;" and, as such, warred against with unceasing vigour until, in Prussia, they were almost totally exterminated. But, whether the European Tartars of that period were wholly, or only partially, invaders, and whether their characteristics were Mongolian, or only partly so, *still they had been preceded by countless swarthy hordes . . . .* Earlier still, in the eighth century, *we see the same stock*—in the Huns, the Bulgarians, the

Pagans of Saxony—whom Charlemagne, after many fierce insurrections, overcame. (*my emphasis,* op. cit. 171)

To be sure, all accounts of Gypsies do not jibe with what MacRitchie says about them. Most accounts of Gypsies follow the oft-repeated storyline of their migration from India, through Persia, into the Balkans and then western Europe. Following the popular storyline, the dates for their arrival or, "appearance," in Europe often vary: in *The Gypsies of Eastern Europe,* (ed. By David Crowe and John Kolsti), Ian Hancock lists the first appearance of Gypsies in Europe (Hildesheim, Germany) as 1407 (11); in *A History of Pagan Europe,* Jones and Pennick locate them in Serbia in 1348; *central* Europe in the early 15th century; Zurich, Switzerland, in 1419, and France in 1421 (197). Shortly after their European arrival, or "appearance," their persecution began, an anti-Gypsy law being issued against them in Germany in 1416, shortly after their arrival. More laws and bans against them ensued all over central and western Europe. In 1580, "Gypsy hunts" were encouraged in Switzerland, and Ian Hancock lists a host of decrees, deportations and punishments meted out to them into the 20th century (11-25). Time does not permit a thorough discussion of the inhumane treatment Gypsies suffered, but along with what is presented above, perhaps the following will indicate the utter savagery Gypsy peoples endured:

1726   Johann Weissenbruch describes wholesale murder on November 14 and 15 of a community of Gypsies in Germany: five are organized nationwide in order to expel them from the land. German monarch Charles VI passes a law that any male Gypsy found in the country is to be killed instantly, while Gypsy women and children are to have their ears cut off and be shipped to the nearest foreign border.

1714   An order is issued in Mainz [Germany] sending all male Gypsies apprehended to the gallows, and requiring the branding and whipping of women and children. Frederick Augustus, Elector of Saxony, orders the murder of any Gypsy resisting arrest.

1722   In Frankfurt-am-Main Gypsy parents are branded and deported while their children are taken from them and placed permanently with non-gypsy families. During this period, Frederick William makes it a hanging offense in Prussia merely to be born a Gypsy for all those over the age of eighteen. A thousand armed Gypsies confront German soldiery in an organized fight for their freedom. Nineteen Gypsies arrested at Kaswasser are tortured to death: four broken on the wheel, three beheaded, and the rest shot or stabbed to death. (Hancock 12-13)

A bit further above, MacRitchie states that 13th century Gypsies in Prussia and Baltic territories were referred to as "devils," "heathens," "pagans," the precise terms presumably white-skinned British inhabitants used to describe Norsemen—most notably the black-skinned Danish Vikings—who began plaguing the Isles in the late 8th century. MacRitchie (and he cites others) seems to infer that these fierce Scandinavian warriors were part of a prevailingly Gypsy population inhabiting the northern reaches of Europe from the British Isles into Russia. Included in this vast "Gypsy" population were some of the groups we have discussed as individual tribes or peoples—old Saxons, Picts, Ambrones, Goths, Wends, Skjoldungs (Scyldings), Black Celts, Geats, Scots, and the Tuatha de Danaan, Dani or Danes who were among the confederation of peoples known as Cimbri or Kymry—the group referred to as Skjoldungs, "the royal race" of Vikings or Norsemen.

Historians—almost never describing them racially—have presented the above-mentioned peoples as individual groups, so we readers envision them as dissimilar from one another, not to mention *white* and possessing Caucasian features. We should now have a new understanding, combined with the knowledge that Africans or Egyptian peoples once predominated throughout the whole of Europe until numbers of westward-moving Caucasoid peoples began dispersing them beginning about 1,500 BC - 600-500 BC in western Europe, although Blacks or Egyptians in northern Europe were for the most part unaffected, and would not be until after the Viking Age (800-1100 AD). And regarding the supposed "Gypsies" of northern Europe, MacRitchie states:

> The fiercest division of these, and apparently the most recent in time, was that of the *Danes*, or *Cimbri*, remembered by the Christianized races of Britain as "the black heathen," the *nigrae gentes, the dubh galls*. (*some, my emphasis, Britons* 173)

If the reader finds MacRitchie's equation of Vikings to Gypsies startling or demeaning, know that I had the same reaction at first. But I now understand why: although the Vikings were rapacious, blood-thirsty and often cruel, they have generally been glorified by historians (while asserting they were blond, blue-eyed Whites) for their aggressiveness, fearlessness, military prowess and seamanship. They could certainly be ruthless, but they humbled most of Britain, France and Europe, in general, their blood eventually flowing in the veins of royalty everywhere they went or settled.

When we meet Gypsies in the popular histories, they are vagrant peoples, a despised, powerless race driven out of districts or countries, seeming to have no roots or history. When they can, they earn money by setting up camps outside a village, displaying their musical talents and other abilities. Their women earn money by fortune-telling; their children, some as young as five- or six-years old, move through the crowds—who have come to the Gypsy camp to enjoy the music, dancing, acrobatics and Gypsy men performing with trained monkeys—picking pockets or handbags. Their men fashion knives and other utensils or give advice to farmers in animal husbandry for which they are paid a little money to buy food and supplies for their families. Then a few days later, village officials would tell them to leave, or they would suddenly be attacked by armed townsmen who slaughter numbers of them, and visit upon them some of the punishments mentioned above.

Because Western historians have Gypsies mysteriously "appear" in 14th or 15th century Europe already rootless, vagrant, bedraggled and often hunted, it is difficult to reconcile them with the powerful hordes of Norsemen who made nearly all of Europe quake only a few centuries earlier. However, the presence of a large number of Blacks in western and northern Europe—Blacks primarily of African and Asian stock—is what has been implied from the beginning of this work and can logically account for the presence of significant numbers of black-skinned Gypsies in Europe after the end of the Viking Age and after the Roman Church-inspired Northern Crusades broke the power of and dispersed other once powerful groups of black- and dark-skinned people occupying eastern and northern Europe, whom the Church considered pagans.

Under various nomenclatures and tribal names, the northern regions of Europe and Eurasia were dominated by a multitude of Afro-Asiatic peoples who must have intermingled to some degree with a growing Caucasoid population. MacRitchie, above, asserts that these "Saracens," "Moors," "devils," "heathens," "Huns" and "Bulgarians" were generaly congeneric and connected racially to the Norsemen of Scandinavia—whom even Charlemagne had not dared to seriously assault, despite border clashes with Danes and Danish assaults into northern Germany and France (i.e., Kingdom of the Franks). Norse chieftains and kings often fought against each other over land, broken agreements or other perceived wrongs. But however admixed these northern peoples may have been with Black Hunnish, Tartar, Indic, Finnic or so-called "Gypsy elements," MacRitchie calls them "virtually the same people under different names"—purely black, with Danes being the most royal race of Norsemen.

Perhaps because these "Goths," "Moors" or "Gypsy" peoples were less organized, less martial or less numerous than their cousins in the primary Scandinavian nations, they were more easily defeated and dispersed when more powerful Caucasian tribes infiltrated their territories, especially during the Northern Crusades when invading armies, with the backing of Rome, brutally slaughtered untold numbers of them in order to crush paganism in Europe and gain Christian converts (1200-1562 AD). Even converted

Scandinavians marched under the Christian banner to participate in the carnage of the largely unknown Northern Crusades.

The transformation of the face of Europe from black to white did not occur overnight, in a year, a century, or several centuries, or even a millennium. It took nearly two millennia to denude Europe of its originally African and Egyptian European population, and even afterwards remnants of them, numbering in the many thousands, would remain in the persons of people called Roma and Sinti—popularly known as Gypsies. In addition to the reported six million Jews killed by the Nazis during the World War II era, it is estimated that the Nazis killed 500,000 to 800,000 Gypsies during the same period. In a recent article in *The Epoch Times* (28 Jan. 2011) newspaper entitled "A Forgotten Holocaust Remembered," Gina Csanyi-Robah, executive director of the Roma Community Center in Toronto, states that as many as 1.5 million Roma might have been killed by the Nazis. The same article (by Marco 'T Hoen) states: "Europe is currently home to 12 million Roma and Sinti. These groups are considered Europe's largest minority with a shared history of rejection."

France has made headlines lately in its efforts to deport immigrant Romanian Roma back to Romania, a practice France has been engaged in for years. A *New York Times* article by Steven Erlanger (13 Sep. 2010), entitled "Document Cites French Bid to Oust Roma," estimates that France currently has a population of roughly 400,000 Roma of French nationality. Illegal immigrants of Roma and Sinti extraction from Romania, along with those immigrants from Algeria and Morocco, are blamed for rising unemployment in the country, "and many encampments have been broken up by the police all over France," which expelled 10,000 Roma in 2009.

With perhaps 12 million Roma and Sinti still residing in Europe, it seems that the once dominant black-skinned, pre-Caucasian Egyptian or Egypto-Asian populace has not disappeared from the continent. The greatly lightened complexions of Gypsies in Europe is testimony to widespread sexual abuse—*rape*, to put it bluntly—of Roma women by white European men over the centuries. Although many look Caucasian and could blend into white European society, the vast majority continue to live by the mores of their ancestors, marrying amongst each other and abiding by Roma laws and values that have withstood the hatred, pogroms, and racial oppression white Europeans have subjected them to for at least 600 years.

The eternally white vision of Europe that Eurocentric historians have long presented us with is a myth; there *never* was such a place. Its original dark-skinned African population was supplanted by a fair-skinned one whose Eurasian nucleus was chiefly composed of Africoid (and perhaps early Mongoloid rejects and Neanderthal elements) albinoid rejects whose mutated chromosomal makeup stabilized over centuries of interbreeding to produce a race referred to as Caucasian or white. In their westward migration into Europe they conquered, displaced and absorbed most of the early possessors of the continent, although later invasions by other peoples—Black Huns, Mongols, Moors, Arabs, Turks—would re-inject dark-skinned genes into the genetic makeup of Caucasian peoples.

In turn, Caucasians have mingled their genes with the darker races over the period of their ascendancy—in India, the Near East, Asia and North Africa—lightening the complexions of peoples in those areas over the centuries. However, there has never been an eternally white Europe, and Steve Olson informs us:

> Viewed over a long enough time period, every European culture is the product of a prodigious mixing of past groups. Yet every European country also has pockets of ethnically distinct groups, such as the Roma (also known as Gypsies), which have remained mostly endogamous for many generations. (189)

Endogamy may allow ethnically distinct groups, like the Basques and Roma, to continue to exist as a distinct people but, in the case of the Roma, remember that thousands of their children were kidnapped, raised in white European homes, were prevented from returning to their tribes and culture, and intermarried—or heavily intermingled with—white Europeans, a result of their childhood tragedies, like being forcibly torn from their parents and clans.

A number of them, I am certain, escaped or were re-kidnapped by parents or relatives who survived the massacres and banishments which brought about the separation of Roma children from their families and tribes. But such returns would have been rare; the overwhelming majority of Roma children remaining in the *Gadze* or white world were forced to abandon their Gypsy culture, or never learned of it. And we have to believe that a great deal of Gypsy blood is present in the genetic makeup of hundreds of thousands—if not millions of Europeans we perceive as white; this is in addition to the widespread race mixing that went on prior to the "appearance" of Gypsies when Blacks—like the Huns, Magyars, and Norsemen—were dominant in Europe. In this regard, Olson assures us: "The blending of peoples that has been going on for millennia in Europe seems destined to continue" (190).

Eurocentric historians and scientists have never documented European history honestly. They discuss ancient European peoples colorlessly, omitting racial particulars that would give us a more accurate picture of Europe's past, especially in regard to Africoid populations who once called Europe home. As we have seen with the discovery of the Grimaldi skeletons and the almost perfectly preserved body of the Iceman, they are suddenly dumbstruck when actual evidence of the presence of Africans or Negroids springs up before them. They were, and are, disinclined to investigate the leads that a handful of more honest scholars left for them to follow.

In the latter part of the 19th century, Gerald Massey declared: "Egypt, and not India is the common cradle of all we have in common, east, west, north, and south, all around the world" (*A Book of the Beginnings, vol. 1* 23). Massey cites a number of scholars who also attested to this, providing detailed proof of a much, much more ancient origin of Egyptian civilization for historians to consider. And, recalling for a moment that our Iceman—who would not be discovered until 110 years later—was discovered high in the Alps on the Italian-Austrian border, perhaps five miles east of the Swiss border, Massey cites historian Karl Vogt, who states that, "[historian] Heer has proved that the *cultivated plants in the Swiss Lake-villages are of African, and to a great extent, Egyptian origin*" (*my emphasis,* op. cit.). The Eurocentric Brotherhood of Academia must have had a hearty laugh over Heer's assertion in 1881!

The secrecy of Europe's history is maintained by the racial omissions discussed in the previous two chapters (as well as in most of this work) and the authoritative, repetitive assertions by Eurocentric historians and scientists testifying to the eternal whiteness of Europe's populations—an exercise modern historians, and some DNA researchers, continue. So, the perpetuation of a false image of Europe and its peoples continues, obscuring a considerable number of factual data that would allow us to contemplate a more accurate depiction of Europe as well as the interrelatedness of the human family—which would allow us to open a pathway to begin to examine the root or roots of the plague of racism that has infected the world far too long.

A few more little known facts may be uncovered in the final three chapters, as we revisit (very briefly) a few epochs discussed earlier as a way of finalizing our examination of them. One of these epochs, of course, is the Europe of the Middle Ages and the Norsemen who settled parts of North America 500 years before Columbus but who, for what should now be obvious reasons, are overlooked as America's discoverers—even if only from a European point of view.

CHAPTER 19

FADING TO WHITE

Although the commonly accepted date of the first Viking raid on the future England is 793 AD, *The Anglo-Saxon Chronicle* records the first Viking raid on the future England's territory as taking place around 789 AD (or 787). It is probable that Viking peoples were not unknown to the Anglo-Saxon colonizers of the eastern coasts of the British Isles who must have known of a Pictish or Danish presence farther to the north and seen occasional fleets of their ships off the coast. However, the *Anglo-Saxon Chronicle* (begun more than a century later) reports the first Viking raid as an attack by unknown people. Most significantly, it makes it clear that these early chroniclers understood that Norwegians and Danes were *the same people,* stating:

> **Year 789** In this year . . . came first three ships of *Norwegians from Horthaland* [Hardangerfjord in Norway]: then the reeve rode thither and tried to compel them to go to the royal manor, for he did not know what they were: and then they slew him. *These were the first ships of the Danes to come to England.* (*my emphasis,* see *the Anglo-Saxon Chronicle* entry for 789 AD)

The location of this attack was Portland, along the south shore of England. It is unspecified what other damage the Vikings caused besides killing the king's reeve, but this *Anglo-Saxon Chronicle* entry clearly demonstrates it was evident early on that these Norwegians were *Danes* out of Norway, the *same* people—black-skinned, according to sources cited in this work—despite claims of later historians that Norwegians were fair-skinned.

According to the *Chronicle,* terrifying omens preceded the events to come immediately prior to the Viking attack on Lindisfarne, which the *Chronicle* describes thusly:

> **Year 793** In this year terrible portents appeared over Northumbria, and miserably frightened the inhabitants: these were exceptional flashes of lightening, and fiery dragons were seen flying in the air. A great famine soon followed these signs; and a little after that in the same year on 8 January the harrying of the heathen miserably destroyed God's church in Lindisfarne by rapine and slaughter. (see *The Anglo-Saxon Chronicle* entry for 793)

There may be symbolic flourishes in the above passage. The "fiery dragons . . . flying in the air," for instance, probably symbolize the sails of Viking dragon-ships on the horizon; the "great famine," a period when normal English (Saxon) trade with their brethren across the English Channel on the continent was disrupted, spawning shortages of food and other necessities that had always been obtainable.

Significant as well is that the earliest Viking raids are against churches and monasteries. In 795, Vikings begin similar depredations in Scotland and Ireland. But raids into these territories are somewhat less ferocious than Viking raids against the English (i.e., Saxons, Angles and related Caucasoids). While most historians insist that a lust for wealth and valuables was the primary motivating factor behind these earliest Norse raids, they ignore what may have been an even greater compulsion: a general abhorrence of Christianity and its spread in Britain.

Although the originally pagan Romans had departed from Britain near the end of the 5th century, their lasting legacy was the introduction and propagation of an early form of Christianity—a faith they had initially opposed and tried to eradicate in their own empire. Whatever the early teachings of this religion (it may have been far different from the Christianity we understand today), its forcible spread undermined the resolve and cohesion of the Africoid tribes (early Saxons, Black Celts, Welsh, Britons, etc.) they disturbed during the four-century Roman occupation.

Eurocentric writers give the impression that England was already a unified, sovereign nation at this time, which it was not; it was a land comprised of territorial districts—Wessex, Northumbria, Kent, York, Mercia, and so on—which would not be unified until some three centuries later after the Norman Conquest of 1066. Lindisfarne, Jarrow, the town of York and a dozen other towns along the east coast of the main island were not much more than outposts established to propagate the Catholic faith among the black-skinned Britons and Celts still occupying the areas where churches and monasteries were established. Might not Viking raids on these places of worship have been an attempt to eradicate them and prevent the spread of the new faith to former trading partners? Remember, there was an older commercial world before the rise of the Britain we know; an Africo-Egyptian world dominated by Picts, Black Celts, Americans, continental Gauls, Etruscans, Phoenicians and Scandinavians who had long traded, fought and interacted with each other in an earlier world that has rarely, if ever, been discussed.

Might not Norsemen have noticed how their racially congeneric allies and, perhaps, relatives had been disrupted, dispersed and compelled to abandon their Old Religion by invading Caucasian Saxons, losing their will to fight and defend their territories after being forced to convert to Christianity? Could the initial attacking, looting and burning of monasteries in the earliest Viking assaults (which were also taking place in France) have actually been attacks against what Norsemen considered bastions of this new faith in an attempt to eradicate it? Its arrival in Britain had significantly altered the dynamics of the world they knew, dispersed peoples, demoralized them. First Roman legions, then invading Saxons brought warfare and slaughter to Britain and its inhabitants, peoples Norsemen—in spite of internecine conflicts from time to time—saw, in a general sense, as racially kindred. While invading Saxon peoples were taller and generally more robust than the earlier Romans, it was the alien religion they both imposed upon the inhabitants that was more reprehensible than their white skins. So, it was the symbols of this religion, churches and monasteries, that were targeted in the earliest Viking raids, and the killing and burning of the priests of the religion was no more egregious than the hunting down, torturing and killing of Druidic priests by the Romans and Saxons.

Upon settling in England, however, the Vikings later found it expedient to form alliances with the English rulers of the various territories they had occupied. As mentioned earlier, there was certainly intermarriage among Danes and English for political reasons, and many Danish chieftains converted to Christianity to secure peace in their realms, often at the behest of an English ruler. These conversions, however, drew them (unwittingly, perhaps) under the influence of the popes in Rome whose power and influence had been increasing since the days when Rome had been overshadowed by the former Eastern Roman Empire, now called the Byzantine Empire, whose overlordship had spread west to south Italy, Sicily and Sardenia and threatened to totally eclipse the staggering, empireless Rome.

*   *   *   *   *

During the 7th, 8th and 9th centuries, the religion of Islam had burst out of Arabia, expanding westward across North Africa to Spain; northward to the Caucasus, and eastward through Mesopotamia and Afghanistan into India. Not only was Christianity's influence threatened in the west through Iberia and the Mediterranean, but the spread of Islam threatened to overwhelm the Byzantine Empire in the east (which it would by the onset of the 13th century), with the possibility of a massive Islamic pincer engulfment of nearly the whole continent of Europe and its reoccupation by black- and dark-skinned Afro-Asiatic peoples.

In the north of Europe loomed the black- and dark-skinned Norsemen of Scandinavia, now threatening the Roman Church's advances in the British Isles as well as France, making the 9th century the blackest, most foreboding period of the Dark Ages for Rome, Christianity and emerging white Europe. To somehow convert the powerful Norse hordes to Christianity and bring them under the influence of the papacy in Rome was of paramount importance for the consolidation of an emerging white Europe facing the additional threat of adherents of rapidly expanding Islam.

Swedish Vikings were less affected by Christianity. Their exploits were primarily in the eastern Baltic regions and Russia, distant from the more active areas of the Roman Church's missionary activities in western Europe, although they certainly knew of them.

In the early 11th century, Swedish king Olaf Skot-Konung (also Olave Scotkonung) imposed Christianity on his subjects—an extremely unpopular decree. This resulted in a reversion to the Old Religion en masse in 1060, an expulsion of Christian bishops and, according to Jones and Pennick:

> Even after the destruction of the [pagan] Uppsala temple in around 1100, Paganism continued openly until the 1120s, when the Christian Norwegian king Sigurd . . . declared a crusade against the Pagans in Smaland, south Sweden, and laid the country waste. (137)

The Swedes were the last of the three Viking-era Scandinavian nations to adopt Christianity, although the Old Religion would continue to be practiced secretly for several centuries in all of them—and even after the fire and sword scourges of the Northern Crusades established Christianity in northern regions of Europe.

The fate of primarily black- and dark-skinned pagan tribes in the Baltic territories, Russia and eastern Europe was much the same as the fate those of Britain had suffered earlier, described briefly here by Timothy Baker in *The Normans*:

> The extent to which the English invaders had displaced their various British [i.e., black Briton] predecessors is not known. Some Britons had been exterminated and probably many more had been enslaved, while those who remained independent had been driven into the fastnesses of Cornwall, Wales and Cumberland. (39)

The Northern Crusades of northeastern Europe subjected so-called pagan Blacks to torture, slavery, extermination and dispersion, which affected mostly Ugrian peoples like Balts and Finns and others less known—and would bring about the emergence of the newly formed territories of Prussia, Lithuania, Estonia, and Latvia.

This is not to imply that all northern Europeans were black-skinned during this Period. The mass Caucasoid migrations out of Eurasia had slowed, with a considerable number of them having settled in territories still ruled over by dark-skinned Tartar tribes. Thirteenth century Mongol invasions into Russia, Poland and eastern Europe brought another infusion of dark Asiatic blood to both black- and white-skinned Europeans and disrupted the thrust of the Northern Crusades underway at the time. Mongols would come to rule Russia for two centuries or more, but in territories west of Russia, Mongol domination was vigorously challenged by the newly formed Teutonic Knights—whose military order had germinated in the Holy Land during the First Crusade. When Mongol domination eventually weakened, the Northern Crusades recommenced in Baltic and eastern European territories.

There—eventually weakened and the Northern Crusades recommenced in Baltic and eastern European territories.

By the latter portion of the 14th century, Prussia, Estonia, Latvia and Lithuania would all be ruled over by armies of Teutonic Knights, primarily Germans whose mission was to enlist rulers to serve the crusade and expand Christianity throughout the region. Those northern Saracens, Moors and other so-called pagan tribes (Prussians, Estonians, Latvians and Slavs among them) who resisted and escaped the crusading armies would continue to hold steadfastly to the religions and cultural practices they had always known, some continuing to live in the same general territories they had always inhabited, others moving farther away. It is more than likely (and exceedingly more logical than an unnoticed migration out of northern India into Europe) that these displaced peoples—still black-skinned, still adhering to long entrenched cultural practices, bands of them "appearing" suddenly in numerous European countries during the same general period (i.e., early 1400s)—became the Gypsies, as we call them, or Roma, as they called themselves.

*   *   *   *   *

While early Danish converts were nominally Christian and did not totally abandon their pagan beliefs they had, nevertheless, pledged allegiance to the popes of Rome and were soon constrained to abide by the Roman Church's mandates. While Western or Eurocentric minds might view the conversion of the Norse peoples to Christianity as the inevitable coalescing of the European continent, the less Romantic conclusion is that the Norse conversion was a major coup for Rome and a *re*ascendant white Europe. This stratagem of conversion—invariably accompanied by fire and sword—would be employed to destabilize, subvert and destroy the cultures of dark-skinned peoples wherever white Europeans traveled in subsequent voyages of discovery or trading ventures to other areas of the world.

While fire and sword were used to tame, kill off and convert the black Britons, Celts and Picts of the British Isles, the Black Norsemen had been too powerful, too numerous, too consumed by their own religious beliefs for such methods to be employed against them. Instead, as mentioned earlier, Norse chieftains and kings were psychologically beguiled by the prospect of becoming part of the expanding Christian European family of nations, the support and blessings of the papacy of Rome, the glory of the Kingdom of Heaven, the blessings of the Father, Son and Holy Ghost, and the especial love of the Son, Jesus Christ, who had by now been given a white face.

Depictions of Jesus as a light-skinned Semitic man or a white man had begun cropping up from the 6th century onward, and while they would not outnumber the depictions of the Black Madonna and Child until the onset of the Renaissance, Christianity, certainly by the close of the 9th or 10th century, became associated with whiteness, the official religion of a whitening Europe—a white man's religion.

In reality, Christianity was no more than an extraction and reworking, of the ancient religions of Greater Ethiopia, which took root in southern Europe as the worship of the Egyptian goddess Isis—spreading from ancient Greece to Rome in historical times. Even the new Romans, who had brought an end to the Etruscan civilization, had worshipped Isis and Horus, the Son, who suckled at her breast. Venerated in their blackness by white-skinned Europeans they, as well as the liturgical rites, were transformed, as the connections with the original sources of the new religion were obscured through warfare, the influx of new peoples with variant but related religions, and the dissolution of the ancient territories of Greater Ethiopia. By the onset of the Middle Ages, Rome had become the fount of a nefariously crafted religion called Christianity with a created liturgy—suffused elements of the pagan practices and beliefs it supposedly abhorred. It is not with disrespect that I say this, for an objective examination of the origins of the religion will bear this out.

Most believers of Christianity do not know the origin of the Bible, which had its beginnings at the Council of Nicea (325 AD), under the auspices of the Roman emperor Constantine, King Constantine, ruler of the Eastern Roman Empire. There are a number of sources extant which discuss the Council of Nicea and what took place there. In a minor work entitled, *The Great Red Dragon,* author Hilton Hotema discusses how the early Christian Bible was created:

> "The Fathers of the Church" went into vigorous action for the success of their newly created institution . . . To Alexandria they went, and pulled what they wanted from Ptolemy's vast library of scrolls and manuscripts.
>
> They copied, interpolated, twisted, and distorted these ancient writings for the making of their Bible . . . [T]hey personalized the ancient symbols and literalized the ancient allegories. Then ancient history was re-written by the church, to serve its ends and to hide the facts . . . (qtd. in *The Philosophy of Divine Nutrition,* Rev. Donald Thomas 12)

Added to this creation was the belief that Jesus (the grown-up Child who was originally the black, Egyptian Horus) was killed or crucified on a cross and that he died for everyone's sins.

Dr. Frances Welsing discusses the psychology of the symbolism of some aspects of Christianity. We should bear in mind that most Europeans of the Middle Ages had not recovered from the stultifying ravages of the Dark Ages when learning in Europe—except in monastic enclaves in Britain (primarily Ireland) and, perhaps, Rome, where history would continue to be recorded—practically came to a halt. Whatever resurgence of learning took place came chiefly through the teachings of Roman Christianity and was politically motivated, meant to indoctrinate rather than truly educate the uniformly illiterate European masses. For most white Europeans, the concocted Roman liturgy was their first form of education—an education centered around a man called Jesus Christ, who was the Son of God, died for their sins, and whose life they were told they should emulate.

People emerging from deprivation and subjugation, seeking validation of their lives, would not have been sophisticated enough to understand that there was a hidden message or agenda in the new teaching they were receiving; that the propagators of the religion they were being told to accept had ulterior or nefarious motives and that much of what they were inculcating was symbolic. So, consider what Dr. Frances Cress Welsing has to say regarding the underlying meaning of the Christ story in a chapter of *The Isis Papers,* entitled "The Symbolism of Christ . . .":

> In Christian religious tradition, it is stated that Jesus died on the cross and suffered so that "we" (whites) can be "saved" (survive) . . . . Thus, Christian (white supremacy) theology can be translated: Jesus (a Black man) shed his Black genetic material in a crucifixion . . . so that the white genetic recessive population, in fear of its genetic annihilation, could be saved (genetically survive). Thus, Jesus is called "savior" by the whites. (68-69)

It is doubtful that white-skinned Christian converts to the faith understood the symbolism and psychological ramifications in the manner outlined by Dr. Welsing as Christianity was being spread or imposed upon supposedly pagan people during the Middle Ages. It is certain, though, that the originators of this arcane, insidious and symbolic belief-system—King Constantine and his prelates, and eventually the papacy and its high priests in Rome—engineered the racial animus that resulted from the subliminal undertones embedded in the teachings of early Christianity or Catholicism. While the shapers of this reconstituted religion (whose origins can be traced back to the ancient belief systems of Egypt, the Near East and Greater Ethiopia) may have had other motives for propagating the new faith throughout Europe, transforming the originally black-skinned Isis and Horus into the white-skinned Madonna and

Child psychologically energized emergent white Europeans. This transformation served to validate their desire to overcome the dark-skinned peoples populating a continent they, themselves, might completely possess, and devalued the lives of black-skinned people, promoting a sense of pride in Whites that would eventually infuse the race with feelings of superiority and privilege over people of color—whom they had mostly known as oppressors.

So, the white-skinned, monastic chroniclers of Irish, Welsh and English history referred to the Norsemen of their day as "the black host," "black pagans," "black devils," "black heathen"—particularly the Danes of Jutland, the nucleus and most royal of black—skinned people of the north—and regarded them as people outside the human family. It is very probable that the Norsemen could have conquered and secured all of Britain (prior to the Norman Conquest) had they remained faithful to their gods and religion, had they maintained their irreverent, aggressive, untamed, temperament. Their conquest of Britain and other territories of Europe would have been certain had they somehow consolidated their contentious Danish, Norwegian and Swedish factions during the 10th century when the physical territories they dominated—large portions of Russia, Britain, France, as well as Bohemia and Moravia—comprised nearly *half the continent.*

The *Normans* who invaded and conquered England in 1066 under Duke William of Normandy were descendants of the black-skinned Danish hordes who had carved out the territory of Normandy in northern France in the late 9th or early 10th century under Gongu-Hrolfr, or Rollo. But these Danes had early on accepted the Christian faith, begun to speak French, losing their Danish tongue, and intermarried with presumably white- or lighter-skinned women for five or six generations. We must assume that Normans had lost their purely black complexions and were largely dark- to light-brown-skinned, and often tawny—although Afro-Asiatic physical traits (dark skins, full lips, high cheekbones and curly hair) were still in evidence among most. As important, the Normans brought to England another infusion of Christian souls whose adoration of the now white depictions of Jesus and Mary would unwittingly pass along feelings of white supremacy to their descendants. The Norman Conquest marks the beginning of the England we know, and the early kings of England descend from the Normans, kings who would rule all the territories of England and would later extend English rule to Scotland, Wales and Ireland.

The Norse peoples who began abandoning Scandinavia after 870 fully settled Iceland by 930—the earliest settlers carving out sizeable chunks of territory, doling out portions to family members, faithful servants and thralls—many whom were from the Hebrides, Orkneys and Ireland. While the bulk of Viking Icelanders is said to have been Norwegian, the island—circumnavigated by Gardar, a *"Dane* of Swedish descent," in 860—must have been known to Danish Vikings, and a sizeable percentage of Danes must have settled there as well. Gardar is also referred to as Gardar the Swede by historians but, as earlier mentioned, he had a son called Uni the *Dane* who served Harald Fairhair, and Uni the Dane's mother was Thorunn, a Norwegian, who would settle in Iceland. So, Danes cannot be excluded as Icelandic settlers, whose population may have included a smattering of Swedes, as well, since intermarriage was common in the three primary Scandinavian countries.

In any case, we saw above that *The Anglo-Saxon Chronicle* called the earliest Norwegian invaders of England *Danes from Norway,* so it would seem that the only difference between Norwegians and Danes of the Viking Age is the difference that Eurocentric historians, from the early Irish chroniclers onward, have suggested since, in essence, all Viking peoples of the period were, technically speaking, black-skinned *Danes* who overspread Scandinavia and other areas of northern Europe. Western historians designated them Danes, Swedes and Norwegians according to the *territories* or countries these *Danes* emanated from, inducing us to believe that the inhabitants of these territories were somehow racially different. So, the interpolation of early Irish historians added to the subterfuge of having us equate Norwegian and Norse with *north, Nordic,* and, therefore, *white-skinned* (along with oft-repeated declarations that white skin is essential to survive cold weather) and has effectively beguiled most of the reading public into believing that the Norwegians who settled *Iceland* must have been white, when the truth is that *ethnically,* Norwegians *were* Danes (as were Swedes of the period) and were predominantly black-skinned, as sources cited in this work have attested.

As the Norsemen of all three Scandinavian nations had imported thousands of white women as wives, concubines, slaves and servants, a racially diverse mix of peoples settled Iceland—black Norsemen, male and female, Whites, half-breeds, Whites and near Whites—demonstrating the same general intermingling occurring in Europe. With dwindling influxes of black-skinned peoples into northern Europe, the complexions of Scandinavians continued to lighten, although the black element would remain prominent for a time. But later arrivals in Iceland, say, after the 12th century, would have tended to be lighter-complexioned or near-white (and white) which, over a dozen generations—as in Europe—gradually absorbed most of the black- and dark-skinned elements there so that, over a period of two or three more centuries, most Icelanders would have exhibited brown and tawny, to near-white complexions—darker complexions and other physical traits resurfacing in atavistic regularity down through the centuries into modern times, just as in continental Europe.

Most historians opine that Norsemen sailed west (to Britain and its outer islands, Iceland and Greenland) seeking land to farm and live a more settled life. This may have been true in a general sense when Vikings owed allegiance to district chieftains. But the expanding Scandinavian population of the 9th century would soon fall prey to kings, like Harald Fairhair, whose chief motivation seemed to be greed and personal wealth.

Burdoned with taxes, levies against their homes and farms, forced allegiances to unpopular kings who had come to power by defeating a popular one, many Norsemen and their families began an exodus out of Scandinavia to seek less stressful lives.

While they were not unused to stress—the vagaries of a rugged existence living in a colder climate than other Europeans; the deceit of formerly trusted comrades; the racing of the heart as men plunged into battle against men or against the sea; homicides and fratricides; sudden fierce storms or unexpected death—two centuries of tumultuous intercourse with more settled people had mellowed the Viking spirit. More Norsemen were ready to sheathe their swords, work farms, spend time at home watching their children grow up and accumulate wealth more slowly, patiently, as other Europeans did. All they needed was a little time and space to implement their new appreciation of life. But, for most Norsemen, time and space had run out for them in Europe.

The earliest Caucasians had stormed into Europe with a seemingly natural antipathy toward black-skinned people. Christianity, now with the white-skinned Mary and Jesus at its head, intensified this antipathy into a general hatred, bringing about the racism evident in the Crusades to the Holy Land and in all European adventures into lands inhabited by black- and dark-skinned people thereafter. While the Norsemen could not be wholly defeated militarily, they were compromised by shrewd, scheming minds in Rome who instructed British kings to insist that Viking leaders convert to Christianity as a condition of any formal treaty or alliance. These conversions—of chieftains and kings, who then had to prevail upon their subjects to convert—sowed dissention among Norsemen who did not care to abandon their old gods and way of living; and continuing Roman missions to Scandinavia resulting in the conversion of some chieftains there, brought disharmony into Scandinavia itself—Swedes and Norwegians remaining particularly hostile to the new religion.

Norsemen must have seen that Europe was now dominated by white people and that everywhere, especially in Britain and northern Germany, black-skinned people like themselves were declining. The Danes who had occupied northern France were now called Normans; they were Christian, spoke French, were no longer very black-skinned, and were, essentially Frenchmen, with few ties to Scandinavia. Norsemen could not avoid noticing that the population in their homelands was lightening and that more and more Norsemen were professing the Christian faith, abandoning the Old Religion. The face of Europe had changed.

To remain in Europe would mean more confrontations with white Europeans—even other Scandinavians—backed by the powers in Rome whose tentacles now stretched to the far north, threatening to expunge any belief contrary to the adoration of the White Mother and Child. Norsemen could not even look to their own kings for solace and protection. For the still black- and dark-skinned Norse peoples, abandoning Europe for lands beyond the British Isles seemed preferable to remaining to be shorn of their independence, religion and property. So, black- and dark-skinned Norsemen—*Danes* mostly from Norway—sold their estates or left them in the hands of relatives, loaded their families, comrades, servants, slaves, tools, cattle and horses onto their longships and knarrs and sailed to Iceland and Greenland a full five centuries before Christopher Columbus and his Spaniards set foot on Watling Island in the Bahamas chain—more than 300 miles south-east of the mainland of North America (Florida), which he never set foot upon.

Already mentioned is that Greenland, the world's largest island, is part of North America and that Norse colonies survived there for at least 500 years—perhaps until 1600. The time span between Columbus' initial landing in the Bahamas to the present is 520 years. While Greenland is not the mainland of North America, it is included in the territories that comprise North America (as is the western peninsula of Iceland). We know that a Norse settlement was established at L'Anse aux Meadows on the northern tip of Newfoundland where the mainland could easily be seen across the Strait of Belle Isle, about 30 miles distant. Knowing the Norsemen, of course they crossed the strait and explored the territory which they named Markland. They also sailed the coastline south, exploring Prince Edward Island, Nova Scotia and named the land just to the west of the Nova Scotia peninsula Vinland, where they must have spent time, although there is no record of a settlement being built there.

There is no reason to doubt that these itinerant seafarers reached other parts of the mainland, like Massachusetts or points farther south, or that they sailed throughout the Gulf of St. Lawrence, debarking at points further inland. We certainly don't have knowledge of each and every occurrence in history—any history—and should logically assume that the written history we do possess (of any country, people, migration, genocide, battle) does not necessarily represent all circumstances, aspects and incidents that may have taken place.

A big-city newspaper may report a murder having taken place overnight, which might get widespread television coverage. But in a city like New York, Los Angeles or Chicago, it may be only one of five murders that occurred overnight, reported because of the area it took place in, the brutality, or the notoriety of the perpetrator or victim. The other four murders may never be reported, but they did occur. So, it is probable that unknown Norsemen put ashore farther south on the North American shore or further inland than we know about, their feat, however, unrecorded.

If the Norsemen were Caucasian, white Europeans, as most writers assert, it remains confounding that even Eurocentric historians do not credit them with America's discovery. Others preceded them, of course, which has been discussed. But in regard to the Norse of Scandinavia, who by 1000 AD, held half of Europe under their domination, it is truly perplexing that historians cooly dismiss an opportunity to enhance the stature of white Europeans to place the supposed purest of them—tall, blond, blue-eyed, robust white-skinned Nordics—in America centuries before Columbus. Instead, European (and American) historians often make comments similar to those of C.W. Ceram, who states, in *The First American:*

> [W]e can only say that the landings of the Vikings in America, interesting as they are from many points of view, *did not change Western man's view of the world or have any effect on his economic patterns.* That was accomplished by Columbus . . . by the Spaniards who were destined to conquer the North American continent . . . . (*my emphasis,* 54)

Although the Vikings of Iceland and Greenland did maintain and engage in trade, religious (i.e., Christian conversion) and, to a lesser degree, political ties with their homelands and with merchants in parts of Ireland and Britain, their commerce did not extend to the whole of Europe, rendering it, one would presume from Ceram's comment, negligible.

And, no, there is no record of Vikings conquering the wilderness or the indigenous tribes on the mainland to create a sizeable territory of their own—another prerequisite, it would seem, for legitimacy to be bestowed upon a people (white Europeans) who historically invaded the lands of others for territory and economic gain. If conquest and the acquisition of territory are prerequisites for discovery, then these supposed blond, blue-eyed Nordics fail to meet the Eurocentric standard. How ridiculous!

Setting aside the earlier arrivals previously discussed for which there is less direct evidence, but acknowledging that they did, in fact, occur; and considering that the Scandinavian peoples who migrated to North America emanated from a definite European entity—three northern countries of racially congeneric peoples whose presence here was known by most European rulers including the popes of Rome—there must be some other reason Norsemen are not proclaimed the discoverers of America, even by *Eurocentric* historians.

Author Charles Boland (*They All Discovered America*) asserts that the Celi Dei, who departed Iceland at the arrival of Norsemen there, established a territory he calls "Great Ireland" somewhere in the area of Massachusetts, which thrived for several centuries and absorbed at least two shiploads of Vikings. These Vikings had been blown off course in 982 and 986, due to stormy seas, and Boland states:

> [T]he colony at North Salem [Massachusetts], begun by the Phoenicians . . . and continued . . . by the Irish . . . now had expanded into an international settlement. It also follows that intermarriage took place . . . between Icelander [i.e., Vikings] and Irish . . . [and] with appealing Indian maidens from the Algonquin tribes which lived in the area. (147)

Boland also informs us that runic inscriptions on stones found in the area, like those on the Dighton Rock, have been theorized to be the handiwork of Phoenicians, Scythians, Egyptians and others, and that Great Ireland (whose ancestors most likely were *black* Celtic Irish converts to Catholicism who fled the encroachment and oppression of Caucasian Saxons who had invaded the island) would later be referred to as *Norumbega,* a term implying New England and sometimes "generously applied to the *entire* eastern coast" (op. cit. 151). So, a case can be made for Norse procreation and continuity in North America, proper, albeit not as conquerors and despoilers of civilizations as, presumably, Eurocentric chroniclers prefer to view the exploits of white-skinned explorers and colonizers. (The storm-tossed Vikings Boland says came ashore in Norumbega in 982 might possibly refer to Rolf Tollefson's ship, the ship on which Aben Arou arrived.) But the failure of the Vikings to carve out a territory through conquest is hardly the reason they have not been credited with the discovery of the New World.

Norsemen both explored areas of North America and intermingled their blood with Native Americans in North America, proper—and within the confines of the future United States—a full five centuries before the man given credit for America's discovery. Looking at it another way: the period of time between the Vikings first setting foot on North America (forgetting, for the moment, Iceland) and the arrival of the Spanish is equal to the same intervening span of time between Columbus' initial landing in the Bahamas in 1492 and the present. And the Viking settlements in Greenland survived at least as long—known to exist by knowledgeable Western Europeans—and by the Roman Church from the outset! Who decided to ignore the Norse achievement and credit Columbus? When? And why? That the Norsemen did not subdue the native inhabitants and hold a sizeable portion of North American territory should not negate the arrival of these Europeans on American shores centuries before Columbus. America was a *European* "discovery," and the Norsemen, being the first significant group of Europeans to settle here and endure, should be duly credited with it.

Alexander the Great held onto his vast Asian "empire" for barely a dozen years before his Greeks and Macedonians were killed or driven back to their homelands. He is deified! The empire he ruled is shown as a large splotch from Macedonia to the Indus on historical atlases, suggesting longevity and governance over the black- and dark-skinned populaces, who were, however, only temporarily subdued. True, he renamed cities after himself, established a financial and coinage system, and his Greek and Macedonian mercenaries married and intermingled with the women of the native populations he subdued. But, like the 11th century Kingdom of Canute, his empire began to disintegrate shortly after his death in 323 BC, and his most enduring legacy is the establishment of Greek Ptolemaic rule in Egypt—which lasted barely three centuries—and the establishment of the city of Alexandria on Egypt's Mediterranean coast from which the Ptolemies ruled. Except for Asia Minor, which had been held by the Persian Empire, Alexander's vast Asian empire shortly dwindled, its black- and dark-skinned inhabitants barely lightened by the absorption of Caucasian blood from northern Egypt out to western India (not that Macedonians and Greeks were all what we might imagine to be "pure" Caucasians).

If a later European power, say, the Roman Empire, had come along five centuries after Alexander and conquered the same territory, holding it until even the present time, would that negate the fact that Alexander had been there/done that first? Would the fact that Alexander and his armies failed to permanently secure even a single city he gave his name to; establish a profitable trade route extending from the Indus back to Greece or Alexandria; or did not significantly alter the religious beliefs of his conquered subjects to any degree, diminish his achievement? Would later historians be justified in saying that Alexander's Asian exploits were "interesting . . . from many points of view," but the conquest belongs to the *Romans* because they were able to hold the territory, decimate its inhabitants, add economic vitality to Rome's coffers and open the territory up for European expansion? Would such a scenario justify crediting Romans as the *first* European conquerors of Asia?

Yet, this is precisely what Eurocentric historians have done in regard to the discovery of America: they have conferred this achievement on a man who sailed into North American environs five centuries *after* the Vikings; never set foot on the mainland of the continent; never established a town or settlement worth mentioning, whose arrival and the subsequent arrival of Spanish conquistadors brought about the decimation and ruin of several million inhabitants in the West Indies, Mexico, South America and southern coastal regions of what would become the United States.

Most people do not know that fifteen years before setting out to discover a route to the Indies of Asia, Columbus had sailed to Iceland where he *must have* learned of the existence of a great landmass to the southwest from the Icelanders or seen an Icelandic map depicting Greenland and an even larger body of land west and southwest of it since, according to Michael Bradley, author of *The Columbus Conspiracy*, "most historians now believe from the [Norse] *sagas* that an extensive stretch of the Atlantic seaboard from Nova Scotia to Chesapeake was . . . known to the medieval Scandinavians" (15).

Icelanders might also have informed him that the larger landmass was not China or the Asian continent, for why else would Columbus, an extremely knowledgeable mariner, have chosen to sail so far south—to the Azores, then south-southwest—in his quest for the Orient? This would strongly indicate that Icelanders, Greenlanders—or an expedition from Scandinavia, itself—did, in fact, explore "the *entire* eastern coast" and knew that the giant landmass was not the Asian continent. Columbus' course, in light of his voyage to Iceland in 1477, indicates that he understood he would not reach Asia or its outer islands taking a more westerly course, that he knew a great landmass or continent stretching far to the south existed when he set out on his first voyage. His goal was to discover a route to China or the Indies of India, not to reach land he knew existed.

(The Muslim Ottoman Empire, having expanded its territory into Egypt and North Africa, dominated the eastern Mediterranean, as well as access to the Red Sea and the Indian Ocean. Voyages around the Cape of Good Hope at the southern end of Africa would have been time consuming, so Spain, Portugal and other European nations sought an alternative route to the Indies and China to avoid interference, warfare or high tax levies from the Ottoman Empire.)

While Columbus' motivation for undertaking his first voyage might seem speculative to the reader who is unaware of circumstances in Europe at the time, he *did* visit Iceland, he *did* take a south by southwest route, and it must have been generally known by that time that the earth, indeed, was round. The people

Columbus found in the Bahamas and Caribbean Isles would not have matched depictions he had seen of Chinese, but they resembled the people of India closely enough for him to believe he had reached the supposed outer islands of India, so he designated them Indians. We know the rest of the story.

If the existence of Norumbega or North America was known to Europeans, it was certainly made known by the Vikings. There is no verifiable evidence that the Celi Dei, or Irish monks, ever returned to Ireland or Europe (although it is possible some could have), but Norsemen would continue to regularly traverse the North Atlantic between the two continents for three centuries or more after their settlement in Iceland and Greenland. The general Scandinavian population knew of the territories across the Atlantic as did people in Germany, France, the British Isles and Russia, since Icelanders and, to a lesser degree, Greenlanders, maintained trade relations with merchants in these countries for a time, or had relatives living in them.

And the papacy in Rome certainly knew of these overseas territories since "[the] Norsemen never kept their settlements on Greenland and explorations of Vinland a secret, but immediately passed all important information on to the Church in Rome," according to James Robert Enterline (*Viking America* 175). Enterline also states that Catholic priests lived in *Greenland* from 999 onwards, and already mentioned is that Leif Eiriksson brought a Catholic priest to Greenland on the express order of Olaf, King of Norway. If the general populaces of Europe, mostly illiterate, did not know of the existence of the New World, European monarchs and those associated with them surely did, including the popes of Rome. So, Italy, Columbus' supposed birthplace, can be added to the list of countries that had knowledge of Viking settlements across the North Atlantic. Perhaps all of Europe knew. So, why aren't the Vikings credited with the discovery of America—even by *Eurocentric* historians, who have long insisted that the Norsemen of the Viking Age were blond, blue-eyed and white?

The Norse discovery of the New World is downplayed in favor of Columbus because there is too much surviving evidence—not abundant, but still surviving—that Norsemen of the period were black- and dark-skinned. We have discussed evidence of their occupation of Jutland since at least 200 BC as Cimbri or Kymry and, if Gerald Massey's research is considered, even earlier, Kymry being the descendants of a widely disseminated Egyptian or Africoid race that once overspread the whole continent (peoples Western historians classify as Iberians, Ligurians, Basques, and so on).

Black-skinned Asians, whether from the Near East, India or Central Asia, sent periodic migrations into Europe. Another wave of Egyptians, the Tuatha de Danaan, or Dani, moved into Jutland, becoming so dominant that the Jutland Peninsula would be named after them and they would become known as Danes, a royal race, who went on to occupy Sweden and Norway, disturbing the Goths (a racially similar people) a large number of whom would migrate south, spreading their numerous members into central Europe. Atilla's Black Huns stormed into Europe as well as into Scandinavia, adding a black Mongolian element to the black-skinned, Egyptoid Danes, who would emerge as Vikings three centuries later.

Around the beginning of the Renaissance (c. 1400), the Europe we know began to take shape. After seven centuries of occupation, the Moors had been almost driven out of Spain, with only the small Kingdom of Granada at the southern end of the Iberian Peninsula still under their control. Most of France and Spain were adherents of the Pope in Avignon; the expansive, Germanic Holy Roman Empire extended from western France to Poland, Christianized but independent, not formally aligned with the popes of Avignon or Rome. The northern half of Italy, the Kingdom of Poland, the extensive Kingdom of Hungary, along with England and Ireland were adherents of the pope of Rome, as were the countries of Scandinavia. Modern Europe was coming into focus, but the memory of black northern Europe had not yet been forgotten. At this time, however, the balance of power and influence in Europe had shifted to white Europeans, largely as a result of the decline and Christianizing of Viking Scandinavia, the massacres and forced conversions of the Northern Crusades, the emergence of powerful German principalities throughout the Holy Roman Empire, or central Europe, and the expulsion of the dreaded Moors from Iberia and southern France.

With the demise of the fearsome Scandinavian nations, the expulsion of the Moors from Iberia and southern France, the stamping out of paganism through massacres and forced conversions in eastern and northeastern Europe nearly complete, many thousands of new converts entered the Christian fold. The white-skinned, Greco-Roman Europe under Roman control long ago envisioned by the Roman elite of Julius Caesar's day was finally coalescing with the ascension of Caucasians and the uprooting of black- and dark-skinned people from the continent.

Genetically, however, most of these "Whites" were admixed with the black- and dark-skinned peoples they had comingled with through migrations to and invasions of the areas they emanated from. Depending on the area, most Europeans were admixed with Black Celtic, Turkic, Black Hunnish, Tartar, Old Saxon, Persian, Magyar, Norse, Basque, Finnic, Ugrian, Mongol and other peoples—some more than others; some to a lesser degree than others; some for a longer time than others; some more recently than others. And this racial intermixing of Blacks (whether of African or Asian descent) with Whites has never excluded European nobility—whether in Archaic Greece, whose early gods and goddesses were black and manifests evidence of prolonged racial intermixing; in Rome, whose ancient nobility intermarried and intermingled with Etruscans; in Britain and Ireland, where Saxons mingled their blood with subjugated female Britons; Norse chieftains married fair British or Saxon maidens, or anywhere else in Europe where Blacks were prominent. Time does not permit more a detailed discussion, but the reader is encouraged examine J.A. Rogers' *Nature Knows No Color Line* and the sources Rogers cites for more information in this regard.

In 1400 the impetus for initiating interracial sexual unions in Europe had decidedly shifted from Black males to white males. But something more had to be done to make the dream of a Europe inhabited by Whites resembling the Greco-Roman vision a reality. The Church of Rome now fully sanctioned white images of Mary and Jesus, and many sculptors and painters, like Michelangelo and Giotto, produced religious works illustrating realistic human expressions, gestures and touches that had not generally been approached prior to the Renaissance, which began in 14th century Italy. The Renaissance spread to other European countries, and many brilliantly realized works—often non-religious—would emerge during the period, which cannot be discussed further, except to say that the cumulative effect was the promotion of white ideals of beauty, piety, religion, righteousness and even supremacy of white-skinned people—if only because other races were almost never depicted; if they were, it was never with as much detail, attention or sympathy.

In concert with the transference of sexual initiative from black males to white males was an ominous, unspoken, decree discouraging white women from any romantic or sexual adventures with black- or dark-skinned men. I cannot cite a source for my comment here, but I am absolutely certain that white women were (and still are) made aware—implicitly or explicitly—of this interracial taboo in their early childhood years. As an African-American, I am acutely aware of this taboo existing in the United States: from the strictures imposed in Puritan dominated New England against intercourse with Native Americans; to those imposed by individual states outlawing interracial marriage—particularly between black men and white women, enduring in several states almost to the 21st century; to the general segregation of black and white American society, which continues to exist throughout the nation—particularly preventing the free association of white women and non-white males.

My two-and-a-half-year stint in France and Germany while in the U.S. Army allowed me to see that this racial stigma was nowhere near as rampant in Europe. But there must have been a time when it was, when black men—be they Norsemen, Moors, Huns, Mongols or Gypsies—were feared by Whites throughout the continent—particularly for their sexual proclivities (real or imagined) and their free association with white European women in whatever areas they dominated. Why was Saxon King Alfred so apoplectic toward the black-skinned Danes settling in the future England? Why did the (supposedly) white-skinned, Christian Spanish feel the need to mount a centuries-long campaign against the Moors to rid the Iberian Peninsula of them? As earlier noted, the primarily African Moors were responsible for the improvement of agriculture there; the architecture still to be seen there; the universities built there and the learning that emanated from them, which effectively made Spain the most civilized country of medieval Europe and led to the modernization of the rest of it. The Moors had made Spain *Spain!* When white Europeans gained ascendancy in Europe, why were Gypsy men frequently murdered en masse in sudden raids on their encampments?

Dr. Frances Cress Welsing attributes white rancor and violence toward Blacks and non-white peoples around the world to a general feeling of rejection, self hatred and a fear of genetic annihilation within themselves. The history of Europeans (and white Americans) in their interaction with the non-white peoples of the world is certainly rife with evidence of hatred *toward* such peoples. But Western historians write the histories that most of the world reads, doing so in a way that prevents the reader from fathoming the extent of their hatred and indifference toward people of color: the three century long Atlantic slave trade was initiated, not out of hate, they insist, but for *economic* reasons; the near genocide of Native Americans was necessary for the *expansion* of the United States to the Pacific and access to valuable resources; the undesired Euro-American invasions of Japan, and into China and Korea in the 19th century were merely to "open up" trade with the West, and so on. Much less attention is given to the millions of non-white people who were conquered, abused or killed in these economic adventures, a process continuing today in Afghanistan, Iraq and Pakistan—which may extend to Iran and other nations of dark-skinned people in the near future—under the pretense of "bringing democracy" to those countries, "rooting out terrorists," or "protecting American interests" almost half a world away. The lives of the million or more people of color who have already died as a result of these overseas adventures has still not registered with many Europeans and most Americans.

The pattern of black death and white survival since Whites attained ascendancy in Europe continues to this day. The rampant disregard for the lives of Native Americans that the earliest Spanish and English colonists displayed is evidence that an acute hatred of black- and dark-skinned people originated in Europe. These Europeans (along with the Portuguese and French) felt themselves superior to dark-skinned Native Americans, and their attempts to Christianize them was not out of humane concern for their benighted souls and a heartfelt desire that they know the eternal grace of God. Their desire was to destabilize them, subject them to white authority, take their beautiful, unspoiled lands for themselves, kill them outright for any show of independence or resistance to white authority.

Just as in Europe at an earlier period, black- and dark-skinned people had to die so that white Europeans could live and prosper. Any sexual dalliances between black- or dark-skinned men and white women would certainly result in dark-skinned or non-white offspring in the Caucasian psyche. In regard to the intermingling of races, science writer Steve Olson informs us: "[T]he lesson from history is that physical differences do little to slow the mixing of groups unless *powerful societal forces* keep them rightly separated" (*my emphasis,* 190). After the sexual initiative shifted from black- to white-skinned males in Europe, an additional measure was needed to insure the expansion of Whites on the continent. So white women, already oppressed in Europe, particularly through the teachings of the Christian Church, somehow learned at an early age that rejection, ostracism or other consequences would ensue should they consort with non-white males. Most people who embraced, or aspired to, the concept of "white" came to understand this. And the chief societal force to convey this message of whiteness, equating it with purity, was the Christian Church—predominantly Catholic in 1400—espousing Catholic dogma, with a white Mary and baby Jesus as its holiest icons, along with a suffering white adult Jesus nailed to a cross.

Unknown to most believers was that the origin of white Mary and Jesus was the far older black Egyptian Isis and infant Horus, reworked and transformed to white by the Fathers of the Church of Rome to assist them in their effort to attract enough converts to uproot and displace the continent's long entrenched dark-skinned populations worshipping "heathen" gods and make Europe the home of white-skinned people and civilization. What Rome failed to accomplish with its legions, it accomplished through cunning, subversion, perseverance, chicanery and—when they had gained enough converts to inspire and finance crusades—torture, violence and warfare. The converts the Church had gained made up for the legions of a millennium earlier. Rome had finally conquered all of Europe.

Again, I do not mean to denigrate the Christian religion or people who hold Christian beliefs; this is a historical treatise, and a perusal of the sources utilized in this work or a good encyclopedia will validate my basic assertions—albeit in a less direct manner. Outside of the Christian Coptics of Egypt (the history of whom I have not researched), several early black Christian Fathers (like St. Augustine) and several black or African popes, Christianity was chiefly spread throughout Europe by white men and the vast majority of Christians in Europe were white. Whiteness of skin became the ideal, which believers strove to maintain—or attain. Again, Whites were not without admixtures of other races, darker races. The physical features of those whose ancestors intermingled with Blacks or other dark-skinned peoples longer or more intensely would continue to bear witness to racial mixing, which is why Benjamin Franklin, speaking of immigrants then coming to the American colonies, could write, in 1751, that "Spaniards, Italians, French, *Russians, and Swedes* are . . . of what we call a *swarthy complexion*," adding *Germans* to his list (*my emphasis*, Malcomson 177). In the case of most of the aforementioned, that swarthiness mentioned by Franklin has not yet disappeared—natives of the southern European countries being most frequently mentioned as being swarthy or of dark complexions.

Mostly unmentioned is that *northern* Europeans betray evidence of swarthiness as well (*swarthy* originally meant *black,* but is used today to infer *dark* or brown-complexioned (or *olive-*toned). Eurocentric historians would rather have us believe that northern Europe has always been inhabited by white-skinned people, blonds, *Nordics.* The reader knows better by now, and has been presented with a number of historians testifying to the predominance of Africoid populations in Europe from remotest times into the Dark Ages and beyond, from the British Isles and Iberia into Scandinavia, Greece and Russia.

Alongside the decline and absorption of black- and dark-skinned peoples in Europe are their *omission* from the pages of more popular histories written by Eurocentric historians who make no effort to mention them, choosing instead to present us with a plethora of nondescript peoples moving into and about Europe, leaving the impression that none of these were other than variations of Caucasoids and, therefore, white-skinned. DNA researchers, like the authors of *History and Geography of Human Genes,* blatantly abuse the science by giving credence to the erroneous claims of past and present Eurocentric historians when they declare most human beings outside of sub-Saharan Africa Caucasoids and non-Africans.

In his more layman-friendly *Mapping Human History,* Steve Olson explains how the term "Caucasian" upset many Europeans who resented being included among the millions of black-skinned Indians (of India) who had also been classified as such, and how migrations of early Caucasoids to India and, perhaps, more extensive migrations of Indians into Europe, brought about their physical resemblance which "resulted from their common descent from the modern humans who left Africa for Eurasia" (160-1). Olson goes on to state:

> [T]hey all mixed relatively little with the groups that acquired the typically "Mongoloid" features of eastern Asia. Thus the "Caucasoid" features of various peoples around the world may simply reflect the features of the *northeastern Africans who gave rise to all the people of Europe and Asia.* (*my emphasis,* 161)

While Olson generally follows the hypothesis of Europe being peopled largely by farming peoples out of the Mid—and Near East as do Cavalli-Sforza et al, he uses decipherable language without the complicated statistical data that makes HGHG seem pompous in comparison and nearly unintelligible to the layman.

Olson's assertion that Caucasoid features "reflect the features of northeast Africans" (above), who went on to populate Europe and Asia, is to say that these continents—and in particular, Europe—were populated by peoples who flowed for millennia out of the area in Africa that we have long known as Egypt. Whatever nomenclatures Western historians have attached to the various types or races of peoples emanating from there—Semites, Grimaldis, Ethiopians, Kafruti, Kamruti, Nubians, Cushites, Hamites, and others—they were genetically similar Negroids of varying black to brown complexions and physical types, originating initially and primaarily in Africa over untold millennia, separated from the Negroids of sub-Saharan Africa (so-called *true Negroids*) only by the writings of Western historians and scientists, who insist that they were somehow racially divergent peoples.

Over the millennia, waves of such peoples followed the Negroid Grimaldis into Europe and spread over the entire continent (and the rest of the world). These are the people, under their various tribal names, that Massey, Churchward, Higgins and others refer to as Egyptians—Higgins claiming an Asiatic origin for *his* black migrants into Europe who were, nevertheless, Negroids—who fashioned the earliest images of Buddha in their likeness. The ancestors of these Blacks or Egyptians had arrived in Europe sometime after the Grimaldis became the first fully human beings to occupy that continent. They were still in occupation of Europe when the Great Flood inundated the Mediterranean Basin, relegating countless villages and port towns to watery interment 10,000-12,000 BC; more arrived with the ability to erect stone megaliths, raising them on their northerly populating migrations into and through Iberia, France, Britain, Ireland, Germany and Scandinavia, commencing at least 5000 BC.

They were still in Europe (probably overspreading it) when our previously mentioned Iceman sought refuge from a sudden blizzard in a rocky depression 10,000 feet up in the Alps 5,300 years ago; when the Great Pyramid was being erected in Egypt several millennia after the Sphinx had been; when Caucasian Albinoids began venturing out of Eurasia into areas of the Near East and eastern Europe 4,000 years ago; when the city of Rome began to be built by the Etruscans around 750 BC; when Alexander the Great began his conquest of Asia in the latter part of the 4th century BC; when new, white Romans seized power from the Etruscans and began their rise to empire from the 3rd century BC onward.

The Roman surge from the south and a considerable influx of Caucasians from the east (presumably Caucasian new Celts) displaced much of the Egyptian (Old Saxons, Black Celts, Kymry, ancient Gauls of central Europe and France) population in Europe, beginning c. 600-500 BC. These more ancient black Europeans would continue to occupy western portions of Europe—western Gaul and the British Isles; Scandinavia, where they were least disturbed; portions of Germany, and Baltic regions eastward into Russia. The reader has already been informed about the most powerful remnant of these people, the Danes or Black Norsemen of the Viking Age, who singularly dominated Europe for three centuries or more—six centuries if one considers that they began to make their presence felt from the onset of the Dark Ages, about 500 AD; more than a millennium if we include late 2nd century BC Cimbrian assaults on Roman armies. Western historians follow Roman chronicler Tacitus in calling the Cimbri *Germans*. If they were, they were black Germans, whose occupation of Scandinavia is generally acknowledged since at least the 2nd century BPE. But Massey, as earlier mentioned, dates their presence in Europe far earlier.

*   *   *   *   *

As chivalrous and terrifying as the Norsemen of Scandinavia were to an expanding white Christian Europe during the Viking Age (i.e., 800-1100 AD), their power and vitality as a formidable entity was compromised, first, by the generally tribal nature of their society and failure to unify and, second, by their acceptance of a religion foisted upon them by avaricious chieftains and kings, which forced them to abandon their old gods—who had rendered them practically invincible—for the crucified white Savior of Rome and unknown papal promises. Christianized Norsemen, or *Normans,* were among the Rome-sanctioned Christian armies of the Crusades into the Holy Land and northern Europe (Northern Crusades), and many of their victims—forced to convert to Christianity or die—were remnants of once numerous Egyptians (admixed, of course, with Asiatic peoples) whose presence in northern Europe is obfuscated by the plethora of tribal names Western historians have attached to various peoples from Baltic territories into Russia. Gypsies would begin to "appear" in central, eastern and northern Europe as the Northern Crusades were winding down.

The reader need only peruse MacRitchie's *Ancient and Modern Britons, vol. 1* for a more detailed accounting of Gypsies (see Chapters 8-10) who, despite their eventual persecution, were known as fierce warriors. It is also probable that their persecution did not come about all at once. Late medieval and early Renaissance Europe was not composed of the individual nations of set borders in evidence today; a glance at a historical atlas will show that there were a number of principalities within regions or territories which expanded or contracted over short spans of time through warfare and treaties, and Gypsies were often recruited as auxiliaries or mercenaries—just as Native American Indian tribes were often auxiliaries of American, French and British forces vying for territory in the fledgling United States. MacRitchie, cites Simson's *History,* which states:

> In the thirty years' war [1618-48] the Swedes had a body of them [Gypsies] in the army; and the Danes had three companies of them at the siege of Hamburg in 1686. They were chiefly employed in flying parties, to burn, plunder, or lay waste the enemy's country . . . . Francis von Perenyi, who commanded the siege of Nagy Ida, being short of men, was obliged to have recourse to the Gipsies, of whom he collected a thousand. (*Britons, vol. 1,* 165)

The reader has already been informed that, "the Moors or Saracens, the Danes and other kindred races, and the Gipsies are *virtually the same people* under different names" (*my emphasis,* op. cit. 141), so it is quite reasonable to assume that black-skinned people, the progeny of Egyptians admixed with black Asians, remained numerous in Europe through the Middle Ages, though their numbers would significantly decline after the aforementioned Northern Crusades and horrendous persecution, which included sporadic pogroms targeting Gypsy men and fighting-age boys.

The face of Europe *faded* to white, but most of us think of Europe as having always been inhabited by Whites, largely due to the refusal of Western historians to present an honest depiction—with racial particulars—of all the peoples who have occupied the continent. Black Norsemen, as we have seen, predominated in Scandinavia and other areas only a millennium ago; black-skinned Roma, or Gypsies, were numerous there only five or six centuries ago. In ignoring racial considerations, historians, sidestep the underlying causes of racial hatred that developed in Europe and was transported to America by the Spaniards of Columbus and the Puritans (Pilgrims) of England who began to despoil and murder the beautiful, dark-skinned Native American peoples they found here—the heinousness of their behavior largely unregistered in our minds because of the bounteous riches and territories acquired—apparently far more important than the lives of the people who were abused and murdered to obtain them. Western historians failed to acknowledge the abject racism that developed into a normal infestation in the minds of most Whites, so prevalent that by the time an average white child reaches school age in the United States, he or she displays behavior revealing that the racist germ has already taken root in his or her mind.

The writings of Eurocentric historians have not allowed even knowledgeable Whites to realize that despite their fair skin—and the blond hair and blue or green eyes of some—they have genetic admixtures of the dark-skinned races that were once prominent in Europe. While Western writers may focus on the persecution of Jews in Europe, very few mention the suffering of Roma or Gypsy people, and almost none reveal that Gypsies were once purely black-skinned people, whom MacRitchie states:

> . . . [were] warred against with unceasing vigour until, in Prussia, they were almost totally exterminated. But, whether the European Tartars of that period were wholly, or only partially, invaders, and whether their characteristics were Mongolian, or only partly so, still, they had been preceded by countless swarthy hordes. (op. cit. 171)

*   *   *   *   *

Before moving on to the final chapters, I would like to add a few personal notes and observations, which I hope will not be too much of a digression for the reader.

While I am not widely traveled, when I served in the U.S. Army, I spent almost two-and-a-half years in Europe, nearly two years stationed in northeastern France. Of my travels in Europe: I spent a weekend in Brussels, driving through Luxemburg to get there; on a two-week leave, taking my French girlfriend with me, I drove through the Swiss Alps into Italy, and after reaching Genoa, drove along the Italian Riviera back into France and along the French Riviera, stopping in, or passing through Nice, Cannes, St. Tropez and other towns to Marseilles, where I turned north and headed back to my post near the city of Bar-le-Duc; I spent my last seven months stationed in southwestern Germany near Kaiserslautern; three months before I was to return to the States I used up my remaining leave days, spending two weeks in Copenhagen, Denmark, finding the Danes, generally, to be the friendliest Europeans I had encountered (speaking from an African-American perspective). That sums up my European travel.

For some reason, there were many Poles living in France and working on U.S. Army posts. Some were tall, some were short, but all were white. One evening after work I drove to a small village I had never been to before, stopping at a small, unremarkable bar to have a couple of drinks. There were only two or three people in the place other than the female bartender. A boisterous, muscular swarthy man sitting at a table began talking to me, inviting me to sit down with him, which I did. I can't remember what we talked about. He spoke English with an accent I could not place but which I knew was not French. He told me he was Polish, looked to be about 40, had dark, curly hair and wore a short-sleeved Banlon shirt revealing a muscular build, though he was slightly thick around the middle.

He told me he had once been a circus performer and bet me a drink (or was it 10 Francs?) that he could lift the table we sat at with his teeth. It was a 4'x4' oakish table sitting on four legs, the top of which was at least an inch thick. Folding several napkins and placing them in the center of one side of the heavy table, he crouched down, carefully clamped his teeth over the folded napkins, braced himself for the right moment, and began to rise, lifting the table (which remained straight) with him to his full height (about 5'8"). Then he lowered the table in the same manner. I bought him a well-earned drink (or gave him 10 Francs).

Anyway, compared to the typically ashen-complexioned Poles I had seen, he was dark—lighter-skinned than I, but very swarthy, in modern parlance. I have encountered several similarly swarthy-complexioned Poles with *blond* hair in my life, and noticed a number of white Americans (whatever their ethnic makeup) who exhibit these same traits—dark skin, blond hair.

About fifteen years ago, I worked part-time as a driving instructor and learned from a female co-instructor that she was of Scottish ancestry, though she was born in the U.S. She claimed to be a descendant of Robert the Bruce, who was king of Scotland from 1306-1329. She was white, with a slight hint of swarthiness, which rendered her complexion what I would call bright ivory. She had short hair, kinky short hair, indistinguishable from the *Afros* that a typical African-American woman used to wear during the late 1960s and '70s.

I also worked (but not closely) with a swarthy-complexioned man at a stock brokerage company in the late '70s. He worked in an office adjoining mine. He looked to be in his late 50s, was tall, bespectacled, well built, and always had a serious look on his face. Outside of my supervisor, he rarely spoke to anyone in my office. Everyone called him Mac, and because there were many Irish people employed by the brokerage house, I assumed he was Irish as well. One Friday afternoon Mac came in to consult with my supervisor over some detail. As he was leaving, I asked, "Hey, Mac? Are you Irish?" He turned and said slowly in his typically serious, rather stern manner: "My name isn't M-c. It's M-*a*-c." Then he walked back into his office, leaving me puzzled over his somber response. Years would pass before I realized that Mac was telling me he was not Irish, but Scottish—the *Mc* before Irish surnames equivalent to the *Mac* before many Scottish surnames, both indicating *son of.* Mac was a Scot I will not forget.

On a late afternoon seven or eight years ago on Third Avenue in midtown Manhattan, I waited for the light to change so I could cross. A short, slightly stout woman in a soiled black trenchcoat trundled over to me. I remember her face clearly. She was dark—*very* swarthy—not black, but considerably darker than I am. Her eyes were almond-colored. She had a thickish mat of black hair streaked with gray down to the lower nape of her neck. My initial feeling was that she might be a dark-skinned Hispanic, but a second later I rejected that conclusion. A native New Yorker, I am very familiar with Latino appearances, and Latino didn't fit. Native American, I wondered. Perhaps Caribbean. No. She didn't fit those types, either, so I just gave up trying to place her.

My first impression was that she was homeless, although she did not strike me as totally homeless—dirty and disheveled with no place to go. But she was certainly down at the heel. She didn't ask for money right away. I don't recall what she asked or said to me when she first approached, but we talked for a couple of minutes before she asked me if I could spare a dollar. I never give beggars more than a dollar if I *do* give them anything, but something told me to be more generous with this woman, and I slipped her two or three dollars from my pocket, and we continued to talk.

Her English was good, spoken with a slight accent that I couldn't place. I'm usually on target or at least close when determining accents, but hers escaped me. After another minute of chatting, I gave up and politely asked her where she was from. "Can't you tell?" she asked seriously, looking up at me as if I should know. I told her I was usually good at placing accents but couldn't figure hers out. "I'm Swedish," she said a bit forlornly, looking into my eyes. Then her eyes shifted to a point across the street somewhere. Even though I had recently begun a first draft of this work, I hadn't yet come across information that Viking Age Swedes were uniformly black-skinned, believing that the blackness Gwyn Jones referred to (regarding the Swedes) resulted from a mixture of black Danes from Denmark and Whites occupying Sweden. At the time, I was amazed that someone from Sweden could be so dark-skinned (the woman would not have been distinguishable standing amongst a group of African-Americans, or even some Africans!), but I did not betray my surprise.

Then I wondered what had happened in her life to bring her to this mendicant condition. In no way would anyone—any American, anyway—believe she was from Sweden. We spoke a couple of minutes, I think, about the rudeness of people. I wish I had spoken to her longer, asked her more questions, but doing so would have been awkward. However, as I left her and crossed Third Avenue, I knew unmistakably why success seemed to have eluded her, a Swede, in America, and I wondered if she knew.

Whether the woman was actually a Swede or of Old Norse, Tartar or Roma stock—peoples we now know were racially congeneric—I see her face, clearly remember her complexion, and have no doubt that Scandinavians and other areas of *northern* Europe were originally black-skinned, just as the historians presented in this work have attested. Her complexion did not betray the obvious racial intermixture exhibited in the complexions of many African-Americans, indicating that a grandmother, great-grandmother or grandfather was probably white. Her complexion was not café au lait or doeskin brown; it was a solid, dark brown, more like bronze or burnt almond, with no hint of Caucasian admixture.

Her parents and grandparents had to have been similarly complexioned. She probably had brothers and sisters, aunts, uncles, and great—great—great-grandparents going back who knows how long to a time when her ancestors were purely black. The presence of this Swedish woman suggests that there must be pockets of black- and dark-skinned people still residing in Scandinavia despite the whiteness of most of its inhabitants. The same would be true for other areas of Europe, despite the veneer of whiteness Eurocentric historians have draped over a continent that has, to a significant degree, *faced* to white.

CHAPTER 20

THE DAMNED AND THE DISPOSSESSED

It would have been difficult to demonstrate that Norsemen were black-skinned without considering migrations into Europe after humans began journeying out of Africa. The reader was urged to use his or her common sense and logic while reading, and I feel certain the open-minded reader will find that what has been presented is far more reasonable than the standard histories of Europe promoted by Western writers. That black-skinned people never entered Europe is a rank falsehood that I trust the commentary and quotations from notable historians and scholars have helped make clear.

The relatively recent discovery of the 5,300 year-old Iceman has literally tongue-tied Eurocentric scientists who now want to dispense with racial designations in classifying human beings after classifying human remains by race for some three centuries or so and locking the world into a racially based mindset in the study of anthropology and human evolution. Western historians and scientists have been able to disseminate their view of history because Europeans have dominated most of the world for the last five centuries or more having, collectively, destroyed or undermined nearly all black- and dark-skinned peoples they encountered, along with the writings, cultural practices, traditional learning systems and values of these peoples—while wiping out significant numbers of them through warfare and genocide in the process.

Most of the above has been touched upon earlier in this work, most notably the destruction of peoples. However, a fairly recent *New York Times* article exemplifies the insidious nature of European and American efforts to separate people from their own culture in order to weaken them. The article, "Canada Offers an Apology For Native Students' Abuse" (12 June 2008, A6), reported on the formal apology by the government of Canada for removing 150,000 Native Canadian (Indian) children from their families and forcing them to attend government-sponsored schools where they were forbidden to speak their own languages—from the early decades of the 20th century until the 1970s.

Stephen Harper admitted that the "policy of assimilation" was harmful and wrong. There was also widespread sexual abuse at the schools run by Anglican, Roman Catholic and Presbyterian Christian denominations. Children, who were forced to attend these schools from age 7 to 16, were beaten for speaking their own native languages, and males, as well as females, were sexually abused by school personnel. A number of children died from their experiences, the total unknown. Harry S. LaForme, a Mississauga Indian and judge, stated at the conference: "The policy of the Canadian residential schools wasn't to educate Indian children. It was to kill the Indian in the child, it was to erase the culture of Indian people from the fabric of Canada."

The reader should recall the plight of Roma children who were forcibly taken from their families and made to live with Whites. The United States did the same with Native American children for a number of decades, and Australians did the same with Aborigine children, all in an effort to erase the culture and eventually destroy the people who had survived the outright violence and murder inflicted on their parents, grandparents and great-grandparents only a decade or two before. While apologies do not amount to much for the disaffected people at this stage in history, they are at least an acknowledgement that an egregious wrong was perpetrated by an official government. While the Australians and the Canadians have offered an apology to their Native peoples, the United States did not apologize for the wrongs perpetrated against their Native peoples until very recently, and has only offered a half-hearted apology to African-Americans for the suffering of their ancestors to the brutalities, rapes, tortures and cultural destruction they endured during the period of slavery.

Racism, racial hatred by Whites toward people of color, was the primary motivation behind the genocidal destruction of Native Americans, Native Australians, Native Canadians and the four-century European assault on sub-Saharan Africa to destroy its civilizations and denude it of its manpower, historical glory and natural resources—African peoples, themselves, being one of these—resources which are still largely controlled or dominated by European nations to this day, despite the fact that from the 1950s to 1990 African nations regained their independence from European colonial powers.

Many people, including some African-American historians, are of the opinion that the racism we know today began only 500 years ago with the advent of the African slave trade, while others believe it has been present longer. Historian J.A. Rogers has pointed out that ancient Greece and Rome exhibited little or no racial prejudice, and earlier mentioned was that Africans and Ethiopians fought with white Greeks against the Trojans and Persians and that some of the Greek heroes and peoples Eurocentric historians have led us to believe were white were actually black—Agamemnon, Menelaus, Spartans, Pelasgians and Athenians, among others. Rome had several black emperors and popes and employed black African troops (Numidian, Mauritanian) in her assaults on Gaul, Britain and Germany. By most accounts, Rome was a cosmopolitan city whose streets must have looked much like those of modern Paris or New York City in its variety of inhabitants. But these were the common people.

The ruling elite were predominantly white and had wrested the city and most of the Italian peninsula from the black- or dark-skinned Etruscans, whom they had often intermarried with. And Rome was singularly responsible—although historians don't convey or frame it this way—for the breakup of the Old World domination of western Europe by predominantly Africoid and Egyptian peoples like the Black Celts of Britain and the Carthaginians who, along with Etruscans, Phoenicians and early black Germanic and Scandinavian peoples (who have been likened to Picts) had established a European commercial network that new Romans set out to possess. If the reader understands that the areas the Roman Empire invaded—Etruscan Italy, Spain, Gaul, Britain, Germany—were areas where the most valuable products and resources in Europe (tin, iron, amber, silver, grain, pottery, olive oil) were to be found, the history of the Roman Empire and Europe is at once more comprehensible. Considering what transpired—and now understanding that black- and dark-skinned peoples predominated in these invaded territories—a racial animus must have been present in the predominantly white ruling class of the Roman Empire. After black- and dark-skinned Goths and Hunnish peoples brought about Rome's demise, the Eastern Roman Empire flourished, becoming the religious standard-bearer for Christianity, a position the "illuminated" elite and the Roman Church desired to regain after Christianity had been firmly established in Byzantium by the Eastern Roman Empire, whose territory extended from the Balkans, through Asia Minor and into the Holy Land by the 6th century AD.

With the acquisition of power, territory and influence primarily through warfare, the emerging Caucasian monarchs and elites of Rome and Constantinople, along with those emerging in Germany and Britain, began to view themselves as a higher type of human than Blacks who worshipped other gods that they, Caucasians, had never been able to fully fathom. Black- and dark-skinned peoples—whether Viking, Celt, Pict or Goth—generally lived for the day, often devoted themselves to licentiousness and debauchery, celebrated temporary, easily won victories and, other than planting and harvesting and acquiring goods through trade, paid less attention to organization and planning for the future. The ancestors of Caucasians had endured more severe hardships, the colder environment out of which they emanated necessitating planning, cunning and sacrifice to ensure survival.

Although they had entered Europe as barbarians, they learned from those they had vanquished and new Romans, despite their less than glorious preoccupation with pleasures of the flesh, treachery and paganism, finally emerged as an ancient model of Caucasian organization and empire. To be sure—considering the fate of the Etruscans, the demise of the Carthaginians and the invasions of Gaul and Britain—racism was in existence in ancient Rome and would only increase as the centuries rolled forward and more black Europeans were conquered and displaced.

With the advance of Roman Christianity—less spiritual than utilitarian and militarily and politically expedient—emboldened Roman-supported Caucasian European principalities and would-be nations developed a sense of entitlement along with a growing racial superiority. It was not the full-blown racism that evolved during the Renaissance and the African slave trade; many territories were still dominated by powerful pagan black- and dark-skinned peoples, and white European dominance of the continent was by no means certain. But enough white-skinned areas existed to allow a revulsion of black-skinned people (psychologically embedded since their albinoid ancestors were banished to White Forest areas) to develop, and the steady expansion of Caucasian Europe allowed Whites to express their racial antagonism toward all the darker races and to combine forces, as they had earlier in 451 AD, in what author C.D. Gordon (*The Age of Attila*, 107) calls a "great Christian alliance," to turn back Attila and his Black Huns in the heart of France. It had not been a wholly racial battle, for Attila's great army included German (some, presumably white) allies, but the alliance of the primarily Roman, Frankish and Visigothic forces opposing Attila highlights—whatever its catechism or precepts in this epoch—the military expedient that Christianity was able to achieve in the battle that many have acknowledged "saved Europe"—*white* Europe.

This is not to imply that all of Christian Europe was white. With what has been presented in this work, it should now be easier for the reader to envision Europe as a continent of mixed-race people, generally lightening, strongly influenced by a predominantly white-skinned Roman intelligentsia fiercely opposed to any new infringements by black- and dark-skinned people into the continent it saw as theirs for the taking.

The oldest known representations of Jesus and Mary as white-skinned emanate from the 5th or 6th century, although they would not become more widespread until the Renaissance many centuries later and not become the *dominant* representations of these icons of Christianity until several centuries afterward. The unwritten imperative that good and inherently superior Whites must always rule evil, inferior dark-skinned people was disseminated from the Dark Ages onward, and pure, white virginal Mary became representative of white women whose bodies should never again be gazed upon or defiled by dark-skinned men, although in an article by Morton Smith, entitled "The Secret Gospel" (*The Book Your Church Doesn't Want You to Read*, 178), it is noted that:

> Fathers of the Christian church strongly opposed the worship of Mary because they were well aware that she was only a composite of Marianne, the Semitic God-Mother and Queen of Heaven, Aphrodite-Mari, the Syrian version of Ishtar, Juno the Blessed Virgin, the Moerae or trinity of Fates, and many other versions of the Great Goddess. (from *Women in Mythology*)

The Egyptian Isis, as mentioned earlier, is the source of inspiration for all versions of the Queen of Heaven—worshipped even by pre-Christian Greeks and Romans, who adopted the religious practices of the black- and dark-skinned Aegean and Etruscan peoples they eventually overcame and conquered.

Although the Fathers of the Christian Church were concerned with accuracy and attentive to the sources and underpinnings of the Christian faith, the intelligentsia and monarchs of Europe were more concerned with enlisting men and arms into the Christian fold and realizing their vision of a white Greco-Roman Europe finally rid of dark-skinned people worshipping unfathomable deities and repugnant, black-skinned men freely taking and impregnating their wives, sisters and daughters. Then the Moors invaded Iberia in the early 8th century, and at the close of the century, black Vikings began descending upon Britain and France and would export their fury and dominance to every territory their dragon ships could reach.

More than ninety-five percent of books and articles on the Vikings describe them as white, blond-haired and blue-eyed, a description the sources presented in this work never even suggest. What we believe about the history of Europe and the Vikings is a product of decades upon decades of regurgitated assertions, an agreed-upon historical paradigm we have inculcated and accept as factual. While each new book or article might add a new fact or offer new insight on an old one, Western authors never allow these new insights to extend to racial considerations, content to allow the world to believe that all the peoples who played a part in European history were white. We know better now.

It should no longer be doubted that black- and dark-skinned people were numerous in Europe—especially northern Europe—throughout the Viking Age and almost to the end of the Middle Ages under various tribal names. The reader has read the assertions of noteworthy *European* historians that many of them "were the same people" under different names, racially similar, worshipping similar pagan gods and goddesses (having different names in different areas). Their cultures, including that of the early Norsemen, were often matrilineal, and their ancestors had long occupied the northern regions of Europe from the British Isles into Russia, large numbers of them inhabiting Bohemia, Moravia, and areas of the Balkans. If the reader remains doubtful about the presence of Blacks in Europe, or finds difficulty in envisioning such people in the areas mentioned just above, perhaps the following statement from Roland B. Dixon (*The Racial History of Man*), relying on extensive cranial examinations, will be instructive:

> In Neolithic times the population of all of eastern Germany, Bohemia, Hungary, Poland, and southern, western, and northwestern Russia, was predominantly dolichocephalic [i.e., long-headed], the Proto-Australoid type being everywhere apparently fundamental, mixed in the north with Proto-Negroid and Caspian, in the south mainly with Mediterranean types . . . . although among the central and western Teutons this was in larger part Proto-Australoid, whereas in the eastern, such as the Goths and among the Slavs, the Proto-Negroid was in the majority. (118-119)

We earlier noted that the ancient crania and physical types of Finns are so similar to physical types in North Africa that a racial connection cannot be denied (Churchward 136).

My less than extensive research precludes this writer from asserting emphatically, as others have, that Goths, Danes, Picts and Saracens were all the same people; however, it seems very apparent that most of them were the progeny of Egyptian and African peoples who anciently migrated into Europe as Kymry, Kafruti, Cushites, Khefti and ancient Celts or Keltae, whom Gerald Massey asserts came "by land from Egypt to Spain, and thence to Ireland" (*A Book, vol. 1,* 450). In eastern, northeastern and southeastern Europe, these African peoples intermixed with black Asian, Near Eastern and Mongoloid migrants, which would not have significantly altered their physical makeup or complexions, but must have spawned perceptible characteristics in the essentially Africoid peoples occupying territories where extensive intermingling took place. Intermingling with Caucasians would, of course, lighten many of these populations over the centuries, which would eventually occur in most of Europe—though many unmixed Blacks would remain in some areas.

Much later, the Danes who, as has been said, came to Scandinavia after a sojourn in Ireland, emerged as the most powerful of northern Blacks after the Common Era. If they were indeed the Tuatha de Danaan out of Egypt—which seems a more likely probability than their being named after a King Dan—and were a highly advanced race of people who "possessed ships, knew the art of navigation, had a compass or magnetic needle, worked in metals, had a large army," having as well surgeons and a Druidic class of priests, (Churchward 197), it is not surprising that they became the most formidable people in northern

Europe—occupying Denmark several centuries BCE, then spreading into nearby Norway and Sweden, where racially similar Goths (Geats, Jauts) had long resided.

Danes were the most royal representatives of the Norse, spawning legendary rulers, navigators, explorers and warriors, settling in European territories like Normandy, England and other areas in the British Isles, Italy, Russia and Baltic regions. Early historians and later ones who mention race call them black—the black host, black devils and heathens, *Dane* seeming to *signify* black; so when Gwyn Jones states: "The Norsemen in Kiev [modern Ukraine] in 1018, despite their unquestioned Swedish origin, were . . . for the most part Danes" (*A History of the Vikings* 76), we should understand that *purely* black-skinned people is implied.

We have covered the Norse assaults on the British Isles, especially the Danish invasion of fledgling England and Alfred's efforts to limit their advances. Nevertheless, the Danes were there to stay, and over the next two centuries became part of the English fabric. With Moors and Saracens dominating all of Iberia (Spain/Portugal) and harrying the southern coasts of western Europe, Danes and Norwegians (technically, all *Danes*) dominating Britain and northern Europe, and Islamic armies beginning to pressure the Byzanatine Empire and eastern Europe, the intelligentsia of the Christian Church in Rome must have seen the dissolution of their vision of a white, Greco-Roman Europe on the horizon, and the onset of the 10th century must have been the bleakest epoch for Europeans who considered themselves *white*, superior, entitled and unrelated to the dark-skinned people threatening to reconquer a continent new Europeans had begun to see as their own.

The Church knew that Islamic zealotry—barely three centuries old but the ardor of which rendered its adherents unafraid—could not be bargained with. Its inspiration was the Holy Quran, whose words came through Prophet Muhammad (570-632 AD) who—it is said—received them directly from Allah, God, through the angel Gabriel. Unlike the Bible, the Holy Quran was not a compilation of some sixty written works by various people, selected, edited, modified and interpolated by men with a plan of domination. It was sensible, not contradictory, and mixed actual historical events with an outline of how men should order their lives and live in peace with their fellow men. It could be easily understood, and its message spread like a raging wildfire out of Arabia across cultural and racial boundaries into North Africa and as far east as Afghanistan, India and, eventually, China—the fastest spreading religion in history, readily embraced by most of the peoples inhabiting what had once been Greater Ethiopia, despite the oft-stated assertion that Islam was spread by the sword. The teachings of Christianity would not sway Islamic adherents.

But there *had* been instances of Norse chieftains converting to Christianity, so the Roman Church pressed Christian monarchs to insist that conversion to the faith be a part of any agreement or alliance with Norse kings and chieftains who had also to swear allegiance to the pope in Rome. The Christian faith, or Catholicism, was abhorrent to the Norse peoples who once reveled in burning churches to the ground after looting them of any valuables. Although some chieftains and kings would convert, more than half of 9th century England was under the Danelaw. Anglo-Saxon monarchs still resented their presence, and author David Keys, in a *Smithsonian* article entitled "A Viking Mystery," states: "there was undisguised hatred for the Scandinavians, who were described by contemporary writers as 'a most vile people,' 'a filthy pestilence' and 'the hated ones,'" and that "the Danish community in England (a substantial percentage of the population) was targeted for mass murder, akin to a pogrom," by King Aethelred (965?-1016) in 1002.

In the article, Keys discusses two recently unearthed mass graves and skeletal remains of well-built, youngish men who had been decapitated. Radiocarbon dating of the remains places their deaths within the range of the St. Brice's day massacre, which the *Anglo-Saxon Chronicle* mentions, stating in part:

> ". . . the king gave orders for all the Danish people who were in England to be slain on St.Brice's day [13 November], because the king had been told that they wished to deprive him of his life by treachery and all his councillors after him, and then seize his kingdom"

It is unclear how widespread this massacre was, but perhaps it occurred in only two or three districts (I have not researched the event further). A year after the massacre, King Svein of Denmark arrived with a huge Viking fleet, invading Anglo-Saxon England in revenge for the massacre. Then in 1016, King Svein's son, Canute, led a huge Viking invasion fleet to England, subdued the whole country, and was crowned king in 1017.

When William I, Duke of Normandy, crossed the English Channel from France in 1066 to claim the English throne, he is said to have arrived with an armada of 1,400 vessels (Durant 494). These *Normans* were originally and primarily men of Danish descent, though intermarriage among the French (West Saxons) had surely lightened their complexions over the 150-plus years they had sojourned in Normandy—but not to the point where they were not recognizable as essentially Danes.

H.G. Wells calls the Norman invasion of 1066 "a third wave of the same people," linking Angles, Jutes and Saxons of the 5th and 6th centuries to the Danes of the 9th and the Normans of the 11th, stating: "[A]ll these peoples were the same people, *waves of one Nordic stock.*" Wells refers to them as Hunnish-Turkish peoples out of Asia, while making no mention of their complexions (*The Outline of History* was first published in 1920), which has been established by other historians mentioned in this work. Other than Wells' omission of the complexions of Norsemen, an admixture of Black Huns and Turks will not be denied here. Wells also connects the Goths to Norsemen, stating that Scandinavians and other Germanic peoples were "[a]ll . . . fundamentally Gothic and Nordic peoples" (527)—peoples we now understand were black-skinned.

Wells' inclusion of Saxons, Jutes and Angles as belonging to the same race as the Norsemen is to say that these were also black- and dark-skinned people (which Wells does *not* say, but other historians, like MacRitchie and Higgins *do*). I have assumed that Saxons (whom I have referred to as *new* Saxons) and Angles were Caucasian as a way of accounting for the whitening of the English and Irish populations; Roman intermingling with black- and dark-skinned Britons during their subjection of England (they never went to Ireland) could have considerably lightened the population but, as mentioned, they were generally not tall, so another incoming people or peoples must account for the taller stature of Englishmen, and an influx of white-skinned, taller Germanic peoples seems a reasonable conclusion. If black-skinned Danes were the next major wave of people to arrive in England, where would white-skinned people have come from if the Germanic Jutes, Saxons and Angles were of the same general race as the Norsemen of Scandinavia?

A possible answer might be the Celts, whom I have referred to as new Celts, the enigmatic Celts who, it seems, show up in any area of Europe they are needed. They are believed to have made their way to Iberia and the British Isles by 600-500 BC, so if they were white, as I have also presumed, *they*—along with Romans and later arriving Saxons—may most account for the lightening of the British and Irish populations. Donald A. Mackenzie (*Ancient Man in Britain*) calls them fair-skinned, seeming to make a distinction between Celts and *Celtiberians,* whom many historians believe resulted from an intermingling of Iberians and incoming new Celts. However, Mackenzie states: "The fair Celts and the darker Celtiberians were invading and settling in Britain before and after the Romans first reached its southern shores" (127). Mackenzie implies an African origin for the earliest peoples that settled Britain, calling them, however, *Cro Magnons,* and stating that they had migrated from some North African cultural center. He believes that they arrived by way of the Italian landbridge, calling it unlikely that many entered Europe from eastern areas, like Asia Minor (15).

As mentioned, the population of the British Isles remained predominantly black-skinned and *Africoid,* despite the coming of new Celts, and in regard to whether the Roman occupation significantly lightened the complexions of the inhabitants of Britain, Mackenzie asserts:

> During the Roman period, the ruling caste was mainly of south-European type, but the Roman legions were composed of Gauls, Germans, and Iberians, as well as Italians. *No permanent change took place in the ethnics of Britain during the four centuries of Roman occupation.* (*my emphasis,* 127)

And it was noted earlier that new Celts had no hand in the erection of the megalithic monuments littering the Isles, many erected several millennia before the arrival of new Celts. Mackenzie mentions W.J. Perry's findings that these monuments were erected in areas that were mined or worked for lead, flint, copper and pearls (op. cit. 82).

Western historians have fraudulently associated fair-skinned new Celts with more ancient Black Celts to credit Whites with achievements they had no part in, although it is not unreasonable to presume there was racial intermixture between the two peoples and that new Celts—fair-skinned Celts—adopted the religious practices of Black Celts, which many modern-day Irish, Welsh, Scottish and English folk still celebrate.

Similarly, Western historians have attached *new* Saxons to black Saxons (Higgins' Sacae), noted to have anciently inhabited northwestern Germany. However, it remains debatable whether these new Saxons—those entering England in the 4th and 5th centuries—were, in fact fair-skinned, but I will not spend much more time with this issue except to note that Wells infers that they were dark-skinned, like the Norsemen and Goths; Higgins asserts they were related to black Asiatic Scythians. Roland B. Dixon divides them into South, East and West Saxons and, concerning the Anglo-Saxons entering England, makes the following comments:

> From the fifth century onward for some time, a stream of Anglo-Saxon conquerors and colonists poured into the south and east of Britain . . . The crania from the Saxon graves of the south of England and of the Angles . . . show that these immigrants were, like the invaders of Neolithic times, primarily dolichocephalic [long-headed] . . . having a large factor of the Mediterranean type . . . They were, moreover, of tall stature, and had fair hair and light-colored eyes . . . The Angles have an unexpectedly large element of the Proto-Australoid type . . . The West Saxons formed . . . the point of the wedge which the newcomers were driving into the older population, and might thus be expected to show, more clearly than the others, the effects of intermixture with the ancient British population. (67-68)

In the above comment, Dixon intimates that the Saxons who settled in the south of England were what would be called Caucasian—tall, fair-haired, with light-colored eyes. The Angles who settled in the north—possibly Caucasian—had a considerable degree of Proto-Australoid (i.e., Negroid) elements; while the West Saxons—possibly Caucasian, as well, settled between the two aforementioned groups, intermixing more heavily than the others with the black- and dark-skinned British inhabitants in the area they settled. However, each group must have come from the continent already possessing Mediterranean, Proto-Australoid and Caspian racial elements, having acquired them, presumably, in Germany which, as we have seen, Picts, Cimbrians, Teutons, Goths, Sacae or black Saxons, earlier inhabited (and were *still* inhabiting when new Saxons and Angles emigrated to England). If Angles and new Saxons were Caucasian, they were *predominantly* so, not completely untouched by intermixture with the black and dark-skinned peoples who were, even then, still inhabiting areas of Germany.

So, I am of the opinion that, along with the new Celts and Romans who preceded them, the 5th century AD Anglo-Saxon invasions—assuming that at least the *new Saxon* elements were predominantly Caucasian—contributed to the general lightening of the populations of England and Britain—hastened by the wanton killing of untold numbers of Black Celts and Britons from the moment they began arriving. If, as some historians assert, Angles and Saxons were racially akin to black-skinned Goths and Norsemen, why did Alfred, a new Saxon, so detest Danes settling in England, and battle unceasingly to drive them out? And why were Danes considered "a most vile people," and "a filthy pestilence," a century after Alfred—when perhaps half the population of England was Danish or had a Danish ancestor—if Danes were racially congeneric to Anglo-Saxons and, presumably, resembled them? A racial hatred toward Danes is strongly suggested, and perhaps it had arisen in the breasts of new Saxons as they slowly worked their way westward through Germany (though Western historians never reveal their *actual* origin).

Their 5th century arrival in Britain would have coincided with the invasions of Attila's Black Huns into western Europe—including Germany and Scandinavia—which may have precipitated the Anglo-Saxon exodus to the British Isles. But we will leave the issue for the reader to contemplate.

*   *   *   *   *

Along with the African Moors and Arabs occupying Spain and dominating the Mediterranean, the Black Norsemen, chiefly descendants of *black* Nordic occupiers of Scandinavia, seriously threatened the free existence of a whitening, Christianized western Europe. The Church's stratagem of inducing them to convert to Christianity eventually proved a more effective weapon than a protracted military campaign by Church-sanctioned Anglo-Frankish armies, who might ultimately have been defeated—especially if the Vikings had somehow unified for the greater good of the three Scandinavian nations. However, the Norse peoples were divided—the *Danes* of Denmark, Sweden and Norway each desiring their own sovereignty—and within each, or in the territories each controlled outside of Scandinavia, chieftains vied with other chieftains for more territory and influence. And having Christianity foisted upon them by kings who had converted to the hated faith engendered more division, which filtered down to the common man, leading many to emigrate to the New World far to the west across the North Atlantic.

By about 1120, all the Scandinavian nations were officially Christian and part of the fledgling European family of nations. Much of northeastern Europe—areas surrounding the Baltic, including Russia—remained pagan. But all nations of western Europe now swore fealty to either pope of the Roman Church, which now, finally, viewed Europe as a definitive entity with the promise of vast numbers of men for any adventure it sanctioned. The fury of the Norsemen had finally abated, and Christianized Norsemen would thereafter be referred to as Normans—unless *Norman* is another term bestowed by later Western historians.

One of the last major conquests of these Norse progeny was of southern Italy, subjugating the southern end of the Italian peninsula from just south of Rome to Sicily. The territory was called the Norman Kingdom in South Italy and would eventually include Corsica, Sardinia and all of Sicily. Normans had begun venturing to Italy in the early part of the 11th century, mostly looking for employment as mercenaries but seeking any lands or booty they could acquire. In an article entitled "Singing Swords & Charging Warhorses" (*Military History*, April 2004), author Terry Gore mentions a letter to Pope Leo IX from the Abbot of Fecamp which said in part:

> "The hatred of the Italians against the Normans has reached such a degree that it is impossible for a Norman, even if a pilgrim, to travel in Italy without being stoned, beaten or thrown into irons, even if he escapes being murdered in prison."

Although the pope was allied with the Byzantine Empire, then at war with invading Pechenegs and Seljuk Turks, he felt he needed more assistance to contend with the ambitious Normans and convinced Italo-Lombard princes to aid him. Intrigues would follow within the Italo-Lombard factions, but they had been pretty much resolved by the time the Normans marched on Salerno [just south of Naples] and captured the city in a great battle. The pope then went to Germany to recruit troops, appealing to Henry III, the Holy Roman Emperor, who turned him down. The pope did persuade 700 Swabian [German] infantry and a number of mercenaries to join him on his return to Italy, where he increased the size of his army with Italians, Lombards and Byzantines eager to join the campaign. Although the Norman army is said by some to have had 3,000 horsemen, Gore believes that number should be half that size or less, adding that "[t]he Normans were badly outnumbered even facing a single portion of the alliance."

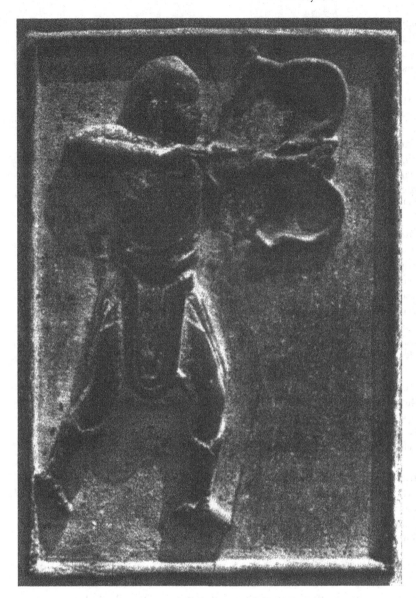

Fig. 21
Norman warrior in Italy
using recurved bow, seen
on a cathedral door. Note
Negroid/African features
of his face in profile.

Knowing that they would be destroyed if they lost the impending battle, the Normans sent an envoy of a dozen knights to the camp of the pope to pledge loyalty to the "Vicar of Christ" if he would put off the battle and allow them to remain. Regarding the Norman proposal, Gore states:

> Pope Leo did not intend to back down . . . In response to the Norman proposals, he acceded to Frederick of Lorraine who, according to William of Apulia, boasted that with a mere one hundred "effeminate" German knights, he would destroy the Normans and that "long-haired Germans, because of their tall bodies, derided the smaller stature of the Normans and paid no attention to the envoys of a race whom they deemed their equal neither in numbers nor physique."

Here we see further confirmation that the Vikings were not the tall human specimens they have long been purported to have been. Confident in the superior numbers of Pope Leo's alliance and the physical stature of the German contingent, Frederick of Lorraine told the Normans they should depart Italy or perish, and the Germans shouted for the death of the Normans as the Norman envoys departed for their camp.

The great battle took place on June 18, 1053 around the town of Civitate on the banks of the Fortore River. The Papal forces numbered from 3,000 to 5,000 men and horse. The Normans, greatly outnumbered, drew up a complex battle plan. Humphrey de Hauteville, Count of Apulia, was the commanding Norman leader; his brother, Robert de Hauteville, or Robert Guiscard, led one contingent of Norman troops, which had to be held back until a critical moment in the battle, or to cover a Norman retreat if retreat became necessary. A contingent of Norman knights under the command of Richard Aversa charged out from behind a hill into the much larger Italo-Lombard forces, who broke and fled, casting their weapons away. The Normans rushed onward, slaughtering those who were not crushed by their own fleeing comrades and their horses.

An attack by Humphrey's horse contingent drove into the German cavalry, but superior Swabian numbers stalled the attack, forcing the Normans to withdraw. The Normans charged the considerably larger Swabian (Germans) contingent seven times but were unable to break them. The Normans under Humphrey found themselves surrounded amidst the powerful mounted Germans; they were tiring, overwhelmingly outnumbered, and began to be cut down. It was then that Robert Guiscard ordered his hundred knights to charge into the German flank. Robert and his men tried to cut and hack their way to their falling brethren in whose midst he had seen his brother struck down. Gore quotes William of Apulia as stating that Robert was cursing and threatening the Swabians as he and his knights waded into them and describes the carnage thusly:

> [V]aried [were] the means he employed; some [Swabians] had feet lopped off at the ankles. Others were shorn of their hands, or their heads sliced from their shoulders. Here was a body split open, from the breast to the base of the stomach; here was another transfixed through his ribs, though headless already. Thus the tall bodies, truncated, were equaled in size [with that of the smaller statured Normans].

Tiring from their efforts, the Normans were being cut down, losing; even their mounts were tired from the charges. Then Richard of Aversa, whose contingent had routed the Italo-Lombards, returned, and led his knights into the German rear. The Germans were also tiring, but were told to dismount and continue fighting. Falling back into panting groups as other Normans continued to fight, Norman horses got badly needed rest. Then the rested Normans remounted with lances, again savagely attacking the Germans, eventually cutting the remaining several hundred Swabians down. As the pope looked out from the walls of Civitate, he watched the remainder of his army being slaughtered as the Battle of Civitate drew to a bloody end.

The battle almost has an eerie echo of the second Punic War, when Hannibal's forces, often outnumbered—fighting in the same general area of the Italian peninsula—always found a way to seize the victory. Knowing that Civitate could not defend itself against these valiant, bloody, dark-skinned warriors, Gore informs us:

> Leo sent out a letter asking them to make penance for the lives they had destroyed while at the same time offering his own surrender. The townspeople of Civitate delivered him to the Normans, who suddenly fell to their knees and begged his forgiveness for their sins.

The Normans, after all, were *Christians.* Following the Battle of Civitate, the Normans would capture Sicily and invade areas of the Byzantine Empire. In 1084, Guiscard besieged and sacked Rome with a contingent of Sicilian Muslims (usually called Saracens) as part of his fighting force. The Norman Kingdom carved out by Robert Guiscard and his son would become part of the Holy Roman Empire by 1230 under the rule of Emperor Frederick II of Germany.

*   *   *   *   *

By 1100, the Moors of Iberia had lost the northwest quadrant of the peninsula to Christian armies and would continue to cede territory until their expulsion from Spain by King Ferdinand and Queen Isabella in 1492, the year Columbus embarked on his first storied voyage to the New World. But that world was not new to Icelanders who had occupied that North Atlantic island for 600 years by 1477, when Columbus visited it to be captivated by tales of a huge island to the west and an immense continent southwest of it, which many of their ancestors had sailed to, some never returning.

When Columbus dropped anchor off the island in the Bahamas he would name San Salvador, the Norse settlements in Greenland were 500 years old and, by many accounts, still inhabited by a dwindling Norse population. The descendants of Aben Arou and the Norsemen who had washed ashore in Maine 500 years earlier were fully Indian, Native American, their blood mixed with other Native American tribes throughout the New England region and, probably, eastern Canada. How many other Norse ships came ashore on North American coasts, put in on riverbanks, trekked inland seeking timber or food only to be captured, enslaved or adopted by Native American peoples is unknown. What *is* known is that Norsemen in numbers—whether Dane, Norwegian or Swede—preceded Columbus to North America, proper, by at least five to six centuries, a fact known to many Europeans at the time and by the Roman Church, which began sending bishops to Iceland as early as the beginning of the 10th century, during the reign of King Harald Fairhair of Norway.

As mentioned, the Vikings are often discussed as if they were non-European and emerge after the Europe we know—white Christian Europe—had, presumably, come into existence (in the historiography of Western writers), so that they are viewed as unwelcome strangers, intruders, invaders, a "black heathen" menace that plagued the Roman-civilized continent for three centuries before their fury subsided. Their discoveries of Iceland, Greenland and an immense continent across the Atlantic are disregarded in favor of Columbus precisely because Eurocentric, Western historians—ancient or modern—almost never discuss Norsemen as if they were true Europeans. The question is, why not?

The answer as to why they are not credited with the European discovery of America can only be that Norsemen were an overwhelmingly black-skinned people. Ongoing, irrational, deeply rooted white racism prohibits Western historians from revealing this information, or offering an objective, honest presentation of European history. Their insistence that European peoples have always been white—going so far as to assert that Norsemen were white, despite significant historical evidence to the contrary—is fallacious. Their continuing insistence on an eternally Caucasian Europe, injecting Caucasians into more ancient black civilizations to obscure their accomplishments and make them appear inferior, has been instrumental in the maintenance of white racism and superiority in Europe and the United States.

The Norse peoples *were* Europeans. Their African and Egyptian ancestors—under various nomenclatures—had anciently occupied Scandinavia and adjacent territories for several millennia. Their discoveries of territories across the Atlantic must have been known to most Europeans, since the Fathers of the Church in Rome maintained an interest in their colonies—evinced by bishops sent to Iceland and more distant Greenland to augment their Christian progress. They long maintained trade and family ties to Scandinavia, Ireland and Britain long after settling in the New World. And the origin of the royal houses of several European nations began with them—most notably in England and Russia.

The first half of the Middle Ages—referred to as the Dark Ages, were not so called because Europe experienced a period of freakish, overcast weather that shrouded the continent in gloomy mist; saw the emergence of mysterious hooded monks in black garb trekking through the darkened land spreading sinister beliefs (although this is partially true); had only pockets of inhabitants in sparsely populated towns, where people living in dreary hovels prayed for the half-light of dawn to return; and where mythmakers concocted supernatural tales in the moonlight which were set down to writing and passed along to future generations as factual occurrences.

The term "Middle Ages" was applied to the epoch during the period of the Renaissance in Europe by Italian Humanists to enhance cultural and artistic expressions taking place in 14th century Italy to greater distinguish them from European art over the thousand-year period of time since the decline of Rome. Later historians, however, made use of the term in their writings, injecting "Dark Ages," and "Early Middle Ages" into the first half of the millennium-long epoch, to express the nadir of the period—roughly 500-1100 AD. Other than the writings of the Goth, Bede, the *Anglo-Saxon Chronicle,* and Irish and Welsh histories of the period (not consulted for this work), there is almost no definitive chronological rendering of events taking place in Europe during the Dark Ages, and much of the history we have of the period is shrouded in mythology.

The Dark Ages were dark primarily for white Europeans whose ascendancy was thwarted by the demise of the light that Rome had shone. The faceless, black-garbed monks walking through the gloom that we envision when the term Dark Ages is mentioned are the mythological representations of the actual black men and women who were still inhabiting major areas of Europe during the epoch. These men and women saw no darkness and moved about Europe attempting to reorder their lives after the turmoil the dominance of new Romans and the invasion of Huns under Attila had produced throughout most of Europe had waned. They were real and still numerous—with thousands of Black Huns remaining in areas of Europe after the death of Attila—their presence foreboding a reclamation of Europe by black- and dark-skinned people and the death of the new Roman dream of a white Europe under their domination. In this regard, the *True Myth* of the title of this work is aptly in accord with MacRitchie's assessment that the Dark Ages in Europe were "*dark* in a double sense."

Some historians, however, attribute the darkness of the Dark Ages to the Roman Church, a belief I will only comment upon briefly. After Roman emperor Constantine convened the Council of Nicea (325 AD) in an effort to merge eastern religious beliefs with beliefs in the west, the Roman Church in the west would eventually come to dominate Christianity. During or immediately after the Council of Nicea, the books that would make up the Holy Bible were assembled, and religious writings from the east, as far away as India, were purloined or destroyed so that the Bible authorized by King Constantine would become the preeminent religious doctrine. These matters have been written about but are not widely known or disseminated because they would reveal that early Christianity was not the altruistic, peace-seeking, quiescent faith we have been taught to believe it was, but that it began in militancy for the purpose of domination. Along with the militancy, torture and forced conversions spoken of earlier regarding the Northern Crusades, Prof. Hilton Hotema, in a work entitled *Mystery Man of the Bible,* states, regarding the beginnings of the early Roman Church: "With the establishment of the church in the 4th century, all schools were closed, libraries demolished, research work banned, and science was branded as 'magic'" (52).

The advent of the Vikings several centuries later was a threat to Roman dominance and the expansion of Greco-Roman civilization on the continent. The Roman Church feared the Norsemen, and later Eurocentric historians who looked back on the epoch—which also saw the Muslim-dominated Moorish occupation of the Iberian peninsula—understood how close white Europe had come to total dissolution. After the ascension of white Europe to dominance and her collective subjugation of dark-skinned people around the world, Western scholars could not allow the dark-skinned world it now dominated to know how close white Europe had come to eradication. Europe had to be made to seem eternally Caucasian, ever-unified, ever-powerful, the primary engine of world civilization. The civilizations and cultures of dark-skinned peoples were destroyed or diminishing, their written works in ashes, long buried, or secreted in restricted archives. With the exception of a few honest historians that would emerge, Eurocentric historians wrote their version of history, erasing black-skinned people from European soil and history by omitting them from their works. They ignored the discovery of the African Grimaldi skeletons unearthed in Mentone; they mentioned European peoples—Goths, Danes, Gauls, Britons, etc.—without racial or ethnic descriptions of them so readers would assume they were white, blond-haired, or "Nordic"; and they instituted the practice of declaring black-skinned people *Caucasian*—ancient Egyptians, Ethiopians, Indians, Persians, modern-day Australian Aborigines, to name a few—by standards which defy comprehension.

Like the authors of *History and Geography of Human Genes*, Eurocentric DNA scientists are attempting to validate assertions of pre-DNA scholars regarding the demography, ingenuity and intrinsic superiority of white people. While they admit their studies show that all humans retain a gene or genes which indicate an African origin, they imply that Caucasians are somehow an advanced type in human development—even though a study of all Caucasians would reveal admixtures of various black- and dark-skinned peoples in their genetic makeup. Even if the genetic makeup in some Caucasians does not reveal admixture with black- or dark-skinned people in the last 100, 200, 500, 1,000, 2,000 or 5,000 years, then the African gene or genes would still be present from the long ago epoch when African albinoids, who had lost the ability to produce melanin, were cast out of black-skinned societies in ancient Europe, Asia, and Africa—which DNA research has confirmed was the birthplace of all modern humans.

The deliberate distortions of pre-DNA Eurocentric historians, the propagation of a white-skinned Jesus and Mother Mary, along with the dominance Europe and the United States have exercised over most of the world for the last three centuries, has imbued Whites with an unwarranted feeling of superiority over the dark-skinned races of man because Western historians and scientists have, in effect, eliminated black- and dark-skinned people from any meaningful contribution to world history—which some DNA scientists, like the authors of HGHG are attempting to "finalize"—employing what can be termed *intellectual* racism—with curious, unintelligible data classifying upwards of two-thirds of the world's population *Caucasian*. If, in their numerous charts depicting genetic variations, alleles, blood groups, polymorphisms and gene frequencies in various peoples, they do not specify which are of black African, black Asian or Caucasian origin; and if they discuss, say, Scandinavian, Portuguese or Greek peoples without revealing the same; how is the reader to comprehend the racial intermingling that has always taken place when racially distinct peoples have encountered each other? How would they explain the dark-skinned Swedish woman I encountered a few years ago? When they undertook the racial history of humans, were they even aware that black-skinned people once predominated in Scandinavia and consider tracing evidence in this regard during their research in Sweden, Norway, Germany, or other areas of Europe? Cavalli-Sforza et al do acknowledge that research into man's genetic makeup can be improved, and warn:

> [T]he usefulness of living populations is being destroyed by a rapid increase in the rate at which human populations are vanishing. The mixing of formerly isolated groups is especially damaging for future research. (xii)

However, the dark-skinned Swedish woman I met is proof that more such people still exist in Sweden and probably other areas of Scandinavia, and if, as the authors state, "social changes taking place in developing countries are rapidly destroying the identities—if not the very existence—of the most important aboriginal populations" (op. cit., xi), there still seems to be enough time to locate other dark-skinned Swedes or Scandinavians. The question is: would they present their genetic findings in a way that would establish the ethnicity of such individuals, revealing that it is attributable to an Egyptian, Hunnish or Tartar ancestry, or merely lump their findings with other blood groups, alleles and polymorphisms on an incomprehensible chart, and present them as members of the Caucasian family? I suggest they would do the latter and not disturb long-stated Eurocentric assertions that only "non-African" people have ever resided in Europe.

Chapter 21

NEW WORLD OBSERVATIONS

The over-riding reason why the Vikings or Norsemen of the Early Middle Ages have not been accorded their due credit for the European discovery of America can only be due to ongoing, pervasive, collective white racism—racism perpetrated by Whites against black- and dark-skinned people all over the world, which exists on every stratum of political and societal interaction. Fundamental to the proliferation of racism are the writings of Western or Eurocentric historians who have presented readers with an incomplete and, therefore, inaccurate and often falsified assessment of history—particularly European history—which attributes nearly all the wonders and innovations of archaic civilizations to Caucasian ingenuity.

To admit that only a millennium or so ago numerous black- and dark-skinned people still resided in Europe would call into question the supposed "purity" of the white race, deeply embedded at the root of racist sentiments. The Eurocentric historians and scholars who have promoted these sentiments, on the other hand, never seem to present definitive information on the origin of *Caucasians*, other than a general consensus that they emerged from somewhere in the Caucasus region of Eurasia and that they expanded in all directions. How and why they became white is never addressed other than the oft-stated assertion that living for millennia in a cold climate with less direct sunlight was responsible—although many millennia living in the same type of environment somehow did not affect Native Americans and Inuit peoples. The evidence of the civilization they created *in their supposed homeland* and where it is to be found is never discussed—its buried cities, monuments, art, aarchitecture. Eurocentric scholars brazenly attach Caucasians to all the ancient civilizations, from Iberia to the Pacific islands, contending they were responsible for the archaic, wondrous, inscrutable works known to have existed in all the lands between them—in Ethiopia, Egypt, Sumer, Persia, India—the fabled and extensive territory of Greater Ethiopia.

To admit that only a millennium ago the Norsemen of Scandinavia were predominantly black-skinned would call into question the purported preeminence of Whites and their supposed eternal presence in Europe. It would mean that black-skinned Europeans were the authors of the feudalistic societies that would become prominent in medieval Europe; demonstrate that Blacks were the preeminent mariners of the epoch; the preeminent warriors of the age, who had nearly the whole continent under their dominance. Such an admission would be an admission that Black Norsemen were involved in the heraldry and pomp that would be adopted by later European royalty, and were the innovators of the *thing*, the earliest organized courts to settle legal disputes in trials by peers—a judicial procedure that was duplicated by other Western nations and would lead to the prevailing modern systems of jurisprudence in Europe and in the Americas.

So, Western historians converted Black Norsemen into blond, blue-eyed, white *Nordics*, an assertion the evidence presented in this work has shown to be a fabrication. This fallacy and others regarding the history of Europe and its peoples was able to be perpetuated because the written works of civilizations and cultures of peoples and nations white Europeans and Americans trampled upon were desecrated, vandalized, destroyed or hidden—replaced with a Eurocentric outline of history that the descendants of peoples divested of their cultures and history are taught in educational systems established by the descendants of the very peoples who subjugated their ancestors and benefit most from the injustices of the past.

While the Vikings were not the first people to reach North American shores, they did so long before Columbus and, in regard to European exploration, should be credited with America's "discovery." Iceland still exists and is considered the westernmost nation of Europe. But Norse colonies in Greenland are believed to have survived for at least five centuries—or about the same period of time from Columbus's 1492 adventure to the present. If the reader feels that the United States has a long and storied history, the Viking colonies in Greenland endured more than twice as long!

In *Viking America,* James Robert Enterline discusses a map depicting the western portion of Alaska (the Seward Peninsula) and part of Siberia across the Bering Strait, drawn in 1427 by a Roman named Claudius Clavus. Enterline asks: "How did such a map make its way from the Bering Strait to Rome in 1427?" (90). Enterline as well questions how the map made it from Alaska to Greenland, speculating that if Vikings drew it, they had to have explored the Alaskan coastline (and must have viewed the easternmost coastline of the Asian continent) and returned to Greenland—the map eventually ending up in Rome (another indication that Rome knew of European settlement in North America prior to Columbus' first voyage). He theorizes that while Norse settlements in Greenland were deteriorating, Norsemen had not ceased exploring and may have ultimately "gone Eskimo" (89-90). In the same vein, Patrick Huyghe (*Columbus Was Last*) lends support to Norsemen reaching Alaska, and even beyond, when he states:

> There is also some lore to suggest that one Norse expedition may have sailed through the maze of islands and passages that form Canada's Northwest Passage, then south through the Bering Strait all the way to Mexico. (161)

Huyghe mentions a tribe of Native Americans called the Seris on the island of Tiburon in the Gulf of California who mention the "Came from Afar Men" coming to their island long ago where they were worshiped as if they were gods (op. cit.). However, Huyghe, typical of most chroniclers who mention Norse contact with Native Americans in North America, states that the Viking men who landed "had blue eyes and white or yellow hair" (op. cit.), which I can only attribute to deliberate interpolation by Western writers to Caucasianize Vikings and any other groups of people—Egyptians, Phoenicians, Carthaginians—who are rumored to have made contact with Native American tribes in North, Central or South America. They seem to be always white-skinned, white garbed, with long, flowing beards; they are always assumed to be gods by Native Americans, and they always promise to return one day.

If the Native American peoples so visited had a written language, the Western authors who make assertions of visitation by the white gods never present the actual native writing stating that these visitors were white-skinned or blue-eyed. The average reader may not understand the written language or its symbols, but some intrepid readers might undertake to study the language, compare them with other native writings or ancient scripts, become familiar enough with the symbols to discern whether particular words *do,* in fact, translate to "white men," or "blue eyes," as the historians allege—just as Champollion and others deciphered ancient or dead languages, Runic symbols or the Dead Sea Scrolls in more modern times. In the case of ancient white mariners visiting Native American tribes, we are presented only with the assertions of the writers.

The assertion that Native Americans likened the visitors to gods serves as another tool of Western historians who do not offer us the actual Native American writings.

In effect, these repeated assertions surreptitiously equate *whiteness* to *godliness* in the minds of readers, reinforcing the Christian ethos which associates God, Jesus and Mary with whiteness and, therefore, white-skinned people with God, holiness, power, purity and superiority. Most of the world has been tormented with such assertions since the emergence of Christian Europe.

Yet, the visited Native Americans never seem to have taken the time to paint, sculpt or erect images of these white-skinned, god-like visitors. On the other hand, Blacks—conspicuously African, and sometimes Asian—often *were* so deified, in sculptures as small as marbles, or tremendously large like the gigantic Olmec heads unearthed along the coast of the Bahia de Campeche in southern Mexico. We are informed by Alexander von Wuthenau, in an article entitled "Unexpected African Faces in Pre-Columbian America" (*African Presence in Early America*):

> From around 1000 B.C. until the Post-Classic era in the 16th century we have an abundant testimony of African portraitures in clay, stone and jadite on the American continent . . . . [N]obody can "invent" a Negroid face if he has not seen one, on a continent where Africans were never native. (57)

The article offers more than two-dozen photographs of pre-Columbian Native American sculptures, and more than one hundred such photographs are to be found in German-born researcher Wuthenau's major work, *Unexpected Faces in Ancient America,* published in 1975.

The reader is probably more familiar with the giant stone heads at Tres Zapotes and La Venta in the area of Vera Cruz, Mexico—heartland of the ancient Olmec culture—that exhibit distinct African features. A few of these heads are estimated to be 3,000 years old and, states Ivan Van Sertima, in an article entitled "Egypto-Nubian Presences in Ancient Mexico" (*African Presence in Early America*):

> These heads . . . were placed on a north-south axis. So was the pyramid at La Venta, the first to be found anywhere in ancient America. This north-south axis corresponds to the axial orientation of the pyramid complex in Egypt and the Sudan. (34)

Fig. 22
Three views of large stone head at Tres Zapotes in Southern Mexico, unearthed in 1862.

Fig. 22.A
Shows frontal view.

Fig. 22.B
Shows side view. Note African features—wide lips and nose,
high cheekbones.

Fig. 22.C
Shows Ethiopian—type braids on the figure.

Extensive excavations of Olmec sites (very near to where the Mayan civilization would later emerge), begun in 1938, spearheaded by archeologist Matthew Stirling, found that the Tres Zapotes head was carved from a single block of basalt (volcanic rock), was 8 feet high, 18 feet in circumference, weighed more than 10 tons and had a helmeted dome covering the head. Of this head, Stirling wrote:

> Cleared of the surrounding earth, it presented an awe-inspiring spectacle. Despite its great size, the workmanship is delicate and sure, its proportions perfect. Unique

in character among aboriginal American sculptures, it is remarkable for its realistic
treatment. The features are bold and *amazingly Negroid* in character. (op. cit. 30)

While it is not certain that the models of these representations were worshipped as gods by the natives
who presumably sculpted them, one is prompted to inquire about similar representations—sculpted
depictions, artifacts, *evidence*—of the supposedly w*hite-skinned*, god-like men Western writers have long
asserted arrived in areas of pre-Columbian America, and where these representations may be found.

Like the unsubstantiated assertions of Western writers that pre-Columbian, god-like white men arrived
in various parts of the Americas, long-repeated, unsubstantiated assertions that the Vikings or Norsemen
of the Early Middle Ages were tall, blond, blue-eyed, Caucasian *Nordics* have painted a false picture of
these people, as well as of Europe. The reader has been presented with abundant evidence, some of it
from ancient sources, or sources quoting ancient works, that the Vikings of the Dark to Early Middle Ages
were black-skinned people—the most powerful of numerous other black- and dark-skinned people still
inhabiting Europe only a millennium ago. We should realize by now that ongoing white racism toward
people of color is the reason the Vikings have not been accorded their due recognition for the European
discovery of America.

After the turmoil and rapaciousness of the Viking Age subsided (or after the ferocity of the Norsemen
had been neutralized by Christianity), they are referred to as Normans—those remaining in Europe having
become acclimated to European politics and sensibilities. At the onset of the 12th century, according to
Rosalind Mitchison:

> The Normans were the men of business of all Europe . . . providing the tools of
> government, a literature, and a common standard of values from Sicily northward. They
> understood things in terms of a mixture of military force, law, and organization. (20)

They introduced a feudal system of law to England, which was eventually adopted by most European
states, and Normans would participate in the First Crusade (1096-1099) to wrest Jerusalem from the
Muslim Saracens. In fact, so many Normans participated in the adventure under Robert of Normandy
that more than one chronicler likened their procession to a "Christian Viking expedition." And a
significant portion of primarily Danish and Swedish Normans participated in the Northern Crusades,
undertaken, as mentioned, to subdue and convert remaining pagan peoples in Europe—Wends, Slavs,
Finns and Baltic groups—through warfare, attrition and torture, extending into Russia. The Northern
Crusades (c. 1100-1500) are almost never discussed by historians, but when they ended, Christianity was
the predominant religion throughout Europe—spread primarily by terror, torture and slaughter.

Although Vikings are first seen as pirates, marauders and bloodthirsty heathens, their impact upon
Europe was more widespread than is generally acknowledged, but Eurocentric historians would rather
convert these brutish, abominable oppressors into Caucasians than admit the extent of their influence on
the continent and bestow upon them credit as the European discoverers of America. White racism toward
black-skinned people became so rampant, especially after the commencement of the African slave trade,
that Western historians felt compelled to deny black- and dark-skinned peoples credit for any contribution
to civilization and world history in order to insinuate a more prominent role in civilization and history for
themselves. White-skinned people were in the process of subduing most of the world and its dark races; to
maintain their dominance, they could not let it be known that Blacks were once preeminent in Europe.

To be sure, the population of Scandinavia began to lighten in complexion, perhaps from the mid-11th or
12th century onward—although there are probably no historical writings or records specifically delineating
this process there. But, the sources presented in this work have shown that Scandinavia was heavily
populated by purely black-skinned people during the Viking Age and such a process, understandably,
would not take place swiftly, like in two or three centuries. As mentioned, in the mid-18th century, a

middle-aged Benjamin Franklin was concerned that America would become mongrelized by numbers of Spanish, Italian, French, Russian, Swedish and German immigrants, noting their "swarthy" complexions.

Like the Puritans who had colonized most of New England, Franklin and American Whites of English ancestry, were of the opinion that Anglo-Saxons were the only true Whites. This racial sentiment was at the core of the idea of "America" from its inception, and as immigration of Europeans into the United States increased over the next century and a half, "Whites wrestled with whether the Irish, Germans, and others were actually white; the dominant opinion held that they were, if somewhat differently so" (Malcomson 346).

While one would be hard pressed to locate information on the lightening of the population of Scandinavia and Europe in general, such a process obviously occurred. The Christian Church—whatever crude doctrinism it was espousing at the commencement of the First Crusade, and the Northern Crusades that would soon follow—had long associated blackness with the Devil, "the Black One," coming to equate blackness of skin with sin and evil (Malcomson 137). This belief would only have intensified during the fierce clashes of the Crusades. Time will not permit a detailed account of the causes of the Crusades, but Will Durant (The Age of Faith) cites three primary reasons for the First Crusade: the oppression of Christian pilgrims and desecration of their icons by the Seljuk Turks who had wrested Jerusalem from the Fatimids; the weakening of the Byzantine Empire due to internal discord and heresies; and the desire of important Italian cities, like Genoa and Venice to extend their commercial enterprises (585-586). None of these seems to merit the large scale military campaign that ensued, but the Church of Rome saw a threat to white Christian European expansion from the Islamic world, and a collapse of the Christian Byzantine Empire would eventually bring an end to Rome's resurgence.

Although a sizable proportion of dark-skinned European conscripts marched under the Christian banner toward the Holy Land, many were formerly pagans, forcibly converted. Now they envisioned a suffering white Jesus, a pure, and white-skinned Holy Mary, a Holy Ghost they could not fathom but who must have been as white and stern as the rosy-cheeked priest who stared intently into their eyes as they were lashed, strangled, nearly crushed under the weight of heavy stones, or burned with glowing fire tongs until they screamed out in agony that they Saw Him! Accepted Him! Loved Him! Would love his Son! Would love His Mother!

These Christian converts, like their white-skinned overlords, came to regard their black- and dark-skinned Muslim and Saracen foes (Arabs were considerably darker-skinned than they are today, some tribes black; and black-skinned Africans fought in Turkish armies) as a dark, evil pestilence that had to be removed from Spain and the Holy Land. Western historians, in addition to their other historical omissions, seem never to outline the violence with which Christianity was spread in Europe. Regarding the First Crusade (1096-1099), the most successful of these European military campaigns, when Jerusalem was taken by Christian armies, Malcomson notes:

> Christian powers from Jerusalem to Gibraltar, Scotland to Riga, had been conquering local pagans, converting them, and then exploiting their resources from late Roman times. They had done it with savage Britons and wild Lithuanians, shaggy Goths, godless Germans. This was the story of Christianity's advance . . . . (147)

The full story of how pagans were forcibly converted to Christianity might never be known, or, if it has, might possibly be stored in a number of restricted archives in various European cities. Eric Christianson's The Northern Crusades, however, does provide a poignant view of Christianity's bloody expansion. How many thousands of so-called pagans were exterminated is generally unknown, as are the fates of pagan women, who may have been subjected to torture and—if they were not killed, or did not take their own lives—repeated and organized rapes. Any children that resulted from such horrors would be baptized Christians, adding many thousands more to the European Christian fold over the duration of the Northern Crusades, which lasted from about 1100 to 1500.

As mentioned, large contingents of Norman knights and warriors took part in the Northern Crusades into Baltic and Slavic territories, as well as into the Holy Land. They, too, performed their mandates for Holy Mother, crucified Son and Holy Ghost, but their immediate ancestors had been much too powerful and fearsome to suffer torture and forced conversion—at least by Roman, English or German oppressors. Norsemen had been victimized by their own leaders and kings—Canute, Svein Forkbeard, Harald Fair-hair, Saint Olaf, and various other chieftains—although it still remains a mystery precisely what persuaded these powerful kings to convert and then impose Christianity on their subjects. Assessing the results of their efforts, the Roman Church formulated a stratagem that it and later white Europeans would perfect and employ repeatedly over the centuries—even down to today—to achieve their aims, and while there may be slight variations of the strategem, Malcomson sums it up quite clearly when he states:

> Invaders terrorize the populace until they can scare up some turncoats in the local leadership; the target elite splits; sooner or later a new leadership is installed by force, persuasion, and intermarriage; and history has a new Christian people. (147-148)

(Substituting only a word or two in the above quotation—for instance, "operatives" for invaders, and "government" for Christian people—reveals the basic operational strategy of secret governmental agencies.) The Vikings were not terrorized, but they, or their leaders, were certainly targeted, and dissention arose amongst their populations. While some kings, like Hakon the Good, wavered and reverted to the Old Religion when he realized how repulsive Christianity was to his followers, others, like King Canute and Saint Olaf used harsh methods, even torture, to compel their subjects to convert. The increasing pressure to convert is perhaps the primary reason thousands of Norsemen abandoned Scandinavia and sailed west to areas of Britain, Iceland and points beyond. Vikings who remained in the countries of Scandinavia resisted conversion as long as they could but eventually succumbed. The hated religion would soon come to torment émigrés in the New World and, as earlier mentioned, Norsemen were the first major black-skinned people the Church of Rome's stratagem was employed against.

The abandonment of their gods and religion looms paramount as the cause of the Norse demise, an unwitting blunder on the part of their leaders, which Norsemen never recovered from. The reader may disagree, feeling that one's belief has no bearing on what one might accomplish. He or she might believe everything he or she has been taught and inculcated from a very young age, viewing Christianity as a religion of love, brotherhood and peace, beneficial to all men: However, it did not begin for altruistic purposes; was not spread by gentle words; and the destruction it has brought to dark-skinned peoples and societies is quite evident to an objective inquiry As should now be obvious by the few bits of information presented in this work, Christianity was, in effect, a means of politically assembling the culturally disparate groups residing in Europe into a potential military confederacy to achieve the objectives of the Roman Church. Popes organized armies, bestowed titles and territories for political gains, instigated and sponsored wars, and worse. While Christianity would experience schisms leading to the advent of Protestantism, which eventually dispersed into numerous denominations, it was initially a religion created by the Fathers of the Church in Rome with an aggressive militaristic design, responsible—historically speaking—for shedding more blood than any of the revealed faiths. Much blood was spilled over many centuries in converting pagan Europe to the religion; the marshaling of armies to invade the Holy Land and take Jerusalem spilled more; and subsequent European adventures of conquest into the Caribbean and the Americas accounted for more bloodshed and death. Even today—continually vilifying Arabs and the religion of Islam—the United States continues its decade-long wars in Afghanistan and Iraq that have spilled into other Muslim countries; the average American or American politicians now and again mentioning God and "our Christian values," which seem to have draped a veil of sanctimony and justification over the bombing and killing of people the country is engaged in. I should not have to cite a source here.

Looking back and considering the dynamics, the First through the Fourth Crusade (there were a total of seven, and Christian armies were driven out of Jerusalem in the Third, 1189-1191) might be looked upon as "world wars"—with armies from various European countries converging on Asia Minor and The Levant to seize control of the Holy Land in order to dominate the area and open a gateway into the rest of Asia.

Although the Crusaders were unsuccessful in the end, the seed of future European world domination was planted. Being denied a foothold in the Middle East is what prompted European nations like Portugal to round the Horn of Africa to reach the promising markets of Asia; Spain to finance Columbus' first voyage to the west; the French, English and Dutch to invest energy into settlement of the Caribbean and the Americas once they had been "discovered."

Christianity has waged an assault on black- and dark-skinned peoples for more than a millennium, beginning with the Vikings, who had to be subdued if Rome's vision of a unified Europe—a unified white Europe—was to be realized. Norsemen were the first major black-skinned people to be effectively subdued by the Christian ethic; in the future, Europeans would impose their religion on black- and dark-skinned people more forcefully.

During the Middle Ages, the typical European—except, perhaps, for English and German Saxons—might not have paid attention to skin complexion, since many were swarthy and could remember darker-skinned ancestors. Many inhabitants might have remembered or heard of a black, ancestor—grandparent, great-grandparent, great-great grandparent or great-great uncle—in their family tree. But as the population of Europe lightened, truly black-skinned people became a rarer sight, and in countries where Blacks had been prominent, like the Iberian Peninsula, southern Italy, Greece or Scandinavia, swarthy-skinned inhabitants would make a conscious choice to be white to conform to Catholic dogma and cultural imperatives.

The Moors of Spain (in their varying shades of complexion), who were instrumental in rescuing Europe from the doldrums of the Dark Ages, were cast in "blackness," considered licentious, primitive, undesirable in the new European mindset, as would be newly-discovered, dark-skinned Native Americans—a number of whom Columbus had kidnapped and brought back with him to Spain as gifts to the king and queen. Future Native American captives would end up in Portugal and other European countries, author Jack D. Forbes, in *Africans and Native Americans*, stating that "at least 3,000 [Native] Americans are known to have been shipped to Europe between 1493 and 1501, with the likely total being possibly double that" (24). While the Europeans who saw them marveled at their dark copper and bronze complexions, long hair and graceful physiques, many would "show up in the slave markets as negros without a place of origin being mentioned" (op. cit.). To European Whites, all black- and dark-skinned people had become equal: all were primitive, sub-human, and heathenistic; benighted commodities to be captured, bought and sold into slavery; idolaters needing of the grace of the true God.

In *The Falsification of Afrikan Consciousness*, the late Dr. Amos Wilson—my ex-professor who gave me the New York Times article on the work of Dr. Luca Cavalli-Sforza—refers to the European writing of history as historiography—historical writing of history that is not often honest and meant to distort history and promote European world domination. Dr. Wilson ties this domination to power and economics, and asks:

> [I]f there were not a direct relationship between history and money, a direct relationship between history and power, history and rulership, history and domination, then why is it that the European rewrote history? Why is it that the European wants to take our history away from us? Why is it that the European wants to rewrite our history and distort it? Why is it that he doesn't want to present it at all? (15)

Several of Dr. Wilson's questions concur with assertions made earlier in this work, namely, European scholars rewriting history to suit European aims to project an appearance of superiority; the transformation of black- and dark-skinned people into Whites to "take our history away from us"; and European historians rewriting history in a way that erases black people from it, leaving readers to assume Blacks were not participants on the world stage; in effect, restricting Blacks to sub-Saharan Africa and slavery.

In his work, Dr. Wilson presents a psychological analysis of political, social and economic motivations of white racist mentality and the way white authors "[present] so-called facts and information as if they have no political connections or implications" (op.cit.).He refers to European history, or historiograghy, as European *mythology* in the way it is presented, which can only work against black people if Blacks have no knowledge of African history, which encompasses the entire world, as I have endeavored to show. The Eurocentric presentation of history, dispensing with the race and ethnicities of the many peoples who positively and dynamically contributed to civilization, allows Caucasians to be viewed as the primary innovators of all the processes and sciences that have moved civilization forward, increased human knowledge, improved human life—a view that is as false as the notion of white purity. If black- and dark-skinned peoples do not know their past history, are left to inculcate European historiography—the purpose of which is to promote white superiority and maintain European domination—they will continue to believe in their own inferiority, leaving the business of running the world and improving it to Whites who—despite positive contributions to science, medicine and technology—have, collectively, brought the world to near ruin through warfare, pollution, avarice and ongoing racism. Offering an example of how European historiography has distorted history, Dr. Wilson explains:

> [Whites] may do this by the pure falsification and concealment of history, by omission and by commission. It may do it by what I call a "theft of history." We, in studying Egyptology, are trying to take back what European historiography has stolen, completely falsified; to erase the new false identities it placed on the Afrikan Egyptian people . . . [W]hen there isn't a direct lie we get a history book that's written about Egyptians without any reference to ethnicity. (25-26)

Long-promoted assertions that the ancient Egyptians were Caucasian is tantamount to a myth crediting Whites with the building of the Great Pyramid and Sphinx, originating astronomy and other sciences, charting the constellations, developing geometry, and all other inventions, arts and innovations associated with ancient Egypt. Conversely, black Egyptians have been erased from the equation, dismissed, assumed to have been idly languishing along the banks of the Nile, depicted as slaves of white-skinned Egyptians in our minds—fostered by Hollywood biblical movies, like the film "Cleopatra" (1963)—doing the heavy menial work or performing servant duties in royal settings.

Eurocentric historiography has obscured other black- and dark-skinned people, and the Black Norsemen of the Early Middle Ages—who would come to dominate the affairs of Europe for three centuries, from c. 800-1100 AD—are significant in this regard. Despite the reluctance of Western historians to reveal their race, the reader has been shown that Norsemen were not the tall, blond, blue-eyed Caucasians we have always been told they were. This image of Norsemen is the revised one, revisionist, historiography, devised and propagated through numerous books Eurocentric historians have written about the Vikings; assumed as accurate because predominantly white-skinned people live throughout Scandinavia today; promoted by films, newspaper comic strips, commercials, and the tall, blond contestants representing Scandinavian countries in beauty pageants; believed, because of the insistence of Eurocenric scientists that only people with white skins could survive in colder European environs.

But since the melting of Wurm glacial ice c. 10,000-12,000 years ago, temperatures worldwide have fluctuated and, in Scandinavia 8,000 BC to 5,000 BC "the average summer temperatures . . . were about twenty degrees warmer than they are today" (Luke, Egypt vs. Greece 100). Temperatures would become even warmer so that during the Bronze Age in Denmark, roughly 3,000-500 BC, "[b]ronze age girls . . . sometimes wore the cord skirt and nothing else, just bare legs and a bare top . . . The weather during the bronze age was much warmer than it is today; it was drier, summer practically the whole year round" (Lauring, Palle, *A History of Denmark*, qtd. in Luke, op. cit.). Even during the period of the Viking Age (i.e., 800-1100 AD) the temperatures in Denmark and the rest of Scandinavia averaged 5-10 degrees warmer than today. Nevertheless, Eurocentric historians have painted Europe in general as an eternally snow-prone, frigid continent that black-skinned people could never have survived in—a belief hopefully dispelled in an earlier chapter regarding the millennia-long migrations of the majority of Native Americans out of northern Asia over the Bering landbridge who, along with dark-skinned Inuit or Eskimo peoples, survived arctic weather conditions for millennia, melanin still intact into the 20th century. If Caucasians were so adaptable to snow and cold climates, it is surprising that millions of them did not "go Eskimo" and embrace the Inuit culture and lifestyle.

*   *   *   *   *

Some form of racism has probably existed ever since human beings differentiated into varying types, sizes, dispositions and complexions in the relative isolation of the areas they found themselves in. Encountering a different type of human may have led to conflict as well as intermingling, which engendered a new type or race, though all human beings were genetically and intellectually equal—a human being from one area of the world able to adopt the culture, habits, abilities and language of a human being from another. As a major people or race, Caucasians, Whites, came late to civilization, but being human (and probably more heavily intermixed with ancient Neanderthals than scientists have so far admitted), adopted the ways of the cultures and civilizations they encountered after bursting out of Great White Forest areas in barbaric fury—retaining, however, the pent up anger passed down to them from their ancestors.

At first, it would be more anger than racism that drove them to invade areas of Greater Ethiopia; for racism implies the power to dominate other human beings, subject them to governance, slavery, laws, deprivation and undesired sexual license. And while all of these would occur to varying degrees when Caucasians began invading the world of black-skinned peoples, their dominance was not total. In fact, they had to learn the ways of civilization from black-skinned people, whom they sometimes came to admire, assimilate and intermingle with, as in the ancient Near East and in Greece, regarding which, J.A. Rogers (Sex and Race, vol. I) states:

> Grecian civilization was the offspring of the Egyptian one. This fact has been clearly proved by Sir Arthur Evans, who, through his excavations on the island of Crete, has established that island as 'the vital link between the civilizations of Egypt and Southeastern Europe' . . . . The earliest Greek gods, like the Egyptian ones, were black. (79)

The reader has heard much regarding Blacks in ancient Greece in an earlier chapter, but here the point is that the pattern of invading Caucasians adopting the customs, languages and religions of the peoples they initially invaded occurred nearly everywhere, although a warlike quality would often be instilled in those societies. In some areas, as in India, a caste system based on race would emerge early on, the blackest Indians being deemed "untouchables," relegated to the lowest rung of society. Generally, though, amalgamation and a degree of racial intermingling occurred, and racially differing tribes lived side by side, speaking the same language, worshipping the same gods, aiding each other in times of war—until Whites gained ascendancy, especially after the advent of Roman Christianity and the Roman Church's military crusade to stamp out paganism in Europe.

It was during this period, about the last quarter of the Middle Ages, that whiteness of skin became the paramount determinant of privilege, power, superiority and assumed "purity," no doubt stoked by Christian tenets equating blackness—and by inference, black- and dark-skinned people—with evil, Satan, idolatry and lasciviousness. A poem by German-born Notker Balbulus (ca. 840-912) seems to crystallize the medieval white, Christian attitude (or Christian Church attitude) toward black men ostensibly removed from dominance. I have not researched this poem to discern whether Balbulus is referring to Blacks in Germany, Moors then occupying Iberia, or Norsemen in nearby Denmark. Although there is an allusion to Eve's fall from Grace, the poem is speaking of more than this, and there is mention of "an Ethiop brandishing a drawn sword" (a footnote states Ethiop implies the Devil). The poem proclaims a triumph of Christianity, and certainly a seeming demise of Blacks, who previously had operated with impunity, especially in regard to taking women. Although the poem was written long before the period of the Crusades, it seems to express an over-arching remonstration that could span the entire duration of the second half of the Middle Ages. Following is the middle portion of the poem, entitled "A Hymn to Holy Women" (Norton Anthology of Western Literature, pp. 1387-1388):

6. This is the ladder the love of
         Christ
    made so free for women
    that, treading down the
         Dragon
    and striding past the Ethiop's
         sword.

7. By way of torments of every kind
         they can reach heaven's
              summit
    and take the golden laurel
    from the hand of the strength-
              giving king.

8. What good did it do you,
         impious serpent,
    once to have deceived a
         woman,

9. Since a virgin brought forth
         God incarnate,
    only-begotten of the Father:

10. He took your spoils away
    and pierces your jaw with a hook.

11. To make of it an open gate
         for Eve's race, whom you long
              to hold.

12. So now you can see girls
    defeating you, envious one,

13. And married women now
         bearing sons who please
              God.

14. Now you groan at the loyalty
    of widows to their dead
         husbands,

15. You who once seduced a girl
         to disloyalty towards her
              creator.

16. Now you can see women made
         captains
    in the war that is waged against
    You,

17. Women who spur on their sons
         bravely to conquer all your
              tortures.

I cannot say how widely extant Balbulus' poem became in Europe, but if it is an indication of the sentiments of the Catholic clergy and white Europeans of the day, proscriptions against marriages or dalliances between black men and white women—and the fear of reprisals in individuals who entertained such a thought—must have resulted. Such a prohibition—officially or unofficially—through the remainder of the Middle Ages would accelerate the lightening of Europe whose existence as an emergent Caucasian domain would again be seriously challenged by another wave of dark-skinned Asians—the 13th century invasion of the Mongols under Genghis Khan.

The branch of Mongols known as the Golden Horde swept westward into eastern Europe and the Balkans inflicting much the same terror and destruction as their ancestors (Attila's Black Huns) had in the 5th century, if not more. The Mongols, as well, invaded much of the Muslim world, India and China, and at its height the Mongol Empire would stretch from Poland and the Balkans in the west to Korea in the Far East. It was an immense territory, and historian Leon Poliakov, author of *The Aryan Myth* states:

> The dream of a world empire never came so near to fulfillment as in the middle of
> the thirteenth century, when the power of the Mongols stretched from Vietnam to the
> Adriatic Sea. Genghis Khan . . . had a plan of action and a code of values. By virtue of a
> divine decree . . . the Mongols had been charged with the mission of bringing peace and
> order to the whole world. (109)

Poliakov does not reveal what this divine decree was or who issued it; however, Russia was overrun by the Mongols in 1240 and "[i]t was the Khan, therefore, who became the first real Tsar of All the Russias and who is so designated in the earliest writings" (110). Russia would be ruled by Mongols for two-and-a-half centuries—almost to the end of the 15th—bringing another significant infusion of dark-skinned blood to Europe's lightening population.

Scandinavia, however, would not be touched by this last great wave of black Asians, and Christian Normans participated in the defense of Germany and the Baltic region against the Mongol onrush. Western Europe, not directly affected by Mongol inroads, continued to coalesce as fledgling independent nations emerged and formed tenuous alliances with others that were often short-lived. Largely unaffected by the racial intermingling taking place in eastern Europe and Russia, lightening Western Europe was more concerned with expulsion the Moors in Spain, which finally came in 1492, 781 years after their initial occupation. Soon afterwards, the New World was rediscovered, and the more maritime European nations felt confident enough to begin exploring it and other parts of the world. In doing so, Europeans became more conscious of their whiteness, though all Europeans were not as white as, say, a modern German. According to Scott Malcomson (One Drop of Blood):

> Whiteness, beginning in the fifteenth century, was a puzzlement. Light Europeans, going
> ever farther from home to expand their wealth and power, confronted people apparently
> different from themselves—darker. This caused some Europeans . . . to marvel not only
> at the diversity of human life but at their own whiteness. (278)

Imagine what light-skinned Europeans (in the 15th century all Europeans were not what we presently consider white, especially early maritime nations like the Portuguese and Spaniards who must have still been very swarthy) must have felt finding black- or dark-skinned populations wherever they dropped anchor—in the Americas, the Caribbean, Africa, India, China or Indonesia. Malcolmson believes that the relative "whiteness" of Europeans, compared to the darkness of the peoples they encountered, was confusing to them, stating, "[t]heir self-understandings came from political loyalty, language group, home culture, religion—not from whiteness . . . White racial solidarity was almost non-existent in early imperial days" (op. cit. 278-279).

While I generally concur with many points Malcolmson makes in his work (which borders on monumental), I find it difficult to believe that white-skinned Romans did not view themselves as white and Etruscans, Carthaginians, Iberians, Gauls and Britons as black, or dark, and different, and that race or racism played no part in Rome's destruction and/or subjugation of these peoples. Equally difficult to accept is that the rancor of Alfred the Great and white Anglo-Saxons in England toward black-skinned Danes had no racial significance—considering that Danes were referred to as "black gentiles," "black devils," and "black heathen" throughout the Viking Age, and that Whites in England were never comfortable with their presence, even after Danes converted to Christianity. However, the English or Anglo-Saxons of the period (assuming they were predominantly white) cannot be assumed to have been "racist"; their animosity toward the black-skinned Danes and other Norsemen was certainly race-based, but they exercised no power over these Blacks. They could not defeat them in war; they could not prevent Danes from consorting with their women; they could not subject Danes to English law or prevent them from taking towns or territories as they chose. The English lacked the necessary power to be racists. Clearly, though, a racial hatred festered in their bosoms.

And what drove European Whites to oppress black-skinned Roma peoples, or Gypsies? What, if not racial hatred, drove them to enact laws against their presence in or near towns when they were first "noticed" in the 15th century; to torture those they captured, brand them with hot irons, slice off the ears of women, enslave both women and men, organize pogroms to decimate all Gypsy males they could find?—activities that would continue into the 19th century, even later in some areas of Europe.

Malcolmson, as do many other historians—including African-American historians who have written about American slavery and the origin of race hatred—seems to feel that the racism of Whites is relatively recent, informing us that:

> It was not until social power took racial form—when the West African seagoing slave trade began in the middle of the fifteenth century—that white skin became socially valuable as a token of group membership. (278)

To imply that Whites only became cognizant of their whiteness after the advent of the African slave trade and, presumably, did not generally nurture racial animosity toward black- and dark-skinned people prior to this period is an evasion of demonstrated racial animosity displayed long prior to this period. It is to intellectualize the matter, like rationalizing the European enslavement of West Africans as an economic choice: *"Europeans had new, vast, fertile lands to exploit. There were millions of strong Africans who could endure the rigors of hard labor in the hot climates of the Caribbean, Central America and the southern U.S. So, maximizing profits was the chief motivation for the African slave trade."*

Malcolmson seems not to address a history of European aggression and hatred of black-skinned people in Europe which has been apparent at least since the rise of the new Roman Empire—after they dispensed with the original Romans, the more ancient Etruscans, who taught them the ways of civilization. The same can be said of Greece in an earlier time—barbaric white Greeks or Hellenes invading an area inhabited by a black-skinned Aegean civilization, composed chiefly of highly civilized Mycenaeans and Cretans, doubtlessly of Egyptian origin. After initial warfare and destruction, these incoming Whites amalgamated with these peoples, intermingled with them, acquired civilization from them, their scholars traveling to Egypt—the ancient fountain of knowledge—for higher learning and initiation into the Mystery Systems. A millennium or so later, after what is called a "dark age," a brash young Macedonian named Alexander unites presumably white, or white-minded Greeks, and invades Egypt and most of Greater Ethiopia to bring this territory under Greek domination (though Greeks, generally were heavily intermixed with Blacks and would continue to lighten over many centuries).

So, it is difficult for this writer to ascribe to an intellectualization that Whites suddenly became aware of their whiteness a mere 500 years ago and became, all at once, racist. Degrees of racism in Whites had long existed. What occurred 500 years ago was that Whites—rid of the Moorish presence in Iberia—fully realized that they had finally gained ascendancy in Europe. They had more freedom to sail the western Mediterranean—though the eastern Mediterranean was still denied them because the Islamic Ottoman Empire dominated most of eastern Europe, Asia Minor, the Middle East, Egypt and Arabia. But the ships of Spain, Portugal, France, Holland and England had become seaworthy enough to round the Horn of Africa to reach the Indies and other Asian destinations, and these maritime European nations wasted no time in venturing to the Indies for trade, and to the Caribbean and the Americas for territories—and people—they could exploit for economic gain.

Trade conflicts and warfare would often break out among these nations in Europe as well as in the Americas when they established colonies or land claims there. However, European expansion revealed a collective racial hatred and a flagrant disregard for the black-, brown-, and red-skinned peoples whose territories they invaded and colonized for their resources. Collectively, whitened European nations began a 500-year offensive against the world's black-, red-, and dark-skinned peoples for the wealth their lands contained, an offensive that continues to this day with the 21st century, United States-instigated "wars" in

Iraq and Afghanistan (extending at this writing into Pakistan). Several reasons have been floated for the primarily U.S. invasions of these nations, but most thinking people understand that the primary reason is to secure vast oil repositories and build oil pipelines to procure them. While the American press bemoans the loss of perhaps 5,000-plus American military personnel, two independent monitoring groups estimate that at least 1,000,000 Iraqis, alone, have died since that war's inception in 2003. Yet, hardly anyone in the media decries the loss of Iraqi lives in the war, which was begun under false U.S. allegations. The number of Afghani and Pakistani people who have died as a result of these adventures is also considerable, many civilians being killed by drone attacks on supposed "terrorists."

The point is that the racial hatred that Europeans and white Americans display toward people of color has become so calloused and ingrained that it, rightfully, should be regarded as a severe mental disorder. How can white scholars, whose goal as academicians and historians should be to present us with a truthful impartation of our world and its history deliberately distort their works so that it appears that white people were responsible for the world's oldest civilizations, have exclusively occupied the continent of Europe since homo sapiens came into existence, and that black-skinned people never resided in Europe, and the Vikings or Norsemen were all white, blond, blue-eyed people—ignoring significant historical evidence to the contrary?

Even more than skin complexion, whiteness is a mental outlook, a state of mind, and racism is the ultimate product of a dissociated mental state. For whatever reason, Whites, generally, seem especially susceptible to this mental condition or imbalance. I do not believe it is innate, that white babies are born this way. But something in the Caucasian makeup renders them particularly receptive to societal dictates of superiority over dark-skinned people. With effort, some are able to overcome these feelings, but most cannot (or do not because of societal pressures) and mentally disconnect themselves from the majority human family which happens to be dark-skinned. They cannot exist among this human family, but must be above it, superior. They resist being taught by members of this human family and believe they must be the teachers; they should have the final word in any conversation, not content to let stand the last word or bit of advice from a person of color.

This attitude of superiority over dark-skinned people has been so ingrained in them that their behavior seems normal, and they don't realize that they are infected with what I can only describe as the mental disease of racism. It certainly infects most Whites—American Whites more than European—regardless of profession, education, or social or economic class. Unfortunately, it also infects historians and other learned people. So rampantly has racism spread, for instance, that even Scandinavian nations from which the Vikings sprang—Norway in particular—have not challenged the EBA on the issue of Norsemen being the true European discoverers of America. Historians and translators of Icelandic sagas—even those of Scandinavian descent—have helped to obscure the race of the Viking Age men and women who put Scandinavia on the map, so to speak. By their reticence on the issue, even they have conspired to promote the belief that Norse peoples were Caucasian and evade the issue of ethnicity in their works by often outlandish rationalizations (see Luke, Egypt vs. Greece, 109-115). Have those supposedly racially liberal, once black-skinned Scandinavian nations so succumbed to the overbearing dictates of Eurocentrism that they would forego a valid claim of a Norse discovery of America? If so, why? Why allow Columbus to be universally credited with this achievement?

While this work does not claim to resolve every issue or racial aspect involving the peoples who established themselves in Europe, it has presented considerable information demonstrating that Europe has never been the exclusive domain of people we refer to as white, and that the overwhelming majority of Norsemen who dominated Europe throughout the Viking Age were black-skinned and referred to as such by historians and commentators of the period, as well as by more modern historians who are mostly overlooked. It has also shown that numerous black-skinned Europeans have been obscured by Eurocentric historians who have littered their works with nomenclatures—Goths, Britons, Gauls, Basques, Pelasgians, Cretans, Ligurians, Celts—bereft of racial descriptions. We have been led to assume that all the just-named peoples were white, or, at most, concerning some, tawny or near-white. We have been left to associate these peoples with the present populations of European nations today. But even within these nations populated by predominantly white-skinned people, there are ethnic minorities whose complexions and physiognomies hint at once larger, racially divergent populations having previously lived in them. As well, a percentage of the dominant populations in these nations often betray evidence of the racial intermingling of the past—which, in some cases, took place not so very long ago.

Western historians have continually endeavored to evade any notion of black- and dark-skinned peoples inhabiting Europe—African or Asian; however, Asian migrants into Europe have been numerous, and if historians must account for some seeming anomaly in Europe—evidence of Buddha worship, megalithic structures—Asians are typically cited as responsible for them over black Africans or Egyptians.

Combined with the anti-black Christian dogma that emerged during the Crusades and white renderings of Jesus, Mary and, therefore, God, Himself, in peoples' minds (since Jesus is called God's "only begotten son"), Eurocentric writers have generally infested most people in the world with anti-black sentiments—primarily toward Africans and African-Americans. Some black- and dark-skinned Indians (of India) resent being associated with, or thought of as Blacks, although many are nearly as black as sub-Saharan Africans, and three or four millennia ago the Indian population was wholly so. But Western historians and scientists have written that Indians are Caucasians for two or more centuries, and Indians who have absorbed Western ideas through literature and Western-influenced historical works would rather be associated with Whites than with Blacks because they have inculcated this fallacy and view black Africans and African-Americans as the backward, evil, lazy, uncivilized, ape-like people the works of Western authors have long insisted they are.

Closer to these shores, many Hispanic or Latino peoples have learned to think of Blacks (African and American) in the same way, regarding them negatively, feeling that their generally lighter skin, more wavy hair, "Indian" physiognomy is more precious, "better"—even though many of these have darker complexions than African-Americans and a large percentage of them are historically mixed with black Africans—those brought to the Caribbean by the Spaniards (and perhaps some who pre-dated these), made slaves, who yet are responsible for replenishing the depleted Native American populations in the Dominican Republic, Cuba, Puerto Rico, the Caribbean in general, and areas of Central and South America. But today they are Christian, the vast majority Roman Catholic, with framed white Jesuses in their homes, and they have inculcated the anti-black sentiments of Christianity to the point where even very dark-skinned or black Hispanics or Latinos (widely accepted by Spanish speakers in the Americas as an acceptable descriptive term) feel they are superior to Africans and African-Americans. This is what Europeans and Christianity have wrought—the primary reason black and dark-skinned people in Latin America and the United States fail to see their interrelatedness and blood ties.

Fifty years ago in the United States and in Latin America black and Latino people were burdened with the same prevailing Eurocentric ideologies that the rest of the world has been saddled with, and Latinos, generally, viewed Africans and African-Americans in the same way that the white, Christian, Western world regarded them—although actual white people never considered even white-skinned Latinos white. These negative views of black-skinned people, though less pronounced than half a century ago, have not quite disappeared. Much more can be said regarding the foregoing, but further discussion in this area is for another time, perhaps by another writer.

CHAPTER 22

A SUMMARY, AND OTHER CONSIDERATIONS

The intent of this work is to demonstrate that the Vikings, generally referred to as Norsemen, were predominantly black- and dark-skinned peoples during the Middle Ages. This could not have been effectively demonstrated looking at Vikings in exclusivity—solely during the period of the Viking Age (800-1100 AD). Most readers, having heard that only Caucasians have ever inhabited Europe, would immediately want to know how black people could possibly have been living so far north in Scandinavia—having been long indoctrinated with the falsehood that Norsemen were blond, blue-eyed, white warriors and knowing that the preponderating percentage of Scandinavians today are Caucasian. Except for Normans, known to be direct descendants of Norsemen—and primarily Danes—who would remain influential in several areas of Europe for two or three centuries after the end of the Viking Age, Scandinavians have hardly been known as "warriors" since the end of the Middle Ages (i.e., 1500).

To allay any doubts about Blacks inhabiting northern Europe, it was necessary to begin this journey with Africa and the peopling of the earth in remote times; to journey through southern Asia to Australia and the Pacific; to take the reader over ice age land-bridges; and sail the Mediterranean and the western coast of Europe to demonstrate how the earliest Homo sapiens migrated to different regions of the earth and how Africans assuredly journeyed into the northern regions of Europe from remote into historical times. The earliest migrants never "died out" in the sense that Eurocentric historians profess; instead, fresher waves of African and Egyptian migrants into Europe over long millennia dispersed earlier ones. Much later, racially similar black Asiatic tribes would enter the continent, here and there intermingling with the dominant African and Egyptian element—blendings which eventually resulted in Greater Ethiopia, long before any significant influx of Caucasians, or Whites, arrived in western Europe.

It was also necessary to consider the ancientness of the Egyptian civilization and to question the time frames Eurocentric scholars and Egyptologists have assigned to it. The reader has to understand not only that Egypt (the northeast quadrant of Africa) was the gateway to Asia and the rest of the world but that the world was anciently peopled by black-skinned humanity who established the earliest civilizations, sciences, religious systems (from an original Egyptian one) and erected monumental structures which can still be marveled at today. Egyptians constructed the earliest seagoing ships in a long ago epoch that later Viking dragon-ships seemed to be duplications of and advancements upon.

The most ancient megalithic structures and standing stones, according to most accounts, date to 5000 BC and are located in the Iberian Peninsula (Spain/Portugal), Ireland, Scotland, England, France, southern Italy, Denmark, western and northern Germany through northwestern Poland. Others, dating from roughly 2000-4000 BC, are even more widely distributed in Western Europe—overlapping the most ancient megaliths and extending over two-thirds of Spain, most of France, northwestern Germany and southern Sweden. The distribution of the older megalithic structures and standing stones (i.e., 5000 BC, if not even older) strongly indicates that the erectors moved south to north, were a sea-borne people who had mastered navigation and the transport of huge stones over land and sea, and certainly moved northward along the western coast of Europe to areas of the British Isles and up to Scandinavia. But they moved inland, as well, erecting structures in central France and northwestern Germany. Two historians cited assert that only Egyptians had the ingenuity to cut, transport by sea and erect such huge stones in these remote epochs, and we must allow that there had to have been great numbers of these people in Western Europe, including Scandinavia. Megalith-building endured for several millennia, with perhaps hundreds of men engaged in single major constructions in every individual area over the duration of the megalithic age. Women surely accompanied them, children were born, forests were cleared and towns would have been established wherever megalith-building occurred. There would have been hundreds of thousands of people (if not several million) occupying western Europe—people who would have resembled the 5,300 year-old, Ethiopian-looking Iceman unearthed high in the Alps on the Italian-Austrian border, a man who lived during the same remote epoch that megalith building took place.

The earliest human remains found all over Europe, including Germany, Finland and both the European and Asian portions of Russia, are essentially Negroid and Proto-Australoid. Later Africoid arrivals in Europe, probably Proto-Egyptian, would establish the civilizations of the Neolithic and earliest historical periods, civilizations we can only view through shadow, myth and rumor. But fresher civilizations arose in Europe, and the tribal names of the peoples they were comprised of—Basques, Cimbri, Firbolgs, Iberians, Goths, Mycenaeans—are more familiar to us, though the extent of their territories and the periods of their emergences and dominance are not precisely known. What is hidden is that they were black-skinned, predominantly African and Egypto-Ethiopic and that they continued to overspread Europe into historical times. They were often maritime peoples and maintained cultural ties with Egypt and points farther east like Mesopotamia and the Indus Valley.

Over the same period Egyptoid peoples of the earlier megalithic culture would endure until they were replaced or replenished by an influx of people called Cimbri or Kymry in northern Europe—who were probably racially akin to people Western historians call Goths (Western historians never divulging that the Cimbri, Picts, Goths and other ancient peoples were black-skinned and predominantly Africoid or Egyptian, invariably calling them Asians). Western scholars never mention the Cimbri until the late 2ⁿᵈ century BC, when historical maps show them occupying northern Germany, Denmark and Sweden. But their arrival in Scandinavia was in a remote epoch impossible to assign any time frame to. For instance, in *A Book of the Beginnings*, vol. 1, Gerald Massey asserts:

> The Kymry [Cimbri] were the first known people in Scotland; they preceded the Pict, Scot, and Gael; the appearance of the Picts in the north of the country is strictly connected with the disappearance of the Kymry . . . The disappearance is but the submergence of the name of the Kymry in that of the Picts and Scots. (my emphasis, 471)

If Massey is correct, the Kymry or Cimbri have a presence in Europe far older than other Western historians have divulged, and if they were the first people to occupy Scotland, they would have been the erectors of the megalithic structures there as well as in the rest of western Europe—whatever their tribal names. And if the Picts, who emerged out of the Kymry, were also Scandinavians, as MacRitchie opines in Ancient and Modern Britons, vol. 1—citing a historian who asserts, "it is generally acknowledged that the Picts were Germans, and particularly from that part of it bordering upon the Baltic Sea" (Britons 110)—it evidently implies that the Cimbri (Cimmerians, Kymry) were also Egyptians, the term Kymry a general designation for a numerous division of racially kindred people who very anciently overspread at least northern and western Europe as long ago as the megalithic age, out of which other kindred peoples—Picts, Scots, Scandinavians, ancient Goths, Germans and some tribes of Britons emerged.

The names of some Africoids are more familiar, peoples Western historians have designated Iberians, Basques and Ligurians—the extent of their territorial occupation of Europe differing, open to continued speculation. However, they were essentially Africans or Egyptians, kindred peoples whose territories spanned southern, western and central Europe—peoples generally referred to as Mediterraneans—whom Sergi refers to as Eurafricans. These black- and dark-skinned Negroid peoples once overspread all of Europe and were still occupying the continent when Caucasians arrived. The contention of this writer is that a late westward migration of Caucasians into Europe dispersed and gradually replaced an essentially African European occupation. That Caucasians were late arrivals in Europe is validated in an earlier statement by Michael Bradley (*The Iceman Inheritance*) and is repeated here for the reader's consideration:

> Eurasian Neanderthal-Caucasoids existed from the end of Wurm I, but their population did not reach a level permitting expansion in force until about 1500 B.C . . . These people began to invade the area of the Mediterranean basin where the Egyptian civilization had long been established. (141)

The Cimbri or Kymry, or a segment of them still known by that name, would come to be called Dani or Danes after the martial, highly civilized, and maritime Tuatha de Danaan—according to legend, out of Egypt—settled themselves in Denmark after a supposed sojourn in Ireland. The precise year of their entry into Denmark and Sweden is not certain but, according to historians, they make their presence known in the 2nd century BC (i.e., 113 BC) as Cimbri, when they march south and defeat Roman armies in several major battles. They are often referred to as Germans, as are their allies the Teutons and Ambrones. All of the above-mentioned peoples (except, of course, new Romans) have been described as black-skinned by several historians in this work who discuss racial particulars.

*   *   *   *   *

If white racism is a relatively recent phenomenon which emerged only five centuries ago—supposedly inspired by the advent of the trans-Atlantic slave trade—there should be abundantly more evidence of racial intermixture in Europe among Whites and dark-skinned peoples up to that time. Most Europeans would have been brown- or tawny-complexioned when Columbus set sail for the New World, demonstrating centuries of the free intermingling of light and dark races. While this might have been true to varying extents in some areas of Europe—Greece, Spain, Portugal, Scandinavia, Russia, and areas of Eastern Europe—it was largely not the case in Western Europe, where an organized process of overcoming and eliminating Blacks seems to have emerged from the time of the Roman Empire and steadily extended over the breadth of Europe during the Middle Ages as Whites gained ascendancy and the reach of Roman Christianity expanded. That the Scandinavian Viking hordes who invaded the British Isles were called "black heathen" and "black Devils"; that the Moors who overran the Iberian Peninsula were black- and dark-skinned and considered equally repugnant before most were finally driven out in the late 15th century; that the Northern Crusades were implemented to rid northern Europe of a multitude of dark-skinned adherents of so-called paganism; and that there was a protracted persecution and murder of originally black-skinned Gypsies, is clear proof that a racial line had long been drawn in western Europe and that racism did not begin a mere 500 years ago.

The economic advantages of the African slave trade may have been realized after it had been set in motion. But the fact that Africa was chosen as the storehouse from which to procure slaves suggests an already existing racial animus toward black-skinned people. White Europeans had already come to believe that they were a more deserving race and that black Africans were fit only to serve them. Perhaps this mental posture was tempered by deeply-rooted memories of subjugation by European Blacks—Norsemen and Moors more recently. Such resentment seems peculiar, coming so shortly after the Moors were expelled from Spain. The reader may recall that the Moors—predominantly African, but including numbers of Arabs and Sephardic Jews—were singularly responsible for the civilizing of Spain (and, by extension,

Europe) and elevating it to preeminence on the continent. How was it that upon their expulsion Spain and Portugal decided to seek slave labor in the very continent that most Moors emanated from?

The assertion that modern racism emerged only five centuries ago out of economic necessity can be filed under intellectualized racism—scholarly Eurocentric rationalization that absolves Whites of any feelings of guilt and culpability in the enslavement of Africans and the degradation, forced separation, dehumanization, suffering and death this institution brought to millions of Africans over a four-century span. Good, God-fearing people would not kidnap, enslave, torture, rape, dehumanize and murder other human beings, and Whites believe, or need to believe, they are good people. So, the trans-Atlantic African slave trade has been rationalized, transformed by Western historians into a practical, efficient, economically sound method of simply securing the manpower needed to enable Europe and later the United States to become the world's most dynamic and foremost economic spheres. Many African-American scholars have bought into this rationale, widely disseminated in books and in educational institutions, along with an equally misleading assertion that Africans "sold their own people into slavery," another evasion of European culpability and guilt that has gained prominence over the last three or four decades.

Whites, generally, have yet to acknowledge their past or present racism; very few Whites would admit to holding racist sentiments. So, it is peculiar that white hate groups and arms-bearing militias thrive unhindered in the United States. In a nation that boasts the highest living standards and wealth, and where Whites overwhelmingly dominate all state governments, as well as the national government (despite current president Barak Obama being the first African-American president), these hate groups espouse a visceral hatred toward Blacks, Jews, Catholics and immigrants in evidence since the emergence of the Ku Klux Klan after the end of the Civil War in 1865. However, most of their venom is directed toward Blacks. With Nazi-like zeal, they openly advocate race war against Blacks, who comprise no more than 13 percent of the U.S. population. One might understand people oppressed and murdered by invaders holding such racial sentiments, believing the total annihilation of all the invaders would lead to freedom. But what threat can white Klansmen, skinheads and militias—numbering in the many thousands—feel from a long oppressed, out-gunned, African-American minority to warrant a call for a race war to wipe them out?

Neo-Nazi hate groups have also arisen in a number of European nations over the last couple of decades, and there have been reports of African immigrants being beaten in Italy and Russia by skinhead types. As I write, just recently (July, 2011) a white, blond-haired, 32 year-old Norwegian man was arrested for setting off a huge fertilizer bomb in downtown Oslo killing eight people, then going to a small island where he methodically shot down at least 68 young people (most, presumably, white Norwegians) who were on an annual Labor Party retreat there. He reportedly told authorities he was on "a mission to save Europe from a 'Muslim takeover'" (The Wall Street Journal, 26 Jul. 2011, "Gunman is Ordered Held, Warns of More Terror Cells"), a growing concern for a number of European countries over the last decade or two.

The threat to Whites is psychological, a mental alienation or malfunction most refuse to admit they have, which their learned professionals—scientists, psychologists, psychiatrists—have never seriously addressed. Dr. Frances Cress Welsing assesses this disorder accurately when she states: "The white personality, in the presence of color [i.e., non-whites] can be stabilized only by keeping blacks and other non-whites in obviously inferior positions" (9). But it is deeper than that. In the extreme, this white personality disorder has driven Whites to resort to the wanton murder—and sometimes the genocide, or near genocide—of black- and dark-skinned peoples who pose no obvious threat to them—Gypsies, Native Americans, Australian Aborigines, Africans, African-Americans.

In the case of African-Americans, this destructive personality disorder is most obvious in the number of black men killed by white police officers in most major cities throughout the U.S., killings that have steadily risen since the early 1970s. Time does not allow a detailed sketch of such killings—often of unarmed Blacks, male but sometimes female, occurring on streets, in cars or in their own homes. Even if police misdeeds are caught on tape—like the beating of Rodney King in Los Angeles in 1992, where someone video-taped several white police officers beating this African-American man with nightsticks for several minutes after a chase—white police officers are almost always absolved of any crime. The jury watched replays of the King beating many times, yet acquitted the officers of any wrongdoing, sparking two days of rioting by Blacks not only in Los Angeles but in several other cities. In one or two cities, even some incensed Whites took part in the rioting.

But on the whole, Whites in the U.S. have exhibited a predilection to abuse, cheat, humiliate, punish, beat and kill Blacks and other people of color without compunction. All Whites are not predisposed to such behavior. There were white Abolitionists who opposed slavery in the United States in the 19th century; Whites who assisted talented Blacks in their quests for education or careers that were mostly closed to them; Whites who championed civil rights for Blacks and Native Americans. There are courageous white women who marry or consort with black men who face the ignorance of the general white populace, which often includes family members; and there are Whites who endeavor to simply treat Blacks and people of color as they, themselves, would like to be treated. But such Whites have always been in the minority in the United States, while the vast majority of Whites harbor the same racial antipathy toward Blacks and people of color that has been inexorably passed down for generations—many of them without being aware of it, so ingrained has racism become, especially in American society. White antipathy and racism toward Blacks and other peoples of color has been evident since the Puritans and Pilgrims debarked at Plymouth Rock in 1620, soon afterwards going about the business of killing Native Americans and acquiring their lands tribe by tribe.

During the Viking Age, as mentioned, Norsemen were too powerful and numerous to be militarily assaulted, though their presence in northern Europe was clearly unsettling to fledgling white European nations. The perfidious conversion strategy the Roman Church employed divided and eventually subdued them—a "divide-and-conquer" stratagem European nations would later adopt and employ in all their dealings with non-white peoples wherever they went in the world. It worked in Africa, the Americas, and is currently being employed in the Middle East. In the case of the latter region, religious conversion is not the stated goal. Muslims are far too staunch in their adherence to Islam for the West to effectuate religious change. However, seeds of distrust have been sewn among Muslim nations preventing their unification, which Arab leaders like Egyptian president Gamel Abdel Nasser tried to achieve in the late 1950s and early '60s.

The stratagem of internal disruption, sowing seeds of disharmony within nations to bring about brother-against-brother conflict, was first employed against the Vikings—the militant early Roman Church achieving its aim of Norse destabilization and the eventual dissolution of once powerful Norse peoples. Citing reputable historians, I have endeavored to identify some black- and dark-skinned peoples Western historians have never taken the time to describe, least of all the Black Norsemen, fearsome warriors who impacted affairs in Europe for more than three centuries, while remaining militarily unassailed in their northern realms.

In the Shetlands, as mentioned, the Norwegian invaders were described as "swarthy," or black. In the British Isles (Ireland included) Norsemen were called "black heathen" and "black gentiles," and one has to wonder when and why Irish historians began calling Norwegians Finn gaill or "white foreigners," unless the term is a later affectation of Eurocentric historians, since the Irish Chronicles refer to them as "dub gint" and "dubh Gennti" (see Charles ix). They were black whether Danes, Norwegians or Swedes—Swedes later referred to as Rus, Rhos, or Varangians in Balkan and Russian regions; however, the term Dane seems to have applied generally to all Vikings, not just those of Denmark. They were black when they invaded Normandy under Rollo in 911 (or possibly earlier); still essentially black when they invaded England under William the Conqueror in 1066; and still noticeably Negroid when, as Normans, they carved out the Norman Kingdom in South Italy during the mid-11th century.

So, Vikings, Norsemen, were unquestionably black when they began to venture across the North Atlantic to Iceland and Greenland from 870 AD onwards—Greenland for certain, part of North America—some 600 years before Columbus and his Spanish fleet waded ashore on Watling Island in the Caribbean. From Norse artifacts found scattered in several locations of what is now Canada, it is understood that Vikings sailed farther afield, establishing a settlement at L'Anse-aux-Meadows (Newfoundland) and exploring the

North American coastline and rivers. They sailed north into Baffin Bay and perhaps Baffin Island; sailed south to Massachusetts and farther south; and sailed west across northern Canada leaving an indication, in the form of a map, that they reached Alaska and the Pacific Ocean.

Columbus, on the other hand, set neither eye nor foot on the North American mainland, yet he is credited with "discovering" America, a continent some Europeans, and certainly the Fathers of the Church, learned the existence of from the Vikings more than five centuries before. The rationale we have been given for Columbus being accorded America's discoverer is ludicrous and, frankly, dishonest in light of what the reader has been presented with in this work. It is hoped that the reader can now fathom the extent that Eurocentric Western historians, scholars and scientists have gone to—will go to—to diminish or ignore the achievements of black-skinned peoples in the history of the world, if not erase them from history altogether. In this regard, they have been most successful in expunging their presence in Europe. Their motivation is simple: a collective and consuming racism toward black- and dark-skinned people and the need to uphold the myth of white superiority and dominance in the world—with little regard for truthfulness.

The Caucasian psyche seems unable to tolerate the thought of black people on an equal plane with them—a deep-rooted psychosis that most Whites seem to suffer from, including their scientists and historians, who have resorted to converting black-skinned peoples into Whites in their works—from ancient Egyptians to Norsemen—in order to assuage any negative psychological perceptions of inferiority. When Caucasians emerged from the Great White Forest, they found advanced cultures in almost whatever direction they went. They found the civilizations they stormed into wondrous, terrifying—along with the black-skinned people responsible for producing them and endeavored to destroy what they had never conceived and could not understand.

As they gradually acquired civilization, they were determined to dominate the peoples whose territories they had invaded. When they learned to write, they recorded history from the point they found themselves in its midst. As the centuries wore on white historians, knowing there was no evidence of civilization to speak of in the Caucasian homeland of the Great White Forest, began asserting that Caucasian invaders were the founders of the ancient civilizations in Greece, Egypt, Mesopotamia and India (i.e., Greater Ethiopia). Western historians—merely because Caucasian invaders intermingled with the original inhabitants—have long asserted that the ancient Egyptians were Caucasian; ancient Mycenaeans and Greeks were Caucasians; ancient Dravidians and Indians were Caucasian, although the peoples in these areas remained essentially black- and dark-skinned, albeit lightened in complexion and unalike in nature to actual Caucasians whose aggression has led to dominance over the modern world. Historian Michael Bradley (*The Iceman Inheritance*) aptly describes the destructive impact on humanity that Caucasians have wrought since their emergence when he states: "The Caucasoids manifestly expanded culturally and geographically, often at the expense of other races of men" (28).

Whites continue to exhibit a callous indifference to the lives of black- and dark-skinned people, unconcerned with bombing nations of civilized dark-skinned inhabitants "back into the Stone Age"—feasting on bombs, bullets, pain, blood and death, savoring the taste. In earlier times there were different weapons, but the Caucasian appetite for blood was the same concerning Blacks and peoples of color once Whites became dominant in Europe and set out to possess the world's riches.

Historians attaching Caucasians to ancient civilizations while denying the actual builders credit for their achievements has psychologically infused Caucasians with a feeling of superiority over the dark-skinned races which they are determined to maintain. Most Blacks and people of color, disinherited by Eurocentric historians of their glorious past achievements, unable to locate their ancient role in civilizing the world in the books authored by Western historians, believing in a religion imposed upon them when Europeans invaded the Mother Continent and other areas of the world, have been psychologically damaged—in their hearts, most convinced that their inferior stations in the Western societies they live in are somehow justified.

Such feelings would not be sustainable if Eurocentric historians had presented a true outline of history; if they had always written that the ancient Egyptians were, indeed, black-skinned Africans who very anciently charted the universe, developed advanced mathematics, measured the circumference of the earth, built stupendous monuments, including the perfectly constructed Great Pyramid with all its mathematical and astronomical properties; spread themselves throughout most of the world, carrying civilization with them; and built the earliest ocean-going vessels which were able to transport huge stones to far away shores long before Caucasians made their way into Europe.

Such feelings of inferiority would not be sustainable if Eurocentric historians had always let it be known that Hellenes or white Greeks invaded a black-skinned, Egyptian-oriented, highly civilized world, which they largely destroyed, but from which they received an early dose of civilization, as they would when they descended in barbaric fury into the Indus Valley, the eastern extremity of Greater Ethiopia, which had contacts with China, Southeast Asia and Indonesia—lands inhabited by predominantly black-and dark-skinned, racially similar peoples. The Romans—new Romans—emerged to prominence after the Hellenic Greeks, but both these predominantly Caucasian entities would continue to abide the worship of black Isis and uphold the black gods of Egyptian origin already existing in the lands they would eventually come to dominate.

Feelings of inferiority in Blacks and non-white peoples would not be sustainable if Eurocentric historians had always let it be known that the Vikings were predominantly black- and dark-skinned peoples, numerous northern black Europeans who had long inhabited Scandinavia and completely dominated affairs in Europe throughout most of the Middle Ages (i.e., 500-1500 AD). The knowledge just outlined—knowledge that black-skinned peoples were empire builders, innovators, explorers, scientists, seafarers, warriors—would have infused Blacks and people of color with a more positive spirit and they would have long ago broken the mental chains that continue to restrict them. So, of course, Eurocentric historians have always kept such information hidden in order to maintain the psychological advantages they have imbued themselves with. But this psychological edge is built on deception and falsehood.

*   *   *   *   *

Some readers, even non-white readers, may resent this writer's attaching them or their ancestors to "black- and dark-skinned" peoples, a term used often in this work. They may be especially offended over the term Negroid or black being applied to their ancestors, the term having been long applied to people from sub-Saharan Africa—Africa and Africans having been so long associated with primitiveness, ignorance, savagery, immodesty, and ape-like, sub-human humanity. The stigma attached to Negroid and black is the product of the writings of Western historians, scientists and scholars who needed to denigrate black-skinned Africans during the period of the trans-Atlantic slave trade as a way of justifying their involvement in it. Negativity toward black-skinned people has been disseminated throughout the world. But Africa was—is—the Mother Continent of all humanity, the original source of the world's earliest civilizations. Ancient Egypt (i.e., northeast quadrant of Africa), the most advanced civilization for millennia, dispersed colonists who spread Egyptian knowledge, ingenuity, religion and civilization over most parts of the habitable earth.

Eurocentric Western historians are most responsible for the negativity attached to blackness, a contrivance that worked so well that most people resent being associated with the continent or its people. However, a minority of more honest historians, in particular Gerald Massey, Sergi and Churchward (not to forget modern African and African-American historians like John Henrik Clarke, J.A. Rogers, Cheikh Anta Diop and others) have demonstrated the falseness of the negative images attached to Africa and Africans. Neither Hellenic Greeks nor Romans would have agreed with such negative sentiments, nor did any other invaders of Egypt. My use of the terms Proto-Australoid, Negroid or black to describe the originally African people who settled Australia, India, Europe, Mesopotamia, the Near East, Finland or Central Asia is in conformity with these more honest historians—scholars and scientists who demonstrate that humanity is interconnected and that racially different types of humanity ultimately share the same ancient origin and ancestry. The reader is encouraged to regard Africa in the context of being the origin of explorers, colonizers, builders and disseminators of civilization and to at least make a serious mental attempt to put aside the negative feelings and concepts that Eurocentric writers have engendered over the last several centuries regarding Africans and black skin.

Most historians seem to believe that Caucasians emanated from somewhere in Eurasia—the area I have designated the Great White Forest. No one would doubt that Caucasians—however they lost the ability to produce melanin—eventually expanded into areas of Asia, the Near East and North Africa once they emerged. For whatever reason, they were most successful in overspreading western Europe where they eventually dispersed an earlier settled Africoid population before spilling over to the Americas, virtually displacing the original inhabitants of North America over the last five centuries. While racial demographics are changing, we can say that Whites or Caucasians predominate in the United States and Canada as well as in Europe into Russia. Although Caucasians are composed of varying genetic mixtures, Western historians contend that white-skinned peoples predominate in the abovementioned lands.

DNA research has now validated what a number of mostly ignored historians and anthropologists have argued for two centuries or more: Africa was the birthplace of Homo sapiens or modern man and black-skinned humanity spread from there to most parts of the earth in remote times—continuing to send waves of humanity into Europe down to historical times. Yet, Western historians have generally restricted Africans to the Mother Continent—implying that Ethiopians, Egyptians, Hamites and other North African Blacks were not really black-skinned; that the earliest migrants out of North Africa into the Middle East, Mesopotamia and India on their long journey to Australia beginning at least 100,000 years ago, were not really black but somehow Caucasian; that Negroid Grimaldis "died out" in Europe to be suddenly replaced by Cro Magnon men out of nowhere; and restrict black Africans to sub-Saharan Africa so that no one can fathom the extent of the ancient black African dispersal over most of the earth—including the northern reaches of Europe, where Goths, Cimbri (Kymry), Basques, Britons, Picts and Danes would remain the most prominent remnants of once predominant African peoples in western Europe after the arrival and expansion of significant numbers of Caucasians into the continent.

The assignation by Western historians of various tribal names to these peoples has obscured the fact that they were racially similar and originally of African ancestry as several authors cited in this work have attested. So, while Western historians declare peoples from Russia westward through Europe and into North America Caucasian, their colorless, tribal designations of peoples—particularly in Europe—has prevented readers from visualizing the extent of African expansion into that continent, Asia and other areas of the earth, restricting Africans to Africa, alone in our minds. To further restrict our visualization of African expansion, Western historians generally declared Africans who migrated out of the northeast quadrant somehow non-African as soon as they left the continent, assigned them tribal names—Medians, Elamites, Mesopotamians—and call them Asians. They do this after having initially confused us by dividing peoples within the northeast quadrant of Africa into Semites, Hamites, Kushites and other designations, asserting that they were lighter-skinned than sub-Saharan Africans, even though ancient Greek writers referred to Ethiopians—coming out of the same northeast quadrant of Africa—as black, sun-burnt, sable-skinned, and despite the evidence that all such peoples emanated from points farther south, or sub-Saharan Africa.

The proliferation of tribal names employed by Eurocentric historians has clouded our understanding of the peoples who anciently overspread Europe—black-skinned, Africoid peoples, perhaps predominantly Egyptian—whose presence is attested to by the Negroid remains unearthed from Europe into Asia and the megalithic structures found throughout western Europe up through Scandinavia into Sweden, which only Egyptians had the ingenuity to erect.

*   *   *   *   *

If a minor historian like this writer has found sufficient evidence demonstrating that the Norsemen of the Viking Age were predominantly black- and dark-skinned—the remnant of essentially African peoples who once predominated in Europe—it is certain that more authoritative historians, particularly those who have published histories on the Vikings, must have come across this same evidence and chosen to ignore it—hoping no one would ever challenge their oft-repeated assertions that the Vikings were blond, blue-eyed and white. The reader might feel that the information offered regarding Norse "color names" does not provide convincing evidence that Vikings were comprised of black-and dark-skinned peoples and continue to believe that references to black in these names referred to hair color, dispositions or the color of the chain mail they often wore into battle. Undoing the effects of what one has inculcated and accepted as truthful over a lifetime can be a terribly stressful, guilt-ridden undertaking. One must also question and judge the honesty of the authoritative sources, or the society responsible for impressing upon him his original, long-held assumptions and seriously consider the new and provocative information now thrust his way.

Norse color names are not something dreamed up by this writer; they are derived from historians far more authoritative than I, like David MacRitchie and Don Luke, who spend considerable time discussing individuals who bore such names and demonstrating that hair color was not a factor behind sobriquets like—the Black or—the Red (see Luke, Egypt vs. Greece, "Preserving the Eurosupremacist Myth," 110-115). If the reader is now able to fathom that the Caucasian psyche seems unable to accept black-skinned people being on equal footing with Whites, he or she might now understand why Columbus is accorded recognition as the discoverer of America over the Vikings, whom the Fathers of the Church knew to have been the discoverers from the outset—nearly 600 years before Columbus' first voyage.

Besides Norse color names, there are the chronicles to consider, chronicles from the Viking Age referring to Norsemen as "Dubh Gaill" (the black foreigners), "gentiles nigri" (the black heathen), and "y Normanyeit duon" (the black Normans) that historian B.G. Charles plainly affirms (*Old Norse Relations with Wales,* ix), while asserting that the Welsh saw no difference between the complexions of Norwegians and Danes—Danes styled emphatically black by chroniclers imprudent enough to discuss the race of Norsemen.

Regrettably, these people of Viking Age Scandinavia are mostly faceless unless the reader, weighing the evidence that has been presented to him or her against what he or she now understands was inaccurate and false information, has made an effort to envision black faces under Viking helmets and coats of mail, the piercing eyes of black men trained on the shores their dragon-ships approached—one hand holding a decorated, round shield, the other a long sword of temper that could slice a foe from shoulder to waist with one mighty stroke. If the reader can then envision a thousand such men on twenty dragon-ships slinking onto a beachhead, debarking, and sloshing through the surf to attack an unsuspecting town, he or she will have begun to undo the false image of Vikings that Eurocentric historians have long promoted and to understand the terror Norsemen evoked for more than three centuries in a fledgling, whitening Europe through the first six or seven centuries of the Middle Ages.

The Norse conversion to Christianity and the end of the Viking Age seems to have inaugurated the onset of a collective, protracted assault by European nations against black- and dark-skinned people throughout the European continent. When the Northern Crusades drew to a close and the New World was rediscovered by Columbus, the most powerful European nations of the day began to invade areas of the black- and dark-skinned world which, though interrupted for brief periods, has not relented since Whites and Christianity gained ascendancy in Europe.

Europe, itself, has seen its internecine conflicts: the Hundred Years' War; wars between Spain, England and France for dominance in Europe as well as in the New World; the Napoleonic Wars; World Wars I and II. But when the dust of war settled, European nations resumed their economic and military stranglehold on the black- and dark-skinned nations of the earth, still glaringly in evidence today in Afghanistan, Iraq, Pakistan, as well as in the threats against Iran (ancient Persia) and behind the scenes in a number of other conflicts in Africa, Asia, and Central and South America.

Sadly, the United States has taken over the role of chief imperialist oppressor from European countries who were once the primary imperialists and colonizers in the dark-skinned world. Most Americans are content with their wide-screen TVs, iPods, Blackberrys, and the assortment of games and websites accessible on their computers. Watching sports, reality shows and nonsensical sitcoms on television satisfies them more than reading and, perhaps, uncovering the origins of some of the world's ongoing conflicts.

Many young people, especially African-Americans, spend far too much time listening to music, some even believing that they can obtain knowledge through the lyrics in a song. While a song or rap may mention a history-related reference or a historical personage or two in its lyrics, it is only a phrase and does not teach the listener about anything—unless the listener seeks more information in an encyclopedia or book when the song is done. Reading among younger people, in general, has seriously declined, and listening to hours of music, although pleasurable, severely limits the ability to focus on matters of more importance. For younger African-Americans the distaste for reading is extremely regrettable considering that just over a century-and-a-half ago enslaved Blacks in the U.S. considered learning to read and write of paramount importance—a gateway to knowledge and freedom.

Most people have heard of the Jewish Diaspora out of the Near East and the African Diaspora to the Caribbean and the Americas during the period of the African Slave Trade. Little is said of the earliest migrations of modern man out of Africa into Europe, Asia and other areas of the earth. Almost unknown is the predominance of black- and dark-skinned people in western Europe and that such people—called ancient Celts, Britons, Iberians, Basques, and in northern Europe Picts, Scots, Cimbri, Goths, Danes and Norsemen—remained a dominating presence in northern Europe up to a millennium ago. What can also be called a Diaspora took place when Blacks—after Scandinavian nations became Christianized and part of a reconstituted Europe—were systematically killed or expelled from Europe, a process that would continue for several centuries, generally ending with the expulsion of the Moors from Iberia, but technically continuing with the ostracization and/or expulsion of now mostly light-skinned European Gypsies taking place in several European countries—most recently in France.

There is a need devote more time to studying history, but not the standard Western histories we have become accustomed to and always considered unassailable.

The popular historical works—the works one finds in libraries and on bookstore shelves—have generally not presented a completely honest picture. As the reader has hopefully seen, Western historians have not given us an accurate historical recitation, deliberately omitting a significant portion of mankind from their historical works. While many African-Americans, Afro-Caribbeans, Latinos or Latin Americans aspire to be singers, rappers, athletes and assorted entertainers, there is certainly a need for more of these black and non-white peoples to pursue careers as teachers, zoologists, biochemists, nurses, doctors—but as importantly, historians, anthropologists, writers, and DNA scientists to counter-balance the information received primarily from one race of people, which we have been programmed to accept without challenge. Those who have benefited from the injustices of imperialism, exploitation, war, racism and murder continue to thrive, passing along their ill-fashioned wealth to their children and others of their race. Those whose ancestors suffered the loss of their lands, dignity, wealth, cultures and lives seem not to fathom the precariousness of their repressed condition, content to allow others to run a world their forebears once explored and civilized. Such dynamism must be rekindled, with the guiding light of truth shining in the breast of those who hope to bring justice and equanimity to a world long poisoned by racism and unrestrained arrogance. Hopefully, this work will inspire others, regardless of race, toward this noble goal—a journey that one might begin by remembering: The only reason the Vikings or Norsemen are not credited with discovering America is because they were black-skinned peoples.

WORKS CITED

Sagas Cited and/or Consulted

Egil's Saga. Trans. Christine Fell. London and Melbourne: J.M. Dent & Sons Ltd., 1975.

Eyrbyggja Saga. Trans. Paul Schach and Lee M. Hollander. Omaha: University of Nebraska Press, 1959.

Gisli Sursson's Saga and The Saga of the People of Eyri. Trans. Leifur Eiriksson. London: Penguin Books, 1977.

Laxdaela Saga. Trans. Magnus Magnusson and Hermann Palsson. London: Penguin Books, 1988.

Njal's Saga. Trans. Magnus Magnusson and Hermann Palsson. London: Penguin Books, 1960.

Orkneyinga Saga. Trans. Magnus Magnusson and Paul Edwards. London: Penguin Books, 1978.

The Sagas of the Icelanders. Trans. Katrina C. Attwood, George Clark, Ruth Ellison et al. New York and London: Penguin Books, 2000.

Saga of King Hrolf Kraki. Trans. Jesse L. Byock. London: Penguin Books, 1998.

Sturluson, Snorri. *Heimskringla.* Trans. Lee M. Hollander. Austin, Texas: University of Texas Press, 1991.

—.*King Harald's Saga.* Trans. Magnus Magnusson and Hermann Palsson. New York: Dorset Press, 1986.

—.*The Prose Edda.* Trans. Jean I. Young. Los Angeles and London: University of California Press, 1992.

The Vinland Sagas. Trans. Magnus Magnusson and Hermann Palsson. London: Penguin Books, 1965.

WORKS CITED (General)

Amen Ra Un Nefer. *Metu Neter.* vol. 1. Brooklyn, New York: Kamit Publications, 1990.

AMERICAN EXPERIENCE. *The Massie Affair.* WGBH-TV Education Foundation, 2005.

Anglo-Saxon Chronicle. Trans. G.N. Garmonsway. London: J. M. Dent & Sons Ltd., 1967.

Ardrey, Robert. *African Genesis.* New York: Atheneum, 1961.

Asante, Melefe Kete, and Anna Mazama, eds. *Egypt vs. Greece and the American Academy.* Chicago: African American Images, 2002.

Baker, Timothy. *The Normans. USA:* The Macmillan Company, 1969.

Balbulus, Notker. "A Hymn to Holy Women." *Norton Anthology of Western Literature,* 8th Edition. New York: W.W. Norton & Company Inc., 2005.

Bernal, Martin. *Black Athena.* 2 vols. New Brunswick, New Jersey: Rutgers University Press, 1991.

Birley, Anthony. *Septimus Severus.* New Haven: Yale University Press, 1968.

Blakely, Allison. *Russia and the Negro.* Washington: Howard University Press, 1986.

Boland, Michael. *They All Discovered America.* Garden City, New York: Doubleday Company, Inc. 1961.

Booth, William. "New Evidence of 'Eve.'" *Washington Post 27* Sept. 1991: A1. Print.

Bradley, Michael. *The Black Discovery of America.* Toronto: Personal Library, 1981.

—. *The Iceman Inheritance.* New York: Warner Books, 1978.

Braund, David. *Georgia in Antiquity.* New York: Oxford University Press, 1994.

Breasted, James. *A History of Egypt.* New York: Charles Scribner's Sons, 1909.

Brunson, James. "African Presence in Early China." *African Presence in Early Asia.* Ed. Ivan Van Sertima. New Brunswick, New Jersey: Transaction Books, 1985.

—. "The African Presence in the Ancient Mediterranean Isles and Mainland Greece." *African Presence in Early Europe.* Ed. Ivan Van Sertima. New Brunswick, New Jersey: Transaction Books, 1985.

Burrows, Edwin G. and Mike Wallace. *Gotham.* New York: Oxford University Press, Inc., 1999.

Bury, J.B. *The Invasion of Europe by the Barbarians.* New York: W.W. Norton & Company, 1967.

Cavalli-Sforza, L. Luca, Paulo Menozzi and Alberto Piazza. *The History and Geography of Human Genes.* Princeton, New Jersey: Princeton University Press, 1994.

Ceram, C.W. *The First American.* New York: New American Library, 1972.

Chandler, Wayne. *Ancient Future.* Baltimore, Maryland: Black Classic Press, 1999.

—. "The Jewel in the Lotus: The Ethiopian Presence in the Indus Valley Civilization." *African Presence in Early Asia.* Ed. Ivan van Sertima. New Brunswick: Journal of African Civilizations, Ltd., Inc., 1985.

Charles, B.G. *Old Norse Relations With Wales.* Cardiff: The University of Wales Press Board, 1934.

Childress, David Hatcher. *Lost Cities of Atlantis, Ancient Europe & the Mediterranean*. Telle, Illinois: Adventures Unlimited Press, 1996.

Christianson, Eric. *The Northern Crusades*. London: Penguin Books Ltd., 1967.

Churchward, Albert. *The Origin and Evolution of Religion*. (1920) *Bensenville*, Illinois: Lushena Books, Inc. 2003.

—. *Signs and Symbols of Primordial Man*. (1912) Brooklyn, New York: A&B Publishers Group, 1994.

Clegg, Legrand II. "The First Invaders." *African Presence in Early Europe*. Ed. Ivan Van Sertima. New Brunswick, New Jersey: Journal of African Civilizations, Ltd., Inc., 1985.

Cohane, John Phillip. *The Key*. New York: Schocken Books, 1976.

Collins, Roger. *Early Medieval Europe 300-1000*. New York: St. Martin's Press, 1995.

Davies, John. *A History of Wales*. London: Penguin Books, Ltd., 1993.

De Las Casas, Bartolome. *A Short Account of the Destruction of the Indies*. London: Penguin Books, 1992.

De Costa, B.F. *The Pre-Columbian Discovery of America by the Northmen*. Albany, New York: Joel Munsell's Sons, Publishers, 1890.

Diop, Cheikh Anta. *The African Origin of Civilization*. Westport, Connecticut: Lawrence Hill & Company, 1974.

—. *Civilization or Barbarism*. Paris: Presence Africaine, 1981. Trans. Yaa-Lengi Meema Ngemi. New York: Lawrence-Hill Books, 1991.

Dixon, Pierson. *The Iberians of Spain*. London: Oxford University Press, 1940.

Dixon, Roland B. *The Racial History of Man*. New York and London: Charles Scribner's Sons, 1923.

Dorsey, George A. *Why We Behave Like Human Beings*. New York: Harper & Brothers, 1925.

Dyck, Lugwig Heinrich. "Wolves at the Border." *Military History,* June 2003:40. Print.

Durant, Will. *The Age of Faith*. New York: MJF Books, 1950.

Enterline, James Robert. *Viking America*. Garden City, New York: Doubleday & Company, Inc., 1972.

Farb, Peter. *Man's Rise to Civilization*. New York: E.P. Dutton, 1978.

Fell, Barry. *America B.C.* New York: Quadrangle/The New York Times Book Co., 1977.

—. *Saga America*. New York: Times Books, 1980.

Finch, Charles S. III. *The Star of Deep Beginnings*. Decatur, Georgia: Khenti Inc., 1998.

Forbes, Jack D. *Africans and Native Americans*. Urbana and Chicago: University of Illinois Press, 1993.

Fox, Hugh. *Gods of the Cataclysm*. New York: Dorset Press, 1976.

Fraser, Angus. *The Gypsies*. Oxford, UK: Blackwell Publishers, 1993.

Frazer, James George. *The Golden Bough*. New York: Macmillan Company, 1944.

Funck-Brentano, Fr. *A History of Gaul*. Trans. E.F. Buckley. New York Barnes & Noble Books, 1993.

Gadalla, Moustafa. *Egyptian Romany*. Greensboro, North Carolina: Tehuti Research Foundation, 2004.

Gibbon, Edward. *The Decline and Fall of the Roman Empire*. London: Encyclopedia Britannica, Inc., 1952.

Gladwin, Harold Sterling. *Men Out of Asia*. New York: McGraw-Hill Book Company, 1947.

Gordon, C.D. *The Age of Attila*. New York: Barnes & Noble Books, 1993.

Gordon, Richard. "Stopping Attila: The Battle of Chalons." *Military History*, Dec. 2003: 34. Print.

Gore, Terry. "Singing Swords & Charging Warhorses." *Military Heritage*, Apr. 2004: 50. Print.

Greizer, Axtol. "Rediscovery of a Lost Tribe." *Scientific American*. American Features Syndicate, Ltd., Oct._Dec., 1997.

Greizer, Axtol. "Viking Heritage in Maine: The Rediscovery of a Lost Tribe." Chicago American Features Syndicate, Ltd., 2000.

Grundberg, Sven, Vanessa Fuhrmans and Nicolas Rolander. "Gunman is Held, Warns of More Terror Cells." *The Wall Street Journal* 26 July 2011, A10. Print.

Guerber, H.A. *Myths of the Norsemen*. New York: Dover Publications, Inc., 1992.

Hancock, Graham. *Underworld*. New York: Three Rivers Press, 2002.

Herm, Gerhard. *The Celts*. New York: St. Martin's Press, 1975.

Herodotus. *The Histories*. Trans. Aubrey de Selincourt. London: Penguin Books, 2003.

Hertz, Friedrich. *Race and Civilization*. 1928. USA: KTAV Publishing House, Inc., 1970.

Higgins, Godfrey, Esq. *Anacalypsis*. 2 vols. 1836. Brooklyn, New York: A&B Books Publishers, 1992.

—. *Celtic Druids*. London: Ridgeway and Sons, 1829.

Hoen, Marco T. "A Forgotten Holocaust Remembered." *The Epoch Times*, 29 Jan. 2011. Print.

Hotema, Hilton. *Mystery Man of the Bible.* Mokelumne Hill, California: Health Research, 1956.

Howarth, David. *1066 The Year of the Conquest.* New York: Penguin Books, 1978.

Huyghe, Patrick. *Columbus Was Last.* New York: MJF Books, 1992.

Ivimy, John. *The Sphinx and the Megaliths.* London: Turnstone Books Ltd., 1974.

Jablonski, Nina G. *Skin.* Los Angeles: University of California Press, 2006.

Jackson, John G. *Introduction to African Civilizations.* Secaucus, New Jersey: The Citadel Press, 1980.

—.*Man, God, and Civilization.* New Hyde Park, New York: University Books, Inc. 1972.

James, George G.M. *Stolen Legacy.* 1954. San Francisco: Julian Richardson Associates, 1976.

Jones, Gwyn. *A History of the Vikings.* London: Oxford University Press, 1968.

—. *The Norse Atlantic Saga.* New York: Oxford University Press, 1986.

Jones, Prudence and Nigel Pennick. *A History of Pagan Europe.* New York: Routledge, 1995.

Keller, Werner. *The Etruscans.* New York: Alfred A. Knopf, Inc., 1974.

Keys, David. "A Viking Mystery." *Smithsonian,* Oct. 2010: 64. Print.

Knight, Franklin. *The Caribbean.* New York: Oxford University Press, 1978.

Kuper, Leo. *Genocide.* New Haven and London: Yale University Press, 1981.

Lancel, Serge. *Carthage: A History.* Trans. Antonia Nevill. Oxford: Blackwell Publishers, 1995.

Leedom, Tim C., ed. *The Book Your Church Doesn't Want You to Read.* San Diego: Truth Seeker Books, 2003.

Leland, Charles G. *Fusang.* 1875. London and New York: Curzon Press Ltd. And Barnes & Noble, 1973.

Levathes, Louise. "A Geneticist Maps Ancient Migrations." *The New York Times* 27 July 1993: C1. Print.

Lissner, Ivar. *The Silent Past.* New York: G.P. Putnam's Sons, 1962.

Luke, Don. "African Presence in the Early History of the British Isles and Scandinavia." *African Presence in Early Europe.* Ed. Ivan Van Sertima. New Brunswick, New Jersey: Transaction Books, 1985.

Mackenzie, Donald. *Ancient Man in Britain.* London: Senate/Random House, 1996.

MacManus, Seumas. *The Story of the Irish Race.* 1921. Old Greenwich, Connecticut: The Devin-Adair Company, 1990.

MacRitchie, David. *Accounts of the Gypsies of India.* 1886. New Delhi: New Society Publications, 1976.

—. *Ancient and Modern Britons.* 2 vols. London: Kegan Paul, Trench & Co., 1884.

—. *The Testimony of Tradition.* London: Kegan Paul & Trench & co., 1890.

Maenchen-Helfen, Otto. *The World of the Huns.* Los Angeles and London: University

Malcolmson, Scott L. *One Drop of Blood.* New York: Farrar Straus Giroux, 2000. of California Press, Ltd., 1973.

Marrs, Jim. *Rule by Secrecy.* New York: Harper-Collins Publishers, 2000.

Massey, Gerald. *A Book of the Beginnings.* 2 vols. 1881. New York: A&B Books Publishers, 1994.

Mitchison, Rosalind. *A History of Scotland.* London Methuen & Co., Ltd., 1982.

Mowat, Farley. *The Farfarers.* South Royalton, Vermont: Steerforth Press, 2000.

Niderost, Eric. "The First Korean War." *Military History,* August 2002: 30. Print.

NOVA: *Iceman.* WNET-TV. New York. Nov., 1992.

Olrik, Axel. *Heroic Legends of Denmark.* Trans. Lee M. Hollander. New York: The American-Scandinavian Foundation, 1919.

Olson, Steve. *Mapping Human History.* New York: Houghton Mifflin Company, 2002.

Oxenstierna, Eric. *The World of the Norsemen.* Cleveland and New York: The World Publishing Company, 1957.

Perry, W.J. *The Children of the Sun.* London: Methuen & Co., 1923.

Picard, Barbara Leonie. *Tales of the Norse Gods and Heroes.* London: Oxford University Press, 1980.

Poe, Richard. *Black Spark, White Fire. USA:* Prima Publishing, 1997.

Pohl, Frederick J. *Atlantic Crossings Before Columbus.* New York: W.W. Norton and Company, 1961.

Poliakov, Leon. *The Aryan Myth.* New York: Basic Books, 1974.

Pritchard, Evan. *Native New Yorkers.* San Francisco: Council Oak Books, 2002.

Reader's Digest. *The World's Last Mysteries.* Pleasantville, New York: 1978.

Rice, Patty C. *Amber: The Golden Gem of the Ages.* New York: The Kosciuszko Foundation, Inc., 1987.

Rodney, Walter. *How Europe Underdeveloped Africa.* Washington: Howard University Press, 1982.

Sanders, Ronald. *Lost Tribes and Promised Lands.* New York: Harper Collins, 1992.

Schoch, Robert M. *Voyages of the Pyramid Builders*. New York: Penguin Group (USA), 2004.

Scobie, Edward. "The Black in Western Europe." *African Presence in Early Europe*. Ed. Ivan Van Sertima. New Brunswick, New Jersey: Journal of African Civilizations, Ltd., 1985.

Scullard, H.H. *The Etruscan Cities and Rome*. Ithaca, New York: Cornell University Press, 1967.

Sergi, G. *The Mediterranean Race*. London: Walter Scott, Paternoster Square, 1901.

Sertima, Ivan Van. "Egypto-Nubian Presences in Ancient Mexico." *African Presence in Early America*. Ed. Ivan Van Sertima. Piscataway, New Jersey: Tut-Ra-Ma Books, 1987.

Shaw, Karl. *Royal Babylon*. New York: Broadway Books, 1999.

Skene, William F. *Celtic Scotland*. Edinburgh: Edmonston & Douglas, Princes Street, 1876.

Spindler, Conrad. *The Man in the Ice*. New York: Harmony Books, 1994.

Stannard, David E. *American Holocaust*. New York:/Oxford: Oxford University Press, 1992.

Tacitus. *The Agricola and The Germania*. London: Penguin Books, 1970.

TERRA X. *The Golden Fleece*. The Discovery Channel, 1995.

Thomas, Bertram. *The Arabs*. Garden City, New York: Doubleday, Doran & Co., 1937.

Thomas, Donald. *The Philosophy of Divine Nutrition*. New York: Vantage Press, 1977.

Vanderwerth, W.C. *Indian Oratory*. Norman, Oklahoma: Oklahoma University Press, 1982.

Waddell, L.A. *Phoenician Origin of the Britons, Scots and Anglo-Saxons*. London: Williams and Norgate, Ltd., 1924.

Wells, H.G. *The Outline of History*. 1940. New York: Doubleday & Company, Inc., 1956.

Welsing, Frances Cress. *The Isis Papers*. Chicago: Third World Press, 1991.

Williams, Chancellor. *The Destruction of Black Civilization*. Chicago: Third World Press, 1976.

Wilson, Amos. *The Falsification of Afrikan Consciousness*. New York: Afrikan World InfoSystems, 1993.

Wuthenau, Alexander von. *Unexpected Faces in Ancient America*. New York: Crown Publishers, Inc., 1982. "Unexpected African Faces in Pre-Columbian America." African Presence in Early America. Ed. Ivan Van Sertima. Journal of African Civilizations Ltd., 1987.

General Index

A

Aben Arou, 122-124, 179, 283, 303

Abnaki, 123

Aborigine(s), (Australian), 2, 48, 61, 190, 293-294, 324

Aesir, 78

Aestii, (also see Estonians), 71

Afghanistan, 235, 246, 277, 287, 312, 319, 329

Africa, 1, 3-4, 10-11, 20, 48, 51,53, 63, 75, 89, 144, 178, 186, 194, 212, 215-217, 235, 317, 323, 327-329

African-Americans, 213, 294, 318, 320, 324, 330

African(s), 1, 31, 33, 47-48, 62-64, 68, 75, 86, 89, 182-186, 233, 237, 242-246, 255, 271, 294, 303, 320, 323-324, 327-329

African Slave Trade, 182, 185, 194-195, 234, 294, 310, 318, 324, 327, 330

Africoid(s), 33, 35-36, 42, 64, 70, 245, 252, 260, 265, 273-274, 285, 288, 294, 322, 328

Albinoids (albinism; albinos), 11, 16-20, 231, 233

Alexander (the Great), 21-22, 43, 76, 220, 234, 283, 289, 318

Alfred (the Great), 90, 100, 127, 173, 286, 299, 317

Algonquian, 123

Althing (also *Thing;* early Norse public court assembly), 173, 306

Amber, 65, 69

America (the Americas), 73, 75, 112, 177-179, 182, 184, 186, 194-195, 235, 244, 283, 310-311, 313, 317-319, 328

Americans, 243, 261, 330

Angles, 44, 57, 118

Anglo-Saxon(s), 47, 175, 310, 317

Anksar, 97

Aquitania, 89, 98, 253, 255

Arabia, 5, 10-12, 273, 318

Arab(s), 53, 61, 63, 89, 101, 104, 181, 236, 299, 312, 323

Arngrim (Killer-Styr) Thorgrimsson, 154-156

Aryan(s), 18, 54, 66, 83, 71-72, 111-112, 215, 236, 241, 255-256

Asia, Asian (Asiatic), 9, 14, 18, 48-50, 53, 63-64, 66, 70, 73, 75, 84, 86, 99, 113, 144, 177-178, 195-196, 212, 235-236, 246, 259-260, 273, 283-285, 313, 320, 328-329

Asia Minor (Turkey), 3, 37, 60, 69, 84, 102, 214-216, 221-222, 284, 313, 318

Asiatic Blacks, 42, 84, 244, 259-260, 277, 285, 317

Asuras, 247-248

Ativism, 130

Atlantic (Ocean), 32, 65, 67

Atlantic Slave Trade (see also African Save Trade), 287, 323

Atli (various), 147-148

Atilla (Khan; the Hun), 42-44, 50-51, 57, 70-71, 85, 87, 116, 147, 260, 285

Aud Ketilsdottir (the Deep-Minded), 100, 146, 149-150

Aurignacian Age, 9

Australia, 48, 217, 228

Australoid(s), Proto-Australoid(s), 5, 9, 11, 15, 48, 71, 84, 177-178, 181, 215, 229, 234, 238, 248

Austrasia, 97

B

Bahamas, 181, 303,

Basque(s), 36-37, 51, 54, 61, 103, 176, 225, 241, 258-259, 268, 273, 285, 322, 328

Bede, 71,

Beowulf, 86-87, 92

Beringia, Bering Strait (also see Landbridges), 307

Bjorn the Black (a berserker), 156-157

Bjorn Buna, 148

Bjorn Ketilsson (the Easterner), 148-149

Black Celts (Black Celtic),44, 47, 51, 69, 71, 94, 97, 103, 112, 118, 161, 251, 255, 261-262, 276, 278, 299

Black Douglasses (of Scotland), 161-162

Black Dwarfs (Black Elves) 6, 49, 79, 87-88, 116, 121, 160-161, 187, 208-209

Black Gentiles (*Black Foreigners; Black Strangers*), 46, 94, 98-99, 105-106, 132, 144-145, 161, 173, 272, 317

Black heathen(s); devils; pagans; 303, 317, 323, 325

Black Hungarians, 93, 106

Black Huns, 43, 44, 50, 70-72, 87, 93, 99, 106, 116, 171, 260, 266, 273, 285, 304

Black Madonna (Madonna and Child), 118, 176, 184, 232, 278,

Black Norsemen (Black Vikings; also see Vikings). 90, 101, 105, 144, 173, 278, 299, 306, 314, 325

Black Vikings, 79, 91, 173

Blacks, 12, 18-19, 23, 30-31, 36, 45, 54, 57, 60, 62-63, 80-81, 85, 87, 89-90, 176, 182, 184, 238, 258, 262, 274, 277, 286, 288, 294, 296, 306, 310, 313-317, 320, 323-325, 327, 330

Blue-eyed, 22, 42, 72, 121, 145, 176, 190, 192, 194, 321, 329

Britain, (British Isles), 1, 13, 22, 46-47, 60, 64, 67-69, 71, 75-76, 79, 86-87, 89, 92, 94, 97, 106-107, 115, 117-118, 176, 192-193, 240-241, 245, 253-254, 257, 259, 261, 276-278, 280-282, 288, 312, 322-323

British, 234-235

Briton(s) (Bretons), 22, 51, 77, 94, 97, 103, 106, 175, 251-253, 258, 261-262, 276, 278, 298, 317, 328

Buddha, 10, 37, 48, (corruption of *Ptah*, 50), 51, 57, 64, 113, 244, 246, 248, 254, 289

Buddhism, 50-51, 106-107

Bulgars, 108-110, 272

Burma, (Myanmar), 52

Burmese, 1

Byzantine Empire (also see Eastern Roman Empire), 70, 89, 101, 107, 113-114, 116, 124, 129, 276-277, 297, 300, 302, 311

C

Caesar, Julius, 68, 106, 286

Canute (Knut) Sveinsson (King; the Great), 125, 139-142, 284, 298, 312

Caribbean, 2-3, 181-192, 195, 235, 285, 313, 317-318, 320, 330

Carthage, 38-39, 43, 56, 64-65, 67-69, 89, 104, 178, 234

Carthaginian(s), 38, 64-65, 67, 69-70, 79, 178, 180, 193, 294, 317

Catholic (also see the Roman Church), 188

Caucasian(s), 1, 12, 16, 19, 30, 36-37, 39, 44, 50-51, 54, 59, 63, 69, 72, 76, 83-86, 89-90, 100-103, 105, 112, 130, 144, 172, 176, 193, 215, 220, 227, 230, 234, 237, 255, 263, 270, 273, 281-282, 285, 287-288, 294-295, 303-306, 310, 314-315, 320-321, 323, 326, 328-329

Caucasian Negroes, 81-82

Caucasoid(s), 16-17, 54, 69, 101, 112, 220-222, 225, 227-234, 238, 251, 255, 259, 265, 288

Cavalli-Sforza, (Dr. Luigi), 213, 237

Celts (black; also see Black Celts), 240, 250-254, 258, 276

Celts (Caucasian; new or later), 65, 240, 251, 259

Central America, 2, 185, 318, 320, 329

Chalons (Battle of), 42-43, 50, 70

Charlamagne, 85-86, 96-97, 110, 124-126, 272

Charles Martel, 85, 89

Children of the Sun, 178-179, 248, 254, 264

China, 6, 9, 48-49, (*Negroids* in, 48-49), 51, (pyramids in, 75), 190, 234-235, 244, 284, 287, 316, 327

Chinese, 6, 18, 52, 61, 178, 221, 233, 241

Christ (*white*), 118

Christ, Jesus, 54, 118, 143-144, 181, 185, 278-281, 295, 305, 311, 320

Christian(s), 176, 181, 186, 279, 288, 302-303, 307-308, 313, 320

Christianity (also Roman Christianity; Catholicism), 51, 70, 83, 87, 96, 106, 113, 124, 127-128, 143-144, 185, 187-188, 251-254, 263, 276-282, 288, 294, 297, 300, 310-313, 315-317, 320, 329

Church, The, (also see Roman Church), 187-188, 286-287, 311-312

Cimbri, (Cimbric; Cimmarians; also Kymry), 45, 57, 70, 87, 92, 105, 112, 239, 245-246, 261, 272, 285, 322-323

Hudson, Henry, 123

Hui-Shen, 178

Hungarians (black), 63

Huns (Hunnish Empire; see also Black Huns), 42-44, 51, 53, 56-57, 63, 69, 70-71, 84-86, 90, 109-110, 147, 274, 285, 304

I

Iberia (Iberian Peninsula; Spain), 60, 62, 68, 73, 88-89, 99, 101, 102, 104, 117, 183, 232, 238, 240, 257-259, 285, 288, 306, 313, 323

Iberian(s), 21-22, 26, 36-37, 44, 51, 54, 69, 109, 132, 193, 241, 258-259, 285, 317, 322

Ice age, (Great Ice Age; Wurm glacial), 3, 177, 216, 230, 239, 314

Iceland, 73, 95, 104, 117-119, 121-122, 126, 138, 175-181, 187, 193, 255, 280-285, 307, 312, 325

Icelanders, 280, 283-284, 303

Iceman, The, 26-31, 40-41, 161, 230, 274, 289, 293, 322

Illugi the Black, 153

India, 4, 36-37, 48, 51, 64, 89, 107, 109, 111-112, 116, 179, 194, 217, 234-235, 243, 248, 271, 273, 277, 284-285, 315-317, 327

Indians (of India; Asuras, Dravidians), 54, 63, 320

Indians (Native Americans), 112, 177, 190-192, 285, 303

Indies (The), 186, 318

Indo-European(s), 78, 111-113, 176, 242-243, 256

Indonesia(ns), 3, 5, 9, 51, 317, 327

Indus Valley (Indus River), 12-13, 48, 111-112, 248, 283-284, 322, 327

Inuit (Eskimos), 121, 187-188, 194, 234, 306, 315

Iran, 287, 329

Iraq, 235, 287, 312, 319, 329

Ireland, (and Celtic Irish), 75-76, 93, 99, 114, 117-118, 174, 251, 253, 255, 276, 280, 282, 285, 323

Irish, 192, 252, 255, 283, 311

Isis (Egyptian; Great Mother), 287, 295

Islam, 51, 89, 101, 277, 312

Italy, 31, 37, 39, 52, 180-181, 223, 232, 241

J

Japan, 235

Jason and the Agonauts (film), 201

Jews, 101, 181, 257, 261, 273, 323-324

Judaism (Jews), 51, 101, 290

Jutes, 44

Jutland Peninsula (see Denmark), 44

K

Karlsefni, Thorfinn, 120

Ketil Flatnose (Caitill Finn), 99-100, 146, 148-149

Khazars, 108, 110

King Harald (of England), 175

King Kong (film), 201-205

Korea, 52, 235

Koreans, 48, *Fig. 9*, p. 52, 52-53

Ku Klux Klan, 324

Kushites (see Cushites)

Kveldulf (Ulf) Bjalfason, 164

Kymry (see Cimbri)

L

Landbridge(s) (i.e., Beringia), 177, 192, 194, 229, 234, 315

Lapps, 9, 87, 92, 225, 234

Latin America, 320

Latino(s), 320, 330

Leakey, Louis, 212

Levant, The (i.e., eastern end of the Mediterranean; also see Near East), 230, 244, 246, 248

Libya, 16

Liguria (Ligurians), 36, 51, 64, 241, 258, 285

The Long Ships (film), 199

Lucius Tarquinius Priscus, 39

M

Madonna and Child, 279-280 (also see Black Madonna)

Magyars, 63, 69, 110, 274

Maliseets, 122-124, 179-180